Those Bloody Kilts

The Highland Soldier in the Great War

Thomas Greenshields

Helion & Company

Helion & Company Limited
Unit 8 Amherst Business Centre
Budbrooke Road
Warwick
CV34 5WE
England
Tel. 01926 499 619
Fax 0121 711 4075
Email: info@helion.co.uk
Website: www.helion.co.uk
Twitter: @helionbooks
Visit our blog http://blog.helion.co.uk/

Published by Helion & Company 2019
Designed and typeset by Mach 3 Solutions (www.mach3solutions.co.uk)
Cover designed by Paul Hewitt, Battlefield Design (www.battlefield-design.co.uk)
Printed by Gutenberg Press, Tarxien, Malta

Text © Thomas Greenshields 2018
Images © as individually credited

Every reasonable effort has been made to trace copyright holders and to obtain their permission for the use of copyright material. The author and publisher apologize for any errors or omissions in this work, and would be grateful if notified of any corrections that should be incorporated in future reprints or editions of this book.

ISBN 978-1-912390-26-7

British Library Cataloguing-in-Publication Data.
A catalogue record for this book is available from the British Library.

All rights reserved. No part of this publication may be reproduced, stored in a retrieval system, or transmitted, in any form, or by any means, electronic, mechanical, photocopying, recording or otherwise, without the express written consent of Helion & Company Limited.

For details of other military history titles published by Helion & Company Limited contact the above address, or visit our website: http://www.helion.co.uk.

We always welcome receiving book proposals from prospective authors.

Contents

List of Illustrations		iv
List of Colour Plates		vii
List of Tables		ix
Introduction		x
1	Heroes of Empire	15
2	Organisation and Service	51
3	Noble Causes, Nagging Doubts	87
4	The Men Who Marched Away	113
5	The Kilt: Mystique and Tradition	142
6	The Kilt: Fighting the Elements	172
7	The Kilt: The Hazards of War	200
8	The Pipes	228
9	Discipline	256
10	Hierarchy	283
11	Comradeship	308
12	Lines of Support	337
13	Identity	363
14	Self-image and Reputation	392
15	Ferocity and Compassion	410
16	Courage and Failure	439
17	Final Thoughts	468
Bibliography		482
Index		504

List of Illustrations

The pre-War Regular Army overseas: Ration stand, 2nd Cameron Highlanders, Baird Barracks Bangalore (1909-1913). (From a contemporary postcard by The Picture House, Bangalaore, author's collection)   16

The pre-War Regular Army overseas: a soldier of 2nd Cameron Highlanders in Bangalore (1909-1913). (Author's collection)   16

The pre-War Territorial Force: Liverpool Scottish at camp, Caerwys, 1909. (Author's collection)   25

The pre-War Canadians: 72nd Canadian Militia regiment (Seaforth Highlanders of Canada) on parade c.1912. (from a contemporary postcard, publisher unknown, Author's collection)   30

The romance of the pipes: Piper Findlater wining the V.C. at the heights of Dargai in 1897, illustrated by H. Montague Love, on a popular pre-War series of postcards by Tucks depicting V.C. winners. (Author's collection)   35

The commemoration of the Highland regiments: statue of a Cameron Highlander outside Inverness railway station, sculpted by George Edward Wade and erected in 1893. (photograph author)   40

Disaster! Gordon Highlanders and friends flee Majuba Hill 1881. Not the typical image of the Highland soldier. Illustration by Melton Prior, published in the *Illustrated London News*. (Copyright Mary Evans Picture Library)   41

An encampment of 1st Seaforth Highlanders at Shabkadar during the Mohmand Expedition, 1908. (from a contemporary postcard, publisher unknown, Author's collection)   44

Boer War memorial at Alloa, sculpted by William Birnie Rhind and erected in 1904. (Photograph author)   47

The pre-War Volunteers: The London Scottish at the Royal Volunteer Review Edinburgh, 1905. (from a contemporary postcard by the Mezzotint Company, Author's collection)   48

Monument at Dingwall to Sir Hector Macdonald, a flawed Highland hero, opened 1907. (Photograph author)   49

A sergeant of the Black Watch says goodbye to his family before entraining for the front. Did he see his family again? From a contemporary postcard, publisher unknown. (Author's collection)   52

Regular battalions return from overseas. Soldiers of 2nd Black Watch photographed at Marseilles, where they disembarked on 12th October, 1914 still in tropical kit. From a contemporary French postcard published by E.L.D. (Author's collection)   54

Highland soldiers of the Territorial Highland Division compete in a dancing competition at a Highland Games at Bedford in 1915. From a contemporary photographic postcard by Blake & Edgar. (Author's collection)   55

List of Illustrations

Soldiers of 1st Garrison Battalion Seaforth Highlanders in Salonika. Not the ideal representatives of a martial race (Author's collection)	62
Kilted Canadian officers of the First Canadian Contingent on Salisbury Plain shortly after their arrival, from a contemporary postcard by Tuck's. (Author's collection)	64
South African Scottish march through Marseilles on 8 May, 1916, after returning from the Western Desert to deploy to the Western Front. Their reception was riotous. From a contemporary French postcard, published by E.L.D. (Author's collection)	66
A Highland soldier at Lagny-Thorigny on 3 September, 1914, at the end of the Great Retreat, with the British Army about to turn and fight. A contemporary French postcard by local company Ensch Rochat. (Author's collection)	67
Men of the 16th Battalion C.E.F. (Canadian Scottish) moving up to the front line, 27 September 1918. (IWM CO3289)	71
Other theatres: soldiers of 2nd Black Watch practise marksmanship across sandbag defences on the Palestine coast near Arsuf. (IWM Q12485)	73
Other theatres: soldiers of 5th Argylls helping to make a breakwater at Cape Helles, Gallipoli, 1915. (IWM Q13517)	74
Other theatres: Mesopotamia. Two soldiers of 1st Seaforth Highlanders with a local Arab under escort in 1917. (Author's collection)	74
Less than glamorous temporary uniforms typical of those worn in training by Highland soldiers before receiving their kilts. (Author's collection)	146
A Seaforth Highlander in a khaki kilt, probably from 7th Battalion, one of the few battalions to wear them. (Author's collection)	152
Trousers worn in training by Gordon Highlander Kitchener recruits. They are wearing non-regimental Glengarries. (Author's collection)	156
Mandatory studio photo of a young Seaforth Highlander in kilt while training. This photo was taken at Ripon, where the T.F. training battalions were based. He is wearing boots and puttees, as issued from 1915 onwards. How old is he? (Author's collection)	157
Riding a horse in a kilt was not recommended for comfort. (Author's collection)	163
The curiosity of the public. French civilians eye a soldier of the London Scottish on L.O.C. duties in 1914. The ladies seem enchanted; the young lad in centre photo seems less than impressed. From a contemporary postcard published in France by C.C.C. & C. (Author's collection)	168
Studio photograph of two soldiers of the Black Watch, illustrating the khaki Tam o' Shanter which replaced the Glengarry, and sporting the famous red hackle worn proudly by the regiment. (Author's collection)	174
A Scots Guardsman helping a Highlander in the mud, 1916. (IWM Q17499)	178
A soldier of the Royal Engineers collecting the identity disc from the wrist of a Highlander killed by a shell on the edge of a water filled crater. (IWM Q3963)	179
2nd Battalion Argyll and Sutherland Highlanders, Bois Grenier Sector, winter, early 1915. (IWM Q48955)	182
Soldiers of the Gordon Highlanders putting on rubber thigh boots, Bazentin-le-Petit, November 1916. (IWM Q4474)	191
Gordon Highlanders preparing barbed wire entanglements north of Arras, 24 April, 1917. (IWM Q65400)	209
The romance of war: dead Highland soldier. (Author's collection)	224
More romance. Another dead Highlander, from the Tynecot visitor centre. (Photograph, author)	225

The pipers' memorial at Longueval. (Photograph, author)	232
During the Battle of the Somme, a piper of the 7th Seaforth Highlanders pipes men back from the front after the attack on Longueval, 14 July 1916. (IWM Q4012)	237
Pipe band playing to resting troops after the capture of Longueval on 14 July 1916. (IWM Q4001)	241
Pipers of 2nd Black Watch pipe the battalion into Beirut, 10 October 1918. (IWM Q12407)	243
Comrades. Men of 9th Royal Scots. (Author's collection)	311
Comrades. Captain Hyslop DSO and Hutchinson, 2nd Argylls, in cellar of farmhouse that formed part of frontline, Christmas Day 1914. (IWM HU128734)	327
Support from home. Harry Lauder, in a contemporary fund-raising photograph, dressed as a soldier to perform his wartime song, 'The Laddies who Fought and Won.' Harry's son John was killed during the war while serving in 1/8th Argylls. Harry devoted himself to the war effort, famously visiting the troops at the front in June, 1917. (photographic card, Author's collection)	346
Support from family. A long-serving soldier of the Seaforth Highlanders with his family. Would he still be there for them at the end of the war? (Author's collection)	350
Support from religion. The Scottish Churches Hut at Montreuil depicted on a contemporary postcard. (Author's collection)	357
Identity. Memorial to 1st Black Watch and 1st Cameron Highlanders erected at High Wood to commemorate their losses September, 1916. From a contemporary postcard, publisher unknown. (Author's collection)	382
Identity. Men of the Black Watch celebrating New Year's Day in the hutments at Henencourt, 1917. (IWM Q4642)	386
Identity. Men of the Liverpool Scottish enjoy a tug of war in Games at Tunbridge Wells. (Author's collection)	389
Image. Soldiers of 8th Black Watch practice a bayonet attack at Bordon Camp, 1915. (IWM Q53939)	394
Hate. The Germans shell a church being used as a hospital on the retreat from Mons, according to an illustration by F. Matania, which appeared in *The Sphere* and is reproduced here on a contemporary French postcard by l' Atelier d' Art photographique. (Author's collection)	420
Ruthlessness. Battle of the Scarpe. Patrol of 6th Seaforth Highlanders demonstrate firing into a dug-out in a deserted German trench to dislodge any remaining Germans, 29 August, 1918. (IWM Q7013)	423
Lucky man. South African Scottish troops carrying a wounded German on a stretcher during the Battle of the Menin Road Ridge, 21 September 1917. (IWM Q2869)	431
The fortunate ones. Troops of 51st Highland Division with German prisoners during the battle of Cambrai 20 November, 1917. (IWM Q6276)	432
Memorial to Sergeant John Meikle, V.C., outside Dingwall railway station, erected by his railway comrades. Meikle was a railway clerk at Nitshill station before he enlisted. He was killed in action on 20 July, 1918. (Photograph, author)	441
'The Jock on the Rock.' 51st Highland Division memorial, Newfoundland Park, Beaumont-Hamel. (Photograph, author)	469
Diagram 1: Factors influencing Morale	471

List of Colour Plates

The glamour of the kilt: superb illustration by Harry Payne from a set of postcards depicting the Gordon Highlanders, published by Tucks shortly before the war. Such uniform sets were collected by boys and both reflected and contributed to the popularity of the Army, the Empire and the Highland regiments. (Author's collection) — i

The Highland soldier as Imperial icon. In a popular illustration of 1914 by Lawson Wood, Britain's defiance of the German invasion of Belgium is characterised by a soldier of the Black Watch. From a contemporary postcard published by Dobson, Molle & Co. (Author's collection) — ii

Bronze low-relief at the South African memorial, Delville Wood, shows a soldier of the South African Scottish leaving the wood. (Photograph author) — iii

Swank. 'The Cock o' the North': illustration by Reg Maurice on a contemporary postcard by the Regent Publishing Co. (Author's collection) — iv

Ascending the outdoor stairs on trams and buses was a risky business when wearing the kilt. A cartoon by D. Tempest on a postcard published by Bamforth & Co. (Copyright Bamforth & Co.) — v

The hazards of winter: a classic contemporary postcard by Donald McGill published by the Inter Art Co. (Author's collection) — vi

The idealised image of the piper at war. Piper Laidlaw of the K.O.S.B. winning the Victoria Cross at Loos, an illustration by E.F. Skinner, providing the frontispiece to Volume 4 of *The War Illustrated*. — vii

Comforts from home. Perhaps not the most appropriate gift for Highland soldiers and likely to be thrown into No Man's Land once lice-infested. A contemporary comic postcard by the Inter-Art Co. (Author's collection) — viii

Support from home. Many soldiers maintained frequent communication with family, friends and sweethearts at home through an excellent postal service. A sentimental contemporary postcard by Tuck's. (Author's collection) — ix

Identity. Scottish pride. A contemporary postcard published by J. Salmon. (Copyright J. Salmon Ltd, England) — x

Image of the bayonet-toting Highland soldier. A contemporary postcard of the Seaforth Highlanders by Ernest Ibbetson, published by Gale & Polden (Author's collection) — xi

Popular image. 'The charge at St Quentin 1914.' The stirrup charge that never was. Imaginary repetition of the legendary feat at Waterloo, painted by Harry Payne for a contemporary postcard published by Tuck's. (Author's collection) — xii

To see ourselves as others see us. A Highland soldier personifies Britain in this unflattering Italian postcard, produced no doubt before Italy joined the war on the side of France, Britain and Russia. (Author's collection) — xiii

To see ourselves as others see us. A contemporary German postcard in the Kriegs Erinnerungs Karte series demonstrates German satisfaction at taking Highland soldiers prisoner. (author's collection)   xiv

Corporal Pollock of 5th Camerons wins the Victoria Cross at Loos. A contemporary advertising card by Walker, Harrison & Garthwaites Ltd. (Author's collection)   xv

War Memorial, Dornoch. Many men from Dornoch served and fell in 5th Seaforth Highlanders. (Photograph, author)   xvi

List of Tables

1.1	Amalgamation of regiments 1881	17
2.1	Early deployment of Territorial battalions to France and Belgium	58
9.1	Non court-martial offences recorded in Part II Orders 1/8th Argyll & Sutherland Highlanders May 1915 to December 1916	258
9.2	Appropriate punishments listed by Captain Thomas Young, 3/6th Black Watch, Ripon, 1915-1916 (Source: BWA)	259
9.3	Punishments for disobedience, insubordination and violence towards superior officers recorded in miscellaneous sources	265

Introduction

This book has two distant origins. The first lies over sixty years ago, when mum and dad first presented me with a box of lead soldiers. This small section gradually grew into an army of about 150, mostly plastic warriors, in which Romans curiously did battle with Roundheads and Desert Rats on the living room floor. This was the rather un-scholastic beginning of my love of military history. The second spur came rather later, perhaps 45 years ago, when I took my first walking holiday in the Scottish Highlands, in Glencoe, and fell in love with the mountains. From that grew a love of the Highlands and an interest in their history and that of Scotland in general. At an early stage I read J.D. Mackie's paperback History of Scotland, a revelation for an Englishmen, as I became aware that, heavens above, Scotland had its own history before 1603. How pleased I was to find much later that Mackie served as an officer in 14th Argylls during the Great War. I gobbled down John Prebble's books on Glencoe, Culloden and the Clearances, and after an interesting related chat with the staff at Dunrobin Castle became aware of the delicate sensitivities which attach to Highland history. I walked in awe around the Scottish United Services Museum as it then was, visited the great bulwark of Fort George, and admired the impressive military memorials at Edinburgh, Stirling, Aberfeldy and elsewhere.

I took early retirement in 2008, largely for reasons of health, but also because I realised that in my career, I had really missed my vocation: I should have devoted myself to the study of military history. I then launched myself into this project, combining my interests in military history and Scotland with a growing interest in the Great War. The inspirations for the project were really three. First, I had hugely enjoyed reading the books of Lyn Macdonald,[1] Max Arthur[2] and Derek Young,[3] in which the eye-witness experiences of serving soldiers are linked together with a skilful narrative. Second, Diana Henderson's ground-breaking study of the Highland Soldier between 1820 and 1920[4] demonstrated a new social approach to military history. Finally, Richard Holmes' analytical approach to the soldier's life in *Tommy*[5] offered a broad model for similar study of the Highland soldier in the Great War.

There is no monograph on the Highland soldier in the Great War, but there is much mythology about the Highland soldier. The centenary of the Great War is an appropriate time to offer a review. It has been my intention in this review not to de-bunk the image of the Highland soldier, but to examine the reality and in the process subject the mythology to critical review.

---

1   For example Macdonald, Lyn, *1914* (London: Penguin, 1987).
2   Arthur, Max, *Forgotten Voices of the Great War* (London: Ebury Press, 2003).
3   Young, Derek, *Forgotten Scottish Voices from the Great War*, (Stroud: Tempus, 2005).
4   Henderson, Diana M, *Highland Soldier 1820-1920*, (Edinburgh: John Donald, 1989).
5   Holmes, Richard, *Tommy* (London: HarperCollins, 2004).

The intention is to provide a 'warts and all' picture of the Highland soldier and in so doing not to diminish him, but to show him in his essential humanity. Only if we understand this humanity and the reality of his experience can we really appreciate his contribution and sacrifice. The hugely impressive Scottish National War Memorial in Edinburgh Castle, the famous 'Jock on the Rock' at Beaumont-Hamel and the many impressive memorials dotted around the Highlands at Forres, Dornoch, Dingwall and elsewhere mean nothing if they are based on bombast; everything if we recognise the reality of the Highland soldier's experience.

In this book, therefore, we clinically dissect this experience, starting with a review of the position of the Highland soldier on the eve of War. We then review the organisation and deployment of the Highland battalions during the War. This is followed by an examination of why soldiers joined up and specifically why they joined Highland regiments. We then look at the prime distinctive features of the Highland soldier. We examine the mystique of the kilt and its practicality in war, as well as the role of the pipes, including how they were really used in battle and behind the lines. From these very tangible elements we move on to look at the way discipline and hierarchy operated in the Highland regiments. Was there really a more informal relationship between officers and men based on mutual respect? We look at the way comradeship operated within the Highland battalions, and the support both officers and men received from home, the community and religion. We next examine identity and reputation, before considering ferocity and compassion on the battlefield and finally courage and failure. Finally, we draw some conclusions about the cultural significance of our findings, before examining their military significance in the light of morale, for if the Highland soldier enjoyed some differences from his other Army colleagues, it is argued that their significance was chiefly felt in terms of morale.

This is not an operational history. Many battles are mentioned, but the reader wanting a detailed examination of the Highland battalions at Loos, Arras or Cambrai will need to look elsewhere. Like Henderson's pioneering study, it covers elements of social history, such as the regional and social origins of the soldiers and the relationships between officers, N.C.O.'s and men. But it is much more than a social history, for, alongside these elements, we consider, for example, the practicality of the kilt, the use of the pipes on the battlefield, and less tangible elements like ferocity and courage on the battlefield. Many of these elements as we have remarked contributed to morale, and morale is a primary military consideration. In that respect the study has some relationship with Holmes' *Tommy*. As far as possible I have used the words of the soldiers themselves to describe their experience, although at times I have had to suppress or paraphrase them to meet demands on space or avoid infringing copyright. In defining the Highland soldier, I have embraced all the kilted soldiers of Britain and the Empire, including those of Canada and South Africa. I have specifically included the kilted 6th and 9th Highland Light Infantry (H.L.I.) and 9th Royal Scots, but I have not included the non-kilted battalions of the H.L.I. Likewise I have included both the London and Liverpool Scottish but not the non-kilted Tyneside Scottish. No doubt I risk being 'persona non grata' in Glasgow and Newcastle!

The best existing treatment of the subject is an excellent pithy chapter by Edward Spiers,[6] which addresses many of the themes I have explored, albeit for the Scottish soldier as a whole, not just the Highland soldier. Diana Henderson's ground-breaking study does extend to

---

6 Spiers, Edward, 'The Scottish Soldier at War,' in Cecil, Hugh and Liddle, Peter H., *Facing Armageddon, The First World War Experience*, (Barnsley: Pen & Sword Select, 2003), pp.314-335.

embrace the Great War.[7] However, her scope is vast, covering 100 years, during which there was great change and her sources for the Great War are very limited. Derek Young[8] provides a useful and readable compendium of original sources arranged to illustrate the life of the Scottish soldier in the war, but he covers all Scottish soldiers, and his book is descriptive of life rather than analytical of character. The overall Scottish experience of the war is usefully examined by Trevor Royle[9] and by Macdonald and McFarland.[10] There are of course a number of Divisional and regimental histories of which those for the Black Watch and the Cameron Highlanders are remarkably comprehensive. Recent useful monographs include Colin Campbell's new history of 51st Highland Division[11] and a string of regimental or battalion histories, by Derek Bird[12] (6th Seaforths), Hal Giblin[13] (Liverpool Scottish), Mark Lloyd[14] (London Scottish), Patrick Watt[15] (4th Camerons) and Alec Weir[16] (Glasgow Highlanders). On the pre-War background, the work of Spiers[17] and Allan & Carswell[18] is invaluable. For the pipes the work of Seton & Grant[19] is still important, while Murray[20] provides a more recent perspective.

As source material I have of course made use of regimental histories and many published memoirs which effectively constitute primary eye-witness accounts. As far as possible, however, I have used original letters, diaries, written memoirs and recordings in the various archives. Many, including all the recordings, have come from the Imperial War Museum and the Liddle Collection at Leeds. I have also been delighted to find much material in the archives of the various regimental museums, including the Gordon Highlanders Museum at Aberdeen, The Highlanders Museum at Fort George (for both the Cameron and Seaforth Highlanders), The Black Watch Museum at Perth, the Argyll and Sutherland Highlanders Museum at Stirling and the Royal Scots Museum in Edinburgh Castle. More material was obtained from the National Library of Scotland. Regrettably, for lack of time, I was not able to examine the archives of the London Scottish, Liverpool Scottish or H.L.I. I would like to place on record my appreciation to the curators and staff of all the institutions I did visit for their unfailingly friendly assistance. I have been particularly grateful for the freedom of access given to sources in the regimental museums, with no constraints on use. Regimental museums of course have two objectives; to preserve the records of the regiment, but also to preserve the reputation of the regiment.

---

7 Henderson, *Highland Soldier*.
8 Young, *Forgotten Scottish Voices*.
9 Royle, Trevor, *The Flowers of the Forest: Scotland and the First World War*, (Edinburgh: Birlinn, 2006).
10 Macdonald, Catriona M.M. and McFarland, E.W. (ed) *Scotland and the Great War*, (East Linton: Tuckwell Press, 1999).
11 Campbell, Colin, *Engine of Destruction: The 51st (Highland) Division in the Great War*, (Glendaruel: Argyll Publishing, 2013).
12 Bird, Derek, *The Spirit of the Troops is Excellent*, (Eastholme, Moray: Birdbrain Books, 2008).
13 Giblin, Hal, *Bravest of Hearts*, (Liverpool: Winordie Publications, 2000).
14 Lloyd, Mark, *The London Scottish in the Great War* (Barnsley: Leo Cooper, 2001).
15 Watt, Patrick, *Steel and Tartan* (Stroud: The History press, 2012).
16 Weir, Alec, *Come on Highlanders!* (Stroud: Sutton Publishing, 2005).
17 Spiers, Edward M., *The Scottish Soldier and Empire, 1854-1902* (Edinburgh University Press, 2006); Spiers, Edward M, 'Scots and the Wars of Empire,' in Spiers, Edward M., Crang, Jeremy A. and Strickland, Mathew J., *A Military History of Scotland* (Edinburgh University Press, 2014).
18 Allan, Stuart & Carswell, Allan, *The Thin Red Line* (Edinburgh: NMSE Publishing, n.d. [c.2000]).
19 Seton, Sir Bruce & Grant, John, *The Pipes of War* (Glasgow: Robert Maclehose & Co., 1920).
20 Murray, David, *Music of the Scottish Regiments* (Edinburgh: Mercat Press, 2001).

Liberal access to such records inevitably risks exposing dirty washing, but I hope and believe that nothing I have written will damage regimental reputations, although these are in any case sufficiently secure to resist minor pin-pricks. It was my intention also to search the archives in Canada and South Africa, but in the end, time was against me, and I have had to leave this task for another day. Some original material on the soldiers of both countries is available in published form as well as some unpublished papers in the IWM and Liddle Collection. Fortunately, some of the relevant regimental histories are outstanding.

The material used has been of varied value. Contemporary letters and diaries are of most value, although some contemporary letters were clearly written with an eye on publication, while others might deliberately sanitise life at the front to avoid causing alarm at home. Eye-witness memoirs may well be influenced by the time at which they were written. The most reliable are likely to be those written either during the war or immediately after. From the 1930's there is a danger that memoirs reflect the evolving reappraisals of the war, rather than the thoughts of the writer during the war itself. The same risk is even truer of any account written since 1960, and of all recordings of interviews with veterans, all made since the 1960's, and all potentially influenced by later opinion. Many of these interviews took place between the 1970's and 1990's, with veterans who were frequently in their eighties or nineties. Sometimes their memory clearly fails them, or they retain idealised or romanticised impressions of their experiences. But often they speak with crystal clarity and directness, with a truthfulness that exposes modern prejudices. We owe a huge debt to the pioneers of recording, like Peter Liddle, without whom we would not have these valuable records.

1

Heroes of Empire

We are a little apt to magnify the deeds of our soldiers[1]

Introduction

On the eve of the Great War, kilted corps were found in both Britain and the Empire. Within Britain, the battalions were provided by the Regular Army, the Special Reserve and the Territorial Force. Within Canada they were provided by the kilted Canadian Militia regiments, and within South Africa, by two kilted regiments of the Active Citizen Force. In this first chapter we will examine each of these in turn. We will look at their two defining characteristics, the kilt and the pipes. We will then consider questions of identity, reputation, internal character and their relationship with society at home. The chapter will conclude with a look at the service of the Highland regiments in the years from 1899 to 1914, and at significant events which affected them during that time.

The British Army

Within the British Army, the old Regular, Militia and Volunteer battalions had, by 1908, if not in most cases much earlier, been brought together in a common regimental system, in which each regiment contained its own Regular, Special Reserve and Territorial Force (T.F.) battalions.

In 1914, there were five Regular kilted regiments in the British Army. These were:

The Black Watch
The Seaforth Highlanders
The Gordon Highlanders
The Queen's Own Cameron Highlanders
The Argyll and Sutherland Highlanders

---

1 *Glasgow Herald*, 9 May, 1899, quoted by Spiers, *The Scottish Soldier and Empire*, p.148.

The pre-War Regular Army overseas: Ration stand, 2nd Cameron Highlanders, Baird Barracks Bangalore (1909-1913). (From a contemporary postcard by The Picture House, Bangalaore, author's collection)

The pre-War Regular Army overseas: a soldier of 2nd Cameron Highlanders in Bangalore (1909-1913). (Author's collection)

Each regiment contained two regular battalions. In each regiment, as was usual, one of these battalions was on home service, while the other was on service abroad, garrisoning some distant part of Empire.

These two-battalion Highland regiments were in fact a fairly recent creation, having been created by amalgamations in 1881. Before that date there were just five single-battalion regiments of kilted Highlanders. These were the 42nd, 78th, 79th, 92nd and 93rd Regiments.

In 1881, in the Childers reforms, came the creation of the two-battalion system,[2] by which existing regiments were combined to form the 1st and 2nd battalions of new two-battalion regiments, to be known by name, not number. In these reforms, all the pre-reform kilted regiments survived intact,[3] each being amalgamated with a non-kilted regiment. Moreover, in every case the old non-kilted regiment was effectively absorbed as a battalion of the kilted regiment, even when it had been the more senior of the two. Exceptionally, the Camerons remained the only single battalion regiment in the British Army, until their second battalion was eventually raised in 1897. The result was to double the number of kilted battalions in the British Army virtually overnight from five to 10.

Table 1.1 Amalgamation of regiments 1881

Previous designation	New Designation
42nd (kilted)	1st Battalion The Black Watch
73rd (non-kilted	2nd Batttaliion The Black Watch
72nd (non-kilted)	1st Battalion Seaforth Highlanders
78th (kilted)	2nd Battalion Seaforth Highlanders
75th (non-kilted)	1st Battalion Gordon Highlanders
92nd (kilted)	2nd Battalion Gordon Highlanders
79th (kilted)	Cameron Highlanders (initially single battalion)
91st (non-kilted)	1st Battalion Argyll & Sutherland Highlanders
93rd (kilted)	2nd Battalion Argyll & Sutherland Highlanders

Astonishingly, this was done at a time when, even though there were just five kilted battalions, it was already proving impossible to fill their ranks with Highland recruits. The steady decline in the population of the Highlands in the nineteenth century meant that long before the 1881 reforms, the Highland regiments were having to recruit from areas outside the traditional Highland counties and beyond the Highland line[4], although of course some soldiers recruited from outside the Highlands might be second or third generation Highland emigrants.[5]

---

2 See Henderson, *Highland Soldier*, p.27.
3 On resistance to amalgamation of kilted regiments, see Newark, Tim, *Highlander, The History of the Legendary Highland Soldier* (London: Constable & Robinson, 2009), pp.155-157.
4 Henderson, *Highland Soldier*, p.15. Henderson defines the traditional Highland counties as Sutherland, Ross, most of Inverness, Cromarty and Argyll, including the Inner and outer Hebrides. These, together with further areas of Inverness, part of Moray, Banff, Aberdeen, Angus, Perth, Stirling and Dumbarton, fell within the Highland Line.
5 Ibid., p.18.

A second feature of the 1881 reforms, however, was to allocate new Regimental Districts to the reformed Highland regiments,[6] which were themselves to transform recruiting. Under the new system, the Seaforths, with their depot at Fort George, and the Camerons, with their depot at Inverness, both had recruiting districts which were almost exclusively Highland, although when the second battalion of Camerons was eventually raised in 1897, shortage of potential recruits required that the regiment was permitted to recruit from the whole of Scotland, not just its Highland district. By contrast, the recruiting districts of the other three regiments all straddled Highlands and Lowlands, with depots respectively at Aberdeen (Gordons), Stirling (Argylls) and Perth (Black Watch), none of which were strictly Highland. Their recruiting areas extended way outside the Highlands, bringing in more highly populated areas, including for example, Fife and Dundee for the Black Watch, and part of the Glasgow hinterland for the Argylls. In some ways this was fortunate, for there were now insufficient Highlanders left to fill the ranks of the regiments, and they became increasingly dependent on recruiting from the large urban centres.[7] In effect, by Ministerial decree, the kilted Highland regiments had become the unique representative regiments of north and north-central Scotland, embracing areas which were not strictly Highland. Thus, 1881 was a significant landmark, with implications not only for the regiments themselves but also for the cultural identity of the areas they came to represent. Of course, many Highlanders, including some Gaelic-speakers,[8] still remained in the Highland regiments, for the recruiting districts of the Seaforths, Camerons and Argylls still extended to surviving Gaelic-speaking areas, but by 1914, their overwhelming composition was Scottish, not specifically Highland.

By 1914, whatever their origins, socially the officers of the Regular Highland regiments had been largely absorbed into mainstream army culture.[9] Regular Highland officers on the outbreak of war generally came from a limited exclusive officer class, embracing military families, the gentry or the professional classes; the term 'professional' encompassing, for example, the law, publishing, the Indian Medical Service, and planting in Ceylon. The normal route to obtain a Regular commission was from a well-established public school, generally English, through Sandhurst, but it was also possible to obtain a Regular commission via service in the Special Reserve, as in the case of James Cunningham.[10]

Most were of Scottish descent, although some of these were born overseas in India and Ceylon. Some, like I.M. Stewart, in 2nd Argylls and Alexander Stewart, of 1st Gordons, although both born in India, were of old Highland families, in their case, the Stewarts of Athnacone, the senior cadet branch of the Stewarts of Appin.[11] Some officers who actually came

---

6   See ibid., pp.26-29. Note that in the case of the 93rd, this meant losing their traditional recruiting ground in Sutherland.
7   Spiers, 'Scots and the Wars of Empire.'
8   Henderson, *Highland Soldier*, p.36; Mackay Scobie, Maj I.H., *Pipes and Pipe Music in a Highland Regiment* (Dingwall: Ross-shire Printing & Publishing Co., c.1934), p.55.
9   Allan & Carswell, *The Thin Red Line*, p.99. See also Spiers, 'Scots and the Wars of Empire,' pp.460-461.
10   IWM 10909 Cunningham, loc. cit.
11   LC GS 1535 Stewart, Brig. I.M., Tape 359, interview with Liddle, 1976; LC GS 1534 Stewart, A.D.L., *Memoir of the Late Captain Alexander Dugald Lorn Stewart, M.C., The Gordon Highlanders, Younger of Achnacone*, compiled by his father Lt.-Col. Alex. K. Stewart of Achnacone.

from the Highlands were Gaelic speakers.[12] In other cases, the Highland connection might be more immediate but, in reality, more spurious. Thus, John and Alan Fowler,[13] of respectively 2nd Seaforths and 2nd Camerons, were the sons of a baronet who owned a Highland estate at Lochbroom. But the family was not Highland; their money was from engineering, the grandfather being the engineer who designed and constructed the London Underground Railway and the Forth Bridge. A few were from England.[14] In many cases a previous family attachment was important for choice of regiment (and possibly acceptance), as with Alexander Stewart and James Cunningham.[15] Promotion from the ranks, while not exceptional, was not frequent, a list of the officers of the Black Watch (both battalions) in 1891 revealing only three who were so promoted.[16]

Few junior officers in 1914 had actually seen action, although some in the Seaforths might have seen service in the Zakka Khan and Mohmand expeditions of 1908.[17] More senior officers had often seen service in the South African War and possibly on the North West Frontier or the Sudan.[18]

As regards the other ranks, in 1914, the regiments remained essentially Scottish, but, as we have seen, not exclusively Highland, with variations in their composition related to recruiting districts and the import of men from outside those districts, especially from southern Scotland. Thus, according to MacKay Scobie, on the outbreak of war, 1st Seaforths, then in India, were two-thirds Scots, including a fair number of men from Lewis.[19] Douglas Gillespie wrote, after visiting 1st Seaforths in 1915, "They tell me that 90 percent of them are real Highlanders from Stornoway and Ross-shire."[20] By contrast, Gillespie observed in March and June, 1915, that there were hardly any real Highlanders in his own battalion, 2nd Argylls, the men being mostly from Glasgow, Falkirk and thereabouts,[21] This observation is supported by H.J.D. Clark[22] and by Cavendish.[23] Wauchope claims that 1st Black Watch on mobilisation had 92 percent Scottish officers and men.[24]

Amongst the pre-War Regular soldiers serving in 1914 encountered in our research, some had come from their regimental districts.[25] Hugh Ross, however from Lairg in Sutherland,

---

12 Henderson, *Highland Soldier*, p.119-120.
13 *Captain Sir John Fowler, Bart, Captain Alan Fowler* (Dingwall: Ross-shire Journal, n.d.), pp.5-8; Fraser, Edith, *Records of the Men of Lochbroom who fell in the European War 1914-1918* (Glasgow: Robert Maclehose & Co., 1922, pp.13-14, 18-19.
14 GH PB242 Stansfield, Lt. Col. John R.E., extract from 'British Roll of Honour.'
15 See also Henderson, *Highland Soldier*, p.90.
16 Ibid., p.112.
17 *Lieut.-Colonel Robert Horn*, passim.
18 like Standish Crauford, CHM PB2093 Crauford, Sir George Standish, record of service.
19 Mackay-Scobie, *Pipers*, p.55.
20 Gillespie, *Letters from Flanders*, p.272, letter home, 12 August, 1915.
21 Ibid., p.44, letters home, 12 March, 6 June, 1915.
22 LC GS 0315 Clark, interview.
23 Cavendish, *An Reisimeid Chataich*, p.239.
24 Wauchope, *Black Watch*, Vol.1, p.3.
25 see: ASHM N-E2 Aiken, Sgt J, notes dated 18 December, 1914; ASHM N-E2 Macfarlane, Cpl F.A., 'A brief sketch of my experience in the British Army from 11/5/09 to 21/1/21.' apparently written 12 March, 1921; IWM Books Parke,'Memories of an 'Old Contemptible.' pp.9-24; THM Camerons 91-119, Documents relating to Pte Alexander Macleod/2Lt A.C. Macleod.

chose to enlist in the Regular Camerons at Inverness in 1900.[26] Others came from southern Scotland.[27] Alan Watts,[28] who joined the Camerons, exceptionally came from England, having been born in Sandhurst, but he was a soldier's son with three brothers in the regiment. Indeed, a significant number of pre-War Regulars came from military families.[29] Those with non-military backgrounds include a miner, the son of a trawler-master, a farmer's son, and a railway porter. Most would be regarded as working-class, but although there were no doubt some rough diamonds in the Army, any notion that the Regular Army was the last refuge of the unemployable does not hold water. Indeed, a trawler-master and a farmer might possibly aspire to middle-class status. It was boredom and a sense of adventure that induced nineteen-year-old farmer's son Andrew Anderson to enlist, not poverty or desperation.

One characteristic, perhaps not unconnected to the ready acceptance of under-age boys by recruiting sergeants during the war, was that enlisting young in the pre-War army appears to have been remarkably common. Harry Ditcham was just 14½ on enlistment, Alan Watts 15 and Charlie Parke just 16. Another characteristic was that a number of their men had seen service in the South African War.

The Special Reserve battalions provided the first reserve for the regular infantry. In the event of war, both officers and men were liable to be drafted to the Regular army. Each infantry regiment had a Special Reserve battalion attached to it as a 3rd Battalion, although in the case of the Argylls, there were two Special Reserve battalions, numbered 3rd and 4th, based respectively at Stirling and Paisley.

The Special Reserve battalions had been created from the Militia battalions in the Haldane reforms of 1908. The Militia had been reactivated after an invasion scare in 1852, and had remained in being since. In 1870. out of 16 regiments of Militia, four claimed association with the Highlands. In the Childers reforms of 1881, the Militia battalions became the reserve of the regular army and were each given a parent regiment, to which they were attached as the 3rd and/or 4th Battalion/s. The regular depot became also the Militia headquarters. In 1908, Haldane created the Special Reserve from them.[30]

Socially, the Special Reserve officers were drawn from a similar set to their regular counterparts, that is the gentry or the professional classes, although, unlike their regular counterparts, they had frequently attended university. "Militia officers represented society in uniform to an even greater extent than did Regular army officers," writes Wood.[31]

Scottish descent was usual but not exclusive. Some, like the Hon. A.A. Fraser,[32] 3rd Gordons, were of Scottish aristocratic descent. But, as in the Regulars, Highland ancestry might be somewhat spurious. Angus Macnaghten,[33] of 3rd Black Watch, for example, had all the attributes of

---

26 THM C78-87a, Notes on service details of the Ross family, donated by Miss U. Ross.
27 See: GHM PB1428 Spence, C.S.M. Robert, Account Book and Pocket Ledger; THM Camerons 89-44, Anderson, Brig. A., typescript memoir, 'A Well Trodden Path', pp.1-10.
28 THM Camerons 02-111 Notes on various Cameron Highlanders by Mr J.A. Leszczuk of Fife.
29 See: IWM 374 Recording Ditcham, Charles Harry, IWM interview, 1974; THM Camerons C502, 'The Fine History of the Fighting Guns', *Daily Sketch*, Mon., 11 Oct 1915.
30 Wood, *Scottish Soldier*, pp.62-64, 75, 78; Henderson, *Highland soldier*, p.31.
31 Wood, *Scottish Soldier*, pp.62-64.
32 GHM PB97 Fraser, 2Lt. A.A., 'Manuscript Account of the 1st Bn the Gordon Highlanders in the Le Cateau area August 1914.'
33 IWM 3696 Macnaghten, letters, passim.

a Highland gentleman. He was a landowner at Balquhidder in Perthshire, the grandson of the Chief of Clan Macnaghten, a member of the Highland Society of London and a Gaelic speaker. But this Highland background was illusory. His own branch of the Macnaghtens had settled in Ulster in the sixteenth century during the Plantation and had only been offered the chieftainship of Macnaghten after the surviving Scottish line became extinct, and after the disintegration of the clan system. His grandfather, Sir Francis, came, like his ancestors, from Dunderave in County Antrim, but had built his career in the law in India. Angus's father, Stuart, was born in India, followed his father into law, but became Deputy Lieutenant of Hampshire and Chairman of the Southampton Dock Company. Clearly Angus's attributes as a Highland gentleman were acquired rather than inherited.

Most of the ex-Regular Reservists in 1914 had honest respectable working-class jobs; postman, policeman, miner, driller, engine-fitter, school-janitor, for example. In age, they ranged from the late twenties to their forties, with most probably in their thirties.[34] A number had married and started families.[35] Many of these Reservists were living in the Lowlands, some of them having abandoned their Highland birthplace.[36] Unsurprisingly, a number of them had seen action.

We know less about the Special Reservists, but they were, like the Territorials, local to their Regimental areas. One such was Donald MacDonald, who was born on South Uist in 1892, the son of a crofter and fisherman. He had joined 3rd Camerons, but around the end of 1913 had gone to sea.[37] Some Special Reserve men came from non-Regimental areas. 34 Lewis men died serving with the Gordon Highlanders during the war. As Lewis was strictly speaking within the Seaforth recruiting area, this is surprising, but Charles Reid, a volunteer at the Gordons' Museum, has shown that, due to their own local recruiting difficulties, 3rd Gordons were given permission to recruit from Lewis in 1911 and 1912, when, it appears, most of these men were taken on.[38]

The Militia and Special Reserve undertook more training than the Volunteers and Territorials, and in the case of some officers, this could equip them with useful experience. Thus, Alec Wade joined the Militia as an officer in 1903, having served as a Volunteer in the Imperial Yeomanry during the South African War. When he began his service, he undertook six months training at the depot. He notes how much service a Militia officer could actually put in.

> Between the years 1903 and 1910 I had spent over three years at the depot. I had been attached to Regular line regiments for training when they were on summer and autumn manoeuvres. I had passed through the School of Musketry at Hythe, a long course, and the Gunnery School at Golden Hill, Isle of Wight. I had attended seven annual trainings of my own battalion, and, as Musketry Instructor, I always took the recruits to fire their course

---

34 Fraser, *Lochbroom*, p.35 (Roderick Maclean); Wilson, *Biographical List*, p.166 (Alexander Fraser).
35 GHM PB2586 Morrison, loc. cit.; THM Camerons 02-40 Johnston, CSM Thomas, background notes; ASHM N-E2 Todd, Capt H.B., manuscript memoirs (James Macintosh).
36 See: Fraser, *Lochbroom*, pp.8-9 (Norman Morrison).
37 LC Transcripts Tape 526, interview with Donald MacDonald.
38 GHM PB1046, Men from the Isle of Lewis, note by Charles Reid, 2009.

prior to the arrival of the Battalion for the annual training. I also attended three other battalion annual training camps, on Salisbury Plain, at Stensall, and at Richmond, Yorks.[39]

The men too did a month's training a year, but for many the principal motive was the extra money. Captain Russell comments on the composition of the 3rd Camerons in 1914.

At the commencement of the War the Third battalion consisted of about six hundred or so Special reservists, the bulk of them hailing from the Western Isles, Lewis, Harris, Skye and Barra. Most of these were Highland crofters, who joined principally for the five pound bounty then awarded to Special reservists, and their training was fitted in to the period in the Summer when work was slackest, usually the beginning of July. Many of these men could speak very little English, and Gaelic-speaking senior NCO's and officers were few and far between.[40]

One such man was Donald McKay from South Uist, who joined 3rd Camerons in 1909, "just to earn a little bit of money, and the pay at that time was 6 pence a day. Three shillings a week; that was our pay."[41]

In 1914, there were within the five Highland regiments, alongside the Regular battalions, a total of 17 battalions of the Territorial Force (T.F.), all volunteer soldiers, as follows:

4th to 7th Black Watch
4th to 6th Seaforth Highlanders
4th Cameron Highlanders
4th to 7th Gordon Highlanders
5th to 9th Argyll and Sutherland Highlanders

In addition, there were a number of kilted T.F. battalions outside the five principal Highland regiments. These are considered later.

The Territorial infantry battalions had been created in 1908, out of the pre-existing Volunteer Force. Their soldiers were part-time volunteers, who trained on drill-nights, weekends and at annual camp, and were liable for home defence only, not for overseas service. It was nevertheless possible for Territorial soldiers to volunteer their availability for overseas service in an emergency, and those who did so were entitled to wear an Imperial Service brooch.[42] The Volunteer movement was popular and widely supported in Scotland and became an important part of Scottish and Highland social life in the second half of the nineteenth century.[43]

---

39   Wade, Maj. A.G., *Counterspy* (London: Stanley Paul & Co., 1938), pp.99-101.
40   THM Camerons 97-22, Russell, S.C., of Aden, typescript memoir, p.179.
41   LC Transcripts Tape 526 McKay, D., interview with Liddle, 1978.
42   Westlake, Ray, *British Territorial Units 1914-1918*, (Oxford, Osprey Men-at-Arms 245, 1991); Spiers, *The Scottish Soldier and Empire*, pp.209-210.
43   On the popularity of Volunteering in Scotland, see Henderson, *Highland Soldier*, p.31; Spiers, *The Scottish Soldier and Empire*, p.114.

Most of the 17 T.F. battalions aligned to the five Highland regiments could trace their origins back to the early days of the volunteer movement in 1859 and immediately after.[44] But they had not always been either Highland battalions or kilted, having for the most part started life as independent corps of Rifle Volunteers. Their affiliation to the Highland regiments essentially came only after 1881, when in principle the volunteer battalions were attached to the regular regiments in whose Regimental Districts they lay, although the process was not completed until 1908. In some cases this affiliation meant a complete transformation in character from Lowland to Highland. Thus, all the volunteer rifle battalions in the largely or entirely Lowland areas of Dundee, Angus, Fife, Renfrew, Stirlingshire, Dunbartonshire, Clackmannan and Kinross were turned into Highland battalions at a stroke, when these areas were allocated to the Black Watch and Argylls. In this way, many T.F. Highland battalions had now been established in Lowland counties and recruited wholly or largely from Lowlanders. The 7th Black Watch for example were recruited from Fife, entirely outside the Highlands, and were in fact the successors of the 1st Fifeshire Rifles.[45] By contrast, in some cases the T.F. battalions' recruiting areas were almost exclusively Highland, notably in the case of the 4th Camerons (Inverness-shire), 4th Seaforths (Ross-shire), 5th Seaforths (Caithness and Sutherland), and 8th Argylls (Argyllshire) and the effect was to create Territorial battalions which were probably more effectively Highland in composition than any Regular battalions had been for a century.

Indeed, a fundamental characteristic of the Territorial battalions was their territorial organisation. In the Seaforths, for example, the men were recruited on a territorial basis as follows:[46]

Battalion	Headquarters	Recruiting area
4th	Dingwall	Highland-Ross-shire
5th	Golspie	Sutherland and Caithness
6th	Elgin	Morayshire

Within the battalions, companies would also be recruited on a regional basis. In 4th Seaforths, for example, which recruited in Ross-shire, with its headquarters at Dingwall, companies were distributed as follows:[47]

A Company	Tain
B "	Dingwall
C "	Munlochy
D "	Gairloch
E "	Ullapool
F "	Invergordon

---

44 Grierson, Maj. Gen. J.M., *Records of the Scottish Volunteer Force 1859-1908*, (Uckfield: NMP reprint, 2004), passim. For some useful additional comment on the Volunteers, see Allan & Carswell, *The Thin Red Line*, pp.34-35, 106-107; Wood, *Scottish Soldier*, pp.64-65; Henderson, *Highland Soldier*, p.31.
45 Grierson, *Records*, p.254, Plate XXVII; Wauchope, Maj Gen A,G,. *A History of the Black Watch (Royal Highlanders) in the Great War, 1914-1918* (London: Medici Society, 3 vols, 1925-1926), Vol.2, pp.239, 244.
46 Fairrie, *Queen's Own Highlanders*, pp.97-103.
47 Haldane, Lt-Col M.M., *History of the Fourth Battalion The Seaforth Highlanders* (London: H.F.&G. Witherby, 1927), p.36.

G " Alness
H " Maryburgh

Such territorial organisation even extended below company level. Thus, for example, in 6th Gordons, Glenbuchat, Corgarff and Strathdon together formed the Strathdon section of F Company, centred on Alford.[48]

Alongside the 17 T.F. battalions which formed in 1914 part of the five principal Highland regiments, there were five kilted T.F. battalions with no such allegiance. These were:

9th Royal Scots (Highlanders), the "Dandy Ninth"
6th Highland Light Infantry
9th Highland Light Infantry (Glasgow Highlanders)
The London Scottish
The Liverpool Scottish

These battalions had rather different origins. Two of them were early creations; the London Scottish and the Glasgow Highlanders. The London Scottish[49] was raised in 1859, under the impetus of the expatriate Scottish community in London, the principal drivers being Lord Elcho, the Highland Society of London and the Caledonian Society. In 1908, they became the 14th Battalion, County of London Regiment (London Scottish). Recruitment was confined to Scotsmen resident in the metropolis, with initially an entrance fee and annual subscription. Although the entrance fee was subsequently abolished, the unit remained socially elite, with a large proportion of professional, public school and university men in the ranks. Officers were appointed only from the ranks. Initially, the unit was very much a rifle corps, with six companies, all clad in Hodden Grey, only one of which was kilted, which wore the unique London Scottish kilt of the same colour. However, with the active backing of Sir Hope Grant, the Honorary Colonel at the time, the entire corps was clad in the kilt by 1872; an astonishing and rapid transformation.

The Glasgow Highlanders[50] were raised in 1868, with the support of the Celtic Society, as a result of the desire of Highlanders who had settled in Glasgow to raise a specifically Highland volunteer unit. The unit was named the 105th Lanarkshire (Glasgow Highland) Rifle Volunteers. In order to avoid identification with any particular "clan", and partly because some of the movers and shakers came from Aberfeldy, in Black Watch country, the Black Watch tartan was selected, along with a suitable Gaelic motto; "Clanna nan Gaidheal ri guelibh a cheile" ("Highlanders, shoulder to shoulder.") In 1908 the battalion became the 9th Battalion, Highland Light Infantry (H.L.I.), within the Territorial Force. Despite the fact that the battalion was affiliated to the H.L.I., who since 1881, wore trews of Mackenzie tartan, the Black Watch tartan was retained. At its inception, at least, the battalion was of genuine Highland character. It had

---

48 GHM. PB2984, Strachan, Albert, memoir written in 1976.
49 Grierson, *Records*, pp.336-341; Lindsay, Lt. Col. J.H., *The London Scottish in the Great War* (London: RHQ London Scottish, 1926), pp.1-15; Lloyd, *London Scottish*, pp.9-24.
50 Grierson, *Records*, pp.272-274, 234-235; IWM Books Reid, Col. A.K., 'Shoulder to Shoulder, The Glasgow Highlanders 9th Bn Highland Light Infantry 1914-1918', unpublished typescript, 1988, edited by Alex Aiken, Preface 1 and 2; Weir, *Come on Highlanders!* pp.1-29.

The pre-War Territorial Force: Liverpool Scottish at camp, Caerwys, 1909. (Author's collection)

companies with specific Highland origins, 'F' Company being drawn from natives of Islay, and 'G' Company from natives of Argyllshire. There were too a fair number of Gaelic speakers in the battalion, and some at least of this character was retained.[51]

The South African War was the spur for the raising of two additional kilted units; the Liverpool Scottish and the 9th Royal Scots. The Liverpool Scottish were raised in 1900, on the initiative of Mr G. Forbes Milne, and with the support of leading local businessmen and the Scottish community, the Battalion to be called the 8th (Scottish) Volunteer Battalion, The King's Liverpool Regiment. From the start the unit was tilted towards the middle-classes, for in addition to the annual subscription of ten shillings, each man on joining had to pay an entrance fee of two pounds. Later the entrance fee was reduced to ten shillings, but each man paid a clothing subscription of one pound. In 1901, Highland dress was officially sanctioned for the battalion and the Forbes tartan was chosen. In 1908, the Liverpool Scottish were re designated the 10th (Scottish) Battalion The King's (Liverpool) Regt.[52]

While the Liverpool Scottish were forming, a similar movement was taking place during the South African War to raise a Highland corps in Edinburgh[53]. The new battalion was designated the Highland Battalion, Queen's Rifle Volunteer Brigade, Royal Scots. The battalion wore kilts of the regimental tartan, Hunting Stewart. In 1908, its name was changed simply to the 9th

---

51 IWM Books, Reid, 'Shoulder to Shoulder', Preface.
52 Grierson, *Records*, p.200, McGilchrist, A.M., *The Liverpool Scottish 1900-1919* (Liverpool: Henry Young & Sons, 1930), pp.3–9, Giblin, *Bravest of Hearts*, pp.1-5.
53 Grierson, *Records*, pp.177-181, 198-199; Royal Scots RHQ, *9th Battalion (Highlanders) the Royal Scots (The Royal Regiment)* (Edinburgh: RHQ Royal Scots, 1925), pp.1-2.

Battalion (Highlanders) The Royal Scots, but, owing to its distinctive dress, it enjoyed the nickname "the Dandy Ninth."

The last of the exceptional kilted Territorial battalions was the 6th Battalion H.L.I.[54] This battalion had been raised in 1860 as the 6th Battalion Lanarkshire Rifle Volunteers. It had not been formed as a kilted battalion and in fact its members did not wear tartan at all until 1906, when, unlike their regular counterparts, who wore tartan trews, they adopted the kilt, joining the Glasgow Highlanders as the second kilted battalion of the H.L.I. The battalion's title was changed to the 6th Battalion H.L.I. on formation of the Territorial Force in 1908.

Officers commanding Territorial battalions in 1914 were like their regular counterparts generally drawn from the upper echelons of society. Some might have a purely Volunteer background, like Sir Alexander Leith-Buchanan, commanding 9th Argylls since 1911,[55] One at least, David Mason-Macfarlane, commanding 4th Seaforth Highlanders since 1913, was acting as virtually a full-time officer.[56] Others were former Regular officers, who were also members of the local Highland gentry, like John Campbell of Kilberry, commanding 8th Argylls since 1912.[57] Yet another was a retired Indian officer; Hugh Allen, who in 1913 took command of 7th Black Watch.[58] Of the regimental officers, the great majority encountered in the study were from professional and other middle-class backgrounds, although, unlike their Regular counterparts, they were not dominated by the major English public schools, and some had attended university. With the inclusion of, for example, a distillery manager from Islay[59] and a partner in a firm of tanners from Paisley,[60] the middle-class element was more inclusive than in the Regulars. There were also some ex-Regular soldiers who had made their way up through the ranks.[61] Such men might bring with them some experience of active service. As one might expect, the great majority of Territorial officers were born, or living, in their Territorial districts. In the case of the Territorial battalions from Highland districts proper, they might include members of distinguished old Highland families, like the brothers Ian and William Mackay, both members of 4th Camerons, descended from the Mackays of Achmonie in Glenurquhart.[62]

It was customary for Territorial battalions to have Regular officers attached as adjutants. The appointment was not universally popular amongst the Regular officers concerned, an attitude based at least partly on professionalism.[63]

Territorial soldiers[64] were of course recruited specifically from their regimental districts, although, even before the War, 6th Black Watch, strangely, had detachments in Belfast and

---

54 Grierson, *Records*, pp.262-264.
55 *Roll of Officers Dunbartonshire*, pp.23, 76.
56 Butler, Ewan, *Mason-Mac, The Life of Lieutenant-General Sir Noel Mason-Macfarlane* (London: Macmillan, 1972) pp.1-14.
57 Malcolm, *Argyllshire Highlanders*, pp.15, 27.
58 IWM 114 PP Allen, Lt Col H.H., introductory notes, and letters to wife, 22 April, 1915, 2 July, 1916.
59 LC DF 148 Campbell, Dr A.M., manuscript memoir.
60 Maclean, *On Active Service*, Vol.2, pp.104-105.
61 GHM PB179 Marr, Joseph, record of service and miscellaneous documents.
62 THM Camerons 94-8 Typescript, ed. By Donald Mackay, 'Tell Them of Us; Ian and William Mackay, 4th Bn QOCH, letters from the trenches 1914-1918', biographical notes; THM Camerons 91-7, background information on Maj Ian Mackay.
63 BWA Gordon, Brig. Gen. C.W.E., letters home 14, 18-19 June, 1915.
64 This analysis is largely based on details of 23 pre-War Territorial soldiers encountered in the sources.

Dublin, which joined the battalion on mobilisation.[65] The Liverpool and London Scottish, both recruiting locally in England, imposed rules requiring Scottish descent, although grandparents' rights would of course allow in recruits who were only a quarter Scottish.

Socially they were of varied background. Outside the London Scottish, the only representative of the higher orders in our sample was Robert Johnston, whose father was an officer in the Royal Scots, and who joined the 'Dandy Ninth' as a drummer boy before his fifteenth birthday.[66] The rest of our sample came from varied working-class and lower middle-class backgrounds; blacksmith, ploughman, tailor, photo technician, apprentice tenter, and workmen in the biscuit or timber trades. It is true that on balance Territorials were generally of higher social status than their regular counterparts, but there were significant variations in social composition between the different kilted battalions. Thus, for example, as originally constituted in 1914, 7th Black Watch, reflecting its recruiting area, contained 60 percent Fife miners, and contributed a large number of volunteers to support the Royal Engineers tunnellers in 1915.[67] Other battalions with a high proportion of miners were 5th Black Watch[68] and 7th Argylls.[69] By contrast, the London Scottish, with a banker, stockbroker and tailor amongst our three source examples, was essentially a middle-class regiment. almost certainly the most socially elevated of the Territorial kilted battalions.[70] The London Scottish were not, however, unique in their elevated social status.[71] Similar claims were made for the Glasgow Highlanders[72] and the 'Dandy Ninth,'[73] while the famous 'U' Company of 4th Gordons, was formed exclusively of students from Aberdeen University.[74] These units grouped together in the ranks a large number of men who were potential officer material.

As in the Regulars, there was a tendency to join the Territorials at a tender age. Robert Johnston joined aged 14, while four others in our small sample joined aged 16, again shedding light on the ready acceptance of under-age recruits during the Great War. Ex-Regular N.C.O's were welcome for the experience they brought, none more so than Donald Farmer, V.C., who had won his Victoria Cross in South Africa with the Camerons, and disembarked at Boulogne as R.S.M. of 1st Liverpool Scottish in November, 1914.[75]

Finally we should note that, if Territorial Scottish miners provided useful tunnellers, another specifically Highland occupation, that of ghillie, provided an excellent source of snipers in the true Highland battalions.[76]

The Territorials' commitment to training was less than the Special Reserve, and although some officers and men took their duties very seriously, there must be a question about their

---

65   Wauchope, *Black Watch*, Vol.2, p.126.
66   LC Transcripts etc Johnston, loc. cit.
67   Wauchope, *Black Watch*, Vol.2, pp.242, 255.
68   Ibid., Vol.2, p.48.
69   Walker, Tom, *Tom Walker Remembers* (privately published, n.d., c.1981), p.5.
70   See, for example. IWM 6702 Low, letter to wife Noanie, 18 June, 1915.
71   IWM 10529 Stanford, memoir, p.20.
72   IWM 3460 Macmillan, diary preface.
73   LC Transcripts etc Johnston, memoir. See also, IWM 13586 Johnston, interview.
74   Fraser, *Doctor Jimmy*, pp.vii-viii, 5-7, 38-48; Rule, *Students*, pp.2-3.
75   THM Camerons 91-62 Farmer, autobiography.
76   ASHM N-E8 Munro, narrative of life in trenches, compiled late June, 1915; Sutherland, Capt. D., *War Diary of the Fifth Seaforth Highlanders* (London: John Lane, 1920), p.62.

overall readiness for battle. Colonel David Mason-MacFarlane, who was personally convinced that war was coming, was appointed to command 4th Seaforths in February, 1913. He found his battalion unready, realising that

> officers, N.C.O.s and men were physically and mentally as good as had ever been seen in uniform, but that with a few exceptions, had not learnt the rudiments of their job. The Battalion depended almost entirely upon the eight regular Colour-Sergeant Instructors, one of whom was attached to each company.[77]

Although patriotic feelings were important, many young men joined the Territorials as much for the social life as for the soldiering. James Rodger joined 6th Black Watch at Auchterarder in December, 1908, aged just 16. To a large extent, he joined for the social side, "for the fun of the thing," "a kind of club, you might call it." Compulsory training only started in the Spring, with a drill evening every Wednesday. One had to do drill and one compulsory shoot a year on the range. Annual camps lasted a fortnight, and one had to put in one week unless one's employer refused.[78] Similarly, Albert Strachan joined 6th Gordons before the War. "It would be nice to say we joined to protect our country, but I am afraid that would just not be true. We joined to have a friendly time with our mates at drills in Spring and a week annually at camp."[79]

Kilted regiments of the Empire

The formation of Scottish units within the Empire is a fascinating phenomenon.[80] Both Canada and South Africa deployed kilted troops in the First World War, and we will concentrate on the regiments in these two countries.

In 1914, Canada had a very small regular army, officially known as the Permanent Force of the Active Militia of Canada. The force contained just one regiment, the Royal Canadian Regiment, organised in 1883, and no Highland battalions. Alongside this regular force was the Volunteer Militia, or more correctly, the Non-Permanent Active Militia. This was, by contrast, a large force, consisting of about 75,000 men with about 110 single-battalion infantry regiments.[81] Of these Militia regiments, in 1914 eight were kilted. Of these eight regiments, only three existed as kilted regiments before 1900. These were the 78th Pictou Highlanders, 94th Victoria Regiment, Argyll Highlanders and the 48th Highlanders of Canada. Two of these, the 78th and the 94th, had not been Highlanders on formation, and had only been re-designated as

---

77 IWM 12311 PP Mason-MacFarlane, Lt. Gen. Sir Noel, typescript account by his father, Col David Mason-MacFarlane.
78 IWM 373 Recording Rodger, James Grant, IWM Interview, 1975.
79 GHM PB2984 Strachan, Albert, diary. See also: IWM 495 Recording Pratt, James Davidson, IWM interview, 1974; IWM 15345 PP Fleming, Rev. J.G.G., typescript memoir, 'World War 1 and other Army Memories', pp.2-3.
80 For a general discussion, see Ugolini, Wendy, 'Scottish Commonwealth Regiments,' in Spiers, Crang & Strickland, *Military History*, pp.485-505, p.485. Newark, *Highlander*, pp.192-196, has a brief consideration of the Canadians.
81 Chartrand, Rene, *The Canadian Corps in World War 1* (Oxford: Osprey Men-at-Arms 439, 2007), pp.3-5.

Highlanders in 1879. By contrast the other battalion, the 48th, had been raised specifically as a Highland regiment in 1891.[82]

The period between the South African War and 1914 saw the creation of five new kilted regiments. One of these was a conversion. In 1904, the long established Royal Scots of Canada became affiliated with the Black Watch and adopted the kilt, changing its title to the Royal Highlanders of Canada in 1906.[83] The four completely new creations, by contrast, were the 91st Canadian Highlanders[84], formed in Hamilton in 1903, the 72nd Seaforth Highlanders of Canada[85], formed in Vancouver in 1910, the 79th Cameron Highlanders of Canada[86], formed in Winnipeg in 1910, and the 50th Gordon Highlanders[87], formed in Victoria, British Columbia, in 1913. This was an astonishing burst of enthusiasm, which continued the process begun with the raising of the 48th in 1891, each successful establishment encouraging others. It does seem that the South African War acted as a catalyst to the creation of these regiments. The war demonstrated an enthusiasm for volunteering, and encouraged a pride in Empire and its common defence; Canada had supplied many volunteers, including a detachment from the 48th Highlanders. Imperial enthusiasm was demonstrated by the donation of colours to both the 91st Canadian Highlanders and the 72nd Seaforths by the Ladies of the Imperial Order of the Daughters of the Empire. Common to the raising of all these regiments was the initial participation of the local societies of expatriate Scots; the Gaelic Societies, the Sons of Scotland, St Andrew's and Caledonian Societies. Common also was the desire for the regiment to be kilted and Highland, even when the original Scottish settlers in an area came, for example, from Selkirk. In selecting tradition, evidently self-image outweighed historical truth. Indeed, the trappings of tradition had to be instantly created. Tartans had to be chosen, and the selection was rather arbitrary. In the 48th, the Davidson tartan was chosen, in honour of its first commander; in the 79th, the choice of Cameron title and tartan was made simply in appreciation of the enthusiastic way in which Mr D.C. Cameron, President of the St Andrews Society, was supporting the project. Ancient sounding Gaelic mottos were devised; "Dileas Gu Brath" ("Faithful Forever") for the 48th, "Buaidh No Bas" ("Victory or Death") for the 50th. Badges were designed, the 50th, who had adopted the title Gordon Highlanders, incorporating a version of the Gordons' stag in the cap badge. Pipe bands were created and regimental marches were chosen; "Hielan' Laddie" for the 48th. Regimental numbers were deliberately

---

82 Beattie, Kim, *48th Highlanders of Canada 1891-1928* (Toronto: 48th Highlanders of Canada, 1932), pp.1-16; Beal, George W., *Family of Volunteers*, (Toronto: Robin Brass Studio, Toronto, 2001), pp.9-18, 36-42, 136-138.

83 Anon, *The Royal Highlanders of Canada, allied with the Black Watch (Royal Highlanders)*, (Montreal, London: Hugh Rees Ltd, 1918), pp.6-10; Wauchope, *Black Watch*, Vol.2, p.349.

84 Bruce, Lt. Col. Walter H., Turnbull, Lt. Col. William R. & Chisholm, Lt. Col. James, *Historical Records of the Argyll and Sutherland Highlanders of Canada etc., 1903-1928*, (Hamilton, Ontario: Robert Duncan & Co., 1928), pp 7-31.

85 McEvoy, Bernard & Finlay, Capt A.H., *History of the 72nd Canadian Infantry Battalion, Seaforth Highlanders of Canada*, (Vancouver: Cowan & Brookhouse, 1920), pp.1-9.

86 Craig-Brown, Brig Gen E, ed., *Historical Records of the Queen's Own Cameron Highlanders*, Vol.4, (Edinburgh: William Blackwood & Sons, 1931), pp.1-7.

87 GHM PB1506 Beaton, Capt D.B., 'A Concise History of the 50th Regiment (Gordon Highlanders of Canada),' one page extract from *The Falcon* magazine, date not stated (received 1995); Urquhart, Lt Col H.M., *The History of the 16th Battalion (The Canadian Scottish) Canadian Expeditionary Force in the Great War, 1914-1919* (Toronto: Macmillan, 1932), p.362.

The pre-War Canadians: 72nd Canadian Militia regiment (Seaforth Highlanders of Canada) on parade c.1912. (from a contemporary postcard, publisher unknown, Author's collection)

chosen to reflect the old numbers of the Highland regiments in Scotland; thus 72nd for the Seaforths, 79th for the Camerons. Scottish sentiment was assiduously cultivated. In the 91st, for example, Hogmanay was regularly celebrated while Scottish dancing was fostered by classes for the officers.[88]

Affiliation to the home regiments was eagerly sought, and perhaps surprisingly, for untested upstart units, was readily granted. Thus the 48th obtained an alliance with the Gordon Highlanders; the 72nd were affiliated with the Seaforths; the 79th with the Camerons; the 91st with the Argyll and Sutherland Highlanders; and, as we have seen, the 5th Regiment changed their affiliation to the Black Watch in 1904. Detachments even trained for short periods with their British Army counterparts. Presents were exchanged. The Argylls presented the Canadian 91st with a silver tup's head snuff mull, while the 91st returned the compliment with a moose head. The new Canadian regiments were keen to be taken seriously. The 48th provided a contingent for the coronation of King Edward VII in 1902, while the 79th were represented at the coronation of King George V in 1911. In 1897, a team went overseas to represent the 48th at the Islington Military Tournament. Great public interest was aroused by the victory of the bayonet fighters of the 48th over a team of Guards; "the outstanding event in years of militia activity in Canada."

With regard to nationality, Captain Leckie, commanding the 72nd Seaforth Highlanders of Canada in 1911, commented;

---

88   Bruce, Turnbull & Chisholm, *Historical Records*, pp.30-31.

> In selecting the officers, my first consideration was efficiency … Nationality came next in consideration, and as this is a Canadian regiment, my first choice in this particular would lie with Canadians of Scotch descent, after which, of course, would come Scotsmen born in the Old Country … Of those already selected, twenty are Scottish Canadians, or Scottish by name. Five Canadians of Irish parentage but partly Scotch, four English, three of whom I believe are partly Scotch. So you see we have an overwhelmingly strong representation of Scottish blood among the officers, more so, I think, than any Scottish regiment in the Imperial service … With respect to the non-commissioned officers and men we have had to take pretty much what we could get in the way of recruits, having regard to a high standard of physique. Here also, however, Scotsmen greatly preponderate in numbers, as may be seen from the regimental rolls.[89]

While, as we shall see, there may have been a tendency to exaggerate the Scottish-ness of some Canadian Militia regiments, this was in some cases manifestly not the case. It is probably justifiably claimed that the 94th Regiment, recruited in Nova Scotia, "was at the commencement of hostilities perhaps the most distinctively Highland Battalion in the forces of the Empire, inasmuch as the Gaelic language was the mother tongue of eighty per cent of its personnel."[90] When in autumn, 1913, Cameron of Lochiel visited Winnipeg, and inspected the 79th Cameron Highlanders of Canada, he said prophetically: "Our young blood is all leaving the old land and coming out to the new country. I see them here … this means that in the event of the necessity arising for recruiting up to war strength we might have to draw upon you, 'the 5th Battalion.'"[91]

By 1914 the Canadian Highland Militia regiments were keen but untested. The 48th provided a small detachment to the Canadian contingent in the South African War, and the regiment was also called out to provide aid to the civil power on the occasion of the Toronto Railway Company strike (1902) and the Sault Saint Marie riots (1903).

In South Africa, the enthusiasm for Scottish volunteering in the late nineteenth and early twentieth Centuries gave rise to two kilted infantry regiments; the Cape Town Highlanders[92], formed as early as 1885, and the Transvaal Scottish[93], formed considerably later in 1902.[94] The Transvaal Scottish regiment was raised under the Volunteer Ordinance of 1902 which allowed for the creation of volunteer regiments at the conclusion of the Boer War. This movement, and the creation of a specifically Scottish regiment, was promoted by, amongst others, a group of influential Scots including most notably the Marquis of Tullibardine, who had commanded the Scottish Horse during the war.

In both cases the local Scottish community and Caledonian societies played a significant role in promoting and supporting the regiments from their inception. In the Transvaal Scottish at

---

89 McEvoy & Finlay, *Seaforth Highlanders of Canada*, pp.4-5.
90 Hunt, Capt M. Stuart, *Nova Scotia's Part in the Great War* (Uckfield, NMP reprint, no date) (first published c.1920), p.263.
91 Craig-Brown, *Historical Records*, Vol.4, p.7.
92 Orpen, Neil, *The Cape Town Highlanders 1885-1970* (Cape Town: The Cape Town Highlanders History Committee, 1970), pp.1-72.
93 Juta, H.C., *The History of the Transvaal Scottish*, (Johannesburg: Hortors Ltd, 1933), pp.1-74.
94 There were a number of other apparently Scottish companies formed in different units, but none appear to have survived beyond 1913. For a brief consideration of the South Africans, see Newark, *Highlander*, pp.184-189.

least, a degree of exclusivity was practised, it being customary initially to insist upon a recruit producing a recommendation from one of the Caledonian Society branches. Likewise, both regiments were to be not only Scottish but kilted Highlanders, and soon adopted the full panoply of traditional Highland regalia. It was felt that the lure of the kilt was a great help to recruiting. Where traditions did not exist, they had to be invented or imported. The Cape Town Highlanders adopted the tartan of the Gordons, though the reason why is not stated in their history; the Transvaal Scottish chose the Atholl Murray tartan, given the support provided by the Marquis of Tullibardine. The Transvaal Scottish also chose to have a suitably ambiguous Gaelic motto, 'Alba nam Buadh.' Finally, in 1887, Sir Donald Currie presented the Cape Town Highlanders with a splendid mascot; a stag, which was called Donald!

Highlights of the regiments' service before the Great War included providing contingents for the coronations of King Edward VII in 1902 (CTH only) and King George V in 1911 (both regiments). In 1913, in a rationalisation of defence forces, somewhat akin to the Territorial Force reforms of 1908 in Great Britain, both regiments became part of the Active Citizen Force of the Union of South Africa under the terms of the Defence Act of 1912. Importantly, for the forthcoming conflagration, this force was only permitted to serve in southern Africa.

The kilt

The Highland regiments had two blatantly distinctive characteristics; the kilt and the pipes, and we will deal with both in turn. What was truly astonishing was the rise to dominance of the kilt from the middle of the nineteenth century right up to 1914. The kilt, of course, and the great plaid before it, had been the traditional dress of the Highlanders. Effectively extinguished as everyday wear by ordinary Highlanders after Culloden, it had remained in use in the British Army, as the government tapped into Highland manpower, both to divert the Highlanders from revolt and to use them to support the wars of empire. By 1815, the Highland regiments had, through their exploits in Egypt, the Peninsula and Waterloo, as well as in earlier campaigns, moved 'from threat to pet.' However, the Highland Clearances, in which the ordinary Highland people were betrayed by their clan chiefs to make way for sheep, were gradually denuding the land of people and therefore recruits. This process had started with the destruction of the 'clan system' after Culloden and continued through the nineteenth century. By the middle of that century, as we have seen, there were not even sufficient Highlanders to fill the ranks of the five surviving kilted regiments.

In those circumstances, it might reasonably be thought that, either the Highland regiments would be done away with, as representing a past era, or the number of battalions would be reduced to fit the number of recruits available from the Highlands themselves. Instead, as we have seen, in the Childers reforms of 1881, quite extraordinarily, the number of kilted battalions was doubled, from five ultimately to ten. The process of 'tartanisation' in 1881, by which the Lowland regiments were stuffed into tartan trews has long been recognised as part of the creation of the image of Scotland.[95] What has received less attention[96] is the parallel triumph of

---

95 e.g. Wood, *Scottish Soldier*, p.76; Carswell, Allan, 'Scottish Military Dress,' in Spiers, Crang & Strickland, *Military History*, pp.627-647, p.641.
96 except perhaps by Allan & Carswell, *The Thin Red Line*, p.33, and Carswell, Allan, 'Scottish Military Dress,' in Spiers, Crang & Strickland, *Military History*, pp.627-647, p.640

the kilt, in a process we may describe as 'kiltification.' The Childers reforms were a significant landmark in the cultural history of Scotland, with strong implications for identity. Moreover, as we have seen, by the extension of the Regimental districts into the Lowlands, the process also affected the Volunteers, as the associated battalions were transformed between 1881 and 1914 from Lowland Volunteer riflemen, clad originally in subdued grey or rifle-green rifle uniforms into kilted clones of the Highland regiments to which they were now attached as Territorial battalions.[97]

While this process continued, we also see the establishment of specifically kilted Volunteer battalions within the Lowland regiments, which occurred as we have seen, in the formation of 9th Royal Scots ('the Dandy Ninth'), 9th H.L.I. (the Glasgow Highlanders) and 6th H.L.I. There were no parallel trousered battalions formed within the kilted regiments. Moreover, when Scottish units were formed in England and overseas, they all ultimately chose to wear the kilt,[98] even if this process was sometimes convoluted, and even when the original Scottish settlers in an area came, for example, from Selkirk! Traditions were invented to order. Thus in 1901, in the Liverpool Scottish, according to the regimental history, the Forbes tartan was chosen as a compliment to the first Commanding Officer, C. Forbes Bell. In fact, Forbes was only one of his Christian names, and it appears that his own first choice of tartan was Lamont. When it was pointed out to him that the only tartan available in the required quantity in the time available was Forbes, he acquiesced.[99] Thus the choice of tartan was quite providential, arguably spurious, just as only a proportion of those Scots who joined could claim Highland origin in the first place. But reality would not be allowed to interfere with self-image. In Canada and South Africa, the trappings of tradition had to be instantly created, and we have already seen the splendidly arbitrary way in which tartans were selected.[100]

Many of these kilted units, both at home and overseas, were formed during or after the South African War, the last, the 50th Gordon Highlanders of Canada, being formed only in 1913, demonstrating that the process of 'kiltification' was still in full swing on the eve of the war. Yet at the same time, the practicality of the kilt was coming into question. In 1902, when khaki was adopted as the official service dress for the army, there was a rumour that the government was considering abolishing the kilt and clothing all Highland regiments in standard British Army uniform. When the Highland Society of London heard rumours of this, they began an active campaign to oppose it. The Secretary of State for War was visited by the President of the Society and several clan chiefs. The 'Glasgow Evening News' fulminated, "We are not yet prepared to sacrifice the one sartorial feature which has, for a century and a half, made Scots regiments different." Questions were asked in the House of Commons. Was this being done by the War Office in revenge for Bannockburn? When the Secretary of State replied that "Of course the distinctive tartans of the Highland regiments will be preserved," there were loud cheers from the House.[101] It was a foretaste of arguments to come.

---

97 5th Seaforths stubbornly retained their Sutherland tartan. This analysis is based on information extracted from Grierson, *Records*, passim.
98 Ugolini comments on this phenomenon, op.cit., pp.489-490.
99 McGilchrist, *Liverpool Scottish*, pp.3-9.
100 Beattie, *48th Highlanders*, pp.1-16; Craig-Brown, *Historical Records*, Vol.4, pp.1-7; Juta, *Transvaal Scottish*, pp.1-74.
101 Newark, *Highlander*, pp.176-177; Lloyd, *London Scottish*, p.21; Henderson, *Highland Soldier*, p.139, n.6.

The Pipes

In 1914, the bagpipes were fundamental to the life of a Highland regiment.[102] They were by no means unique to the Highland regiments, playing an important part too in the lives of their Lowland counterparts[103], but it is the former which concern us, and here they permeated every aspect of life. It had not always been so. Although strongly associated with Highland regiments, they did not come to dominate Highland regimental music until the latter part of the nineteenth century. They had always been present, encouraged by the regiment, but only tolerated by the authorities. Only after 1854, when an official establishment was created in Highland regiments for a pipe major and five pipers, did the pipes come to dominate, as pipe bands, combining pipers with drummers, were established, and grew in importance. By the early twentieth century, the process was complete, and Highland battalions were consolidating their pipes and drums in massed displays.

As the role of the pipes evolved, so did their music. Initially the pipers had played traditional pipe music, which consisted of Ceol Mor, or Piobaireachd, and Ceol Beag, or light music, which included strathspeys, jigs and reels. With the combination of pipes and drums, marching tunes were added to the repertoire, regimental marches being formally sanctioned in 1881. Thus the Black Watch, Gordons and 2nd Argylls would march past to 'Highland Laddie,' the Seaforths and Camerons to 'The Pibroch o' Donuil Dubh,' and 1st Argylls to 'The Town of Inverary' ('The Campbells are coming!').[104] Marches might be formalised down to company level.[105]

By 1914, the pipes were integral to the life of a Highland regiment. "Day in, day out, from morning to night, the soldier is dependent on the piper."[106] They controlled the daily routine of the regiment with duty pipe calls, for example at reveille, meal-times and 'lights-out.' They entertained the officers at formal mess dinners. They were used on the march, for parades and inspections, for beating Retreat, for recruiting, for competitions and for entertainments. They were played at funerals, when the laments 'Lochaber no more' and 'Flowers of the Forest' would be heard. They would also be used for special occasions. For example, at the memorial service for King Edward VII in Malta in 1910, the ceremony was brought to a close by the pipers of the 1st Argylls playing 'Lochaber No More'[107].

Last, but not least, they were used in battle, with the most celebrated instance being the winning of the Victoria Cross by Piper Findlater of the Gordons in 1897 on the heights of Dargai. Wounded in both legs, he continued to encourage his comrades to storm the heights with the old Gordon tune, 'The Cock of the North.' Piper Milne, wounded in the chest, similarly

---

102 For the use of the pipes before 1914 see Henderson, *Highland Soldier*, pp.234-262; Malcolm, Charles A., *The Piper in Peace and War*, (London: Hardwicke Press, 1993) (first published 1927), passim; Murray, *Music*, passim; West, Gary J, 'Scottish Military Music', in Spiers, Crang & Strickland, *Military History*, pp.649-668; Murray, Lt.-Col. D.J.S., 'The Great Highland Bagpipe and Scottish Military Music' in Baynes, John, *Soldiers of Scotland*, (New York: Barnes & Noble, 1997) pp.96-106.
103 And the Scots Guards. They were also used in many non-kilted Canadian battalions, also outside the remit of this study. See, Malcolm, *The Piper*, pp.217-226.
104 For regimental marches, see Murray, *Music*, pp.190-192.
105 Malcolm, Lt Col G.I., *Argyllshire Highlanders 1860-1960* (Glasgow: The Halberd Press, 1960), p.16.
106 Malcom, *The Piper*, p.16.
107 Anderson, Brig. R.C.B., *History of the Argyll and Sutherland Highlanders 1st Battalion 1909-1929* (Edinburgh: Constable, 1954), p.3.

The romance of the pipes: Piper Findlater wining the V.C. at the heights of Dargai in 1897, illustrated by H. Montague Love, on a popular pre-War series of postcards by Tucks depicting V.C. winners. (Author's collection)

played on and received the D.C.M., in "an imperial epic immortalised in poetry, paintings and imperialist iconography."[108] But there were other examples of great courage. At the Atbara in 1898, Piper James Stewart of the Camerons played 'The Cameron Men' to encourage his colleagues, presenting an easy target. When he fell, he had been hit seven times. Pipe tunes were composed to commemorate significant events or battles. Thus, from the late nineteenth and early twentieth centuries, we have, for example, 'The Highland Brigade at Tel-el-Kebir,' and from the Boer War, 'The 91st at Modder River,' and 'Magersfontein,' a rare case of a pipe-tune commemorating a defeat.[109]

Both officers and pipers played a considerable part in retaining, encouraging and preserving pipe music. Some regimental pipers were musicians of a high calibre and made a substantial contribution to contemporary composition, particularly in Ceol Beag, while at the same time maintaining the tradition of Ceol Mor. Their officers meanwhile played a considerable role. The bagpipe was widely considered in the nineteenth century to be the instrument of a gentleman, closely associated with the Highland revival and acceptable for an officer not only to

108 Spiers, 'Scots and the Wars of Empire, 1915-1914,' p.473. And see Spiers, *The Scottish Soldier and Empire*, pp.120-128.
109 Murray, *Music*, pp.287-290.

listen to, but also to play, and many could. Highland officers were responsible for liaising with the Piobaireachd Society, to which many belonged, to start the first official tuition of Army pipers, ultimately to become the Army School of Piping. The classes which began in 1910 at Cameron Barracks, Inverness, under John MacDonald of Inverness, were primarily designed for improving Piobairaechd playing.[110] In this way regimental pipers and their officers contributed to the survival of the cultural tradition. This contribution transcended the purely military significance of the Highland regiments and made them also guardians of Highland culture.

Everywhere that Highland regiments were formed, the pipes were deemed essential to their existence, so that the practice of maintaining pipe-bands was duplicated with expatriate fervour in the Highland regiments raised elsewhere in the Empire, notably amongst the many Canadian Militia regiments and in the Transvaal Scottish and the Cape Town Highlanders in South Africa.[111] During the Zulu Rebellion in Natal in 1906, the Transvaal Scottish provided recruits to form a company of the Natal Rangers to meet the emergency, and "The pipes of the Transvaal Scottish were much in demand."[112]

As "one of the 'icons' of Scottishness,"[113] the pipes emphasised Scottish identity, while, through the use of particular pipe tunes, they stressed regimental identity too. David Murray even claims that the regimental bands "played the major part in the projection of the regiment or battalion as a distinct and separate military entity."[114] He also makes an extraordinary claim for the bagpipes. "Like the sound of most other instruments, that of the Highland pipe can move to laughter, joy and tears, but the sound of the Highland pipe has one unique quality not shared with any other instrument – it can make men feel brave."[115]

Discipline, Hierarchy and Family

Apart from the tangible elements of kilt and bagpipes, another characteristic of the Highland regiments is sometimes held to be a more humane attitude to discipline, a certain informality in the relations between officers and men, and a friendly camaraderie between officers. These areas of discipline and inter-personal relations have been examined for the period 1820 to 1920 in Henderson's ground breaking-study, which really demands to be supplemented by more in-depth studies.

With regard to discipline, Henderson stresses that in the 19th Century, the scope for a separate liberal approach to discipline in the Highland regiments was actually limited by a formal military code of discipline which applied to all soldiers in the Army. This laid down strict and explicit rules, and also defined the required scale of punishment for breaches of the rules.

---

110 For School of Piping, see Henderson, *Highland Soldier*, p.252; West, 'Scottish Military Music', p.658.
111 Apart from refs cited below, see Fetherstonhaugh, R.C., *The 13th Battalion Royal Highlanders of Canada 1914-1919*, (13th Bn, Royal Highlanders of Canada, 1923), p.7; Beattie, *48th Highlanders*, pp.5, 10; Bruce, Turnbull & Chisholm, *Historical Records*, p.22; McEvoy & Finlay, *Seaforth Highlanders of Canada*, p.8; Urquhart, *Canadian Scottish*, p.362; Craig-Brown, *Historical Records*, vol.4, pp.4, 6; Orpen, *Cape Town Highlanders*, p.7.
112 Juta, *Transvaal Scottish*, p.72.
113 West, 'Scottish Military Music', p.653.
114 Murray, *Music*, p.214.
115 Murray, 'The Great Highland Bagpipe and Scottish Military Music,' p.96.

There was more freedom with regard to minor offences, where the scale of punishments was at the discretion of Commanding Officers. The most prevalent offences in the Highland regiments in the nineteenth Century would appear to have been desertion and drink, while venereal diseases were common. Even though some men were total abstainers, heavy drinking remained an essential part of regimental life, up to the Great War. There does seem to have been on occasion a sympathetic view taken by officers of such offences. Henderson also notes, with regard to discipline, that deprivation of rank was an important part of punishment, while promotions were used for reward and encouragement. She claims that Highland regiments were early in appreciating the benefits of incentives and praise in discipline.[116]

Henderson believes that a characteristic of Highland regiments was the ability of officers and men to converse across rank on the basis of mutual respect, with no damage to discipline. Furthermore, pastimes such as music, dancing and sports often involved both officers and men together, while common socialising between officers and men at New Year was frequent.[117] She writes:

> These occasions may have been contrary to all the rules of discipline, but they represented the very essence of the spirit of Highland regiments. Here was discipline that permitted legitimate release without loss of respect on either side, a vital but intangible quality now accepted as one of the keystones of morale.[118]

She further stresses the importance of the 'Regimental Family.'[119] Officers provided patronage, financial and otherwise, to their men, and subscribed to charities and funds. At the same time, their wives provided support to the men's wives and children. Many officers became deeply attached to their men and their regiments, while in return there could be a close attachment to officers who were considerate. The regimental family too extended beyond service to ex-soldiers. Thus we see the development of Regimental Associations, and the provision of support through them. The Highland Regiments too contributed heavily in funds in the years immediately before the War to found the Scottish Naval and Military Veterans Residence, Whiteford House, Edinburgh, in 1910 and Queen Victoria School, Dunblane.[120] Within the family, however, harmony did not always prevail. There were squabbles between officers, some of them bitter. However, theses squabbles would be 'kept in the family,' and "carefully omitted from regimental records."[121] It would be wrong to regard these features of Highland regiments as necessarily unique, for the notion of the 'Regimental Family' has been central to the regimental system of the entire British Army for many years. What they do is provide pointers for investigation in the study to follow.

---

116 Henderson, *Highland Soldier*, pp.265-282.
117 Ibid., pp.267-268, 275, 279, 284-285.
118 Ibid., p.279.
119 Ibid., pp.126-127, 156-157, 288-292.
120 Ibid., p.292.
121 Ibid., pp.128-138.

Identity and Reputation

It is evident from the discussion of kilt and tartan above, that the Highland regiments played a significant role in what has been described as the reinvention of Scotland in the nineteenth century in the image of romantic 'Highlandism.'[122] It is equally clear that, although they remained predominantly Scottish, the Highland regiments had by the end of the nineteenth century, for the most part ceased to be regiments composed of real Highlanders, but had in effect become 'cultural entities' called 'Highland Regiments' which retained elements of Highland culture but existed in their own right, semi-detached, to a greater or lesser extent, from their actual Highland origins. In some respects, they became guardians of ancient Highland culture; in other respects, this culture became a pastiche. As Allan and Carswell put it, they had established "an identity that could flourish independently of the society that produced them."[123]

What is equally significant is the role that they had come to occupy in the public imagination. By the end of the nineteenth century, they had become icons of Empire,[124] at a time when Scots overall were relatively comfortable with their position within it. There was more too. For despite Scots' acquiescence in their position within the Empire, Scotland still remained a nation within a nation, and, with their distinctive kilts and bagpipes, Highland soldiers had also become arguably the most tangible expression of Scotland's national identity. As Spiers puts it, they "embodied the country's national identity within the union."[125] Spiers further shrewdly observes that it was this identification of the Scottish soldier with the nation that distinguished his support from that of his English county counterpart.[126]

The exalted position of the Highland regiments had developed through their success in battle, especially during the Napoleonic Wars, in Egypt, the Peninsula and Waterloo, but subsequently in the Crimea and the Indian Mutiny and in a string of colonial campaigns thereafter. Spiers describes the conduct and evolving reputation of the Scottish soldier, from the Crimea and Indian Mutiny, through the Ashanti campaign, Afghanistan, Tel-el-Kebir, the Sudan, the North-West Frontier, and Omdurman up to the South African War.[127]

Since, as we have seen, the triumph of the kilt and tartan in the military followed on only after the Crimea and the Mutiny, the reconstitution of the Militia (1852) and the commencement of the Volunteer movement (1859), and reached its most definite affirmation in the Childers reforms of 1881, it is tempting to identify this transformation of the Highland soldier into national icon as a late nineteenth century phenomenon, related to, but in a sense separate from, the earlier expression of romantic 'Highlandism.' Spiers indeed believes it was the Indian Mutiny which established the iconic significance of the Scottish soldier,[128] and it is interesting to observe that the great battle paintings of the Highland soldier at Waterloo are all later nineteenth century creations and retrospective. Whatever the case, Allan and Carswell are surely

---

122 See Allan & Carswell, *The Thin Red Line*, p.24; Spiers, *The Scottish Soldier and Empire*, pp.2-3; Ugolini, 'Scottish Commonwealth Regiments,' p.486.
123 Allan & Carswell, *The Thin Red Line*, p.32.
124 Spiers, 'Scots and the Wars of Empire,' p.476; Spiers, *The Scottish Soldier and Empire*, p.1.
125 Spiers, 'Scots and the Wars of Empire,' p.476.
126 Spiers, *The Scottish Soldier and Empire*, p.213.
127 For a discussion of this process, see Allan & Carswell, *The Thin Red Line*, pp.20-30; Henderson, *Highland Soldier*, pp.8-9 and Spiers, *The Scottish Soldier and Empire*, passim.
128 Spiers, *The Scottish Soldier and Empire*, p.7.

right when they state that "during the Victorian period the reputation of the highland regiments really became an article of faith for Scottish patriots."[129] After Omdurman, Hector Macdonald, the crofter's son who had enlisted as a private in the Gordons and risen to be Major-General, to command Sudanese troops decisively at that battle, became the new Scottish hero. He was seen as the epitome of the qualities of the Highland soldier.[130]

Highland soldiers came to be known for their ferocity in battle, their keen use of the bayonet, and the 'Highland charge.' They came to be epitomised as a martial race and at times the language of adulation became, in retrospect, embarrassingly racial. As Spiers points out, "Both journalists and officers embraced fashionable ideas of racial superiority and Social Darwinism, and regarded moral and not materiel factors as the ultimate arbiter in battle." In this context, "they eulogised the warrior ethos of the Victorian soldier, including the Highlander."[131] The perceived qualities of the Highland soldier were of course entirely consistent with the Victorian concept of manliness.[132] Highland soldiers certainly received great support from the people at home, which was reflected in the crowds that gathered whenever regiments left or returned to Scotland.[133] Henderson stresses that additionally, "as a result of history, literature and culture, soldiering was widely looked upon as a respectable profession in Scotland," and she suggests that the large number of army pensioners living in the Highlands may have had a favourable influence on the perception of the army.[134]

The exploits of Highland soldiers were commemorated in paintings, monuments and in popular culture. Paintings[135] included, for example, Robert Gibb's 'The Thin Red line.' (1881), Alphonse de Neuville's 'Tel-el-Kebir' (1883), William Barnes Woollen's 'The Black Watch at Bay, Quatre Bras' (1894), and Stanley Berkeley's 'Gordons and Greys to the Front, Incident at Waterloo' (1898). Some of these paintings were produced almost immediately after the events they depict; others, depicting especially Quatre Bras and Waterloo, were retrospective. Popular prints and engravings were based on such paintings, which were hung in messes, clubs, schools and institutes. They also appeared in the press, in school textbooks and on cigarette cards.[136] The image of the Highland soldier was even used in advertising, most famously on the label of 'Camp Coffee,' a chicory-based drink made in Scotland from 1885.[137]

They were also commemorated in monuments.[138] In this respect we may note first the laying up of old Scottish Regimental Colours in St Giles, Edinburgh, in 1883. Otherwise, stone memorials were produced. One of the first was the Celtic cross on Edinburgh Castle esplanade

---

129 Allan & Carswell, *The Thin Red Line*, p.23.
130 Spiers, *The Scottish Soldier and Empire*, pp.146-150. On the career of Macdonald, see Montgomery, John, *Toll for the Brave*, (London: Max Parrish, 1963); Royle, Trevor, *Fighting Mac* (Edinburgh: Mainstream,1982).
131 Spiers, *The Scottish Soldier and Empire*, p.14.
132 Ibid., pp.115-116.
133 Spiers, 'Scots and the Wars of Empire,' pp.476, 478; Henderson, *Highland Soldier*, p.220.
134 Henderson, *Highland Soldier*, pp.44, 32.
135 See Harrington, Peter, 'The Scottish Soldier in Art,' in Spiers, Crang & Strickland, *Military History*, pp.688-705; Spiers, *The Scottish Soldier and Empire*, pp.9-10, 82, 126.
136 Spiers, *The Scottish Soldier and Empire*, pp.14-15.
137 Newark, *Highlander*, p.229; Spiers, *The Scottish Soldier and Empire*, p.117.
138 McFarland, Elaine W., 'Scottish Military Monuments,' in Spiers, Crang & Strickland, *Military History*, pp.748-775; Allan & Carswell, *The Thin Red Line*, pp.35, 39-40; Spiers, *The Scottish Soldier and Empire*, pp.112, 113.

erected in 1862 to honour the 78th Highlanders who fell in the Indian Mutiny. In 1884, the Aberdonians raised a memorial cross to the Gordons in Duthie Park. A particularly impressive monument commemorating the raising of the Black Watch, depicting a soldier of the original regiment, was unveiled at Aberfeldy in 1887, and in 1893 came the unveiling of the Cameron Memorial at Inverness, depicting a contemporary soldier of the regiment.

There was also the publication of a number of books on the Scottish military tradition, following Archibald Murray's *History of the Scottish Regiments* in 1862,[139] such as James Cromb's *The Highland Brigade: Its Battles and its Heroes*. Highland heroes appeared on the stage in melodramas,[140] as well as in juvenile literature with its prominent themes of adventure and imperialism.[141] In 1893, William Britain began to manufacture model soldiers. They proved immensely popular with boys in the early twentieth century. In their first year of production two of their twelve sets of toy soldiers were devoted to the Black Watch and the Argylls.[142]

The commemoration of the Highland regiments: statue of a Cameron Highlander outside Inverness railway station, sculpted by George Edward Wade and erected in 1893. (photograph author)

Amidst the exploits of the Highland regiments, there were nevertheless some mishaps. Three companies of the 92nd (Gordon Highlanders) were involved in the catastrophe at Majuba Hill in 1881,[143] described as "one of the most humiliating defeats the British were to suffer during Queen Victoria's 64-year reign."[144] The soldiers of course were not necessarily themselves to blame for the debacle, and Scots commentators were determined that the disaster should not reflect on the gallantry of the 92nd. Instead, "defeat could be dressed for popular

---

139 Allan & Carswell, *The Thin Red Line*, pp.30-31.
140 Spiers, *The Scottish Soldier and Empire*, p.116.
141 Ibid., p.115.
142 Newark, *Highlander*, p.231.
143 On Majuba, see Spiers, *The Scottish Soldier and Empire*, pp.57-61; Cowan, Paul, *Scottish Military Disasters* (Glasgow: Neil Wilson, 2008), pp.129-135; Henderson, *Highland Soldier*, p.128. For more extensive treatment of Majuba, see Lehmann, Joseph, *The First Boer War* (London: Jonathan Cape, London, 1972), pp.223-262; Laband, John, *The Transvaal Rebellion*, (Harlow: Pearson Education Ltd, 2005), pp.198-212.
144 Cowan, *Disasters*, p.129.

Disaster! Gordon Highlanders and friends flee Majuba Hill 1881. Not the typical image of the Highland soldier. Illustration by Melton Prior, published in the *Illustrated London News*. (Copyright Mary Evans Picture Library)

consumption as highland heroism in adversity", as in the pamphlet, *The Majuba Disaster, a Tale of Highland Heroism*, by James Cromb, published in 1891.[145]

Another near disaster, in 1884, was the so-called breaking of a British square by the Mahdists at the battle of Tamai,[146] celebrated by Kipling, for which the Black Watch were subsequently mercilessly held accountable. What appears to have happened is that the 1st Black Watch formed the front face of a brigade square, which was thus not a Black Watch square per se. When ordered to charge, they left a gap between themselves and the remainder of the square. Through this gap, hundreds of the enemy got into the square, and the rear rank of the Black Watch were forced to turn about to defend themselves, until the threat was effectively dealt with. No square was 'broken,' for the way in was apparently left wide open. The real issue is, who was culpable for such tactical ineptitude? Nevertheless, for many years afterwards, it was a common taunt in public houses and canteens for soldiers of other regiments to order, within the hearing of Black Watch soldiers, a pint of 'Broken Square,' at which a fight became inevitable.

In any case, such mishaps could not be allowed to tarnish the image of the Highland soldier, as to do so would be to tarnish the image of Scotland. Much more likely was an over-indulgence of praise. Naturally, this inspired some resentment. As Spiers points out:

> The martial qualities and values reflected in the reportage and imagery generated by these wars, especially the gallantry, comradeship, resolve, offensive zeal, esprit de corps and good officer/men relations, were not the exclusive preserve of the Highland regiments. Any proficient Lowland, English, Welsh or Irish regiment claimed similar qualities.[147]

And as the 'Glasgow Herald' observed on 9 May, 1899:

> We are a little apt to magnify the deeds of our soldiers; the depreciation which English regiments suffered by comparison with the Gordons at Dargai and the Camerons at Atbara was eminently absurd and offensive.[148]

Allan and Carswell recognise the problem, noting that after the Crimean War and the Mutiny:

> the Scottish aspect of British military endeavour was beginning to be acclaimed in print and imagery quite out of proportion to its practical impact, sometimes to the irritation of non-Scottish regiments who could find their own comparable battlefield successes, even those achieved side-by-side in highland company, overshadowed by the cult of the highland soldier.[149]

And Wood states, with regard to the Highlanders in particular:

---

145 Allan & Carswell, *The Thin Red Line*, p.37. See also Spiers, *The Scottish Soldier and Empire*, p.115.
146 On Tamai, see Henderson, *Highland Soldier*, p.128 and note 44, p.141; Spiers, *The Scottish Soldier and Empire*, pp.92-94; Newark, *Highlander*, pp.147-150. For a more extensive treatment, see Schofield, Victoria, *The Highland Furies*, (London: Quercus, 2012), pp.520-528.
147 Spiers, *The Scottish Soldier and Empire*, p.10.
148 Ibid., p.148.
149 Allan & Carswell, *The Thin Red Line*, p.24.

With their tartan kilts and feather bonnets, with pipers and broadswords, the Highland regiments were the object of much bemused and often bitter, envy from men of non-Highland regiments. It was felt, occasionally justifiably, that the Highlanders' part in any action tended to be disproportionately reported because their outlandish appearance and awful noise made them more noticeable.[150]

It was felt, for example, that disproportionate credit was claimed for Highlanders in the Crimea,[151] who did not have to serve in the trenches before Sevastopol, and for the Gordons at Dargai.[152] On the other hand, the Highlanders were keen to ensure that their own achievements did get recognised, and there was criticism of Wolseley's despatch after Tel-el-Kebir, which, it was claimed, gave too much credit to the Irish regiments.[153] On balance, though, it is undoubtedly true that the Highland regiments received more than their fair share of credit.

From South Africa to the Eve of War 1899-1914

Between 1900 and 1914, the principal action seen by the Highland regiments was in the South African War (1899-1902). Otherwise the regiments were called upon occasionally for aid to the civil power and served in three small colonial wars. The first of these wars occurred in Natal, where in 1906 there was a serious Zulu rebellion. Both the Cape Town Highlanders and the Transvaal Scottish provided detachments to assist; the Cape Town Highlanders provided a detachment to the Natal Active Service Contingent of volunteers from the Cape, while the Transvaal Scottish provided an entire kilted company to a newly formed regiment of volunteers, the Natal Rangers. As part of this regiment, they participated in the decisive action at the Mome Gorge on 10 June 1906 when the Zulu leader Bambata was killed. 2nd Camerons, who were stationed in Pretoria at the time, were moved to Pietermaritzburg in readiness, but were not called upon for service in the field.[154] The other two small wars occurred on the North West Frontier of India; these were the Zakka Khel and Mohmand expeditions of 1908, in which 1st Seaforths took part.[155] Otherwise, 2nd Camerons served as part of the international force in China between 1908 and 1909, amongst other duties guarding the British Legation in Peking.[156] All other episodes involved aid to the civil power. In Canada, 48th Highlanders were called out on the occasion of the Toronto Railway Company strike (1902) and the Sault Saint Marie riots (1903).[157] In South Africa, in 1907, 2nd Camerons, stationed at Pretoria, sent a contingent to Johannesburg during strikes in the gold-fields, and in the same year nearer

---

150 Wood, *Scottish Soldier*, p.76.
151 Spiers, 'Scots and the Wars of Empire,' p.468; Spiers, *The Scottish Soldier and Empire*, pp.5-6.
152 Spiers, *The Scottish Soldier and Empire*, pp.123-125.
153 Ibid., pp.71-77
154 Orpen, *Cape Town Highlanders*, p.65; Juta, *Transvaal Scottish*, pp.68-72; Fairrie, Angus, *Queen's Own Highlanders (Seaforths and Camerons) An Illustrated History* (Trustees of the Queen's Own Highlanders Amalgamation Trusts, 1998), p.74.
155 Fairrie, *Queen's Own Highlanders*, p.63.
156 Ibid., p.74.
157 Beal, *Family*, pp.136-138.

An encampment of 1st Seaforth Highlanders at Shabkadar during the Mohmand Expedition, 1908. (from a contemporary postcard, publisher unknown, Author's collection)

home, 1st Camerons were called to assist during an outbreak of rioting in Ulster.[158] In 1911, 1st Gordons were ordered to Sheffield to guard stations during a railway strike.[159] Finally, in January 1914, both the Cape Town Highlanders and the Transvaal Scottish were briefly mobilised when industrial troubles on the Rand and in the Natal coal-mines snowballed into a general strike. In preventing an attempt to blow up a railway line at Denver, one private of the Transvaal Scottish was killed.[160] Much sterner tests were to come.

The principal war service experienced by the Highland regiments, however, in the years before 1914, was in the South African War. This was not a small war. It involved a huge national and imperial effort, both military and financial. 450,000 troops were committed to South Africa; the largest number of troops ever sent abroad by Britain up to that time. 22,000 died, two-thirds of them from disease.[161] These deaths pale into insignificance compared with those of the Great War, but they were nearly fifty times greater than British deaths in our recent campaign in Afghanistan. The war had a correspondingly huge impact on the people of both Britain and the Empire

---

158 Fairrie, *Queen's Own Highlanders*, pp.72, 74.
159 Henderson, *Highland Soldier*, p.218.
160 Orpen, *Cape Town Highlanders*, p.74; Juta, *Transvaal Scottish*, p.18.
161 Corrigan, Gordon, *Mud, Blood and Poppycock*, (London: Cassell, 2003), p.53.

For the Highland regiments themselves it was not a comfortable experience. Their most notable battle was the disaster at Magersfontein[162], on 11 December, 1899, during "Black Week." In this battle, the Highland Brigade attempted a night march and dawn attack to take the Boer position at Magersfontein. In order to keep formation they advanced in quarter column. As they deployed into extended line prior to the attack, they were caught in a fusillade of fire from the Boer trenches. Pinned down throughout the day, they began to melt away, until eventually the retreat became a rout. The Highland Brigade had broken. A shocked observer wrote:

> Then I saw a sight that I hope I may never see again: men of the Highland Brigade running for all they were worth, others cowering under bushes, behind the guns, some lying under their blankets, officers running about with revolvers in their hands threatening to shoot them, urging on some, kicking on others; staff officers galloping about giving incoherent and impracticable orders.[163]

It was a catastrophe. Lord Methuen, the Army commander, came in for much criticism, and stoically accepted his role as scapegoat. But the battle plan was sound, if risky. Probably most responsible was the Highland Brigade commander, "Andy" Wauchope, who delayed the order to deploy into line. But he was a brave man who was killed early in the action, and remained a hero in the eyes of the public. As for the soldiers, it is quite possible that other soldiers, put in that position would have behaved in the same way. What is important is that the Highland soldier, in this spectacular instance, had demonstrated his fallibility, his normalcy. Highland soldiers, after all, were human.

Nevertheless, in the eyes of the public, the Highlanders' reputation remained unsullied. The Highland soldier had become such an icon that he was immune to criticism. Reality could not be allowed to obscure the image. Instead the disaster was portrayed as a tragedy, which of course it was. Richard Caton Woodville's painting, 'All That was Left of Them. The Black Watch after the Battle of Magersfontein 1899' portrayed nobility in defeat.[164] The monument to the Highland Brigade erected at Magersfontein, subscribed for by readers of the 'Glasgow Herald,' proudly proclaimed, "Scotland is poorer in men but richer in heroes."[165] Fortunately there were no more disasters, at least to the Highland Brigade. Another Highland hero, Hector Macdonald, or 'Fighting Mac' as he was known, the hero of Omdurman, was sent in to command the brigade and rebuild its morale. The reputation of the kilted Highland soldier survived unscathed until 1914, when it would be available still to inspire young, and not so young, volunteers.

---

162 On Magersfontein, see Spiers, *The Scottish Soldier and Empire*, pp.157-181 Pemberton, W. Baring, *Battles of the Boer War* (London: Pan Books, 1969), pp.77-116; Kruger, Rayne, *Goodbye Dolly Gray*, (London: Pimlico, 1996) (1st published 1959), pp.125-135; Pakenham, Thomas, *The Boer War*, (London: Weidenfeld & Nicolson, 1979), pp.201-206; Carver, Field Marshal Lord, *The National Army Museum Book of the Boer War*, (London: Sidgwick & Jackson, 1999), pp.32-39; Spiers, 'Scots and the Wars of Empire,' p.474; Newark, *Highlander*, pp.167-171; Cowan, *Disasters*, pp.136-145.
163 Roger Poore, quoted in Pemberton, *Battles of the Boer War*, p.105.
164 Harrington, 'The Scottish Soldier in Art,' p.701.
165 Allan & Carswell, *The Thin Red Line*, p.38.

The disaster of Magersfontein was just one of three disasters in one week in December, 1899. "Black Week", with defeats at Stormberg, Magersfontein and Colenso, had a massive impact.[166] On the one hand it united much of the rest of the world in contempt for Britain and the Empire. As Rayne Kruger has written, "the months after Black Week were a revelation to England [sic] of the extent to which she was loathed."[167] Given the bullying nature of this blatant grab for gold, this loathing was not totally unfounded. Be that as it may, the survival of the Empire and of Britain's position in the world seemed under threat. Faced with this threat, the British public and the Empire rallied as never before. There was an astonishing offer of volunteers for the front, both from within Britain itself and from the Empire. Over 40,000 volunteers came from the countries of the Empire, making this "the first time the Empire as whole went to war."[168] Many of these volunteers were cavalry, but there was infantry too and this included some Highlanders. In South Africa itself, the Cape Town Highlanders had been mobilised on the outbreak of the war and notably saw action at Jacobsdal in October, 1900.[169] From Canada came a contingent of the 48th Highlanders.[170] In Britain, the Militia were embodied, and some even served abroad. Thus, for example, the 3rd (Militia) Battalion Seaforth Highlanders volunteered to a man for active service abroad, and the battalion was sent to Cairo in May, 1900, where it served for 18 months alongside the 1st Battalion, allowing the 1st Battalion to provide reinforcements to the 2nd Battalion in South Africa.[171] Otherwise, as we have seen, two new battalions of Highland volunteers were raised, the Liverpool Scottish and the 9th Royal Scots ("the Dandy Ninth"); both in time to supply contingents to the front. In addition, as early as 2nd January, 1900, a special Army Order was issued calling upon the Volunteers to furnish contingents to Volunteer Service Companies, one to be raised for each regular battalion serving in South Africa, the men to serve for a year or the duration. Further companies were raised in 1901 and 1902.[172] In total, the Highland battalions of the Volunteer force, including the Liverpool and London Scottish,[173] which both sent contingents to join the Gordon Highlanders, sent 2,361 men of all ranks to South Africa. Of these, about 65 percent, or a little over 1,500 men, served in the Volunteer Service Companies of the five Highland regiments; the remainder served in other corps, such as the Imperial Yeomanry.[174] Of those serving with the Highland regiments, at least 15 were

---

166 For the reaction to Black Week, the Empire under threat, volunteering and the Empire's response, see in particular Kruger, *Goodbye Dolly Gray*, pp.144-159; also Pakenham, *The Boer War*, pp.242-253; Carver, *Boer War*, pp.50-54.
167 Kruger, *Goodbye Dolly Gray*, p.148.
168 Ibid., p.153. For Scotland's response in particular, see Spiers, *The Scottish Soldier and Empire*, pp.163, 182-197; Spiers, 'Scots and the Wars of Empire,' p.475; Allan & Carswell, *The Thin Red Line*, pp.36-37, 107.
169 Orpen, *Cape Town Highlanders*, pp.41-58. This was not the first time they had been called out. In 1886, they had been called out to help suppress rioting by the Malay Community., and in 1897, they had supplied a contingent to the Bechuanaland Field Force. See Orpen, pp.4-6, 19-39.
170 Beattie, *48th Highlanders*, pp.9-10; Beal, *Family*, pp.36-42.
171 Fairrie, *Queen's Own Highlanders*, pp.63, 76.
172 Grierson, *Records*, pp.92-98.
173 McGilchrist, *Liverpool Scottish*, pp.5-6; Giblin, *Bravest of Hearts*, pp.4-5; Lindsay, *London Scottish*, pp.6-11; Lloyd, *London Scottish*, pp.15-20.
174 These figures are calculated from the individual regimental totals provided by Grierson, *Records*, passim. The calculations exclude 9th V.B. Royal Scots and the two kilted H.L.I. volunteer battalions, which sent volunteers to join their own Lowland regiments in South Africa.

killed, 44 wounded and 25 died of disease.[175] The most fiercely engaged appear to have been the 1st and 2nd Volunteer Service Companies of the Gordon Highlanders, including men of the London Scottish.[176] Generally, the Volunteers were given a tremendous send-off in Scotland and a great reception when they returned.[177]

Spiers considers that, "the South African War had reflected the pervasive appeal of martial values within Scotland."[178] Certainly there were great celebrations and demonstrations in Scotland over the relief of both Ladysmith and Mafeking, and the capture of Pretoria.[179] He also considers that "The South African legacy dominated the early years of the Edwardian era."[180] Indeed, after the war came the memorials.[181] Some were functional. Queen Victoria School, Dunblane,[182] opened in 1908 and was intended as a memorial to both Queen Victoria and to the Scottish servicemen who fell in the South African War. It was instituted to maintain and provide an elementary education for the sons of Scotsmen in naval or army service, and the sons of soldiers of any nationality serving in the Scottish regiments. In Aberdeen a Memorial Institute was created in memory of Lieutenant-Colonel Dick-Cunningham, V.C.[183] And in 1910, troubled by the living conditions of some retired servicemen, two Seaforth Highlander officers began an appeal to create The Scottish Veterans' Residence at Whitefoord House in Edinburgh. It was founded with the help of a significant charitable contribution from a Scottish mother who had lost a son in the South African War.[184]

Boer War memorial at Alloa, sculpted by William Birnie Rhind and erected in 1904. (Photograph author)

---

175 These figures are calculated as above. They may not be complete.
176 Grierson, *Records*, pp.289, 293, 296, 300, 304, 306-7, 340.
177 Spiers, *The Scottish Soldier and Empire*, pp.188-191, 195-197, 203-204.
178 Ibid., p.212.
179 Ibid., p.213.
180 Spiers, 'Scots and the Wars of Empire,' p.477.
181 Spiers, *The Scottish Soldier and Empire*, pp.203-208; McFarland, 'Scottish Military Monuments,' pp.758-760; Allan & Carswell, *The Thin Red Line*, p.36.
182 Allan & Carswell, *The Thin Red Line*, p.38. See also Baynes, John, *Soldiers of Scotland* (New York: Barnes & Noble, 1997), pp.201-202; Henderson, *Highland Soldier*, p.37; Spiers, *The Scottish Soldier and Empire*, p.211.
183 Spiers, *The Scottish Soldier and Empire*, p.205.
184 Allan & Carswell, *The Thin Red Line*, pp.38-39.

The pre-War Volunteers: The London Scottish at the Royal Volunteer Review Edinburgh, 1905. (from a contemporary postcard by the Mezzotint Company, Author's collection)

Other memorials were more conventional. In Dingwall, a twenty-foot high cross in pink granite was erected to the Seaforths in 1904. A fine statue of Highland soldiers was erected at Alloa in 1904, and others at Falkirk in 1907 and outside Stirling Castle the same year. In Edinburgh a statue to the Black Watch was erected on the Mound between Waverley and the Royal Mile in 1910. In South Africa itself, the sacrifice of the Highland Brigade was commemorated by a Celtic cross at Magersfontein. As we have seen, the war also encouraged the creation of more volunteer Highland battalions in the Empire in the following years; the Transvaal Scottish in South Africa and a veritable flowering of battalions in Canada. In several respects, the public response to the Boer War pre-figured that of 1914; the sense of the Empire under threat, the great rush of volunteers and the willing contribution of the Empire. And the subsequent memorialisation found even greater expression after the Great War. To consider the response to the war in 1914 without considering the response to the South African War is to miss a vital part of the jig-saw.

Public support for, and identification with, the Highland soldier, continued unabated. Highland soldiers maintained their position in popular art on picture postcards, with splendid sets of regimental uniforms. A notable event for the Volunteer Highland battalions was the review of the Scottish Volunteer Force by King Edward VII at Edinburgh on 18 September 1905. Popular support was also shown in the remarkable turnout for the funerals of distinguished Highland soldiers 'Fighting Mac', Sir Hector Macdonald, in 1903,[185] and Sir Archibald Alison in 1907.[186] The former case is astounding. Sir Hector had tragically committed suicide in

---

185 On Macdonald, see Spiers, *The Scottish Soldier and Empire*, pp.203, 206-207. For a fuller discussion see Montgomery, *Toll for the Brave*, pp.130-169 and Royle, *Fighting Mac*, pp.124-162.
186 Spiers, *The Scottish Soldier and Empire*, pp.203, 207-208.

Monument at Dingwall to Sir Hector Macdonald, a flawed Highland hero, opened 1907. (Photograph author)

Paris, possibly on the advice of the King, after being accused of interfering with boys in Ceylon, a charge of which he was almost certainly guilty. The Scottish public simply chose to disregard the charges and turned out in their thousands to show their respects to their hero. A huge monument was erected to him in Dingwall, and a smaller one at Dean Cemetery in Edinburgh. Nothing could be allowed to besmirch the name of a Highland soldier hero. Since the Highland soldier represented the Scottish nation, and the Scottish people saw in him the personification of their virtues, he could not possibly be allowed to have failed. Indeed, on the eve of the Great War, few things demonstrate better than the reaction to Macdonald's death the robust survival of the image of the generic Highland soldier, who retained his status as an icon of Empire and as the most tangible expression of Scottish national identity.[187]

---

187 See ibid., p.203; Allan & Carswell, *The Thin Red Line*, pp.19, 40; Carswell, 'Scottish Military Dress,' p.642 Spiers, 'Scots and the Wars of Empire,' p.478.

Conclusions

In 1914, then, kilted Highland regiments were found not only in Scotland, but also in England and overseas in Canada and South Africa. In Britain, the Highland regiments were divided between the Regular Army, Special Reserve and Territorial Force. Their form had been strongly influenced by the reforms of Childers in 1881 and Haldane in 1908. The Highland regiments had emerged triumphant from these reforms, but since 1881 their Regimental districts had straddled large tracts of the Lowlands. The Regular regiments remained predominantly Scottish, but were no longer filled with Highland-born recruits. Alongside them the Special Reserve had emerged from the Militia as a useful first reserve. The Territorial battalions meanwhile had evolved from the Volunteer regiments which had been raised in an astonishing outburst of popular enthusiasm after 1859, and even included some units in both England and Scotland which were separate from the five principal Highland regiments. The Territorials, intended for home defence only, were not as professional as the Special Reserve, with many members joining primarily for the social life. Their fitness for battle was questionable. In parallel there had been a remarkable formation of kilted regiments elsewhere in the Empire in Canada and South Africa, with an associated invention of tradition. These regiments were testimony to the remarkable triumph of the kilt in the nineteenth century, although its practicality for war was beginning to be questioned. Equally fundamental to the life of the Highland regiments in all corners of the Empire were the pipes, and we shall examine their use in the Great War carefully. The regimental family was highly valued in the Highland regiments, and there may be evidence for an approach to discipline based essentially on mutual respect. We will need to put this to the test too. Identity was central to the Highland regiments. By the end of the nineteenth century they had become not only icons of Empire, but also the most tangible expression of Scottish national identity. While they were not infallible, given their iconic status they could not be seen to fail, and were rather subjected to excessive praise, a practice which unsurprisingly aroused some resentment. Their most significant test in the years before the Great War was the South African War, the response to which in many ways pre-figured that to the greater conflict. Despite the disaster at Magersfontein, the reputation and iconic status of the Highland soldier remained intact. In the following chapters we will pick up all these threads as we examine the experience of the Highland soldier in his greatest test ever.

2

Organisation and Service

"I am looking forward to my new adventures."[1]

Introduction

The kilted regiments which fought in the First World War were drawn from three countries of the Empire; Great Britain, Canada and South Africa. In the first part of this chapter, we will deal with each in turn, before considering the deployment of these battalions to the Western Front, and to several separate theatres overseas. In the second part of the chapter, we will look in more detail at some specific aspects of organisation and service, in particular, volunteering for overseas service amongst the Territorials, the completion of the Territorial Highland Division with recruits from London, the question of 'time-expired' Territorials, the problems of recruiting prior to conscription, and the anguish caused by transfers, amalgamations, absorptions and reductions of both Territorial and New Army battalions.

The British Regular Battalions

At the opening of hostilities, the following Regular kilted battalions were on home service:

1st Black Watch	Aldershot[2]
2nd Seaforths	Shorncliffe[3]
1st Camerons	Edinburgh Castle[4]
1st Gordons	Plymouth[5]
2nd Argylls	Fort George[6]

1　IWM 8192 PP Lawson, R.K., 14th Argylls, letter to Bessie, 23 April, 1918.
2　Wauchope, *Black Watch*, Vol.1, p.1.
3　Fairrie, *Queen's Own Highlanders*, p.88.
4　Craig-Brown, *Historical Records*, Vol.3, p.25.
5　Falls, Cyril, *The Life of a Regiment, Vol.4, The Gordon Highlanders in the First World War* (Aberdeen: The University Press, 1958), pp.2-3.
6　Cavendish, Brig Gen A.E.J., *An reisimeid chataich; The 93rd Sutherland Highlanders 1799-1927* (Frome: Butler and Tanner, 1928), p.239.

On mobilisation, the Regular battalions at home had first to be completed to full strength with Reservists. It is astonishing how many were required; at least 650 to 1st Black Watch,[7] for example, 700 each to both 1st Camerons[8] and 2nd Argylls,[9] and over 500 to 1st Gordons.[10] In general these men, although trained, were not sufficiently fit for the active service on which they were almost immediately deployed.[11] But this was an Army-wide problem, not unique to Highland troops.

There was also an issue of integration, as the home service battalions were effectively reconstituted around a pre-war cadre. Sergeant Macpherson, in 1st Camerons, noted in his diary: "The reservists are a mixed lot. Some had been out of the service 12 to 13 years & were out of date… the web equipment was a monkey's puzzle to the majority of the reservists." [12] Likewise, Lance-Sergeant Andrew Anderson, who had enlisted in 1910, found the reservists very rusty. But, after a relatively short space of time, "we, the young regular soldiers, had become acquainted with the old soldier reservists who with a few exceptions turned out to be excellent fellows. And jolly good companions. In time we became a happy and I think a very efficient battalion."[13] H.J.D. Clark, then a junior officer in 2nd Argylls, observed later that on mobilization:

A sergeant of the Black Watch says goodbye to his family before entraining for the front. Did he see his family again? From a contemporary postcard, publisher unknown. (Author's collection)

> We absorbed 600 reservists, many of whom had been in civilian life for quite a number of years … and if it hadn't been that all our Company commanders knew their men, the

---

7   IWM 3696 PP Macnaghten, A.C.R.S., Capt., letter to wife, n.d.; BWA, Hitchman, Sgt Peter, diary, 6, 7, 8, 11 August, 1914.
8   Craig-Brown, *Historical Records*, Vol.3, p.27; IWM 43 Recording Dunton, Arthur Naylor, IWM interview, 1973 (Dunton says about 600).
9   Cavendish, *An reisimeid chataich*, p.239; ASHM N-E2 Hyslop, Lt. Col. H.G., typescript war diary, 7, 8 August, 1914.
10 Falls, *Gordon Highlanders*, p.2.
11 Ibid., p.2; ASHM N-E2 Hyslop, diary, 25 August, 1914.
12 THM Camerons 99-87, Macpherson, H., diary, 18-20 August, 1914.
13 THM Camerons 89-44 Anderson, Brig. A., memoir.

retired ones as well as the serving ones, it would have been a harder problem than ever, but thanks to our knowing them, and the Company Commanders being so well versed in the characters of these reserving chaps, the machinery worked like clock-work.[14]

It was therefore an experienced but unfit Army which was deployed to France. All the home service Regular Highland battalions arrived in France between 14 and 23 August. They did not form a Highland Brigade but were spread about the various divisions of the B.E.F.[15]

The remaining Regular kilted battalions, on service overseas, were stationed as follows:

2nd Black Watch	India; Bareilly[16]
1st Seaforths	India; Agra[17]
2nd Camerons	India; Poona[18]
2nd Gordons	Cairo[19]
1st Argylls	India; Dinapore and Dum Dum[20]

All were recalled for service in France. Unlike their home service counterparts, these battalions had in principle been kept up to strength, and for the most part therefore consisted of fit seasoned soldiers. They nevertheless benefitted from a number of reservists recalled to the colours in India. William Robertson, who was with 1st Seaforths in Agra, when war was declared, remembered, "reservists recalled to the Colours from jobs on the State Railways, mines, the plantations, grass farms and extra-regimentally employed in the Telegraph Service and Staff Offices throughout the land."[21]

2nd Gordons, coming from only Cairo, were first to arrive, and landed at Zeebrugge on 7 October.[22] 2nd Black Watch and 1st Seaforths disembarked at Marseilles on 12 October,[23] while 2nd Camerons and 1st Argylls arrived in England in November and disembarked at Le Havre on 20 December, 1914.[24] Thus the overseas Regular battalions were all deployed to Belgium and France between 7 October and 20 December, 1914, the initial deployment being well over a month after the last of the home battalions.

---

14 LC GS 0315 Clark, H.J.D., Tape 356 Interview with Liddle, 1976.
15 Wauchope, *Black Watch*, Vol.1, pp.1-2; Craig-Brown, *Historical Records*, Vol.3, pp.21-32; Falls, *Gordon Highlanders*, pp.2-3; Fairrie, *Queen's Own Highlanders*, pp.90-92; Cavendish, *An reisimeid chataich*, pp.238-40, 253, 270-3.
16 Wauchope, *Black Watch*, Vol.1, p.161.
17 Fairrie, *Queen's Own Highlanders*, p.90.
18 Craig-Brown, *Historical Records*, Vol.3, p.295.
19 Falls, *Gordon Highlanders*, pp.13-14.
20 Anderson, *1st Argylls*, pp.15-21.
21 IWM 1134 PP Robertson, William S, typescript memoir, 'Reminiscences of an Old Soldier', written 1983, 7pp, p.2.
22 Falls, *Gordon Highlanders*, pp.12-14.
23 Wauchope, *Black Watch*, Vol.1, pp.161-165; Fairrie, *Queen's Own Highlanders*, pp.88-90.
24 Craig-Brown, *Historical Records*, Vol.3, pp.295-296; Anderson, *1st Argylls*, pp.24-26.

Special Reserve Battalions and Depots

The Special Reserve battalions were also mobilised at the outbreak of the war and generally had two duties; to provide local defence, and to train and provide drafts for the regular and service battalions in the front line. Initially composed of those men who had been members of the Special Reserve before the war, the battalions were soon composed largely of either new recruits or of casualties who had returned to the regiment after hospitalisation. To give one example of the scale of their activity, during the war 3rd Black Watch supplied some 1,200 officers and 20,000 other ranks to reinforce the regiment's battalions in the war theatres.[25] Thus, although never 'fighting battalions', many of the officers and men who appear in this study passed through one or other of these battalions at some stage, and their experiences with the 3rd battalions figure in their thoughts and observations.

After mobilisation the Special Reserve battalions moved to their initial stations, principally on coastal defence. Some of these battalions subsequently changed their locations in Britain, while three were to move to Ireland in 1917, as we shall see. None served overseas in an operational theatre. Meanwhile, The Regimental Depots served throughout the War as receiving points for new recruits. Recruits reported to the Depot for medical inspection and issue of uniform before being sent to the Reserve battalions for training.

Regular battalions return from overseas. Soldiers of 2nd Black Watch photographed at Marseilles, where they disembarked on 12th October, 1914 still in tropical kit. From a contemporary French postcard published by E.L.D. (Author's collection)

The Territorial Force Battalions

As we have seen, at the outbreak of war, there were 22 kilted Territorial battalions, of which 17 were provided by the five principal Highland regiments and five were exceptional, such as the London Scottish.

The Territorial battalions were all originally destined for home defence. Accordingly, on mobilisation, they took up their home stations. Many (but not all) deployed to Bedford where,

---

25 Wauchope, *Black Watch*, Vol.1, p.345.

Highland soldiers of the Territorial Highland Division compete in a dancing competition at a Highland Games at Bedford in 1915. From a contemporary photographic postcard by Blake & Edgar. (Author's collection)

with the exception of the Black Watch, the Territorial battalions of the principal Highland regiments were concentrated as the Highland Division, consisting of 12 battalions.[26]

Thus, unlike the Regular Army, the Territorial Force was to provide a uniquely Highland division. The remaining kilted Territorial battalions took up their war stations around the country, mainly on coastal defence.[27]

At an early stage, the government called on the Territorial Force to volunteer for overseas service. Many men did so, but not all, and we will return to this issue later in the chapter. The overseas volunteers were then separated from the "home service only" men and the battalions split. The overseas men constituted the 'First Line' Territorial battalions, while those who stayed behind and others recruited to them became the 'Second Line' Territorial battalions, which took the place of the original battalions in home defence. Thus, for example, the overseas and home defence battalions formed from 4th Gordons were designated 1/4th and 2/4th Gordons respectively. After the second-line battalions had been formed, 'third-line' or reserve battalions were created in order to train and supply drafts to the others, but principally to the first-line battalions. These were designated for example 3/4th Gordons. The second and third-line 'home service' Territorial battalions are considered below.

---

26 Campbell, *Engine*, p.18.
27 Wauchope, *Black Watch*, Vol.2, pp.3-6, 39-42, 125-128, 239-250; Ewing, Maj. John, *The Royal Scots 1914-1919* (Edinburgh: Oliver & Boyd, 1925), pp.6, 8; IWM Books, Reid, 'Shoulder to Shoulder,' pp.2-18; Weir, *Come on Highlanders!* pp.30-53; Lindsay, *London Scottish*, pp.16-27; Lloyd, *London Scottish*, pp.25-32; McGilchrist, *Liverpool Scottish*, pp.13-21; Giblin, *Bravest*, pp.6-11.

At the opening of hostilities, most of the Territorial battalions were under strength. With the commitment to overseas service, and the formation of the first-line battalions, the problem was exacerbated as some men were too young, too old or too infirm to serve overseas. In addition, not all men were willing, and a proportion remained behind on home service duties. Part 2 Orders for 1/8th Argylls record the extent of these shortfalls in one battalion. On 23 March, 1915, 82 men were struck off the strength of the battalion at Bedford and sent to 2/8th Battalion at Dunoon, while orders dated 26 April list 175 men who were to proceed to Scotland the following night, and identifies the reasons as follows:[28]

For Imperial Service, but under 19 years of age	20
Men who have never accepted Imperial Service	108
For Imperial Service but medically unfit	47

Consequently, the first-line battalions had to be rapidly recruited to strength. As a result, the Territorial battalions sent overseas did not by any means consist solely of pre-war trained Territorials. Many of the men who went out on initial deployment had been recruited after the war began. One useful source of recruits to the Highland Division in Bedford was London, from where a significant number of recruits were drawn, many of them being surplus recruits to the London Scottish. This phenomenon is examined in depth later in the chapter.

Corners were cut in the need to fill the battalions going overseas. Albert Strachan, a 19-year old pre-war Territorial in 1/6th Gordons describes the most cursory of medical examinations when the battalion was finally warned for foreign service.

> We were to have a medical examination which we thought would be strict and many would not pass. One would hardly credit what took place. In batches we were put in a room, took off all our clothes and marched naked along a passage and came to a door at which a clerk sat and the Medical Officer stood by. The Clerk asked Name and Number. The M.O. said, "Are you all right?" "Yes, sir". Gave you a tap with his instrument, said "A1" and you was passed for foreign service. No-one who wished to go was rejected. In front of me was a boy of 16 yrs. "How old are you?" asked the M.O. "19", the boy replied. "Do you wish to go to France?" "Yes, sir", "A1" shouted the Dr and off he went.[29]

Norman Macmillan describes how the strength of 1st Glasgow Highlanders was made up before departure overseas in November, 1914, by drafting 400 untrained men from the 2nd Battalion. "We who were selected for these drafts had never worn regimental uniform or equipment, had never handled a Service rifle in drill or fired a shot from one on the range. We were, without doubt, almost completely untrained militarily."[30] Similar expedients were adopted to ensure that both the London Scottish[31] and Liverpool Scottish[32] were able to deploy quickly to France. The

---

28 ASHM NE 8.4 1/8th Bn Argyll & Sutherland Highlanders, Part 2 Orders, 23 March, 26 April, 1915.
29 GHM. PB2984, Strachan, memoir.
30 IWM 3460 PP Macmillan, Wg Cdr N., diary, author's preface.
31 Lindsay, *London Scottish*, pp.20-21; Lloyd, *London Scottish*, pp.28, 163.
32 McGilchrist, *Liverpool Scottish*, pp.15, 24.

implication of this practice is that Territorial battalions were being dishonestly declared fit for service when their Commanding Officers must have known otherwise.

It is indeed quite evident that at the beginning of the war, most Territorial battalions were woefully under-trained, ill-equipped and not really prepared for the job they had to do. Much could be written about the Highland battalions in this respect, but there is no reason to believe that this lack of preparedness was any more applicable to them than to the rest of the Territorial Force. Those seeking confirmation can do no better than study the diary of Sir Arthur Grant, who was in command of 5th Gordons at the outbreak of the war. From the very start he had reservations about the professionalism of himself, his officers and his N.C.O.'s.[33] There are numerous other references.[34] Norman Macmillan of the Glasgow Highlanders, who subsequently rose to the rank of Wing Commander in the R.A.F, wrote retrospectively in damning terms regarding the Territorials; "War Minister Lord Kitchener regarded this Force insufficiently trained for immediate active service; from my own experience I know that he was right."[35] Only the desperate need to fill gaps in the line could have justified their early deployment at all.

Initial deployment of T.F. battalions

However, with the urgent need for reinforcements at the Front, an early call was made on the Territorial battalions, and between September, 1914 and February, 1915, 12 kilted Territorial battalions were deployed overseas piecemeal as they were deemed ready and distributed amongst the divisions according to need.[36] These are listed in Table 2.1 (see next page).

Six of these battalions were removed from the Highland Division, still in training at Bedford.[37] This represented half its infantry strength, leaving only six of its original battalions. In order to make up the deficit, six replacement battalions were drafted into the division. Two of these battalions were Highland, the 1/6th and 1/7th Black Watch, which had previously been

---

33 GHM PB107.1 Grant, Arthur, diary, passim.
34 For 5th Black Watch, see BWA Quekett, Hugh Scott, typescript memoir, 'Jottings of an ordinary man. From childhood to the end of the Great War 1914-1918,' 32pp, pp.12-14. For 6th Gordons, see GHM PB3309 Pelham Burn, Henry, letters to father, 12 October, & to mother, 23 October, 1914. For 4th Gordons see GHM PB1699 Anon, 'As We Go Up the Line to Death, The Story of the University of Aberdeen Company of the 4th Battalion of the Gordon Highlanders in the Great War of 1914-1918', 83pp, pp.23-24, quoting diary of J.F. Knowles, 21 December, 1914; GHM PB3279 Matthews, James, diary, 6, 12 January, 1915.
35 IWM 3460 Macmillan, diary, author's preface.
36 Lindsay, *London Scottish*, pp.22-27, 46; Lloyd, *London Scottish*, pp.29-32, 45; Wauchope, *Black Watch*, Vol.2, pp.3-7, 39-42; McGilchrist, *Liverpool Scottish*, pp.16-21; Giblin, *Bravest*, pp.6-11; IWM Books, Reid, 'Shoulder to Shoulder,' pp.17-18; Weir, *Come on Highlanders!* pp.42-53; Fairrie, *Queen's Own Highlanders*, pp.97-99; Haldane, Lt Col M.M., *History of the Fourth Battalion The Seaforth Highlanders* (London: H.F. & G. Witherby, 1927) pp.47-63, Falls, *Gordon Highlanders*, pp.31, 34; Morrison, A.D. (text), *7th Battalion The Great War 1914-1919* (Alva, Scotland, Robert Cunningham, n.d.), pp.9-18; Watt, *Steel and Tartan*, pp.14-27; Craig-Brown, *Historical Records*, Vol.3, pp.421-450; Fairrie, *Queen's Own Highlanders*, pp.103-105; Forrester, James & Crawford, Watson, *The War Diary of the 9th Argyll & Sutherland Highlanders, Dumbartonshire Men at the Front* (Glasgow: History Department, Jordanhill College, 1978); Ewing, *Royal Scots*, pp.6, 8, 86; Royal Scots RHQ, *9th Battalion Royal Scots*, passim.
37 Bewsher, Maj. F.W., *The History of the Fifty First (Highland) Division 1914-1918*, (Uckfield: NMP reprint, n.d.), p.7.

Table 2.1 Early deployment of Territorial battalions to France and Belgium

Battalion	Date disembarked
1st London Scottish	16 September 1914
1/5th Black Watch	2 November 1914
1st Liverpool Scottish	3 November 1914
1st Glasgow Highlanders	5 November 1914
1/4th Seaforths	6 November 1914
1/6th Gordons	9 November 1914
1/7th Argylls	16 December 1914
1/4th Gordons	20 February 1915
1/4th Camerons	20 February 1915
1/9th Argylls	20 February 1915
1/4th Black Watch	26 February 1915
1/9th Royal Scots	26 February 1915

employed on coastal defence. The remaining four battalions were provided by an entire brigade from Lancashire. The overall result was that, when the Highland Division deployed to France at the beginning of May, 1915, its infantry was actually one third English! It was very soon re-designated as 51st (Highland) Division and included the following Highland battalions.[38]

152nd Brigade
1/5th Seaforth Highlanders
1/6th Seaforth Highlanders
1/6th Argyll and Sutherland Highlanders
1/8th Argyll and Sutherland Highlanders

153rd Brigade
1/5th Gordon Highlanders
1/7th Gordon Highlanders
1/6th Black Watch
1/7th Black Watch

1/5th Argylls and 1/6th H.L.I meanwhile sailed from Devonport in May, 1915 with 52nd (Lowland) Division, and landed at Cape Helles, Gallipoli, on 3 July, the last of the First Line kilted Territorial battalions to enter a theatre of war.[39]

Three new Highland battalions, of Territorial origin, were actually created later in the war in Egypt, by converting Yeomanry regiments into infantry. The first two of these battalions were created in September/October, 1916; 10th Camerons, from the Lovat Scouts,[40] and 13th Black Watch, from the Scottish Horse.[41] Despite their new official identities, both battalions retained their original uniforms and identities for the rest of the war, did not adopt the kilt, and should not truly be considered Highland regiments at all. Both were almost immediately sent to Salonika, where they arrived in October, 1916. The third 'converted' battalion was 14th

---

38 Ibid., pp.7, 8, 11, 18; Campbell, *Engine*, pp.22-25.
39 Malcolm, Lt Col G.I., of Poltalloch, *The History of the Argyll and Sutherland Highlanders (Princess Louise's) 1794-1949* (Edinburgh: Mclagan & Cumming, 1949), pp.82-83.
40 Craig-Brown, *Historical Records*, Vol.4, pp.389-390.
41 Wauchope, *Black Watch*, Vol.3, pp.293-300.

Black Watch, created in January, 1917, from the Fife and Forfar Yeomanry. This battalion was committed to the Palestine campaign. Unlike 13th Battalion, they would ultimately adopt the kilt.[42]

Second Line Battalions
When the 'Second Line' Territorial battalions were established a parallel divisional organisation was set up to accommodate them. For the principal Highland regiments, this was the 2nd Highland Division, later numbered the 64th. Initially based in Scotland, the division moved to East Anglia in 1916. Then, during 1917 and 1918, a major restructuring took place, in which the 'Second Line' units were withdrawn and replaced by the Graduated Battalions we describe below. The fate of the other Second Line Territorial battalions is rather more interesting: four were deployed to Ireland, in view of the security situation there, and two were actually deployed direct to the Western Front. Thus, 2/9th Royal Scots, 2/6th H.L.I. and 2/9th H.L.I. (Glasgow Highlanders) all moved to Ireland in 1917.[43] 2nd London Scottish, meanwhile, had already moved to Ireland at the end of April, 1916, but after a very short stay deployed to France in June.[44] 2nd Liverpool Scottish followed them to France in February, 1917.[45]

Third Line Territorial battalions
The 'third-line' or reserve battalions were created in order to train and supply drafts to the others, but principally to the first-line battalions. Initially, there was one Third Line battalion for each First Line battalion in a regiment. Thus, in the Seaforths, for example, there were 3/4th, 3/5th and 3/6th Battalions. These battalions were generally constituted at their home bases, but from about November, 1915, those of the Seaforths, Gordons, Camerons and Argylls were concentrated at Ripon in Yorkshire, to be joined by those of the Black Watch in 1916. This concentration of the kilted Territorial training battalions at Ripon had the effect of attracting a significant number of Yorkshiremen into their ranks. In 1916, within the regiments, the separate Third Line battalions were amalgamated. Thus, for example, the 3/4th, 3/5th and 3/6th Seaforths were amalgamated to become the 4th Reserve Training Battalion Seaforth Highlanders. The Ripon reserve training battalions were all moved to stations nearer home in 1918.[46]

Kitchener Battalions

At the commencement of hostilities, Lord Kitchener realised that a much larger army would need to be raised than could be supplied by the existing Regular and Territorial battalions. He determined to expand the Army considerably. In so doing, he decided not to use the existing

---

42   Ibid., Vol.3, pp.315-323; Ogilvie, D.D., *The Fife and Forfar Yeomanry and 14th (F. and F. Yeo) Battn, R.H. 1914-1919*,(London: John Murray, 1921), pp.41-119.
43   Ewing, *Royal Scots*, pp.778-779; Aiken, Alex, *Courage Past, A Duty Done*, (Glasgow: privately published, 1971), pp.125-126.
44   Lindsay, *London Scottish*, pp.225-233; Lloyd, *London Scottish*, pp.161-173.
45   McGilchrist, *Liverpool Scottish*, pp. 189-197; Giblin, *Bravest*, pp.92-94.
46   Wauchope, *Black Watch*, Vol.2, pp.344-345; Fairrie, *Queen's Own Highlanders*, pp.110-111; Haldane, *Fourth Seaforths*, p.329; Craig-Brown, *Historical Records*, Vol.3, pp.463-468; Rorke, F, *Roll of Officers 1st Dumbartonshire Volunteer Rifle Corps* (1937), p.29.

Territorial Force organisation as a basis, but to raise separate 'New Army' or 'Kitchener's Army' battalions. Sensibly, however, instead of creating brand new regiments, he chose to create new battalions of existing regiments, their battalion numbers following sequentially from the Territorials.

Two specifically Scottish divisions were raised as part of Kitchener's Army; 9th Division, the first of the New Army divisions to be raised, and 15th Division. Both divisions were about half Highland and half Lowland. 9th Division initially included six Highland battalions (8th Black Watch, 7th Seaforths, 8th Gordons, 5th Camerons, 10th Argylls, plus 9th Seaforths, who formed the divisional Pioneers).[47] 15th Division included seven Highland battalions (9th Black Watch, 8th Seaforths, 10th Gordons, 6th and 7th Camerons, 11th Argylls, plus 9th Gordons, who formed the divisional Pioneers).[48] The two Pioneer Battalions had tasks which included building roads, communication trenches, strong points, trench mortar emplacements, drainage and field tramways. In addition, 26th Division included two Highland battalions; 10th Black Watch and 12th Argylls. 9th Division arrived in France in May, 1915, 15th Division in July, 1915,[49] 26th Division, with its two Highland battalions, in September, 1915.

More Kitchener battalions were raised, also intended for overseas service. But in 1915 these were converted to reserve training battalions, to act as feeders to the Kitchener battalions at the front. In September, 1916, these reserve battalions lost their regimental designations and became instead Training Reserve Battalions.[50] At least in the Black Watch and Cameron battalions, the staff continued to wear their regimental uniforms, but from summer, 1916, for example, the men in 38th Training Reserve Battalion (formerly 11th Black Watch) wore khaki kilts. Some of these battalions were reconstituted later as Gordon Highlanders young soldier battalions.

In addition, two Highland Labour Battalions were created; 12th (Labour) Battalion The Black Watch[51] and 9th (Labour) Battalion Queen's Own Cameron Highlanders.[52] These battalions were ironically drawn from men unfit for service in the front line (mostly category B2), as a rule elderly and not physically strong. 9th Camerons were not issued with kilts, and it seems unlikely that 12th Black Watch were either, the regimental history being silent on this point. The battalions moved to France in June and September, 1916, respectively.

Finally, there were a number of late creations of Kitchener battalions. 2/9th Black Watch was formed after the original 9th Black Watch had been absorbed by 4/5th Battalion in May, 1918, and arrived in France on 30 July, 1918. 11th Camerons exceptionally were raised in theatre in France in June, 1918, as we shall see. There were also several additional battalions of Argylls raised. Most importantly, 14th Argylls were formed in early 1915, but did not land at Le Havre until June, 1916. Reduced to a cadre it moved back to England in June, 1918. There it was reconstituted, by absorbing 17th Battalion, and returned to France in July. Three other late-formed Argyll battalions (15th, 16th and 17th) did not see service overseas.

---

47 Ewing, John, *The History of the Ninth (Scottish) Division*, (London: John Murray, 1921), p.6.
48 Stewart, Lt Col J., & Buchan, John, *The Fifteenth (Scottish) Division 1914-1919*, (Edinburgh: William Blackwood & Sons, 1926), pp.1-15, 286-288.
49 Ibid., pp.225-226 1-17, 286-288.
50 Wauchope, *Black Watch*, Vol.3, pp.269-277; Fairrie, *Queen's Own Highlanders*, p.116; Addison-Smith, Lt Col C.L., *10th Battalion The Seaforth Highlanders in the Great War* (Edinburgh: privately published, 1927), passim; Craig-Brown, *Historical Records*, Vol.3, pp.375-386.
51 Wauchope, *Black Watch*, Vol.3, pp.285-288.
52 Craig-Brown, *Historical Records*, Vol.4, pp.387-388.

The Graduated and Young Soldier Battalions

In October, 1917, three Graduated or Young Soldiers Battalions were designated as Gordon Highlanders; 51st Graduated Battalion, 52nd Graduated Battalion[53] and 53rd Young Soldier Battalion. These battalions were allocated to the training of young conscripts. The recruits would first attend the Young Soldiers battalions, from where they would be sent on to the Graduated Battalions to complete their training. The Gordons battalions were created by re-designating existing battalions which had lost their regimental identity, though all had previously existed as Highland battalions. For example, 51st Graduated Battalion Gordon Highlanders was created from 202nd Graduated Battalion. Before that it had been 38th Training Reserve battalion, and up to September, 1916, had been the 11th (Reserve) Battalion of the Black Watch.[54] The change in regimental allegiance on creation of the Gordons battalions was not entirely welcome.[55] In March and April, 1919, all three battalions were deployed to Germany, where they joined the Army of Occupation.[56]

Garrison Battalions

Two Highland Garrison Battalions, of Seaforths and Gordons, were raised from men who were below the normal standard of fitness. They were intended to serve as Garrison troops abroad, to relieve other fitter troops for fighting. Sym comments on the composition of the Seaforths battalion.

> These men, for the most part, belonged to categories who were, for various reasons, not up to physical standards demanded by the War. Some failed to reach the standard by reason of age, some as the result of wounds, and from other causes. Many were seasoned old soldiers … The Officers, for the most part, were drawn from categories similar to those of the men.[57]

1st Garrison Battalion Gordon Highlanders was formed in 1916 and known as the 12th Battalion for a short time. The Battalion departed in January, 1917, for India, where it arrived in March, and where it was based at Rawalpindi.[58] 1st Garrison Battalion Seaforth Highlanders

---

53 Craig-Brown, *Historical Records*, Vol.4, pp.375-386.
54 Anon, *The 51st Battalion The Gordon Highlanders 1914-1920* (Mansfield: F. Willman, n.d.), passim; Wauchope, *Black Watch*, Vol.3, pp.277-280.
55 On feelings regarding the conversion of former 11th Black Watch to 51st Gordons, see: *51st Battalion*, p.9; BWA Paul, Phil, letter to Miss May Merrett, 1 November, 1917. On same regarding conversion of former 8th Camerons to 52nd Gordons, see: Craig-Brown, *Historical Records*, Vol.3, pp.384-386.
56 *51st Battalion*, pp.17-24; GHM PB507 Wallace, Col. H.R., Diary 53rd Bn Gordon Highlanders
57 Sym, Col. John, ed, *Seaforth Highlanders* (Aldershot: Gale & Polden, 1962), pp.226-227.
58 GHM PB 2459 Williams, Cpl J., 'Diary of my voyage from Plymouth 20/01/1917 to Bombay, India, 14/3/1917'; GHM PB3112 Blinco, Sgt H.A., manuscript memoir, 'Rough Diary of a Voyage with D Coy 1st F.S. Garr. Battalion Gordon Highlanders to the Far East', 50pp; GHM PB2788/1 Emslie, Henry, diary.

Soldiers of 1st Garrison Battalion Seaforth Highlanders in Salonika. Not the ideal representatives of a martial race (Author's collection)

was formed in July 1916 and in August moved to Salonika.[59] Although intended for duty in the city, the battalion was sent up to the Struma front and spent 18 months of duty in the trenches facing the Bulgarians, "contrary at least to the letter of their enrolment, but not to the spirit of the men." Captain Wyllie notes both their unsuitability for such service and their exceptional vulnerability to malaria.[60] After the armistice with Bulgaria, the battalion served in garrisoning Constanza, and various towns in the Dobrudja province of Romania. Later it was moved to Constantinople, disembarking on 2 January, 1919. It was soon given the task of guarding the Anatolian Railway. Demobilisation was nevertheless well under way by March and by July the remains of the battalion had been broken up.[61]

Canadian Highland regiments

On the outbreak of war, as we have seen, Canada had a very small regular army, with no Highland units, and a large number of volunteer Militia regiments, amongst which were a number of

---

59 Fairrie, *Queen's Own Highlanders*, p.116; Sym, *Seaforth Highlanders*, pp.226-227. For accounts of this battalion, see LC SAL 059, Shipton, Charles Eldred Curwen, diary; IWM 7508 PP Wyllie, Capt. A.T., diary, passim; IWM PP 12688 MacKay, Maj. G.S., letters, January to August, 1917, passim.
60 IWM Wyllie, diary, 5, 16 August, 1917.
61 Ibid., passim from 30 December, 1918; Fairrie, *Queen's Own Highlanders*, p.116; Sym, *Seaforth Highlanders*, pp.226-227.

Highland units. Rather than build on the existing Militia regiments, the Minister for Militia, Sir Sam Hughes, opted to create an entirely new structure for the Canadian Expeditionary Force (C.E.F.), inviting the Militia regiments to send contingents of volunteers which would then be combined into completely new battalions, without necessarily any allegiance to the old Militia regiments.[62] In some respects, by ignoring the existing volunteer structures, he was mirroring the creation of the New Armies in Britain by Lord Kitchener. In two important respects, however, his approach was different. First, Kitchener did not disband the Territorial units in being, but allowed them to continue, and, indeed, to expand; by contrast, Hughes looked to the Militia only as a source of recruits. Second, Kitchener was careful to create his new battalions within the existing regimental structure, such that regimental pride could be inherited by the New Army soldiers; by contrast, Hughes was in principle creating totally new entities, with no inherited tradition.

Of course, in many of the Highland Militia battalions this "tradition" was a fairly recent invention. Nevertheless, Hughes' decision to ignore the existing Militia regiments provoked considerable resentment. Some Militia commanders had already offered their complete battalions for service at the outbreak of war, and a number fought so hard to keep their unit identity that the government finally agreed to let them proceed overseas as units.[63] In these cases, they acquired a new C.E.F. battalion number, but retained their identity in both their uniform and a suffix to their title. Thus, for example, the 79th Militia Regiment provided the 43rd Battalion C.E.F. (Cameron Highlanders of Canada). In due course, a number of additional C.E.F. Highland battalions were raised without any previous Militia associations. In the end, out of 260 infantry battalions raised for the C.E.F. a total of 23 were Highland.

Only eight of these Highland battalions actually served at the front. It was found that, given the attrition rate, and despite the introduction of conscription in 1917, Canada was unable to sustain more than four divisions, comprising 48 infantry battalions, at the front. Thus, after the fighting divisions had been provided for, the C.E.F. battalions which arrived in Britain were either broken up or incorporated into reserve battalions in England which were used to supply drafts to reinforce battalions at the front. Although reinforcement from sister battalions was common, the practice was not universal and reinforcements might be provided from non-Highland battalions. Similarly, Highland battalions once broken up were not drafted universally either to sister battalions or other Highland battalions.

The eight Highland battalions which survived to serve at the Front were as follows:

> 13th Battalion C.E.F. (Royal Highlanders of Canada)
> 15th Battalion C.E.F. (48th Highlanders of Canada)
> 16th Battalion C.E.F. (The Canadian Scottish)
> 42nd Battalion C.E.F. (Royal Highlanders of Canada)
> 43rd Battalion C.E.F. (Cameron Highlanders of Canada)
> 72nd Battalion C.E.F. (Seaforth Highlanders of Canada)
> 73rd Battalion C.E.F. (Royal Highlanders of Canada)
> 85th Battalion C.E.F. (Nova Scotia Highlanders)

---

62 For a useful discussion of the formation of the C.E.F., see Chartrand, *Canadian Corps*.
63 Those Highland Militia regiments which did not succeed in raising affiliated C.E.F. battalions were 50th (Gordons), 78th (Pictou) and 94th (Argylls).

Kilted Canadian officers of the First Canadian Contingent on Salisbury Plain shortly after their arrival, from a contemporary postcard by Tuck's. (Author's collection)

Of these eight battalions, despite Sam Hughes' policy, no fewer than six had been formed and provided by single Militia regiments and maintained their Militia title and uniforms. These were 13th, 42nd and 73rd Battalions, all formed by the 5th Royal Highlanders of Canada, 15th Battalion, formed by the 48th Highlanders of Canada, 43rd Battalion, formed by the 79th Cameron Highlanders of Canada and 72nd Battalion, raised by the 72nd Seaforth Highlanders of Canada. Of the other two battalions, the 16th Battalion (The Canadian Scottish) was formed by amalgamating contingents of four different Highland Militia regiments; 50th (Gordon Highlanders), 72nd (Seaforth Highlanders), 79th (Cameron Highlanders) and 91st (Argyll & Sutherland Highlanders). There were challenges in forming a cohesive unit from these disparate elements, which at times became quite acute.[64] The final battalion was a new one raised in Nova Scotia. Authorisation to raise a Highland battalion in the province, the 85th Battalion C.E.F., was granted on 14 September, 1915, and recruiting was so successful, that it was decided to create an entire Nova Scotia Highland Brigade of four battalions. The Brigade arrived in England in October, 1916, but, in the end, only the 85th were sent to France.[65]

64 Urquhart, *Canadian Scottish*, pp.6-44, 323-331.
65 Hayes, Lt Col Joseph, *The Eighty-Fifth in France and Flanders*, (Halifax, Nova Scotia: Royal Print & Litho Ltd, 1920) passim; see also Hunt, *Nova Scotia's Part*, pp.99-115.

The Canadian battalions deployed to France via England as follows; February, 1915 (13th, 15th and 16th Battalions[66]), October, 1915 (42nd Battalion[67]). February, 1916 (43rd Battalion[68]), August, 1916 (72nd and 73rd Battalions[69]) and February, 1917 (85th Battalion[70])

The South Africans

In South Africa, the two kilted volunteer regiments, the Cape Town Highlanders and the Transvaal Scottish, were both mobilised on the outbreak of war.[71] Both regiments were committed to the campaign in German South West Africa and were afterwards disbanded by August, 1915. A 2nd Battalion of the Transvaal Scottish was formed on the outbreak of the Boer rebellion at the end of September 1914. After service against the rebels, it was also committed to German South West Africa and subsequently disbanded.

By July 1915, the Imperial government had accepted an offer from Botha to provide a contingent for service in Europe. For this purpose, new forces had to be raised. Neither the Cape Town Highlanders nor the Transvaal Scottish, as part of the Active Citizen Force, were eligible for service outside southern Africa. Accordingly, four completely new battalions were raised to form a South African Brigade. As soon as the British government had accepted the offer, the local expatriate Scots got to work once more, in a continuation of pre-war practice, and proposed that one of the battalions should be kilted. The British government undertook to equip the battalion in Highland dress, and permission to use the Murray-Atholl tartan, already the tartan of the Transvaal Scottish, was obtained from the Duke of Atholl.[72] Thus the 4th South African Infantry battalion came to be the South African Scottish.[73] It was drawn largely from the 1st and 2nd Transvaal Scottish, the Cape Town Highlanders, and from the Caledonian societies throughout South Africa. The brigade formed and trained at Potchefstroom. By October, 1915, the whole brigade had sailed for England, where, on arrival, it was quartered at Bordon.

The South Africans were not destined for immediate service on the Western Front, however. On 30 December 1915, as a result of the Senussi revolt in the Western Desert, the South African Scottish embarked with the brigade at Devonport for Alexandria, where they arrived in January 1916. When the rebellion was over, they returned to Alexandria, and in April 1916 sailed for Marseilles, from where in May, the entire brigade joined 9th (Scottish) Division on the Western

---

66 Fetherstonhaugh, *13th Battalion*, pp.4-32, 305-318; Wauchope, *Black Watch*, Vol.2, .349-372; Beattie, *48th Highlanders*, passim; Beal, *Family*, pp.43-67; Urquhart, *Canadian Scottish*, pp.6-44, 323-331.
67 Topp, Lt Col C. Bereseford, *The 42nd Battalion, C.E.F., Royal Highlanders of Canada, in the Great War*, (Montreal: Gazette Printing, 1931), pp.3-20, 301-309. See also Wauchope, *Black Watch*, Vol.2, pp.349-372.
68 Craig-Brown, *Historical Records*, Vol.3, pp.7-10, 34.
69 McEvoy & Finlay, *Seaforth Highlanders of Canada*, pp.12-22, 172-191; Wauchope, *Black Watch*, Vol.2, 349-359; Fetherstonhaugh, *13th Battalion*, pp.175-176; Topp, *42nd Battalion*, p.135.
70 Hayes, *Eighty-Fifth*, passim; Hunt, *Nova Scotia's Part*, pp.99-115.
71 Orpen, *Cape Town Highlanders*, pp.75-81; Juta, *Transvaal Scottish*, pp.75-106.
72 Juta, *Transvaal Scottish*, pp.105, 122.
73 For the service and organisation of the South African Scottish see Orpen, *Cape Town Highlanders*, pp.81-92, and Juta, *Transvaal Scottish*, pp.105, 122-134.

South African Scottish march through Marseilles on 8 May, 1916, after returning from the Western Desert to deploy to the Western Front. Their reception was riotous. From a contemporary French postcard, published by E.L.D. (Author's collection)

Front.[74] Meanwhile, other men of the Transvaal Scottish joined a Scottish company of the 9th South African Infantry battalion which served in German East Africa.[75]

Deployment: the Western Front

As we have seen there were many varieties of kilted battalions committed to the Western Front; the Regular battalions, five initially from home and, later, another five brought back from overseas, all of which had been committed by the end of 1914; the first Territorial battalions, twelve in all, committed early in an emergency response, between September, 1914 and February, 1915; the Territorial Highland Division itself, including a further eight kilted battalions, in May, 1915; later even two second line Territorial battalions, 2nd London Scottish in May, 1916, and 2nd Liverpool Scottish in February, 1917; the New Army divisions, 9th (Scottish) Division with a further six Highland battalions, in May, 1915, 15th Division, with seven Highland battalions, in July, 1915, and 26th Division, with its two Highland battalions, in September, 1915; two Labour Battalions in 1916; the late formed 14th Argylls in June, 1916; the eight Canadian kilted battalions, which arrived in theatre between February, 1915 and February, 1917, and the South African Scottish who arrived in April, 1916. This makes a total of 59 kilted battalions deployed to the Western Front, and there were more to come, arriving from lesser theatres to supplement the forces in France and Belgium, especially in 1918. At the same time,

74 Orpen, *Cape Town Highlanders* pp.82-84; Juta, *Transvaal Scottish*, pp.123-124.
75 Juta, *Transvaal Scottish*, pp.105-106.

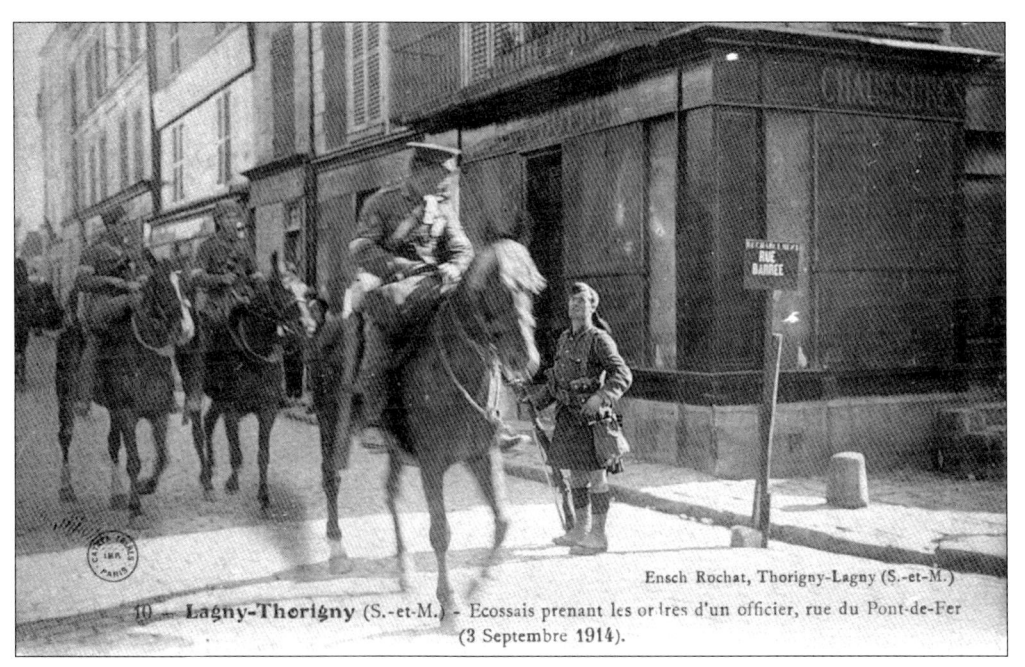

A Highland soldier at Lagny-Thorigny on 3 September, 1914, at the end of the Great Retreat, with the British Army about to turn and fight. A contemporary French postcard by local company Ensch Rochat. (Author's collection)

there were losses. A number of battalions deployed from the Western Front to lesser theatres, while others were disbanded, absorbed or amalgamated.

Of the ten regular battalions, five remained on the Western Front throughout the war (1st Black Watch, 2nd Seaforths, 1st Gordons, 1st Camerons, 2nd Argylls,) but five were subsequently deployed overseas. Thus, in November, 1915, both 2nd Camerons and 1st Argylls moved to Salonika,[76] while in December, 1915, 2nd Black Watch and 1st Seaforths moved to Mesopotamia.[77] Finally, 2nd Gordons moved to Italy in November, 1917.[78] Thus, quite astonishingly, half of the most effective kilted fighting battalions were removed from the principal theatre of war, where one might have considered their presence essential to stiffen resolve, and were sent to lesser theatres. None would see service on the Western Front again. Interestingly, too, the battalions which were sent to the lesser theatres were exactly those which had been brought home from overseas at the opening of hostilities, while the original home-based battalions all remained on the Western Front.

Of the 22 kilted Territorial battalions committed directly to the Western Front, only two were subsequently deployed to lesser theatres (although two had already been deployed direct from Britain to Gallipoli), in marked contrast with the Regulars. The first of these were 2nd London Scottish, who, having arrived in France in June, 1916, were quickly whisked away in

76 Craig-Brown, *Historical Records*, Vol.3, pp.316-320; Anderson, *1st Argylls*, pp.45-47.
77 Fairrie, *Queen's Own Highlanders*, p.88; Wauchope, *Black Watch*, Vol.1, pp.198-206.
78 Falls, *Gordon Highlanders*, pp.176, 232.

November to Salonika.[79] The second was 1/6th Argylls. They had arrived in France with the Highland Division, but in June, 1916, had transferred to 5th Division as a Pioneer Battalion. In November, 1917, they moved to Italy with the division.[80] Meanwhile, three Territorial battalions had actually been left behind when their divisions departed for other theatres; thus, unlike their Regular counterparts, neither 1/4th Black Watch nor 1/4th Seaforths went to Mesopotamia with the Meerut Division in December, 1915, nor did 1/9th Royal Scots go to Salonika with 27th Division in November. Instead, all three battalions, after temporary transfers to other divisions, joined 51st Highland Division between January and March, 1916.[81]

Through losses and recruiting difficulties, the Territorial battalions were subject to some disbandments and amalgamations, again in contrast to their Regular colleagues. Three battalions were effectively disbanded; 1/4th Camerons, broken up in 1916,[82] 1/9th Argylls, which had by April, 1916, effectively ceased to function as an infantry battalion.[83] and 2nd Liverpool Scottish, who were absorbed by their 1st Battalion in April, 1918.[84] Otherwise, four battalions were amalgamated to create two new merged battalions; 1/4th and 1/5th Black Watch were amalgamated in March, 1916, to form a new battalion, designated 4/5th Black Watch,[85] while 1/6th and 1/7th Gordons were amalgamated to form 6/7th Gordons, in October, 1918.[86]

The remaining 13 kilted Territorial battalions continued to serve on the Western Front until the end of the war. In 51st Highland Division, the Lancashire battalions departed in January, 1916, and were replaced by 1/4th and 1/5th Black Watch, 1/4th Seaforths and 1/4th Camerons, four of the Highland battalions which had arrived in France before the division.[87] The Highland Division thereby regained its ethnic purity. Further changes took place in February, 1916, when 1/4th and 1/5th Black Watch were detached, subsequently to be amalgamated, and 1/4th Camerons detached and subsequently broken up. These battalions were replaced by 1/9th Royal Scots, 1/4th Gordons and 1/7th Argylls.[88] When in June, 1916, 1/6th Argylls were, as already observed, transferred as a Pioneer Battalion to 5th Division, they were replaced by 1/6th Gordons.[89] When 51st Division went into action on the Somme, therefore, it was totally Highland in composition, including nine of its original mobilisation battalions and three replacement battalions, all Highland. The Division was obliged to shed three battalions (1/9th Royal Scots, 1/5th Gordons and 1/8th Argylls) when, along with the rest of the army, its brigades were reduced from four to three battalions in early 1918.[90]

---

79   Lindsay, *London Scottish*, pp.233, 240-243; Lloyd, *London Scottish*, pp.173, 176-177.
80   Malcolm, *History Argylls*, pp.82-83; Bewsher, *Fifty First*, p.72.
81   Wauchope, *Black Watch*, Vol.2, pp.23-24; Stewart & Buchan, *Fifteenth Division*, p.55; Bewsher, *Fifty First*, p.53; Fairrie, *Queen's Own Highlanders*, pp.97-99; Haldane, *Fourth Seaforths*, pp.141-153; Ewing, *Royal Scots*, pp.102, 257; *9th Royal Scots*, passim.
82   Watt, *Steel and Tartan*, passim; Craig-Brown, *Historical Records*, Vol.3, pp.421-450; Fairrie, *Queen's Own Highlanders*, pp.103-105.
83   Forrster & Crawford, *9th Argylls*, passim.
84   McGilchrist, *Liverpool Scottish*, pp. 189-197, 219; Giblin, *Bravest*, pp.92-94, 104.
85   Wauchope, *Black Watch*, Vol.2, pp.3-24, 39-51, 67-68; Bewsher, *Fifty First*, p.53; Stewart & Buchan, *Fifteenth Division*, p.55.
86   Falls, *Gordon Highlanders*, pp.31, 44, 73, 230; Bewsher, *Fifty First*, pp.7, 10, 72, 373.
87   Bewsher, *Fifty First*, p.53.
88   Ibid., p.53; Morrison, *7th Argylls*, p.18; Ewing, *Royal Scots*, p.257.
89   Malcolm, *History Argylls*, pp.82-83; Bewsher, *Fifty First*, p.72.
90   Bewsher, *Fifty First*, pp.271-272; Malcolm, *Argyllshire Highlanders*, p.45; Ewing, *Royal Scots*, pp.553-554.

Finally, in October, 1918, when 1/6th and 1/7th Gordons amalgamated, 1/6th Argylls, who had returned to France from Italy with 5th Division in April, 1918, was converted back to an infantry battalion and transferred back to the division.[91]

Apart from 1/6th Argylls, we must also note a number of battalions brought back from lesser theatres overseas. Both 1/5th Argylls and 1/6th H.L.I., which had been deployed direct from home to Gallipoli, returned from Egypt in April, 1918,[92] while 2nd London Scottish, arrived from Alexandria in July, 1918.[93] The 'converted' ex-Yeomanry battalions were also brought back: 10th Camerons,[94] and 13th Black Watch[95] returned from Salonika in June, 1918, while 14th Black Watch arrived from Palestine in early May, 1918. In August, unlike the other two 'converted' battalions, the whole battalion was finally issued with kilts.[96]

As we have seen, 18 kilted Kitchener battalions were committed directly to the Western Front, from May, 1915 onwards; six with 9th Division, seven with 15th Division, two with 26th Division, two Labour Battalions, and the late arrivals, 14th Argylls. To these we may add the replacement 2/9th Black Watch, and a new battalion, 11th Camerons, exceptionally raised in theatre. Only two of these battalions were subsequently deployed to lesser theatres. These were the two battalions (10th Black Watch and 12th Argylls) in 26th Division, which arrived in France in September, 1915, only to be quickly despatched to Salonika in November.[97]

Otherwise the Kitchener battalions suffered from similar reductions and amalgamations to the Territorials. No fewer than six (about one third of them) had ceased to exist by the end of the war, while two had miraculously secured resurrection. The two resurrected battalions were 9th Black Watch and 14th Argylls. The original 9th Black Watch in 15th Division were absorbed by 4/5th Black Watch, a Territorial battalion which had joined the division, in May, 1918. After a short period training American troops, the cadre from 9th Black Watch returned to Aldershot in May, 1918, where a new battalion, designated 2/9th Black Watch, was raised, which arrived in France in July, 1918.[98] 14th Argylls had arrived in France quite late, in June, 1916. In April, 1918, the battalion was reduced to a cadre, after posting about 500 men as drafts, and in June, the cadre crossed to England, where the battalion was reconstituted by absorbing 17th Battalion. In July, it returned to France.[99]

The six reduced New Army battalions were 12th Black Watch, 8th and 10th Gordons, 7th and 9th Camerons, and 11th Argylls. Two of these were the Highland Labour Battalions, 12th Black Watch and 9th Camerons, which had ceased to exist in May, 1917, when the Labour Corps came into being.[100] In May, 1916, as a result of recruiting difficulties, 8th Gordons were amalgamated with 10th Gordons to form the 8/10th Battalion. In June, 1918, 8/10th Battalion

---

91   Malcolm, *History Argylls*, pp.82-83.
92   Ibid.
93   Lindsay, *London Scottish*, pp.337-343; Lloyd, *London Scottish*, pp.231-234.
94   Craig-Brown, *Historical Records*, Vol.4, pp.389-390; Fairrie, *Queen's Own Highlanders*, p.106.
95   Wauchope, *Black Watch*, Vol.3, pp.297-300.
96   Ibid., Vol.3, pp.315-330; Ogilvie, *Fife and Forfar Yeomanry*, pp.119-142.
97   Wauchope, *Black Watch*, Vol.3, 211-213.
98   Ibid., Vol.3, pp.173-175; Stewart & Buchan, *Fifteenth Division*, pp.225-226.
99   ASHM N-E11 BOW.2 Bowie, LCpl J.M. diary, April, 1918 (for sending of drafts to 11th Battalion).
100 Wauchope, *Black Watch*, Vol.3, pp.285-288; Craig-Brown, *Historical Records*, Vol.4, pp.387-388.

itself was absorbed by 1/5th Gordons, a Territorial battalion.[101] In June, 1918, 7th Camerons were absorbed by their 6th Battalion,[102] and in June, 1918, 11th Argylls were absorbed by 1/8th Argylls, another Territorial battalion.[103]

As with the Territorials. with the exception of those battalions which were either deployed to other theatres, disbanded or amalgamated, the remaining Kitchener battalions continued to serve on the Western Front until the end of the war. Most served in either 9th or 15th Scottish Divisions. These two divisions underwent some significant changes, notably the attachment of the South African Brigade (including the South African Scottish) to 9th Division. Otherwise, the most significant change to 15th Division, affecting kilted troops, was the introduction of four Territorial battalions. These were 4/5th Black Watch, which joined in May, 1918 and absorbed 9th Black Watch, and three battalions which joined in June, 1918, having been detached from 51st Division when it reduced its brigades to three battalions each. These were 1/5th Gordons, 1/8th Argylls and 1/9th Royal Scots, of which the first two absorbed 8/10th Gordons and 11th Argylls respectively.[104]

We must also note that 10th Black Watch was brought back to France from Salonika in July, 1918, but was disbanded in October.[105]

Finally, one Highland battalion, exceptionally, was actually raised in France. This was the 11th Camerons, which was formed at Etaples in June, 1918, at first as a Labour battalion. The reason for its designation as Cameron Highlanders is a mystery. The men, drawn from Category B, were from 29 separate labour companies, and were mainly English and Irish. However, an attempt was made to give the battalion a more Scottish character, with 251 Scotsmen joining in exchange for 221 Englishmen and Irishmen who were distributed to other units. "These Scotsmen had been given the option of transferring to the 11th Camerons, or of adopting the uniform of the English battalions to which they were then attached." Several replacement Scottish officers were also brought in at the same time. On 16 July, the role of the battalion was changed from a Labour to a Service battalion, and about the same time the men were issued with kilts. The battalion then served in the line from August 1918 until the Armistice.[106]

We have already noted the deployment of a total of eight kilted Canadian battalions to the Western Front between February, 1915 and February, 1917, battalions which after their arrival continued to receive reinforcements from Canada via reserve battalions in England. All but one of these eight battalions remained in being on the Western Front throughout the war. The exception was 73rd Battalion C.E.F (Royal Highlanders of Canada) which was broken up after the battle for Vimy Ridge in April, 1917. Their place was taken by 85th Battalion (Nova Scotia Highlanders), which had disembarked at Boulogne in February.[107]

---

101 Falls, *Gordon Highlanders*, pp.76-77, 206; Ewing, *Ninth Division*, pp.81-82; Stewart & Buchan, *Fifteenth Division*, pp.68, 225-226.
102 Craig-Brown, *Historical Records*, pp.346-348; Stewart & Buchan, *Fifteenth Division*, pp.225-226; Macleod, Lt Col Norman, *War History of the 6th (Service) Battalion, Queen's Own Cameron Highlanders* (Edinburgh: Wm Blackwood & Sons, 1934), pp.104-105.
103 Stewart & Buchan, *Fifteenth Division*, pp.225-226; Malcolm, *Argyllshire Highlanders*, p.47.
104 Stewart & Buchan, *Fifteenth Division*, pp.225-226; Wauchope, *Black Watch*, Vol.2, p.97, Vol.3, p.173; Falls, *Gordon Highlanders*, p.206; Malcolm, *Argyllshire Highlanders*, p.47; Ewing, *Royal Scots*, p.641.
105 Wauchope, *Black Watch*, Vol.3, pp.250-255.
106 Craig-Brown, *Historical Records*, Vol.3, pp.391-396.
107 Wauchope, *Black Watch*, Vol.2, pp.349-359; Fetherstonhaugh, *13th Battalion*, pp.175-176; Topp, *42nd Battalion*, p.135.

Men of the 16th Battalion C.E.F. (Canadian Scottish) moving up to the front line, 27 September 1918. (IWM CO3289)

The South African Scottish had been brought back to France after helping to suppress the Senussi Revolt. They joined 9th Division, with their brigade, and remained on the Western Front for the remainder of the war, their most memorable battle being the slaughter at Delville Wood in July, 1916.[108]

Deployment outside the Western Front

Although the principal experience of the kilted soldier in the Great War relates to the Western Front, kilted soldiers actually served in many different theatres outside the Western Front, thus ensuring experience of a wide range of climates, landscapes, peoples, insects and diseases, which will figure in our later chapters.

In terms of battalions engaged, the principal theatres which involved Highland troops were Salonika and Palestine. As many as eight Highland battalions were deployed to the Salonika Front. First to arrive, in November, 1915, were the two Kitchener battalions in 26th Division,

---

108 Orpen, *Cape Town Highlanders*, pp.84-92; Juta, *Transvaal Scottish*, pp.124-134; Ewing, *Ninth Division*, pp.81-83, 332-333.

10th Black Watch[109] and 12th Argylls.[110] Next to arrive, in December, were the two Regular battalions in 27th Division, 1st Argylls[111] and 2nd Camerons.[112] They were joined, in August, 1916, by 1st Garrison Battalion Seaforth Highlanders.[113] In October there arrived from Egypt two of the converted 'Yeomanry' regiments, 13th Black Watch,[114] and 10th Camerons.[115] Finally, 2nd London Scottish arrived from England in November, 1916.[116] This last battalion embarked in June, 1917, to move to Egypt. Then in June and July, 1918, three battalions were despatched urgently to meet the crisis in France; 10th and 13th Black Watch, and 10th Camerons. This left four battalions which served on till the end in Salonika. After the armistice with Bulgaria, 12th Argylls were deployed to Ruschuk on the Danube. From there they were deployed in the occupation of Constantinople. Likewise, 1st Garrison Battalion Seaforth Highlanders served in garrisoning Constanza, and various towns in the Dobrudja province of Romania. Later it too was moved to Constantinople, departing on 31 December, 1918. After the armistice with Turkey, 1st Argylls were detached from 27th Division and embarked for Constantinople in December, 1918. The Division itself was sent by sea to Trans-Caucasia, 2nd Camerons embarking with the brigade on 24th December, 1918.

As regards Egypt and Palestine, setting aside the South African Scottish, who deployed to Egypt for the Senussi campaign, and any battalions passing through on transit, five kilted battalions were deployed to theatre, and three Highland battalions were actually created there. First to disembark in Egypt were two Territorial battalions, 1/5th Argylls[117] and 1/6th H.L.I., which arrived from Gallipoli with 52nd Division. Next was another Territorial battalion, 2nd London Scottish, this time from Salonika, which disembarked at Alexandria in July, 1917.[118] The two Regular battalions from Mesopotamia, 2nd Black Watch[119] and 1st Seaforths,[120] arrived in Egypt in January, 1918. All these battalions were committed to the Palestine campaign. Of the three Highland battalions created from Yeomanry in Egypt, two, as we have seen, were almost immediately sent to Salonika; the third, 14th Black Watch, was committed to Palestine. However, of the six kilted battalions actually committed to the Palestine campaign, only the two Regular battalions, 2nd Black Watch and 1st Seaforths, saw out the war there. The other four battalions were all sent to France in response to the crisis there, between April and June, 1918.

Elsewhere, we have already noted the deployment of the Transvaal Scottish and Cape Town Highlanders to German South West Africa in 1914 and 1915, the use of the Transvaal Scottish

---

109 Wauchope, *Black Watch*, Vol.3, pp.211-213, 250-251.
110 LC GS 0456, Dick, Rev Dr, typescript memoirs, pp59-70, diary, 7 November 1918 to 6 January, 1919.
111 Anderson, *1st Argylls*, p.84.
112 Craig-Brown, *Historical Records*, Vol.3, pp.316-355.
113 Fairrie, *Queen's Own Highlanders*, p.116; Sym, *Seaforth Highlanders*, pp.226-227. For accounts of this battalion, see LC SAL 059, Shipton, diary; IWM 7508 Wyllie, diary, passim; IWM PP 12688 MacKay, letters, January to August, 1917, passim.
114 Wauchope, *Black Watch*, Vol.3, pp.293-297.
115 Craig-Brown, *Historical Records*, Vol.4, pp.389-390.
116 Lindsay, *London Scottish*, pp.240-243, 258-261; Lloyd, *London Scottish*, pp.176-177, 187-189.
117 Malcolm, *History Argylls*, pp.82-83.
118 Lindsay, *London Scottish*, pp.258-261, 337-343; Lloyd, *London Scottish*, pp.187-189, 231-234.
119 Wauchope, *Black Watch*, Vol.1, pp.268, 271-272, 290-293.
120 Fairrie, *Queen's Own Highlanders*, pp.88-90.

Other theatres: soldiers of 2nd Black Watch practise marksmanship across sandbag defences on the Palestine coast near Arsuf. (IWM Q12485)

against the Boer rebels in 1914, and the deployment of a Scottish company of the 9th South African Infantry to German East Africa. We have also noticed the deployment of the South African Scottish against the Senussi in the Western Desert. Two Highland battalions served in the Gallipoli campaign; 1/5th Argylls and 1/6th H.L.I., who landed at Cape Helles on 3 July, 1915 with 52nd (Lowland) Division. In January, 1916, both battalions were evacuated from Gallipoli and arrived with the division in Egypt in February.[121] Just two Regular Highland battalions were sent to Mesopotamia. Both 2nd Black Watch and 1st Seaforths arrived in Mesopotamia in December, 1915, with the Meerut Division. Both battalions left Mesopotamia for Egypt on 1 January, 1918.[122] Finally, two kilted battalions were sent to Italy in November, 1917; 2nd Gordons[123] and 1/6th Argylls[124] 1/6th Argylls returned to France in April, 1918, but 2nd Gordons remained in Italy for the rest of the war.

Less well known, perhaps, is the transfer of a number of Highland battalions to Ireland in view of the uncertain security situation there. These were either second-line Territorials or Special Reserve battalions. The first to be sent over, at the end of April, 1916, were 2nd London Scottish. Their headquarters were at Tralee, but their stay was short, as they returned to

121 Malcolm, *History Argylls*, pp.82-83.
122 Wauchope, *Black Watch*, Vol.1, pp.199-200, 204, 222, 232, 268; Fairrie, *Queen's Own Highlanders*, pp.88-90.
123 Falls, *Gordon Highlanders*, pp.176, 266.
124 Malcolm, *History Argylls*, pp.82-83.

Other theatres: soldiers of 5th Argylls helping to make a breakwater at Cape Helles, Gallipoli, 1915. (IWM Q13517)

Other theatres: Mesopotamia. Two soldiers of 1st Seaforth Highlanders with a local Arab under escort in 1917. (Author's collection)

England in May.[125] Next to arrive between January and Spring, 1917, were 2/6th H.L.I, 2/9th H.L.I.[126] and 2/9th Royal Scots.[127] They were based variously at the Curragh, Dublin, Tralee and Limerick. All three battalions had been disbanded in Ireland by July 1918. Finally, three Highland Special Reserve battalions were moved to Ireland in November, 1917, in exchange for Irish battalions, to reduce the chances of stolen weapons. These were; 3rd Camerons, stationed at Birr and Ballynovare,[128] 3rd Argylls, stationed at Kinsale,[129] and 3rd Black Watch, stationed first at Queenstown Harbour, then the Curragh.[130]

Finally, a number of deployments took place after the various Armistice agreements. Thus, 2nd Camerons were sent by sea from the Salonika theatre to Trans-Caucasia, disembarking at Batum in December, 1918. The battalion then moved to Tiflis, from where it finally demobilised by May, 1919.[131] Meanwhile, 1st Argylls[132] disembarked in December, 1918, at Constantinople, as G.H.Q. troops, having sailed from Salonika. From here they were gradually demobilised. Surplus personnel of 1st Argylls were transferred to 12th Argylls,[133] who came down from Ruschuk on the Danube, to relieve them. 12th Argylls were also eventually demobilised from Constantinople. 1st Garrison Battalion Seaforth Highlanders[134] was also brought down to Constantinople from Rumania, disembarking in January, 1919. They were soon given the task of guarding the Anatolian Railway. Demobilisation was nevertheless well under way by March and after July the remains of the battalion were broken up. A significant number of battalions were also allocated to the occupation of Germany. No attempt is made to describe this process here, but it is worthy of note that in March and April, 1919, all three Gordons young soldiers' battalions (51st, 52nd and 53rd) were deployed to Germany, to serve during the occupation.[135]

General Observations

The Territorials and Overseas Service
It might be thought that as alleged representatives of a 'martial race' Highland Territorial soldiers would have unquestioningly volunteered for overseas service. In fact, this was not the case, despite immense pressure placed on them to do so.

---

125 Lindsay, *London Scottish*, pp.232-233; Lloyd, *London Scottish*, pp.170-173.
126 Aiken, *Courage Past,* pp.125-126.
127 Ewing, *Royal Scots*, pp.778-779.
128 Craig-Brown, *Historical Records*, Vol.3, pp.394-399.
129 See IWM 3449 PP Cordner, Charles, typescript memoir; IWM 5251 Sound Anderson, Ronald Charles Beckett, IWM interview, 1981; Fraser, Dr James Fowler, *Doctor Jimmy* (Aberdeen: University Press, 1980), pp.60-66.
130 Wauchope, *Black Watch*, Vol.1, pp.351-355.
131 Craig Brown, *Historical Records*, Vol.3, pp.355-361.
132 Anderson, *1st Argylls*, pp.84-89.
133 LC GS 0409 Cunningham, J.C., notes written by him 1976; LC GS 0456, Dick, memoirs, pp59-70; IWM 7508 Wyllie, diary, from 30 August, 1919.
134 IWM 7508 Wyllie, diary, passim from 30 December, 1918; Fairrie, *Queen's Own Highlanders*, p.116; Sym, *Seaforth Highlanders*, pp.226-227.
135 Falls, *Gordon Highlanders*, p.265; *51st Battalion*, pp.17-24; GHM PB507 Wallace, Diary 53rd Bn.

Thus, Commanding Officers might make impassioned appeals which took real courage to refuse.[136] James Rodger was a member of 6th Black Watch. After mobilisation, two companies of the battalion were addressed at South Queensferry by the C.O., Sir Robert Moncrieff.

> He said in front of the two companies, he says, words to this effect, 'Step out those men who *won't* go to France with me,' which of course took a lot of courage for anybody who didn't want to step out in front of the others and face up to what he had to say to them about not going with him. He didn't mince his words, believe me.[137]

He had some support. Alick Guthrie, a Senior N.C.O. in the same battalion, notes that at the time when the men had to decide about overseas service, some of the local people, "were blaming me for making their boys volunteer."[138]

Albert Strachan, a 19-year old pre-war Territorial in 6th Gordons, describes in some detail the pressure put on T.F. soldiers to volunteer for overseas service. Initially at least, "except a few who received £1 a year for signing for overseas none of us thought of volunteering." When the battalion reached Perth, however, the C.O., Colonel McLean, urged the men to volunteer for foreign service, stating that it was likely to be for garrison duty or lines of communication, that everyone would get a week's leave before going, and that he would guarantee that those who volunteered would get home sooner than those who didn't. "He got on horseback and with what he thought were stirring words he shouted 'Men of the 6th Gordons who are to volunteer for foreign service follow me.' About 40 followed him. He got what he deserved." Strachan felt they were being deceived, but, in fairness, at that stage of the war, McLean was probably telling the men what he believed to be true.[139] Hugh Quekett, for example, gazetted to take a commission in 5th Black Watch in September, 1914, wrote, "Never in our wildest dreams did we ever envisage leaving the country for any purpose other than the relief of regular troops serving in garrisons overseas."[140] But Colonel McLean's approach was evidently naive, and failed to take into account the sensitivities and concerns of his volunteer soldiers. The battalion then moved to Bedford, where they had another parade. On this occasion, the Colonel told all volunteers for overseas service to stand fast; the remainder to fall out on the left. This time, having had more time to consider, a half remained and a half fell out. Many however kept going back in small parties. "The Strathdon boys fell out waiting for a lead. They got it. John Philip crossed over and all from the Section followed him. In the end all volunteered except thirty, so McLean was pleased." Strachan notes pressure to volunteer from their attached Regular Instructors. He also observes that "it took a bolder man to say no than yes to all his mates [who] were volunteering." He felt that many of the older men were "forced" into joining, that is to say by the obligation of duty. They had been many years in the volunteers and Territorials and had risen in rank and they were supposed to show the young men an example. When the battalion was finally warned for foreign service, several more of the

---

136 See for 4th Seaforths, IWM 12311 Mason-Macfarlane, memoir by David Mason-Macfarlane, p.7. For 5th Gordons see GHM PB107.1, Grant, diary, 13, 24, 25 August, 5 September, 4 October, c.5 November, 1914, 26 April 1915.
137 IWM 373 Rodger, interview, 1975.
138 BWA Guthrie, A.C., letter to wife Crissie, 6 January, 1916.
139 GHM PB2984 Strachan, memoir.
140 BWA Quekett, memoir, p.11.

men dropped out on apparent medical grounds,[141] while some soldiers who had been cajoled by peer pressure into volunteering for foreign service might subsequently have second thoughts, like a young lad from Alford in Albert Strachan's company, cajoled into volunteering by his comrades.[142]

But it should not be thought that many men were not delighted to go. Harry Strachan from Banchory joined his local T.F. unit, the 7th Gordons, two days after the war began, aged 18, and moved to Bedford with the battalion. He recalls that most of the men volunteered for foreign service.

> One day the Adjutant … held a parade of all under 19 in order to select the likeliest for imperial service. About 100 paraded in single line while Capt. Maitland went along selecting. Each picked man was told to take one step forward. This stickler for discipline had never been seen to smile, yet, when he got to the end of the line and turned round & found that all had stepped out and were standing rigidly at attention. Heavens! He smiled and gave up. Later he became Brigade Major but was never known to smile again.[143]

But what proportion of the men did not volunteer for overseas service? The sources are a little coy on this point, and in some cases inexact. There is an obvious reluctance to acknowledge the number who did not volunteer. Thus, according to the Camerons' regimental history, when the C.O. of 4th Battalion paraded his men in Inverness on 12 August, and called for volunteers, "the whole battalion responded in the affirmative", but according to the battalion's more recent historian, the total was "over 80 per cent", a significant difference.[144]

We do have some more reliable indicators.[145] Sir Arthur Grant, commanding 5th Gordons, was able to note in early November, 1914; "29 officers, 982 men, 86.4% Volunteers for Active Service,"[146] that is 14 percent who had not. On 13 September, 1914, Henry Pelham Burn, adjutant of 6th Gordons, noted that "819 out of 994 have volunteered for active service," that is 82 percent, leaving 18 percent (175) who had not. And on 12 October, there were 150 non-volunteers with the battalion at Bedford, waiting to be sent back to Keith.[147] Part 2 Orders for 1/8th Argylls at Bedford for 26 April, 1915, note 108 men who had not accepted overseas service waiting to proceed to Scotland.[148] In the London Scottish, in the papers of Claud Low, a company commander on the outbreak of the war, is an undated note recording the names of 27 members of "Number 2 section." Of these men, 22 were willing to serve overseas, while two were doubtful and three were not willing, indicating from a pitifully small sample a refusal rate of 11 to 19 percent.[149] Finally, in the Liverpool Scottish, those who declined to volunteer

---

141 GHM PB2984, Strachan, memoir.
142 Ibid.
143 LC GS 1549 Strachan, H.J., typescript memoir.
144 Watt, *Steel and Tartan*, p.15; Craig-Brown, *Historical Records*, Vol.3, p.421.
145 Apart from the evidence quoted see also: for 1st Glasgow Highlanders, IWM 3160 Macmillan, diary, Introduction; IWM Books, Reid, 'Shoulder to Shoulder,' pp.4, 9, 11-12: for 4th Seaforths, Haldane, *Fourth Seaforths*, pp.48-49: for 5th Seaforths, IWM PP 16335 Racine, J., transcribed memoir, written 1920's., p.8: for 6th Seaforths, Bird, *The Spirit*, p.27.
146 GHM PB107.1, Grant, diary, c 5 November, 1914.
147 GHM PB3309 Pelham Burn, letters to mother, 27 August, 13 September, 12 October, 1914.
148 ASHM NE 8.4 1/8th Bn Argyll & Sutherland Highlanders, Part 2 Orders, 26 April, 1915.
149 IWM 6702 PP Low, Major C.J., manuscript note. See also Lloyd, *London Scottish*, p.28.

were formed into two new companies, which did their training separately from the rest of the battalion.[150] It seems likely that that these companies contained some 150 to 200 men.

Overall, it seems that about 10 to 20 percent, say 15 percent, of existing Territorial soldiers did not volunteer for overseas service, a considerable total, which is not truly consistent with the notion of the Highland warrior-ethos. Nevertheless, the great majority of Territorial soldiers, probably about 85%, did choose so to volunteer, an action which, we must remember, the majority of them were under no obligation to take.

Those who did not volunteer were often older married men with families,[151] and one wonders how many family men felt obliged to volunteer by peer pressure, against their better judgment.

Some younger men, possibly of an age when they should not have been going anyway, could not get permission from their parents."[152] Even some officers decided not to go and were castigated for it.[153]

In fact, quitting jobs and businesses, to deploy overseas, could involve considerable sacrifice for Territorial soldiers. In a paper written after the war, Major Claud Low, who served in the London Scottish, noted that Territorial Force regulations had left no time for volunteers to settle their affairs on mobilisation,[154] although, according to their regimental history, the businessmen of the London Scottish were at least given time to consider the implications of volunteering before making their decision.[155] When the war broke out, Alex Campbell's father was a captain in the Territorials, commanding the Islay company of 8th Argylls. He was also a distillery manager and had been employed by the distillery company for thirty years. The family lived in the Manager's house, which belonged to the Distillery, and after his father was mobilised, they were required to vacate it in order to accommodate a 'temporary' manager. The family had to move to Glasgow, where they lived with relatives throughout the war at no small inconvenience to both. After demobilisation, his father hoped to resume his former employment as distillery manager but was told that his post was no longer available to him. Then followed a period of some years unemployment with considerable hardship until eventually he secured a post as a security officer with the Canadian Pacific Steamship Company.[156]

The soldiers were not the only ones to make sacrifices.

> A letter came from a lady who explained that she had three sons who were all joining up and pleaded that the one in the London Scottish might remain on Home Service. After the Battle of the Somme on 1st July 1916, it was necessary to write to this lady and tell her

---

150 McGilchrist, *Liverpool Scottish*, pp.11-12; Fennah, Alfred, *Retaliation*, (London: Houghton, n.d.), pp.20-21.
151 LC GS 1549 Strachan, memoir; BWA Quekett, memoir, p.12; LC Transcripts etc, Johnston, Lt Col R.W.F., typescript memoir, 'Some experiences of the Great War of 1914-1918', & Tape 992, Summary, interview with Johnston, 1975; McGilchrist, *Liverpool Scottish*, pp.11-12; GHM. PB2984, Strachan, memoir.
152 McGilchrist, *Liverpool Scottish*, pp.11-12.
153 GHM PB107.1, Grant, diary, 25 August, 1914; GHM. PB2984, Strachan memoir.
154 IWM 6702 Low, paper on mobilisation, no date.
155 Lindsay, *London Scottish*, pp.19-20.
156 LC DF 148 Campbell, Dr A.M., manuscript memoir.

that her son had been killed in action, and I then learned, to my sorrow, that all her three sons had been killed.[157]

There was frequently some ill-feeling between those who volunteered for overseas service and those who did not. Sir Arthur Grant is vitriolic about those members of 5th Gordons who chose not to go. Of Captain Reid, who refused to go, he wrote, "I trust that he will be branded as a skunk for life."[158] Alfred Fennah is equally scathing about those men of the Liverpool Scottish who did not enlist for overseas service and observed that the split severed some friendships. "The excuses of some of them that I knew were lamentable, and absolutely deplorable; in a few cases they did not handle a rifle abroad right through the whole war from start to finish." The two special companies of home service men were nick-named 'Mother's Own Fireside Borderers' or 'The Fireside Rangers.' In 6th Gordons, at a medical inspection prior to deployment overseas, two of the Strathdon men complained of symptoms and were excused service. "We looked down on them, but we were wrong. It was entirely their own affair. They didn't want to go and took the chance of getting off."[159] In one case, at least, such ill-feeling was not kept "within the family." An indignant Colonel Blair, commanding 1/9th Royal Scots at the Front, wrote to *The Scotsman* in July, 1915:

> I see in one of the Edinburgh evening papers an article … in which it is stated that 'one or two of the officers at the head of the Second Battalion object to the title "Dandy Ninth", and wish it dropped. Will you kindly let it be known that none of the officers and men of the real Dandy Ninth object to it in the least; in fact, we are proud of it and try to live up to it. We are the real 9th Royal Scots, and no others have any right to speak for us, or indeed to have any say in the matter, until they come out here and do their share like men.[160]

As late as February, 1916, Alick Guthrie, in France with 1/6th Black Watch, could write to his wife that the 2/6th "are not held in much respect by the men of the 1st. But as they are to be brought in under the new scheme they will get a chance to redeem themselves before the war is finished."[161]

London Recruits to the Highland Division
As we have seen, one useful source of recruits to the Highland Division in Bedford was London, from where a significant number of recruits were drawn, many of them being surplus recruits to the London Scottish. 4th, 5th and 6th Seaforths, 4th Camerons and 8th Argylls all definitely benefited in this way, and interestingly all these five battalions were theoretically amongst the most Highland in composition. The London Scottish history puts the total recruits provided to the Highland Division through their headquarters at Buckingham Gate at an astonishing 1,200.

---

157 IWM 6702 Low, paper on mobilisation, no date.
158 GHM PB107 1, Grant, diary, 25 August, 1914.
159 GHM. PB2984, Strachan, memoir.
160 Springer, Shaun & Humphreys, Stuart, *Private Beatson's War*, (Barnsley:Pen & Sword, 2009), pp.21-22.
161 BWA Guthrie, letter to wife Crissie, 2 February, 1916.

It is quite possible that these recruits were mostly at least a quarter Scottish, as the London Scots at this time were still applying their eligibility rules based on grand-parents' rights.[162]

It is evident that battalions may have individually received at least up to 300 London recruits from London Scottish surplus. 4th Camerons obtained 250 between 4 and 11 September.[163] Likewise, although the regimental history is silent on numbers,[164] 4th Seaforths received as many as 200.[165] One of these men was Archie Tweddle, who enlisted at Buckingham Gate in August, 1914.[166] As many as 300 Londoners were recruited to 1/6th Seaforths.[167] When A.R.Walker joined them in 1916 as a newly commissioned officer, he found that, "A Coy, curiously enough, was composed entirely of cockneys who had flocked to enlist in the battalion which was under strength at Bedford before going overseas."[168] As far as 8th Argylls are concerned, the battalion history is reticent on this point. But Alex Campbell recalled that his father, commanding the Islay company, "acquired in his company a draft of Cockneys from London and for these men he developed a great admiration and respect"[169]

We have no figures for 5th Seaforths, but we do have records left by four 'Londoners' who joined. One such was James Racine, who actually lived at Guildford. On the outbreak of the war he was enrolled as a Special Constable, his duty being to guard a railway bridge in the town.

> My friend, Ernest Gyatt, and I had discussed offering our services to the Army and we decided to go to London the next day and enlist in a regiment. On Saturday, 12th September, 1914, we arrived in London, strolled up Victoria Street, and found ourselves at Buckingham Gate [London Scottish HQ]; we were informed that a certain number were required to complete the strength of the 5th Battalion of the Seaforth Highlanders. After a short conversation, my friend and I decided to offer ourselves for service.[170]

Another was Oswald Croft. He was about 18 when the war broke out, lived in Hampstead and was a trainee at a tobacco firm in Piccadilly. He had no military background at all but felt very loyal to his country. He joined 5th Seaforths on 14 September.

> I happened one day went out round Buckingham Gate somewhere. There was recruiting going on when the war broke out and I didn't say anything to my parents at all about it. I made a few enquiries and they were recruiting and I joined up and told them afterwards.[171]

---

162 Lindsay, *London Scottish*, pp.21-22, 225-226.
163 Watt, *Steel and Tartan*, p.16; Craig-Brown, *Historical Records*, Vol.3, pp.422-423.
164 Haldane, *Fourth Seaforths*, p.49.
165 IWM 12311 Mason-Macfarlane, memoir by David Mason-Macfarlane, p.8.
166 THM Seaforths 96-36 Tweddle, Archibald Thomas, manuscript 'Extracts from the letters of a Seaforth Highlander'; also manuscript account, 'The Son of the Father', written by his widow, Dorothy Tweddle, 1977.
167 Bird, *The Spirit*, p.26.
168 IWM 13230 PP Walker, A.R., typescript memoir, written 1978.
169 LC DF 148 Campbell, memoir.
170 IWM PP 16335 Racine, memoir, pp.6-7.
171 IWM 4440 Recording Croft, Oswald, IWM interview, 1979.

A third London recruit was S.G. Gyton. He was under age when the war broke out, on holiday with a boys' camp. When war was declared, the camp broke up and he returned to London where he was resident in a club in Westminster.

> Actually, most of us lost our jobs, so I went and enlisted. Tried to get into the Imperial Yeomanry at Westminster. They were full up, not taking anybody, so my colleague at the club, oh, he says, I'll get you into the London Scottish. So he went over to the London Scottish. Of course, they were full up, so they recruited to other units, Scotch units, so that was that. From then on you see we received our shilling from the recruiting people and proceeded to come under their jurisdiction, which we had to report and go down by train to Bedford. Having reached Bedford, you see, that was that… Amongst the London boys were all more or less spread about through each company of the Scotch. We became the 5th Seaforth Highlanders.[172]

Our fourth recruit was Johnnie Strang, born in Upminster, Essex, in December, 1895. He was involved in farming, although it is not certain if he was a farm-hand or perhaps a farmer's son. By November, 1914, he was training with 5th Seaforths at Bedford.[173]

One upshot of this recruiting policy was that in February, 1915, in France, in 4th Seaforths, it was possible to arrange within the battalion "a very exciting football match between Scotland and England, England being the Scots who joined as Recruits at Bedford. It was a great match, and as was fit and proper Scotland won by 3 goals to 2."[174]

Time Expired Men
One of the lesser known features of service in the Territorial Force was the ability of soldiers recruited before the war, whose contractual period of service ended during the war, to return home from the front "Time Expired" when their contractual period of service ended. George Murray was a sergeant in 1/4th Seaforths. On 23 February, 1916, he wrote to his sister Alex, in Glasgow;

> Jim Wilson is 'time expired' in a month & I think he is not taking on again. Our Coy Sgt Major, John Smith, Avoch, left us last night, also time expired, & a sergeant in my platoon is going away tonight for good. All the old hands, all N.C.O.'s, are gradually leaving us. They are quite right to get clear of the Army, as they can get better jobs at home, & get the same thanks in the end.[175]

Some measure of the extent of this practice is provided by Part 2 Orders of 1/8th Argylls, of which a virtually continuous set survives for 1915-16. These Orders record the departure of

---

172 IWM 15596 Recording, Gyton, S.G., interview, 1982.
173 LC GS 1551 Strang J.S., letter to brother Willlie, November, 1914, & part completed AF E536.
174 IWM 12311 Mason-Macfarlane, memoir by David Mason-Macfarlane, p.61.
175 THM Seaforths 81-180 Murray, Sgt George, letter to sister Alex, 23 February, 1916. For other examples of this practice, see THM Camerons 93-123 McLeod, Pte Duncan, letter from Sgt John McLeod, 11 April, 1916; IWM 14340 PP McArthur, H, diary, 4-7 December, 1915; IWM 3460 Macmillan, diary 27 February, 1916.

time expired men together with re-engagements by those who chose instead to re-engage for four years or the duration. The first departure of a time-expired man is recorded on 20 August, 1915, the man's service having expired on 7 August; the last is recorded on 27 May, 1916, the last five men's service having expired on 24 May. After that date the practice seems to have been stopped. During this period from 20 August, 1915 to 10 June, 1916, a total of 93 men went home, time-expired, while 41 chose to re-engage. In other words, 69 per cent of time-expired men in 1/8th Argylls chose to quit the war. If this percentage was typical of T.F. battalions, it posed a real threat to force numbers at the Front, and it is hardly surprising that the practice was stopped. We do not know the motives of those who left. Some of them may have been near, at or over the age-limit for service; others may have felt that they had done their bit, and that it was time for the "shirkers" at home to step up to the mark; others may have been induced by peer pressure to volunteer for overseas service, and come to feel that their first duty was to their wives and family; still others may have found the grim reality of war far different from their romantic imaginings. In any case, this was not the action of a martial race. After the procedure was stopped, we find instead apparently all men whose time expires recorded as "continuing to serve under the Military Services Act (Session 2) 1916". 23 such men are recorded between 31 July and 31 December, 1916.[176]

One such "Time Expired" man was Alick Guthrie, who was a veteran senior N.C.O with 1/6th Black Watch. He was born in November, 1864, and had served with the Volunteers long before signing up to the new Territorial Force on its formation on 1 April, 1908. His term of service did not expire until the end of March, 1916, but he was looking forward to his discharge from October, 1915, when he was shortly to turn 51. He was clearly feeling the conditions in the trenches. In November, 1915, he was concerned that his discharge might not be possible. "I'm afraid there's not much chance of any of our Territorial or other soldiers getting home 'time expired' now, as the Government have a bill in hand to keep them till the end of the War. It's like not respecting a 'Scrap of Paper' on the part of the Government." A little later he was more optimistic: "My term of service expires on March 31st and … it is not my intention if am spared till then to re-engage. I believe I will be able to claim my discharge then even if a bill for the prolongation of service of time expired men should become law." He was worried about what his seniors would think. "I had a talk with the S,M. now and Q.M. Wilson today, and told him of my intention to quit at March. He says I am quite right in doing so, so that's part of the ordeal over, as I was wondering how he would take it." He was eventually discharged time-expired on 31 March, 1916. Shortly beforehand, he wrote, "I hear there will be about fifty of us taking their discharge at this time so we will have a happy squad coming the homeward journey."[177]

Recruiting
We have already observed how heavy losses and a shortage of recruits led to a number of reductions and amalgamations in both Territorial and New Army battalions. In effect, Scotland had raised more Highland battalions than it was possible to sustain, at least with voluntary recruiting.[178] We have already noticed this phenomenon in relation to the Canadian battalions, and

---

176 ASHM NE 8.4 1/8th Bn Argyll & Sutherland Highlanders, Part 2 Orders, 1915-1916.
177 BWA Guthrie, letters to wife Crissie, passim, but particularly letters of 20, 27 November, 26 December, 1915, 14 March, 1916.
178 See for example, Ewing, *Ninth Division*, pp.81-82.

recruiting remained a problem until the introduction of conscription. An early appreciation of the problem is revealed in a letter from Colonel William Wells, Chairman of the County of Aberdeen T.F. Association to the War Office, dated 14 June, 1915.[179] In this he notes that 1/6th Gordons are threatened with amalgamation, states that the recruiting area of the 6th Gordons cannot sustain three battalions (1/6th, 2/6th and 3/6th), and advocates that the second and third line battalions should simply be used as draft-producing units for the 1/6th. He also argues strongly that the 1/6th Battalion does not deserve amalgamation.

The problem is also illustrated by letters from Colonel Gunn, commanding 8th Camerons, a New Army battalion at Inverness, to Colonel Haig, commanding 7th Battalion in the field, written shortly after 8th Battalion was reduced from a Service to a Reserve battalion: In a formal letter of 22 April, 1915, he writes.

> Now the function of the 8th Bn has been established to be that of a Reserve Bn to the other Service Bns, it is more than ever in the interests of the Regiment as a whole that recruiting for the 8th Bn should be brought about on a large scale. Efforts have been made by personal appeals from officers, N.C.O.'s & Men of the 8th Bn addressed to likely men or localities, and have met already with considerable success. I enclose 6 copies of a post card, 1,000 of which were obtained for 50/– from Gale & Polden. The stock is nearly exhausted, but you may possibly think it worthwhile to help on recruiting by means of some similar appeal through your officers & men and you might possibly think it worthwhile to obtain a supply of a similar card worded at your discretion.

And in a less formal covering letter he adds;

> Many of the men in your Bn have friends who contemplate joining the army, and they are likely to know the addresses of such men. Might I therefore suggest that they should be issued with a number of these cards (adapted to suit the case of your Bn)… In the Lowlands especially there is a tremendous competition among all the new units (Territorials and others), and so it behoves all ranks of the Cameron Hrs to make special efforts among their own friends. Inverness-shire and the Northern Counties are almost depleted in consequence of the number of new Territorial Units. I may mention that a new 3/4th Bn (Territorials), under Major Kemble of Knock, is now being recruited in the County, and so, there is small room left for us to work up here… I should be most grateful if you would help the 8th Bn as well as the Regiment as a whole, by getting your men to fill up these cards, and having them issued to their friends.[180]

Similar recruiting difficulties are noted in Dunbartonshire for 1/9th Argylls before they were broken up in March, 1916.[181] In June, 1915, too, the Glasgow Highlanders were threatened with possible disbandment, but successfully enlisted the support of Sir Thomas Dunlop, Lord

---

179 GHM PB24 Brown, Brig Gen P.W., letter from Colonel William Wells, Chairman of the County of Aberdeen T.F. Association to the War Office, dated 14 June, 1915.
180 THM Camerons C102, letters from Lt Col G.Gunn to Lt Col Haig, 22 and 23 April, 1915.
181 *Roll of Officers Dunbartonshire*, pp.25-27, 29.

Lieutenant of the County of Glasgow. Their historian even suspected a desire to destroy the Territorial Force.[182]

Problems of reductions and amalgamations
The transfers, reductions, absorptions and amalgamations were not always well received. The disbandment of 1/4th Camerons, the only first-line Territorial Camerons battalion, despite the pleas of its Commanding Officer, Colonel Murdoch Beaton, for it to be saved, and arguably despite the existence of potential reinforcement drafts at home, was not well received in Inverness, and led to the question being raised in Parliament by Annan Bryce, MP for Inverness Burghs, a measure of the strong relationship between the Territorial battalions and their local community.[183] At another level, John Matheson, in 1st Camerons, which received drafts from the 4th Battalion, wrote despairingly in June, 1916 of their quality. "We get drafts from the 4th now and the majority of the men are enough to make a good soldier weep. They know nothing and won't try to learn."[184]

The absorption of 11th Argylls, a New Army battalion, by the 1/8th Battalion of Territorials, in June, 1918, was not well received by Lance-Corporal John Bowie of the 11th Battalion.:

> We are now called the 8th A. & S.H., a Territorial battalion with many Gaelic speakers in it. Most of the men come from Campbeltown and the Kyles of Bute … the 8th had command in the 'Commissary' department … Much animosity or spite were cast up between the two Battalions. The Coy Qr Master Sergeants were all inefficient. One could not write his name. The troops described him as being so STUPID or HIELAN. The heather grew out of his ears was their Proof. However we soon got over this spite because nearly all the 8th men went away to Hospital sick, and were poor Stickers.[185]

Lieutenant Robert MacKay in the same battalion also had reservations but felt that the absorption was conducted with some sensitivity.[186] Similar reservations were expressed when 7th Camerons were absorbed into the 6th,[187] when 1/4th Black Watch were threatened with amalgamation after Loos,[188] and when 8th Gordons were transferred from 9th Division to be amalgamated with 10th Battalion in 15th Division.[189]

There was also regret when the Territorial battalions were transferred out of the Regular divisions they had joined on early deployment back to Territorial divisions, even to the 51st

---

182 IWM Books, Reid, 'Shoulder to Shoulder,' pp.71-73, 112.
183 Watt, *Steel and Tartan*, pp.110-121; Craig-Brown, *Historical Records*, Vol.3, pp.443-448.
184 THM Camerons 10-25 Matheson, John, letter to father, 16 June, 1916.
185 ASHM N-E11 Bowie, diary, 8 June, 1918.
186 IWM 11144 PP MacKay, Lt R.L., diary, 16 May, 1, 10. 14 June, 1918. See also: IWM 15017 PP Wilson, Lt Col G.L., privately printed biography, p.31, this section, 'The Lieutenant Colonel' written by Capt George F. Macleod.
187 Burns, Robert, *Once a Cameron Highlander* (Bognor Regis: Woodfield Publishing, 2000), p.157; Craig-Brown, *Historical Records*, pp.346-348.
188 IWM 5525 PP Steven, Lieut S.H., MC, typescript extract from Rollo Steven's history of the Steven family, letter from Lt Harvey Steven, 28 September, 1915.
189 GHM PB 1639 Kemp, Capt William, typescript memoir, 'The Great War 1914-1918 My Experiences', pp.22-23.

Highland Division, which did not really begin to acquire its reputation until Beaumont-Hamel, in November, 1916. Thus, for example, Captain R.L.McKinnon regretted the transfer of 1/4th Gordons from the regular 3rd Division, where they had served and been accepted alongside their own 1st Battalion, to the Territorial 51st Division in February, 1916:

> We heard the news with real regret. For nearly a year we had been with this regular Division; they had mothered us when we had come to them raw and inexperienced, we had been privileged to fight side by side with them in the line, and now going, we knew they recognised us as one of themselves, an equal comrade in arms.[190]

Similarly, the transfer of 1st London Scottish from the 1st Division to the 56th Division, composed of London Territorials, in February, 1916, caused some angst, as Stewart Jordan recalled many years later:

> We felt we'd been downgraded. Instead of being the sort of – what shall I say? – the ones that, you know, we were more or less looked after by the senior regiments in a sense, we became the senior regiment, well, we became what we called the Black Watch of the 56th Division. We were the only Scottish one in it, you see, and I think we had some of the rough bits to do. We were the Scottish of the 56th Division … I didn't think we had a lot of respect for *some* of the other regiments. Mind you, we were brigaded with the Kensingtons; the Kensingtons were good. But it was one or two of the, what do they call them – Oh, I forget – they were a pretty rough lot you know, they came from the sort of central London, Whitechapel; compared with us who were up there were … you'd understand what I mean (laughs).[191]

Jordan clearly had a difficulty with the social composition of some of the other battalions! Similar regrets were expressed when 1st Liverpool Scottish were transferred from 3rd Division to the 55th, in January, 1916,[192] and when 1/4th Seaforths were left behind when the Meerut Division deployed to Mesopotamia in November, 1915, taking with it their regular colleagues in 1st Battalion.[193]

The conversion of Yeomanry regiments to Highland infantry battalions also caused some discontent. Ogilvie summarises the views of the men of the Fife and Forfar Yeomanry on their conversion to Black Watch:

> We were all very sorry to see the demise of the Yeomanry and to close, though only temporarily, the records of a Regiment which had had an honourable career, and of which we were all so proud. At the same time we realised that, in our capacity as dismounted yeomanry, we were not pulling our weight either as yeomanry or infantry, and no other regiment

---

190 GHM PB583 McKinnon, Capt R.L., manuscript memoir, 'Two years with the 4th Gordons in France', p.46.
191 IWM 10391 Sound Jordan, Stewart, IWM interview, 1988. See also Lindsay, *London Scottish*, pp.93-94.
192 McGilchrist, *Liverpool Scottish*, p.61; Giblin, *Bravest of Hearts*, p.30.
193 Haldane, *Fourth Seaforths*, pp.141-142.

certainly appealed to us as much as our own Territorial Infantry Regiment, and we were proud to link our record to the long and glorious record of the Black Watch.

In fact, unlike the Scottish Horse, the Fife and Forfar Yeomanry acquiesced in their conversion sufficiently to finally change completely into Black Watch kilts in August, 1918.[194]

Indeed, soldiers could prove adaptable. Bob Lawson, a signaller who was in hospital when his battalion, 14th Argylls, was broken up in April, 1918, wrote on 23 April: "The old batt. is no more and for some reason has been bust up. Where I will land I don't know … I hope to meet some of my old chums wherever I go, but I am looking forward to my new adventures." By 12 May, he could write,

> I can tell you I was right sorry when the old batt. was done away with, but I have met quite a few of my old chums here. At present, I am attached to a batt. of Gordons; not as a signaller but on a trench-mortar battery … This transfer of course will only be temporary & I may be returned to the batt. any day, but I am in no hurry to go as I have made quite a few pals in the 'Gay Gordons' and had a very good time.

And by 16 June he could write; "This last week, owing to a few alterations, I have met a good number of chaps who were in the old batt. I am now quite at home in this batt. and it is quite a change to be a soldier again."[195]

Conclusions

In this chapter we have seen that a large number of kilted battalions were committed to the Great War, drawn not only from the Regular, Special Reserve, Territorial and New Army battalions of the British army, but also from South Africa and particularly from Canada. We have seen how existing army organisation in all three countries was part ignored, part adapted and part supplemented to provide these battalions. We have also seen how, while the principal experience of these battalions was acquired on the Western Front, they also experienced campaigning in many other theatres, and some were even sent to Ireland to help keep the peace there. Certain features of organisation stand out: the large number of reservists required to complete the home service Regular battalions; the reluctance of some Territorials to undertake overseas service, and the desire of many to end their service when their original terms of enlistment expired, neither of which exactly supports the notion of a warrior-race; the unpreparedness of many Territorial battalions for war at the time of their deployment overseas; the extraordinary influx of London recruits into the Highland Division; the problems of recruiting before conscription for both the Territorial and New Army battalions; and finally the distress caused by the sometimes associated transfer, amalgamation, absorption and reduction of battalions. In the next chapters we will examine who exactly were the men who provided the officers and soldiers for these battalions and why they went to war.

---

194 Ogilvie, *Fife and Forfar Yeomanry*, pp.41, 126; Wauchope, *Black Watch*, Vol.3, p.294. For Scottish Horse, see BWA Stratton, Sandy R., letter to sister Betty, 20 September, 1916.
195 IWM 8192 Lawson, letters to Bessie, 23 April, 12 May, 16 June, 1918.

3

Noble Causes, Nagging Doubts

When I think of Belgium, I think of a child being abused by a hulking brute.[1]

In this chapter we consider why men joined up, and their evolving attitude to the war. Of course, the main issue for us is why men joined specifically Highland regiments, and we address this issue separately in the second part of the chapter. But in gathering data on the latter question, it was found to be almost inseparable from the first. It is not assumed that the general reasons for enlistment were in any way different to those of the average Tommy or his officer. But it is nevertheless useful to understand this background, for commitment to the cause or otherwise was a vital component of morale, and if we are to set other elements of morale in context we need to understand this component. The record is inevitably somewhat distorted, being dominated by the statements of those who joined up voluntarily or under the Derby scheme. Many of the Highland soldiers who marched off to war in 1914 had enlisted before that date, either as Regulars, or as Special Reserve, or had re-joined as Reservists, so they were simply discharging the duty they had taken on when they first enlisted. Later in the war too, once conscription was introduced, men were simply called up by age-group. This did not mean that they were necessarily without enthusiasm, but that they had no reason to record it as a reason for joining. They joined up because they were called up. So the surviving record of 'reasons for joining up,' is almost by definition biased in favour of volunteers. What nevertheless does it tell us?

Here, there is little doubt that the primary motive, cited by innumerable sources,[2] was duty, often couched in patriotic terms, but quite distinguishable from 'jingoism.' The fact that the

---

1   Ross, D.M., *a Scottish Minister and Soldier*, (London: Hodder & Stoughton, 1917), pp.19-23.
2   Apart from specific sources cited, see: Andrews, Linton, *The Autobiography of a Journalist*, (London: Ernest Benn Ltd., 1964), pp.80-81; IWM 16335 Racine, memoir; IWM 12311 PP Mason-Macfarlane, Lt Gen Noel, typescript memoir by Col David Mason-Macfarlane, 90pp, p.9; IWM 4440 Croft, interview; Gillespie, 2Lt A.D., *Letters from Flanders*, (London: Smith, Elder & Co., 1916), p.2, letter home, 2 August, 1914; One of the Jocks [Capt Alex Scott], *Odd Shots*, (London: Hodder & Stoughton, 1916) p.12; GHM PB507 Wallace, anonymous essays by soldiers of 10th Gordons, December, 1914; GHM PB1937 Dawson, Robert, letter to mother, 1 November. 1914; GHM PB2644 Anderson, James, letter to sister Nellie, 27 March, 1915; LC GS 0084 Barclay, Brig. C.N., manuscript recollections, written, 1973; IWM 576 PP Bowser, Lt H.F., typescript memoir, written 1969, pp.47-53; IWM 6702 Low, letter to wife Noanie, 29 November, 1914; IWM 11739 PP Sangster, W.J.C., Memorial volume compiled by parents, letter to father 7 July, 1915; IWM 10529 PP Stanford, Lt.-Col. J.K., typescript

majority of the Highland soldiers who marched off to war in 1914 had enlisted before that date does not diminish the sense of duty they felt[3] or the sacrifice they made. Lieutenant Angus Macnaghten was a pre-war Special Reserve officer in 3rd Black Watch and joined the 1st Battalion at Aldershot on mobilisation He was 31 when the war broke out and had married his wife Hazel in 1911. Their only child, a son also called Angus, had been born on 29 May, just over two months before he reported for duty at Aldershot. His baby son was still not six months old when his father was killed at First Ypres.[4] As we have discussed in a previous chapter, the Territorials had a choice to make regarding overseas service, and while most felt their duty was to serve overseas, a significant minority chose legitimately to stay at home and put family first.

John Cooper in Dundee was 17 when the war broke out, and still at school a year later, when he signed up under the Derby scheme. "Don't call it heroism, it was nothing of the sort, it was merely the natural desire of all young fellows to be doing the accepted thing in the circumstances." He was called up to join the local Black Watch Territorials in May, 1916, just short of his nineteenth birthday.

> Many people went into no end of a flurry about their young lads joining up. It was really all very senseless, I thought. The right way to look at it was the way that the boys themselves looked at it, and they went joyfully, most of them, even although they may occasionally have had misgivings about the probable end of the adventure. Not that young lads ever thought morbidly of death in battle – we had all a pathetic faith that we should come through somehow.[5]

Another wartime Territorial volunteer was William Paterson from Wick, who joined 5th Seaforths in the summer of 1915. He wrote to his parents in November, 1917, in case of his death:

> I know that when I joined the army I caused you much worry & anxiety, but I think you will admit I did the right thing. If I had not done so, I should never have been satisfied, & perhaps you won't think it credible, but I was satisfied & content when wading through muddy Flanders, & sitting under ear-splitting shellfire, – satisfied, because I knew it was where I ought to be at this time.[6]

---

memoir, 'Essays of a Non-Soldier', written c.1968. pp.13-24; IWM 10391 Jordan, Stewart, interview; LC GS 1783 Wood, T.W., manuscript recollections, written 1970's, & Transcript Tape 310, interview with Liddle 1975; Lyon, Thomas M., *In Kilt and Khaki*, (Kilmarnock: The Standard Press, 1916), pp.31-32; IWM 7408 PP Lorimer, Capt. J.B., typescript transcription of memoir of his life by A.R.S. (at end of typescript transcript of his letters, pp.229-233) and letter to mother, 19 April 1915; *George Buchanan Smith 1890-1915*, (Glasgow: privately published, 1916), passim; IWM 926 PP Mackenzie, J.B., letters dated 18 June, 3 July, 1915; LC Transcripts, Tapes 728 and 744, Davies, Harry, interview with Liddle 1989; LC Western Front Recollections, MacKenzie, Dr W., manuscript memoir, c.1980; BWA, Paul, background notes and letters to Miss May Merrett, 14, 19 November, 1915.

3   IWM 3696 Macnaghten, letters, passim.
4   Ibid.
5   IWM Books, Cooper, John, 'Domi Militaeque', unpublished book written 1926, 368pp, biographical note & pp.1-8.
6   Paterson was killed four days later on 20 November, 1917. See THM Seaforths 89-122 Paterson, William, transcript of manuscript memoir, 'Life in the Army, Experiences at Home and Abroad', November, 1917.

Similarly, Frank Brooke, a Yorkshiremen, living in Leeds, had a number of reasons for enlisting in the Seaforth Highlanders in November, 1915, but beneath them all was the realisation that, "It seemed the decent thing to do since the war had become too big for the professional soldier to handle."[7] Alex ('Sandy') Macmillan was one of three brothers who served in various capacities. Mother lived at Cambuslang, near Glasgow. In December, 1915, he enlisted underage in the Argylls as a private soldier. Despite his mother's misgivings, he saw it as his duty to go:

> I am ready to go & wouldn't be at home in ease & comfort for anything. It is my duty to go & I am glad I am old enough to do my bit & have decent companions to go out with. You mention I may find myself shortly in 'Eternity.' I know that. I didn't join to wear a uniform & *surely* you didn't imagine that, Mother.[8]

H.P Samson was born on 13 July, 1898 and attended Robert Gordon's College, where he won a bursary to King's College, University of Aberdeen. In 1916, not quite yet 18, he lied about his age and joined the Gordon Highlanders. "There was consternation when I arrived home. My reasons for joining? I thought I was 'doing my bit' for King & Country. Up to my joining I was a sergeant in Gordon's College O.T.C."[9]

L.A. Lynden-Bell was 17 when the war broke out. His father was a regular officer, so unsurprisingly he went straight to Sandhurst and was ultimately commissioned into 1st Seaforths. His principal motive appears to have been a simple sense of duty. "Really I didn't go to the war with any enthusiasm … we had just got to face it."[10] Likewise, Duncan McDougall was aged 18 when he was killed at Aubers Ridge on 9 May, 1915, serving as a subaltern with 1st Seaforths. At the outbreak of war he had gone from Rugby to Sandhurst to obtain his commission. Four days before his death he wrote a "last letter" to his mother, which illustrates beautifully his sense of duty:

> At first I thought it was horribly sordid to die amongst the squalor and stench of the trenches and be taken away after dark and have a foot of earth thrown over me, but I have gradually come to realise that it is a glorious death; a ration box and an honourable death is far better than the most expensive marble coupled with the fact that you have failed to do your duty, as many have and will I hope live to realise it.[11]

The same sense of duty was felt by Britons overseas and Imperial cousins. A large number of Britons returned from the Empire, including, for example, Canada,[12] South Africa,[13]

---

7   IWM Books, Brooke, Frank C., typescript memoir, 'Wait for it', 315pp, pp.1-3.
8   IWM 3460 Macmillan, letters from Alex Macmillan to mother, 15 December, 1915, n.d., 26 February, 1916.
9   LC DF 148 Recollections, Samson, Dr H.P.
10 LC GS 0993 Lynden-Bell, L.A., transcript of Tape 488, interview with Liddle, 1977.
11 IWM 1/133 PP McDougall, Duncan, letter to mother and Norah, 5 May, 1915.
12 LC Western Front Recollections G5, Gillespie, Capt. Ronald Dave, typescript record of an interview by 'J'; Wilson, Col Maurice J.H., *Biographical List of Officers (other than Regular, Militia and Territorial) The Queen's Own Highlanders (published in Ten Supplements in each issue of the '79th News' from September, 1957, to September, 1960, inclusive)*, p.1 (H.D. Alexander), p.36 (D.T. Croal), p.41 (Gordon Hamilton).
13 Levyns, J.E.P., *The Disciplines of War*, (New York: Vantage Press, 1984), pp.1-28; Wilson, *Biographical List*, p.4 (Sir Archibald A.A. Campbell).

British East Africa,[14] Sudan[15] and the Federated Malay States.[16] Others came from the rest of the world, including Portuguese East Africa,[17] the Argentine,[18] the United States,[19] St Petersburg[20] and 'the East.'[21] Some joined the ranks, although several of them were subsequently commissioned. Others were commissioned directly. Alan Shewan is an interesting case. He was born in 1891, educated at Fettes, and, after preliminary training in accounting, joined his Uncle Bob's firm in Hong Kong. This was an import/export business with offices also in Shanghai and Canton. On the outbreak of the war he volunteered to return home to join the Army, and did so, having been recommended for a commission by the G.O.C. South China Command. He joined 11th Argylls in France in October, 1915.[22] The letter from the G.O.C., Major General Kelly, to the War Office is indicative of Government involvement in volunteering from the Empire:

> I have the honour to forward an application from Mr A.D. Shewan for a temporary commission in one of the new Service Battalions. I have seen this gentleman and consider that he is likely in every way to become an efficient officer. As, however, his age is rather under the 25 years laid down in the telegram dated 11th November from the Secretary of State for the Colonies to the Governor of Hong Kong, I have not felt justified in granting him a commission … The Colonial Government have however provided him with a passage in the P. & O. S.S. 'Nubia' sailing today and I strongly recommend him for a commission as 2nd Lt in one of the new Service Battalions.

Ross McIntyre was born in 1892, in Ontario, a second generation Canadian, whose grandfather had settled in Canada. Ross was a farmer who had owned a farm since he was 16 years old. When he decided to join up, he wished to join the Canadian Flying Corps. But he was unable to do so because he wore glasses and because Canada was not taking any more men for flying at the time. He then chose to join the Black Watch, because his grandfather had served in it. He could easily have joined the Canadian branch of the Black Watch and received the pay of a Canadian soldier, which was much greater, but he preferred to serve with one of the British Army battalions. He embarked for Britain in March, 1916, and enlisted in the Black Watch in April, 1916. He was immediately dubbed "Canada". After training at Nigg, at the end of August he was drafted to France, where he joined 1st Battalion. Two years later, in August, 1918, he left France having been recommended for a commission. He had been interviewed by the Brigadier. "'When the General', explained McIntyre, 'leaned that I was a Canadian and what

---

14 GHM PB19 Blunt, Henry Staveley, miscellaneous papers.
15 Wilson, *Biographical List*, p.131 (William Cattanach).
16 ASHM N-E8 Munro, Hugh, letter to sister Effie, 1 October, 1914.
17 Wilson, *Biographical List*, p.146 (Percy Male).
18 Ibid., p.72 (James Miller), p.93 (M.C. Pearson).
19 BWA Logie, Col. Marc James, papers.
20 Wilson, *Biographical List*, pp.76-77 (A.W and R.D. Macpherson).
21 Ibid., p.105 (A.A. Macdonald).
22 IWM 6444 PP Shewan, Capt. A.D. biographical notes by his niece, Jennifer May, 1977, letter from Shewan to his brother Ian, 30 October, 1915, letter from G.O.C. South China command to War Office, 20 November, 1914.

I had sacrificed to be in my grandfather McIntyre's regiment, he wrote, I understand, "Black Watch only" across my papers.'"[23]

Robert Ashburner was from North Lancashire but had gone out to join his father in South Africa. When the war broke out he was in his third year as an engineering student at the School of Mines. "There didn't seem to be anything else to do but join up. I can't remember anybody thinking of anything else. Any educated people and young fit fellows, they all thought, well, it's our duty to go, which we did." He was 20 when he joined up in September, 1914. He served in South West Africa, then after the Germans surrendered, transferred to the South African Scottish and went to France with them.[24]

Brian Brooke was born in Aberdeenshire in 1889, the third son of Captain H.V. Brooke, formerly of the Gordon Highlanders. His three brothers were in the services, two in the Army, one in the Navy. Brian had hoped to be a soldier but, because his eyesight prevented him passing the medical exam, he resolved to go the colonies. By rigorous training, he developed into an enormously strong youth of six feet 2 ½ inches. At the age of 18, he made his way to British East Africa, where he settled on land his father had bought for him there. He became a big game hunter and a blood-brother of the Masai, to whom he proved his worth by killing a leopard with a spear. By the Masai he was christened 'Korongo' ('The Big Man'), the name under which he wrote his poetry; by the Europeans he was known as 'The Boy.' After an unsatisfactory attempt at a career as a planter in Ceylon, he returned to British East Africa, where, at the outbreak of war, he was acting as a transport officer on the Jubaland frontier. He immediately enlisted as a trooper in the ranks of the British East Africa force. He rose quickly from private to captain. In a night attack he was wounded losing two fingers. When he learned of the death in action with the Gordons of his brother, Captain J.A.O. Brooke, who was awarded the posthumous V.C., he returned home and was made a captain in 2nd Gordons. He joined them in France in early 1916 and died of wounds received at Mametz on 1 July, 1916. His desire to play an active part in the war is shown in his poem, 'Waiting for News on the Frontier,' written in Africa, before his return.

> Oh, whirlwind and wind and vulture, I asked for the news of war
> …
> Did I ask you for weeping and crying, did I ask you for tales of woe?
> When my people perhaps are dying, and I long to be striking a blow?
> I know that our country will win it, but send us some news how they fare,
> And give me a chance to be in it, and send me a chance to be there.[25]

Peter Stewart had served in the Gordons for 21 years and fought with them at Elandslaagte and Ladysmith. He had retired in 1912 and settled in India to work on the Kolar Goldfield. He had married twice, with several children by his first marriage and seven by his second. When the war broke out he felt duty bound to volunteer. He finally arrived in Aberdeen in March, 1915, and was appointed Company Sergeant Major in 8th Gordons, a Service battalion. His frequent

---

23 BWA McKay, Janet Haggard, typescript, 'Canadian Loyalty to Scottish Tradition and the British Empire', passed to Museum, 1965.
24 IWM 24887 Recording Ashburner, Robert, interview, 1975.
25 Brooke, *Poems by Brian Brooke (Korongo)*, (London: John Lane, 1917), pp.10-18, 163-166.

letters to his wife in India show his keen sense of duty, and also the risk to his family. On the eve of the Battle of Loos he wrote to his wife, Lil:

> Now darling this may be the last time I will be privileged to write to you. I am going out without any thought of myself, only of you, my little ones, and my regiment. Pray to God darling that I may be worthy of you all. Kiss my little ones for me darling. I wish I could see you all just to say Good-bye before I go, but perhaps it is as well as it is for all will be over before you know about it. My only regret darling is that should this be my last fight you will be left with so many helpless little ones on your hands. I know love you will do your best by them. Well Good-bye my darling wife and may God protect and shield you and the Bairns, and always remember love that I left home not that I did not value you but because I could not stay to face you and my children knowing that my place was here. Whatever the result I thank God you can all say, He was not afraid to do his bit.[26]

Alongside this keen sense of duty, there was often a clear perception of the justice of the cause.[27] Grant Fleming, a pre-war Territorial, who turned 19 in 1914, served at Gallipoli, where he was wounded, and was afterwards given a commission in 1st Gordons. Much later he wrote:

> Materialistic, arrogantly militaristic yet subservient to autocracy, almost worshipping the Kaiser as the 'All Highest.' making a pretence at democracy, paying lip-service to Christianity yet anti-democratic and at heart anti-Christian, the Teutonic cult was ripe for expansion. However unprepared, whatever horrors war might bring, that we should rise as a people to halt this barbarism was itself an act of grace.[28]

James Sloan was 16 when the war broke out. The invasion of Belgium left a lasting impression on him.

> Even today [1979] I can find nothing but condemnation for the militaristic leaders who ordered their armies to march across the virtually undefended frontiers of the little nation that ventured to stand up for itself and defy the German ultimatum … Within days we had completely un-investigated but implicitly believed stories of German atrocities. Doubtless some were true but we had the inevitable erotic garnish of nuns being raped on tables in the High Street.

He joined the London Scottish, still under age, in 1916, and was drafted to 1st Battalion in France in July, 1917.[29]

---

26   GHM PB2021 Stewart, Peter, letter to wife Lil, 24 September, 1915, and research notes by Charles Reid, 26 November, 2008.
27   Apart from specific sources cited, see also: IWM 6702 Low, letters to wife Noanie, 29, 30 November, 1914, 4 July, 1915; *George Buchanan Smith 1890-1950*, passim; IWM 13511 PP Macgregor, Lt. R., letter to mother 11 June, 1916; IWM 926 Mackenzie, letters to wife Minnie, 18 June, 3 July, 1915.
28   IWM 15345 PP Fleming, J.G.G., typescript memoir, 'World War 1 and Other Army Memories,' written post 1945, 201pp, pp.2-3, 8, 19-26.
29   LC Western Front Recollections S18 Sloan, J.A.C., typescript memoir, 'Master of None,' written 1979, age 82.

Oswald Croft was one of the Londoners who joined 5th Seaforths in September, 1914, through Buckingham Gate. "I never liked war. I can't say that I liked it, but it was essential: we had to stop the Germans, whatever happened they had to be stopped, and whether we got killed or not, it didn't make any difference, but we had to stop them."[30]

Harry Taylor joined the Liverpool Scottish in July, 1915, aged 18 and four months. He had a very personal reason for joining.

> I have been giving further consideration as to why I joined the Army in 1915 when I was under age. Maybe I was influenced by the sinking of the 'LUSITANIA' in May of that year at which time I was with the Cunard Line Mediterranean Outward Freight Depot in Rumford Street. On the day following the disaster the basement of a building in Rumford Street had been converted for the purpose of displaying Press type photographs of the bodies of passengers (and crew) lying on the shore where they had come to rest as the tides receded. One I particularly remember was of a young mother still holding a baby in either arm, but many of the photographs were too horrible for words. Each incoming tide floated in a further pathetic quota.
>
> The entire staff became more or less on continuous duty for several days, and I was given the onerous responsibility, working through the night, advising by telephone to next of kin or relatives that passengers with whom they were connected had been identified, and I then had to break the sad news.

All this at age 18.[31]

George Ramage joined 1st Gordons at the front in April, 1915. After he was wounded he gave his reasons for joining:

> Tho' war is a hellish travesty of humanity, yet as long as one nation is prepared by force of arms & by the consequent slaughter, disfigurement & devastation to overthrow the liberties & destroy the lives of other nations, each nation must be prepared & ready to resist to death.[32]

Such thoughts were shared elsewhere in the Empire. J.E.P Levyn's family had had to change their German name from Kuhlmann to Levyns following Lusitania riots in South Africa. Notwithstanding his German background, J.E.P. signed up for the South African Scottish in 1916 before his nineteenth birthday.

> I was mainly moved by the same spirit of idealism that caused so many thousands of my doomed generation to offer their lives to their country. I believed with them that this war was like no previous one and that Great Britain had taken up arms to defend the noblest ideals of democracy against the grossest form of military tyranny and aggression that the world had seen since the defeat of Napoleon.[33]

---

30 IWM 4440 Croft, interview.
31 LC GS 1579 Taylor, LCpl Harry S., typescript memoirs, 'Reminiscences' and 'Further Reminiscences of the Great War 1914/1918.'
32 NLS MS944-947. Ramage, George, diary, passim, in particular MS 947, following 18 June, 1915.
33 Levyns, *The Disciplines of War*, pp.1-28.

By contrast, Bernard Blaser poured scorn on the justice of the German war in contrast to what he perceived as a crusade, as he marched with 2nd London Scottish from Gaza into Palestine:

> It was now, as we passed along one of the oldest routes in history, … we began to feel that we, too, were Crusaders engaged upon a task similar to that held so sacred by our gallant predecessors of the Middle Ages. Here in Palestine there could be no empty and fallacious reasons for the war we were waging against the Turks, no selfish aims to commercial supremacy, no 'Remember Belgium' and other shibboleths which had so sickened us that they became everyday jokes, but the purest of all motives, which was to restore this land, in which Christ lived and died, to the rule of Christian peoples. Apart from any sense of duty, it seemed to me a privilege to take part in such an undertaking. To free the Holy Land from a policy of organised murder, a tyranny so awful and despicable as to cause the hearts of the most apathetic to revolt in disgust, was in itself sufficient to urge us to great efforts, to suffer increased hardships without complaint. Such thoughts as these came to me as we plodded along this ancient way, and I could clearly see in my mind Cooper's picture of Richard Coeur de Lion, swinging his great battle-axe above his head, engaged in mortal combat with Saladin at the battle of Ascalon.[34]

He had evidently not had to deal with victims of the 'Lusitania,' while the purity of motives in dismantling the Ottoman Empire is somewhat questionable.

The soldier poet John Dunning MacLeod ('Jock') demonstrates his belief in a just war in his poem 'In Defens,' written retrospectively in 1932.

> 'Tis not to gain undying fame
> Nor have an epic-glorious name,
> But to right wrong and fight for 'hame'
> That we must fight aggressors.[35]

Douglas Gillespie was commissioned into the Argylls and joined 2nd Battalion at the front in February, 1915. In June he wrote: "To be killed fighting for a cause like ours is the greatest honour a man can win, and that is how we should try to look at it, as something far greater than a V.C. or any other honour to the living."[36] Almost identical feelings were expressed at the same time by Lieutenant Lionel Sotheby in 2nd Black Watch, in a farewell letter written to be opened in the event of his death:

> Never have such wonderful & heroic private soldiers assembled in such masses … as today. To die with such is an honour. To die for the safety of one's home is an honour. To die for one's country is an honour. But to die for right & fidelity is a greater honour than these. And so I feel it now. When it is an honour to die, then be not sad, rather rejoice & be thankful that such an opportunity was given one … Floreat Etona[37]

---

34 Blaser, Bernard, *Kilts across the Jordan* (London: H.F. & G. Witherby, 1926), p.97.
35 Macleod, John Dunning, *Poems* (privately published, 1958), p.20.
36 Gillespie, *Letters from Flanders*, pp.viii-xii, and p.210, letter home, 25 June, 1915.
37 LC GS 1507 Sotheby, Lionel F.S., farewell letter, 4 June, 1915.

Both men got their reward. Both were killed on 25 September. Standish Crauford meanwhile welcomed the war, which, rather like Rupert Brooke, he felt would be "a cleansing purge to modern civilisation."[38]

Quite remarkably, a number of Church ministers of various persuasions considered it their Christian duty not simply to serve as chaplains, but to join up as fighting men.[39] Several joined the ranks, some were subsequently commissioned, and some were commissioned directly. Cecil Barclay Simpson, for example, born in Aberdeen-shire in 1885, was minister of Moss Street Church, Elgin in the United Free Church of Scotland. In February, 1916, he went up to London to join the Inns of Court O.T.C., and a year later was given a commission in the Seaforths. In April, 1917, he was sent out to France and was killed by a shell on 7 October. In a sermon delivered on a visit to Elgin just before he went to France, he stated. "I … entered the army full of fervour, rejoicing that … I was permitted to obey what I felt to be the call of God, and to serve as a soldier in the great war for justice and freedom."[40]

The Reverend Dr Robbie Macmillan was the son of the Reverend John Macmillan of Ullapool. In 1913, he was appointed minister of St John's Presbyterian Church, Kensington, where he was serving at the outbreak of war. He was appointed chaplain to 2nd Camerons in France in November,1915, and moved with them to Salonika. There, in March, 1916, he was hospitalised with fever and a touch of pleurisy. He returned home, and in July, 1916, started training as an officer cadet at Worcester College, Oxford, wearing initially a chaplain's uniform! He received his commission as an infantry officer, was posted to 1/6th Seaforths in France in February, 1917, but soon transferred to 2nd Battalion. He was killed at Arras on 11th April, aged 33. John Buchan spoke at his memorial service at Kensington: "I remember many talks I had with him while he was still trying to find where lay his main duty. He did excellent work as a chaplain on various fronts, but I knew that would never content him. He was a happy man when he joined his beloved regiment as a combatant officer."[41]

Ross Husband was born in Dundee on 7 February, 1886. In the autumn of 1914, he became assistant at the High Church, Edinburgh. On the outbreak of war, he became convinced that it was his duty to join up and serve as a fighting soldier. His views are expressed in a draft letter he wrote to a fellow student in autumn, 1914:

> I simply can't avoid the conclusion that the war was deliberately provoked by Germany … We did not declare war on Germany till after the German Government had sent a brutal ultimatum to Belgium, and the King of the Belgians had addressed a pathetic appeal to King George, and German troops had already entered Belgian territory. What else could we do? How could we disown our obligations? How could we refuse to help the little country that trusted in us, and called for our aid? … Talk about non-resistance seems

---

38 GHM PB2093 Crauford, Sir George Standish, letter to father, 2 August, 1914.
39 ASHM N.F.5 Main, Capt D.M., letter to wife, 21 April, 1918; IWM 12643 PP Ferrie, Capt. W.S., Cataloguer's notes; IWM 1862 PP Craig-Brown, Ernest, letter, 28 March, 1916; Craig-Brown, *Historical Records*, Vol.4, p.379; Wilson, *Biographical List*, p.58 (John Morison).
40 *Cecil Barclay Simpson, A Memorial by Two Friends*, (Edinburgh: Turnbull & Spears, 1918), pp.7, 20.
41 NLS Acc.11627/87 Buchan Papers, Macmillan, Rev. Dr R.A.C., Obituary from *The Times*, 28 May, 1917, description of memorial service, and letter to Walter Buchan, 5 February, 1917; Fraser, Edith, *Records of the Men of Lochbroom who fell in the European War 1914-1918*, (Glasgow: Robert Maclehose & Co., 1922), pp.56-58.

strangely remote from the real facts of life. When I think of Belgium, I think of a child being abused by a hulking brute. In such circumstances even the most peace-loving wishes to strike a blow … Is that an entirely unregenerate, unsanctified, un-Christian temper?[42]

Declared unfit for military service because of varicose veins, he underwent an operation to cure the problem. When still declared unfit, he returned briefly to ministerial service before finding a military doctor who passed him fit for service on 22 November, 1915. He began his military training in December, 1915, initially at the Inns of Court O.T.C. in London and then at 9th Cadet Battalion at Gailes in Ayrshire. In July, 1916 he was commissioned into the Black Watch. He landed at Boulogne on 5 September, joined the 1st Battalion and was killed when attacking the German trenches on 26 September.[43]

Alongside the sense of duty and just cause, so clearly expressed by these ministers, was sometimes a somewhat naïve enthusiasm, excitement and sense of adventure.[44] Lionel Sotheby, for example, was commissioned at the beginning of the war and posted to 1st then 2nd Battalions Black Watch. In his diary, in February, 1915, he reveals his enthusiasm for the war. "It's awful in a way, and yet I am revelling in it, and would not have peace declared for any money. It is simply heavenly this life. I suppose my exuberance will wear off in time, but at present nothing can stay it." "This life I am still adoring, and count it dearer than anything else. I cannot imagine people being fed up, it's glorious, and I sometimes feel I am living in a sort of heaven at times, which may be rudely shattered any minute." Even after his eyes had been opened to the reality of war by the slaughter at Aubers Ridge on 9 May, 1915, as we have seen, he still retained his idealism and commitment to the cause.[45]

William Darling, a 29-year old insurance worker in Dundee, was very keen to enlist when war was declared.

> I decided that I must, somehow, get into uniform – the war would be over very soon, and I would have missed a lifetime's opportunity! What an urgency there was in these days! How eager men were to enlist! Was it that they were bored with their civil occupations or was it because there had not been any opportunity since 1900 to take part in the war? The excitement was general and it possessed me.[46]

Captain McKinnon of 1/4th Gordons recalled that when they left Bedford

---

42 Ross, *A Scottish Minister*, pp.19-23.
43 Ibid, passim.
44 Apart from specific sources cited, see: LC GALL 066 Nicol, 2Lt Alexander, letter to mother, postmark 15 May, 1915; LC GS 0890 Kershaw, Kenneth.R.B., letter to his father, 30 June, 1915; LC GS 1026 Maclean, G.F., typescript memoir written from diary, 1977, pp.2-7, Tape 495, interview with Liddle, 1978; LC Western Front Recollections C15 Cormack, E.W., typescript memoir, 'World War 1 Recollections, My Undistinguished Career,' written c.1970's; ASHM N-E11 Bowie, diary; IWM 8192 Lawson, letters to sister Bessie, 4 March, 3 June, 1916; GHM Not yet accessioned, Beaton, Norman, manuscript memoir, pp.8-15; IWM 10533 PP Reid, Maj Gen D.W., manuscript memoir; IWM 12043 Recording Collins, Norman, IWM interview, 1991; Rule, Alexander, *Students Under Arms*, (Aberdeen: The University Press, 1934), pp.38, 47.
45 LC GS 1507 Sotheby, diary, 2, 5 February, 1915.
46 Darling, Sir William Y., *So it looks to me*' (London: Odhams Press Ltd., n.d.), pp.122-125.

> In this parting the spirit of adventure was uppermost in the minds of nearly all. For we were embarking on an adventure, a great adventure from which we knew some would never come back. And I think that this spirit of adventure was uppermost in the minds of nearly all of us.[47]

When the war broke out, Howard Bowser was aged 19, and articled to a firm of chartered accountants in London. He decided to join the London Scottish. He received permission from his employers, who promised him that his place in the firm would be available on his return. "As I left the building my spirits rose – I felt like a schoolboy going on holiday. I should like to have thrown my hat in the air! I felt so elated that I nearly did."[48]

Henry Coates likewise left a city office to join up in November, 1914.

> Well, it was the idea of glamour, the ignorance. Battle always seemed to be something that was rather gallant and attractive. The fact that people round about were killed or badly wounded, mangled, was not a recognised fact until you were actually there and it was happening, and then it was too late to have second thoughts. It was a terrible shock really.[49]

Such feelings of enthusiasm were not confined to the volunteers of 1914-1915. Dave Harrison was born in Carradale in Scotland, but emigrated with his father to Canada years before the war began. Dave enlisted in the 72nd Battalion C.E.F., but once in England, in June, 1916, he was put on a draft of 300 men to join the 16th Battalion (Canadian Scottish) who had lost heavily in recent fighting.

> I was one of the lucky ones picked and we leave for the trenches in the morning. The psychology of war is a strange thing. Those of us who are picked are whooping it up tonight like a lot of schoolboys on their first picnic, and those who are left behind are very sore; one would think we were going to a glorious picnic in place of bloody battle and all the horrors of war, and I am just as bad as the rest. I feel very glad to go and very proud to be one of those chosen.[50]

J.K. Robertson, a junior subaltern in the Black Watch, was ordered to join a draft for France in April, 1917:

> Well can I remember the jubilation with which the news was received by all of us who were going to help our comrades at the Front at last … The majority of us … were light hearted boys like myself, who had been compulsorily kept for nearly a year with the home battalions owing to our extreme youth & who all that time had been fretting, worrying & cajoling the adjutant to let us get out to a theatre of war. For myself, I was overjoyed to learn that I had been picked for France.[51]

---

47 GHM PB583 McKinnon, memoir, p.1.
48 IWM 576 Bowser, memoir, pp.47-53.
49 IWM 9833 Recording Coates, Henry Bloomfield, interview, 1985.
50 IWM 16841 PP Harrison, D.C., letters to 'Joe', n.d., to daughter Gertrude, 11 June, 1916.
51 LC GS 1367 Robertson, J.K. Argyle, manuscript book, 'Twelve months as a Platoon Commander in France & Belgium', written 1920, 61pp, pp.1-2, 6-7.

Otherwise, professional officers might, like Graham Seton Hutchison, in 2nd Argylls, believe they had "found now the opportunity to put my professional training to the test, and in contemplation experienced a thrill of satisfaction.," but also "a vaguely realised patriotic sense."[52] There were even some professional adventurers from abroad. One such was Marc James Logie, a native of New York City. He served with the U.S. Navy from 1911 to 1915, taking part in the Nicaragua Expedition and the occupation of Vera Cruz in Mexico. He enlisted in the Black Watch at Perth in August, 1915, and is said to have served with them as an N.C.O. in Belgium, France, Mesopotamia and Macedonia. In June, 1918 he was released from British service to enlist in the American Expeditionary Force, in which he was subsequently commissioned.[53]

Patriotic sentiment was not new or unique to 1914. It had already been exhibited in 1899 and during the course of the South African War when many volunteers had signed up for duty. It is possible that the example of volunteering during the South African War (and the popularity of the volunteers themselves) was recent enough to have itself influenced the patriotic fervour of 1914. Many of the personalities involved, known and beloved by the public, were the same, most notably of course Lord Kitchener and Sir John French. Indeed, the whole military and Imperial panoply of Late Victorian and Edwardian Britain had a stirring effect on impressionable young boys.[54] Frank Brooke, who lived in Leeds, enlisted in 3/5th Seaforths in November, 1915, inspired partly by his boyhood love of things military.

> Almost from when I could read, my reading had been mainly of military history, story, and incident. I had a passion for things military. Where a boy usually collected stamps or birds' eggs, I collected scraps of information, pictures and postcards having to do with soldiers. I had the 'scarlet fever' in a much more virulent form than usually the case. I had a scrapbook filled with soldier pictures and photographs; I had a notebook containing all British regiments and their battle 'honours.' I entered into conversation with every ex-soldier I came across; I knew the dates of every battle since Hastings.[55]

Young boys played proudly with their favourite toy soldiers on the nursery floor.[56]

Certainly, the South African War formed the basis of childhood games for boys who would be of prime military age when the Great War began. James Fraser was born in 1893 in Aberdeenshire. At school he played 'Boers and Britons.'

> As the Boer War was in full flow the Boers were the unpopular side to be in; we all wore little buttons with the heads of the various famous people, viz. Kitchener, Roberts, Sir John French and our favourite in the North-East, General Sir Hector Macdonald, the crofter's

---

52　Hutchison, Lt.-Col. Graham Seton, *Warrior*, (London: Hutchinson, 1931), pp.29-46.
53　BWA Logie, papers.
54　Apart from specific refs cited, see: LC AIR 258A Low, P.V.C., extracts from typescript autobiography; *Lieut.-Colonel Robert Horn, D.S.O., M.C., 1st Seaforth Highlanders, a Sketch by his Mother*, (privately published, 1933), passim; IWM 7593 PP Harper, Cecil Gordon, transcription of *A Subaltern's Memoir of the 10th Battalion Gordon Highlanders, from July1914 to July 1915*, edited by Beryl & Stuart Blythe, January 1998.
55　IWM Books, Brooke, 'Wait for it', pp.1-6.
56　IWM 7593 Harper, memoir; IWM 15345 Fleming, memoir, pp.5-6; *Lieut.-Colonel Robert Horn*, passim.

son who became a General. We also had several little buttons with the heads of the Boers. There was Kronje, Kruger, de Villiers and de Wet.[57]

J.K. Stanford, born about 1892, Cecil Harper, born in 1893, and Grant Fleming, born in 1895, did the same.[58] Boer War veterans were idolised,[59] in the case of Stanford, his uncle Arthur, who had been a 'despatch-rider' during the war. Boys were also influenced by ripping Boys' Own tales of gallant heroes performing brave deeds in South Africa and elsewhere, for them to emulate.[60] These were powerful role-models. Douglas Gillespie, holding a wartime commission in 2nd Argylls, wrote a touching letter to his mother from the trenches in April, 1915:

> I … can remember very well the night when I cried myself to sleep. You were asking why it was – and it's a strange coincidence that you should ask me now, and that I should write and tell you from the trenches. Someone had been talking about what I was going to be, and it was suggested that I should be a soldier, but you said that 'Bey would never be a soldier, for he was not that sort,' and I took it as a great insult – but you were quite right, for it's not really a profession which suits me very well, though I am very glad to be an amateur soldier now.[61]

Self-image, indeed, was a powerful inducement to enlist. Thomas Lyon, who volunteered for service in the Glasgow Highlanders in September, 1914, recognised this, in describing their recruiting marches through Glasgow. "Oh, yes, we knew that we presented a very impressive sight as we swept through the city streets, each man trying to adopt the air of a martial hero, and wondering in his heart if the onlookers noticed the remarkable resemblance between him and Lord Kitchener or Napoleon." They were soon brought down to earth by the local youngsters, when marching to drill practice on Glasgow Green:

> "Aw, luk at that big yin there; the Germans'll tak' 'um for a telegraph powl." – "Hi, sir, ye'd better tak' yer mither's paurlour carpet wi' ye for a kilt!" – "Haw, here's speccy Dan! Kill yin or twa Germans fur me, purfessor!" – "Dis yer mither ken ye're oot wi' the bald heid?" … Yah! Luk at the tin sodgers wi' their badges – H.L.I. – Harry Lauder's Infants – Heluva Long Idle!"[62]

The influence of friends was also important. Many recruits joined up with pals, having discussed the options with them.[63] Frank Brooke, a Yorkshireman living in Leeds, had been enthusiastic

---

57   Fraser, Dr James Fowler, *Doctor Jimmy*, (Aberdeen: University Press, 1980), pp.vii-viii, 5-7, 38-48
58   IWM 10529 Stanford, memoir, pp.8-11; IWM 7593 Harper, memoir; IWM 15345 Fleming, memoir, pp.5-6.
59   IWM 10529 Stanford, memoir; LC MES 093 Recollections, Ballantyne, A.R., Tape 509, transcript of interview with Liddle 1978; IWM 13586 Recording Johnston, R.W.F., interview with grandson James, 1975.
60   IWM 10529 Stanford, memoir; IWM 12043 Collins, interview.
61   Gillespie, *Letters from Flanders*, p.94, letter home, 10 April, 1915.
62   Lyon, *In Kilt and Khaki*, pp.1-7, 11.
63   Apart from specific refs cited, see: Bogle, Kenneth R., *Walter Sutherland, Scottish Rugby Legend 1890-1918*, (Stroud: Tempus, 2005), passim; LC WF recollections D8 Denham, Dr R.H.S.H., manuscript

since boyhood about the military and the Highland regiments in particular, but it was the suggestion of his friend that induced him finally to join up in November, 1915:

> Harry Johnson, my chum from boyhood, suggested our enlistment. I had been friends with Harry since meeting him at my first place of employment. He was about my own age, fond also of reading military stuff ... I agreed with his suggestion; it seemed the decent thing to do since the war had become too big for the professional soldier to handle.[64]

W.S. Macdonald was born in 1897, and was at school at George Watson's Academy, where he joined the O.T.C. Artillery unit. He was told that if he waited six weeks he could get a commission in the Artillery. But he and his pals decided that by that time the war would be finished, so in 1915 they all decided as friends to join up in the ranks together in the 14th Argylls, of which a company was then being formed at Edinburgh. At that time, he could have been barely 18 years old.[65]

Others fell victim to pestering and white feathers. Alex Campbell, from the Isle of Islay, attended High School at Glasgow. "I was big for my age and although I was only 14 years old at the time I was one day accosted by a woman who told me I should be 'at the front.'"[66] J.W. Drury was aged 15 when the war broke out, living at Dewsbury Moor in Yorkshire. "I was tall and probably looked older than I was. Possibly that accounted for numerous remarks intended for me and one or two friends, also 'under age,' that, 'we seemed old enough to go' etc etc." Accordingly, he enlisted in November, 1915 at Bradford, joining the Seaforth Highlanders at Ripon. In January, 1916, however, he fell ill after a 20-mile route march. During his hospital spell, his real age emerged and he was discharged in February, 1916, just before his seventeenth birthday.[67] Another case was a misfit soldier in 1/4th Seaforths, recorded by Frank Brooke:

> Dicky Binks ... was a queer fellow. He had a nickname – very appropriate – 'Missus Binks.' He never resented it, for he was the mildest-mannered man in the battalion ... There was every reason for his nick-name, and he would have earned a fabulous salary as a pantomime dame. He was exceedingly shy, and retired modestly to the rear whenever any boisterous frolic was in being. He was particularly girl-shy, and sweated in agony at an invitation to be near a member of the opposite sex ... Two years ago [i.e. c.1933] I was passing a huge multiple provision shop in Bradford. From its interior plunged an assistant ... It was Dicky. There was a real 'Missus Binks now, and two or three little Binks. 'I was never a soldier, Jack,' he said, bitterly, 'I was never patriotic. I joined to avoid so much of the rotten talk that

---

recollections, c.1970's?; LC GS 0084 Barclay, recollections; LC WF Recollections S18 Sloan, memoir; Levyns, *The Disciplines of War*, pp.1-28; LC Transcripts, Tape 324, Jordan, Charles Kenneth, interview with Liddle, 1976; BWA Brown, George Murray, 'George Murray Brown His Story 1896-1980', privately produced 2009, 93pp; IWM 16335 Racine, memoir; IWM 10786 Recording Hood, David L.S., IWM interview, 1989.

64 IWM Books, Brooke, 'Wait for it', pp.1-3.
65 LC Tape 630/647, Macdonald, W.S., interview with Liddle, 1981.
66 LC DF 148 Campbell, memoir.
67 IWM 20852 PP Drury, J.W., manuscript memoir, 'Experiences of the European Great War Aug 1 1914 – 1918 Nov 11th Armistice Day', begun 1919.

was flying around and the white feather business – you know. I did nothing much to win the blasted war and I'm proud of it.'[68]

Charles Cordner worked in an office in Glasgow as a shorthand typist. He decided to enlist in November, 1915, when he was jostled in his civvies by a mass of uniformed members of the H.L.I. leaving the Glasgow Coliseum, where they had been entertained by Harry Lauder.[69] Hal Kerridge enlisted in the London Scottish some time in 1916, aged just 16. One reason was his annoyance at being constantly pestered in the streets.

> There were these various regiments, the East Surreys and the Royal West Kents, and they sent their sergeants out on the streets to try and get young fellows who were walking about to join the army … If you were out for a walk at any time you'd find a sergeant who'd come up behind you and say, 'Well, what about you, young lad. You're a fine looking young man, why don't you join the army? We want your sort.' It's no good telling them that you're only 16 and you've just left school. That's one thing. You got fed up with these people coming up to you all the time and you ended up feeling like a shirker.[70]

Another reason for joining up was unemployment. When Linton Andrews, a journalist in Dundee, first attempted to enlist in the Black Watch in the first week of the war, it became a struggle:

> A mob clamoured around the recruiting office in Dundee. At first I thought it a wonderful demonstration of patriotism … But the people competing to reach the recruiting sergeant had more than punitive thoughts. One of them looked suspiciously at my white collar, unfrayed tie and dark suit, and asked, 'Are *you* out of work, chum?' I replied that I had a goodish job. Thereupon my questioner told me to make way for lads without jobs. I was hustled to the back of the crowd as if I had been an impudent queue-jumper. After an hour or two of the hubbub and confusion I returned in disappointment to my desk at the office.[71]

One such man who was out of work when the war broke out was Charles Forman. He joined the Black Watch as a Regular soldier in November, 1914.[72] Another was David Hood, who was born in June, 1897, and worked at a Singer sewing machine factory in Glasgow. The work was reduced to about two days a week in 1914 due to loss of contracts, and when the war broke out he was unemployed. "Unemployment at that time was pretty bad. It was quite awkward to get a job anywhere." When the war broke out, his pal, Tommy McDermott, who was also pretty unfortunate in his family life, suggested they join up. So they joined the Argylls on 23 August, 1914. David was still just 17.[73]

---

68 IWM Books, Brooke, 'Wait for it', pp.230-231.
69 IWM 3449 PP Cordner, Charles, typescript memoir.
70 IWM Misc 234 Item 3338 Western Front Memories: 80 Years On Transcriptions, interview with Sgt Hal Kerridge, 1998.
71 Andrews, Linton, *Autobiography* p.81.
72 BWA, Forman, Charles, manuscript memoir, 'My Life', 1965.
73 IWM 10786 Hood, interview.

While soldiers may have enlisted with notions of adventure, patriotic duty, or the justice of the cause, these feelings did not always survive. Russell observed that, at Invergordon, in 3rd Camerons, in autumn, 1914,

> Everyone was keen to get out to France to fight the Germans, and men were even known to have concealed themselves on the train, in order to join the draft. This state of affairs continued until some of the wounded men and officers from the 1st Battalion were discharged from hospital and rejoined. It was then realised that active service was anything but a picnic, especially when the Germans attacked in force in November, 1914, at the first battle of Ypres, and many of the personnel of the 1st Battalion were either killed or missing.[74]

For some, the disillusionment and disgust were almost total.[75] George Martin, from Clapham, serving with 1/4th Seaforths in France, and presumably one of their 'London' entrants, wrote to a friend as early as January, 1915:

> I cannot convey the general impression better than repeating the words of a sergeant in the Gurkhas, who said 'This is not war, it's --- murder!' They will not stop till there is only two men and a dog on each side and they would not stop while they could stand up. You will excuse me talking like a veteran but I have already seen and heard enough to know that the romantic side only exists in the eyes of journalists.[76]

Lieutenant Alan Shewan, an officer with 11th Argylls, wrote on 18th December, 1915, after only two months at the front:

> The papers may talk of the 'glories of war,' but I have yet to discover them! I can see nothing 'glorious' in sitting in a mudhole that the average buffalo would despise, laying the foundations of a rheumatic old age and seeing good men blown to pieces – and to what end? God knows, I don't.[77]

Arthur Wrench, who joined 1/4th Seaforths in France in November, 1915, records his evolving bitterness towards the war as his diary unfolds. On 10th April, 1917, after the opening day of Arras, he wrote:

> It is all so sickening and if the folks away behind the lines could only see this, surely there would be no more war. But this is not war. It is only licensed murder, the sport of nations, by

---

74 THM Camerons 97-22, Russell, S.C., of Aden, typescript memoir, p.182.
75 Apart from specific refs cited, see: IWM 21092 PP McGregor, Peter, letters to wife Jen, 5, 17 July, 6 August, 8 September, 1916. For more retrospective comments, possibly influenced by later post-war attitudes, see: IWM 15175 White, Capt. R., retrospective 'General Remarks on war'; LC WF Recollections D8 Denham; IWM 10414 Recording McGregor, James Wallace, IWM interview, 1988.
76 Wheatley, Lawrence, ed., *Echoes from Hell Letters from the Western Front*, (Hitchin: The Dodman Press, 1982), letter from George Martin to Mrs Dorothy May Bonney, 8 January, 1915.
77 IWM 6444 Shewan, letter to his uncle Robert Shewan, 18 December, 1915.

a lot of ambitious and unscrupulous politicians and munition makers who urge on the war to their own profit and ends without the necessity of having to engage in it themselves.[78]

Frank Brooke, as we have seen, enlisted in 3/5th Seaforths in November, 1915, inspired partly by his boyhood love of things military. After being wounded at Arras in April, 1917, he found himself back at Ripon in early summer, 1917. By then his disillusionment was fairly complete:

> The reality was different … I experienced the drab, dull monotony of trench life, the weary 'waiting', the loathsome lice, the filthy conditions under which our food was prepared and eaten, the lack of the everyday little comforts only fully appreciated when they were absent, the forced intimate companionship of loose-talking, foul, animal-like brutes (in the main), the misdirection and inane 'strategy' of the fools set in authority, the moans, cries and groans of sadly, cruelly mutilated humans and animals, the absence of anything truly meant by 'religion', the mockery of both sides believing in, and exhorting, the same 'all-powerful Being.' Such things had been withheld or been camouflaged by Press and Pulpit. I knew now, and knowing, hated the whole wretched sordid business of warfare.[79]

Lieutenant Guy Macgregor, although he had joined up in September, 1914, had only seen war through the eyes of a front-line fighting unit since October, 1918, with 1/6th Argylls. He wrote on 29 October:

> I suppose there is an end to it all but I've lost the capacity for believing in it. It's all a loathsome treadmill – shambles & stink & filth & exhaustion – never a gleam of truth or beauty – just filth & stink & shambles & exhaustion over again.[80]

Private 'Jock' Low, in 9th Gordons, in his early twenties, wrote to his young pen-pal Mary, about seven years old, in Tebay, Westmoreland, in a string of letters, none of which, sadly, are precisely datable. Her brother Robbie seems to have been in the Boys Brigade.

> You may think that you would like to be a man, so that you would have a chance of having a shot at the Germans, if so I would like to say that this is murder not fighting and it's horrible. I am not allowed to write as I would like to do, but I think, little friend, that you will have heard how it is.
> Your Village has done very well, I think, contributing £5 10/– and I've no doubt but what the Boys Brigade did their Duty well. When I was eleven years old I joined the Boys Brigade, and I can remember the night when I was handed my Belt, Haversack and Hat, and I put them on, and my idea was that I was of some importance, and I longed to be a soldier, but I find now that I'm a soldier, that I would rather be the Boy again, for sham fighting is a great deal different to the real thing.[81]

---

78 IWM 3834 PP Wrench, A.E., diary, 10 April, 1917. See also entries for 11, 18 November, 1916, 21 January, 21 July, 4 August, 1917, 11 November, 1918.
79 IWM Books, Brooke, 'Wait for it', p.206.
80 IWM 8592 PP Macgregor, Lt A.E., letter to his wife Dulcie, 29 October, 1918.
81 LC GS 0981 Low, LCpl J.B, letters to pen -pal Mary, not precisely datable.

For others, the romance had been blown away, but the sense of necessary duty remained, and so they were sustained by the need to 'stick it.' Henry Pelham Burn, a regular officer with 1st Gordons, wrote to his mother as early as November, 1914, "I am sure the war would not last much longer if the people in London, Berlin & Paris could know the truth and see what war is."[82]

Charles Fettes, who served with 1/4th Gordons, did not shirk his duty but expressed qualms about killing in March, 1915.

> I often wonder how long men will be allowed to go on murdering one another. It is not that I flinch from my duty in the least. I would have felt a great coward if I hadn't volunteered, but the idea of taking other men's lives is repugnant to me.[83]

D. Dick deployed to France with 14th Argylls in June, 1916, and was invalided home during the winter of 1916-1917 with trench feet, frost-bite and dysentery. Recovered and returned to 3rd Argylls in 1917, he noted,

> By that time the glamour of war was over – I had enlisted in the spirit of the knights of old, fired on with ambitions to get the chance of being a hero – and gaining a medal. War, I now knew was a matter of doing one's duty, of standing by your comrades and not letting them down under any circumstances, and of keeping your fears to yourself.[84]

Likewise, Captain Don Main of 1/5th Argylls, en route from Gallipoli to hospital in Alexandria, wrote on 13 August, 1915, "If this cruel game of scientific murder would only cease how happy we would all be, but God's will be done, and we must put duty first."[85]

Whatever their thoughts about duty and justice, there was clearly a difference in attitude within drafts between those cheerfully going out for the first time, and those who had been recycled and were being sent back for a second or third time into the maelstrom. Stewart Thomson, in 1st London Scottish, was hospitalised home from France with septic cuts and abrasions about the end of January, 1915. He wrote to his brother David in New Zealand in May, 1915: "Nobody who has been literally at the front can honestly want to go back. It's the chaps who have 'cushy' jobs at the base etc who are not yet fed up."[86] William Ferrie, newly commissioned in 3/9th Argylls at Dumbarton Castle, wrote to his brother in September, 1915; "A draft of 100 men leaves here (probably tomorrow) for the front. They have all been there before and don't want to go back."[87] And J.K. Robertson, a junior subaltern in the Black Watch, watching his mixed draft embarking at Folkestone in April, 1917, recognised the different attitudes of the soldiers:

> It is very interesting to note the different expressions on the men's faces … from which one is able to judge the length of service abroad of each man. One will look thoroughly dejected

---

82 GHM PB3309 Pelham Burn, letter to mother, 15 November, 1914.
83 GHM PB1726 Fettes, Pte Charles, diary, 14 March, 1915.
84 LC GS 0456 Dick, memoirs, p.47.
85 ASHM N-E5 Main, letter to wife, 13 August, 1915.
86 IWM 12968 Thomson, 2Lt J.S., letter to brother David, 22 May, 1915.
87 IWM 12643 Ferrie, letter to brother Allan, 21 September, 1915.

& miserable at the thought of going back again perhaps for the 4th or 5th time. Another will be laughing & joking & asking questions by the dozen of the older soldiers who have been out before.[88]

Robert Greig was a journalist who enlisted in 1916, and served in 2nd Seaforths. In an article written for the 'Shetland Times' in 1920, he wrote that routinely the troops at the front were 'fed up.'

After the first novelty of being in the war zone wore off, the men just got 'fed up' and stayed 'fed up.' When they were leaving the trenches for a rest they felt less 'fed up,' and consequently more cheerful, but the depression settled again when the time came to resume duty in the line. The spirits of the troops were excellent only when they got leave, and the excellence of their spirits dropped considerably when they had to go back.[89]

Captain A.H. Macdonald of 6th Seaforths makes an interesting observation on the same phenomenon.

Being 'fed up' was better than having the 'wind up,' and both were infinitely preferable to having a 'gloom up,' All three were infectious and depressing, but none so acutely as the last, some men (one has heard) and some officers (one knows) were past masters in the art. Excellent fellows when the mood was off, but when grovelling in it (and enjoying it, mark you, in their own way, like an undertaker at his first funeral, which you were attending out of respect for the deceased) they set the pace towards miseries, real and imagined, and seriously impaired the efficiency of their neighbours.[90]

Perhaps we should leave the last word to Private Percy Taylor, of the Black Watch, who wrote in the autograph book of Jean Leslie, a V.A.D. at Drumossie Hospital:

'Tis a Bloody War is this
We'll be glad when it's all done
For I might have killed a Mother
When I killed a Mother's Son[91]

More specific to this study is why men chose to join Highland regiments. The kilt and uniform itself was an attraction to some. Captain Robert Horn was adjutant of 1st Seaforths, aged 33, when the war broke out. Many years before, when he was five years old in Edinburgh, he first saw a Highland regiment swinging across the Dean Bridge in Edinburgh, and announced solemnly that he was going to join a Highland regiment. He remained true to his resolution, went to

---

88 LC GS 1367 Robertson, memoir, pp.1-2, 6-7.
89 Cluness, Alex, ed., *Doing his bit, A Shetland Soldier in the Great War*, (Lerwick: The Shetland Times Ltd, 1999), p.41.
90 Peel, Capt R.T & Macdonald, Capt. A.H., *The Great War 1914-1918 6th Seaforth Highlanders Campaign Reminiscences*, (Elgin: W.R.Walker & Co., 1923), p.48.
91 GHM PB564 Leslie, Jean, autograph book.

Sandhurst after Winchester, and in 1900 was gazetted to 1st Seaforths.[92] J.C Cunningham, from Kelso, joined the Argylls Militia and afterwards transferred to the Regulars. He joined the Argylls, not only because his brothers had served in the regiment, but because "it was a very fine uniform."[93] Another Scotsman who acknowledged the lure of the uniform was Alexander Rule, a native of Huntly, and a student at Aberdeen University who joined 'U' Company in November, 1913. While he states that he was "attracted mainly by the good fellowship in U Company's ranks," he concedes that the uniform was also an attraction.

> The kilt in itself is sufficiently attractive – provided one's legs are reasonably proportionate and, even with the lowly status of a private of the line, one can bask fully in the reflected glory of regimental traditions. The kilted recruit enters into a particularly colourful inheritance, that dates from "battles long ago."[94]

The Englishman Norman Collins wanted to join a Scottish regiment, although his family connection with Scotland was apparently limited to two great-grand-parents. He was clearly attracted to the idea and conceded that "the uniform appealed to a boy."[95] Another Englishman who appears to have been attracted by the uniform was young William Newton, who joined up aged 15. When the war started he was a messenger boy at the Post Office in Torquay. He went to join up at the Town Hall, but the recruiting sergeant recognised him. So he took his Post Office bicycle to the recruiting office at Paignton. Outside was a picture of a Highlander in full regalia.

> I told the recruiting sergeant I wanted to join that particular regiment, to which he replied, 'You have to be a Scot,' and I said, 'Well, I am.' But I wasn't: I was born in Torquay. However, he said, 'Where was you born?' I said, 'Ayr,' and when I put it on my application form I spelt it AIR. However, in due course my papers came through and I was sent to Aberdeen.[96]

The kilt may nevertheless have attracted some undesirable characters. James Sloan joined the London Scottish in 1916 and found himself under canvas in Richmond Park. Here, the kilt;

> may also have played its part in attracting to the regiment a particularly undesirable kind of recruit. The glamour attached to the uniform plus the convenience of Richmond Park for getting up to the West End brought in a few pansies of the chorus-boy type and there were some scandalous reports of extra-military activities in Piccadilly and Shaftesbury Avenue.[97]

In fact, the kilt and uniform did not necessarily attract just for their own sake, but because they were part of the overall attraction of joining a Highland regiment, which, as we have seen,

---

92 *Lieut.-Colonel Robert Horn,* passim.
93 LC GS 0409 Cunningham, notes written 1976, and Tape 363, transcript of interview with Liddle, 1976.
94 Rule, *Students Under Arms,* pp.2-3.
95 IWM 12043 Collins interview.
96 IWM 24855 Recording Newton, William James, interview, 1975.
97 LC WF Recollections S18, Sloan, memoir.

depended on the somewhat overblown reputation which they had earned during the previous century. Thus, before Charles Forman, from Burton-on-Trent, joined up in November, 1914, "I'd asked my eldest brother Jim … what regiment I should join. He told me, 'Join the Black Watch! You'll see more fighting with that lot.'"[98] In November, 1915, Frank Brooke and his chum Harry Johnson enlisted in the 3/4th Seaforths, which, with other Highland regiments, had been brought from depots in Scotland to Ripon, near Leeds, their home town. The romance of the Highland regiments undoubtedly played a part in Frank's decision to join the Seaforths.

> I have mentioned my fondness for military history. In this all the Highland regiments figured largely. Who, indeed, even among people who ignored or who had forgotten such history, hadn't heard, or read, of the Black Watch, the 'gay' Gordons, the Seaforths, the Camerons or the Argylls? There was a fascination about the kilted soldier. His records of fighting were 'won' in India, in South Africa, in Egypt, in Europe – all over the world. Inspiring poetry and exuberant music had been composed in his honour. His place during battle was in the forefront: his was the first bayonet in the attack. The 'Thin Red Line', the Highland Brigade in South Africa, the square at Waterloo, the zarebas of Atbara and Tel-el-Kebir, the Relief of Lucknow, all were indelibly part and parcel of the Highlanders' traditional battle prowess. Round his head was a halo of valour, and the Victoria Crosses won in action, though granted to individuals, were won by, and for, the 'kilties' generally.[99]

Cecil Harper was commissioned into the 10th Battalion Gordon Highlanders before Christmas, 1914. On the outbreak of war he was a medical student at London University. When he was not quickly called up, Cecil lost patience, and began to pull strings using his Scottish family connections. For although he had himself been born in England, in Bromley, in 1893, his father Peter had been born at Kincardine o'Neil, on Deeside. Peter had become a journalist and moved to England, but had himself, while working at Aberdeen, enlisted in the Aberdeen Rifle Corps, which later became 4th Gordons. Thus, as a boy, Cecil and his brothers' favourite regiment of lead soldiers was the Gordon Highlanders, in their red coats and feather bonnets, which conjured up their father's Scotland, which the boys had never visited. They had a picture of the Gordons storming the heights of Dargai in 1897, urged on by Piper Findlater, and when the Gordons were in the thick of things in South Africa, the boys acted out the dramas of Ladysmith, Modder River and Magersfontein. Cecil's Scottish connections worked wonders.

> One of Mother's close friends was Mrs Grant of Bickley, the widow of General Grant, who had seen much service in India … Somehow I was Mrs Grant's blue-eyed boy. She immediately wrote to her old friend General Hamilton Gordon at Aldershot. Within a few days I was offered a temporary commission in any of the Scottish regiments I might chose to name, but preferably a Highland regiment. Inevitably my choice was the Gordon Highlanders. The recruiting territory included the region from which my Father came, and we had been brought up in its love and legend.[100]

---

98 BWA, Forman, memoir.
99 IWM Books, Brooke, 'Wait for it', pp.2-3; see also THM S98-11 Brooke, Frank C., typescript memoir, 'A Yorkshire Kiltie', written 1973, pp.1, 8. These memoirs are not identical.
100 IWM 7593 Harper, memoir.

Harold Judd was born in 1898 in Walthamstow. He was unusual in that he was a volunteer, not a conscript, in 1917. He was a railway worker, but volunteered aged 18, before being called up, in order to get into the regiment he wanted – the London Scottish. He had read about their exploits in France at Messines and was determined to join them. "I didn't want to be pushed into some county regiment – I wanted to get into the London Scottish!"[101] By contrast, Hal Kerridge joined the London Scottish because, when some of them had been billeted on his family in East Sheen, just outside Richmond, "I thought what a lot of jolly nice fellows they were, and if ever I had to join the army … I thought well I would like to join the London Scots."[102]

> Now in the London Scottish it's not a question of joining the army, it's more a question of will they accept you in the London Scottish, if you don't meet their standards well they'd say sorry. That was another reason, I thought if I'm going to join the army I don't want to join the Stepney Gurkhas or anything like that! I wanted to go into a decent regiment where there are a nice lot of fellas.[103]

Chaplains or Medical Officers might be delighted to be posted to Highland regiments. Johnathan Bates was an English Medical Officer who found himself posted to 8th Black Watch in May, 1916. He was delighted with the posting; "When I come back on leave I shall have to wear a kilt and pretend to enjoy the bagpipes!"[104] Similarly, in June, 1917, after a few days in France with 12th Royal Scots, Coll Macdonald was delighted to be posted as chaplain to the same battalion.[105]

Of course, many men joined Highland regiments because it was natural to join their local regiments. John Cooper was born in Broughty Ferry, Angus, on 5th June, 1897, but was brought up by his aunt and uncle in Dundee. Both were in Black Watch territory. He enlisted in November, 1915 under the Derby scheme. "When the clerk asked which regiment I wished to join, I said 'The Black Watch,' and when asked which I should prefer if that were not open, I said 'Any other Highland Regiment.' But 'Black Watch' was written at the top of my attestation form." Accordingly, he was called up on 10 May, 1916 for service with 3/4th Battalion Black Watch.[106] William Paterson lived in Wick. He joined up voluntarily but did not do so until early summer, 1915. He was torn between service in the Army or the Navy.

> So, I was still undecided, but it was not for long. News came to hand that our local battalion, the 5th Seaforth Highlanders, had been in action and up against the Hun in France [no doubt at Festubert]. Many brave boys had made the supreme sacrifice, amongst them two comrades of my own, with whom I had spent many carelessly happy days. The die was cast. I had decided to enlist in the Army.

---

101 LC Several Fronts Recollections Judd, H,C., Transcript of Tape 1545, interview for Liddle Collection, 1997.
102 LC Tape 1618/1619 Kerridge, Hal, interview, 1998.
103 IWM Misc 234 Item 3338. Kerridge interview.
104 IWM 2854 PP Bates, , Maj J.V., letter to fiancée, 3 May, 1916.
105 BWA, Macdonald, Coll, letters to wife, 6, 7 June, 1917.
106 IWM Books, Cooper, 'Domi Militaeque', biographical note & pp.1-8.

In early summer, 1915, He went to the depot at Golspie to enlist and was posted to 3/5th Seaforths.[107] Linton Andrews was a Yorkshireman, born in Hull, but had taken a job as a journalist on the Dundee Advertiser. He saw it as his duty to enlist, and duly joined 4th Black Watch, the Dundee Territorial battalion.[108]

Englishmen or Anglo-Scots joining kilted regiments, and particularly the London Scottish, would often do so on the basis of legitimate Scottish ancestry. Others might make extraordinary claims to Scottish ancestry to justify their decision. Norman Collins justified his choice of a Scottish regiment (the Seaforths) by his having two Scottish great-grand-mothers. "Well, I wanted to join a Scottish regiment, because my father's side, his grandmother was a Hay and another was a Henderson, so I felt that I had enough Scottish blood in me to justify joining a Scottish regiment."[109]

For some, it was family connections which determined their choice of regiment. J.C Cunningham, as already noted, joined the Argylls before the war because his brothers had served in the regiment. "I had always intended to become a soldier, and of course only an Argyll."[110]

Friends may also have influenced choice of regiment. D. Dick studied at St Andrew's University and served in the O.T.C. there. When he had completed his degree exams, he decided that, instead of applying for a commission, he would enlist as a private soldier. He enlisted in Dundee into 14th Argylls. "Two of my teachers in Greenock had enlisted in the Greenock Bn of the Argylls and perhaps that swayed with me; for the Black Watch was the regiment of my native Fifeshire, and many of my friends were serving in the B.W."[111] Walter Sutherland, Scottish rugby international from Hawick, had joined the Lothian and Border Horse soon after the outbreak of war. But, frustrated at being kept at home, like others in July, 1915, he deserted and enlisted in the 14th Argylls, giving a false name. He seems to have chosen this battalion as his friend and team-mate from the Hawick First XV, Geordie Johnstone, had already joined it.[112] Dr R.H.S.M. Denham was a medical student at Aberdeen University when the war commenced.

> Notwithstanding the fact that I was a member of the University O.T.C. and was also wearing a naval armlet awaiting call up to the Navy as a surgeon probationer, I eventually enlisted in the 4th Battalion of the Gordon Highlanders. The reason for this was that the father of a friend of mine had become Lord Provost of Aberdeen and was vigorously recruiting on behalf of this regiment. I succumbed to my friend's constant persuasion and we agreed to join together.[113]

C.N. Barclay, a trainee civil engineer of Scottish descent chose to join the London Scottish partly because several of his friends were joining the same regiment.[114] Harry Taylor joined the

---

107 THM Seaforths 89-122 Paterson, memoir.
108 Andrews, Linton, *Autobiography*, pp.80-81.
109 IWM 12043 Collins, interview.
110 LC GS 0409 Cunningham, loc. cit.
111 LC GS 0456 Dick, memoirs.
112 Bogle, *Walter Sutherland*, passim.
113 LC WF Recollections D8 Denham.
114 LC GS 0084 Barclay, Brig. C.N., recollections.

Liverpool Scottish in July, 1915. "Although not a Scot, I knew personally many members of the Battalion, older than I of course, who lived in Waterloo, so I had in mind the possibility of joining them in France in the year 1915."[115] Charles Jordan was born in Sunderland in 1897, the son of a policeman. "When it came to my [nineteenth] birthday there were a few pals of mine that were going to join The Black Watch. So I joined up with them."[116] E.R. Savage had enlisted in the Army Service Corps (A.S.C.). Sent to the remount depot at Romsey, "I was there about a year when a chum said what about putting in for a transfer to the Black Watch, which three of us did and got through."[117] George Murray Brown joined up aged 19 in December, 1915, opting for the Black Watch under the Derby scheme. Disappointed in his desire to join the Royal Flying Corps, he decided to follow his friends. "Three Twynholm lads were already in the Black Watch so I thought if I went now I could join up with them. That would be better than joining up with a lot of strangers. So to Dumfries I went and took the Oath."[118] J.A. Douglas was born in Fourstones, near Hexham, but was living in Walker-upon Tyne, when he received his calling up papers under the Derby Scheme on 13 March, 1917. He had opted to join the Argylls. "Alex White, a relation of mine on my mother's side, had joined up at the outbreak of the war, and with having a strong Scottish connection had joined the A. & S.H. and he was my main inspiration for me wishing to go into the A. & S.H."[119]

In Cape Town in 1916, when J.E.P. Levyns failed his first half-year exams at the South African College, he teamed up on the spur of the moment with a pal in the same predicament and, "arm in arm, we went back down the avenue together to the recruiting office in the old Supreme Court building at its foot. We were both eighteen years of age." There he joined the South African Scottish.[120]

Others might need the help of friends to get into their regiment of choice. Lionel Ferguson recalls how, on the afternoon of 5th August, 1914,

> "I decided to join the Liverpool Scottish. At the … HQ things seemed hopeless; in fact I was giving up hopes of ever getting in, when I saw Rennison, an officer of the battalion, and he invited me into the mess, getting me in front of hundreds of others. I counted myself in luck to secure the last kilt."[121]

In some cases, the regiment joined bore little relation to first choice. William Cameron would have preferred to join the Glasgow Highlanders, but failed to be accepted for service when he turned 18 in 1915. He was ultimately called up in May, 1916, and after another abortive attempt to join the Glasgow Highlanders, was posted to the Scottish Horse. Yet the day after arriving at Etaples in January, 1917, he was transferred to 7th Black Watch. "I always had a great liking for the kilt," he stated, so at least, in that respect, he got his way.[122] H. King was from Kilwinning

---

115 LC GS 1579 Taylor, memoirs.
116 LC Transcripts, Tape 324, Jordan, interview.
117 LC Middlebrook Somme 1918, Savage, E.R., letter 6 July, 1976.
118 BWA Brown, His Story.
119 IWM 4586 PP Douglas, J.A., manuscript memoir, 'Khaki Apron', 1578pp, pp.1-12, 680.
120 Levyns, *The Disciplines of War*, pp.1-28.
121 Quoted in Brown, Malcolm, *Tommy goes to War* (Stroud: Tempus, 2005), p.10.
122 BWA Cameron, William, manuscript memoir, 'Army Life & Trials of William G. Cameron.'

in Scotland. He managed to secure a commission in the Seaforth Highlanders, but it is evident that the commission was more important to him than the particular regiment. He had hoped to obtain a commission in his local regiment, the Royal Scots Fusiliers, and once commissioned, although he did eventually see service with 2nd Seaforths, he spent most of the war on secondment to the Signals Service.[123]

In some cases, allocation to a regiment was quite arbitrary. Albert Hay lived in the village of Maud in Aberdeenshire. He was called up shortly after turning 18 and reported to Castlehill Barracks in Aberdeen. But from there he was sent for training, not to the Gordons as one might expect, but to 2/2nd Scottish Horse. Finally having turned 19, he 'volunteered' for a draft to France. It was apparently at the Scottish Depot at Calais that he was transferred to the Black Watch, and drafted to 1st Battalion. Evidently, his drafting to that particular regiment was more or less random.[124]

In other cases, the choice of a Highland regiment does not seem to have mattered too much to the individuals concerned. Before he joined the Black Watch, to be with his pals, Charles Jordan had tried to get into the Grenadier Guards, but did not like the terms he was offered. Then, when training at Norwich, he was quite happy to volunteer (albeit unsuccessfully) for the Tanks.[125] George Murray Brown had hoped to get into the Royal Flying Corps. "I had not intended being a rifle and bayonet fighter as I felt I was too wee for that sort of exercise." Finding the R.F.C. was full, he only opted for the Black Watch because some of his local pals had done so.[126] J.A. Douglas was living in Walker-upon Tyne, and in 1917, he was called up under the Derby Scheme. He had opted to join the Argylls, largely through the influence of one of his relations who had joined the regiment at the outbreak of the war. He was evidently not totally committed to the Argylls, however, for while still in training he underwent a trade test as a Royal Engineers draughtsman. However, he was marked 'indifferent', heard no more about it, and continued his progress in the Argylls.[127] In the case of Alexander Braes, his choice of regiment appears to have been dictated more by his keen desire to get to the front than to an attachment to any particular regiment. He attested for the Army at Glasgow on 3 September, 1915. Four days later, at Maryhill Barracks, he volunteered to join a draft for the Seaforths.

> The news that 32 Seaforths were wanted soon brought crowds to fall in on the Seaforth marker. So anxious was I to get away that I took up my position seventh in the front rank at 10 a.m. and stood there until the Commanding Officer selected the men required at 3 p.m. By standing on two stones I was able to give myself another inch and was fortunate enough to be selected to be one of the 32 to proceed that night to join the Seaforth Highlanders at Fort George.[128]

---

123 LC GS 0895 King, H., manuscript memoir, 'Recollections of the War', pp.1-5.
124 BWA Hay, Albert A, manuscript memoir, 'Soldiering', written, 1935, 318pp, pp.6-62.
125 LC Transcripts, Tape 324, Jordan, interview.
126 BWA Brown, 'His Story.'
127 IWM 4586 Douglas, memoir, pp.1-12, 21-24, 680.
128 THM 2013-072(S) Braes, Alexander, typescript memoir, 'My Experiences during the Great War', 54pp, pp.1-11.

To conclude, it is maintained that the principal reason why men chose to enlist, and which subsequently motivated them, was a sense of duty, which extended not just to Britons but also to expatriate Scots from distant parts of the Empire. Related to this keen sense of patriotic duty was a strong feeling of the justice of the cause, which even attracted church ministers to join the ranks to do their bit. This sense of duty was quite distinct from jingoism, with which it is sometimes confused. There were of course some less noble sentiments. There was a degree of naïve enthusiasm, as well as a degree of patriotism of the flag-waving type, inspired by the power and military panoply of the Empire, with which youngsters had been brought up. There was also a strong element of self-image. To be seen in uniform was the thing to do. Some joined under the influence of friends; others in response to pestering and white feathers. Some joined simply to escape unemployment. Inevitably, when ignorance of the true face of war was confronted with reality, there was some disillusionment, even amongst those who had accepted service as a necessity of duty rather than naively as a jolly adventure. But beneath the bitterness, there remained generally a remarkable commitment to duty, a determination to 'stick it' through the awful realities of war until the necessary job was done. Overall the soldiers believed in the justice of the cause and the necessity to fight and win.

As regards joining Highland regiments, some were attracted by the glamour of the kilt and uniform; others by the reputation gained by the Highland regiments in the wars of Empire. Some of course simply joined their local regiments, especially the Territorials, as the natural thing to do. Some simply followed their families into regiments. Scottish ancestry was one driver, although some Highland identities were sometimes assumed and problematic, while some Englishmen might make spurious claims to Scottish ancestry to justify their decision to join kilted regiments. Others simply followed friends into Highland regiments. Finally, a significant number of soldiers were drafted to Highland regiments for quite arbitrary reasons. By no means all were there because they specifically chose to be. In the next chapter, we shall consider just who these men were who made up the kilted battalions.

4

The Men Who Marched Away

> It means the thinning out of an ancient race, the fading of one of the old languages of Europe, and a great unbridged blank in a generation.[1]

Introduction

In this chapter we look at the composition of the kilted battalions which marched away to war. We examine the social background of all ranks, as well as where they came from, including the extent to which they were Highland or even Scottish. We look in turn at the Commanding Officers, the regimental officers and the Other Ranks, distinguishing between the Regular, Territorial and Kitchener battalions, considering at the same time the impact of continuous change through casualties and reinforcement. We then consider some specific groups; under-age soldiers, Gaelic-speakers, mere Englishmen, and then the Canadians and South Africans, before offering some summary conclusions.

Commanding Officers

Commanding Officers for the new Kitchener battalions were initially found from retired Regular officers[2] or Special Reserve officers.[3] C.O.'s for the newly raised second and third line Territorial battalions were partly found by recycling Territorial officers not fit for overseas service,[4] possibly after retiring from the front. Otherwise, retired officers might be employed.[5]

---

1. Watt, Lauchlan Maclean, *In France and Flanders with the Fighting Men*, (London: Hodder & Stoughton, 1917), .90-91. See also BWA, Macdonald, Coll, letter to wife, 4 November, 1917.
2. Wauchope, *Black Watch*, Vol. 3, p.3 (Sempill), p.107 (Lloyd); IWM 7593 Harper, memoir (MacDougall of Lunga).
3. NLS Acc.6028 Addison Smith, C.L., biographical details; Addison-Smith, *10th Seaforths*.
4. *Roll of Officers Dunbartonshire*, pp.23, 76 (Leith-Buchanan); IWM 12311 Mason-Macfarlane, memoir by David Mason-Macfarlane; Wauchope, *Black Watch*, Vol.2, pp.135, 345 (Moncrieffe).
5. Maclean, *On Active Service*, Vol.1, p.84 (Macalpine-Downie).

114 Those Bloody Kilts

In the Regular battalions, replacement C.O.'s were generally found from within their own caste and regiment.[6] Not all C.O.'s of Regular battalions however were home-grown, especially as the war progressed, severe casualties were incurred, and there was a need both to promote talent and to appoint officers to the job who were sufficiently capable and experienced.[7] The situation required both tact and strength of character.

In the Territorials, some C.O.'s were found on the outbreak of war to be physically unfit for service overseas and had to be replaced.[8] Replacements for such officers were found from former officers, prised out of retirement,[9] sometimes older than the men they replaced. Afterwards, some replacement C.O.'s came from the Territorials themselves,[10] However, both Territorial and Kitchener battalions received replacement Regular and Militia officers to command them, and, as the war progressed, officers with Temporary Commissions, who had proved themselves in battle. Indeed, a significant number of replacement Territorial commanders were Regulars, reflecting perhaps the need to instil greater professionalism. Sometimes these were drawn from the same regiment.[11] In other cases, Regular officers were appointed from different regiments,[12] sometimes even cavalry, reflecting the availability of cavalry officers in an infantry war. Such external postings could create dissent, requiring great tact to overcome, not always successfully.

Kitchener battalions likewise received replacement C.O.s from the Regulars,[13] or from the Militia,[14] Still others had temporary wartime commissions.[15] Notable was Laurie Wilson, gazetted in September, 1914 to 11th Argylls, who remarkably took command of that Kitchener battalion in March, 1918, aged only 23, and later commanded the Territorial 1/8th Battalion.[16] Finally, there was even the possibility for talent to rise from the ranks. William Morrison, who became acting Lieutenant-Colonel of 1/5th Seaforths in August, 1918, was a former private in the Gordons who had transferred to the Reserve in 1908. When the war broke out, he was

---

6   See for example: GH PB242 Stansfield, Lt.-Col. John Raymond Evelyn, extract from 'British Roll of Honour'; GHM PB2093 Crauford, record of service; IWM 10909 PP Cunningham, Brig, J.C., typescript memoir, 14pp, pp.1-8.
7   ASHM N-E2 MacMillan, Gordon H.A., notes written by him, 31 January, 1976.
8   *Roll of Officers Dunbartonshire*, pp.23, 76 (Leith-Buchanan); Wauchope, *Black Watch*, Vol.2, pp.126-7 (D.C. Campbell).
9   *Roll of Officers Dunbartonshire*, p.93; Maclean, John, *On Active Service with the Argyll and Sutherland Highlanders in Belgium and France*, Vol.1, (Edinburgh: The Scottish Chronicle Press,, n.d.), p.83 (James Clark); Wauchope, *Black Watch*, Vol.2, pp.126-7 (Sir Robert Moncrieffe).
10 *Roll of Officers Dunbartonshire*, pp. 76, 93, 98, 121; Maclean, John, *On Active Service*, Vol.2, pp.100-101 (Neil Diarmid Campbell).
11 *Roll of Officers Dunbartonshire*, p.98.
12 Wauchope, *Black Watch*, Vol.2, p.135; IWM 3249 PP Montgomerie, Maj. E.W., letter to W.O., 27 January, 1917; ASHM N-E8 Maclachlan, Capt .T.K., letter to him from Gen. Sir Douglas Baird, n.d.
13 *Lieut.-Colonel Robert Horn*, passim; Wilson, *Biographical List*, p.48; BWA Gordon, Brig. Gen. C.W.E., notebooks containing letters from France, Vols 1-3, passim; GHM PB3309 Pelham Burn, Henry, biographical notes and letters to parents, passim.
14 Maclean, *On Active Service*, Vol.1, p.84; GHM PB507 Wallace, Col. H.R., Record of Service, and diary, 31 August, 1915.
15 Apart from G.L. Wilson, see also Wilson, *Biographical List*, pp.19, 51, 161.
16 IWM 15017 Misc Wilson, G.L., *Lieutenant-Colonel Gavin Laurie Wilson, D.S.O., M.C., 11th Battalion Argyll and Sutherland Highlanders and later 1/8th Battalion Argyll and Sutherland Highlanders*, (privately printed, no date).

called up for duty with the Gordons and served with 1st battalion in France. Commissioned in the Gordons in June, 1915, he took command of 1/5th Seaforths in August, 1918.[17]

Noteworthy in this process is the degree of interchange between regiments and battalions, and the degree of infiltration of the Territorials by non-Territorial C.O.'s. Further, while most of our examples were drawn from the officer class, the professional class and even the minor aristocracy, we see also promotion on merit alone, as a headmaster's son and a former Regular private soldier rise to command Territorial battalions, the former at the remarkable age of only 23.

Officers

At the commencement of the war it was necessary to provide officers for the newly raised Kitchener battalions, as well as for the second and third line Territorial battalions. It was subsequently necessary, in the face of casualties, to keep battalions at the front up to strength through the constant supply of new officers.

When the Kitchener battalions were formed, most of the junior officers were newly commissioned Temporary Officers, with no previous experience. We consider these officers below. As we have seen, however, their Commanding Officers were brought in from outside, while the C.O.'s were reinforced on formation by a small cadre of Regular officers.[18] Subsequently, some junior Regular officers were posted to both Kitchener and Territorial battalions,[19] but more usually such postings were made to provide some additional backbone.[20] These Regular transferees were supplemented by the commissioning of ex-Regular Senior N.C.O.'s and by the filling of more senior posts by bringing in ex Regulars, Militia and former Volunteers, some with service in the South African War.[21]

In the Regular battalions, the first reinforcement occurred when a significant number of Special Reserve officers were taken on the strength of the Regular battalions in August, 1914 and afterwards to bring them up to strength.[22] The arrival of these Reserve officers was not universally popular.[23] Other officers continued to arrive with Regular commissions. These generally came from the same caste as pre-War entrants and followed the same entry route.

---

17 GHM PB2586 Morrison, Col. William, biographical notes, and anonymous manuscript, 'A Dumfriesshire Soldier Lieutenant Colonel W.J. Morrison 1881-1932.'
18 Wilson, *Biographical List*, p.58 (Milne); THM Camerons 81-7, typescript memoir, 'The Story of my Life' by Archibald J.A. Douglas, pp.1-35.
19 See: IWM 4771 Recording Stitt, John Heslop, IWM interview, 1980; LC GS 1203 Oldham, diary, passim; LC AIR 258A Low, loc. cit.
20 See: LC Transcripts Tape 356/367, Hay-Young, Lt. Col. J., interview with Liddle, 1976 ; LC GS 0731 Hay-Young, letter to unknown, 23 February, 1917, to sister Margaret, 4 March, 1917, to father, 30 December, 1917, *Lieut.-Colonel Robert Horn*, passim; GHM PB3309 Pelham Burn, biographical notes and letters to parents, passim.
21 See: IWM 4370 Christison, memoir, p.29; IWM 7593 Harper, memoir.
22 See: Barber, *My Diary*, pp.1-7; IWM 3696 Macnaghten, letters; *Gilbert M. Mackenzie*, preface by 'A.M.M.'; IWM 156 PP Williamson, 2Lt A J N., extract from 'The Bond of Sacrifice', Vol.1, p.446; GHM PB97 Fraser, memoir; Buchanan Smith, George, *George Buchanan Smith 1890-1915* (Glasgow: privately published, 1916), passim.
23 GHM PB97 Fraser, memoir.

Unsurprisingly, several followed their family in choosing a regiment.[24] Other routes to Regular commissions were however possible. Commissioning from the ranks was surprisingly common, given its rarity before the war. In total during the war an astonishing 61 men of 1st Black Watch and 28 men of 2nd Battalion were commissioned from the ranks. Of the 61 1st Battalion men, 36 were Regular soldiers, while 25 had enlisted for wartime service. Of the Regulars, 28 were given commissions in the Black Watch and 14 of them served subsequently in the 1st Battalion; the remaining eight went to other regiments. Of the 25 war-time men, only four were posted to Black Watch battalions, the bulk going to other regiments.[25] The figures show both a willingness to promote proven N.C.O.'s from the ranks, and a preference to keep Regular soldiers so commissioned within the regiment. Similar practices are recorded in the Seaforths[26] and Camerons,[27] with other examples found in the Gordons.[28] Other officers might receive commissions into the Regulars after officer training in France at St Omer,[29] or transfer from a temporary to a Regular commission,[30] although those applying for Regular commissions might find themselves directed towards the Indian Army.[31] Finally, some retired officers were recalled for service at home.[32]

Most Regular officers were of Scottish descent, although some of these were born overseas. Few were actually born in the Highlands, but as we have already observed in Highland regiments before the war, things were not always as they appeared. Hugh Grant, born in England at Chelford in Cheshire, was actually of impeccable Highland background, being the grandson of John Grant of Glenmoriston. By contrast, Douglas Wimberley, born in Inverness, was actually an incomer, by descent only half Scottish, of a British Imperial family. He nevertheless felt a strong attachment to the Highlands. This was not make-believe. His paternal grandfather, born in India, had served as an officer of the Camerons during the Mutiny, and had afterwards settled in Scotland, ultimately at Inverness. While Douglas's father served in India, in the Indian Medical Service, as a small boy Douglas was left for long periods with his grandparents in Inverness. His grandfather generally wore the kilt, and Douglas himself wore it on Sundays. As he grew older, his grandfather would tell him of actions fought in Indian Mutiny days and sometimes they would visit the field of Culloden together. Hector Macdonald was his boyhood hero. Douglas became imbued with Highland culture, a Highlander by adopted culture and only partly by descent.

---

24 ASHM N-E2 MacMillan, loc. cit; Goldsmith, Anne, ed., *Gentle Warrior, A Life of Hugh Grant, Soldier, Farmer and Kenya Administrator*, (Whitebridge, Inverness-shire: Anne Goldsmith, 2001), pp.xiii, 1-23; IWM 430 PP Wimberley, Maj Gen D.N., typescript memoir, pp.1-26.
25 Wauchope, Vol.1, pp.104-129, 156-157, 295-321, 342. See also: IWM 681 PP Mitchison, Naomi, undated letter from brother, Lt J.B.S. Haldane, March, 1915.
26 Sym, *Seaforth Highlanders*, pp.222-224.
27 THM Camerons 99-87 Macpherson, H., diary, 22 September, 1914; THM Camerons 97-22, Russell, memoir, pp.186-187; THM Camerons 10-25 Matheson, John, letters to father, 16 June, 1916 & to mother, 26 October, 1916, 22 February, 1917.
28 GHM PB207 Pirie, Alexander, miscellaneous documents, and letter from Capt. C. Boddam-Whetham to his widow, 13 December, 1914; GHM PB2586 Morrsion, loc. cit.
29 LC Several Fronts Recollections, Kingsley, E.D., typescript memoir. 'The Great War 1914-1918.'
30 LC GS 1203 Oldham, E.A.S., diary, passim.
31 LC Tapes 636/653 Cowan, D.T., interview with Liddle, 1982.
32 THM Camerons 97-22, Russell, pp.184-185.

Later, Regular regiments received also numbers of newly commissioned Temporary Officers.[33] Faced with such change, Regular officers might feel the loss of their cosy pre-War social world.[34] In time though, even Regulars could come to accept the mixture of backgrounds as a fact of life, and resented moves to separate 'outside' officers from battalions where they had become essential cogs in the machine.[35] We will return to this issue in a later chapter, when we consider comradeship and the social relations between officers.

In the Territorials, it was necessary not only to replace casualties in the first-line battalions but also to find officers to direct the second and third-line battalions. As confirmed by an analysis of 118 officers who joined 9th Argylls after the declaration of war, the great majority of these were newly commissioned, with a few previously commissioned officers being transferred from Kitchener battalions and the Regulars. About half were commissioned on application, without previous service in the ranks; about half by promotion from the ranks.[36]

It is evident that a significant number of new Territorial officers, whether commissioned on entry or from the ranks, were drawn from outside their Territorial areas, even though they might be still of Scottish descent.[37] Some wartime entrants were even received from overseas, dutifully returning to join up from the Federated Malay States, the Sudan, a Consular post in the East and from Vancouver.[38] Of those commissioned from the ranks, some were commissioned into their local battalions,[39] while by contrast we find Guy Macgregor, from London, Norman Collins, from Hartlepool, and Gordon Crask, a Yorkshireman, commissioned into 2/9th Argylls, 1/6th Seaforths and 2/5th Seaforths respectively.[40]

Socially, new Territorial officers, whether commissioned on entry and from the ranks, generally mirrored the professional or middle-class background of their pre-War colleagues. There was even in some quarters a desire to maintain some exclusivity.[41] As one would expect, public school, university and O.T.C. training were useful passports to commissions. From the ranks we find Harvey Steven, a solicitor, while the father of Hugh Quekett,[42] commissioned into 5th Black Watch, was actually chairman of the London Stock Exchange. More inclusively,

---

33 See: GHM PB19 Blunt, miscellaneous papers; Gillespie, *Letters from Flanders*, pp.viii-xii, 11; Craig-Brown, *Historical Records*, Vol.4, p.379 (John Morrison).
34 LC GS 0731 Hay-Young, letter to sister Margaret, 11 August, 1915.
35 IWM 114 Allen, letter to wife, 4 October, 1915.
36 Based on analysis of 118 officers from *Roll of Officers Dunbartonshire*, and of Territorial officers encountered in the sources.
37 Like, for example, Alan Mackintosh: Campbell, Colin & Green, Rosalind, *Can't shoot a man with a cold*, (Glendaruel: Argyll Publishing, 2004), passim.
38 ASHM N-E8 Munro, letter to sister Effie, 1 October, 1914; Wilson, *Biographical List*, pp.105, 131; LC Western Front Recollections G5, Gillespie, Capt. Ronald Dave, typescript record of an interview by 'J.'
39 THM Seaforths 89-122 Paterson, memoir; IWM 5525 PP Steven, Lieut S.H., MC, typescript extract from Rollo Steven's history of the Steven family, IWM introduction.
40 IWM 8592 PP Macgregor, Lt A.E., letters to his fiancee (and subsequently wife) Dulcie Newling, passim; IWM 12043 Collins, interview; THM Seaforths 89-26 Crask, Lt William Gordon, diary, 29 April, 1915, letters to parents, 18, 22 May, ?12, 13, 17, 20, 21, 28 June, 1, 10 July, 20, 25 August, 25 September, 1915, 30 August, 1916.
41 GHM PB107.1 Grant, diary, 14 April, 1915. See also the experience of R.E. Badenoch: BWA Badenoch R.E., typescript memoir, 'My Recollections of the First World War 1914-1918', written 1978, 22pp.
42 BWA Quekett, memoir, pp.1-11.

we find William Paterson from Wick, son of a seaman, but of sufficient standing to be 'Naval Agent' there, commissioned to 5th Seaforths, Norman Collins, an apprentice to a marine engineering company, and 'Guy' Macgregor, a journalist. We also find more experienced ex-Regular soldiers,[43] including Donald Farmer, V.C.,[44] commissioned to the Liverpool Scottish.

The great majority of Territorial officers commissioned from the ranks had come from the ranks of the Territorials themselves. About half appear to have come from the same regiment as that in which they were commissioned, the rest from outside. More frequently than not, however, newly commissioned officers, while possibly remaining in the same regiment, were posted to different battalions after commissioning. There was thus a continued preference in the Territorials for home-grown officers, but while Territorial affiliation remained a force, it was being steadily eroded by the influx of new officers from outside the battalion or regiment and from outside the Territorial area.

Within the Territorial battalions, not all officers held Territorial commissions. There was also a number of Temporary Officers posted to Territorial battalions.[45] In addition, some junior Regular officers were posted to Kitchener and Territorial battalions,[46] although perhaps more usually such postings of Regular officers were made to provide some additional backbone.[47] Territorial officers themselves generally stayed in Territorial battalions but might also find themselves transferred to non-Territorial posts,[48] notably when their battalions were disbanded.[49] The result of such change was that cosy pre-war Territorial structures were eroded.

Turning next to Temporary Officers, Colonel Maurice Wilson lists over 400 officers receiving Temporary Commissions to the Camerons during the Great War.[50] These have been analysed by the author, along with the available data for 53 officers encountered randomly in the sources.

Apart from a number of officers already holding commissions in other regiments who transferred, it appears about half to two-thirds of Highland officers obtaining Temporary Commissions were direct entrants, about half to one third commissioned from the ranks.

---

43   *Roll of Officers Dunbartonshire*, p.97 (Andrew Fenton), p.113 (Frederick Angus); Wilson, *Biographical List*, p.149 (Frederick Oakley).
44   THM Camerons 91-62 typescript memoir, 'The Autobiography of Donald Dickson Farmer, VC', 29pp, written after 1945; Giblin, *Bravest*, p.200.
45   See: LC Tape 606, Douglas, Sir Sholto, interview with Liddle, 1980; IWM 233 McKechnie, memoir, passim.
46   See: IWM 4771 Recording Stitt, John Heslop, IWM interview, 1980; LC GS 1203 Oldham, diary, passim; LC AIR 258A Low, loc. cit.
47   See: LC Transcripts Tape 356/367, Hay-Young, Lt. Col. J., interview with Liddle, 1976 ; LC GS 0731 Hay-Young, letter to unknown, 23 February, 1917, to sister Margaret, 4 March, 1917, to father, 30 December, 1917; *Lieut.-Colonel Robert Horn*, passim; GHM PB3309 Pelham Burn, biographical notes and letters to parents, passim.
48   See: BWA Badenoch, memoir; IWM 233 PP McKechnie, Maj. E.A., 'Reminiscences of the Great War 1914-1918', passim; NLS Acc.11627/87 Buchan Papers, Macmillan, Rev. Dr R.A.C., Obituary from *The Times*, 28 May, 1917, description of memorial service, and letter to Walter Buchan, 5 February, 1917; Fraser, *Lochbroom*, pp.56-58.
49   See: Wilson, *Biographical List*, p.106 (Ian Mackintosh); THM Camerons 94-8 Mackay, 'Tell Them of Us,' biographical notes, and letters from Ian Mackay, from 7 May, 1916, passim; THM Camerons 02-111, Notes by Leszczuk (Roderick McErlich).
50   Wilson, *Biographical List*.

Of the direct entrants, most were young and inexperienced, but a number had previously served in the Regulars, Militia or Volunteers. Some were aging retired pre-War Regular officers,[51] or ex-Regular S.N.C.O.'s.[52] Others had served with the Volunteers or Militia.[53]

Those commissioned from the ranks may either have served at home only, sometimes for a very short period, before being recognised as potential leaders, or they may have demonstrated their capability on active service during the war, perhaps by displaying conspicuous gallantry, like Corporal James Dalgleish Pollock, who won the Victoria Cross at Loos.[54] It is notable that over half of these men were drawn from the Territorials, 20-30 percent from Kitchener battalions, and the rest from the Regulars, Special Reserve and regiments of the wider Empire. About a third appear to have come from the same regiment to which they were promoted, and about 60 percent in all from kilted battalions; the remainder came from other sources. Although the net effect would be some dilution, there was clearly some attempt to maintain both regimental and Highland identity. Some Temporary Officers were commissioned from the ranks of serving Regular soldiers.[55] Others were drawn from ex-Regular S.N.C.O.'s serving with the Kitchener battalions.[56] A few were commissioned from overseas battalions.[57]

A relatively small proportion of Temporary Officers actually transferred their commissions from other regiments, generally in order to get into active service with the infantry.[58] Some of these transferred commissions from overseas regiments.[59]

Overall, Temporary Highland officers were largely Scottish or of Scottish descent, but a significant number were drawn from England. It is evident that Highland regiments were unable to find most of their officers in their regimental areas and had to draw the deficit from the rest of Scotland, England and overseas.[60] As we have already observed amongst Regular officers, Highland identity took interesting forms. Douglas Edward Brodie was born in 1873, the fourth son of Brodie of Brodie, of Brodie Castle in Morayshire. He was educated at Winchester and became Secretary of the British South Africa Company in 1905. In June,

---

51 Ibid., p.140 (Sir James Home).
52 Ibid., pp.46 (Angus Maclean), 74 (Edwin Wilkins), 132 (Frank Colledge).
53 Wade, *Counterspy*, pp.21-118; Wilson, *Biographical List*, pp.50 (Ludovick Cameron), 71 (Maitland-Makgill-Crichton), 173 (Macleod).
54 Wilson, *Biographical List*, p.77.
55 Ibid., p.115 (John Cameron); LC GS 1761 Wilson, Douglas J,B., typescript memoir, 'A Flanders Fling. A 1918 episode', 117pp, pp.91-92 (Kennie Cameron).
56 Wilson, *Biographical List*, pp.9 (John Fraser), 74 (Arthur Macdonald), 166 (Alexander Fraser).
57 O'Kiely, Elizabeth, *Gentleman Air Ace, The Duncan Bell-Irving Story,* (BC Canada: Harbour Publishing, 1992), pp.15-55, 207-210; Wilson, *Biographical List*, pp.105 (Patrick Jenkins), 72 (Douglas Moir).
58 Wilson, *Biographical List*, p.75 (McDonnell). See also LC GS 1021 Mackie, J.D., Application for Temporary Commission, 24 December, 1914; IWM 4370 PP Christison, Sir Philip, typescript memoir, 'Life and Times of General Sir Philip Christison, Bt', 217pp, pp.1-.28.
59 Brooke, *Poems*, pp.10-18. See also GHM PB2990 Gordon, Maitland Lockhart, miscellaneous documents; Wilson, *Biographical List*, p.179 (Charles Sheringham).
60 For overseas entrants, see GHM PB19 Blunt, miscellaneous papers; LC GS 1635 Turing, Sir John, privately published memoir, written c.1963; IWM 6444 Shewan, biographical notes by his niece, Jennifer May, 1977, letter from Shewan to his brother Ian, 30 October, 1915, letter from G.O.C. South China command to War Office, 20 November, 1914; Wilson, *Biographical List*, p.1 (H.D. Alexander), p.4 (Sir Archibald Campbell), p.36 (D.T. Croal), p.41 (Gordon Hamilton), p.72 (James Miller), pp.76-77 (A.W. and R.D. Macpherson), p.93 (M.C. Pearson), p.146 (Percy Male).

1915, he received a temporary commission in the Camerons, joining 1st Battalion in October.[61] He was of Highland origin, but a member of the British Imperial ruling class. The soldier-poet John Dunning MacLeod ('Jock') was descended from the ancient line of the MacLeods. He was nevertheless born in India in 1894, and his father worked for the Indian Civil Service. Jock enjoyed the perfect English upper-class education, attending Rugby School and winning a scholarship to Corpus Christi College, Cambridge in 1913. He obtained a commission in the Camerons in August, 1914 and joined 2nd Battalion in France in February, 1915.[62] Although of impeccable Highland stock, he was also really a product of the British Imperial ruling class. Another apparent Highlander was Donald Macintyre, the son of John Macintyre, who was head of Clan Macintyre. In fact, Donald was born in Glasgow in 1893, and educated at Glenalmond and Clare College, Cambridge. He was commissioned into 6th Camerons in September, 1914 and went to France with them in June, 1915. He survived the war and became head of Clan Macintyre himself on the death of his father.[63]

Yet another apparent Highlander was Philip Christison, who famously won the Military Cross after rallying his men at the battle of Loos by singing to them in Gaelic 'The March of the Cameron Men.' Unlike MacLeod, however, he was not of Highland stock. He was the son of Alexander Christison, a distinguished surgeon from Edinburgh, who had pursued a career in India and risen to be Principal of Agra Medical College. When he returned to Edinburgh, he finished his career as Superintendent of the Royal Victoria Hospital. Philip's mother, was English, from Somerset. Philip himself was born in Edinburgh in 1893, and was educated at Edinburgh Academy, from where he entered University College, Oxford, in 1912. From Oxford, he was accepted for a commission in 6th Camerons. But, he was manifestly not a Highlander. He was actually half-Scots, half-English, a member of the Edinburgh professional classes, with, like Jock MacLeod, a British Imperial family background. Nevertheless, he had acquired some impeccable Highland cultural credentials. Every year since 1902, he had spent his summer holidays at a farmhouse in the Highlands, where he immersed himself in the culture, taking pains to learn Gaelic. He joined the Edinburgh Gaelic Choir in 1911, singing with them in the national Mods of 1912 and 1913. He also took up the pipes, although he was not an accomplished player, so instead played both the tenor drum and the bass drum in the Edinburgh Academy pipe band. Perhaps unsurprisingly, he subsequently became Pipe President of his battalion. His embrace of Highland tradition is interesting because it was through cultural learning rather than inheritance.[64]

In terms of social background, whether commissioned directly or from the ranks, the overwhelming majority of those commissioned were from the professions, including military families, or other middle-class families (government, business, office, school-teachers), with a smattering from the aristocracy or gentry.[65] Public school education was normal, and university education frequent. Connections and influence, which of course went hand in glove with social

---

61 Wilson, *Biographical List*, p.34.
62 LC GS 1027 MacLeod, Lt. J.D., Notes by his sister, and letter to mother, 10 August, 1914; Macleod, John Dunning, *Poems*, (privately published, 1958), pp.iii-vi.
63 Wilson, *Biographical List*, p.17.
64 IWM 4370 Christison, memoir, pp.1-.28.
65 For the aristocracy, see Wilson, *Biographical List*, p.75 (McDonnell), 140 (Sir James Home of Blackadder) and p.4 (Sir Archibald Ava Augustus Campbell).

standing, could be a passport to a temporary commission, or to admission to a particular regiment. Such a system, of course, had been in operation before the war in the Regular Army. There are numerous cases in the sources of applicants using connections to obtain commissions in both Territorial and Kitchener battalions. Another passport to a commission was past attendance at O.T.C. This also reflected and reinforced social background as a determinant, for the O.T.C. flourished at the public schools and universities. Sometimes potential officers sought training through the Inns of Court O.T.C., which acted as a sort of Sandhurst for Temporary Officers.[66]

There is some evidence that the social net was cast wider for those commissioned from the ranks, but only a small percentage could be described as 'working-class,' and a number of these had been commissioned from the ranks of the Regulars. Many Temporary Officers would have been perfectly at ease socially with their Regular counterparts; others, from the lower end of the middle-class social spectrum, less so. If there was snobbery towards such 'Temporary Gentlemen' it was directed less towards the working class than towards the lower middle-class. The soldier poet William Fraser Mitchell, who served in 1/4th Seaforths, in his poem 'From the Ranks' wrote perceptively of the inverse snobbery that might be felt towards 'Temporary Gentlemen' by the ranks:[67]

'E don't 'ave a gentleman's way;
'E came from a grocery store;
And 'is tone of command seems to say:
'Are you sure you don't want nothin' more?'

'E's not for an officer, – im!
Though I'm not saying but wot in the ranks
'E'd do just like any old Jim,
But the officers I knewed were swanks!

As the war progressed, officers did not necessarily remain within their own caste, but were increasingly posted to battalions independent of origin and according to need. Postings between battalions of the same regiment were common.[68] Officers might often be posted to different regiments than their own.[69] It was indeed not uncommon for officers to have multiple postings between different regiments or battalions.[70] Temporary officers might well find themselves

---

66 Gillespie, *Letters from Flanders*, pp.viii-xii, 11, and p.2, letter home, 2 August, 1914; LC GS 1635 Turing, memoir; THM Seaforths 81-2 Cooper, Leslie G., typescript memoir, 'Before I came of age', 188pp, pp.2-21.
67 Mitchell, William Fraser, *Off Parade and other Verses*, (Dundee. A.B. Duncan, 1919), p.9.
68 See: LC Several Fronts Recollections, Kingsley, memoir; *Diary and Letters written during the War in France, Belgium and Mesopotamia by the late Captain Gilbert M. Mackenzie, B.A., Cantab., 3rd Seaforth Highlanders*, (privately published, no date), preface by 'A.M.M.'; THM Camerons 97-22, Russell, memoir, pp.201-219.
69 See: GHM PB3309 Pelham Burn, biographical notes and letters to parents, passim; IWM 4370 Christison, memoir, pp.71-75; IWM 8503 Byrom, memoir, p.33.
70 See: IWM 8503 PP Byrom, Capt J.A., typescript memoir, 'Somewhere East of Suez', pp.1-33; THM Camerons 97-22, Russell, memoir, passim; LC GS 1203 Oldham, diary, passim.

commissioned in one regiment but posted to another.[71] Such mixing and intermingling of officers could be disconcerting for both individuals[72] and battalions, as their original identity was eroded. Thus, the arrival of outsiders might be resented, although sometimes the objections were more to their social status, quality or youthful inexperience.[73] Constant casualties and changes of officers potentially had a severe impact on battalions' efficiency.[74] In particular, command structures were disrupted as the link between officers and men was broken.[75] Otherwise, the net effect of constant change was that battalions became increasingly polyglot, as the distinction between the officers of the Regular, Territorial and Kitchener battalions became increasingly obscure. With the tendency for the most effective officers to rise to the top (unless killed on the way), and the need for all involved to learn the real business of warfare through experience at the front, the result was by 1918 to significantly reduce the distinction between the different types of battalion.

Other Ranks

As for officers, there was an initial need to fill the ranks of the Kitchener battalions, together with the second and third line Territorial battalions. Once the battalions had been made up to strength and deployed, there was a need to provide continuous reinforcement drafts to replace casualties. A few men joined as Regular soldiers, but most reinforcements were provided initially by Volunteers for wartime service, to the Territorial, Kitchener and Regular Battalions, then by 'Derby' men and finally by conscripts.

As early need was to provide a cadre for the Kitchener battalions, otherwise raised from new volunteers. A number of experienced ex-Regular S.N.C.O. reservists were posted to them to provide a cadre of experience.[76] Such old timers might become father figures for the new recruits.[77] Some Special Reservists, surplus to the initial requirements of the Regulars, were also sent to join the Kitchener battalions, to which they supplied at least an element of experience.[78]

---

71 See IWM 524 PP Macfarlane Reid, Sir Ranald, memoir 'Fly Past', written 1972, pp.1-5; LC GS 1507 Sotheby, diary, passim; Campbell, Ivar, *Poems by Ivar Campbell*, (London: A.L. Humphreys,1917), pp.7-28, memoir by Guy Ridley.
72 McDermott, R.K. *Robert Keith McDermott, Captain 3rd Battn Seaforth Highlanders (attached 1st Battn)* (London: Walter McDermott, 1930), letters of 4 and 8 December, 1914; BWA Gordon, letters, Vol.2, 7 December, 1915, Vol.3, 1 March, 1916; LC GS 1507 Sotheby, diary, introductory notes, 3 January, 1915, letters to unknown, 8 March, 1915, to parents, 2 August, 1915.
73 GHM PB3309 Pelham Burn, letters to father, 26 December, 1914, 19, 26 January, 1915, to mother 25 June, 1915; ASHM N-E5 Brown, Ronal, letters home, 29 December, 1917, 24 January, 1918; Craig-Brown, *Historical Records*, Vol.3, pp.106, 128; IWM 1862 Craig-Brown, letter, 27 May, 1915; LC GS 1507 Sotheby, introductory notes, 3 January, 1915, letters to unknown, 8 March, 1915, to parents, 2 August, 1915.
74 See IWM 1862 Craig-Brown, letter, 1 February, 1915 and Field Message books, ECB to Colonel, 13 November, 1914.
75 THM Camerons 81-203 Mackay, Ian, letter to father, 21 May, 1915.
76 Wilson, *Biographical List*, p.9 (John Fraser), 166 (Alexander Fraser), 74 (Arthur Macdonald). Some, as we have seen, were given commissions.
77 LC Western Front Recollections A9, Andrew, I.G., photocopied account; see also on Willie Watt, *Souvenir Booklet of the Sixth Cameron Highlanders* (Glasgow: The Glasgow Herald', 1916), pp.39-40; IWM 7593 Harper, memoir. See also: Addison-Smith, *10th Seaforth Highlanders*, p.8; GHM PB2021 Stewart, letter to wife Lil, 4 May, 1915.
78 LC Transcripts Tape 526, McKay, D., interview by Liddle, 1978.

At the beginning of the war, the Reserve and Special Reserve were mobilised. They were used initially to bring the Regular battalions up to strength. They then provided the first reinforcement drafts, through to early 1915, along with re-enlisted old soldiers.[79] The standard of the Special Reservists sent out as first reinforcements was lamented by some regular officers.[80] Subsequently, we have many examples of soldiers who were posted to the Regulars during the war, but most of these had not joined as Regulars. In several cases their status is uncertain.[81] We have in fact only one definite example of a soldier who joined up as a Regular. This was Charles Forman who lived in Burton-on-Trent in the English Midlands and was out of work when the war broke out. He joined the army on 5 November, 1914.[82] Otherwise, Regular battalions received a supply of volunteers, Derby men and Conscripts.

The Territorials continued to recruit to their own battalions as the war continued. They did of course need to bring their battalions up to establishment, replace those men who chose not to opt for foreign service, replace those who were too young, old or infirm to go abroad, and fill the ranks of the second and third line battalions, quite apart from the continuous need to replace casualties. In some cases, territorial allegiances remained strong.[83] Nevertheless, of the individual recruits encountered in the sources,[84] only about 60 percent came from their own regimental areas, such that the regional distinctiveness of the Territorial battalions was clearly being eroded.[85] More evidence of this comes from the roll book of No.13 Platoon, D Company, 1/4th Black Watch, which provides a picture of the platoon at 21 November, 1914, that is while training and manning the Tay defences prior to deployment to France in February, 1915. The roll lists 54 soldiers, of whom only 16 were serving in the battalion before the start of the war. In other words, this platoon was 70 percent composed of new recruits. All the pre-War members of the platoon were drawn from Dundee or its immediate vicinity, which was the battalion's recruiting district. But only 49 percent of the new recruits came from Dundee. The remainder came largely (38 percent) from the wider Black Watch areas of Angus and Fife, with the rest from southern Scotland or England.[86] The platoon nevertheless remained both overwhelmingly Scottish and overwhelmingly from the Black Watch area.

This dilution reflected the difficulties of recruiting from the Highland battalions' own recruiting districts, on which we have already commented. At an early stage, the Highland

---

79 Anderson, *1st Argylls*, p.29; IWM 1862 Craig-Brown, diary, 20, 26, 27 January, 1915; THM Camerons 97-22, Russell, memoir, p.180; ASHM NE-2 Collier, Frank, journal, 6 September, 1914; Craig-Brown, *Historical Records*, Vol.3, pp.96, 114; GHM PB3309 Pelham Burn, letter to mother, 1, 15 November, 1914, to father, 24 November, 1914; IWM 681 Mitchison, letter from brother Capt J.B.S. Haldane, 2 September, 1914.
80 IWM 1862 Craig-Brown, diary, 17 November, 18, 28, 30 December, 1914, draft letter to Brigade Major, 1st Brigade, 12 January, 1915; letters 11, 15, 17 January, 1915; Craig-Brown, *Historical Records*, Vol.3, pp.106, 114; GHM PB3309 Pelham Burn, letter to mother, 15 November, to father, 24 November, 1914.
81 See: LC MES 093 Ballantyne interview; BWA McKay, Janet Haggard, typescript, 'Canadian Loyalty to Scottish Tradition and the British Empire', passed to Museum, 1965; IWM 860 Recording, Mabbott, Henry, interview, 1976.
82 BWA, Forman, Charles, manuscript memoir, 'My Life', 1965.
83 See for example, THM Seaforths 89-122 Paterson, memoir.
84 a sample of 32.
85 See for example NLS Acc.12872 Wood, Murdo, letter to brother, 13 December, 1914.
86 BWA Roll Book of No.13 Platoon, D Company, 1/4th Black Watch, last entry 21 November, 1914.

Territorial battalions began to cast their nets wider for recruits, with 3/4th Camerons recruiting from the north of England,[87] and the Seaforths attracting a large number of recruits from Northern Ireland.[88] Other battalions too looked to the north of England. The Dandy Ninth, for example, collared a large number of disappointed recruits from Manchester, when an attempt to start a Manchester Scottish had failed.[89] 7th Gordons also enrolled between 200 and 300 from Manchester.[90] In fact, a significant number of recruits came from England. Some of these were those Londoners who were passed on to the Highland Division at Bedford from the London Scottish in 1914. Most of the rest came from the north of England. In this respect the proximity of the Highland Territorial training battalions at Ripon was certainly an inducement.[91] Malcolm feels that 8th Argylls, one of the most Highland of Territorial battalions, succeeded in obtaining reinforcements of its own,[92] but that cannot explain the presence of, for example, Ernest McGuinness, from Manchester, who enlisted in January, 1915,[93] or Jack Gunn, from Bromley and latterly San Francisco, who joined at Christmas, 1914.[94] Nevertheless other witnesses describe the Reserve Battalion of the Argylls at Ripon in 1917[95] and 1/6th Seaforths in 1916,[96] as containing men largely drawn from their regimental areas. In the London and Liverpool Scottish, the need to cast a wider net resulted in a less rigorous application of rules on nationality. While many of those who joined during the war could claim legitimate Scottish ancestry,[97], the claims of other recruits were much more spurious.[98]

One result of the hierarchical territorial organisation of the Territorial battalions was to make the communities which supplied the men particularly vulnerable to concentrated casualties when a particular section or company was badly hit. This was especially the case in the early battles of 1915, before the strict territorial structure of the battalions had been diluted by reinforcement drafts. Thus Wullie Murison notes the effect on the Alford district of the participation of 1/6th Gordons at the battle of Neuve Chapelle in 1915. "This was a devastating battle as 60 men from the Alford district were in this battle and only 10 returned."[99] Similarly, 1/4th Camerons suffered heavily at the Battle of Festubert on 16 and 17 May, 1915. From the town of

---

87 Craig-Brown, *Historical Records*, Vol.3, pp.464-467.
88 THM Seaforths 89-122 Paterson, memoir; IWM 12043 Collins, interview; THM Seaforths 89-26 Crask, letter to parents, 25, 26? April 1915, diary, 29 April, 1915.
89 IWM 24879 Recording, Fidler, John P., interview 1975.
90 LC GS 1549 Strachan, memoir.
91 LC GS 0771 Hirsch, F.B., various documents.
92 Malcolm, *Argyllshire Highlanders*, p.29.
93 ASHM N-E8 McGuinness, Ernest, notebook.
94 IWM 15990 PP Gunn, J.A., letter to a pal, surname Pite, 16 April, 1915.
95 IWM 4586 Douglas, memoir, p.15.
96 IWM 13230 Walker, memoir.
97 LC Tapes 621/641 Pollock, Henry, interview with Liddle, 1981; LC GS 0084 Barclay, recollections; IWM 576 Bowser, Record of Service in Cadets, Discharge Certificate from London Scottish, and memoir, pp.47-53; IWM 13263 PP Bryden, W.N., explanatory note; IWM 13262 PP Bryden, R.E.C., introductory notes; IWM 10391 Jordan, interview; NLS Acc.7658 No.2 Angus, Archie, Introductory notes; LC WF Recollections S18 Sloan, memoir.
98 IWM Misc 234 Kerridge interview; IWM 12007 PP Wilson, Capt. J.K., typescript memoir, written post 1971, p.22; IWM 10529 Stanford, memoir, pp.13-24, 72; LC GS 1783 Wood, recollections; LC GS 1579 Taylor, memoir, p.1.
99 GHM PB3712 Murison, William John, typescript recollections, written c.1985.

Portree alone in Skye, 26 boys lost their lives, and losses throughout the rest of the island were proportionate.[100] 4th Battalion Black Watch, as we know, was drawn largely from the city of Dundee, and the town was particularly hard hit when the battalion suffered appalling losses at Loos on 25 September 1915.[101]

Socially, outside the rather exclusive London Scottish, three-quarters of the individual wartime Territorial recruits encountered in the study were drawn from the middle-class. This is an astonishingly high figure, which almost certainly exaggerates the general case and probably reflects imbalance in the surviving papers, especially given the high proportion of miners in some battalions before the war we have already noted. We should not forget that a number of men joined because they were unemployed. And a certain desperation in recruiting, even greater than recruiting Englishmen, was shown by 3/5th Argylls who, in 1915, admitted 27 men from the nearby prison, who had been allowed out on ticket-of-leave, provided that they immediately joined the Army.[102] More normal volunteers were a bakery worker from Banchory,[103] a naval agent from Wick[104] and a Clyde riveter originally from Donegal.[105] The abundance of Fife miners in 7th Black Watch allowed them to support the Royal Engineers tunnellers in 1915.[106] A more specifically Highland occupation, that of ghillie, provided an excellent source of snipers in the true Highland battalions, as Hugh Munro observed in 1/8th Argylls.[107] Meanwhile, the social uniqueness of battalions like the London Scottish, where the recruits encountered in the sources were almost all middle-class, evidently survived well into the war,[108] such that the subsequent drainage of men to take commissions was a major worry, notably to the C.O. of the London Scottish.[109]

Other than those volunteers recruited direct into the Territorial battalions, many others went to the Kitchener battalions or to reinforce the Regulars. An analysis of Kitchener volunteers encountered in the sources shows that the great majority came from outside the recruiting district of the regiment they joined, in stark contrast to the Territorials. The volunteers were overwhelmingly Scottish, albeit with a useful English contingent, but only one man out of 22 came from the Highlands proper.

The composition of Kitchener battalions might vary according to how they were raised. The raising of the Camerons battalions is particularly worthy of note, for its strong and particular Glasgow contingents. In response to Kitchener's request, an astonishing four battalions were raised by Cameron of Lochiel, head of Clan Cameron and commander of 3rd Camerons. He launched an extraordinary recruiting effort in Glasgow. As a result an entire company of

---

100   Macdonald, Martin, *Skye Camanachd, A Century Remembered*, (Portreee: Skye Camanachd, n.d.), p.71.
101   Wauchope, *Black Watch*, Vol.2, pp.3, 21.
102   LC WF Recollections C15 Cormack, memoir.
103   LC GS 1549 Strachan, memoir, and Soldier's Pay Book.
104   THM Seaforths 89-122 Paterson, memoir.
105   ASHM N-E8 Jordan, Patrick, miscellaneous documents.
106   Wauchope, *Black Watch*, Vol.2, pp.242, 255.
107   ASHM N-E8 Munro, narrative of life in trenches, compiled late June, 1915. See also Alan Mackintosh's skittish poem 'Sniper Sandy,' in Sutherland, Capt. D., *War Diary of the Fifth Seaforth Highlanders* (London: John Lane, 1920), p.62.
108   See for example: IWM 13262 Bryden, letter to mother, 22 May, 1916; LC GS 0731 Hay-Young, J, letter to sister Margaret, 4 March, 1917.
109   IWM 6702 Low, letter to wife Noanie, 14 August, 1915.

5th Camerons was formed of members of the Glasgow Stock Exchange, while Highlanders from the University of Glasgow formed another company within 6th Battalion.[110] There were no "Pals" battalions of Highlanders, but these were effectively Pals' companies. Although his own battalions were largely raised from Glasgow, Lochiel stipulated that all recruits should be Highlanders or of Highland descent. Eventually, the four companies of 5th Battalion were constituted as follows;

> A Company: Gaelic-speaking company; men from North Uist, Harris, Lochaber and Strathspey
> B Company: Men from Inverness and the North, Skye, South Uist and Benbecula
> C Company: Highlanders from the rest of Scotland
> D Company Glasgow Stock Exchange Company.[111]

It is indeed possible that Lochiel managed to achieve ethnic purity in 5th Battalion, the first raised.[112] In the next battalion, 6th Camerons, standards were slipping, for "two companies of Gaelic speaking Highlanders from the West coast and Western Isles, and two companies composed mostly of students from Glasgow University" were "complemented by some tough Glasgow men who had been discarded from the 5th Battalion."[113] In 7th Camerons, a large proportion of recruits were students and young professional men from Glasgow, while a considerable number came from Inverness-shire. By this time it was apparently a rule in 7th Battalion that no man was admitted unless he was a Scotsman,[114] implying that the more specific requirement to be a Highlander had been relaxed. Finally, by the middle of 1915, the last of Lochiel's battalions, the 8th, which never deployed to France, had to acquire several hundred of its recruits from the populous centres of Lanarkshire.[115] It seems that while Lochiel's battalions maintained their Scottishness and continued at least for a time to receive recruits from the Highlands, the initial desire for battalions of Highlanders was not sustainable. In any case, parents' or grandparents' rights must have applied from the outset, as evidenced by a number of the volunteers encountered in the sources.[116]

Other regiments might struggle to maintain their local identity. Thus we find in the Seaforths,[117] men from Glasgow, Edinburgh, Lanarkshire, Dunfermline, and Lancashire in England. Harry Strachan claimed that the Gordons' Kitchener battalions, 8th, 9th and 10th,

---

110 McEwen, *Fifth Camerons*, pp.2-6; Macleod, *6th Camerons*, pp.1-4.
111 McEwen, *Fifth Camerons*, pp.4-6.
112 See THM Camerons 81-7, Douglas, memoir, p.32.
113 IWM 4370 Christison, memoir, p.29.
114 Craig-Brown, *Historical Records*, Vol.4, p.273.
115 Ibid., Vol.4, pp.377-379.
116 IWM 926 PP Mackenzie, J.B; LC Transcripts Tape 432, Brown, G.W., interview with Liddle, 1976; THM Camerons 89-17 McFarlane, Daniel, typescript memoir, written 1969-1971; Burns, *Once a Cameron Highlander*, pp.17-19; LC Tapes 963 and 1316, Burns, Robert, interviews 1994 and 1996; IWM Misc 234 Item 3338, Burns, Robert, two interviews 1998; IWM 22743 Recording, Burns, Robert, interview, 1996.
117 IWM 3460 Macmillian, letters from Willie Macmillan to mother, 15 May, 21 July, 1915; THM Seaforths 95-125 Sharp, Pte William, background notes; THM 2013-072(S) Braes, memoir, pp.1-11; Addison-Smith, *10th Seaforth Highlanders*, pp.8, 35.

were chiefly recruited in Lanarkshire.[118] But there were also in the Gordons Durham miners from Hartlepool,[119] not forgetting young William Newton from Torquay who joined the Gordons aged 15.[120] Our information regarding the Argylls relates mainly to 14th Battalion, which we will consider below. Otherwise, it does seem that, with a recruiting area embracing a large chuck of the populous lowland belt. the regiment was able to recruit substantially from its own area or nearby.[121]

For the Black Watch, we are fortunate in possessing a set of nominal rolls of the four companies of 10th Battalion,[122] essentially indicating the composition of the battalion as it deployed overseas in November, 1915. 814 men are listed with legible addresses, providing a sound basis for analysis. We find that only 27 percent of the battalion came from the Black Watch regimental district, compared with 63 percent from the rest of Scotland and 10 percent from elsewhere, mostly England, but some from Ireland, Wales and the Empire. These figures support the notion that regional affiliation was of relatively minor importance for the Kitchener volunteers. Significantly too, of those recruited in the Black Watch area, the greater part (62 percent) came from the densely populated Lowland area of Fife. However, if regional allegiance was weakened, then despite the helpful influx of 10 percent non-Scots, at least the battalion remained overwhelmingly Scottish (90 percent) and in this respect mirrors the figure from our small sample of individual volunteers.[123] With their regional composition diminished, the Highland Kitchener battalions still retained their national identity.

An analysis of Kitchener volunteers encountered in the sources[124] reveals 63 percent from the 'middle-class' and 37 percent from the 'working-class,' But these figures are scarcely truly representative: the sample size is small, Lochiel's Camerons are over-represented, and middle-class soldiers are likely to be disproportionately represented in the surviving papers. In any case, as with regional origins, the social background of recruits is likely to vary between battalions. We have already seen that there was a distinct middle-class input into Lochiel's Camerons, which we find reflected in our individual sources.[125] But there were working-class elements, 6th Camerons being complemented as we have seen by some tough Glasgow men discarded from the 5th Battalion.[126] In 7th Camerons, at its inception, though a large proportion were students and young professional men from Glasgow,[127] some individuals were not, like Daniel

---

118 LC GS 1549 Strachan, memoir. Partly confirmed by IWM 7593 Harper, memoir
119 IWM 7593 Harper, memoir.
120 IWM 24855 Newton, interview.
121 LC Tape 921 Stuart, interview; IWM 3460 Macmillian, letter from Alex Macmillan to mother, 15 December, 1915, and to James (a pal), 26 December, 1915.
122 BWA Nominal Rolls of A, B, C and D Companies, 10th Black Watch, c. June, 1916.
123 For evidence from individual Black Watch volunteers, see Darling, *So it looks to me*, pp.122-125; LC Transcripts, Tape 324, Jordan, interview; BWA Macdonald, Coll, letter to wife Mary, 17 June, 1917.
124 based on a sample of only 19.
125 THM Camerons 96-52 Laidlaw, Petra, 'Grandpa's War, The War Correspondence of Thomas Douglas Laidlaw', written c.1996; LC WF Recollections A9, Andrew; LC GS 0259 Cameron Highlanders. Memoir by R.A. Muir; IWM 6933 PP Moir, K.P.; LC Transcripts Tape 432, Brown, interview; Burns, *Once a Cameron Highlander*, pp.17-19; LC Tapes 963 and 1316, Burns, interviews; IWM Misc 234 Item 3338, Burns, interviews; IWM 22743 Recording, Burns, interview.
126 IWM 4370 Christison, p.29.
127 Craig-Brown, *Historical Records*, Vol.4, p.273.

MacFarlane, from a working-class family in Glasgow.[128] The initial recruits to 8th Camerons, recruited in 1914, were of high quality: "Of the first batch of fifteen men to be promoted to corporal, twelve were certified school teachers in Scotland or university graduates," but by the middle of 1915, the battalion was encountering acute recruiting difficulties, which was reflected in the origins of its recruits.[129] Perhaps a better impression of the overall composition of new Cameron recruits is given by those witnesses who passed through the depot at Inverness or 3rd Battalion at Invergordon, who recorded a sizeable number of rougher elements.[130]

Recruits to the Seaforths appear to have been a mixed bag.[131] As regards the Gordons, Cecil Harper found in 1914 that his own company of 10th Gordons, recruited in Glasgow and its environs, were predominantly miners and colliers, ironworkers, stevedores and general labourers. He also had a group of Durham miners from West Hartlepool.[132] As for the Argylls, 10th Battalion was initially raised in 1914 in Stirling, and a large percentage of the men were miners.[133] Amongst the Kitchener volunteers generally, some were ex-Regulars who re-enlisted.[134] One battalion which was rather unique, equivalent in some ways to the Stock Exchange and Glasgow University companies of the Camerons, was 14th Argylls. This battalion, which recruited nationally in Scotland, was, as their recruiting circular demonstrates,[135] quite deliberately socially exclusive,[136] and perhaps unsurprisingly, members are disproportionately represented among the sources.[137]

Finally, some breakdown of the social composition of Kitchener volunteers is possible from the roll book of No.16 Platoon, D Company, 9th Black Watch,[138] which effectively provides a picture of the platoon in April, 1916. This battalion had been in France since July, 1915, and had suffered severely at the Battle of Loos in September. The roll book therefore includes a significant number of drafts received since that battle. The recruits were over two-thirds 'working-class,' but with over 30 percent 'middle-class' representation. There was a significant number of miners. These divisions are imprecise, but they do reverse the proportion of middle- and working-class found among our individual recruits from the sources, emphasising the bias of the latter. It seems in any case that social composition varied very much between Kitchener battal-

---

128 THM Camerons 89-17 McFarlane, memoir.
129 Craig-Brown, *Historical Records*, Vol.4, pp.377-379.
130 Chambers, Heather (ed), *Diaries of World War 1 written by William Liddell Chambers June 1914-October 1916*, (Eglinton, Australia, c.2000), pp.9-10; THM Camerons 97-22, Russell, memoir, pp.179-182.
131 Addison-Smith, *10th Seaforth Highlanders*, p.8.
132 IWM 7593 Harper, memoir.
133 Sotheby, Lt.-Col. Herbert G., *The 10th Battalion Argyll and Sutherland Highlanders 1914-1919* (London: privately published, 1931), p.xvii; Wade, *Counterspy*, p.120.
134 GHM PB91 Flockhart, Sgt George, miscellaneous documents; GHM PB2021 Stewart, letters, passim, extract from 'Hamilton Advertiser,' 30 October, 1915, research notes by Charles Reid, 26 November, 2008.
135 IWM 21092 McGregor, Recruiting circular for 14th Argylls, 26 July, 1915.
136 LC GS 0456 Dick, memoir. See also: LC Transcripts, Tape 619, McCrow, G.W., interview 1981.
137 LC Tape 700, Gilmour, Andrew, interview with Liddle, 1979; Gilmour, Andrew, *An Eastern Cadet's Anecdotage*, (Singapore: University Education Press, 1974), pp.10-20; Bogle, *Walter Sutherland*, passim; IWM 21092 McGregor, letter to wife Jen, 10 May, 1915; LC Tape 630/647, Macdonald, interview; LC GS 0456 Dick, memoir.
138 BWA Roll Book of 16 Platoon, D Company, 9th Black Watch.

ions, that a significant proportion of volunteers in the ranks were drawn from the middle-class, and that their ranks were a remarkable social melting-pot, possibly on balance less middle-class than their Territorial counterparts.

We have less information about Derby scheme men; only five of the volunteers encountered in the study definitely joined under this scheme, the precursor of conscription, whereby, on registering for future call-up, a volunteer could have his choice of regiment. Derby men might be posted to Regular, Territorial and Kitchener battalions, but four out of our five men were posted to Territorial battalions. Possibly this was because the Territorials were suffering from the exodus of Time Expired men when the Derby scheme was at its height. Three of these men joined their local regiment,[139] while one was a Yorkshiremen who joined the Camerons at Ripon.[140]

Information on conscripts in the individual sources is rather scarce. There seems to be a tendency to mask conscription under volunteering or perhaps the Derby scheme. Only one certain conscript has been identified[141] and a few problematic cases.[142] A much better indication comes from the roll of No.4 Platoon of the 4th (Reserve) Battalion Seaforths, dated 30th July, 1918.[143] This battalion was the reserve training battalion for the Territorial Seaforths. 65 recruits are listed; all aged 18, all single and all enlisted in June or July, 1918, so this is clearly a platoon of young conscripts. Only 18 percent of the recruits came from the Seaforths' own recruiting district. Of the remainder the great majority came from the recruiting districts of the other Highland regiments, mainly the Black Watch and Argylls. Only 3 recruits fell outside these limits; one Scotsman, one Welshman, and one Englishman. While 97 percent of the recruits were Scottish, only 27 percent were actually from the Highlands proper, a large proportion being drawn from the southern recruiting areas of the Black Watch and Argylls, in particular Dundee and Fife, Renfrew and Dumbarton. These figures suggest the successful maintenance of Scottish identity, alongside a failure to maintain recruiting from the Highlands.

With regards to occupation, the recruits were predominantly working-class, with a smattering of lower middle-class representation. A high proportion, being young, were either unskilled or apprenticed. Not all conscripts, however, were young. Captain Don Main in 5th (Reserve) Battalion Argylls, wrote on 21 April, 1918, of the older conscripts: "It is realised now that every man worth having has volunteered when the country called in 1914 and 1915, and that we must do the best we can with the remnants of humanity who have funked up till now."[144]

Conscripts, of course, were sent to Regular, Territorial and Kitchener battalions. By the middle of 1918, especially after the heavy losses in the German offensive, and the desperate reinforcement of the Army with young soldiers from home, battalions at the front were increasingly composed of conscripts, as Private Douglas remarks of 8th Black Watch in early June, 1918.[145]

---

139 BWA Junks, Herbert, 'The Diary of a Soldier in the Great War', typescript; IWM Books, Cooper, 'Domi Militaeque', biographical note & pp.1-88; IWM 14335 PP Mair, J.R., word processed memoir, written in Winnipeg, Canada, pp.1-20, 38.
140 IWM 2528 PP Bradbury, S, typescript memoir written 1923, pp.1, 7, 14.
141 LC GS 1516 Stables, Sgt G., letter to Liddle, 5 February, 1979.
142 BWA Hay, memoir, pp.6-62; IWM 10414 McGregor, interview.
143 THM Seaforths 80-12 4th (Reserve) Bn Seaforth Highlanders, A Coy, No.4 Platoon Roll, 30th July, 1918.
144 ASHM N-E5 Main, letter to wife, 21 April, 1918.
145 IWM 4586 Douglas, memoir, pp.605-606.

From 1915, all types of battalion were being reinforced by drafts first of volunteers, then of Derby men and finally conscripts, in addition to wounded men returning to the front and 'comb-out' men or 'dugouts' transferred from cushy posts at home. In the Territorials, the principal complaint in 1915 and later was that drafts were sent out either insufficiently trained or unfit.[146] The volunteers sent to Regular battalions, like George Ramage, who joined 1st Gordons at the Front in April, 1915,[147] were generally well-regarded by the battalions which received them,[148] but gradually changed the character of those battalions.[149] By contrast, there is some condemnation in the Kitchener battalions themselves of the inadequate training of reinforcement drafts.[150] Later in the war, a number of "comb-out" men arrived.[151] Such men were often resented. Not only were they looked down upon for their cushy existence at home, their arrival could be resented for the blight cast by their seniority on the situation of long-serving officers at the front.[152] Their practical inexperience of trench-warfare was nevertheless the cause of some amusement. From 1916, battalions received Derby men,[153] and perhaps unsurprisingly, early Kitchener volunteers sometimes complained of their spirit.[154]

Finally, from 1917 came the conscripts. There was some contempt for conscripts,[155] coupled with a recognition that some were fine men.[156] There was some resentment from the old hands towards Derby men and Conscripts for not having enlisted at the start of the war, although this was not directed towards the young drafts called up when 18 and innocent of any hanging-back.[157] Many such boys were deployed in response to the 1918 German offensive, often under 19 years of age.[158] The spirit of these young lads was often seen to be exemplary,[159] although some did find it physically hard to cope.[160] A noticeable feature as the war progressed was the increasing mixing of Territorial and Kitchener battalions and men. We have already noted

---

146 See: IWM 14269 PP Cooper, Capt Charles Miller, letter to mother, 8 May, 1915; LC GS 1536 Stewart, G, letter to mother, 18 January, 1917; THM Seaforths 05-87 Hope, A.H.C., typescript of diary, 22 March, 21 April, 1915; IWM 114 Allen, letters to wife, 11 July, 1915, 5 March, 1916; IWM Books Reid, *Shoulder to Shoulder*, pp.144-145; IWM 6702 Low, undated paper on mobilisation.
147 NLS MS944, Ramage, diary, 13 April, 1915.
148 IWM 1862 Craig-Brown, letter to 1st Brigade, 18 January, 1915; GHM PB3309 Pelham Burn, letter to mother, 31 January, 1915; Craig-Brown, *Historical Records*, Vol.3, p.195; GHM PB242 Stansfield, letter home, 6 June, 1915; GHM PB375 Pailthorpe, memoir, p.40.
149 LC GS 1026 Maclean, memoir, p.8. See also ASHM N-E2 MacMillan, memoir, 1976.
150 GHM PB507 Wallace, diary, 31 August, 1915; ASHM N-E11 Bowie, diary; IWM 2854 Bates, letters to fiancée, 21 September, 12 November, 1916.
151 THM Seaforths Laurie, John Emilius, diary, 4 September, 1918; GHM PB1892.3.18 McDonald, Lt.-Col. Sam, unpublished typescript, 'Uncle Harper's Duds,' p.93.
152 LC GS 1203 Oldham, diary, 28, 30 April, 5 May, 1917; LC GS 1536 Stewart, letter to mother 10 January, 1917.
153 LC GS 1551 Strang, letter to brother Willlie, 20 March, 1916.
154 IWM 7668 PP Escombe, Capt W.M.L., letter from C.B.Anderson, 1 August, 1916.
155 GHM PB1639 Kemp, memoir, pp.39, 94.
156 GHM PB375 Pailthorpe, memoir, p.49.
157 IWM Books, Cooper, 'Domi Militaeque', pp.92-93; IWM 4586 Douglas, memoir, p.80.
158 ASHM N-E5 Main, letters to wife, 24, 27, 31 March, 3, 7. 10, 14, 18, April, 1918; BWA, Macdonald, letters to wife, n.d. c.April, 1918 and 29 April, 1918.
159 GHM PB1892.3.18 McDonald, 'Uncle Harper's Duds,' p.93; Buchanan-Smith, Alick, *The Gordon Highlanders Loos and Buzancy* (Aberdeen: Univerity Press, 1981).
160 IWM 4586 Douglas, memoir, pp.323-327; BWA Foreman, memoir.

under Organisation the transfer of four Territorial battalions to the 15th Division in May and June, 1918, and the absorption of Kitchener battalions by three of them. Additionally, for example, near the end of June, 1916, 1/5th and 1/7th Gordons, both Territorial battalions in 51st Highland Division, received drafts of all the Gordons in 11th Entrenching Battalion, a battalion which had been formed partly from the men left over after the amalgamation of 8th and 10th Gordons, both Kitchener battalions.[161]

In the face of a continuous drip of casualties and reinforcements, battalions were subject to constant change throughout the war. Sometimes this was sudden and dramatic; the consequence of particular battles when casualties were so heavy that battalions had to be heavily reinforced or reconstructed and effectively transformed. Such transformations affected, for example, 1st Camerons after their losses sustained in the battles of the Aisne and First Ypres in 1914, when losses of Regulars were replaced by Special Reservists and others.[162] Likewise, 5th Camerons were transformed after the battle of Loos,[163] when the original volunteers were lost, as were the Glasgow Highlanders after High Wood in July, 1916, which marked the first really big break from the battalion of 1914.[164] 1/7th Black Watch suffered such enormous losses in the German 1918 offensive that by May it was practically a new Battalion.[165]

For individual soldiers, as for officers, whatever battalion they had originally joined, it was very common for them to be posted to another battalion of the same regiment. In some cases this was a continuation of the process by which ex-Regular N.C.O.'s from the Reserve had been posted to provide a cadre of experience for the Territorial or Kitchener battalions, or possibly a consequence of evicting dug-outs from home service.[166] In some cases, transfers occurred because the battalion recruits joined at home, originally destined for foreign service, was never deployed overseas.[167] In other cases, the transfers were the result of disbandments.[168] Perhaps most frequently, this practice occurred when soldiers were posted to battalions overseas after recovery from wounds or sickness at home.[169] Many wartime entrants were, of course, drafted from home straight into Regular battalions.[170] In fact, soldiers would not necessarily be drafted to the same type of battalion (Regular, Territorial or Kitchener) they had served in previously.[171] There are numerous examples.

---

161 GHM PB 1639 Kemp, memoir, p.28.
162 Craig-Brown, *Historical Records*, Vol.3, p.114.
163 McEwen, *Fifth Camerons*, p.54.
164 IWM Books, Reid, *Shoulder to Shoulder*, pp.142, 153-154.
165 Wauchope,, *Black Watch*, vol.2, pp.301, 305, 306.
166 See: THM Camerons 78-87a, Notes on Ross family; IWM 4586 Douglas, memoir, p.329.
167 See: IWM 3449 Cordner, memoir.
168 See: LC GS 0771 Hirsch, various documents.
169 See: THM Seaforths 98-113, Wilson, Pte John, notebook.
170 See: IWM 3449 Cordner, memoir; IWM 10786 Hood, interview; NLS MS944-947. Ramage, diary, passim, in particular MS 947, following 18 June, 1915; LC GS 0280 Chamberlain, Tom, interview with Liddle, 1978; Chambers, *Diaries of World War 1*, pp.3-5, 7-9, 11; BWA Marshall, Pte James McGregor, manuscript reminiscences, written 1937.
171 See:IWM 3449 Cordner, memoir; LC GS 0280 Chamberlain, interview; LC Several Fronts Recollections Munro, memoir; LC Transcripts Tape 432, Brown, interview; THM Seaforths S796(R) Cartmell, John, typescript memoir, 'Some memories of my service with the 'Seaforth Highlanders' during the Great War'; IWM 3460 Macmillan, letters from Willie Macmillan to mother, 1

Likewise, sometimes soldiers were drafted to or from completely different regiments from their own.[172] In other cases, soldiers were transferred into Highland regiments from completely different regiments. Sometimes they appear to have transferred in order to see service with the infantry, perhaps impelled by conscience or a sense of adventure.[173] Others transferred partly at least for family reasons.[174] We have already noted, in considering organisation, the conversion of Yeomanry units into 'Highland' infantry units. In addition to these conversions, a large number of men of both the Lovat Scouts and the Scottish Horse were drafted to the Cameron Highlanders[175] and Black Watch[176] respectively.

The drafting of recruits from one regiment to another actually became the most potentially contentious issue in reinforcement. Astonishingly mixed drafts were supplied to 2nd Gordons[177] and to the Glasgow Highlanders[178] during the Somme, and to other battalions at other times, through to 1918.[179] A draftee to 1st London Scottish, when asked why he joined the regiment, replied "I didn't, Sir. I was numbered off and marched from the Base Camp to make up a draft."[180] This bewildered soldier effectively demonstrates how, in some cases, regimental identity appears to have been of little or no concern in drafting soldiers to battalions from the base. Kilted soldiers, for example, might be drafted to non-kilted battalions, and vice versa, sometimes almost simultaneously. The drafting of soldiers to battalions irrespective of regiments became a bone of contention to regimental officers.[181] The issue even became the subject of a little-known mutiny at the Scottish depot at Calais in July, 1918, when men refused to entrain for the front unless they were given assurances that they would serve with their own regiments.[182]

It does seem that the authorities at the base at times pursued a policy of providing reinforcements simply according to numerical need and not according to regiment or battalion, at least for new drafts arrived from England.[183] Some officers and men felt that by following this prac-

---

December, 1915, 30 January, 21 March, 1916; THM Seaforths 02-138 Alexander, Pte Thomas, typescript diary; LC GS 0456 Dick, memoirs.
172 See: LC POW 056 Millar, W, manuscript memoir, 'My experience on the Somme & after at age 18', written c.1976; LC Tape 921 Stuart, interview; LC Tape 1618/1619 Kerridge, interview.
173 See: LC Middlebrook Somme 1918, Savage, letter 6 July, 1976.
174 See: IWM 14321 PP Small, P.M., letters to Ethel Shaw, 31 August, 14 October, 14 , 27, 28 November, 3 December, 1914, 22 February, and postmark 8 July, 1915.
175 THM Camerons 94-8 Mackay, 'Tell Them of Us', letter from Ian Mackay to mother, 6 August, 1916; Craig-Brown, *Historical Records*, Vol.3, pp.464-467; IWM 7408 Lorimer, letter to mother, 2 November, 1916.
176 LC POW 056 Recollections, Sheppard, Dr H.J., typescript memoir, 'Dr Herbert James Sheppard, An Account of part of his life as recalled by his younger daughter Mrs Jillian Craig Peckham', 1984; Wauchope, *Black Watch*, vol.2, pp.80, 277; IWM Books Cooper, 'Domi Militaeque', p.121; BWA Cameron, memoir; BWA, Macdonald, Coll, letter to wife, 9 June, 1917.
177 GHM PB375 Pailthorpe, memoir, pp.17, 20, 23. See also GHM PB2183 Watson, memoir, pp.7-8.
178 IWM Books, Reid, *Shoulder to Shoulder*, p.144.
179 Macleod, *6th Camerons*, pp.72, 103; LC GS 1203 Oldham, diary, 5 September, 1918; IWM Books, Cooper, 'Domi Militaeque', p.64.
180 IWM 6702 Low, undated paper on mobilisation.
181 IWM Book, Reid, *Shoulder to Shoulder*, pp.168-170; IWM 4370 Christison, memoir, pp.65-66; Macleod, *6th Camerons*, pp.83-84; THM Camerons 97-22, Russell, memoir, pp.250-251; IWM 4586 Douglas, memoir, pp.315, 492-493; Hutchison, *Warrior*, p.141.
182 IWM 4370 Christison, memoir, p.72.
183 See: IWM Books, Cooper, 'Domi Militaeque', p.47.

tice, the authorities were ignoring 'esprit de corps,' and indeed regarding it as an embarrassing impediment to the necessary flexibility in drafting.[184] On this particular issue, it is hard not to take the part of the regimental officers, concerned with maintaining happy and effective fighting units, and conscious all the time of the need to manage individual human strengths and weaknesses. Equally, however, one's sympathies must also extend to the staff officers who had to cope with huge organisational problems in keeping up to strength battalions which did not conveniently all lose casualties at a constant rate at the same time. It was a question of striking the right balance, and in so doing, some tensions were necessary and inevitable, even without the wrong decisions which were sometimes made. We will return to the question of identity in a later chapter.

Under Age soldiers

An astonishingly large number of Highland soldiers were recruited under-age. Nor was the practice confined to enlisted men; some officers were also commissioned very young.[185] This phenomenon was not, however, a peculiar feature of kilted battalions, so, despite the wealth of source material, will be dealt with only briefly.

Although we have seen that in principle under-age pre-War Territorials were left at home, it is nevertheless true that some were taken out under-age.[186] Amongst new Kitchener volunteers under-age enlistment, giving a false declaration of age, was very common.[187] There were some cases of boys enlisting as young as 14 or 15.[188] There was wilful collusion by some recruiting teams,[189] as there was a wilful blind eye turned by doctors on medical inspection.[190] Parental permission was usually sought by the youngsters and given, either willingly[191] or reluctantly.[192]

---

184 LC WF Recollections S18 Sloan, memoir; Hutchison, *Warrior*, p.141; Macleod, *6th Camerons*, pp.83-84; THM Camerons 97-22, Russell, memoir, pp.250-251.
185 Wilson, *Biographical List*, p.97 (Christian Boulton), p.106 (Ian Mackintosh, Robert Macleod). See also: LC AIR 258A Low, autobiography; GHM PB2183 Watson, Richard Jackson, typescript memoir, probably written 1943, pp.1-6, 13; LC GS 1026 Maclean, memoir, pp.2-7, Tape 495, interview with Liddle, 1978; THM Seaforths 81-2 Cooper, memoir, pp.2-21.
186 Walker, *Tom Walker Remembers*, pp.1-5; GHM PB3253 Gray, John, miscellaneous documents.
187 LC Tape 700, Gilmour, interview; Gilmour, *An eastern cadet*, pp.10-19; Dingwall Museum Trust, *Portrait of a Soldier, Sgt John Meikle, V.C., M.M., 4th Bn Seaforth Highlanders 1898 1918*, (Dingwall Museum Trust, Local Studies No.4, 1992); LC Several Fronts Recollections Munro, Archibald M., 'Recollections of the First World War with the Gordon Highlanders.'; LC DF 148 Recollections, Samson; GHM unaccessioned, Beaton, Norman, manuscript memoir, pp.8-15, 101; LC WF Recollections S18 Sloan, memoir; LC WF Recollections M3 McLeavy, J.C., manuscript recollections, probably written 1970's; IWM 24552 Recording McLeavy, J.C., interview 1988; LC WF Recollections C15 Cormack, memoir.
188 Craig Brown, *Historical Records*, Vol.4, p.372; IWM 24855 Newton, interview; LC GS 1470 Silvester, Victor M, transcript of interview with Liddle, 1973.
189 IWM 10786 Hood, interview; LC Several Fronts Recollections Munro; IWM 20453 Recording Pring, W., interview 1992.
190 LC GS 1470 Silvester, transcript; LC WF Recollections S18 Sloan, memoir.
191 LC WF Recollections, MacKenzie, memoir; LC Tape 700, Gilmour, interview, Gilmour, *An eastern cadet*, pp.10-19; LC Several Fronts Recollections Munro.
192 IWM 3460 Macmillan, letters from Alex Macmillan to mother, 15 December, 1915, n.d., 26 February, 4 August, 5 September, 1916, from Alex to James (a pal), 26 December, 1915; LC Tape

Sometimes parents objected after enlistment, but often to little or no effect.[193] Other parents were more successful.[194] In fairness, even without parental intervention, once the boys had enlisted under-age, they were often held back from drafting overseas until they were older, if not 19.[195] A number of under-age soldiers were released by the Army. Some were discharged from home before seeing service in France.[196] Other men were sent down to the base from the Front when discovered to be under-age.[197] Many young soldiers, of course, were sent out under age in 1918 in the wake of the German offensive.[198]

Gaelic speakers

One group of soldiers worth singling out are the Gaelic speakers. We have already noted how the most truly Highland regiments in terms of composition were the Seaforths and Camerons with the addition of 8th Argylls, the only truly Highland battalion of Argylls. Not all Highlanders were Gaelic speaking, with those to whom Gaelic was the primary tongue largely concentrated in the Northern and Western Highlands and the Hebrides. But the great majority of these Gaelic speakers were concentrated in the regimental areas of the battalions above. Numerous sources attest to the presence of Gaelic-speaking Highlanders in the ranks of the Seaforths,[199] the Camerons[200] and the 8th Argylls.[201] Of course, a few Gaelic-speakers would be found in other battalions, such as, for example, 8th Black Watch,[202] and the Gordons.[203] We must also

---

1618/1619 Kerridge, interview; LC WF Recollections M3 McLeavy, memoir; IWM 24552 McLeavy, interview; GHM PB3712 Murison, recollections.
193 IWM 10786 Hood, interview; LC Tape 922 McLean, Alexander, interview with Isobel Farrow, 1993; NLS Acc.7658 No.2 Angus, Archie, Introductory notes.
194 LC WF Recollections M3 McLeavy, J.C., memoir; IWM 24552 McLeavy, interview; LC WF Recollections C15 Cormack, memoir; LC GS 1516 Stables, letter to Liddle, 5 February, 1979.
195 LC WF Recollections, MacKenzie, memoir; LC GS 1470 Silvester, transcript; LC AIR 258A Recollections, Murray, H.G.F., typescript memoir; LC Tape 1618/1619 Kerridge, interview; LC DF 148 Recollections, Samson.
196 IWM 20852 Drury, memoir.
197 ASHM War Diary 1/6th Argylls, 31 July, 1916, 31 January, 30 November, 1917; LC GS 1470 Silvester, transcript.
198 LC POW 031, Hain, John, letter to him from Mrs May Dewar, 20 February, 1919.
199 THM Seaforths 89-26 Crask, letter to parents, ?29 April 1915; IWM 12043 Collins, interview, 1991; IWM 3608 PP Anderson, Maj. A., manuscript memoir; Campbell, Ivar, *Letters of Ivar Campbell written between May 1915 & January 1916*, (privately published, 1917), p.25, letter of 16 June, 1915; Fraser, *Lochbroom*, pp.xiii-xiv; IWM 12311 Mason-Macfarlane, memoir by Col David Mason-Macfarlane, p.8.
200 THM Camerons 89-17 McFarlane, memoir; THM Camerons 93-35, Welsh, D, Typescript, 'Memoirs of an S.B.,' p.23; McEwen, *Fifth Camerons*, p.14; IWM 4370 Christison, memoir, p.46; Craig-Brown, *Historical Records*, Vol.3, p.422, Vol.4, p.378.
201 Malcolm, *Argyllshire Highlanders*, p.13; IWM 15990 Gunn, letter to pal, 16 April, 1915; IWM 14340 McArthur, memorandum, 1914, and diary, 20 March, 20 August, 1915.
202 BWA, Macdonald, Coll, letters to wife, 13 June, 14, 15, 20, 22 July, 12 August, 2 September, 29 November, 1917.
203 GHM PB2790 Graham, Murdo, poem, 'Gordon Highlanders, 1914, aged 18'; GHM PB375 Pailthorpe, Maj D.W. ('Sassenach') typescript memoir, 'With the Highlanders', p.40.

remember the survival of Gaelic culture in Canada, and particularly Nova Scotia, which strongly influenced the composition of the Nova Scotia Brigade.[204]

Private Douglas noted that in March, 1918, at Ripon, in the reserve training battalion of the Argylls:

> Now and again I would meet a REAL HIGHLANDER amongst us, the very few and they were only a few, I could number them on one hand, who spoke Gaelic, and very little English, … Generally speaking they did not chum up with the other Scotsmen, but sought each other out in the other huts, and when two or three of them, there was never more, they spoke nothing else but Gaelic amongst them. The few Gaelic speaking Highlanders I came into contact with came from the Western Isles, one of them was a road man, on the Isle of Mull, as he could only speak a few words of English, he was unable to chum up with anyone in the hut, I used to think it was a shame to drag him away from his lonely island to a strange world of danger & death and amongst associates who to him would be almost foreigners.[205]

Private Douglas, a Geordie, was both perceptive and understanding, but the situation he described was splendidly ironic; 'Real Highlanders' feeling out of place in a Highland regiment.[206] The Highland regiments which had originally all been composed of Gaelic-speaking 'real Highlanders,' had been transformed during the nineteenth century into cultural entities which retained elements of Highland culture but in many cases retained very few real Highlanders. While the inclusion of Gaelic-speakers in essentially English-speaking battalions could give rise to some genuinely amusing incidents,[207] it was somewhat tragic that many such battalions were now so detached from their origins that the descendants of the men who created them could feel out of place in their ranks.

There was a significant number of Gaelic-speaking officers in the Highland battalions,[208] including, for example, Lieutenant Angus Macnaghten in 1st Black Watch,[209] and Father MacNeill,[210] the Catholic padre of 5th Camerons. One fascinating group were those officers who had learned the language as a cultural attribute, without being born Gaelic-speakers or even Highland. We have already noted the case of Philip Christison. Another example was the celebrated soldier-poet, Alan Mackintosh, who served as an officer in 5th Seaforths. He was actually born in Brighton in 1893, of a Scottish father, and was from the Anglo-Scottish bourgeoisie. He attended Brighton College, St Paul's and Christ Church, Oxford.[211] While

---

204 Hunt, *Nova Scotia's Part*, pp.123, 263.
205 IWM 4586 Douglas, memoir, pp.296-297.
206 On this see also: Burns, *Once a Cameron Highlander*, p.29.
207 IWM 2902 PP Munro, Lt. H.A., letter to mother, 10 June, 1915; IWM 430 Wimberley, memoir, p.108.
208 Apart from Macnaghten and MacNeill, see Craig-Brown, *Historical Records*, Vol.4, p.378; THM Camerons 02-111, Notes by Leszczuk; THM Camerons 94-8 Mackay, 'Tell Them of Us', letters from William, 27 March, 1915, and Ian, 4 April, 1915; Wilson, *Biographical List*, pp.58, 73, 90; IWM 4370 Christison, memoir, pp.1-.28.
209 IWM 3696 Macnaghten, A.C.R.S., Capt., letters.
210 McEwen, *Fifth Camerons*, p.14.
211 Campbell & Green, *Can't shoot*, passim.

at Oxford, he visited the Highlands, and cultivated his interest in Highland culture. In his poem 'Mallaig Bay', written in 1912, he turned his back on his country of birth and started a romantic attachment to the Highlands.[212] He learnt to play the bagpipes and speak Gaelic. References to Highland culture abound in his poems and in effect he redefined himself as a cultural Highlander.

Finally, we have already noted how the Highland Territorial battalions made individual communities vulnerable to losses, and how, for example the town of Portree was hit by the losses of 1/4th Camerons at Festubert. Since the Gaelic-speaking world was itself marginal and fragile, threatened linguistically and culturally by the march of English, arguably such losses potentially threatened the survival of Gaelic culture itself. At least this was a perception. Chaplain Lauchlan Maclean Watt voiced his concern for the future.

> And it means for us, the children of the Gael, something which I think is more than for other folks. It means the thinning out of an ancient race, the fading of one of the old languages of Europe, and a great unbridged blank in a generation. The changes which have taken place in the Highlands in a century have been vast, but this war means something as swift and sudden as the blowing out of a candle, or the drawing of a curtain – for many wide districts, indeed, the end of an old song.[213]

Englishmen

We have already noticed in a previous chapter the large number of Londoners who joined the Territorial Highland Division at Bedford after being sent on by the London Scottish. Englishmen did indeed make a significant contribution to the ranks of the Highland battalions. There was some sensitivity about this situation.[214] In fact, as we have seen, while Highland regiments did often rely on inputs of Englishmen to make up their strength, they remained overwhelmingly Scottish, if not overwhelmingly Highland in composition. Our kilted Englishmen should be regarded not as a dangerously subversive element, destroying the character of Highland regiments, but generally as a useful and willing supplement to numbers, which enabled some battalions to maintain their strength, and indeed in some cases, to be deployed overseas at all.

Along with the Londoners who joined the Highland Division through Buckingham Gate, there was one other major source of English recruits, and this was Yorkshire. A large number of Yorkshiremen joined the Territorial training battalions at Ripon through a combination of enthusiasm and convenience.[215] Otherwise, the arrival of Englishmen in Highland regiments

---

212 Mackintosh, E.A., *A Highland Regiment*, (London: John Lane, 1918), p.59.
213 Watt, *In France and Flanders*, pp.90-91. See also BWA, Macdonald, Coll, letter to wife, 4 November, 1917.
214 Watt, *In France and Flanders*, pp.32-33.
215 IWM 3834 PP Wrench, A.E., diary, Introduction, and, 15 May, 1917; Craig-Brown, *Historical Records*, Vol.3, p.441; IWM 322 Recording Reid, J.P.O., interview, 1966; IWM 20852 Drury, memoir; IWM Books, Brooke, 'Wait for it', pp.1, 13-14, 16; see also THM Seaforths 98-11 Brooke, Frank C., 'A Yorkshire Kiltie', pp.1, 8.

was a little more haphazard, but there was a significant number from the north of England,[216] a few from the Midlands,[217] and, apart from the Londoners who joined the Highland Division at the beginning of the war, a trickle of recruits from the south.[218]

Englishmen were not always welcome.[219] There were misgivings about the number of Yorkshiremen joining 3/4th Camerons at Ripon,[220] and the ultimate drafting of these men to 1st Battalion when 1/4th Battalion was broken up, caused annoyance to their C.O., Ernest Craig-Brown.[221] When Private Douglas from Walker-on-Tyne was drafted to 8th Black Watch, in April, 1918, he felt he was discriminated against by his lance-sergeant.[222] But probably much more typical was the experience of Hal Kerridge from East Sheen, who was drafted from the London Scottish at Etaples to join 1st Gordons and felt he was accepted very well.[223] Indeed, good-natured banter in the face of shared adversity was probably the norm.[224]

As we have seen, some officers even pre-War Regulars, were English, like the distinguished Gordons officer 'Johnnie' Stansfield.[225] Those posted to Highland battalions during the war were not always welcome,[226] with Major Montgomerie, an English officer of the Norfolks removed from command of 1/5th Seaforth Highlanders.[227] Nevertheless, Englishmen Frederick Chandler, who served as M.O. to 2nd Argylls, Johnathan Bates, M.O. 8th Black Watch, and Hugh Quekett, who joined 5th Black Watch from the London Scottish, all found themselves well received and in excellent company.[228]

---

216 THM Seaforths 89-26 Crask, diary, 21 April, 1915; letters to parents, ?26 April, 5, 25 May, ?4, 9, 15 June, 1915; IWM 3460 Macmillan, letter from Willie Macmillan to mother, 21 July, 1915; ASHM N-E8 McGuinness, notebook; GHM PB227 Sergeant, James, miscellaneous documents; LC Transcripts & Tapes, Reynoldson, W., Tape 99, interview with William Redford; LC Transcripts, Tape 324, Jordan, interview; LC Transcripts, Tapes 728 and 744, Davies, interview; IWM 4586 Douglas, memoir, pp.1-12, 21-24, 680; Andrews, Linton, *The Autobiography of a Journalist* (London: Ernest Benn Ltd., 1964); THM Seaforths 91-27 McIntosh, Pte John, background notes; IWM 2294 PP Fraser, J., letter to Gwen Howell, 12 September, 1916; IWM 12043 Collins, interview.
217 BWA, Forman, memoir.
218 IWM 20453 Pring, interview; LC AIR 258A Recollections, Murray, memoir; IWM 24855 Newton, interview.
219 See for example, IWM 1862 Craig-Brown, letter, 27 March, 1915; Andrews, *Autobiography*, pp.82-83; LC Transcripts & Tapes, Reynoldson, interview; THM Seaforths 89-26 Crask, letter to father, 5 May, 1915.
220 THM Camerons 94-8 Mackay, 'Tell Them of Us', letter from Ian Mackay to mother, 7 May, 1916.
221 IWM 1862 Craig-Brown, letter to Mackintosh of Mackintosh, 30 June, 1916. See also his diary, 20 May, 12, 13 June, 27 July, 13 August, 13, 25 September, 1916.
222 IWM 4586 Douglas, memoir, p.331.
223 LC Tape 1618/1619 Kerridge, interview.
224 IWM 12043 Collins, interview; IWM 24855 Newton, interview, 1975; ASHM N-E11 Bowie, diary.
225 GHM PB242 Stansfield, extract from 'British Roll of Honour.'
226 IWM 1862 Craig-Brown, letter, 31 January, 1915; diary 1 February, 1915. And see his letter to Sir Spencer Ewart, n.d., c. April, 1916.
227 IWM 3249 Montgomerie, letter to W.O., 27 January, 1917.
228 IWM 15460 PP Chandler, Capt F.G., letter to future wife Marjorie Raimes, 31 December, 1914; IWM 2854 Bates, letter to fiancée, 3 May, 1916; BWA Quekett, memoir, pp.1-11.

138 Those Bloody Kilts

Canadians and South Africans

For the Canadians, we are fortunate in possessing a tabulation by Urquhart of the country of birth of officers and Other Ranks (O.R.) serving in the 16th Battalion C.E.F.(Canadian Scottish), which permits a statistical analysis and comparison between the composition of the battalion on formation, and the composition of subsequent drafts.[229]

In the battalion on formation 35 percent of O.R. were actually born in Scotland. Of the rest, only 16 percent were born in Canada, with 44 percent born in the rest of the old country (Britain and Ireland), most of these (39 percent) being born in England. Of course, an unknown quantity of those born both in Canada and England may have had Scottish ancestry, but this cannot be assumed. What is most remarkable is the proportion of old country-men (79 percent) compared with native born Canadians (only 16 percent). Of the rest, a number came from elsewhere in the Empire, while there were also representatives from the United States and other countries, no doubt including some non-British immigrant settlers as well as some adventurers,[230] found also in other battalions.[231]

In the case of the officers, compared with the O.R., a significantly higher proportion on formation were born in Canada (48 percent), with a smaller proportion (20 percent) born in Scotland, and 26 percent born in the rest of the old country, mostly in England. Interestingly, as the war progressed, there were many officers promoted from the ranks. In the closing stages of the war, in 16th Battalion, out of a total of 47 platoon commanders, 30 had served in the ranks of the battalion.[232]

Some confirmation of the dominance of old country-men in the Canadian Highland battalions is offered by Fetherstonaugh, who states, regarding the 5th Royal Highlanders of Canada, which formed the core of 13th Battalion, that about 65 to 75 percent of the recruits were old countrymen, the remainder native Canadians, with a small scattering of total outsiders; these proportions being reversed for the officers, all but four of those appointed being Canadian born.[233] In addition, the Camerons regimental history claims that both the Cameron company of 16th Battalion C.E.F. (Canadian Scottish) and the 43rd Battalion (Cameron Highlanders of Canada) itself, were predominantly Scottish born.[234] This may well be an exaggeration, but does suggest, consistently, that most, at least, were old country-men rather than native Canadians.

When we compare the statistics for the Canadian Scottish on formation with those for the much greater number of their subsequent reinforcements, we find that the situation regarding the officers did not change significantly. As far as the O.R are concerned, however, there are significant changes. First, the percentages born in Scotland and the rest of the old country declined substantially to 21 and 36 percent respectively, while there was a significant parallel increase in the percentage of Canadian-born to 34 percent. With the influx of reinforcements, the Canadian Scottish battalion was therefore becoming progressively less Scottish, less Old Country and more Canadian. Some explanation may be provided by the introduction of

---

229 Author's statistics; data from Urquhart, *Canadian Scottish*, Appendix V and VI.
230 Urquhart, *Canadian Scottish*, pp.15, 99, 148.
231 Fetherstonhaugh, *13th Battalion*, p.259.
232 Urquhart, *Canadian Scottish*, p.240.
233 Fetherstonhaugh, *13th Battalion*, p.6.
234 Craig-Brown, *Historical Records*, Vol.4, pp.36-38.

conscription in Canada in 1917.[235] Another perspective is provided by Urquhart's list of reinforcements: only 24 percent came from Highland battalions, the remainder from units with no Highland or Scottish allegiance. This suggests that the reinforcement system itself, which we have considered in the previous chapter, progressively diminished the Scottish composition of the kilted Canadian battalions.[236] In the sources, we find example of Scots,[237] English[238] and Canadian-born[239] soldiers.

Of the 1,282 men of all ranks who formed the South African Scottish when first formed at Potchefstroom, 46 percent were born in South Africa, 26 percent in Scotland, 20 percent in England, and seven percent elsewhere including Ireland and Wales.[240] Like the Canadian figures, these percentages indicate the significant contribution of men from the Old Country to the Empire's war effort. They also indicate, like the Canadian figures, that the South African Scottish were by no means of universal Scottish descent.

The handful of examples encountered in the sources add a little colour to this bare outline. We find a native born South African, J.E.P. Levyns, ironically of German extraction, who joined the South African Scottish after failing his engineering exams in 1916,[241] Scottish-born James Blount-Dinwiddie, who served with the Transvaal Scottish in German South West Africa in 1914,[242] English-born Arthur Betteridge, from Birmingham, who joined the South African Scottish[243] and Robert Ashburner, from North Lancashire, an engineering student who joined up in September, 1914, served first in South West Africa, and afterwards transferred to the South African Scottish with whom he went to France, serving first in the Senussi campaign.[244] There was also an American adventurer in the South African Scottish called Veitch.[245]

Finally, there was the remarkable Hugh Boustead. Born in 1895, the son of a Ceylon planter, in 1914 he was serving as a Midshipman on board H.M.S. Hyacinth on the Cape station. Determined to get into an area of active service, in August, 1915, he deserted his ship and joined the South African Scottish at Potchefstroom as a private soldier, giving the false name of McLaren. In late September, he arrived with them in England. Discovered by the authorities, they turned a blind eye through family connections (his cousin Maurice Hankey, was secretary to the Imperial Defence Committee). Hugh continued with the South African Scottish and changed his name back to Boustead. He went on to serve with them against the Senussi and

---

235 Chartrand, *Canadian Corps*, pp.11-13.
236 See for impact on Canadian Scottish, Urquhart, *Canadian Scottish*, pp.88, 176, 195.
237 Urquhart, *Canadian Scottish*, p.99; IWM 16841 Harrison, letters to 'Joe', n.d., to daughter Gertrude, 11 June, 1916; McMillan, David, *Trench Tea and Sandbags*, (R.McAdam, 1996), pp.1-9; Fraser, *Lochbroom*, p.68.
238 LC Transcripts &c, Tape 850, Henley, R.E., interview with Liddle, 1992; IWM 7200 PP Maxwell-Scott, H.F., Maxwell-Scott, Susan, *Pa's Wartime Letters and This & That*, (privately published, 2010), Introduction; IWM 10819 PP Brittan, S.V., introductory notes; IWM 10117 Recording, Bartholomew, William George, IWM interview, 1987.
239 O'Kiely, *Gentleman Air Ace*, pp.15-55, 207-210.
240 Based on figures in Orpen, *Cape Town Highlanders*, p.81.
241 Levyns, *The Disciplines of War*, pp.1-28.
242 IWM 2221 PP Blount-Dinwiddie, extract from Ruvigny's *Roll of Honour*.
243 LC GS 0132 Betteridge, Arthur H., typescript memoir, 'Combat in and over Delville Wood,' written 1974, passim.
244 IWM 24887 Ashburner, interview.
245 Boustead, Col. Sir Hugh, *The Wind of Morning*, (London: Chatoo & Windus, 1971), p.27.

on the Western Front, where he was wounded at Delville Wood, after which he was awarded a commission in the regiment.[246]

Conclusions

In general officers in the Highland regiments were Scottish or of Scots descent, but for the most part drawn from outside the Highlands, with some from England and overseas. Likewise new recruits, whether volunteers or conscripts, remained overwhelmingly Scottish, despite the remarkable number of Englishmen who joined Highland regiments. There was however a steady erosion of the local affiliation of the Territorial battalions. There was also an increasing difficulty in finding Highland recruits to fill Highland battalions. The most truly Highland battalions were those of the Seaforths and Camerons, especially their Territorial battalions, and the 8th Argylls. It was in these battalions that most Gaelic speakers were found. In other battalions they might ironically feel themselves outsiders in Highland regiments which retained the militarily standardised trappings of Highland culture but not the actual Highlanders to whom they owed their origin. Some officers possessed a genuine Highland background, if not still living there, but other apparent Highland officers had assimilated elements of Highland identity as a cultural attribute, including Gaelic. In the early years the territorial organisation of the T.F. battalions made local communities vulnerable to high casualties in individual actions. Potentially this was a real challenge to the survival of Gaelic-speaking communities and therefore to Gaelic. As regards the kilted battalions of Canada and South Africa, we may notice that many of the men had actually been born in the Old Country, though by no means exclusively in Scotland.

With regard to social status, amongst all types of officers, but most especially of course amongst the Regulars, there was a tendency still to recruit from the military and professional classes, but evidence too of promotion on merit independent of background. A remarkable number of Regular soldiers were commissioned from the ranks. A large number of Territorial and Temporary officers were also commissioned from the ranks. However, both those granted commissions directly and those commissioned from the ranks were still middle-class; only a small percentage were working-class, and the snobbery directed at Temporary Officers (from both directions) was essentially directed towards the lower middle class. Amongst the O.R.'s there was a large middle-class representation amongst the Territorial volunteers. Some Kitchener volunteers too were distinctly middle-class, but possibly on balance less so than their Territorial counterparts. Such class bias necessarily ended with conscription. As in the rest of the Army, a large number of boys enlisted under-age, a continuation in war-time of legitimate pre-war peacetime practice, through blatantly hypocritical collusion.

It is evident that the composition of battalions was constantly changing throughout the war as reinforcement drafts arrived to replace casualties. Regular battalions, initially composed of serving Regular soldiers, but in some cases brought up to strength by large numbers of reservists, received increasing numbers of wartime volunteers, Derby men and then Conscripts as reinforcements. Territorial battalions, initially brought up to strength by wartime volunteers, were sustained by the same suite of reinforcements, and increasingly lost their original Territorial

---

246 Ibid., pp.11-37.

character. Finally, Kitchener battalions, wartime volunteers from the start, with a cadre from the Regulars and Reserve, received reinforcements from the same sources, and with them disappeared some of the boyish enthusiasm with which they had gone to war. With amalgamations and disbandments, and a flexible approach to drafting at the base, many battalions at some time received drafts from other types of battalion, with Kitchener men and Territorials being drafted to the Regulars, and so on. They also received men from completely different regiments, as a result of both the exigencies of war and the somewhat blasé attitude to regimental affiliation adopted by the authorities at the base. Amongst the officers too there was considerable interchange between regiments and battalions

The constant change in itself was disruptive. In addition, battalions became increasingly polyglot. They also became hardened and moulded by the common experience of European war, for this type of war was almost as new to the Regulars as to the others. Gradually, the distinctions between Regular, Territorial and Kitchener battalions, which would have been strikingly evident in 1915, became unclear, if they did not disappear entirely. The battalions as they were composed at the Armistice were very different from those that deployed to France in 1914 and 1915. Increasingly they had come to resemble each other, however much they kept alive their own 'esprit de corps.'

5

The Kilt: Mystique and Tradition

"I know of no inspiration to be got from trousers"[1]

The most distinctive feature of the Highland soldier was his kilt. In this chapter, we start to examine the experience of the Highland soldier wearing the kilt, including his first introduction to it, custom and tradition for wearing it, and its use in training. The Highland soldier's pride in the kilt is considered, and its impact on identity, 'esprit de corps' and morale. The chapter considers the practicalities, risks and challenges of wearing the kilt at home in training and behind the lines. It also considers the public response to the kilt in England, in France and Belgium, and in other places overseas, especially its undeniable attractiveness to the ladies. The rather less romantic experience of wearing the kilt in the trenches and in battle is considered separately in the chapters which follow.

Initiation and Pride

The men were provided with their uniforms; the officers were not. Officers were expected to obtain their kilt and uniform from an allowance. Some did so in the West End or Edinburgh.[2] In other cases they had kilts made for them by the regimental tailor.[3] In the ranks, new volunteer recruits to the Highland regiments were understandably keen to be issued with the kilt.[4] "I yearned to behold myself in the much dreamed-of uniform," wrote Frank Brooke, who had joined the Seaforths in November, 1915.[5] William Murison and his fellow recruits to 6th Gordons "longed to swap our civilian suits for the kilt."[6] The excitement was shared by the family. Lizzie Nimmo wrote to her brother Peter Nimmo in 1/7th Argylls on 16 October 1914,

---

1   Macleod, Lt Col Norman, in appendix to Mackay, John G., *The Romantic Story of the Highland Garb and Tartan* (Stirling: E. Mackay, 1924).
2   IWM McKechnie, memoir, p.7; THM Camerons 97-22 Russell, memoir, pp.177-178.
3   Wade, *Counterspy*, p.118; IWM 7593 Harper, memoir, p.9.
4   Apart from refs cited below, see: Linklater, Eric, *Fanfare for a Tin Hat* (London: Macmillan, 1970), pp.45-46; IWM 8592 Macgregor, letter to his fiancée dated 6 Oct 1914.
5   IWM books Brooke, 'Wait for it,', pp.22-25.
6   GHM PB3712 Murison, memoir.

"Have you got your *kilt* yet? I would very much like to see you in one."[7] Many were to be disappointed in their eagerness.

In the early part of the war the supply of uniforms could not keep pace with the sudden enlistment of large numbers of recruits. This was particularly the case in the Kitchener battalions, which were created from scratch, and which had no pre-existing stocks of kit. As we will see below, there was also the knotty issue of khaki kilts to be resolved. Most Kitchener battalions were affected by the delays.[8] For example, when 10th Seaforths were formed at the end of October, 1914, according to their C.O., "there were no uniforms available, and so the recruits as they came up were issued with a blue emergency suit, a civilian greatcoat, and Bedford cord pantaloons; as rifles were also lacking, it can readily be understood that it took a great deal to keep up their enthusiasm." When, in January, khaki jackets and Mackenzie kilts arrived, "this naturally pleased the men very much, and made them keener and more enthusiastic in their work, as they then felt that they were soldiers in the real sense of the word.[9]

The problem could also be acute in the Territorial battalions,[10] for although they had some stocks of kit, they were unable to keep up with demand in the early stages of the war. Second and third line Territorial battalions might be particularly badly affected, as we find amongst both 2/6th Argylls[11] and 2/6th Gordons.[12] The problem was also felt amongst kilted Canadian battalions. When 92nd battalion C.E.F. was raised in Canada, beginning in August, 1914, at first training was carried on "in rather motley garb, mostly Civilian raiment". Still in November;

---

7   IWM 1375 PP Nimmo, P., letters from Lizzie, 16 October, and Bessie Nimmo, 2 December, 1914.
8   McEwen, *Fifth Camerons*, p.6; Craig-Brown, *Historical Records*, pp.272, 275, 377, 379; David, Saul (ed), *Mud & Bodies, The War Diaries and Letters of Captain N A C. Weir, 1914-1920*, (London: Frontline Books, 2013), p.13; Sotheby, *10th Argylls*, p.xix; THM Seaforths 02-138 Alexander, diary, 8, 12 September, 1914, January, 1915; Addison Smith, *10th Seaforth Highlanders*, pp.8, 11-12; THM Camerons 97-22 Russell, memoir, pp.180, 181, 188; IWM 7593 Harper, memoir, pp.11,20; GHM PB493 Pearson, Maj. N.G., 'The 10th and 8/10th Battalions of the Gordon Highlanders August 1914 – June 1918,', written 1938, p.2; LC WF Recollections, A.9, Andrew, memoir; *The 11th Battalion Gordon Highlanders*, (Glasgow: Maclure, Macdonald & Co., 1916), pp.6, 9; *Souvenir Booklet 6th Cameron Highlanders*, (London: Spottiswoode & Co. Ltd, 1916), p.13; THM Camerons 89-17 McFarlane, memoir; Darling, *So it looks to me*, p.128; ASHM, N-E11 Bowie, diary; THM 2013-072 (S) Braes, memoir, 3,8,11, 28 September, 12, 31 October, 1914, February, 1915.
9   Addison-Smith *10th Seaforth Highlanders*, pp.8, 11-12.
10 Andrews, William Linton, *Haunting Years*, (Uckfield: NMP reprint, n.d.) p.14; GHM PB107, Grant, diary, 21& 24 October, 12 November, 1914; 13 March, 1915; IWM 8592 Macgregor, letters to his fiancée, 1, 23 September, 1,6,17 & 19 October, 1914; Craig-Barr, Lt. Col J., *Home Service*, (Paisley: Alexander Gardner, 1920), pp.30-31; LC GS 1551 Strang, letter to brother Willie, n.d. [1914]; THM Seaforths 87-141 Heriz-Smith, Mrs, photocopy extract from 'Noon Star', the family journal of Mrs Heriz-Smith; IWM 16335 Racine, memoir, pp.8, 13; IWM 132 PP Paterson, W., typescript transcript memoir, 'Life in the Army, Experiences at home and abroad,' p.15; Collins, Norman, *Last Man Standing* (Barnsley: Leo Cooper, 2002), pp.38, 41, 44, 45, 49; IWM 12043 Recording, Collins, interview; GHM PB2815, McWilliam, Pte John, letter to mother, 12 December, 1914; IWM Books Stitt, Capt J.H., typescript 'History of the Sixth Gordons,' written 1933, p.37 ; LC Tapes 621/641 Pollock, Henry, interview with Liddle, 1981; LC Tapes 481/519 Napier, Joseph, interview with Liddle, 1977; LC GS 1579 Taylor, memoir, p.1; IWM 24552 McLeavy, interview 1988; IWM 3460 Macmillan, diary, preface; IWM 3608 Anderson, memoir; Wauchope, *Black Watch*, Vol.2, pp.126-7, 244.
11 Craig-Barr, *Home Service*, pp.30-31.
12 IWM Books, Stitt, *History of the Sixth Gordons*, p.37.

> Shortage of kilts was lamentable and an irritation, in these early days of the life of the Battalion, especially to those Highlanders going on leave. What Highlander appreciates furlough without the swank and swing of the kilt? The owners of kilts and sporrans made many a bright bawbee by renting theirs. During the winter the shortage was fully made up.[13]

Even later in the war, the issue of kilts could be substantially delayed. Charles Cordner enlisted in November 1915 and was posted to 15th Argylls then stationed at Gailes in Ayrshire. He notes that even then, "For the first six weeks we paraded doing squad drill, and formation marching … in civilian clothes, as uniforms were not available due to the onrush of recruits in response to Lord Kitchener's appeal for 300,000 volunteers."[14] And S. Bradbury, who joined the 3/4th Camerons at Ripon on 1st April, 1916, recalled that, "It was over three weeks before I received my uniform."[15]

Even when the supply of tartan cloth had been resolved, there might still be a delay before kilts made to measure could be supplied. Alex ("Sandy") Macmillan was issued with his kit at the Argylls regimental depot at Stirling Castle on or about 16 December 1915, less his kilt, for which he was measured. From the depot, he joined 13th Battalion at Richmond, where "we have breeks and puttees on & till we receive our kilts … we may not leave the camp." He had still not received his kilt by 31 December. As a result, "I & most of our hut were thoroughly fed up. No kilts & can't get out." In desperation, he arranged to borrow a kilt just to get out of camp. When he was finally issued with his kilt, he immediately "went down town after tea with wee Bill."[16]

While waiting, recruits in both Kitchener and Territorial battalions performed drill in civvies,[17] possibly for a period of months. James Racine was recruited to 5th Seaforths through the London Scottish on 12 September, 1914. He notes that initially at Bedford, "We were without uniforms and looked strange when drilling in our civilian clothes; some men wore bowler hats and others caps and soft hats." He did not receive his kilt and tunic until October.[18] A little later improvised military dress was provided, much derided, consisting often of red jackets, blue trousers and caps.[19] "No more military than the London fire brigade," felt Daniel McFarlane of the Camerons;[20] "the funniest dress that could be worn," thought John Bowie in

---

13 Beattie, *48th Highlanders*, pp.407-409.
14 IWM 3449 Cordner, memoir.
15 IWM 2528 Bradbury, memoir, p.2.
16 IWM 3460 Macmillan, letters from his brother Alex (Sandy) to his mother 15, 17, 20 & 31 December, 1915, and undated.
17 Craig-Brown, *Historical Records,* Vol.4, pp.272, 275; Andrews,, *Haunting Years*, p.14; Craig Barr, *Home Service*, pp.30-31; LC Tapes 621/641 Pollock, interview; LC Tapes 481/519 Napier, interview; IWM 3460 Macmillan, diary, preface; Wauchope, *Black Watch*, Vol.2, pp.126-7.
18 IWM 16335 Racine, memoir, pp.8, 13.
19 Craig-Brown, *Historical Records,* Vol.4, pp.377, 379; THM Camerons 97-22 Russell memoir, pp.180, 181, 188; IWM 4370 Christison, memoir, pp.28, 29; GHM PB107, Grant, diary, 21& 24 October, 12 November, 1914; 13 March, 1915; IWM 7593 Harper, memoir, pp.11, 20; GHM PB493, Pearson, p.2; LC, WF Recollections, A9, Andrew, memoir, pp.6, 9; *Souvenir Booklet 6th Cameron Highlanders*, p.13; Darling, *So it looks to me*, p.128; ASHM, N-E11 Bowie, diary; THM 2013-072 (S) Braes, memoir, 3,8,11, 28 September, 12, 31 October, 1914, February, 1915.
20 THM Camerons 89-17 McFarlane, memoir.

11th Argylls.[21] In September 1914, Cecil Harper took up a commission in 10th Gordons, then at Rushmoor. He remarks that,

> The men were kitted out with red coats of uncertain age with tartan trews; or when the supply of these ran out, blue trousers with a red stripe down the seam and buff belts. For head-dress a cap comforter was rolled up into some semblance of a forage cap. Later there was an issue of "Broderick" peaked caps, such as were worn by English line regiments. These offended Highland tradition. The recipients promptly dubbed them "Salvation Army", and that night a quantity of them was consigned to a bonfire at the head of the lines. Although no doubt the C.O. (a Highlander of Highlanders) sympathised with the sentiment, a stern view had to be taken officially of this wanton destruction of government property which of course had to be paid for. Eventually we got glengarries.[22]

Major Pearson, in his history of the battalion, has a slightly different version:

> The uniform of the men was red tunic, postman's breeks, and cap comforter! This last was removed in October in favour of a Salvation Army hat, better suited for keeping at bay the rays of the sun, but not meeting with favour among the men, who formed themselves that first evening into a Salvation Army band and paraded round the camp with song and tin cans.[23]

Kilts were only issued after the battalion moved to Cirencester in February, 1915. Similarly, Ian Anderson recalled the indignity of such temporary dress in 6th Camerons. "To add insult to injury we passed on this march our hated rivals in the 5th Camerons, trimly dressed in their newly issued khaki. The gibes of "Little Tin Soldiers" and worse hurled at us in passing were almost more than we could bear.[24] Only after the battalion had moved to Basingstoke, in the Spring of 1915, did they finally receive their kilts.

When leave was granted, many recruits regretted that they could not go home proudly in the kilt, unless they could borrow or hire one for the purpose.[25] Fortunately, in 7th Camerons, for example, at Aldershot:

> there was, happily, a nucleus of Regulars at the Barracks who boasted the coveted garb. A tentative suggestion that these proud wearers of the kilt might perchance hire them out to their New Army brethren who were going on leave, met with a ready acquiescence, and so rapidly did the idea catch on that kilts were often booked for weeks ahead.[26]

---

21   ASHM, N E11 Bowie, diary.
22   IWM 7593 Harper, memoir, pp.11,20.
23   GHM PB493, Pearson, p.2.
24   LC WF Recollections, A9, Andrew, memoir.
25   LC GS 1579 Taylor, memoir, p.1; *Souvenir Booklet 6th Cameron Highlanders*, p.15; IWM 3460 Macmillan, letter from his brother William to mother, 10 December, 1914.
26   Sandilands, Col. J.W. & Macleod, Lt Col Norman, *The History of the 7th Battalion Queen's Own Cameron Highlanders*, (Stirling: Aeneas Mackay, 1922), p.20.

Other recruits might borrow or hire a kilt to have their photograph taken, or to swank. Robert Burns, who joined 7th Camerons on 6 November 1914, had still not been issued with his uniform when the battalion moved to Aldershot the following month. Nevertheless, he managed to borrow a kilt, "rushed down into Aldershot to be photographed and wasted no time in sending copies back home."[27] Norman Collins in 3/4th Seaforth Highlanders in June 1915 was lent a kilt by his corporal, "to go swanking up to the YMCA tent in the Cameron Highlanders' camp."[28] Otherwise, recruits might find themselves embarrassed in their 'Salvation Army' uniforms. Alexander Braes, in 8th Seaforths at Aldershot went to visit a pal in the Scots Guards at Wellington Barracks. "Looking the picture of a soldier, he thoroughly enjoyed the sight of me done up like a pillar box."[29]

It was, however, a red letter day when kilts were finally issued. To most, this was a completely new experience. Few recruits, even Scots, had worn the kilt before they enlisted, although there were exceptions. H.P. Samson, for example, from Aberdeen, who joined 4th Gordons, had worn the kilt until he was 14,[30] while Robert Burns, who joined the Camerons, and Alec Thomson, who joined the Seaforths, had both worn the kilt as children.[31] Most recruits by contrast had to be initiated into wearing the kilt.[32] James Marr, for example, was called up under the Derby Scheme in June, 1916. He joined the Gordon Highlanders at Castlehill Barracks, in Aberdeen, where he was issued with his kilt.

Less than glamorous temporary uniforms typical of those worn in training by Highland soldiers before receiving their kilts. (Author's collection)

> So far we had not been supplied with the kilt, and wondered if we were going to be allowed to wear it yet. Late that afternoon, however, an old regular sergeant appeared in the room with a supply of kilts and puttees and proceeded to instruct us in the proper method of

27 Burns, *Once a Cameron Highlander*, p.32; LC Tape 963, Burns, interview.
28 Collins, *Last Man Standing*, pp.38, 41, 44, 45, 49; IWM 12043 Collins, interview.
29 THM 2013-072 (S) Braes, memoir, 3, 8, 11, 28 September, 12, 31 October, 1914, February, 1915.
30 LC DF148, Recollections, Samson,
31 LC Tape 1316, Burns, interview; IWM 11460 Recording, Thomson, Alec, IWM interview, 1990.
32 Apart from refs below, see: LC Tape 744, Gaffron, Horace, interview with Liddle, 1989; IWM 6926 PP Dennis, R.V., typescript memoir, pp.258-259; IWM Books, Cooper, *Domi Militaeque*, pp.8, 9; LC Tape 921 Stuart, Archie, interview with Isabel Farrow, 1993; THM Seaforths 89-26 Crask, diary, 22 April, 1915.

putting on and wearing the tartan … They all remarked how warm it was round the waist, but did not anticipate how cold it would be in other parts of the body when standing on parade some cold winter's day in Flanders. After we all felt we understood the intricacies of the Highland dress the Sergeant took off his cap and handed it round. I suppose he got enough to get a good drink that evening in the canteen, for that is where he usually spent his spare time.[33]

In 11th Argylls, kilts were first issued to John Bowie and his fellow recruits shortly before they were to go on New Year's leave in 1915.

In came the Regimental uniforms so we got the first of them and went home respectable looking. It was some fun trying to dress ourselves, I for one put the pleats of my kilt to the front instead of the back. After being shown how to dress, we had all to strip and redress ourselves in the presence of an officer. After you pass him, you shall be punished if improperly dressed whether you plead ignorance or not.[34]

John Bowie was not the only recruit to be baffled by the intricacies of the kilt. When D.W. Reid, who hailed from Inverness, enlisted in the London Scottish, early in the war, he "helped chaps into their kilts etc – most of them wanted to put them on back to front!"[35] Nevertheless, all was vanity, as the recruits wallowed in their self-image. As James Marr observed, "It was amusing to watch the antics of some strutting about like peacocks, turning their heads to see if they were giving the proper swing to the innumerable folds of tartan."[36]

The transition from trousers to kilt for soldiers transferred to Highland regiments might be particularly memorable. In February, 1917, Private William Cameron was transferred from the Scottish Horse to 7th Black Watch:

We suffered very severe cold here and I will never forget the day when the draft was paraded in a field, three inches deep in snow and we were told to get off our slacks as we were being issued with the kilt. The 1916-17 winter was the worst experienced in France, so we were broken in in style.[37]

Ronald Ewert, a Welshman who was transferred from the Machine Gun Corps to 9th Royal Scots in 1917, found that he had to wear a kilt, but "didn't mind in the least,"[38] Albert Hay in the Scottish Horse volunteered in February, 1918 to join a draft for 1st Black Watch in France. At the depot at Calais in March, "it took us some time to become adept at donning the kilt, and I am afraid mine was a little lop-sided during the first few days."[39] R.V. Dennis, was a signaller with 21st Battalion KRRC. Following the dissolution of this battalion in March, 1918, after

33 IWM 14335 Marr, memoir, p.9.
34 ASHM, N-E11 Bowie, diary.
35 IWM 10533 Reid, memoir.
36 IWM 14335 Marr, memoir, p.9. See also: Lyon, *In Kilt and Khaki*, pp.35 36.
37 LC GS 0257 Cameron, W.G., Typescript memoir, written 20 July, 1918.
38 IWM 9930 Wells, interview.
39 BWA Hay, memoir, p.56.

hospitalisation, it was a great shock to find himself transferred to 11th Camerons around June. Nevertheless, "I learned to like the kilt – it was very warm – It was said that the summer time was the best time to adopt a kilt – never in the colder months."[40]

When finally issued with the kilt, the new recruits would be introduced to the particular rules and customs for what went under it. These rules were, of course, inherited from existing practice in the Highland regiments, both regular and Territorial. Charlie Parke was an Old Contemptible, who served in 2nd Gordons at the First Battle of Ypres. He had joined the Regiment in 1909 at Aberdeen as a lad of 16. Recalling his service some 70 years later, he wrote: "strict regulations call for pants to be worn when tossing the caber and doing the Highland fling; at all other times – absolutely nothing!"[41] This general rule is more or less confirmed by Ian Hamilton, who served as a regimental officer with the Gordons in the closing years of the nineteenth century, and later commanded at Gallipoli. Fondly recalling his service as a regimental officer, he wrote that "we didn't wear drawers except at athletics or dancing on a platform."[42] Whatever exceptions were made, the general rule was evidently true also of the Black Watch. Peter Corstophine, from Edinburgh, joined that regiment in 1910, when they were based at the Curragh in Ireland. He was afterwards sent to the 2nd Battalion in India, which arrived in France in October, 1914. He recalls that on joining: "Ye got your first set of uniforms free. That wis, you would get a kilt, a red tunic, a white buff and khaki tunic, two pairs o' socks, two shirts", but "no underpants or anythin' like that. You weren't allowed to wear underpants at that time."[43] It is evident that the general convention in the Regular Army pre-war was for soldiers to wear nothing under the kilt, except when engaged in activities which risked indecent exposure to female spectators.

The same custom was followed in the Territorial Army, at least in 'U' Company of 4th Gordons, which Alexander Rule, a student at Aberdeen University, joined before the war.

> A sudden gust of wind, sweeping across the granite quadrangle of Marischal College, caught us just as our lanky colour-sergeant gave the command 'Company, 'shun.' Our kilts swirled, but we trusted to our sporrans and remained nobly at attention. That was away back in February, 1914. We had fallen-in for church parade, and that treacherous gust caused us some anxious moments, for there is a certain Spartan regulation governing underwear in Highland regiments. Facing us stood six feet odd of perfectly good colour-sergeant, who grinned wickedly at our discomfiture. Luckily it was Sunday and we were the quad's sole occupants.[44]

There is however some evidence that, in some Territorial battalions at least, the tradition was not strictly enforced before the War. Thus, after mobilisation, young Albert Strachan, already a Territorial pre-war, moved with 6th Gordons to Divisional HQ at Perth, where, "We began to get army drill and route marches. One thing we soon found out [was that] pants below the kilt were no good for marching and everybody soon dispensed with them." Clearly Albert and his

---

40 IWM 6926 Dennis, memoir, pp.258-259.
41 IWM Books Parke, memoirs, p.24.
42 Hamilton, General Sir Ian, *Listening for the Drums*, (London: Faber & Faber, 1944) p.42.
43 Quoted in Macdougall, Ian, *Voices from War* (Edinburgh: Mercat Press, 1995), p.4.
44 Rule, *Students under Arms*, p.1.

companions had been used to wearing them before. Nevertheless, after moving to Bedford, "It was a splendid Summer and we soon settled down, wearing the kilt like proper highlanders."[45]

In general, the custom of wearing nothing under the kilt was followed by wartime recruits. In some cases the rule was rigorously enforced. This was, for example, the case in 3rd Camerons, where "no officer or soldier wore an undergarment with the kilt, and indeed ever to do so was a punishable offence, which was enforced."[46] The rule was also enforced in a string of other battalions.[47] When, as a newly joined subaltern in the 8th Seaforths, a Service battalion, in 1915, D.W. Reid attended a map-reading course, "one day the Bite [the regular adjutant] called us together after we had been crawling about … & said he noted that some effeminate [?] young men appeared to wear [some] kind of knickers under their kilts. This is not done in the Seaforths!!"[48] Norman Collins, who enlisted with the Seaforths at Dingwall, recalled that, "We were told not to wear them when we first joined in Dingwall, and if you'd been caught with pants on, I'm afraid life would have been made unbearable by the other soldiers."[49] And James Roy, a subaltern in the Royal Garrison Artillery, describes a battle royal in the guard room at Broughty Ferry, when an English recruit to the Black Watch had his drawers, lovingly knitted by his fiancée to keep him warm, forcibly removed by the Scots corporal of the guard![50]

Otherwise there are numerous statements by Highland soldiers that it was the practice to wear nothing under the kilt, without stating that this was necessarily an enforced rule,[51] and this also applied to the South Africans[52] and Canadians. When Thomas Dinesen, a Dane, joined the Royal Highlanders of Canada in June 1917 in Montreal, "We were also given woollen pants, long heavy ones from which we had to cut off a whole yard in order that we could wear them beneath our kilts. However, we soon discovered that wearing pants beneath your kilts is considered a very serious breach of etiquette."[53] As Hal Kerridge, who served as a private soldier with both the London Scottish and 1st Gordons, put it; "If you wore anything under a kilt you'd have been issued with it. You didn't get that issued so you didn't wear anything."[54] Indeed, no lists of clothing found from 1914 provide for the issue of drawers to kilted soldiers on active service.[55] Nevertheless, a price list for officers' kit, issued by Miller & Smith, Naval & Military Tailors &

45   GHM. PB2984, Strachan, memoir.
46   IWM 430 Wimberley, memoir, Vol.1, p.21.
47   IWM 15990 Gunn, letter to pal, 16 April, 1915; THM S98-11, Brooke, memoir, p.62; IWM 10533 Reid, memoir; IWM 12043 Collins, interview, 1991; IWM 24879 Recording Fidler, John P., interview, 1975; NLS Acc.5415 Roy, James Stewart, typescript memoir, 'Recollections of an Intelligence Officer.'
48   IWM 10533 Reid, memoir.
49   IWM 12043 Collins, interview.
50   NLS Acc.5415 Roy, James Stewart, typescript memoir, 'Recollections of an Intelligence Officer,' p.13.
51   IWM 16455 Recording Hay, William, interview 1984; Walker, *Tom Walker Remembers*, p.5; IWM 18836 Kerridge, Hal, IWM interview, 1999; IWM 24855 Newton, interview; IWM 9756 Manton, interview; IWM 9833 Coates, interview; IWM 21092 McGregor, letters to wife Jen, 16 June, 20, 27 August, 1915, 1 February, 1916; Chambers, *Diaries of World War 1*, p.10.
52   LC GS 0132 Betteridge, memoir, p.7.
53   Dinesen, Thomas, V.C., *Merry Hell!*, (Uckfield: NMP reprint, n.d.), p.32.
54   IWM 18836 Kerridge, interview.
55   THM Seaforths 81-181 4th Batt. Seatorth Highlanders, Clothing etc, worn by the Soldiers; Addison-Smith, *10th Seaforth Highlanders*, pp.70-71; Craig-Brown, *Historical Records*, Vol.3, p.363; IWM 11637 PP Leppan, T.C.

Equipment Makers, of George Street, Edinburgh, includes for Highland regiments "Tartan kilt Drawers."[56] So there were some exceptions! In at least one case, the enforcement of the custom depended upon peer pressure rather than strict direction from above. Harry Strachan's elder brother Joe was a member of 7th Gordons, their local T.F. battalion, before the war. When war broke out, and Joe was called up, Harry joined up two days later.

> Joe, No.2 of our family, and his intimate friend were early on the job. They decided that pants under the kilt were not acceptable, so each arrival was inspected and pants of many kinds, including cut-down long johns, were just stripped off. By the end of the 3rd day all were gathered and a bonfire made it irrevocable. This set a tradition which held throughout the battalion and the war. Pants were 'am strengsten verboten,' – by all ranks.[57]

Englishmen joining Highland regiments might be particularly surprised by the custom. John Fidler was one of the potential members of the Manchester Scottish who were grabbed by 9th Royal Scots in November, 1914, and taken to Edinburgh.

> Then we were issued out with our kit, kilt and all the rest of it, and of course everybody from Manchester anyway, they said, 'Well what about pants for underneath the kilt?' you see. So the reply was, 'You only wear what the army issue you with,' you see, 'and they don't issue you with pants to go under a kilt.' So that settles that argument.[58]

Hal Kerridge observed with some amusement that many new recruits to the London Scottish in 1914 did not realise the custom when they first joined: "after all, we were Londoners, but I knew because I had an association with the Scots at home, but many of the new joiners, they hadn't a clue and they were horrified!"[59] As we have seen a significant number of Londoners also joined the 51st Highland Division to make up its numbers at Bedford.

> The Cockneys fell in love with the kilt at first sight, but when they wore it themselves, they found it fairly trying in cold and wet weather … Another Londoner was discovered wearing braces to hold his kilt up, while underneath he had a pair of civilian trousers, with three-quarters of the legs cut off. The funniest case of all was an English officer who wore a pair of ladies' combinations.[60]

Some soldiers did defy tradition. In some cases, indeed, observation of the rule may have been less than rigorous. When Frank Brooke, a recruit to the Seaforth Highlanders, was issued his kilt at Ripon in November, 1915, and complained about the draught, he was advised by a corporal of a few months service, "Send hame for a pair o' fitba pants an' cut the legs a wee bit shor-rter. Else ye can tuck yer shirt-lap atween yer legs an' fasten wi' a wee safety pin. Yer no'

---

56 BWA, Badenoch, R.E, papers.
57 LC GS 1549, Strachan, memoir.
58 IWM 24879 Fidler, interview.
59 IWM 18836 Kerridge, Interview.
60 GHM PB1892.3.18, McDonald, 'Uncle Harper's Duds,' p.3.

supposed tae wear onnything underneath – it's no' regimental!"[61] Thus some, but by no means all, of the soldiers in the battalion in England "wore football pants and cut down long 'uns."[62] In France, these were dispensed with. Peter MacGregor, who joined 14th Argylls in June, 1915, initially adopted the practice of pinning his shirt-tails between his legs. He soon gave this up and wore nothing, except that "I put on my pants when I go to London; climbing on top of buses." In February, 1916, when there was a snowstorm during a rehearsal for an inspection by the King, he finally gave in and wore underpants.[63] Ronald Wells, a Welshman, who served in 9th Royal Scots, stated when interviewed that under the kilt, "Nobody ever wore anything … There were a couple who wore tartan little pants. I never did."[64] By December, 1917, in a cold English winter at Bramshott, Thomas Dinesen of 42nd Battalion C.E.F. recorded that "most of us have forgone the Highlander tradition and wear thick pants in this cold winter weather."[65]

First impressions of wearing the kilt were varied. Some felt immediately at home in the kilt;[66] to others, at first the feeling was a little strange.[67] Norman Collins, who had joined the Seaforth Highlanders, wrote to his brother, Bolton, "Walking in a kilt at first is just like going to the office with nothing on but your boots, shirt and jacket on and a belt round the middle … Rather draughty as well"[68] "Exceptionally free and easy", wrote S. Bradbury, who joined 3/4th Camerons at Ripon in April, 1916.[69] Some found the kilt cold at first,[70] but others did not. "It is surprising how warm the kilt is," wrote Norman Collins,[71] and Jim Paterson, a Canadian Highlander, wrote, "I feel warmer with kilts than I do in pants with underdress on."[72] There might be a feeling of insecurity,[73] and there was inevitably some embarrassment.[74] "I felt that all of Ripon was gazing at my bare knees," wrote Frank Brooke;[75] "I felt positively indecent," wrote John Turing.[76] They also had to learn the basic lessons of decorum. As Private Jack Gunn, in 1/8th Argylls, wrote to a pal from Bedford, "You have to be careful, of course, if you are with ladies, how you sit down &c for obvious reasons, otherwise one might have to render first aid to a fainting and unspeakably shocked virgin!"[77] And newly commissioned John Turing was told off "for not sitting with my legs crossed!"[78]

61 IWM Books, Brooke, 'Wait for it,' pp.22-25.
62 THM S98-11, Brooke, 'A Yorkshire Kiltie' pp.6, 62.
63 IWM 21092 McGregor, letters to wife Jen, 16 June, 20, 27 August, 1915, 24 February. 1916.
64 IWM 9930 Wells, interview, 1987.
65 Dinesen, *Merry Hell*, p.71.
66 BWA Junks, memoir, 29 July, 1915; LC Several Fronts Recollections, Judd, H.C., Transcript of Tape 1545, Interview for Liddle Collection, 1997.
67 Chambers, *Diaries of World War 1*, p.10; Dinesen *Merry Hell*, p.31.
68 Collins, *Last Man Standing*, p.49.
69 IWM 2528 Bradbury, memoir, p.2.
70 GHM PB1892.3.18, McDonald, 'Uncle Harper's Duds,'p.3; IWM 2528 Bradbury, memoir, p.2; LC GS 1635 Turing, memoir.
71 Collins, *Last Man Standing*, p.45.
72 Stothers, Steven, *Somewhere in France: The Letters of John Cannon Stothers 1916-1919* (2005), p.54.
73 Lyon, *In Kilt and Khaki*, pp.35-36.
74 THM Seaforths 89-122 Paterson, memoir; IWM 233 McKechnie, memoir, p.7; IWM 430 Wimberley, memoir, Vol.1, p.19.
75 IWM Books, Brooke, 'Wait for it,' pp.22-25.
76 LC GS 1635 Turing, memoir.
77 IWM 15990 Gunn, letter to pal, 16 April, 1915.
78 LC GS 1635 Turing, memoir.

In the Service battalions,[79] a major issue was the attempt by government to introduce a kilt made of khaki material rather than regimental tartan. In some respects this was a sensible idea, for all the Highland regiments had, since the Boer War, adopted the rather ungainly khaki kilt cover to wear over the kilt to provide better concealment. The War Office action simply rationalised the situation, and eliminated the need for a cover. But it was widely resented in Scotland, where the War office was accused of "a deliberate attempt – on 'tactical grounds' as was officially averred – to abolish for ever the Highland tartans from the Army."

According to one account this universal kilt "was made of grey-brown cloth, pleated and sewn on to a waist-band of the same material like a girl's skirt. It incorporated all the disadvantages of a kilt without any of the advantages."[80] The Camerons' history claims that opposition was led by Cameron of Lochiel,[81] who, as we have seen, had personally raised four battalions of Cameron Highlanders for Lord Kitchener. While mobilising opinion in Scotland, he succeeded in obtaining a concession for his own battalions. It was not long before all the other regiments had been permitted to wear their own tartans too, and the attempt to impose a universal khaki kilt was dropped. Only, apparently in 7th Seaforths, did the C.O. prefer to keep the khaki kilts.[82] The

A Seaforth Highlander in a khaki kilt, probably from 7th Battalion, one of the few battalions to wear them. (Author's collection)

full story is probably more complex. Thus there is evidence of some serious discussion of khaki kilts amongst the papers of Brigadier General Ernest Craig-Brown, sometime wartime second-in-command and C.O. of 1st Camerons. An undated document, 'The Highland Soldier: as he is and as he might be' proposes for manoeuvre order (i.e. effectively active service) a khaki kilt, although "My idea is a khaki-tartan kilt rather than a plain drab one."[83]

79 I have seen no evidence to suggest that the W.O.'s intention extended beyond the New Army battalions.
80 Craig-Brown, *Historical Records*, Vol.4, p.275.
81 His role of course may be somewhat exaggerated in the Camerons history.
82 McEwen, *Fifth Camerons*, pp.17-19, which contains more detail of the controversy. See also Burns, *Once a Cameron Highlander*, p.32.
83 THM Camerons D242, Craig-Brown, Brig Gen E., papers, 'The Highland Soldier, as he is, & as he might be.'

The decision of C.O. 7th Seaforths to keep the khaki kilts may, in the circumstances, have taken some courage, but unfortunately we do not know his reasons. Nor do we know how long the practice lasted. A photograph of B Company, 7th Seaforths, taken before embarking for France in May, 1915, probably at Bordon Camp, shows the men all wearing khaki kilts except for the pipers and drummers who wear Seaforths (Mackenzie) tartan.[84] A studio photograph held by the author shows a Seaforth Highlander in khaki kilt, and he is probably from 7th Battalion. Douglas Gillespie, serving with the 2nd Argylls, observed on 23 September 1915 some Kitchener Army men in France in khaki kilts.[85] He does not specify which regiment or battalion, but this was probably 7th Seaforths in 9th Division. Finally, a photograph in the regimental history shows 7th Seaforths leaving the trenches during the Somme in 1916 clad now in Mackenzie tartan.[86]

The khaki kilts (probably the unused rejected surplus from the early war) do appear to have been reintroduced in the Graduated Battalions. Thus they were worn at home by 51st (Graduated) Battalion Gordon Highlanders, at least for part of their existence, as their history records "the issue of tartan kilts to replace the khaki" prior to their deployment to Germany in March 1919.[87] The situation was different in the 52nd (Graduated) Battalion Gordon Highlanders, which had been formed in October, 1917, from the 40th Training Reserve Battalion, itself formerly 8th Camerons. Their authorised dress was apparently a khaki kilt, reflecting the practice in the 51st Battalion. However,

> Thanks to the good fight put up by the Commanding Officer and the Quartermaster with the Ordnance Department, the unit up till March 1918 continued to wear the Cameron uniform instead of the authorised drab kilt, while all the officers, W.O.'s, N.C.O..'s, and staff belonged to the Cameron Highlanders.[88]

This practice apparently changed at that time, when the Cameron command cadre was largely re-deployed. It is not certain if the battalion then went into khaki kilts, like the 51st Battalion, or into Gordons kilts. In April, 1918, Coll Macdonald, chaplain to 8th Black Watch in France, noted the quartermaster "busy all day refitting men – giving new kilts to those who joined us on 9th April in Gordon and Khaki kilts and went into action on the 11th."[89] These were presumably drafts from the Gordons Graduated Battalions. Much earlier, in July, 1917, Private Douglas, an Argyll then attached to 4th Entrenching Battalion, noted "a large draft of Gordons wearing a khaki kilt that I did not particularly care for."[90] These men had possibly come from 38th Training Reserve Battalion, a precursor of 51st Gordons, which had apparently been wearing khaki kilts since the summer of 1916.[91]

---

84 THM Seaforths 81-36, photograph of B Coy, 7th Seaforths.
85 Gillespie, *Letters from Flanders*, p.309, letter, 23 September, 1915.
86 Fairrie, *Queen's Own Highlanders*, p.113.
87 *51st Battalion*, p.15.
88 Craig-Brown, *Historical Records*, p.384.
89 BWA Macdonald, Coll, letter to wife Mary, 29 April, 1918.
90 IWM 4586 Douglas, p.36.
91 Wauchope, *Black Watch*, Vol.3, pp.269-277.

Khaki kilts are recorded in at least two other battalions. 10th Black Watch were issued with khaki kilts and leather sporrans early in the New Year of 1915[92], and a photograph reproduced in the Aberdeen *Press and Journal* shows a picture of Lieutenant Patrick Wright Anderson, who served in that battalion, taken in 1915, before deployment to France, wearing khaki kilt and leather sporran[93]. It is not known when the khaki kilts were replaced by tartan, but a photo of the battalion in Salonika in 1916, shows them clearly wearing tartan kilts with khaki aprons.[94] 2/6th Argylls also wore the khaki kilt. According to their C.O.:

> Owing to the fact that tartan could not be obtained for love or money, we instituted the khaki kilt, and this made a very neat and workmanlike garb, and was quite popular with the men, as it did away with the necessity for wearing a kilt apron. The unit retained the khaki kilt until its dispersal in 1918, and had the distinction of being one of only two units of the British Army so clothed.[95]

Khaki kilts were also worn by some Canadian units. When in February, 1915, the Royal Highlanders of Canada, who had already supplied the C.E.F. with one battalion, the 13th, began to raise a second, the 42nd,

> The reserve supply of kilts and other parts of the Highland uniform from the regimental stores had been exhausted in equipping the 13th Battalion. Kilt cloth of The Black Watch tartan could not be obtained … Therefore … to save carrying an apron as an extra article and at the same time with a view to retaining regimental sentiment, a khaki kilt of cloth similar to The Black Watch tartan, with regimental colours, red, blue and green, woven in the pattern of a large check was adopted.[96]

Thus, when Thomas Dinesen joined the Royal Highlanders of Canada on 26 June 1917 in Montreal, he was issued with a khaki kilt, presumably of this pattern. This was not replaced until about February 1918, during training at Bramshott, when he writes, "We have now discarded our ugly khaki skirt for real fine, blue-and-green Black Watch kilts – maybe as a sign that we are now real soldiers and no longer raw recruits!"[97] David McMillan served in the 43rd Battalion C.E.F. (Cameron Highlanders of Canada). He notes that when the battalion disembarked in France in February, 1916, "At the time we wore a khaki coloured kilt which the troops called 'the sandbag' tartan. Later, we wore the Cameron kilt."[98] On 28 April, 1915, the 15th Battalion C.E.F. (48th Highlanders of Canada) received a draft from England wearing khaki kilts.[99]

Khaki kilts were also at the heart of a controversy concerning the identity of 16th Battalion C.E.F. (The Canadian Scottish), which, as we have seen, was formed by amalgamating

---

92 Wauchope, *Black Watch*, Vol.3, p.206.
93 LC AIR 213A Miscellaneous, Item A8, Anderson, P.W., photograph.
94 Wauchope, *Black Watch*, Vol.3, opposite p.218.
95 Craig Barr, *Home Service*, p.32. See also: Maclean, *On Active Service*, Vol.1, p.10.
96 Topp, *42nd Battalion*, p.8.
97 Dinesen, *Merry Hell*, pp. 32, 91.
98 McMillan, *Trench Tea and Sandbags*, p.9.
99 Beattie, *48th Highlanders of Canada 1891-1928*, p.82.

contingents of four different Highland Militia regiments. Initially, at Valcartier Camp in Quebec, each contingent was allowed to wear its own tartan, but in December, 1914, in England, the decision was taken, against some opposition, to adopt a khaki kilt, despite the protest of one MacLure that "he had lived in the Gordon tartan and would die in it." Unless the gallant MacLure was a former Gordon Highlander in the British Army, his protest was somewhat ludicrous – the Canadian Gordons had only been formed in 1913! When, however, the promised khaki kilts arrived in France in June, 1915, they excited so much disgust from the men, that the project was abandoned. Diversity prevailed, and only in 1917 was agreement finally reached to wear the Mackenzie tartan.[100]

For much of their training, recruits did not wear the kilt, but wore trousers instead. Although these were simply ordinary khaki service dress trousers, they were often stubbornly referred to as trews in the Highland regiments, a deliberate verbal distinction to maintain their uniqueness. Trousers were normally worn for drill, fatigues and musketry; kilts for church parades, guards, route marches, and for walking out, when wearing the kilt was generally mandatory.[101] When drafts were designated for overseas service, they had their active service kit made up to current standards, usually ten days or two weeks before departure. In some cases this meant discarding diced hose-tops, spats and glengarries and being issued with khaki hose-tops, puttees, kilt cover and a balmoral or tam o' shanter. Trousers were not taken overseas on active service and were handed in. Recruits normally wore only their field service uniforms after being allocated to a draft.[102] On one occasion at least, in 1918, when there was a need to rush new recruits to the front, there was not time to issue the proper uniform to the draft. George Stables was in this draft which joined 1/6th Gordons on 8th April, 1918 and went into action next day. There were 61 soldiers in the draft and they were called the 'trouser draft' as they hadn't time to give them kilts.[103]

Above all, despite Spartan regulations, embarrassment and cold, from the day it was issued, the kilt was a source of great pride.[104] When, eventually, 6th Camerons were issued with kilts,

---

100 Urquhart, *Canadian Scottish*, pp.16-17.
101 LC GS 0434, Dawson, Robert, diary 21 Oct 1914; GHM PB1639, Kemp, memoir, p.7; IWM Books, Cooper, *Domi Militaeque*, p.22; IWM 14340 McArthur, diary, 13 January, 11 February, 1915; IWM 8192 Lawson, undated letter to mother; IWM 4586 Douglas, memoir, pp.10,12,18, 258, 292; IWM 10414 McGregor, interview; IWM Books Brooke, 'Wait for it,' p.9; THM S98-11, Brooke, memoir, p.62; THM Seaforths 89-26 Crask, letter to parents, probably 29 April, 1915; IWM 16335 Racine, memoir, p.15; Cluness, Alex (ed), *Doing his bit. A Shetland Soldier in the Great War* (Lerwick: Shetland Times, 1999), p.14; LC DF148 Recollections, Samson; IWM 7593 Harper, memoir, p.20; IWM 12678 Kerridge, Hal, Transcription of interview, 1998; IWM 21092 McGregor, letters to wife Jen, 25 August, 3 December, 1915; IWM 2528 Bradbury, memoir, p.2.
102 GHM PB1699, 'As we go up the line to death,' p.44, extract from diary of John Forbes Knowles; LC GS 0434, Dawson, diary 9 February 1915; *11th Gordon Highlanders*, pp.11-12; IWM 4474 PP Johnston, Lt Col R.W.F., typescript memoir, 'Experiences in the Great War of 1914-1918,' written 1983, p.2; IWM Books, Cooper, *Domi Militaeque*, pp.64, 67; Ireland, Lockhart Landels, *Pte John Maclean of the Black Watch and other Stories*, (Kirkcaldy: The Fifeshire Advertiser, 1917), p.17; IWM Books Brooke, 'Wait for It,' p.31; GHM PB3279 Matthews, diary; Cluness, *Doing his bit*, p.14.
103 LC GS 1516 Stables, letter, 5 February, 1979.
104 Apart from sources cited, see: ASHM N-E1 Pringle, 2Lt William B., letter to 'my dear Pilling', 11 August, 1916; IWM 5821 PP Semple. M., letter from Pte Jock McLeod, 8 July, 1915; THM Seaforths 87-141 Heriz-Smith, Mrs, loc. cit.

156 Those Bloody Kilts

Trousers worn in training by Gordon Highlander Kitchener recruits. They are wearing non-regimental Glengarries. (Author's collection)

it "made us feel that we had not lived in vain. With what relief did we hand in that hated emergency clothing. It is true that the kilts were only to be worn on State occasions, but that troubled us not. We could now 'walk out' with the best of them, and mere Lowland regiments were made to feel that they had not a look in."[105] When John Cooper was first issued with his Black Watch kilt, "pride would not allow me to take off the uniform."[106] "Wait till you see me in my kilt!" wrote newly commissioned Argyll, William Ferrie, to his brother.[107] In June, 1915, after he was issued with his kilt in 14th Argylls, Peter McGregor wrote to his wife, "My kilt is very beautiful … I am a real Tommy now … I wish I could show you myself in my full uniform, kilt and all."[108] "I have never forgotten the thrill of wearing the kilt for the first time," wrote Cecil Harper, newly commissioned into 10th Gordons, "when four or five of us raw young subalterns set out across the heather, one late afternoon."[109]

The kilt was, indeed, such a source of pride that at least two American Medical Officers attached to Highland battalions desired to wear it. One at least succeeded. "He was as proud as Punch, but he created a great deal of amusement. The kilt would not sit properly on him. His hind quarters could not make it wiggle waggle. It was no use, the kilt would soon have

---

105 *Souvenir Booklet 6th Cameron Highlanders*, pp.16-17.
106 IWM Books, Cooper, *Domi Militaeque*, p.9.
107 IWM 12643 Ferrie, letter to brother Allan, 21 September, 1915, to mother, 20 February, 1916.
108 IWM 21092 McGregor, letter to wife Jen, 16,22 June, 1915.
109 IWM 7593 Harper, memoir, p.10.

been down on his knees, but for the use of braces."[110] Soldiers transferred from other regiments had mixed feelings. When young Cecil Hodges was transferred from the Royal Scots Fusiliers to the Gordons around February 1918, he looked forward eagerly to receiving his kilt: "I am itching to get one on."[111] Others might have severe reservations. The 3rd Scottish Provisional Battalion was a kilted battalion (later forming the 16th Bn Argylls), and when men were drafted to it not only from English regiments, but also from the Guards, the cavalry and the artillery, a great many of them "heartily detested" the kilt.[112]

Pride required that many new recruits rush to have their photograph taken, to send home to their loved ones, as soon as they had received their kilts.[113] They looked forward to swanking on leave.[114] They took pride in their appearance as a kilted corps. Private Douglas enjoyed a church parade with his training battalion at Ripon in February, 1918, where he had returned after being hospitalised from France. "The sight of the long column of kilted troops when on the march always gave me a great feeling of pride."[115] They wallowed in the public adulation. After a route march in England with 14th Argylls, Peter McGregor felt, "Nothing like the kilties ... What excitement when we go through villages. All the folks come out. Windows fill with heads. It's queer. You feel bucked and strut like a farm-yard cock."[116]

Mandatory studio photo of a young Seaforth Highlander in kilt while training. This photo was taken at Ripon, where the T.F. training battalions were based. He is wearing boots and puttees, as issued from 1915 onwards. How old is he? (Author's collection)

The kilt marked out the Highland soldier as distinct from mere trousered soldiers. The Highlanders knew it, felt it and revelled in it. Norman Collins, training with 3/4th Seaforths in November, 1915, noticed how "The English soldiers here don't show up very well against

---

110 GHM PB1892.3.18, McDonald, 'Uncle Harper's Duds,' p.108. See also IWM 3834 Wrench, diary, 30 September, 1918.
111 IWM 2483 PP Franklin, H.L., letter from Pte Cecil Geoffrey Hodges, 23 February 1918.
112 Craig Barr, *Home Service*, p.215.
113 Stothers, Steven, *Somewhere in France*, pp.33, 34, 36, 43, 45 46. See also. Collins, *Last Man Standing*, pp.38, 41, 44, 45, 49; IWM 12043 Collins, interview; IWM 14321 Small, letters to Ethel Shaw, postmarks 7 and 28 March, 1915; IWM 21092 McGregor, letters to wife Jen, 16, 22 June, to sister Nell, 2 July, 1915.
114 THM Camerons 87-44 Hunter, Peter, letter to sister Polly, 24 September, 1914. See also: Fetherstonhaugh, *13th Battalion*, p.82.
115 IWM 4586 Douglas, memoir, p.270. See also THM Seaforths 89-26 Crask, letter to father, 21 June, 1915.
116 IWM 21092 McGregor, letter to wife Jen, 30 January, 1916. See also Rule, *Students under Arms*, p.18.

the kilties."[117] John Cooper, in the Black Watch, felt that, "It is certain that highlanders always looked smarter than other troops out of the line."[118] When William Kemp received his Military Cross from the king at Aldershot in June, 1918, "as I was one of the only two recipients in kilts you can understand I got a considerable cheer which made me feel very proud of my mother country – Bonnie Scotland.[119] In June, 1916, Phil Paul, with 11th Black Watch at Dunfermline, wrote about a friend winning a commission in an English regiment.

> Yes, Jubb now boasts a sword belt and is in the 3/5 Manchesters. Of course he can't aspire to the swagger glory of a kilt & sporran but we from our exalted position of assistant adjutant 11th Battalion Royal Highlanders will be graciously pleased & condescendingly wish him luck & good hunting.[120]

Hal Kerridge, who served both in the London Scottish and in 1st Battalion Gordon Highlanders, stressed the importance to identity of this difference. "I suppose that is one of the attractions of the kilt. It's different from anybody else. You see whatever other regiments you joined you either wore britches or you wore trousers. We were the odd crowd that wore a kilt and it was different. It was attractive, no doubt about that. It was attractive."[121]

They also took pride in their regimental tartan. "The Gordon tartan is undoubtedly one of the prettiest going," wrote young Cecil Hodges.[122] "The Seaforth uniform beats the rest easily," wrote Norman Collins.[123] "Ever seen the Cameron kilt, Meg? It is admitted to be the finest in the Army," thought Jock McLeod,[124] while Ian Andrew asked himself, "Am I hopelessly prejudiced or is it true that the Cameron tartan with its prevailing warm red and blue tones and its distinguishing yellow stripe is quite the most attractive of all the regimental tartans?"[125] Even the London Scottish could take pride in their uniquely drab grey kilts. "Oh, we were very proud," said Stewart Jordan, "we had a regimental song, 'Way, way, for the Hodden Grey.'"[126] In this way the kilt reinforced identity, not just as a Highlander, but as a member of a specific regiment, and the resistance to universal khaki kilts we have described above becomes perfectly understandable.

When Highland soldiers transferred to other corps, they generally felt some regret at parting with the kilt. When Norman Beaton transferred to the Machine Gun Corps from the Gordon Highlanders about April, 1917, "We had to turn in all our highland uniforms and say 'Au revoir' to our kilts and glengarrys, which I was sorry to part with."[127] Lieutenant William Ferrie, however, was pleased with his move from the Argylls to the same Corps in February, 1916, and

---

117 Collins, *Last Man Standing*, p.65.
118 IWM Books, Cooper, *Domi Militaeque*, p.90.
119 GHM PB1639, Kemp, memoir, Vol.2, p.36.
120 BWA Paul, letter to May Merritt, 29 June, 1916. See also: *9th Royal Scots*, p.36.
121 IWM 18836 Kerridge, interview.
122 IWM 2483 Franklin, letter from Pte Cecil Geoffrey Hodges, 23 February 1918.
123 Collins, *Last Man Standing*, p.64.
124 IWM 5821 Semple, letter from Pte Jock McLeod, 8 July, 1915.
125 LC, WF Recollections, A9, Andrew, memoir.
126 IWM 10391 Jordan, interview.
127 GHM Beaton, memoir, p.195.

felt the "change of uniform is rather a pity."[128] Perhaps most upset was Ian Mackay in 1/4th Camerons, who complained after achieving his captaincy: "One disadvantage that promotion has brought with it is that to my grief I have practically had to discard the kilt. I wear it whenever I can but I am more often than not now in breeks. Until after this spell I had never been in trenches in breeks since we came out."[129] Highlanders might also wish to cling on to their kilts after demobilisation. Colour Sergeant Alick Guthrie was a long serving Territorial in 6th Black Watch, who had served in its predecessor, 4th Volunteer Battalion Royal Highlanders, before the formation of the Territorial Force in 1908. In March, 1916, he obtained his discharge as a time-expired Territorial. He was so proud of his uniform that he requested and obtained from his C.O. the privilege of wearing it after his retirement; "the only one granted in our Bn since mobilisation."[130] Private Douglas in 8th Black Watch was less fortunate. When he was finally demobilised in April, 1919, he retained his kilt and bonnet. "The kilt was a bit of a problem. I did not wish to give it away, but eventually mother gave it to a 'Ragwoman,'… and in exchange got some rather nice cups and saucers."[131]

Highlanders might also resist any attempt to buy or rob them of their kilts when taken prisoner. Although some were prepared to part with their kilts in exchange for trousers, money or bread,[132] others were more resolute.[133] Lieutenant Dudley Stewart-Smith, in 1st Black Watch, was wounded in the defence of Givenchy on 18 April, 1918, and taken prisoner. He was fiercely proud of his kilt. In the German hospital, there was a young soldier from the Seaforths. "Being hard up, he sold his kilt to a German. The cloth of which a kilt is made is very precious in Germany just now and I had several good offers for mine. However, I regarded the sale of any kilt to a German as a direct insult to a man's regiment. To me it would be like parting with my most treasured possession." When he was sent to a prison camp, "The tailor had the temerity to offer me 10 marks for my kilt, which drew a brief but emphatic refusal."[134] They were also ready to resist mockery by their captors. William Hay, in 1/9th Royal Scots, was taken prisoner on 22 March, 1918 at St Quentin. The prisoners stopped for their escort to have something to eat.

> We sat down by the side of a road … So up on the other side of the road came a column of Germans going up to action, going marching up into the line, and they stopped right opposite us and one came over and tried to lift my kilt to see what you wear under your kilt you see, and I gave him a kick in the shins. He hopped around holding his leg, so the others, instead of being set on by them, they started ridiculing him as he was obviously one of these cheeky devils, you see. They didn't like him, I don't think.[135]

128 IWM 12643 PP Ferrie, Capt. W.S., letter to mother, 20 February, 1916.
129 THM Camerons 91 7 Mackay, letter to mother, 2 December, 1915.
130 BWA Guthrie, letters to his wife Crissie, 3/4, 11 March, 1916.
131 IWM 4586 Douglas, memoir, p.1473.
132 IWM 9885 PP Horsburgh, W, diary.
133 GHM PB1755 Young, Andrew, 'Memoirs of Captivity', printed in Largs & Millport Weekly News, June-August, 1929
134 Stewart-Smith, Dudley Cautley, *The Diaries of Lieutenant Dudley Cautley Stewart-Smith, 1918*, (Taunton: Blue Guides Ltd., 2009), pp.22, 25, 49.
135 IWM 16455 Hay, interview.

As the war progressed, quite apart from the problems of its practicality, which we shall examine in the next chapters, there was some disillusionment with the glamour of the kilt. Willie Macmillan had joined the Seaforth Highlanders by November, 1914. In January, 1916, he wrote: "Alec [his brother] seems to give all the details of his soldier life. He seems very proud of his kilt. For me the kilt has lost its glamour long ago. So in fact has war and everything connected with it."[136] When Frank Brooke arrived home on leave from 1/4th Seaforths, at Christmas, 1917, he had no time for the adulation. "I immediately discarded my uniform and assumed 'civvies' – strictly against regulations, of course," to the intense disappointment of his hero-worshipping boy-cousin.[137]

Enough evidence of pride in the kilt has surely now been presented,[138] however, to establish beyond any doubt that the kilt, through its uniqueness, its iconic Scottish status and its historical associations, did much to raise esprit de corps and stimulate morale. Douglas Wimberley, in a paper on the kilt, produced to support a B.B.C. programme 'Ladies from Hell,' broadcast in 1980, felt that pride in the kilt was a crucial factor in the morale of the Highland regiments: "The morale of the Highland Bns became such that all ranks became intensely proud of their very distinctive dress, and also of their consequent World War 1 name, given them by the Germans as 'The Ladies from Hell.'"[139] His fellow defender of the kilt, Norman Macleod, put the advantage very simply. "With reference to morale, I believe that the association of the kilt with the great deeds of valour on the part of the Highland Regiments inspires their members. I know of no inspiration to be got from trousers."[140] Thomas Dinesen notes how, in the Royal Highlanders of Canada, in August, 1917, the kilt could transform the appearance and demeanour of slovenly new recruits,[141] and Major Norman McQueen, writing after the event in 1931, was in no doubt about the significance of the day when the kilt was eventually issued to 10th Argylls at Aldershot.

> That day the Battalion found itself – previously a more or less disorganised body of men, that day it took a hold of itself and became in very truth "Her Royal Highness Princess Louise's 10th Argyll and Sutherland Highlanders", and never forgot the fact during the whole of its existence. In other words, it became conscious of the existence of 'esprit de corps', the very essence of the soul of a Regimental Body.[142]

Practicality

Several sources, including, unsurprisingly, Norman Macleod, claim that the kilt was superior to trousers for marching, apparently due to the extra freedom given by the kilt.[143]

---

136 IWM 3460 Macmillan, letter from his brother William to his mother, 30 January, 1916.
137 IWM Books Brooke, 'Wait for it,' p.285.
138 In addition to references cited, see also: LC, WF Recollections, A9, Andrew, memoir; LC GS 0132 Betteridge, memoir, p.7; THM Camerons 89-17 McFarlane, memoir.
139 IWM 430 Wimberley, 'The Kilt in Modern War', unpublished paper, written 1979.
140 Macleod in Mackay *Romantic Story*.
141 Dinesen, *Merry Hell*, pp.45-6.
142 Sotheby, *10th Argylls*, p.xix.
143 Macleod in Mackay, *Romantic Story*; Lyon, *In Kilt and Khaki*, pp.35-36; LC GS 1635 Turing, memoir.

The Highland regiments also marched normally at a pace attuned to marching in a kilt, slightly slower than that of the bulk of the British infantry. According to Hal Kerridge, who served in both the London Scottish and 1st Gordons, this gave the kilted troops the advantage in endurance.[144] Whether or not this assertion is correct, the difference of pace is said to have caused problems when kilted troops were obliged to march in column with others, for it was difficult for them to march at the 'normal' regulation pace.[145] The kilt could also be less than ideal for marching on a really hot day, causing soldiers to sweat profusely.[146] We will return to this question when we consider the practicality of the kilt at war.

Brambles, gorse, thistles, nettles, thorny hedges and even heather could all prove troublesome to kilted soldiers on exercise.[147] Albert Strachan remembers brigade exercises with 6th Gordons near Bedford in 1914: "There was no fencing in Bedfordshire, all hedges laden with fruit ... You can realise we were more interested in eating the berries than in the supposed battle in which we were taking part. It was not as fine however when the order came to get over the hedge in the kilt minus pants and no opening."[148] Private Peter McGregor, in 14th Argylls complained that, advancing over ploughed fields, through whins and bracken, on a field exercise near Hindhead in January, 1916, his legs were covered with scratches and blood.[149] "You ought to hear the language when the thorns go into the boys' bare knees, wrote Gordon Crask, then a corporal in 3/4th Seaforths, from Fort George in July, 1915."[150] Jock McLeod recorded how, while training with 3rd Camerons near Invergordon in August, 1915, "I tore my knees badly… in dashing thro' the long heather & not turning my hose up first! Hadn't time tho', worse luck!"[151] His statement implies that turning up hose tops may have been a common response to this problem.

As we shall see in another chapter, barbed wire was a genuine problem for kilted soldiers, and this could affect them even while training in the United Kingdom. Jock McLeod was injured on barbed wire while training with 3rd Camerons around March, 1915, and the wound was still giving trouble six months later.[152] Thomas Dinesen of the Royal Highlanders of Canada notes how, while practising putting up barbed wire entanglements at Bramshott in February, 1918, he and his companions "flayed the skin off out hands and knees so that we have to run to the doctor every now and then to have them iodined."[153]

Recruits got a first taste of real cold with the kilt in the British winter.[154] Much worse was to come in the trenches. Phil Paul, a subaltern with 11th Black Watch in training at Catterick in November, 1915, wrote to his sweetheart, May: "Generally the kilt is a rare garment for winter

---

144 IWM 18836 Kerridge, interview. See also: IWM 10786 Hood, interview.
145 IWM Hood, interview; LC Several Fronts Recollections, Judd, interview.
146 IWM 3460 Macmillan, letter from his brother Alex to his mother 18 May 1916.
147 Apart from sources cited below, see: IWM 8192 Lawson, undated letter to his sister Bessie; IWM 10786 Hood interview; Fraser, *Doctor Jimmy*, p.50; GHM PB2021, Stewart, letter to wife, 4 May 1915; Rule, *Students under Arms*, pp.29-30.
148 GHM, PB2984, Strachan, memoir.
149 IWM 21092 McGregor, letter to wife Jen, 16 January, 1916.
150 THM Seaforths 89-26 Crask, letter to mother, 20 July. 1915.
151 IWM 5821 Semple, letter from Pte Jock McLeod, 15 August, 1915.
152 IWM 5821 Semple, letters from Pte Jock McLeod, 29 August, 9 September, 1915.
153 Dinesen, *Merry Hell*, p.88.
154 Apart from sources cited below, see: GHM PB2183, Watson, memoir, p.4; Rule, *Students under Arms*, p.18; IWM 21092 McGregor, letters to wife Jen, 28 November, 1915, 9, 16 January, 23 March, 1916.

on the Yorkshire moors … My knees are a delicate shade of blue but are gradually resuming their normal colour under the influence of the stove which is the centre of life in our hut."[155] Private Anderson, in 2/9th Royal Scots, wrote that at the end of November, 1914, some of the men were suffering from frost-bitten knees after lying on the frozen ground for a long stretch on night manoeuvres, and a year later, in the winter of 1915/16, now at Selkirk, he wrote that even those who should have been well hardened were suffering from badly frosted knees.[156] At Lord Kitchener's infamous inspection at Frensham Common on 22 February 1915 in atrocious weather, "Feet were frozen; kilts, black and heavy with water, dripped icily down blue knees; even the hardiest shivered audibly under the blasts of an Arctic wind."[157]

One activity not recommended while wearing a kilt was riding a horse. The 'mot juste' on this activity was provided by Ian Hamilton, who, as a young lieutenant in the Gordons was obliged to ride kilted to church parade at Mooltan in 1874. As he explained, "you were apt to get the skin of your thighs pinched between the stirrup leathers and the saddle, and anyway it was not very comfortable – I mean bare-back is all very well when applied to the pony, but not to one's own backside."[158] In 1914-18, Highland officers who found themselves a mount behind the lines without having packed their riding trews or britches might find themselves in the same position. Even rankers might find themselves obliged to ride. This was far from comfortable, and riders could suffer from skinned legs.[159] At least the spectacle amused the local inhabitants.[160] Equally amusing no doubt were the exhibition of bare-back riding in kilts arranged by William Kemp in June, 1917, for the children and girls of the village of Fillievres,[161] and the gymkhanas held at intervals behind the lines, featuring "occasional bare-back mule racing for Hindu R.A. drivers and ditto for jocks in kilts!"[162]

Similar awkwardness attended riding a bicycle in a kilt. Generally, runners or despatch riders, who had to ride bicycles routinely, wore trousers instead of the kilt. But any officer or soldier might find himself riding a bicycle behind the lines from time to time.[163] "People here stare at a kiltie riding a bike," wrote Norman Collins after riding a bicycle in the country near Sutton

---

155 BWA Paul, letter to May Merritt, 12 November, 1915.
156 IWM 3608 Anderson, memoir.
157 McEwen, *Fifth Camerons*, pp.21-22. See also: Burns, *Once a Cameron Highlander*, p.34.
158 Hamilton, *Listening for the Drums*, p.42.
159 1026 Maclean, diary, p.18; ASHM N-E10 Gairdner, Charles Dalrymple, letter to mother, 15 September, 1918; LC Several Fronts Recollections, Kingsley, memoir; THM Seaforths 05-87 Hope, diary, 6 June, 1915; LC GS 1761 Wilson, memoir, p.17; IWM 11739 Sangster, letter home, 7 July 1915; IWM 6702 Low, letter to wife Noanie, 4 July, 1915; Burns, *Once a Cameron Highlander*, p.75; GHM PB2788/1 Emslie, H, diary, 12 March, 1918; IWM 11126 Liddell, Capt J.A., VC, diary, 28 September, 1914; IWM 430 Wimberley, memoir, Vol.1, p.35; Davies, Hugh, *The Compassionate War*, (London: Abbotsbury Publications, 1980), pp.24-25; O'Kiely, *Gentleman air Ace*, p. 55; GHM PB2183, Watson, memoir, p.8; LC GS 1027 Macleod, letter to sisters Betty and Molly, 27 May, 1915; IWM 4586 Douglas, memoir, p.1102.
160 LC GS 1203 Oldham, diary, 3 April, 1916; NLS MS 20655 Haldane, J.B.S., letter home, 20 February, 1915.
161 GHM PB1639, Kemp, memoir, p.88.
162 Rorie, Col David, *A Medico's Luck in the War* (Uckfield, NMP reprint, n.d.), p.183; *George Hugh Freeland Bartholomew, 8th June 1896 – 2nd Oct. 1917*, (privately published, n.d.), p.40.
163 LC GS 1507 Sotheby, letter to Elaine, 19 August, 1915; BWA Quekett, memoir, p.13; IWM Books, Cooper, *Domi Militaeque*, pp.148, 149; LC GS 1422 Sanders, 2Lt Spence, diary, 31 January, 1915; GHM. PB2984, Strachan, memoir; IWM 20453 Pring, interview.

Riding a horse in a kilt was not recommended for comfort. (Author's collection)

Coldfield.[164] A soldier of the London Scottish, sent off on a bicycle to find the field cashier behind the lines in France in April, 1915, noted that "the populace took the fact that [he] was riding a bike in a kilt very quietly, with the exception of the infants, who either laughed, expectorated, or threw bricks."[165]

Sports – football, athletics, highland games – were often played in the kilt both in training and behind the lines.[166] While this sometimes provided an amusing spectacle, the kilt was rather too heavy to play football in, and so, while adding to the amusement, it rather detracted from the quality of play. This may explain why, when, in July, 1916, the South African Scottish played a game of football with some French gunners. "the Scotties wore no kilts. It was perhaps as well that there were no females within several miles of the valley."[167]

---

164 Collins, *Last Man Standing*, p.80.
165 cited in Lloyd, *London Scottish*, p.52.
166 IWM 4586 Douglas, memoir, pp.870, 1393; LC GS 0177 Boyle, A.R., diary, 7 August, 1915; LC GS 1026 Maclean, diary, p.12; IWM 16335 Racine, memoir, p.9; THM Camerons 94-8 Mackay, 'Tell Them of Us,' letter from Ian Mackay to mother, 4 April, 1915; GHM PB1639, Kemp, memoir, p.53.
167 LC GS 0132 Betteridge, memoir, Vol 2, extract from an article by him, 'Twenty Years Have Passed', in *The Salstaff Bulletin*, July, 1936, p.79.

Decorum

Quite apart from the ever-present danger of accidental exposure,[168] there were certain rules of etiquette which it was necessary to observe when wearing a kilt in the customary manner. One of these related to sitting or lying down. Newly commissioned Hugh Davies found it a challenge to sit down gracefully at picnics organised by the local girls at Tain.[169] Thomas Dinesen, newly enlisted in the Royal Highlanders of Canada, records that in Montreal on 2nd July 1917, Dominion Day, after taking part in a big parade in the park, the men caused outrage amongst the local citizenry, by not taking sufficient care in gathering their kilts round their knees when throwing themselves down on the sides of a ditch after parade. As a result, they were all confined to barracks.[170]

Care had to be exercised when clambering on and off vehicles.[171] There appears to have been at least some element of truth too in the old tale about Highland soldiers not being permitted to ride on the top deck of trams. William Newton, who served with the Gordons in 1914-15, stated definitely that, "we weren't supposed to go on top of a tram because you could look up and see everything. You weren't allowed. If you did, you had to pull your kilt in."[172] And when R.V. Dennis was issued with his kilt on transferring to the 11th Camerons about June, 1918, he received "a friendly warning from the Q.M. not to go upstairs on the buses when I went home."[173] In London on leave in November 1916, Robert Burns of 7th Camerons recalls, "We did a lot of sight-seeing, but so did others – especially when we climbed the rear winding exterior steps of an open-decked bus. We wondered why so many people were peeping up at us!"[174]

Drill and sports provided opportunities for unintended display. Thomas Lyon, training in the ranks of the Glasgow Highlanders, recalls being drilled by the Regimental Sergeant-Major., "'About turn!' he shouted, and dutifully we 'abouted' – 'Halt!' – We froze to the grass. – 'Heaven help you chaps', said the S.M. then, 'when you get your kilts. They'll be round your necks every time you do an 'about turn', and the whole battalion will be arrested for indecency.'"[175] The Sergeant Major's concerns were not idle. Even in Perth, whose good citizens were surely used to having the Black Watch in their midst, the Territorials of the 6th Gordons "had to wear trousers when drilling in the town as objections were being raised."[176]

Hal Kerridge recalls physical training with the London Scottish,

> We had all this business of physical training, you know all this 'knees bend'… and remember we were a kilted regiment and of course being youngsters we all went down to a full bend and we all started wobbling about and all that sort of thing. And one of the instructors said,

---

168 THM S98-11, Brooke, memoir, pp.5-6; IWM 3834 Wrench, diary, 13 February, 1919; IWM 12007 Wilson, memoir, p.34; Warwick, George W., *We Band of Brothers* (Cape Town: Howard Timmins, 1962), pp.50, 52.
169 Davies, Hugh, *The Compassionate War*, p.11.
170 Dinesen, *Merry Hell*, p.35. See also: McMillan, *Trench Tea and Sandbags*, p.24.
171 Burns, *Once a Cameron Highlander*, p.119; IWM 6926 Dennis, memoir, pp.282-283.
172 IWM 24855 Newton, interview.
173 IWM 6926 Dennis, memoir, p.259.
174 Burns, *Once a Cameron Highlander*, p.120.
175 Lyon, *In Kilt and Khaki*, pp.33-34.
176 GHM. PB2924, Strachan, memoir.

'throw yourself back again and roll it out. Cor blimey', he said, 'you look like a lot of old women pissing!' Now along the road were all these nurses with a lot of kids, of course in those days the nurses with children would take them out for an afternoon with the prams. I've never seen so many nurses disappear so fast in all my life!'[177]

In May, 1917, 1/4th Seaforths held sports at the village of Maizieres, where they were billeted.

> At the sports two of the village maidens were given chairs in a position of honour but, as it proved, much too close to the event where two kilted and therefore untrousered warriors were astride a pole and trying to upset the balance of each other in a pillow fight. As Mademoiselle exclaimed when the position of one man was suddenly inverted shocking!'[178]

Finally, At the 3rd Camerons Battalion Games at Invergordon in summer, 1915, Douglas Wimberley was visited by his cousin, Colin Campbell of Kilmartin, with some of his young female Hay cousins from Edinburgh, accompanied, as chaperone, by their mutual great aunt, Miss Ella Campbell. When the inter-company tug-of war exposed too much bare flesh to view,

> I shall never forget Aunt Ella that day, and the dignified unselfconscious action this Victorian lady took … She at once quietly stood up from out her chair, and turned her back on the whole display, and at the same time firmly told her young ladies with her to do the same, and admire the view of the hills. No more was said, no comment made by any of us; thus did this Victorian deal with what she considered might have been an immodest situation for the girls, in her charge, to undergo.[179]

To see ourselves as others see us

Curiosity and enthusiasm for the kilt was pronounced among the public when Highland regiments first moved south into England.[180] Alexander Rule of the rather unique 'U' Company, 4th Gordons, describes how, in August, 1914, during breaks in their train journey southwards to Bedford, and during their first week there, they danced reels with wild shrieks for the benefit of the locals.[181] He perhaps reveals more about young students cockily wallowing in their self-image than about the true naivety of the locals. When 11th Black Watch marched into Cromer on 12 October, 1917, to take up winter billets, "all Cromer and his wife, not to mention the daughters, turned out to see the 191st (Highland) Brigade march in." Then on 1 December, "This morning the wind is howling and blowing a gale. That was rather embarrassing to kilted

---

177 IWM 12678 Kerridge, Hal, transcription of interview. On gymnastics, see also THM S98 11, Brooke, memoir, p.6.
178 IWM Books, Haldane, M.M., 'A History of the 4th Battalion The Seaforth Highlanders 1914 to 1918,' drafts and typescripts, p.109.
179 IWM 430 Wimberley, memoir, Vol.1, pp.21-22.
180 Apart from refs below, see: *Souvenir Booklet 6th Cameron Highlanders*, p.17.
181 Rule, *Students under Arms*, pp.10-11, 13. See also: GHM PB1699,'As we go up the line to death,' pp.20-21.

men at church parade and I am afraid some of the good people of Cromer were shocked at the airy garb of old Gaul."[182]

On route marches and exercises, hundreds of people would turn out with great enthusiasm to watch the Highland soldiers march past.[183] Audrey Prior, a schoolgirl in Warminster at the outbreak of the war, found it a thrilling and glorious pageant.[184] Visits by individual kilted soldiers on leave to English towns and villages could provoke interest and curiosity to the point of embarrassment.[185] In February, 1915, just prior to his deployment to France, Robert Dawson of 4th Gordons spent the weekend in Coventry.

> I think I was the only one in Highland costume in Coventry so you can imagine how everyone screwed their necks round to have a look at me after I had passed. One little girl when she was passing me asked to touch my coat, and an elderly lady in passing gave a shuddering sound with her mouth thinking I suppose how cold I would be in a kilt … After dinner we went up to Stokes again … his little boys could not understand my kilt at all, one of them asked if I had lost my trousers and another asked if I was a man.[186]

The same enthusiasm, mirth, curiosity and embarrassment was encountered almost universally by kilted soldiers in France.[187] Perhaps no reception was greater than that accorded to the South African Scottish as they marched to the station at Marseilles from their quarantine camp at La Valentine on 8 May, 1916.

---

182 BWA Paul, Phil, letters to May Merritt, 12 October, 1917, 1 December, 1917.
183 GHM PB1937, Dawson, letter to mother, Bedford, 1 November 1914; ASHM N-E8 Munro, letter to sister Effie, 1 October, 1914; IWM 21092 McGregor, letter to wife Jen, 18 April, 1916.
184 LC DF105 Prior, A.E., 'Some Reminiscences of before, during, & after World War I,' p.2.
185 LC GS 1507 Sotheby, diary, 18 November, 1914; IWM 8192 Lawson, undated letter to his sister Bessie; IWM 12643 Ferrie, letter to mother, 4 August, 1915; IWM Books, Brooke, Wait for it,', p.28; IWM 322 Reid, interview; IWM 24855, Newton, interview; IWM 3608 Anderson, memoir; IWM 21092 McGregor, letters to wife Jen, 18, 26 December, 1915; Hutchison, Graham Seton, *Footslogger*, (London: Hutchinson, 1931), p.148; Collins, *Last Man Standing*, p.74.
186 GHM PB1937, Dawson, letter to mother, Bedford, 14 February 1915.
187 LC GS 1507 Sotheby, diary, 2, 3 January, 1915, and letters to mother, 3, 7 January, 1915; BWA Gordon, summary of letter from France, 14 June, 1916; BWA Guthrie, letter to his wife Crissie, 7 March, 1916; IWM 4586 Douglas, memoir, pp.1071, 1136, 1139; Ogilvie, *Fife and Forfar Yeomanry*, p.139; LC GS 0409 Cunningham, letter to mother, 13 September, 1914; LC GS 0456 Dick, diary, 22 October, 1918; ASHM N-E2 Hyslop, diary, 11 August, 1914; ASHM N-E11 Bowie, diary, 16 July, 1915, 22 May, 1917, 16, 21 July, 25 December, 1918; IWM 11144 MacKay, diary, 16 February, 1917; Campbell, *Letters of Ivar Campbell*, p.94, letter home, 18 November, 1915; Hutchison, *Warrior*, p.42; Gillespie, *Letters from Flanders*, p.243, letter 21 July, 1915; THM Seaforths 89-122 Paterson, memoir; IWM Books, Brooke, 'Wait for it,' p.271; IWM 3834 Wrench, diary, 5 June, 1917, 16 July, 1918; Chambers, *Diaries of World War 1*, pp.12, 44; THM Camerons 93-35 Welsh, memoirs, pp.35-37, 39; IWM 1862 Craig-Brown, letter home, 26 September, 1914; Burns, *Once a Cameron Highlander*, p.62; Barber, *My Diary*, p.16; Macleod, *6th Camerons*, p.107; GHM PB3309 Pelham Burn, letter to Ella, 4 November, 1915; GHM PB1639, Kemp, memoir, Vol.2, p.42; GHM PB583 McKinnon, memoir, p.3; GHM PB3712 Murison, memoir; IWM 7593 Harper, memoir, p.26; IWM 13432 Symington, diary, 5, 8, 15, 22 October, 1914; IWM 3460 Macmillan, diary 5 November, 1914; Lyon, *In Kilt and Khaki*, p.127; Stothers, *Somewhere in France*, p.118; Topp, *42nd Battalion*, p.203; Hayes, *Eighty-Fifth*, p.182; Urquhart, *Canadian Scottish*, p.288; Lyon, Thomas, *More Adventures in Kilt and Khaki* (Kilmarnock: The Standard Press, 1917), pp.178-80; Bird, Will R., *Ghosts have Warm Hands*, (Ottawa, Canada: CEF Books, 1968), p.92.

It was a six or seven mile march to the station and we stepped out boldly with the pipes skirling, the Colonel and the field officers riding, and all the young South African Scots cheerful as sand boys. It would seem that no kilted regiment had visited Marseilles since the war began, judging by the ardour of the Marseilles girls who thrust into their ranks, so that by the time we reached the station the fours had broken into single file, and each Jock had great difficulty in seeing the next one ahead of him for the mass of girls in between. Fruit and flowers and red wine and champagne were thrust on us, while the Colonel and the mounted officers were presented with huge bouquets. Each Scottish soldier was hugged by about fourteen girls during his passage.[188]

Even 'The Times' commented on 28 October, 1914 on the extraordinary popularity of the daily patrol of the London Scottish military police in Paris.[189] Not that the kilted men did not have to be on their guard. In May, 1916, at Connaught Camp near Kemmel, some men of the 15th Battalion C.E.F. (48th Highlanders of Canada) washed their kilts "and then foolishly hung them on the fence to dry overnight. The next morning eight blushing Highlanders fell in, clad only in shirt-tails, while ladies who lived near Kemmel were busily making themselves Davidson tartan skirts, the material being obtained at a bargain from thirsty men in the night for five francs or a bottle of champagne."[190]

Only on a few occasions were kilted troops received with fear, suspicion or hostility.[191] When John Gregory moved with his battalion of Argylls to the coast of France on rest in January, 1915, "There was a sulky air about most of the inhabitants ... partly due to the enforced silence and partly to their fear of strangers. As yet they could not make any conversation with British troops and the strange garb of the Highlanders added to their distrust."[192] Charlie Gairdner, an officer in 10th Argylls, notes that in marching through Belgium in November, 1918, after the Armistice:

Instead of the glad welcome I expected, as soon as the first company of Highlanders appears in sight the women dash indoors and bar the door and gaze at us through the chinks. We are the first kilted regiment they have seen and are not sure if we are savages or not! They generally calm down after a bit and merely laugh at us![193]

Kilted soldiers nevertheless had ways of dealing with unkind mockery. Alex Moffat, in 1st London Scottish, met a pal in Abbeville in October, 1914, who "told me how his boxing practice at Headqrs had come in useful here; a Frenchman the other day tried to be funny at his expense and his kilt, but was soon laid out on his back on the floor of the café, from a blow under the jaw."[194]

---

188 Boustead, *The Wind of Morning*, p.29. See also: IWM 11637 Leppan, loc.cit.
189 *The Times*, 28 October, 1914, reproduced in *The Times*, 28 October 2014.
190 Beattie, *48th Highlanders*, p.124.
191 Apart from refs below, see: LC GS 1026 Maclean, diary, p.13; Wauchope, *Black Watch*, vol.2, p.306.
192 [Gregory, John B.], *France 1916-1917-1918*, (Crewekerne: Frank N. Parsons, 1924), p.10.
193 ASHM N-E10 Gairdner, letter to mother, 24 November, 1918.
194 LC GS 1124 Moffat, A., diary, 17 October, 1914.

168   Those Bloody Kilts

The curiosity of the public. French civilians eye a soldier of the London Scottish on L.O.C. duties in 1914. The ladies seem enchanted; the young lad in centre photo seems less than impressed. From a contemporary postcard published in France by C.C.C. & C. (Author's collection)

French troops regarded the kilt with curiosity and amusement,[195] although, as Arthur Betteridge of the South African Scottish remarked, "It was difficult to get them to understand how Scotsmen could possibly come from South Africa."[196] In fact, everywhere that Highland soldiers went, they provoked similar reactions; in Italy,[197] Holland,[198] Dakar,[199] Durban,[200] Palestine,[201] and Mesopotamia.[202] Captain Willie Brown, with 2nd Gordons in Italy, visited St Marks in Venice in September, 1918. "In the Titian Chapel … we found the Sacrament being administered … I regret to say that my kilt proved more than a counter attraction to the transubstantiation which was going on."[203] George Brown records how, en route to India on October, 1916, his draft of Black Watch soldiers disembarked at Dakar for a bathing parade.

195   IWM 4586 Douglas, pp.427, 1035; IWM 3834 Wrench, diary, 10 March, 1916; Fennah, *Retaliation*, p.31.
196   LC GS 0132 Betteridge, memoir, p.38.
197   GHM PB1889 Brown, Capt W.N., letters home 6 August, 6 September, 1918; LC GS 0456 Dick, diary 26 October, 1918; IWM 8592 Macgregor, letters to his fiancée dated 25 December, 1917, 16, 20 March, 1918; IWM 6873 PP Hendry, W.N., manuscript memoir, 'My Experience with the London Scottish 1914-1918', unpaginated.
198   GHM PB1755 Young, 'Memoirs of Captivity.'
199   BWA 'Brown George Murray, His Story', p.33.
200   BWA Drummond, typescript memoir, 'A Journey to India'; IWM 8503 Byrom, memoir, p.6.
201   Blaser, *Kilts across the Jordan*, p.207.
202   IWM 8503 Byrom, memoir, p.22; IWM 511 PP Thorburn, Lt M.M., letters home 17, 28 January, 1916; BWA Cumming, Lieut. A.B., letter, 4 January, 1916.
203   GHM PB1889 Brown, letter home 6 September, 1918.

"As we marched through the village, crowds of natives lined the road amazed at the sight of men wearing kilts. But their amazement turned to terror when they heard the pipes!"[204] In April, 1917, en route to join 2nd Black Watch, Captain Allan Byrom passed through Baghdad:

> The 'Jocks' came in for special attention, especially with the native women. They were quite fascinated with the kilties, and not a little mystified at their feminine attire. It was amusing to see some of the Armenian ladies lift their face masks as the Highlanders swung along so that they might get a better view of them. Having satisfied their curiosity they would show their beautiful white teeth in a pleasing smile.[205]

In Mesopotamia, however, as Lieutenant Thorburn of 2nd Black Watch observed, the local Arab population were only too ready to strip the dead and wounded of their kilts. After the action of 13 January, 1916, he wrote, "Every Arab I would shoot, the devils! Two of our stretcher-bearers – who do not carry rifles – were stripped naked by them the morning after the battle, and in broad daylight too!" And he noted that, after another action on 21st, "a few who never got in at all, and lay out all night and got stripped naked by Arabs, suffered more; but I doubt if there were many such survivors."[206]

In Germany, the reaction of the public to kilts, worn either by prisoners of war or by occupying troops, seems to have been generally one of polite curiosity,[207] especially from the children. There is little evidence, from the eyewitness accounts consulted, that the alleged reputation of the Highland soldier in German eyes generated any hatred amongst the German population as a whole to the kilted soldier in particular. Private Douglas noted the reaction of the local population as 8th Black Watch marched into Germany in December, 1918.

> Although naturally we did not expect any signs of jubilation from the civilian population, nor did I see any signs of hostility as we marched through their villages and towns en route, but what their private thoughts were, could not be happy ones. To the small boys and girls, we kilted troops were obviously a great attraction.[208]

Lieutenant Sholto Douglas was in an officers' P.O.W. camp in Mainz in 1918.

> When the Armistice came, they opened the doors and we could go anywhere we liked. Mainz, anywhere … There was no ill-feeling and one night there was an opera in Wiesbaden. So, I and a friend of mine, also of the Seaforths, we decided to go … and when we came back, we had to wait about ten minutes in Wiesbaden station for the train back and of course, we again only had our kilts, and the people in Wiesbaden, all the people in the station, were most interested. We had a large circle around us, you see, looking at us, you see. However, nobody molested us and we went back in peace to Mainz.[209]

---

204 BWA 'Brown George Murray, His Story', p.33.
205 IWM 8503 Byrom, memoir, p.22.
206 IWM 511 Thorburn, letters home 17, 28 January, 1916.
207 Apart from refs cited below, see: GHM PB1498 Hamilton, Ian B M., diary, 12 May, 1915; IWM 4586 Douglas, memoir, pp.1345, 1443; ASHM N-E8 Humble, Lt Alex. D., typescript diary, 1917.
208 IWM 4586 Douglas, memoir, p.1182.
209 LC Transcripts Douglas, Sir Sholto, transcript of Tape 592, interview with Liddle, 1980.

One constant factor in England and behind the lines in France, Belgium and elsewhere, was the fascination of the ladies with the kilt. There was, unsurprisingly, considerable female interest as to what, if anything, was worn underneath.[210] Lieutenant I.M. Stewart was an officer in 2nd Argylls, who were briefly on L.O.C. duties at Boulogne in August, 1914.

> The excitement in the paper at Boulogne was whether the Jocks wore anything under their kilt or not. They ran leading articles on that, you know, until some lady wrote a letter to the paper and said she knew for certain they didn't. She described how she saw a Highland officer looking into a shop window and she dropped her bag and she bent down to pick it up and she could assure the public that they didn't.[211]

Arthur Betteridge in the South African Scottish considered that curiosity was satisfied by women in different countries in different ways:

> English girls rarely asked, but we noticed when going upstairs on a bus, they suggested the kilty go first, and the few women we met in Egypt were usually in low dives. They had no compunction in making the direct approach, which could be embarrassing. When we marched along French roads behind the front line, where they seldom saw kilted soldiers, young girls would giggle and some of them lift the kilt from behind. The audacious mam'selles were usually defeated in their object, owing to the wide pleats of the kilt.[212]

In some quarters the descent of hordes of kilted soldiers was apparently considered a severe threat to the virtue of susceptible young ladies. Frank Brooke, a Yorkshireman, who joined the Seaforth Highlanders at Ripon, wrote: "We had heard several things about Ripon and the soldiery, particularly when the Bishop of Ripon, through the local newspapers, advised parents to keep a firm hand on their daughters, probably thinking the kilt would prove irresistible to the said daughters."[213] There is no doubt that the kilt was an attraction, and the Highlanders felt that, compared with troops in trousers, they had an advantage with the ladies, which they willingly exploited.[214] On occasion, however, this advantage might be pressed too far. In the early months of 1918, in a village estaminet, Eric Linklater was sitting drinking with some sergeants, when from another room came running their hostess closely pursued by an elderly second lieutenant. "His excitement was obvious, for the front of his kilt was held aloft by an intemperate

---

210 Apart from specific refs cited, see: LC GS 1761 Wilson, memoir, p.17; IWM 6926 Dennis, R.V.,' memoir, p.292; GHM PB1706/2 Robertson, diary, 23 August, 1916; IWM Books Parke, 'Memoirs,' p.35; LC Transcripts, Tape 286, Wilson, J.K, interview with Liddle, 1975; see also IWM 12007 Wilson, memoir, pp.30-31; LC GS 0132 Betteridge, memoir, p.21; IWM 21092 McGregor, letter to wife Jen, 9 September, 1915; NLS MS944-947, Ramage, diary; IWM 11965 Recording, Spencer, Robert Proctor, IWM interview 1991; THM Seaforths 89-122 Paterson, memoir; IWM 233 McKechnie, Reminiscences, p.7.
211 LC GS 1535 Stewart, Tape 359, interview. A slightly different version of this story is given in LC GS 0315 Clark, Tape 356, interview.
212 LC GS 0132 Betteridge, memoir, p.7.
213 THM S98-11, Brooke, memoir, p.1. See also Rule, *Students under Arms*, p.34.
214 GHM PB1639, Kemp, memoir, p.91; Rule, *Students under Arms*, pp.26-27; IWM 21092 McGregor, letter to wife Jen, 27 September, 4 October, 1915.

erection that raised it as if on the ridge-pole of a marquee; and our hostess fled before him with squeals of terror that may or may not have been genuine."[215]

The telling phrase, 'Pour l'amour – bon, pour la guerre, pas bon' was attributed to Marshal Joffre at the time,[216] although it has also been attributed to a General in the Crimea! No wonder that jealous wives worried about the temptations available to their husbands. Jim Cunningham, an officer in 1st Argylls, told how their handsome drum major, Cridland, had been photographed by the press with the girls of Boulogne hanging round his neck, to the extreme annoyance of his wife, who talked of divorce![217] She was right to be concerned, for some of the ladies were very forward indeed. Richard Watson, recently commissioned in the Gordon Highlanders, took advantage of a three-week signalling course at Dunstable, to visit London at the weekends. On his first visit to Piccadilly, surrounded by ladies of easy virtue, he felt an exploratory hand reach up his kilt.[218] George Warwick, in the South African Scottish, was given a pass to visit Marseilles on 6 May, 1916. "In town we were followed by two women who tugged at our kilts, and when we ignored them, I heard one of them say to the other, 'Leave them alone, they are afraid of women!'"[219] Forward ladies were not, however, the only hazard encountered by kilted soldiers. J.K Stanford enlisted in the London Scottish in November, 1914, and was eventually sent to billets in Dorking. "I can recall almost nothing of those months in Dorking except, after our kilts and sporrans came, a battle to resist the advances of a homosexual photographer. He photographed us one by one and then tried to lure selected models into his dark-room to watch them 'being developed.'"[220]

Conclusions

The kilt was a unique dress, ironically, by virtue of extraordinary custom and tradition, the most blatantly masculine dress in the Army, which excited curiosity, amusement, fascination, respect and sometimes adoration from the public, especially the ladies. In terms of practicality, not to say decorum, even in training and behind the lines, it posed certain challenges. But in the soldier who wore it, it inspired great pride, and a strong separate sense of identity as a Highland soldier, himself a national icon. Through the different tartans worn too, it reinforced regimental identity. The net result was to contribute immeasurably to the 'esprit de corps' of the Highland soldier and therefore to his morale. But how would the kilt stand up to the conditions in the trenches and on the battlefield? Was it really suitable for modern warfare? In the next two chapters, we will examine this question.

---

215 Linklater, *Fanfare*, p.61.
216 IWM 114 Allen, letter to wife, 14 October, 1915.
217 LC GS 0409 Cunningham, letter to mother, 13 September, 1914.
218 GHM PB2183, Watson, memoir, p.4.
219 Warwick, *We Band of Brothers*, pp.52-53. On forward ladies, see also: IWM 21092 McGregor, letter to wife Jen, 5 March, 23 April, 1916; Sotheby, Lionel, *Lionel Sotheby's Great War* (Athens, Ohio: Ohio University Press, 1997), p.36.
220 IWM 10529 Stanford, memoir, p.24.

6

The Kilt: Fighting the Elements

'Oh, these kilts! I'd give a thousand pounds for a pair of trousers.'[1]

As we have seen, the kilt was a great source of pride and 'esprit de corps' to Highland solders. But just how practical was it when confronted with the conditions of trench warfare? In this respect, the kilt has not been without its defenders. Douglas Wimberley, a relatively junior officer in the First World War, who went on to command 51st Highland Division in the Second, was a protagonist of the kilt, and prepared a paper prior to a BBC documentary on the subject, entitled "Ladies from Hell", in which he appeared in 1980. His specific points are considered in the discussion below, but importantly, he does not base his argument for the kilt wholly on its practicality but rather on its benefit to esprit de corps.[2] A more extreme defender of the kilt was Norman Macleod, who commanded 6th Camerons during the war. His arguments appear in the battalion histories he wrote or to which he contributed and are summarised in an appendix to "The Romantic Story of the Highland Garb and Tartan", published in 1924.[3] While Macleod like Wimberley correctly stresses the advantage of the kilt to esprit de corps, he insists on its practicality in the face of cold, wet and mustard gas, and acknowledges only one disadvantage; barbed wire. He is not without supporters.[4] Interviewed in 1999, Hal Kerridge, who trained with the London Scottish but served principally with 1st Gordons, stated:

> I wore a kilt for four and a half years and I dreaded the day when I'd got to put trews on again. I love the kilt. I'd wear it today if I could … It's a dress that's fascinating; once you get used to it, it's a fascinating dress. Because it's only a throwback from the original Scots of Ireland … It was a gorgeous dress and I'd wear it today. I wouldn't look so good [as] at the time, mind you! … It was pride of the regiment. Many other people have said the same thing and I suppose that is one of the attractions of the kilt. It's different from anybody else … I love it … It's just a nice dress, I like it. It was different from the ordinary uniforms. It was good for the girls … at 16 or 17![5]

1   IWM 3008 PP McPake, R, diary, 25 October, 1915.
2   IWM 430 Wimberley, unpublished paper, 'The Kilt in Modern War', written 1979.
3   Macleod in Mackay, *Romantic Story*.
4   See: Walker, *Tom Walker Remembers*, p.5; THM Camerons 89-44, Anderson, p.25.
5   IWM 18836 Kerridge, interview 1999; LC Tapes 1618/1619, Kerridge, interview.

Albert Strachan, who served in 6th Gordons, would disagree. "The kilt was a stupid dress. It was said Scots soldiers desired the kilt – perhaps to walk out their lady friends but certainly not for war."[6] Who is right? In the next two chapters, we look in detail at the practicality of the kilt and the Highland uniform.

The kilt was, however, not the only item of Highland dress with which there were problems. There were also problems with headwear. The Glengarry bonnet was found to be unsuitable and was replaced initially by the khaki Balmoral bonnet and subsequently by the khaki Tam o' Shanter. The replacement of the Glengarry generally took place between March and July, 1915, although in 13th Battalion C.E.F. (Royal Highlanders of Canada) it was as late as November, 1916.[7] The Glengarry was considered too conspicuous in the trenches,[8] as Ian MacKay, an officer with 4th Camerons, found out when he received a bullet through his Glengarry on his first day in.[9] Indeed, on 11th October, 1914, well before the issue of khaki bonnets, Major Ernest Craig-Brown, then commanding A Company, of 1st Camerons, instructed his platoon commanders that, "Men on lookout by day are not to wear the blue Glengarry bonnet as it is too conspicuous on the top of a trench. A cap comforter should be worn instead."[10] 4th Gordons were actually issued with cap comforters at Bedford, on 18 November, 1914, long before deployment overseas. They apparently deployed in cap comforters and exchanged them for Tammies in theatre on 10 April, 1915.[11] The Glengarry also provided little protection from the sun, and the Balmoral and Tammy were regarded as an improvement in that respect.[12]

The first sartorial problem encountered in fact concerned the shoes and spats worn by the Highland soldiers who arrived at the front in 1914. Initially, this was as a result of the hard, cobbled roads, although the problem would be compounded later by mud. The regular Highland battalions initially deployed to France in 1914, were all sent over wearing shoes and spats. All found the shoes unable to cope with the cobbled roads traversed on the Great Retreat. In 2nd Argylls, for example, during the retreat from Mons, Captain Hyslop commented that, "the men's boots [i.e. shoes] are giving way and I even saw some poor fellows trying to struggle along in bare feet.". And later, "boots are pretty well worn through and many men have no gaiters." Adam McLachlan in the same battalion similarly describes "a terrible march, some of us with our bare feet 'cause we could not get on our shoes with swollen feet."[13] H.D. Clark, then a regimental officer with the battalion, while defending the Highland uniform, acknowledged the problem, especially for the 600 reservists who had been absorbed into the battalion on mobilisation.

---

6 GHM PB2984 Strachan, memoir.
7 Fetherstonhaugh, *13th Battalion*, p.147.
8 See: THM Camerons 89-44 Anderson, A., p.24; Beattie, *48th Highlanders*, p.44.
9 THM Camerons 90-120, MacKay, Ian, letter to Grant, 1 March, 1915; THM Camerons 94-8 Mackay, 'Tell them of us,' letter, Ian MacKay to mother, 27 February, 1915.
10 IWM 1862, Craig-Brown, Field Message Books, order, Craig-Brown to platoon commanders, 11 October, 1914.
11 GHM PB3279 Matthews, diary, 18 November, 1914, 10 April, 1915.
12 ASHM N-E2 Hyslop diary, 2 September, 1915; Gillespie, *Letters from Flanders*, p.139, letter 9 May, 1915; LC GS 1027 Macleod, letter to father, 14 July, 1915.
13 AHSM N-E2 Hyslop diary, 30 August, 2 September, 1914; LC GS M5 McLachlan, A, Cpl, diary, 25 August, 1914.

On the cobbles it was very hard for the reservists ... The Scottish dress is much better adapted to marching than the English because we don't have Army boots. We have shoes, Highland, and we have fresh air up the kilt and therefore we can march further and we never had anyone fall out ... Certainly, our dress was very helpful from the marching point of view, but the French cobbles, oh dear.[14]

Jimmy Dixon was an Army Service Corps driver attached to 2nd Argylls. He describes their experience on the retreat from Mons:

> They went out when I seen 'em, nice spats on, as if they was going to the pictures, you know, nice and clean, but by the time it was finished, that retreat, they had no shoes at all, they was all worn away, so you may tell me what their feet was like. There was a doctor there, he must have run out of stuff, taking them off and putting the ointment on them ... They couldn't hardly walk.[15]

There is ample evidence that 2nd Seaforths[16] and 1st Camerons[17] also suffered. Sergeant H. Macpherson of 1st Camerons observed that by 5 September, "I had very sore feet, blisters as big as 5/– pieces, owing to my shoes being worn down & also bad socks."[18]

Studio photograph of two soldiers of the Black Watch, illustrating the khaki Tam o' Shanter which replaced the Glengarry, and sporting the famous red hackle worn proudly by the regiment. (Author's collection)

It is quite evident, in the case of all three battalions mentioned, that the problem of the shoes was exacerbated by the fact that the battalions had been brought up to strength with large numbers of reservists, who were not fully fit for campaign, and whose shoes did not in some cases even fit properly. The problem was to get even worse in the winter mud.

14   LC GS 0315 Clark, interview.
15   IWM 10786 Hood, interview.
16   NLS MS 20248, Haldane, General Sir Aylmer, diary, 12, 31 August, 1914; *Gilbert M. Mackenzie*, diary, 26, 30 August, 3 September, 1914; THM Seaforths 98-113 Wilson, notebook.
17   THM Camerons 89-44 Anderson, p.23.
18   THM Camerons 99-87, Macpherson, diary, 25 August, 5 September, 1914.

The frequently wet, muddy and freezing conditions in the trenches are well known.[19] The winter of 1916-17 was one of the most savage in the twentieth century, but all other winters were a trial, especially the first, when there were insufficient troops to man the line and before sensible routines had been established to assist their survival and comfort. Wet and mud could appear too at any time of year, but most especially when rain accompanied the destruction of the landscape by shell-fire. Both water and mud could be ankle, knee or even waist deep, and a number of soldiers actually did drown in the mud.[20] The mud of Passchendaele is legendary, but amongst the worst conditions encountered by Highland troops were those in the area of Courcelette, where 51st Highland Division eked out their sorry existence after the battle of the Somme. Bitter winter conditions were not confined to the Western Front. They could also occur, for example, in Italy[21], and on the Salonika front, where one man died of exposure in 2nd London Scottish,[22] and several in the 1st Garrison Battalion Seaforth Highlanders,[23] whose employment on active campaigning was of questionable judgment. For Highland soldiers dutifully soldiering on in the kilt, it might be expected that the conditions of cold, wet and mud encountered in the trenches of the Western Front would present particular problems.

Excessive water in the trenches could turn the kilt into a source of some discomfort. The kilt would drag in the water or the mud,[24] or spread out on top of the water when it was deep.[25] Sergeant H.E. May of the Gordon Highlanders records advancing in the battle of Passchendaele, 1917, "wading through mud waist deep, with kilts floating on the surface like water lilies."[26] Another nuisance was cold water or mud splashing up inside the kilt.[27] As Private James Campbell of 6th Camerons remarked, in October, 1915, "It's a great sensation when a big splash of cold mud goes up on to your bare legs."[28] It was not pleasant either sitting in a trench, "with the water just dripping up your kilt."[29] Or as Eric Linklater, who joined 4/5th Black Watch in the vicinity of Passchendaele in December, 1917, put it, "Our feet and our arses were sodden wet."[30]

A more important problem was simply the weight of the kilt when it got wet. As William Hay, in 9th Royal Scots, complained, "There are seven and a half yards of material in a kilt so

19 There are innumerable references in the sources to conditions in the trenches. They are only cited when they relate specifically to the practicality of the Highland uniform.
20 Craig-Brown, *Historical Records*, Vol.3, pp.297-298.
21 IWM 8592 Macgregor, letter to wife, 13 January, 1918.
22 LC GS 0731, Hay-Young, letter to mother, 20 March, 1917.
23 IWM 7508 Wyllie, diary, 21 October, 8, 11, 15, 20, 29 November, 4, 13 December, 1918.
24 IWM 3460 Macmillan, diary, 31 December, 1914; THM, Camerons 92-35, Welsh, pp.70, 81; THM Seaforths 89-81, White, Pte Andrew, letter to mother, 9 November, 1915; Royal Scots Museum, Beatson, Cpl James, diary.
25 IWM 5525 Steven, letter to home, 25 March, 1915; LSgt Richardson quoted by Lloyd, *London Scottish*, pp.101-102; LC GS 0158 Bolton, Sir Ian, typescript memoir, 'Reactions to First World War', 6 pp, n.d. but post 1960; IWM 2528 Bradbury, p. 9.
26 May, H.E., 'In a Highland Regiment,' in Lewis, Jon E. (ed), *True World War 1 Stories* (London. Robinson, 1999), p.200.
27 NLS MS 944-947, Ramage, diary, 4, May, 1915. See also: IWM Books Brooke, 'Wait for it', p.126; LC GS 0262 Campbell, J., letter to fiancée 25 June, 1916; IWM 4081 Recording, Douglas, Percy, BBC interview 1963; IWM 9833 Coates, interview.
28 LC GS 0262 Campbell, letter to fiancée 25 October, 1915.
29 LC, Transcript Tape 324, Jordan interview.
30 Linklater, *Fanfare*, p.54.

it's quite heavy. You can imagine what it's like if it gets wet, soaking wet in the trenches, you get a terrible weight hanging on you as well as your gear."[31]

Also serious, was chafing of the knees caused by the friction of a wet kilt. James Sloan, in 1st London Scottish, felt that, "The kilt, when dry, is a comfortable garment, but wet, the lower edge of it chafes the back of the knee and is a misery to march in."[32] Private Douglas similarly describes a march behind the lines by 8th Black Watch in May, 1918, when "the kilt became sodden with rain, and at each step forward was apt to chafe the leg above the knee. Fortunately for me, it did not trouble me much, but some of the chaps in the platoon had sore legs after."[33] As a result, sand-bags might be used to keep knees dry and prevent this chafing.[34]

Another problem was getting kilts dry again after getting soaked. Philip Christison thought, even in the dreadful conditions of the winter of 1916/17, that, "We were better off than the English troops as our kilts shed the rain and dried out quickly."[35] This may have been true of showers. But if a kilt got truly soaked through, it too was difficult to dry, and became a burdensome weight. Lionel Sotheby complained that, when in January 1915 his tent at Le Havre was flooded overnight and his kilt soaked, in the morning, "my kilt is still damp, as the thickness does not allow of quick drying."[36]

The kilt at least did have one real advantage in the wet. When confronted with flooded trenches, the kilt could be raised above water level or even removed entirely, left behind or carried over the shoulder. Solders might leave on their kilt-covers only[37], or simply progress in shirt-tails. There are numerous references in the sources to this practice.[38] Eric Linklater, serving with 4/5th Black Watch recalls how, early in 1918, their commander instructed his company to take off their kilts and wear them as capes about their shoulders. "So we said goodbye to Passchendaele with a flutter of grey shirttails dancing behind our bums."[39]

This ability to discard the kilt easily did give it at least one legitimate advantage over trousers, which could not be removed without removing also boots and puttees. Consequently, trousered troops could only accept that trousers and long drawers would get thoroughly soaked in water-logged trenches and they would have to live with the possibly freezing consequences. This advantage of the kilt has been deployed vigorously by Macleod, but was real and has been reiterated by others, such as Norman Collins.[40]

---

31 IWM 16455 Hay, interview. See also: IWM 5015 PP, Ross, C., letter, Ross to MOD, 12 May, 1981.
32 LC WF Recollections, S18, Sloan, memoir.
33 IWM 4586 Douglas, p.471. See also Walker, *Tom Walker Remembers*, p.5; IWM 9756 Manton, interview; GHM uncatalogued, Beaton, memoir, pp.72-75.
34 IWM 4586 Douglas, pp.523, 732-733.
35 IWM 4370 Christison, memoir, p.51.
36 LC GS 1507 Sotheby, diary, 16 January 1915.
37 LC GS 0262 Campbell, letter to fiancée 25 June, 1916.
38 Hutchison, *Warrior*, pp.58-61; Hutchison, *Footslogger*, pp.138, 147; ASHM N-E2 Hyslop, diary, 10 January, 1915; Collins, *Last Man Standing*, p.82; IWM 926 Mackenzie, letter to wife, 18 June 1915; THM 2013-072 (S), Braes, memoir, 29 October, 1915; Macleod, *6th Camerons*, p.26; Craig-Brown, *Historical Records*, Vol.4, pp.292-293; LC GS 0627 Andrew Gilmour Papers, article by him on 'The Other Enemy' in *The Beam*, September, 1982; IWM 12043 Collins, interview; LC GS 1761 Wilson, memoir, p.82.
39 Linklater, *Fanfare for a Tin Hat*, p.56.
40 Macleod, *6th Camerons*, p.26; Craig-Brown, *Historical Records*, Vol.4, pp.292-293; Macleod in Mackay, *Romantic Story*; IWM 12043, Collins, interview; Collins, *Last Man Standing*, p.82; NLS

Mud was an even greater problem than water, for it affected not only kilts but also shoes. We have already observed how Highland shoes and spats failed on the cobbled roads encountered on the Great Retreat. They were now to encounter Flanders mud, and more battalions were now affected, as to the regular battalions initially deployed with the B.E.F. were added, before the end of 1914, the first Territorial battalions, all still sporting shoes and spats.[41] In 2nd Argylls, for example, Captain Hyslop observes that on taking over the trenches in Ploegsteert Wood, on 8 November:

> The few tracks are so cut up that in places the mud is nearly a foot deep, no wheeled traffic or horses can move in it, and we had to go in single file, slipping and splashing in the mud. The walk is only about 2 miles, but took us at least the same number of hours, and many of the men had to leave their shoes, dragged off and swallowed by the mud. We eventually got the trenches relieved at 2 a.m.[42]

In 5th Black Watch, Hugh Quekett notes how, during the winter of 1914/15, "The straps of the spats, attached between sole and heel of the shoe, would not stand up to its constant immersion in the mud and water with the result that many of our shoes were sucked off without any hope of recovery."[43] The problem was finally resolved in early 1915, when the battalions concerned were provided with boots and puttees to replace the shoes and spats, so it was not repeated the following winters.[44]

As far as the kilt was concerned, mud, like water, would also considerably increase the weight of it.[45] Croft referred to the kilt as "a specially designed mud collector."[46] In those circumstances, it is perhaps not surprising that kilts could be lost in the effort to drag oneself out of the mud. One morning in February, 1917, when C Company, 1st Camerons, came out of the trenches;

> I was a bit surprised to see a Company of men half naked, some without boots, others without kilts or tunics. They had left them in the trenches buried in the mud and were on their way to recover them if possible. It made one shiver to look at them stepping along over the frozen ground, but such is discipline.[47]

    Acc.12729 Wood, Lt Col J.B., letters, letter to brother Willie, 29 June, 1916; Andrew Bowie, Interview in *Reveille*, Vol.75, No.1 Jan/Feb 2002, pp.16-18.
41 Apart from the examples cited, see also; (for 2nd Seaforths) IWM 43, Recordings, Dunton, Arthur Naylor, interview 1973; (for 1st Camerons) THM Camerons 89 44, Anderson, memoir, p.24; Craig-Brown, *Historical Records*, Vol.3, pp.64, 106; IWM 1862, Craig-Brown, diary, 17 October, 18 December, 1914, copy letter to Adjutant 18 December, 1914, letter to mother, 10 January, 1915, letters 13, 14 April, 1915; (for 2nd Gordons) GHM PB242, Stansfield, letters from him, 16, 27 December, 1914, and LC WF Recollections, G5, Gillespie, transcript of interview.
42 AHSM N-E2 Hyslop diary, 8 November, 1914. See also ASHM N-E2, Collier, journal.
43 BWA Quekett, memoir, p.14.
44 References in the sources are too numerous to cite here.
45 THM, Camerons 92-35, Welsh, memoirs, p.13, Beattie, *48th Highlanders*, p.276; LC GS 1761 Wilson, memoir, p.63; Andrew Bowie, interviewed in *Reveille*, Vol.75, No.1 Jan/Feb 2002, pp.16-18; IWM 12678, Recordings, Burns, Robert, transcript of interview, 1998; GHM PB3712, Murison, memoir; Morrison, *7th Argylls*, p.26.
46 Croft, W.D., *Three Years with the 9th (Scottish) Division*, (London: John Murray, 1919), p.158.
47 THM, Camerons 92-35, Welsh, memoir, p.27. See also: IWM 1862, Craig-Brown, Miscellaneous letters, Yeadon to Craig-Brown, 1 March, 1917; Craig-Brown, *Historical Records*, Vol.3, p.224.

A Scots Guardsman helping a Highlander in the mud, 1916. (IWM Q17499)

Mud was also a problem when it accumulated on the back of the kilt and chafed the back of the knees when it dried. Norman Macmillan, who served in the Glasgow Highlanders, explained the problem:

> When we came out of muddy trenches, our kilts were caked and plastered with mud that dried as we marched along and as we moved back to our billets behind the lines we found the swinging kilt rubbing on the back of our thighs and back of our knees under the caked mud, and the kilt cut the skin and made our legs raw at the back, gradually erasing the skin by minute cuts every time the kilt swung.[48]

This was a frequent and serious complaint, acknowledged even by the historian of 51st Highland Division."[49] Youngson notes how in 5th Gordons in December, 1916, around Bouzincourt, the problem was so acute that "many cast their kilts and wore their kilt aprons only."[50]

A major inconvenience also was that the mud would harden on the hair on legs and knees. Douglas Gillespie, in 2nd Argylls, noted in March, 1915, "I find that when I wear the kilt in the trenches, I get quite like 'Rex', for the mud splashes up about my knees, and hardens in little

---

48 IWM 4173 Recording, Macmillan, Norman, BBC interview 1963. See also: LC GS 1579, Taylor, memoir, p.10; GHM PB3712, Murison, memoir; GHM PB375, Pailthorpe, memoir, p.34.
49 Bewsher, *Fifty First*, p.41; GHM PB1892.3.18 McDonald, 'Uncle Harper's Duds', pp.28-30.
50 GHM PB1892.3.1 Youngson, Capt R.W., '1914-1919,' p.28. For other examples, see: Bird, *Ghosts*, p.55; IWM 4081 Douglas, interview; Fraser, James F., 'War Diary, 1915', reprinted from the *Aberdeen University Review*, Vol.46, No.153, Spring, 1975, pp.32-44 p. 44; IWM 24552 McLeavy, interview; IWM 612 PP Gameson, L., typescript memoirs, p.82.

A soldier of the Royal Engineers collecting the identity disc from the wrist of a Highlander killed by a shell on the edge of a water filled crater. (IWM Q3963)

lumps – and when you try to pull them off, out comes the hair too."[51] On the night of 19/20 July, 1918, Douglas Wilson in 5th Camerons was caught with his men in an emergency shallow trench under bombardment and a two-hour downpour of rain.

> While we sat in rising puddles the trench walls slithered down on us. Kilt aprons, at first merely soaking flaps of material, became semi-solid and later solid masses of primordial ooze, drying into thick boards that stood out from our bodies and gave us the appearance of lewd plaster figures. As to our limbs, the more hirsute the man the greater his capacity for attracting and holding coalescing particles. One Lothario ventured the complaint that his prospects of happy marriage had been destroyed.[52]

Unsurprisingly, in these conditions, the kilt was not the most universally popular of garments. Captain R.E. Badenoch was in the Ypres sector during the winter of 1917/18 with 4/5th Black Watch, where he reported that, after Passchendaele, the Salient "was the abomination of desolation ... A kilt was certainly not the most suitable dress for these conditions!!"[53] Private

---

51 Gillespie, *Letters from Flanders*, pp.33, 45, 52 letters 5, 12, 16 March, 1915. See also: BWA Cumming, letter to parents n.d. (October/November 1915); NLS MS 944-947, Ramage, diary, 8 May, 1915, Burns, *Once a Cameron Highlander*, p.88; LC, Tape 963, Burns, interview.
52 LC GS 1761 Wilson, memoir, p.79.
53 BWA, Badenoch, Recollections, p.13.

McPake, in 7th Argylls, complained about the kilt in the cold, wet and muddy conditions in October-November 1915. On 25 October, he complained of, "Rotten weather, and rain all the day and cold that no one could stand. 'Oh these kilts', I'd give a thousand pounds for a pair of trousers." Then on 1st November, "Raining again and 'yours truly' on duty, with it pouring down on top of him, it's not very pleasant when you have to keep wet clothes on, till they dry on you, and 'Oh, these blooming kilts', they hold 'some' water and we have to stick this for ten blooming days, I think." And on 1 December, "We are on all the morning getting the dirt off our kilts & the rest of our clothes & the blooming stuff sticks like glue on our legs. If I was safely out of this war, no more kilts for me. I wish I had been a girl, but mistakes do happen in the best of families, worse luck."[54]

As for water, at least kilts could be removed in muddy conditions for ease of passage. Towards the end of 1915, in the St Elie sector, Douglas Wimberley, in 1st Camerons, records that, "The mud was so bad that the ration parties invariably took off their kilts and waded up wearing rough shorts of sand-bags or the like."[55] And of the winter of 1915/16 generally he comments,

> Our ration parties used to come up the line without their kilts in order to keep them dry, they would wear boots and socks and little white pants – the rest of their legs being bare – and then wash off the mud in billets when they got back; by this means they travelled light, as with the long heavy rubber thigh boots on, walking in the mud was an effort, and if we stood still for long one stuck fast.[56]

The practice certainly occurred at the end of November,1915, in the Aveluy sector, in 6th Black Watch, when "The kilt was temporarily discarded and improvised "shorts", made out of a couple of sandbags, was the usual form of dress for the 6th Battalion during this period."[57] Thomas Lyon similarly recalls that in the wet muddy conditions in the winter of 1915/1916, within the Glasgow Highlanders,

> The battalion orderlies, whose duty it is to carry messages from headquarters to the various companies in the line … have altogether discarded the kilt while in the trenches. They are literally clothed in sackcloth – and mud instead of ashes, for the lower parts of their bodies and the upper parts of their legs are voluminously swathed in sandbags. The appearance they thus present, if not exactly picturesque, is at all events sufficiently quaint and amusing. No comedian of the halls ever appeared in a costume more fantastic or ridiculous to the eye than ours; in pre-war days it would only have been necessary for us to walk on any stage to evoke roars of laughter.[58]

---

54 IWM 3008 McPake, diary, 25 October, 1 November, 1 December, 1915.
55 IWM 430, Wimberley, memoir, p.32.
56 Ibid., pp.36-37.
57 Wauchope, *Black Watch*, Vol.2, p.134.
58 Lyon, *More Adventures*, p.71. See also Young, *Forgotten Scottish Voices*, pp.107-108.

Alternative garments might also be found to replace the kilt. Douglas Gillespie records that in 2nd Argylls, in March, 1915, for service in the trenches, some of the men "have bought baggy blue trousers from Frenchmen, or patched up old garments that they have found lying about."[59]

Cleaning kilts and person was a major operation, normally performed the day after returning to billets from the trenches.[60] Depending on the conditions, mud would have to be scraped, brushed or washed off kilts[61], and the many pleats made this a tiresome operation.[62] Often it took time for kilts to dry[63], and they were not always dry before the next turn of duty. Mud would also have to be washed or scraped from legs.[64] During this operation soldiers would move about in shirt-tails, kilt-covers, greatcoats or blankets.[65]

Not all were as fortunate as Lieutenant Hugh Bartholomew of 14th Argylls. After coming out of their dreadful spell in the trenches at Bouchavesnes on 1st January, 1917, "It took quite four days to get the outer layer of mud off one's clothes. I had to send my kilt home, as Nimmo found it quite an impossible job to clean."[66] The whole performance was not easy, and it was for this reason that sand-bags might be used when going into the trenches to provide protection against mud, to keep puttees and hose-tops clean, and thereby save work in cleaning up.[67]

Apart from water and mud, extreme cold was also a problem. One particular problem, encouraged by the combination of freezing water and mud underfoot, came to be known as 'trench-foot,' often associated with frost-bitten feet and toes. Trench-foot was actually caused by a lack of circulation in the feet and legs, and if untreated, led to gangrene and amputation. Most cases were caught before recourse to the knife, but before treatment was enforced, many soldiers suffered from bad feet which would affect them for the rest of their lives. The problem potentially affected all soldiers at the front, not just Highlanders.

Remedies were of course applied in the Highland battalions as in others. These included rubbing with whale-oil, drying of clothing, provision of thigh high waders, dry socks, hot drinks and rum.[68] By the middle of 1915, a high incidence of trench foot was attributed to officers failing to enforce remedial measures,[69] but trench foot and frost-bite were still common in winter.

---

59 Gillespie, *Letters from Flanders*, p.52, letter 16 March, 1915.
60 Apart from specific refs in this section, see: IWM 1862 Craig-Brown, letter 26 January, 1915; Bird, *Ghosts*, p.33; IWM 4586 Douglas, pp.395-396.
61 Rule, *Students under Arms*, p.90; LC GS 0262 Campbell, letters to fiancée, 12, 15 January, 1917; IWM 4370 Christison, memoir, p.51; IWM 3449 Cordner, memoir, IWM Books Cooper, 'Domi Militacque,' pp.97-98.
62 IWM 4586 Douglas, pp.135, 786; THM, Camerons 92-35, Welsh, memoirs, p.13.
63 Private William Cameron, quoted in Young, *Forgotten Scottish Voices*, p.204; IWM 2528 Bradbury, memoir, p.37.
64 IWM 3008 McPake, diary, 1 December, 1915; Collins, *Last Man Standing*, p.86.
65 BWA, Couston, William, letters to mother, 3 August 1917 & 28 February 1918, and LC, GS 0257 Cameron, memoir; Lyon, *In kilt and khaki*, p.160; LC GS 0262 Campbell, letter to fiancée 28 July, 1916; IWM 3449 Cordner, memoir; IWM Books, Cooper, 'Domi Militaeque,' pp.97-98; IWM Books Brooke, 'Wait for it', p.186; Bird, *Ghosts*, p.84.
66 Bartholomew, p.45, diary 1 January, 1917.
67 IWM 8192 Lawson, letter to Bessie, 12 August, 1917; BWA, Thomson, Alex, narrative, vol. 2, p.63; LC GS 1761 Wilson, memoir, pp 64, 84.
68 References in the sources are too numerous to cite here.
69 Corrigan, *Mud, Blood and Poppycock*, pp.95-96.

2nd Battalion Argyll and Sutherland Highlanders, Bois Grenier Sector, winter, early 1915. (IWM Q48955)

Highland battalions suffered terribly from trench-foot, frost-bite and exposure during every winter from 1914/15 to 1917/18. One example will suffice. About the third week of December, 1916, Private John Cartmell was manning improvised trenches with 7th Seaforths at Sailly-Sallisel.

> About 30% of our men were being carried back with frost bite. Nearly all the men who were frost bitten had lost their boots in the mud, and after the first night their feet had swollen to about twice their normal size. A great many of them burst and quite a lot of chaps died as soon as they got into hospital.

At the end of the fourth day they went back into a reserve position waist deep in icy slush. When relieved:

> Only half the Batt was left and our feet were in such a state with the water and frost that it was nearly impossible to walk. We were told to make the best of our way to Combles where we would find some artillery limbers waiting to take us back. I lost my boots in the mud trying to get to the road, and had to crawl about a kilo and a half to Combles. There were many others in the same plight and the artillery drivers had to help us on to the limbers when we did get to them … more than half the chaps were sent to hospital that night. I

afterwards met some of them in England 6 months later and found that a great many had died or had their feet amputated.[70]

There are many other examples in the sources of individual soldiers affected by either trench-foot or frost-bite,[71] some of them being hospitalized as a result.[72] A few examples will suffice to show the scale of the problem at the battalion level. According to A. Gilmour in 14th Argylls, some 300 members of the battalion were hospitalised with trench foot or pleurisy after standing for four days knee-deep in water in December 1916.[73] According to Norman Beaton, in 7th Gordons, at Le Sars, in front of Courcelette in December, 1916, "more than half of the fellows in the battalion were sent to hospital with frost bitten feet."[74] Coll MacDonald, chaplain to 8th Black Watch, reported that the weather was so severe that on the morning of 5 December 1917, 73 men of 8th Black Watch reported sick, and conditions continued to take their toll well into January 1918.[75]

To what extent was Highland dress a contributor to trench-foot or frost-bitten feet? In one respect it certainly was: the failure of Highland shoes in the mud, which we have already noted. There is little doubt that the failure of Highland shoes also contributed to trench foot and frost-bite in the first winter of 1914/15. At Le Havre, in January 1915, a Tommy, possibly a Munster, back from the front, informed Lionel Sotheby of the pitiable condition of 2nd Argylls in the rigorous weather of November 1914:

> He also went on to say that the brogue shoes worn by the Highlanders were useless in the trenches, as the mud in places reached the knees, & one was stuck in the slime. After a few hours of this suffering the men would try to disengage their limbs from the unwilling embrace & in so doing left their shoes and sometimes their stocking thickly adhered to the mud. Now stockingless and bootless their plight was miserable, and their bare legs rapidly got frostbitten. He said that at this stage, there were more casualties of frost bitten feet than of actually wounded.[76]

While this may be exaggerated, there is no doubt that 2nd Argylls suffered severely from frost-bite in the winter of 1914-15.[77]

---

70 THM S796, Cartmell, memoir.
71 IWM 10819, Brittan, diary, 10 March, 1915; BWA Guthrie, letters to wife, 29 June, 1 July, 3 October, 1915; IWM 5821, Semple, letter from Jock McLeod, 12 December, 1915; IWM 4586 Douglas, memoir, pp.451, 457, 462; ASHM N-E1, Dalziel, LCpl J., diary 26, 27 February, 1915.
72 McDermott, R. K. *Robert Keith McDermott, Captain 3rd Battn Seaforth Highlanders (attached 1st Battn)* (London: Walter McDermott, 1930), pp.8-12, 16, letters from him, 29 December, 1914, 5, 12, 14, 27, 28 January, 1915, 9 July, 1916; LC, Tape 630/647, Macdonald, interview. See also LC GS 1008 Macdonald, W.S., diary, passim, and also letter to father 31 December, 1916; LC GS 0627 Gilmour, article by him in *The Beam*, September, 1982, and LC Tape 700, Gilmour, interview.
73 Quoted by Young, *Forgotten Scottish Voices*, pp.107-108. See also: LC GS 0456 Dick, memoirs, pp.44, 45.
74 GHM uncatalogued, Beaton, memoir, pp.164-168, 170, 178.
75 BWA, MacDonald, Coll, letters to wife 6, 11, 13, 18 December 1917, 2, 4, 8, 16, 17 January 1918.
76 LC GS 1507, Sotheby, diary, 8 January 1915.
77 See: ASHM N-E2 Hyslop diary, 20 November, 1914, 11 & 12 January, 1915; IWM 11126 Liddell, letter to father 26 November, 1914; ASHM N-E2, Collier, journal.

184   Those Bloody Kilts

Similarly, Percy Reid states that in the first four days the 6th Gordons spent in the trenches, in December, 1914, before they were issued with boots and puttees, 100 of the battalion went away with frost-bite.[78] When the right half battalion of 5th Black Watch left the trenches on 9 December, 1914, they could only muster some 150 men, on account of the large numbers who at this time were temporarily unfit for duty.[79]

Another contributor in the first winter was the deployment to France of those regular Highland battalions which had been brought back home from India and Egypt. These battalions could feel the chill even in England[80] before their deployment to France, and there is evidence that they did suffer considerably in the first winter.[81] Ian Grant, a lieutenant in 2nd Camerons states, for example, that on the night of 10 January, 1915, the battalion went into old French trenches, "knee deep in mud" and came out again on the night of the 12th. During that time, "We lost two killed, two died of exposure, 10 wounded, 65 admitted to hospital with frostbite etc." On the 19th he was at Divisional Headquarters, "where all the slight cases of frostbite etc are formed into a composite battalion. We have some 40 men, ourselves."[82] According to the regimental history, the situation was even worse. Not only did Privates Stallard and King drown in the mud, but when on the 13th the brigade marched back to the reserve area, 104 men of the battalion were unable to walk, and had to be carried in wagons. When a composite battalion was formed of men unfit for the trenches but not sufficiently ill to be admitted to hospital – mostly 'trench feet' cases, the battalion contributed 83 NCOs and men to it.[83] On 26 February Lance-Corporal Dalziel of 1st Argylls found himself "sitting in the trenches, crying like a baby with frost-bitten feet."[84] And in his diary for 4 February, 1915, at Dickebusche, Lieutenant Robertson, who had just joined 1st Argylls from home, noted that C Company, to which he was posted, "was 58 strong instead of 100 although it had been in the trenches only five days." Much later, he reflected that at that time, "We still wore the kilt, of all unsuitable kit."[85]

Otherwise, opinions differ on the contribution of the kilt to suffering in the cold. In the face of freezing weather, one undoubted benefit of the kilt was that the seven yards of cloth did at least keep the waist warm. Some veterans indeed became strong advocates of the kilt for this reason. Hal Kerridge, who served throughout the war in both the London Scottish and 1st Gordons, was one:

78 IWM 322 Reid, interview.
79 Wauchope, *Black Watch*, vol.2, p.43.
80 Craig-Brown, *Historical Records*, Vol.3, p.296; THM Camerons 97-22, Russell, memoirs, p.186; LC GS 0177 Boyle, diary, 16 November, 1914; Anderson, *1st Argylls*, p.25; ASHM N-E1, Dalziel, diary, 19 November, 1914.
81 IWM 11334 PP Robertson, W.S., typescript memoir, 'Reminiscences of an Old Soldier', 7pp., p.6.
82 THM Camerons 02-58, Grant, Maj. Gen I.C., letters to father 16 January, and to Aunt Vi, 19 January, 1915.
83 Craig-Brown, *Historical Records*, Vol.3, pp.297-298.
84 ASHM N-E1, Dalziel, diary, 19 November, 1914, 15, 31 January, 19, 20, 26, 27 February, 1915.
85 ASHM N-E1 Robertson, Lt C.B., diary, 4 February, 1915; memoir written 1975. See also on 1st Argylls: LC GS 0177 Boyle, diary, 18 January, 28 February, 1915; Anderson, *1st Argylls*, p.28; THM Seaforths 87-125, Heriz-Smith, letter from Pte J. McDonald, 1st Argylls to Sybil Smith, 3 March, 1915; LC GS.0731, Hay-Young, letter to sister Mag, 11 March, 1915.

> It's one of those things you get used to, because, after all, in wearing a kilt you've got all the protection where it's mostly needed, round the stomach; that's all the pleats around the stomach as you know. I think from memory there's seven or nine yards to every kilt and when it's all pleated up that's a nice big bunch around your waist, and that's the place to keep warm. Your legs and arms and that sort of thing got used to the cold. You didn't notice it.[86]

Norman Collins felt that "it was the best garment to have in the trenches,"[87] while Ronald 'Taffy' Wells who served with 9th Royal Scots on the Western Front from 1917 to 1918, claimed that the kilt kept him "warm as toast".[88] There are several other statements in the same vein, mostly but not exclusively from veterans rather than soldiers writing at the time,[89] and the argument was cheerfully deployed by those great proponents of the kilt, Douglas Wimberley and Norman Macleod.[90] But this view was certainly not shared by Lance Corporal Carter of the Liverpool Scottish, who wrote of the kilt in the winter of late 1914 that, "It may be all right for swank, but at these times you wish you were wearing trousers"[91] In the dreadful conditions encountered after the Somme, in November 1916, Private William Couston felt that, "'breeks' are better than a kilt in this weather. By a long way."[92] W.S. Macdonald, who served as a private in 14th Argylls during the winter of 1916-17, felt, "It seemed ridiculous wearing kilts among all the tough conditions, especially when we were in mud conditions, and we were sometimes on sentry there and the water froze round our [putties?] and after we'd been standing in trenches for a bit we had to break the ice to walk about to get going."[93] J.E.P. Levyns, in the South African Scottish, perhaps summed up the situation most accurately: "my kilt kept my body astonishingly warm under my greatcoat, but my feet were always numb and aching, with the cold penetrating through my boots."[94]

It was indeed above all feet which suffered in the appalling winter conditions in the trenches. Norman Macleod claimed that within 15th Division, the kilted Highland Brigade had fewer cases of trench foot than the other brigades.

> This was partly due to the fact that the men were able to wear an extra pair of hose-tops, which acted like mittens in keeping their feet warm, while the trousered men put on extra socks and forced their feet into boots, thereby directly interfering with the circulation. Again, the puttee worn by trousered regiments tended to shrink, so that the kilt as a fighting dress had its decided advantage.[95]

---

86 IWM 18836 Kerridge, interview.
87 Collins, *Last Man Standing*, p.82. See also: IWM 12043 Collins, interview.
88 IWM 9930 Wells, interview.
89 IWM 4586 Douglas, memoir, p.384; IWM 6926 Dennis, memoir, p.284; IWM 20453 Pringle, interview; IWM 10391 Jordan, interview.
90 IWM 430 Wimberley, 'The Kilt in Modern War'; Macleod in Mackay, *Romantic Story*.
91 Quoted by Giblin, *Bravest of Hearts*, p.11.
92 BWA Couston, letter to mother, 1 August 1916.
93 LC, Tape 630/647, Macdonald, interview.
94 Levyns, *The disciplines of war*, p.63.
95 Macleod, *6th Camerons*, pp.51-52. See also: Craig-Brown, *Historical Records*, Vol.4, p.300; Macleod in Mackay, *Romantic Story*.

But the fact is that Highland battalions did suffer dreadfully at times from both trench foot and frost-bitten feet. In the Glasgow Highlanders, indeed, heavy casualties from frost-bite and trench feet in the winter of 1916-17 were blamed specifically on unfamiliarity with the kilt. In December, 1916, the battalion received drafts of 74 men from 2/7th H.L.I. and a further draft of 175 Lanarkshire Yeomanry who were unaccustomed to the kilt. They then went into the trenches from 18 to 22 December, when they suffered disproportionately from both trench-feet and frost-bite compared with those men who were already used to wearing the kilt.[96] This was clearly an exceptional case. However, if the kilt itself cannot be blamed for a condition which periodically affected all soldiers at the front, it is clear that the extra warmth around the middle provided by the kilt was not sufficient to prevent these complaints.

If frost-bitten feet should not generally be attributed to Highland dress, the same is not true of frost-bitten knees. There is abundant evidence of frost-bitten knees, although apart from two examples, both from January, 1918, one on the Western Front[97] and one in Italy,[98] all the evidence specific to knees relates to the exceptionally cold winter of 1916-17.[99] This does not mean that knees were not frost-bitten on other occasions, but it does indicate that the problem of frost-bitten knees as opposed to frost-bitten feet, became acute only when the cold weather was at its most extreme.

A few examples will suffice. In 1st Camerons, Lieutenant Alastair Jameson wrote on 6 February, 1917: "The weather is the severest I have ever experienced. There is an iron frost & snow everywhere. My legs, from my hips to my hose tops are raw & it is very difficult to keep warm even with all the clothing we can carry." On the 17th he wrote that "I have frost bitten knees & been absolutely perished with cold".[100] Around January, 1917, Welsh confirms that in 1st Camerons, "Frost-bite was getting fairly common, usually on our exposed knees, and a painful trouble it is."[101]

Andrew Bain served as an officer with 7th Argylls and recalls that in January, 1917, after enduring the dreadful conditions at Courcelette:

> we were sent down to the coast for a rest period, and when we came out of the trenches we'd to march back 50 or 60 miles to get down to the place on the coast – I've forgotten the name of it [Le Crotoy] – the mouth of the Somme, and it was during very severe frost and the mouth of the Somme and the Sea were all frozen up – it was just like the North Pole – and we were all wearing kilts at the time and everybody in the Highland Division had terrible chilblains in the knees with all red flesh and the only bandages available were khaki coloured first-aid kit and everybody had their knees wrapped up in these brown,

---

96 IWM Books, Reid, 'Shoulder to shoulder,' p.169.
97 IWM 1659 PP Scammell, F.H., letter to mother and sister Violet, 26 January, 1918.
98 IWM 8592 Macgregor, letter to wife, 13 January, 1918.
99 Apart from the examples cited, see: GHM PB375 Pailthorpe, memoir, p.38; IWM 2528 Bradbury, memoir, p.12; BWA, Couston, letter to mother, 9 February 1917; IWM 14335, Marr, memoir, p.53; Clayton, Anne, *Chavasse Double VC*, (Barnsley: Pen & Sword, 1997), p.180.
100 NLS MS 10305, Jameson, Alastair, letters to mother, 6, 17 February, 1917.
101 THM Camerons 92-35 Welsh, memoir, p.17.

filthy looking bandages, and it really was a sorrowful sight for a time until we got sort of settled down and things healed up again.[102]

And the situation at Le Crotoy is confirmed by the battalion history, which notes that, "The effect on our kilted men was that fully eighty per cent suffered from severe chillblains on the knees."[103]

During the same winter, Private E.R. Savage was training for the battle of Arras with 9th Black Watch when he went sick with frost bitten knees. After hospitalisation and recovery in Britain, he was drafted to France again and posted to 7th Black Watch in time for the Cambrai battle in November. Thus the frostbite had probably put him out of the front line for eight months.[104]

Knees were also affected by ice on kilts cutting the skin, just as we have already observed for dried mud.[105] This problem was most acute in the savage winter of 1916-17 but could occur at other times too.[106] This is amply confirmed in the sources. Percy Reid, for example, describes how the 6th Gordons used field bandages to protect themselves from this chafing on their long march to Arras in January 1917.[107] Second Lieutenant Robbie Macmillan joined 6th Seaforth Highlanders in January, 1917, when they were at rest. On 5 February, they started their march back to the front.

> We started our march today. It has been snowing. The frost is hard everywhere at home, but here I think it is awful … The frost makes havoc with your legs in kilts! Many of us were knocked out for a few days with chafed legs. I saw two men with icicles hanging from their moustaches & the temperature was 16 below freezing point.[108]

Second Lieutenant Grant Fleming, serving in 1st Gordons, describes how, on the night of 10/11 April, 1917, during the Battle of Arras;

> We bivouacked in a wide supply trench we had taken from the Germans – a draughty place and bitterly cold. By morning the temperature had dropped below freezing point and our first task was to beat the ice out of our kilts; frozen stiff as boards, they cut the skin like knives. However romantic the kilt may be as a walking out dress, it was a positive danger in the kind of weather we sometimes had in France.[109]

One soldier directly affected was Private William Couston, of 7th Black Watch, who recorded how his skinned and frost-bitten knees effectively kept him confined to light duties for over a

---

102 IWM 375 Recording, Bain, Andrew Ramsay, IWM interview, 1974. See also [Gregory] *France 1916-1917-1918*, pp.10 11.
103 Morrison, *7th Argylls*, pp.24 26.
104 LC Middlebrook *Somme 1918*, Savage, letter dated 6 July 1976.
105 LC Transcripts, Transcript of conversation between John Richard Gammell, aged 90, and his son-in-law, Michael Wilson.
106 e.g. the Liverpool Scottish in November, 1914. See Clayton, *Chavasse Double VC*, pp.75-76.
107 IWM 322 Reid, interview.
108 NLA Acc.11627/87 letter from Rev R.A.C. Macmillan to Walter Buchan, 5 February, 1917.
109 IWM 15345 Fleming, memoir, p.32.

month between February and March, 1917.[110] It is not surprising that he had asked his mother to send him some Vaseline,[111] presumably as a protection against chafing, and no doubt other soldiers tried this. In any case, assuming that there were other soldiers who suffered from chafing to a greater or lesser extent, it is likely that impact on the battalion would have been noticeable.

In addition to this chafing, icy snow might cut the knees directly. On 8 January, 1918, Arthur Wrench, in 4th Seaforths, moved back from the line to Fremicourt. "I walked down behind a limber-wagon and the snow was blowing a blizzard. The little hard flakes were sharp as scalpels and my knees are all chafed and cut."[112]

One way of keeping knees warm, used for example by R.W.F. Johnston in 9th Royal Scots, was to pull up hose-tops over the knees.[113] Separate woollen knee-hose might be sent out for this purpose from home. In the Glasgow Highlanders, Norman Macmillan records wearing "knee hose" in the trenches on 18 October, 1915.[114] But in January, 1915, George Murray, in 4th Seaforths, complained that they only meant more to carry and were potentially unhealthy. "Please don't send me anything in the way of clothing just now. Knee caps etc are only a nuisance and can't be worn in the trenches. When they get wet they adhere closely to the legs, consequently so many cases of rheumatism."[115] And they did not, initially at least meet with official approval. In 1st Camerons, Craig-Brown noted on 17 October, 1914, that, "An order had to be issued against men wearing woollen coverings over their knees by day, sort of knee mitts, a habit contracted in the trenches at Vendresse,"[116] although a presumably later order found in one of his Field Message Books does permit woollen knee-caps to be worn in the trenches.[117]

Sand-bags might also provide protection from the cold. Their use in 4th Seaforths for this purpose, for example, was apparently considered normal and acceptable.[118] In such circumstances they might even act as a substitute for the kilt.

Douglas Gillespie records the men of 2nd Argylls in March, 1915, with "the most amazing styles of lower garments that you could ever imagine, for to keep their legs warm, in spite of the kilt, they have set to work with sacking and canvas."[119] Percy Reid comments on the measures taken by the soldiers to protect their legs from the extreme cold he experienced on the march with the 6th Gordons in January 1917. On this occasion they used field-bandages rather than sand-bags, and the dressings had the effect not only of providing direct protection from the cold, but also of protecting the knees from the cuts inflicted by their ice-rimmed kilts.

> A couple of days after, we were on the march and it was in the month of January. It was bitter cold; Oh God, it was cold! And we were going up to Arras which was about thirty kilometers, thirty, forty kilometers from this place. Well, we marched and, I always

---

110 BWA Couston, letters to mother, 9, 17, 28 February, 6, 13, 19 March, 1917.
111 Ibid., letter to mother, 9 February 1917.
112 IWM 3834 Wrench, diary, p.174.
113 IWM 13586 Johnston, interview.
114 IWM 3460, Macmillan, diary, 18 October, 1915.
115 THM Seaforths 81-180 Murray, letters to sister Kate, 20, 24 January, 1915.
116 IWM 1862 Craig-Brown, diary, 17 October, 1914; also mentioned in Craig-Brown, *Historical Records*, Vol.3, p.64.
117 IWM 1862, Craig-Brown, Field Message Books, undated order.
118 IWM Books Haldane, '4th Seaforths', unpublished draft, p.76.
119 Gillespie, *Letters from Flanders*, p.52, letter 16 March, 1915.

remember that, our knees were frozen up, you know, with the usual field bandages to wrap up our knees and all up our legs to keep the frost from biting into our legs, our bare legs. However, we got up to Arras.[120]

Willie Macmillan, in 7th Seaforths, wrote home that, in November, 1915, in a shelter in the trenches in front of Zillebeke, "I had a couple of sandbags on each leg and both legs inside the coke-bag, but still my feet would not get warm."[121] Private Douglas, in 8th Black Watch, noted how, "if the nights were either wet or cold, and our legs protruded half out of our cubby or funk-holes, we used to wrap sandbags round our knees and legs to protect them as much as possible."[122] Perhaps the most damning indictment of the kilt in trench conditions was provided by the frequency with which Highland soldiers would use sand-bags or field bandages to protect their bare legs and knees.[123]

Highland soldiers, like other Tommies, were of course issued with fur coats and, later, leather jerkins, as protection against the cold. There is no reason to believe that their experience with these garments was in any respect different to that of their trousered colleagues. Alex Thomson records the issue of fur jackets to 4th Black Watch on 26 February 1915, the day they disembarked at Le Havre. The next day, "It was very funny to see us all running about in the dark with the white jackets on, everyone shouting, 'Baa, baa.'"[124] Not all recipients were impressed,[125] but generally the fur jackets were a great success.

Highland soldiers were also issued with thigh-length trench waders, often referred to simply as gum-boots. These were issued to some battalions as early as January to March, 1915,[126] possibly even by November, 1914,[127] and were distributed widely in the winter of 1915/16 and afterwards.[128] The effect of wearing the kilt with the waders could be quite comical. As Lieutenant-Colonel Allen, commanding 7th Black Watch, commented, "All the men have now got fishermen's boots right up to the top of their thighs. They are very comfortable & serviceable though the men look the most awful buccaneers in them under their kilts."[129] And as Douglas Wimberley in 1st Camerons records of the winter of 1915-16, "In the trenches … the Jocks all wore long rubber gum boots, with their kilts hanging outside them, and goat skin jerkins. In this kit, when unshaved and streaked with mud, they looked awful ruffians."[130] In

---

120 IWM 322 Reid, interview.
121 IWM 3460 Macmillan, William Macmillan to mother, 1 December, 1915.
122 IWM 4586 Douglas, memoir, pp.732-733.
123 Apart from the specific examples cited, see also: THM Camerons 92-35, Welsh, memoir, p.4; IWM 612 Gameson, memoirs, p.82; LC GS 1027 Macleod, letter to mother, 30 March, 1915; LC GS.0456 Dick, memoirs, p.44.
124 BWA, Thomson, narrative. See also: LC GS 1507 Sotheby, diary, 14 January 1915; *Robert Keith McDermott*, p.6, letter from him, 9 December, 1914.
125 Beattie, *48th Highlanders*, pp.39-40.
126 IWM 3460 Macmillan, diary, 23 January, 1915; BWA, Thomson narrative; LC 0177 Boyle, diary, 28 February, 1915; Gillespie, *Letters from Flanders*, pp.26, 29, letters 1, 2 March, 1915; Craig-Brown, *Historical Records*, Vol.3, p.298.
127 IWM 5015 Ross, letter to MOD, 12 May, 1981.
128 Apart from specific instances cited, references in the sources are too numerous to cite here.
129 IWM 114 Allen, letter to wife, 26 November, 1915.
130 IWM 430 Wimberley, memoir, pp.36-37..

fact, the waders were not comfortable to wear with the kilt.[131] Private Bradbury, attached to 2nd Entrenching Battalion, describes the problem.

> We had orders to again parade at three o'clock for the same place but before leaving we were given gum boots which we put on and which stretched up to the thighs; these, however, were very awkward to those of us who had kilts as it was impossible to tuck the kilts into the tops of the boots and there was nothing to keep the boots up owing to their fitting next to our bare legs so that whenever we stepped into any mud our next step left the gum boots stuck in the mud and feet and legs came out of the boots. In addition, by trying to keep the boots on it continually chafed the skin of our legs making them very sore. To us, these boots were an entire failure.[132]

Thomas Lyon in the Glasgow Highlanders records that "while some are content to wear the kilt over these in the ordinary way, others make a desperate attempt to stuff the folds inside the tops of the boots."[133] Ian MacKay noted how in 4th Camerons, "our fellows invented an ingenious idea of sewing two sandbags together like trousers and tucking the kilt into them. The effect was very amusing as it gave them all enormous posteriors."[134]

Private Andrew White in 1st Seaforths also describes how he tied a pair of dry sand-bags round his legs to use as a liner for waders.[135] Yet again we find sand-bags being used unofficially to compensate for the disadvantages of the kilt.

Given the evident disadvantages of the kilt in the extreme conditions in which the soldiers were obliged to live and fight, it might be assumed that the kilt would ultimately be replaced by trousers. In fact, the trousers worn frequently during training were rarely if ever taken on campaign. Both known exceptions, quite separate, curiously relate to 6th Gordons. In the first instance, the Battalion evidently took their trousers with them on initial deployment to France, but they were soon done away with.[136] In the second case, when George Stables joined 6th Gordons on 8 April 1918, with a draft of 61 from a young soldiers' battalion, they were known as "the trouser draft" as they came out in trousers and there was not time to issue them with kilts.[137] Certain battalions, however, may never have been issued with kilts. These were the pioneer or labour battalions, and included 9th Gordons,[138] 9th and 11th Camerons,[139] and 9th Seaforths,[140] who wore trousers.[141] When, in June, 1916, 6th Argylls were converted from a line battalion within 51st Division to a pioneer battalion within 5th Division, they were issued with trousers (cut down to make shorts), for use on working parties and in the trenches, although

---

131 McGilchrist, *Liverpool Scottish*, p.60; BWA, Guthrie, letter to wife, 30 November, 1915; ASHM N-E2 Hyslop, diary, 26 November, 1915.
132 IWM 2528 Bradbury, memoir p.9. The incident took place on 9 January, 1917.
133 Lyon, *More Adventures*, p.70.
134 THM Camerons 91-7 MacKay, letter to mother, 2 December, 1915.
135 THM Seaforths 89-81 White, letter to mother, 9 November, 1915.
136 GHM PB2984 Strachan, memoir.
137 LC GS 1516 Stables, letter from him 5 February, 1979.
138 Charles Bowman, quoted by Young, *Forgotten Scottish Voices*, pp.245, 246.
139 Craig-Brown, *Historical Records*, Vol. 4, pp.387, 392-393.
140 THM Seaforths 81-2 Cooper, memoir, pp.42, 180.
141 Gillespie, *Letters from Flanders*, p.307, letter 21 September, 1915.

Soldiers of the Gordon Highlanders putting on rubber thigh boots, Bazentin-le-Petit, November 1916. (IWM Q4474)

orders insisted that, "the kilt will still remain the parade and fighting dress of the unit."[142] Conversely, when 11th Camerons were converted from a labour battalion to a line battalion in July, 1918, the men were issued with kilts.[143] Charles Bowman, of 9th Gordons, landed in France in June 1916 and was killed in August. At some stage he transferred from the 9th to the 1st battalion, when he was issued with a kilt and rejoiced that "we are the real MacKay again and not half highlanders as when we left King Street."[144]

In addition certain specialists within the Highland battalions, notably the Transport, who would have to ride, routinely wore trousers instead of the kilt. This might also be true of runners or despatch riders, who had to ride bicycles, for which, as we have noted in the previous chapter, the kilt was also not well adapted. Alexander Braes was issued with khaki trousers and long puttees before deploying to France with 8th Seaforths in July, 1915, as he was a cyclist in the signals section.[145] Similarly, when Private Sellar arrived with 4th Black Watch at Le Havre on 26 February, 1915, he was made a despatch rider and given a bicycle. "The sergeant ordered me

---

142 ASHM, War Diary 1/6th Bn, 12 and 13 June, 1916.
143 Craig-Brown, *Historical Records,* Vol. 4, pp.392-393.
144 Quoted by Young, *Forgotten Scottish Voices*, pp.245, 246.
145 THM 2013-072 (S) Braes, diary, 8 April, 9 May, 1915.

to give up my kilt for ever. I did it joyfully. Kilts are no use to despatch riders."[146] And again, as a runner for Brigade, Arthur Wrench, from 4th Seaforths, had to make frequent use of a bicycle, for which for a long time he was permitted to wear trousers. He was not then impressed when on 28 October, 1917 (just in time for winter)

> Up the line an order came through that we are to wear the kilt again instead of breeches for cycling. And after just issuing us with long under-pants too. And imagine cycling with a kilt on in the winter time. I don't like the prospects of being called out of [my] bunk some winter night and getting over a frosty saddle with my bare bottom. However, orders are orders and we've got the gear, so there's nothing we can do about it.[147]

It is evident that at least in some, and possibly all, Canadian kilted battalions, the kilt was replaced by trousers in the winter, sometimes cut into shorts by the men.[148] The practice started in the winter of 1915/16 and continued throughout the war. Generally, trousers would be issued for winter use in October or November and replaced by kilts for summer use in April or May. The practice was certainly true of 13th,[149] 15th,[150] 42nd[151] and 72nd Battalions[152] C.E.F., although there appear to have been some variations. 72nd Battalion, for example, having disembarked in France on 13 August, 1916, appear to have worn the kilt through their first winter, for a raid made on the German trenches on the night of 16/17 February was made in kilts.[153] There is also no indication in the comprehensive regimental history of 16th Battalion (Canadian Scottish), whose Commanding Officer was a great traditionalist, that trousers were ever issued to the battalion for winter use.[154] By contrast, the 85th Battalion C.E.F (Nova Scotia Highlanders) who disembarked in France on 11 February, 1917, initially wore trousers and were only issued with kilts in June/July, 1918.[155]

Not all Canadian Highlanders were pleased to go back into kilts when the time came. Thomas Dinesen was an American Dane who won the Victoria Cross with 42nd Battalion C.E.F. On 4 May, 1918 in France, "we paraded in the grounds and were each given a blue-green kilt and a khaki apron." He was not pleased by the change:

> I sighed with regret as I handed off my tattered trousers and put on the heavy kilt instead. Really there is no sense in letting soldiers go to war in such parade equipment. Tradition bobs up its withered old head again! You can't sleep in a kilt, for all the pleats and folds gather together beneath your body into one big hard knot, so that you have to take it off and

---

146 NLS Acc.8802, No.4, Sellar, R.J.B., Diary, 26 February, 1915. See also: IWM 3460 Macmillan, letter from William Macmillan to his mother, 27 May, 1915.
147 IWM 3834 Wrench, diary, pp.164-165, 28, 29 October, 1917.
148 Beattie, *48th Highlanders*, pp.192, 245, 276, 296.
149 IWM 10819 Brittan, diary, 4 March, 1915; Fetherstonhaugh, *13th Battalion*, pp.73, 90, 146, 216, 235.
150 Beattie, *48th Highlanders*, pp.192, 245, 276, 296.
151 Bird, *Ghosts*, pp.59, 71, 84; Dinesen, *Merry Hell*, pp.31, 94, 169; Topp, *42nd Battalion*, pp.19, 35, 165-166, 193.
152 McEvoy & Finlay, *Seaforth Highlanders of Canada*, pp.37, 52, 83, 93.
153 Ibid.
154 Urquhart, *Canadian Scottish*.
155 Hayes, *Eighty-Fifth*, p.115.

spread it carefully on the ground. You then lie down on it and let your poor bare legs freeze … To merely step across a barbed-wire fence in waving skirts is difficult enough in this place, but what will our lives be with drenched kilts in slushy trenches is more than I care to think about. I have half a mind to apply for transfer to the Flying Corps – as I originally meant to – just to escape wearing these beastly things. [156]

Within the British Army itself, "thanks to a strong appeal made by the officers",[157] the issue of trousers as trench stores for wearing in the trenches (with waders) was finally authorised within 51st Highland Division in November, 1916, in response to the dreadful conditions around Courcelette following the battle of the Somme.[158] Their use that winter in the trenches is confirmed for 9th Royal Scots,[159] 6th Black Watch,[160] 7th Black Watch[161] and 7th Argylls.[162] Interestingly, however, there is no evidence in soldiers' accounts that the practice was continued the next winter, and it seems also to have been confined to trench use, not to the long marches in icy winds which caused the Highland soldiers such grief from frost-bite in the early months of 1917. The issue of trousers was not universally successful. When they were issued to 6th Black Watch, "As the authorities forgot to issue braces, the troubles of the men were little lessened by the change of dress."[163]

Remarkably, only one other instance has been found of trousers being issued to British Highland battalions as a protection against the cold. Trousers and waders were issued to 14th Argylls, in 40th Division, in January, 1917, after their initial dreadful experience in the trenches at Bouchavesnes.[164] As Bob Lawson reports, "Kilts apparently having been found unsuitable for this sector we have now been issued with trousers which are a great improvement, and the spell we have just finished was done in trews, and I got on all right, gum boots and all." Trousers were issued again in January, 1918, and were worn until the following month.[165]

Kilted soldiers might welcome the opportunity to change to trousers if the occasion permitted. Alfred Anderson, who appears to have served in 5th then 4/5th Black Watch, stated when interviewed many years later:

Well the kilt was a bad thing. You were never dry. Dragged in the mud and water and that. The water came up your leg and it never really evaporated. Wherever you walked in the trenches, there were fellers who wore trousers if they wanted. And funny enough, nobody queried it, because they were all glad to get out of the kilt themselves.[166]

---

156 Dinesen, *Merry Hell*, p.169.
157 GHM PB1892.3.18 McDonald, 'Uncle Harper's Duds' p.30.
158 Bewsher, *Fifty First*, p.131.
159 IWM 16455 Hay, interview.
160 Wauchope, *Black Watch*, Vol.2, p.155, IWM Books Cooper, 'Domi Militaeque,' pp.95-98, 100-101, 111-112.
161 Wauchope, *Black Watch*, Vol.2, p.275.
162 ASHM N-E2 Hyslop, diary 5 December, 1916; IWM 375 Bain, interview.
163 Wauchope, *Black Watch*, Vol.2, p.155.
164 LC GS 0627 Gilmour, article by him on 'The Other Enemy' in *The Beam*, September, 1982. See also Bartholomew, p.47, extract from diary.
165 IWM 8192 Lawson, letters to Bessie, 14 January, 1917, 27 January, 14 February, 1918.
166 Anderson, Alfred, Last of the 'Old Contemptibles,' <www.bbc.co.uk/history/worldwars/wwone/last_tommy_gallery_01> (2 June 2018).

During the winter of 1915/16, Alick Guthrie of 6th Black Watch was made Acting R.Q.M.S., partly to give him a rest from the trying conditions in the trenches. He announced with some relief, that "I have got into a pair of trews today, & tomorrow I will increase the comfort by adding a pair of woollen drawers I got from A/Q.M. Wilson so ought to be alright so far as clothing is concerned."[167] While recovering in hospital from dysentery, Lance Corporal Dalziel of 1st Argylls had a pair of trousers issued, and confessed he was "glad to be rid of the kilt for a while."[168] Officers might use the privilege of rank to shed the kilt. Guy Macgregor, in 6th Argylls, disliked the kilt, which he temporarily abandoned for "little yellow shorts", and was pleased when in May, 1918, he was permitted to wear breeches instead of the kilt, because of the problem with mosquitoes. However, when his battalion ceased to be a pioneer battalion, and rejoined 51st Highland Division in October, 1918, he lamented that, "It's the unmitigated kilt in this division, so let us hope it will be a mild winter!"[169]

Quite apart from trousers, it would seem sensible that, in the appalling conditions encountered on the Western Front, at least the wearing of drawers would be sanctioned and tradition temporarily abandoned. There is ample evidence to the contrary.[170] Ronald 'Taffy' Wells served with 9th Royal Scots on the Western Front between 1917 and 1918. When asked what he wore under his kilt, he replied, "Nothing! Nobody ever wore anything … There were a couple who wore tartan little pants. I never did."[171] And asked about the practicality of not wearing pants with the kilt, Norman Collins replied, "We had no use for them, because the kilt was warm, and your shirt came down under the kilt and formed a kind of apron, and there was no point in having pants as far as I can see."[172]

It would appear from these comments that tradition continued to be observed in the trenches. And initially there is evidence that, in some battalions at least, tradition was rigorously enforced. During the winter of 1914/15, for example, an order was put out in the 1st Camerons stating: "It is to be understood that drawers are no part of the Highland Dress and [with the exception of knee coverings worn in the trenches] are on no account to be worn with the kilt."[173] By the next winter, this opposition had been overcome, at least at the staffing level, and drawers, to be worn by Highland soldiers "when recommended by medical authorities", appeared on the scales of winter clothing from October, 1915.[174] It appears that the hardships of the first winter had been taken into account, and that the R.A.M.C. probably had a role in instigating the change. There are, however, very few references in the sources to the issue of these drawers. This does not prove conclusively that they were as rarely issued. There may have been a reluctance to record the infringement of tradition. They were certainly issued in some battalions on some occasions. For example, Lieutenant-Colonel Hugh Allen, commanding 7th Black Watch, in 51st Highland Division, wrote on 18 October, 1915, that, "We got a list the other day of the clothes we are

---

167 BWA Guthrie, letter to wife, 15 December, 1915.
168 ASHM N-E1 Dalziel, diary, 12 February, 1915.
169 IWM 8592 Macgregor, letters to wife, 6 January, 12 February, 9 May, 31 July, 6 October, 1918.
170 See, e.g., Lauder, Harry, *A Minstrel in France* (London: Andrew Melrose, 1918), p.219.
171 IWM 9930 Wells, interview.
172 IWM 12043 Collins, interview. See also IWM 4173 Macmillan, interview; THM, Camerons 92-35, Welsh, memoir, p.57; IWM 11965 Spencer, interview; IWM 16455 Hay, interview 1984; Walker, *Tom Walker Remembers*, p.5.
173 IWM 1862 Craig-Brown, Field Message Books, undated draft order.
174 Great War Forum: post by Joe Sweeney 22 March 2009, <www.greatwarforum.org> (2 June, 2018).

to get for the winter & these include warm vest and drawers, cardigan jacket, leather jerkin, muffler and cap comforter."[175] And Private William Couston recorded the issue of drawers to the soldiers of that battalion probably in October 1916:

> By the way we have been issued with a pair of short flannel pants to wear under the kilt. They look all right but I have not put them on yet. We shall need them I am told. Yon ones you bought may come in handy after all. But don't send anything out until I ask for it as I have so little spare room in my pack for such extras. One must keep things at a minimum here – no other way for it.[176]

Piper Dan McLeod, in 4th Black Watch, then in 15th Division, records that on 25 November 1915, "small kit" was given out, which may have included drawers.[177] At New Year, 1916, 11th Argylls, also in 15th Division, got a rest at Lillers for one month. "During that period, every one man had winter clothing issued; a skin jacket, gloves, semmit and pants."[178] Douglas Wimberley is probably referring to these issued drawers when he comments that "under shorts of extreme brevity" were generally worn under the kilt in winter.[179] Finally, Henry Coates served with 1st London Scottish, in 56th London Division, from 1915 to 1918. He notes that for the most part they did not wear anything under the kilt, but that drawers were issued later on.

> They did later on issue us with some grey flannel little trunks … They were loose horrible things. They did not give us any belts or anything to keep the kilt up and therefore there was no means of keeping these wretched grey flannel – trews they called them – and therefore we only used them for cleaning our rifles. They were no good for protection; they just fell down around your knees. The most stupid thing you ever, well, was ever conceived. It was shocking.[180]

Clearly the regulation Army issue drawers were not a complete success! But the most extraordinary story of all is told by Private G.V. Dennis. He was a signaller with 21st Battalion K.R.R.C. Following the dissolution of this battalion in March, 1918, he was hospitalised for a short time, before being transferred to 11th Camerons at Wormhoudt around June, where he was issued with his kilt. After being dressed,

> I handed in my old cheesecutter after removing my K.R.R. cap badge, my old trousers, puttees … and my underpants. In return I received a chit saying that I had not been issued with the short special type underpants and a friendly warning from the Q.M. not to go upstairs on the buses when I went home. I wondered why I had to have such a chit. Later

---

175 IWM 114 Allen, letter to wife, 18 October 1915.
176 BWA Couston, letter to mother, 13 October 1916. [Note: the pages of this letter are broken up, and it is possible that the page from which this observation is taken belongs to a letter of different date.]
177 IWM 16387 PP McLeod, Pipe Major Daniel Alexander, Diaries transcript, entry for 25 November, 1915.
178 ASHM N-E11 Bowie, memoir.
179 IWM 430 Wimberley, 'The Kilt in Modern War.'
180 IWM 9833 Coates, interview.

on morning parades the officer taking them would flick his cane just under one's kilt to see if the issue pants were being worn. On such occasions I had to produce my chit.[181]

Otherwise, drawers might be supplied through battalion sources. Clayton notes "a special issue of short woollen drawers" to men of the Liverpool Scottish around November 1914.[182] George Murray, a Territorial soldier with 4th Seaforths states that on 30 December, 1914, "We all got supplied with pants and fur coats today," the pants presumably being supplied through some comforts fund.[183] Sometimes well-meaning individuals or organisations at home might send out undergarments of an inappropriate nature. In March, 1915, The Scottish Society in Edinburgh, clearly concerned for the Highland soldiers' welfare in the winter, submitted to the Commanding Officer of the 1st Camerons, then Major Ernest Craig-Brown, a "sample of a new kind of trews for wearing with the kilt." Craig-Brown wrote back, thanking the Society, but pointing out that, "as far as the 1st Battn Cameron Highrs is concerned, the garment is not considered suitable for Kilted Regiments."[184] And on 21 October, 1915, Jock MacLeod in 2nd Camerons wrote:

> Humorous story no rib. At a distributing centre of comforts for the troops, there was a large bale marked 'Flannel Petticoats'. The officials [thought] that they had come by mistake, being probably meant for Belgian refugees. The bale was opened, and among bright red flannel petticoats there was found a note 'For our dear, brave Scottish troops with love from Mrs Smith – !!?[185]

Much more frequently, however, men would either obtain drawers, if they wanted them, through private sources, or be sent them from home, whether they wanted them or not! On 21 September, 1914, Jock MacLeod, as a newly commissioned officer with 3rd Camerons at Invergordon, wrote to his mother on the question of pants: "We do not wear anything under the kilt. We are perfectly warm without, and it is much more comfortable and healthy for marching." But when serving overseas with 2nd Camerons, he asks for pants on 10 and 17 February, 1915, and in an undated letter, he confirms receipt, but asks, "might I have … an old pair of my grey flannel bags for wear under the kilt when in the trenches"?[186] Extraordinarily, a later manuscript note by MacLeod, dated 18 September, 1950, states indignantly: "We wore nothing under the kilt at any time, whether on active service or not. Any mention in these letters of anything to wear under the kilt was a mistake due to my inexperience."! But in reality, there are sufficient accounts of drawers for the winter being requested or supplied from home in the sources to indicate that this was not a hugely unusual state of affairs.[187]

---

181 IWM 6926 Dennis, memoir, p.259.
182 Clayton, *Chavasse Double VC*, p.175. Noel Chavasse makes several references to woolly comforts in his letters home, and it is just possible that these also refer to drawers. See Clayton, *Chavasse Double VC*, pp.66, 73, 77, citing letters by Chavasse to his father, 31 October and 17 November 1914, and to his sister Dorothea, 26 November.
183 THM Seaforths 81-180, Murray, letter to sister Kate, 30 December, 1914.
184 IWM 1862, Craig-Brown, diary, copy letter, Craig-Brown to Secretary, Scottish Society, 12 March, 1915.
185 LC GS 1027 Macleod, letter to sisters Betty and Molly, 21 October, 1915.
186 Ibid., letters to mother, 21 September, 1914, 10, 17 February, 1915 and n.d.
187 See: IWM 12968 Thomson, letters to parents, 22 November, 1914, 3 January, 1915; THM Seaforths 81-180, Murray, letters to sister Kate, 26 November, 19, 30 December, 1914 and to sister Alex, 19

Otherwise, drawers or substitutes might be obtained locally. On 13 November, 1914 when 6th Gordons, newly arrived in theatre, were about to depart from Le Havre, Lieutenant Spence Sanders records that, "Sgt Smith and I nipped out of the station and went into the town and bought some pants to wear under kilts."[188]

But drawers took up extra room in the pack. They also potentially harboured lice. No doubt this was what Norman Collins meant when it was suggested to him that the practice of not wearing drawers might have been unhygienic. "No", he replied, "it wasn't. It was the reverse because there was nothing to get dirty."[189] Frank Brooke, in the Seaforths noted that while in England, in defiance of custom, he had worn football pants under the kilt, "In France, when all underwear became in a few short weeks really 'lousy,' it was far more hygienic to dispense with pants and simply fasten the back lap of the shirt to the front between the legs with a safety pin. Or, more generally, not bother!"[190]

This may explain the resistance to wearing drawers even in the winter. George Murray, for example, having received pants from home and apparently from battalion sources at the end of 1914, had clearly done away with them by the end of January, 1915, as he writes, "Don't send any pants for goodness sake, as the more clothes we wear, the more alive we are."[191] Similarly, Harry Taylor, in the Liverpool Scottish, records that,

> My dear mother, worrying about the physical comfort of her youngest during the very cold month of January, 1917, included in the usual food parcels a pair of brief underpants. Unwillingly, but dutifully, I wore them, but it was only a week or two later, when sitting in a lonely listening post with another soldier, I became so infuriated with lice that I tore the pants off and flung them into no-man's land.[192]

Cold, rain and mud were not the only problems encountered. As William Hay, of 9th Royal Scots, put it, the kilt was "a bit hot in the summer time."[193] George Murray, in 4th Seaforths would have agreed, writing in June, 1915, "The heat is nearly as trying as the cold, but I think that, after the Winter's experience, I prefer the heat, although it makes one very uncomfortable & especially when route-marching or drilling. The best parade we have just now is the bathing parade."[194] As a result, a common practice in summer was to shed the kilt and just wear the

---

December, 1914, 30 January, 1915; IWM 926 Mackenzie, letter to wife 3 July, 1915; GHM PB19 Blunt, letter from father 26 September, 1915; THM Camerons C572, Panton, Howard, letter to brother Tom, 29 September, 1915; BWA Guthrie, letters to wife, 3, 11, 13 October, 1915; THM Camerons 96-52, Laidlaw, 'Grandpa's War,' p.23, letter from Douglas Laidlaw to his wife Bertha, 4 October, 1915; IWM 511 Thorburn, letter to parents, 31 October, 1915; Levyns, *The Disciplines of War*, p.67; IWM 8592 Macgregor, letters to wife, 26 September, 1917, 2 February, 1919.

188 LC GS 1422 Sanders, diary, 13 November, 1914.
189 IWM 12043 Collins, interview.
190 THM S98 11, Brooke, memoir, p.62.
191 THM Seaforths 81-180, Murray, letters to sister Kate, 26 November, 19, 30 December, 1914 and to sister Alex, 19 December, 1914, 30 January, 1915.
192 LC GS 1579, Taylor, memoir, p.8; and see the example of Private Alex Brownie of 4th Gordons in Macdonald, Lyn, *1914-1918 Voices and Images of the Great War* (London: Penguin, 1991), p.264.
193 IWM 16455 Hay, interview.
194 THM Seaforths 81-180 Murray, letter to father, 16 June, 1915.

cotton kilt-cover, or even shirt-tails only.[195] The practice might even be followed to keep kilts dry in torrential rain.[196] Private Sandy Macmillan, at Etaples in a draft for 14th Argylls, in intense heat in August, 1916, noted that:

> When we are dismissed we remove our kilts & meander around in khaki aprons. Having nothing on one's nether limbs but a little cotton rag is really a delicious feeling, & one smiles complacently as English chaps come along in breeches & puttees, leaving a trail of sweat behind them.[197]

And when 4th Seaforths were in billets at Maizieres between 24 April and 12 May, 1917,

> Some days were so hot that the battalion paraded in shirts and kilt aprons only. The result was a spectacle as attractive as a show of the most lithe-limbed beauty chorus on the revue stage … On the tape side of the apron – the left side – the whole length of leg was often visible. On the march the effect was quite dazzling.[198]

A rather more respectable solution was to wear shorts, and these were adopted on occasion in place of the kilt in summer in the trenches in some battalions.[199] As early as August, 1914, when 2nd Argylls were at Boulogne on L.O.C. duties, Captain Hyslop reported that he successfully acquired some shorts but that Colour Sergeant Murray

> returned in triumph with a pair of light blue ladies' knickers with silk bows as being the only thing they could find which would answer the purpose. The Cr-Sgt consoled himself by saying that when he had done with them they would do for his wife.[200]

Another problem encountered in the heat was chafing between the thighs. This rather personal problem understandably does not receive much attention in the sources, but was evidently real. Lance Sergeant Andrew Anderson, in 1st Camerons, states that, on the retreat from Mons, the main trouble of the younger fitter soldiers in the hot and dusty conditions was blistered feet and "chafing inside the thighs."[201] Similarly, Corporal Harry Robertson, in 1stt Gordons, notes on 3 July, 1916, "Move off at two hours notice at 9.0 a.m. Very hot. March for five hours (13 kilometres). Arrive NAOURS. Done up. Legs chaffing owing to kilt rubbing where the sweat and dirt are."[202] Before Frank Brooke set out to march from the railhead to join the 4th Seaforths

---

195 Apart from the examples cited, see: IWM 4586 Douglas, memoir, pp.505-506; Dinesen, *Merry Hell*, pp. 176-177, 196-197; BWA Guthrie, letter to wife, 4 July 1915; NLS MS 944-947, Ramage, diary, 8 June, 1915; IWM 3460 Macmillan, letter to mother, 9 June, 1915, and diary, 24 June, 1915; Aiken, *Courage Past*, p.13; GHM PB1706/2 Robertson, diary, 8 July, 1916; Beattie, *48th Highlanders*, p.312.
196 Sutherland, *Fifth Seaforth Highlanders*, p.40.
197 IWM 3460 Macmillan, letter from Sandy Macmillan to mother, 10 August, 1916.
198 IWM Books Haldane, '4th Seaforths', unpublished draft, p.108.
199 See: Cpl Ian Maclaren, 6th Black Watch, quoted in Young, *Forgotten Scottish Voices*, p.172; Bird, *Ghosts*, p.115.
200 ASHM, NE-2, Hyslop, diary, 17 August, 1914.
201 THM Camerons 89-44 Anderson, memoir, p.15.
202 GHM PB1706/2 Robertson, diary, 3 July, 1916.

about the end of July, 1916, on what promised to be a blistering hot day, he applied boric powder not only to his feet but also between his thighs, to provide some relief. This was obviously something he had done before in training.[203] We also find soldiers requesting or carrying Vaseline in summer, probably as a safeguard against chafing.[204] The problem might not be confined to the summer. Around January, 1917, James Marr, in 4th Gordons, began to be bothered with an irritation of the skin. He reported sick and was ordered to hospital with suspected scabies. There, "the doctor stated that I was just suffering from a kilt rash and ordered me to get a sulphur bath … I was immersed in some kind of liquid which either from its medicinal properties or from my unlimited faith worked wonders. I emerged fresh and wholesome, donned my not over-clean clothes, and set out again for Abbeville."[205]

This chapter has examined the effectiveness of the Highland uniform in coping with the elements. It has been shown that the Glengarry bonnet, being too conspicuous and providing little protection from the sun, proved inadequate and was consequently replaced by the Balmoral and the Tam o' Shanter. Highland shoes could not cope with the cobbled roads on the Great Retreat, and shoes and spats proved completely inadequate when faced with Flanders mud; they too were replaced by boots and puttees. The failure of Highland shoes was undoubtedly responsible for a large number of cases of trench-foot and frost-bite in the first winter of 1914-1915. With regard to the kilt itself, in wet conditions it could prove uncomfortable, but also became very heavy when saturated, and chafed the knees. Once soaked, it was difficult to dry. The thigh-length trench-waders issued for use in wet conditions were uncomfortable when worn with kilts and caused chafing. Mud would also make the kilt heavy, while mud drying on it would chafe the soldiers' legs. Mud would also harden on the hair of men's legs making its removal potentially painful. Cleaning muddy kilts was a major operation. In freezing weather, the kilt cannot really be held responsible for trench-foot and frost-bitten feet, for the lower legs were well enough protected once the inadequate shoes and spats had been replaced. But cases of frost-bitten knees in the extreme winter of 1916-1917 are certainly attributable to the kilt. In addition, the skin could be cut by ice forming on the rim of the kilt, requiring sandbags to be pressed into use to provide protection for the legs against both cold and cuts. Finally, in summer, the kilt could be exceedingly hot and soldiers could experience chafing between the thighs on long marches. In these circumstances it is unsurprising that the Canadian battalions tended to go into trousers for the winter and revert to kilts in the spring. This practice was not followed in the British regiments, although on occasion trousers were issued as trench stores for use in the trenches in extremely adverse weather conditions. For the most part the tradition of no drawers was also followed in the trenches. Although their issue in winter was later authorised, this was not really successful as they became lice-magnets and were frequently discarded or used as cleaning cloths. The kilt did at least have two advantages: it could be removed to wade through water-logged trenches, and in hot weather, it could be discarded and only the apron worn. Altogether, however, despite these minor advantages, the kilt was not the best, nor the most popular, garment in which to face the elements. In the next chapter we will see how it stood up to the other challenges on the battlefield.

---

203 IWM Books Brooke, 'Wait for it', pp.66-67.
204 BWA Couston, letter to mother, 8 June 1917; BWA Guthrie, letter to wife, 9 June, 1915.
205 IWM 14335 Marr, memoir, pp.50-51. See also the advice given to Charlie Parke, before the war, about sweating between the legs: IWM Books, Parke, 'Memoirs,' p.19.

7

The Kilt: The Hazards of War

"a landscape of dead buttocks"[1]

In the last chapter, we considered the practicality of the kilt in the face of the elements. In this chapter we continue the discussion of practicality, considering in turn the challenge of lice, insects (including mosquitoes), barbed wire and the practicality of the kilt for raids and patrols. We then consider mustard gas, deception, some lesser practicalities and the realities of battle. Finally, we consider the overall practicality of the kilt, an attempt to abolish it, and suggest that the real issue is the balance between impracticality and benefit to 'esprit de corps.'

Lice

All soldiers on the Western Front, officers included, became infested with lice. Whatever their origin, the lice became ubiquitous, not just in the trenches themselves, but in billets and camps, where they attached themselves to the soldiers passing through, causing extreme irritation and discomfort, and promoting 'trench fever'. No-one escaped, and Highland soldiers were no exception. In suffering from lice-infested shirts and vests, Highland soldiers were in the same predicament as their English colleagues. Where they differed was in the kilt, which was itself a perfect magnet for lice, which bred in the numerous pleats.[2] The problem was not confined to

---

1 Longley, Michael, *Collected Poems*, (London: Jonathan Cape, 2006), 'Wounds.'
2 References to lice in the sources are ubiquitous and are not cited separately. References to lice-infested kilts are still very numerous and are cited here only where they do not appear elsewhere in this discussion: Clayton, *Chavasse Double VC*, p.76; Hutchison, *Footslogger*, pp.132, 149-50; Robert Burns, quoted in Van Emden, Richard & Humphries, Steve, *Veterans* (Barnsley: Pen & Sword, 2005), pp.49-50; Warwick, *We Band of Brothers*, p.50; Linklater, *Fanfare for a Tin Hat*, p.62 ; Giblin, *Bravest*, p.18; IWM 860 Recording, Mabbott, Henry, interview with IWM, 1976; IWM 24855 Newton, interview ; Rule, *Students*, p.175; Lyon, *In kilt and khaki*, p.152; IWM 21092 McGregor, letter to his wife, 31 August, 1916; IWM Books Cooper, 'Domi Militaeque,' pp.90-91; LC WF Recollections M3, McLeavy, memoir; Mackenzie, Capt D., *The Sixth Gordons in France and Flanders*, (Aberdeen: Rosemount Press, 1921), p.21; NLS MS 944-947, Ramage, diary, 21, 22, 30 May, 16 June, 1915; LC GS 0132 Betteridge, memoir, pp.101, 110; IWM 10391 Jordan, interview; Stothers, *Somewhere in*

the Western Front. Lice made their appearance also in Mesopotamia, Salonika and Palestine,[3] although Private Cooper, serving with 12th Argylls at GHQ Constantinople in July, 1919, found that the Turkish baths at GHQ kept them free of lice![4]

James Fraser, in 4th Gordons, remembered that;

> Once when on leave I hung my kilt on a tree in the sunlight. One of my sisters went to see how it was getting on. She came back in horror. The sun had hatched them out and they were marching down the pleats in column of route.[5]

As William Chambers, a volunteer drafted to 1st Camerons, remarked after six weeks at the front, around March, 1915, "the old hands say they assume a tartan colour after a while," although he conceded that "the great advantage of the kilt lies in the fact that one can explore one's person with the greatest of ease and often catch the blighters on the hop."[6] Private Anderson of 9th Royal Scots could anticipate that on coming out of the trenches in July, 1916, "it is going to be a difficult job standing to attention without scratching."[7] And as Adrian Liddell in 2nd Argylls reported in December, 1914, "One of the Tommies here told me the other day that he'd like to put his kilt and shirt on the Kaiser and handcuff his hands behind him for a week!"[8]

Lice would be hunted and destroyed by hand. Soldiers would spend hours searching their kilts for lice,[9] and trying to destroy them. Douglas Wilson in 5th Camerons wrote of the man in the trenches in 1918 occupied in;

> the pounding of the seams of his kilt with the metal-shod haft of his entrenching tool or other available implement – sometimes the flat of a bayonet. A hot iron run along the seams would be more effective, but there are no hot irons out of civvy-street, so he makes do with cold steel. He enjoys one advantage over the breeched or trousered soldier. A man without his trousers is in a pitiable plight in an emergency. The Jock can gird his loins in a sweep and a wriggle that takes no time at all.[10]

It was generally found that the various powders sent from home to kill the lice, most frequently Harrison's Pomade or Keating's powder, were ineffective.[11] When circumstances permitted,

---

    France, p.82, citing letter, Cannon Stothers to Steve, 18 September, 1917; Cluness, *Doing his bit*, p.19; IWM Books Brooke, 'Wait for it', p.84.
3   BWA Cumming, letter to parents n.d. (October/November 1915); LC Several Fronts Recollections, Judd, transcript of interview; IWM 21511 PP, Nicol, Rev. D.B., letter to wife, 30 January, 1917.
4   IWM Books Cooper, 'Domi Militaeque,' p.309.
5   Fraser, 'War Diary, pp.40, 43, 44.
6   Chambers, *Diaries of World War 1*, pp.18, 44.
7   IWM 3608 Anderson, memoir.
8   IWM 11126, Liddell, letter to mother, 4 December, 1914.
9   Andrews, *Haunting Years*, p.130; Macleod, *6th Camerons*, p.26; GHM PB1639 Kemp, memoir, p.15.
10   LC GS 1/61 Wilson, memoir, p.64.
11   IWM 322, Reid, interview.

candles[12], matches[13], irons[14], heated forks[15] or bayonets[16] were used with varying degrees of success on the seams of the kilt. 2nd Argylls for example set up a bathing and de-lousing centre in the abandoned brewery of Erquinghem:

> Behind trestle tables stood stout-armed Belgian girls, hot iron in one hand, a skewer in the other. No Institute of Industrial Psychology was needed to train the girls in their duties. Two Sappers organised and directed the workshop practice. Like lightning a hot skewer sped up the kilted pleats searing the farthest recesses: then out again carrying its load of dead and wounded lice. Wielded overarm the iron came down like a sledge-hammer upon the remains. Thus twenty women with the precision of machines, thrust and slammed kilt after kilt. And Jock got his own back, even with a fleeting smile, as the worker for an instant lifted an eye and handed back so strange a nether garment.[17]

After a time delousing stations were set up where clothing was fumigated[18], but this was rarely completely successful[19], sometimes destroying the living lice, but hatching out their eggs to leave the kilts still infested. The process could also leave kilts completely disfigured.[20] Some kilts, indeed, may have reached a stage beyond fumigation. Rachel Wilson, a Quaker, who served with the Friends Ambulance Unit at Queen Alexandra Hospital, Dunkirk, between October, 1917 and January, 1919, noted a pile of kilts from a detachment of Cameron Highlanders, so alive with lice as to be beyond 'disinfection.'[21] Noel Chavasse, Medical Officer of the Liverpool Scottish, imaginatively killed two birds with one stone, when he set up a "Sanitary Squad" which performed valuable work including delousing and ironing the kilts of men coming in for a rest after a spell in the front line. It was staffed by men the Doctor could see were weakening under the strain and privations of trench warfare.[22]

12 Linklater, *Fanfare for a Tin Hat*, p.62; IWM 24855 Newton, interview; GHM PB3712, Murison, memoir; IWM 495 Recording, Pratt, James Davidson, interview 1974; IWM 10414 McGregor, interview; LC Several Fronts Recollections, Judd, transcript of interview; IWM 10786, Hood, interview.
13 O'Kiely, *Gentleman Air Ace*, pp.54-55.
14 LC GS 1507 Sotheby, letter from Sotheby, 24 March 1915 – see also his diary entry of the same date; Clayton, *Chavasse Double VC*, quoting Noel Chavasse to Cecily Twemlow, 7 July 1916; IWM 3460 Macmillan, letters to mother, 29 April, to Bessie, 25 June, 1915; IWM 4370 Christison, memoir, p.68; IWM 6926, Dennis, memoir, pp.296, 297.
15 Hutchison, *Footslogger*, pp.132, 149-50; Hutchison, *Warrior*, p.70.
16 Hutchison, *Warrior*, pp.50-51.
17 Ibid., p.57.
18 Gillespie, *Letters from Flanders*, p.295, letter 8 September, 1915; GHM PB1892.3.1 Youngson, memoir, p.15; Fraser, 'War Diary, 1915', pp.40, 43, 44.
19 Chambers, *Diaries of World War 1*, p.44; LC GS 0177 Boyle, diary, 1, 2 October, 1915.
20 Warwick, *We Band of Brothers*, p.50; see also Rule, *Students*, pp.145-146.
21 IWM 10038, recording, Cadbury, Rachel, interview with IWM, 1987.
22 Giblin, *Bravest of Hearts*, p.18; Clayton, *Chavasse Double VC*, quoting Noel Chavasse to Cecily Twemlow, 7 July 1916; Jackson, Frederick, 'Captain Noel Godfrey Chavasse, VC and Bar, MC,' *Army Medical Services Magazine*, Vol.24, No.3, 1970.

One substance which did work was creosol. This would damage the skin if it came into direct contact, as some soldiers found to their cost, but it could be applied safely at least to the external seams of the kilt.[23] Alexander Rule in 4th Gordons noted how,

> I once tried undiluted creosol in a mood of sheer desperation, applying it liberally to the waist portion of my kilt. This drastic remedy caused me agonising hours, for I lost every square inch of skin around my middle. My sole comfort lay in the thought that the lice must also have got pure hell![24]

Robert Burns, in 7th Camerons, reports that one way of getting rid of the lice was to bury the kilt and leave it for an hour.[25] This is the only reference discovered to this procedure. An even less likely remedy was allegedly louse proof reindeer skin underwear, supplied to an American soldier in 15th Battalion C.E.F. (48th Highlanders of Canada).[26] Its effect is not recorded.

Lice were not only a source of discomfort, but also of shame. As Lieutenant Guy Macgregor, in 6th Argylls, complained in January, 1918, "I never can get reconciled to being lousy! It humiliates me & disgusts me each time as if it were the first time. I know it's no fault of mine and everyone in the line is the same, but I loathe it."[27] Private Douglas, 8th Black Watch, was given leave in January, 1919. When he arrived home in Newcastle he was not happy with the state of his kilt and would not wear it to go out. However, "mother suggested that, if she ran a hot iron along each pleat, it would help to kill any lice that might still be alive. After she finished, I gave each pleat a good sprinkling of de-lousing powder along each pleat, and not till then did I feel happy at wearing it while on leave."[28] Will Bryden served with 1st London Scottish from May, 1916 to June, 1918. His daughter later recalled that he told her that, "His kilt hem and his sheepskin coat were full of lice which dropped out in the pub which he visited immediately after disembarking from the train on leave – to everyone's disgust."[29]

Insects

A particular threat to kilted soldiers in theatres outside the Western Front was provided by mosquitoes, which spread malaria. This debilitating and potentially lethal disease was particularly virulent in the Salonika theatre, especially in the Struma and Vardar valleys, but also in Mesopotamia and Palestine. Most soldiers who served in these theatres provide descriptions

---

23 LC GS 0262, Campbell, letter to fiancée 7 October, 1917.
24 Rule, *Students*, pp.145-146. See also NLS MS 944-947, Ramage, diary, 30 May, 1915.
25 Burns, *Once a Cameron Highlander*, p.79.
26 Stothers, *Somewhere in France*, p.82, citing letter, Cannon Stothers to Steve, 12 January, 1918.
27 IWM 8592 Macgregor, letter to wife, 12 November, 1918.
28 IWM 4586 Douglas, memoir, pp.1280-1282.
29 IWM 13263 Bryden, memoir by his daughter Mary Lawton, written 2003.

of the effects of malaria. In Salonika the disease affected 1st Argylls,[30] 12th Argylls,[31] 2nd Camerons[32] and 2nd London Scottish,[33] It also wreaked havoc in 1st Garrison Battalion Seaforth Highlanders. This battalion, which disembarked in Salonika on 24th August, 1916, is worthy of special mention. It was intended for garrison duty only, being composed of men considered, for whatever reason, unfit for front-line service. In the event, no doubt due to the heavy losses from disease in front-line battalions, they were eventually sent up the line to the Struma Front. There, Captain Alistair Wyllie's diary records their consequent inevitable decimation by malaria.[34] In Mesopotamia, it affected 2nd Black Watch[35] and 1st Seaforths,[36] And in Palestine it affected 2nd Black Watch,[37] 14th Black Watch,[38] 5th Argylls,[39] 1st Seaforths[40] and 2nd London Scottish.[41] Flies could also be a nuisance in Salonika,[42] Mesopotamia,[43] Palestine[44] and Constantinople,[45] where 12th Argylls were on occupation duties after the armistice.

30 Anderson, *1st Argylls*, pp.56-77, passim; IWM 10909 Cunningham, memoir, Appendix, p.4; LC GS 0177 Boyle, diary, 24 June, 6 July, 1916; LC GS 0731, Hay-Young, letters to father, 30 May, to mother 13, 28 June 1916; LC Transcripts, Tape 357, Hay-Young, interview; ASHM N-E1, Herbert, Pte Tom, letter to Nell, 28 May, 1917; LC GS 1026 Maclean, diary, pp.29, 35, 40-41, & Tapes 495, 493, interview with Peter Liddle, 1978.
31 ASHM N-E11 Macleod, George, letters to home, 10 February, 29 March, 12, 27 June, 10 August, 1916, and 26 August 1916 to 20 May, 1917, passim; ASHM N-E12, Fisher, Colin, typescript, 'The 12th Battalion Princess Louise's Own Argyll and Sutherland Highlanders,' 26pp, written 1971, based partly on the memories of his grandfather, William Tennant, pp.10-11.
32 LC GS 1027 Macleod, letters home, 11 January, 30 May, 5 June, 9, 13, 18 July, 1916; Craig-Brown, *Historical Records*, Vol.3, p.341, 353-355; THM Camerons 99-55, Coupar, W.A., typescript memoir, 'Memories of the Great War 1914-1919', recording in 1999 information received in discussion with his father, William Waddell Coupar, who died in 1969.
33 IWM 6873, Hendry, memoir.
34 IWM 7508, Wyllie, diary, 1916-1918, passim. See also: IWM 12688 MacKay, letter to mother, 4 June, 1917.
35 BWA Cumming, letter to parents 6 April 1916; NLA MS 20655, Haldane, letter to father 21 January, 1917; IWM 8503, Byrom, memoir, p.31.
36 Sym, *Seaforth Highlanders*, p.181; LC Several Fronts Recollections, Kingsley, memoir; *Robert Keith McDermot*, pp.16, 18, 21, 22, 23 letters from him, 9, 23 July, 29 September, 11, 19, 26 November, 1916; LC MES 013 Bonar, Andrew, letter to H.E.R. Widnell, 2 July, 1917.
37 BWA, Stewart, Lt Col J., letter to wife 11 April 1918.
38 Sommers, Cecil [Down, Norman Cecil Sommers] *Temporary Crusaders*, (London: John Lane, London, 1919).
39 ASHM N-E5, Brown, letter to parents 28 November, 1917.
40 *Robert Keith McDermot*, p.44, letters from him, 15, 25 May, 1918.
41 Blaser, *Kilts*, pp.53, 237, 244 ; LC GS 0330 Clifton, J.G., diary, 16 May, 1918, letter to mother, 5 June, 1918.
42 ASHM N-E11 Macleod, letter to father, 12 June, 1916; LC GS 1027 Macleod, letters home, 11 January, 30 May, 5 June, 9, 13, 18 July, 1916; LC 0177 Boyle, diary, 8, 16 June, 1916; LC GS.0731, Hay-Young, letters to father, 30 May, to mother 4, 13 June, 1916; Craig-Brown, *Historical Records*, Vol.3, p.325; IWM 7508 Wyllie, diary, 2, 4 June, 1917. See also 21 July, 1 August, 3, 5, 6 November, 1917, 6 June, 1918
43 BWA Cumming, letter to parents 6 April 1916; *Gilbert M. Mackenzie*, pp.86, 88, letters to mother, 6 April, & to wife 18 April, 1916; Webster, J.A.C., *Mesopotamia 1916-1917, Letters from John Alexander Croom Webster, Second Lieutenant Seaforth Highlanders* (privately published, n.d.), p.7, letter to mother, 8 October, 1916.
44 Blaser, *Kilts*, pp.53, 237, 244.
45 IWM Books Cooper, 'Domi Militaeque,' pp.309, 314, 318, 335, 354.

G.F. Maclean, then a lieutenant with 1st Argylls, summarised the debilitating effects of malaria:

> Weakness really and absolutely lack of appetite and of course, the trouble was that if you got wounded. Some men in my company were wounded not badly. I mean they were shot through the arm and they would go to hospital and at once they would get malaria and probably die of it. It was a terrible weakener and you were so terribly liable to get it when you were just suffering from wounds and it just came on and it came on so suddenly. We were getting ready for an attack on the Vardar, my company. We were going to attack at one o'clock or something. Some time in the night and one of my Platoon Commanders came in to supper. We were having supper in a little dugout and he literally could hardly stand just with malaria. He was shaking so much.[46]

Standard remedies included the taking of quinine and in Salonika, the seasonal abandonment of advanced positions in the Struma Valley. But the effect on battalions could be severe. In 1st Argylls, between August and October, 1917, admissions to hospital from the battalion averaged 106 per month, while the discharges were over 35. By September, 1918, the ration strength of the battalion was only 237 and of these more than 100 were employed with transport or stores behind the line. By 29 September, the Brigade was so reduced that it could no longer function as such, and it was formed into a composite battalion, with 1st Argylls providing a company.[47] Likewise, by 24 September, 1918, 2nd Camerons had been reduced to two companies, each of only two platoons, owing to malaria and influenza. Then, about 29 September, the brigade being just over 900 strong was amalgamated into a single composite battalion, called the 81st Composite Regiment, with a Cameron company. The battalions had, however, resumed their own identities by 16 October.[48]

Some individual cases will further illustrate the problem. Lieutenant George Macleod served with 12th Argylls in Salonika, arriving with them at the end of November, 1915. By 26 August, 1916, he had fallen sick with dysentery and subsequently contracted jaundice. After hospitalisation, he finally rejoined 11th Argylls in France in May, 1917, his illness having kept him away from the firing line for nine months.[49] Jock MacLeod disembarked with 2nd Camerons in Salonika on 14 December, 1915. By 8 October, 1916, he was in hospital suffering from veldtsores and jaundice and subsequently malaria. After hospitalisation, recovery and retraining he finally arrived in France again, now with the Machine Gun Corps, on 14 October, 1918, less than a month before the end of hostilities. His malaria and attendant problems had effectively kept him away from the front line for two years.[50]

The Highlanders' bare legs were a natural attraction to mosquitoes, and in Salonika this led to the replacement of the kilt at least in 1st Argylls, as James Cunningham records.

---

46 LC GS 1026 Maclean, interview. See also his typescript diary, pp.40-41.
47 Anderson, *1st Argylls*, pp.56-77, passim.
48 Craig-Brown, *Historical Records*, Vol.3, pp.353-355.
49 ASHM N-E11 Macleod, letters to home, 10 February, 29 March, 12, 27 June, 10 August, 1916, and 26 August 1916 to 20 May, 1917, passim.
50 LC GS 1027 MacLeod, letters 8 October, 1916, to 14 October, 1918, passim.

After the usual opposition, the order went forth that we were to wear drawers under our kilts and in due course, the first issue arrived. The drawers were made mostly of 'grey back' flannel. The same material as the men's shirts were made of. A few were actually red and of course, they were said to have belonged to great-grandmothers. Unfortunately, in order to comply with nature, one had to remove one's kilt. The Ordnance were very sorry, they would do better than that. The issue was withdrawn. Presently, along came a better pattern. This was called 'The Elliptical slit pattern'. In fact, they were the original drawers with this curious slit made in them. Of course, these did not protect the knees. Finally, … the kilts were withdrawn and we were issued with good shorts with a very deep turn-up, so deep that when they turned up they buttoned at the waist. In the evening, they were turned down and the legs tucked into the stocking tops, thus making a proper seal.[51]

Hay-Young and Lieutenant G. Maclean confirm the issue of these adaptable shorts, which were certainly in use by the summer of 1917.[52] Photographs of 1st Argylls in the collection of Hay-Young, show the men variously clad in kilts or shorts, depending on time and location.[53] The same anti-malarial protective dress was adopted by the 2nd Camerons, and is illustrated in an excellent photograph in their History, which does not, however, mention the temporary issue of drawers! The same set of photographs also illustrates that in fighting order the Camerons, at least, would still wear the kilt.[54] However, Lieutenant Jock MacLeod, serving with the battalion observed on 9 July, 1916, that his usual uniform at that time was kilt and shirtsleeves,.[55] So the special adaptable shorts may not have been introduced until the following year. The situation amongst the other kilted battalions in Salonika is more obscure.[56]

In Mesopotamia, in July, 1916, Keith McDermott wrote that in 1st Seaforths, "We wear the kilt to go up, and if there is an attack, but in the trenches wear shorts, and shorts only."[57] The letters of John Webster[58] in the same battalion seem to confirm that the usual dress for summer was shorts, but that kilts may have been worn in the winter as the Mesopotamian nights could be very cold. Also, it would appear that kilts were worn when advancing. In 2nd Black Watch, the situation was similar, shorts generally being worn in the trenches. An officer of the battalion writes that: "We always marched up in kilts and marched out in kilts, but during our stay

---

51   IWM 10909 Cunningham, Appendix, p.4.
52   LC GS 1026, Maclean, diary, pp.29, 38; LC Transcripts, Tape 357, Hay-Young, interview.
53   LC GS 0731, Hay-Young, photographs.
54   Craig-Brown, *Historical Records*, Vol.3, p.341 and photograph opp. p.338.
55   LC GS 1027 Macleod, letter to father, 9 July, 1916.
56   Alistair Wyllie records that on arrival at Salonika on 24th August, 1916, 1st Garrison Battalion Seaforth Highlanders paraded in shorts and khaki drill. By 8 October, they were into ordinary serge, but by 12 April, 1917, they had all been issued with light drill. One lieutenant at least of the battalion was wearing a kilt in Constanza in November, 1918, and Wyllie himself was wearing a kilt there in December. See IWM 7508 Wyllie, photograph, and diary, 24 August, 8, 22 October, 1916, 22 March, 12 April, 17 October, 1917, 1 May, 26 November, 15 December, 1918. 2nd London Scottish had kilts inspected on 15 June, 1917, but were issued with shorts on 16th. This was not long before their embarkation for Egypt on 29 June. See: LC GS 0875 Julian, F., diary, 15, 16 June, 1917.
57   *Robert Keith McDermot*, p.17, letter from him, 18 July, 1916.
58   Webster, *Mesopotamia 1916-1917*, pp.3, 14, 29, 31-32, 44, 48, 52, 53, 66, 74, 81, 87, 94, 108, 113, 118, letters home, 13 September, 28 October, 24, 25 November, 22, 25, 28, 30 December, 1916, 18 January, 3, 7, 12, 21 February, 17, 23, 31 March, 1917.

there our clothes were the irreducible minimum, shorts and shirts."[59] This change of clothing is proven by several photographs in his book, which show members of the battalion variously attired in either kilts or shorts. The kilt was worn in battle.[60]

In Palestine, Lieutenant Colonel Jack Stewart, commanding 2nd Black Watch, reluctantly accepted the necessity to discard the kilt for trousers, but could not argue with the logic.

> "Higher Authority" has decided it to discard the kilt for the time being and adopt trousers and short anklet putties. I cannot object for if one single man died of malaria contracted by a mosquito bite on the knee or leg I should hold myself responsible.[61]

14th Black Watch were created in Egypt in 1917, by dismounting the Fife and Forfar Yeomanry. They may never have been issued with kilts, and in Egypt and Palestine wore the special adaptable 'Salonika' trousers.[62] In 2nd London Scottish the evidence suggests that they wore shorts for fatigues, but kilts for marching and fighting.[63] Evidence is scant for 1st Seaforths and 5th Argylls.[64]

Perhaps surprisingly, mosquitoes could be a problem not only in Salonika, Mesopotamia and Palestine, but also on the Western Front. There they were a real nuisance during the summer months from May to August.[65] They attacked faces and hands and played particular havoc with the bare legs and knees of kilted troops.[66] Improvised mosquito nets, perhaps supplied from home, were pressed into action.[67] Many soldiers had to receive medical attention, and some were even hospitalised. In 7th Seaforths, Lieutenant Oldham was sent down the line on 28 July,

---

59 Anon [Blampied, H. John] *With a Highland Regiment in Mesopotamia 1916-1917* (London: The Times Press, 1918), p.39.
60 IWM 511 Thorburn, letters home 15, 28 January, 1916; BWA Dundas, Capt R.H., typed diary, 13 January, 1916.
61 BWA, Stewart to wife 11 April 1918.
62 Sommers, *Temporary Crusaders*, entry for 27 January, 1918.
63 See photographs in Lloyd, *London Scottish*, pp.189, 193, 232; LC GS 0731, Hay-Young, photographs; LC GS 0875 Julian, diary, 3, 9 July, 18 November, 1917; IWM 6873 Hendry, memoir; Blaser, *Kilts*, pp.28, 207, 210-212.
64 In Palestine, in November, 1917, Ronal Brown of 5th Argylls states he is wearing shorts – see ASHM N-E5 Brown, letter to parents 28 November, 1917. They appear to have retained the kilt at Gallipoli – see ASHM N-E5, Letters of Captain D.M. Main, letter, Main to wife, 2 July, 1915. The situation in 1st Seaforths is unknown.
65 Apart from the specific references cited below, see: IWM 3460 Macmillan, letters to mother 4 May, to Tony, 11 May, 1915; IWM 114, Allen, letters to wife, 24 June, 19, 23 July, 13, 18 September, 1915; THM Seaforths 96-36 Tweddle, 23 June, 1915; LC GS 0418, Dane, W.S., typescript diary, 14 August, 1915; IWM 16335 Racine, memoir pp.51, 54; LC GS 1507 Sotheby, letter to mother, 7 August, 1915; IWM 14340, McArthur, diary, 18 August, 1915; BWA, MacDonald, Coll, letter to wife 22 August 1917.
66 NLS MS 944 947, Ramage, diary, 11 May, 5 June, 1915; IWM 14269, Couper, letter to sisters, 7 June, 1915 [NB. This letter is dated 7 May, but this is clearly an error.] ; Gillespie, *Letters from Flanders*, p.225, letter 7 July, 1915; Peel & Macdonald, *6th Seaforths*, p.14; ASHM, N-E10, Gairdner, letters to mother, 15 September, 13 October, 1918; IWM 2854 Bates, letters to his fiancée, 12, 18, 20, 21 May 1916; ASHM N-E6, MacPhie, Lieut. J. diary, 20 July, 1918.
67 IWM 14269, Couper, letters to sisters, 4, 26 July, 2 August, 16 September, 1915; Andrews, *Haunting Years*, pp.145, 151, 155.

1916, having been badly bitten, finally reaching hospital in London, from which he was not released until 21 August. He did not reach the front again until 17 January, 1917, insect bites having apparently kept him away for nearly five months.[68] The kilt might even be abandoned on occasion for breeches, at least by officers.[69]

Another problem on the Western Front was provided by a plague of flies, which, although unhygienic, were more of a nuisance than a threat. Interestingly, all the many references to this nuisance[70] relate to the summer of 1915, when the infestation seems to have been largely related to the number of unburied bodies between the lines. Ivar Campbell, attached to 1st Seaforths, complained of "a plague of flies and bluebottles, bred from corruption, fed on corruption, and carriers of corruption."[71] Likewise, in 2nd Argylls, Douglas Gillespie complained of a plague of flies in June and July, 1915: "I wish I had something which would destroy Bombilius Major, who is holding this trench in great force, and seems to think the sand-bags are put there for him to bask on them."[72] Wasps of course were also an occasional problem for kilted troops.[73]

Barbed wire and other abrasives

Barbed wire was a genuine problem for kilted soldiers. Even the two great defenders of the kilt recognised the problem of the kilt catching on the barbed wire.[74] This at least is true. There are numerous accounts of soldiers' kilts getting caught on the wire[75], and soldiers could find themselves exposed to enemy fire in No Man's Land as they tried to disentangle themselves.

68 LC GS 1203 Oldham, diary, 17, 24 May, 25 July to 5 August, passim.
69 IWM Macgregor, letters to wife, 18, 20 May, 1918.
70 LC GS 1507 Sotheby, letter to mother, 15 June 1915. See also letter to father of same date & to Uncle Booty & Aunt Hennie of 17 June, 1915; Rule, *Students*, p.126; LC GS 0731, Hay-Young, letters to father, 4, 15 June, to mother 25, 30 June, 5 August, and to sister Mag, 30 June 1915; IWM, Allen, letters to wife, 24 June, 19 July, 13 September, 1915; ASHM N-E8 Munro, letters to father, 19 June, and to Winifred, 20 June, 1915; IWM 14340, McArthur, diary, 9 June, 1915; THM Seaforths 81-180 Murray, letters to sisters Alex, 19 June, and Kate, 2 July, 1915; BWA Gordon "Diaries", entries for 8 July, 4 August, 1915 and 2 September, 1916; IWM 6702, Low, letter to wife, 19 August, 1915; IWM 14269 Couper, letters to sisters 4 July and 16 September, 1915; IWM 16335 Racine, p.45; GHM PB10, Blunt, letter to father 18 July, 1915; McKinnell, Bryden, *Diary from November 1st, 1914 to June 14th, 1915* (privately published, n.d.), 28 April, 20 May, 1915; Royal Scots Museum, Beatson, diary; IWM Books Reid, *Shoulder to shoulder*, p.70.
71 Campbell, Ivar, *Letters of Ivar Campbell written between May 1915 & January 1916*, (privately published, 1917), letters of 6 June, 6, 7, 9, 12, 15 July, 1915.
72 Gillespie. *Letters from Flanders*, pp.195, 198, 221, 222, 240, letters 13, 16 June, 2, 4, 17 July, 1915.
73 Ibid., p.270, letter 9 August, 1915. See also: Campbell, Ivar, *Letters*, 10 September, 1915.
74 IWM 430, Wimberley, 'The Kilt in Modern War'; Macleod in Mackay, *The Romantic Story*, Appendix.
75 Apart from those cited in the text, see Private Spencer, quoted in Macdonald, Lyn, *1915 The Death of Innocence*, (London, Penguin, 1997), p.548; Pte Andrew McCrindle and Fred Hollingsworth, quoted in Nicholls, Jonathan, *Cheerful Sacrifice* (Barnsley: Pen & sword, 2003), pp.48-49, 94; Lyon, *More Adventures*, p.115; Craig-Brown, *Historical Records*, Vol.4, pp.285-286; IWM 322 Reid, interview; Urquhart, *Canadian Scottish*, p.233; IWM 12043 Collins, interview; Beattie, *48th Highlanders*, p.375; IWM 16428 Recording, Gaffron, Horace, interview 1995; LC Tape 963, Burns, interview; IWM 12678 Burns, transcription of interview; LC GS 1635 Turing, memoir; GHM PB1889, Brown, letter 17 December, 1918.

Gordon Highlanders preparing barbed wire entanglements north of Arras, 24 April, 1917. (IWM Q65400)

Otherwise the wire could simply cause delay as the soldiers gingerly tried to negotiate it.[76] Harry Robertson, who served in 1st Gordons, recalled that his first experience of barbed wire was at Hooge on 25 September, 1915. "We had fellows hanging all along it – just like clothes on a line."[77] At Arras in April, 1917, William Hay of 9th Royal Scots was buried by a shell when caught on the wire: "I got caught on the barbed wire between the first and the second line. I had a pair of mitts on my hands, you know; my kilt and my mitts caught on the barbed wire and I found myself eventually buried in sand and blinded."[78]

In the process, kilts, covers and hose-tops could be torn to shreds or even torn off.[79] Christopher Haworth, a young soldier in 14th Argylls, left half his kilt on the wire on one occasion during the allied offensive in 1918.[80] William Kemp notes that on 31 July, during the Ypres offensive, 8/10th Gordons reached a feature called Wilde Wood. "The wood was a network of barbed wire

---

76   LC GS 1635, Turing, memoir; IWM 4586 Douglas, p.771; Lyon, *More Adventures*, p.12; IWM Books Brooke, 'Wait for it', p.112.
77   GHM PB1706/2 Robertson, diary, supplementary notes.
78   IWM 16455 Hay, interview.
79   See also: IWM 5525 Steven, letter to home, 17 March, 1915; Lyon, *More Adventures*, p.115; IWM 3008 McPake, diary, 17 January 1916; BWA Couston, letter to mother, 3 August 1917; IWM 8192 Lawson, letter to Bessie, 17 November, 1916; Lieut. Charles Tennant, quoted in Macdonald, *1915*, p.120; LC GS 1579, Taylor, 'Reminiscences', p.15; Bird, *Ghosts*, p.134.
80   Haworth, Christopher, *March to Armistice 1918* (London: William Kimber, 1968) pp.105, 109.

but we tore our way through it in a wonderful manner, coming out at the eastern edge literally in rags." Wounded in the arm, Kemp was taken to the Duchess of Westminster's Hospital at Le Touquet, "my clothes not being fit for wear. I had had my kilt rent to shreds in Wilde Wood."[81]

But arguably much more serious than either torn kilts or the clichéd picture of soldiers hanging on the wire, was the problem that soldiers' bare legs were easily cut on the barbed wire.[82] As Horace Gaffron pointed out, the wire was invariably poisonous,[83] and, as Graham Hutchison observed, in the insanitary conditions in the trenches, "an abrasion quickly became a festering sore: even slight wounds were fraught with the danger of speedy gangrene,"[84] This problem is not even acknowledged by Macleod or Wimberley, but is amply demonstrated by the sources. Private Douglas, newly drafted to France, joined his battalion, 11th Argylls, at Winnezelle on 6 August, 1917. They had just come out of action at Third Ypres. "The 11th … had suffered heavy casualties & most of the survivors of the 11th that I saw walking about the camp had their knees bandaged, due to barbed wire lacerations. As they were wearing the kilt, the bandaged knees gave them a peculiar appearance."[85] In his letters from September, 1916 to April, 1917, Captain Bates, M.O. of 8th Black Watch, records the large number of cuts he had to deal with when the troops came out of the trenches.[86]

Of course, not all abrasions were caused by barbed wire. Even on the Western Front, brambles, gorse, thorns, bushes or woods could prove a nuisance to kilted troops, just as they had in training at home.[87] On 22 July, 1918, for example, when 6th Gordons were advancing in the very dense Bois de Courton,

> They had to leave the tracks and force a way through the tangled brushwood – an almost impossible task. Before the day ended, most of the men's knees were wholly skinned and swollen to twice their normal size, and there was scarcely a man who was not compelled to undo his puttees to relieve the pain of the swelling.[88]

In Salonika, 12th Argylls were "susceptible to sores on their knees often as a result of grazes from thorns"[89] Likewise, in Mesopotamia, John Webster records advancing with 1st Seaforths after the victory at Sanniyat on 22 February, 1917

---

81   GHM PB1639, Kemp, memoir, pp.98, 101.
82   Apart from sources cited, see: NLS MS 944-947, Ramage, diary, 6 May, 1915; Lyon, *In kilt and khaki*, pp.153-154; Lyon, *More Adventures*, p.115; IWM 3460, Macmillan, diary, 9 July, 1915; GHM PB1706/2 Robertson, diary, 18, 25 July, 1916; BWA Couston, letters to sister Jean, 24 September 1916, to mother, 12 August 1917; IWM 8192 Lawson, letter to Bessie, 30 November, 1917; IWM 322 Reid, interview; GHM PB1639, Kemp, 'Narrative of the Fighting at Arras 9th/11th April by Lieut. J.W.T. Leith, M.C.'; IWM 2528 Bradbury, memoir, p.36; THM Camerons 92-35, Welsh, memoirs, pp.80-81; Beattie, *48th Highlanders*, p.375; Sgt Henry Smith, quoted by Lloyd, *London Scottish*, pp.98,101; Hal Kerridge, quoted by Van Emden and Humphries, *Veterans*, p.213; Dinesen, *Merry Hell*, pp.230, 239.
83   IWM 16428 Gaffron, interview.
84   Hutchison, *Warrior*, p.50.
85   IWM 4586 Douglas, memoir, p.44.
86   IWM 2854 Bates, letters to fiancée, 16 September, 1916, 15, 28 March, 18, 20 April, 1917.
87   IWM 14335, Marr, memoir, p.77; ASHM N-E1 Robertson, letter home, 4 September, 1915; THM Seaforths 05-87 Hope, diary, 13 November, 1914; IWM Books Cooper, 'Domi Miliateque,' p.150.
88   Mackenzie, *Sixth Gordons*, pp.166-167.
89   ASHM N-E12 Fisher, 'The 12th Battalion,' p.16.

All the ground is covered in small prickly bushes, like a bramble but smaller, which just cut your knees to bits; then it rains, and your kilt gets wet and that rubs against the cuts, so altogether we have a lovely time.[90]

And in Italy, Captain Brown of 2nd Gordons recorded:

All the dry banks and road sides have dense masses of the acacia… The acacia, though a very fine grower, has the most brutal thorns, often an inch long, which give a poisonous cut, no scratch I can tell you, and the kilt is not the best dress for getting through these thickets.[91]

Some individual examples will show the scale of the problem posed by cuts and abrasions. Eric Knighton served with the Glasgow Highlanders at the Front in 1918.

We used to get caught in the barbed wire a lot too. I got caught on the barbed wire and I got all cut up here and was wearing a kilt and that brought on impetigo and I was in an awful mess, but they just bound me up and dressed it daily. I still had to carry on going up the trenches. I mean I was hoping that I could get put down to light duties or something.[92]

Another soldier to suffer from septic sores, due to cuts from barbed wire, was Linton Andrews in 4th Black Watch. In the summer of 1915, he recalls: "I had not only deafness and mosquito bites, but also, in running through some barbed wire under shelling, I tore my knees and thighs, blood poisoning followed, and great boils made it almost impossible for me to walk. I was pressed to go to hospital but did not want to leave the battalion." Fortunately, as a journalist by trade, he could be usefully employed in the orderly office. Later, he notes that, "My own trouble was impoverished blood and boils, and it was not till ten years later, after I had two grave operations, that I became again the man I was." By summer 1916, he notes that he had "trench-fever and neuralgia behind the eyes and much diarrhoea of blood," and by the end of the year he was still affected by boils and was "hardly able to walk." In November 1917, "On returning from Bodmin Copse I had to run through barbed wire to avoid shells that were hissing out gas on the track. I got a few scratches, and these turned to septic sores that put me out of action for a day or two." Then, on leave, in January/February, 1918, before attending officer training, "I went home to Dundee, and the family doctor was called in to treat my persistent septic sores. Gradually I became more fit than I had been for many months."[93]

Jock McLeod had been injured on barbed wire while training with the 3rd Camerons at home around March, 1915. In September, he was deployed to the Western Front and served in the trenches with the 5th Battalion. Three months later he was in a Casualty Clearing Station with a poisoned leg, apparently from the same wound. Released back to his battalion, he could still write on 6 January, 1916, "I'm sorry to say I'm not quite fit yet. The beastly poison's still there, tho' the leg has healed up A1." And on the 24th, "…my leg is not yet healed up but, of course,

---

90   Webster, *Mesopotamia 1916-1917*, p.94, letter to mother, 21 February, 1917.
91   GHM PB1889, Brown, undated letter from Italy (1917/18).
92   IWM 10263 Recording, Knighton, Eric Leslie, interview 1988.
93   Andrews, *Haunting Years*, pp.152,180,198,207,251,266. See also: Andrews, *Autobiography*, p.90.

I'm able to drill etc, as per usual." The problem became altogether secondary, however, when a few days later he was much more seriously wounded in the right lung.[94] Lieutenant Robert Mackay, in 11th Argylls, recorded on 23 August, 1917, that, "My knees began to give trouble. I had fallen several times on top of barbed wire, which instead of scratching me went in right through the skin. They swelled up greatly, and to crown all, stiffened completely, so that in moving I seemed to be on crutches. They also got a bit painful." The injury effectively kept him out of the line for two weeks.[95]

Cuts and abrasions could in fact keep soldiers out of action for a considerable time. While in the trenches in November, 1917, Private Douglas of 8th Black Watch noticed that he had a nasty cut on his right knee. A week later he had developed a nasty swelling in the groin, and on 30th he was finally sent to hospital. From there he was evacuated to England. After recovery, he reported to the training battalion at Ripon and finally rejoined his battalion at the front on 3 April, 1918. A cut knee had cost him four and a half months absence from the front.[96] Stewart Thomson, in 1st London Scottish was evacuated to England early in 1915 as a result of cuts and abrasions. He did not rejoin the 1st Battalion at the front until about 15 October, 1915, the cuts having kept him away from the front line for about nine months.[97] Finally, S.C. Russell, an officer with 7th Camerons was wounded at Arras on 9 or 10 April, 1917. He was taken back to a Casualty Clearing Station, then to hospital at Le Treport.

> I had only been slightly wounded but was suffering from an infected cut from a barbed wire fence, and shortly afterwards I started to get a succession of boils, an affliction which persisted until well after the war was ended.

Even after hospitalisation and a brief return to the front, the problem persisted and he was removed to hospital again, not returning to the front again until September, 1918, when he joined 1st Battalion Scots Guards. It seems that the effects of the poisoning from the barbed wire in April, 1917, had effectively kept him out of the front line for much of the rest of the war.[98]

One way of reducing the likelihood of cuts was apparently to protect the legs with sand-bags. Colonel Haldane wrote that, in 4th Seaforths, when on the move, sandbags "were most effective in countering the attraction that existed between barbed wire and bare legs."[99] And Captain Robert White noted that the dress of 1st London Scottish on 1 July, 1916, included "Sandbags round legs, 2 per man". It is not clear if this was just a convenient way of carrying them, or if this was for protection against the wire when going into action.[100] Most references to the use of sand-bags for improvised clothing relate to their use in winter as a protection against the cold, and it seems unlikely that this alternative use was widespread.

---

94 IWM 5821 Semple, letters from Pte Jock McLeod, 9 September, 12 December, 1915, 6, 24 January, 1916.
95 IWM 11144 Mackay, diary, 23, 25, 30 August, 3, 8 September, 1917.
96 IWM 4586 Douglas, memoir, pp.183-271 passim.
97 IWM 12968, Thomson, letters to brother David 22 May, & to mother, 15 October, 1915.
98 THM Camerons 97-22, Russell, memoirs, pp.232-256.
99 IWM Books Haldane, '4th Seaforths,' unpublished draft, p.76.
100 IWM 15175 White, memoir.

Raids and patrols

Barbed wire, standing or lying in fragments on the ground, rough vegetation such as thistles, or simply hard rough or frozen ground, were all uncomfortable to negotiate when crawling in a kilt, with the additional risk, as we have seen, that the kilt might be caught on the wire. In September, 1917, Hugh Bartholomew, in 14th Argylls, bemoaned the profusion of thistles in the surrounding country, being "very uncomfortable things to crawl through when out on patrol with bare knees and hands."[101] Grant Fleming, in 1st Gordons, carried out a reconnaissance in April, 1917 and commented that, "the kilt was not a particularly good garment for such snake-like progression on damp and muddy ditches, but, apart from scratches on my face, hands and knees, the going was not too bad."[102] And Private Douglas in 8th Black Watch returned from a night-time patrol in No Man's Land, "our hands & bare knees sore with the constant crawling on the ground."[103] When, on Boxing Day, 1916, Hugh Boustead went out on patrol at 3.00 a.m. to inspect the German wire, he decided, "A kilt was no go for that game. My knees were like two ice blocks on the hard ground."[104] A month later, he had obtained riding breeches from home, which he was using for patrols instead of the kilt, a practice also observed by Douglas Wilson in 5th Camerons.[105]

Trousers were indeed frequently adopted for raids and patrols, as being more practical than the kilt. There are numerous examples of this practice,[106] which may also have been adopted to avoid giving away the identity of the raiding party.[107] Other forms of dress might be adopted. In July, 1918, the scouts of Basil Rathbone, in the Liverpool Scottish took to wearing overalls to facilitate their passage through the undergrowth.[108] Lieutenant Hugh Bartholomew, serving with 14th Argylls, records that in a patrol among the Crassiers on the night of 5 September, 1916, he was wearing shorts instead of his kilt.[109] When the Glasgow Highlanders took part in a raid on the evening of 20 February, 1915, heavy rain had made the communication trenches very wet and muddy. "The Highlanders had discarded the kilt and went over in khaki aprons."[110] And on 9 July, 1918, when 6th Gordons and 6th Seaforths launched a raid, "the kilt was discarded. Faces, hands and legs were blackened. A few men wore shorts, a few wore service dress jackets, but a number went over wearing only a shirt, with equipment above."[111] Most extraordinary, however, were the white camouflage nighties worn by 8/10th Gordons on 30 January, 1917, for their famous raid on the Butte de Warlencourt in the snow.[112]

---

101 *Bartholomew*, p.71, letter, 22 September, 1917.
102 IWM 15345 Fleming, memoir, p.33.
103 IWM 4586 Douglas, memoir, p.129.
104 GHM PB18 Boustead, Hugh, transcript letters, letters to mother, 26 December, 1916, 25 January, 1917; Boustead, *The Wind of Morning*, p.43; LC GS 0165, Boustead, Sir Hugh, transcript of interview with Liddle, 1976.
105 LC GS 1761 Wilson, memoir, p.62.
106 IWM 3608 Anderson, memoir; IWM 6873 Hendry, memoir; McEwen, *Fifth Camerons*, p.73; IWM 3834 Wrench, diary, p.57; THM Camerons 92 35, Welsh, memoirs, p 50; LC WF Recollections, S18, Sloan, memoir.
107 IWM Books Cooper, 'Domi Militaeque,' p.137.
108 Giblin, *Bravest of Hearts*, pp.97, 105.
109 *Bartholomew*, p.30, extract from his diary.
110 IWM Books Reid, 'Shoulder to Shoulder,' p.43.
111 Mackenzie, *Sixth Gordons*, p.160-161.
112 IWM 4370 Christison, memoir, p.52; GHM PB 2183 Watson, memoir, p.10.

Kilts of course were used on raids, especially early in the war. As described above, when this happened, knees and legs would be blackened as well as faces.[113] On occasion, other participating members of the party might don the kilt out of sheer bravado. A group of sappers did so when they joined 2nd Gordons on a raid in July, 1917,[114] and so did an American officer when he (unofficially) joined the Glasgow Highlanders for a raid in July, 1918.[115]

Mustard Gas

Mustard gas[116] was first used against the British Army east of Ypres on the night of 12/13 July 1917. The gas had been introduced by the Germans in the search for a lung irritant with greater persistency than chlorine and phosgene. They knew it as 'Lost' or 'Yellow Cross.' It became known as 'Mustard Gas' to the British because of its faint smell of mustard. It was delivered by shell and dispersed as a liquid with a very low boiling point, the gas forming as the liquid evaporated. As intended, the gas was persistent, and ground impregnated with mustard gas could remain toxic long after the initial shelling had ceased. Although the smell was faint, and detection difficult, the British Army soon found that the delivery of mustard gas was given away by the tell-tale 'plop' sound of the gas-shells. Accordingly in late 1917, the Germans increased the high explosive content of their mustard gas shells, or from April 1918[117] conducted joint bombardments with both gas-shells and HE shells to disguise their arrival. The gas had three effects. Firstly, if inhaled, like the earlier gases, chlorine and phosgene, it attacked the lungs; secondly, it caused conjunctivitis and painful, but usually temporary, blindness; and thirdly, it caused painful burns and blisters on any areas of exposed skin, especially any warm, moist, sweaty areas of exposed skin. It was this last feature of the gas which intuitively, one would think, would make the gas a particular hazard to kilted troops.

Highland troops came under attack from mustard gas from the very start, and the gas remained a threat until the end of the war,[118] large amounts being expended in both 1917 and 1918. Amongst the worst examples were 6th Camerons, in which Captain Rowan's company

---

113 Hutchison, *Warrior*, p.97; Peel & Macdonald, *6th Seaforths*, p.27.
114 GHM PB375 Pailthorpe, memoir, pp.48-49.
115 IWM Books Reid, 'Shoulder to Shoulder,' p.279.
116 See Jones, Simon, *World War I Gas Warfare Tactics and Equipment*, (Oxford: Osprey Elite No.150, 2007), pp.41, 44; Corrigan, *Blood and Poppycock*, pp.170-174. Once the dramatic effects of mustard gas became known, production was also started by the British.
117 Hutchison, *Warrior*, p.299.
118 Apart from specific examples cited, see: IWM 4370, Christison, memoir, p.63; NLS, Acc.9084, No.37, Macleod, George F, letter to father, 9 August, 1917; GHM PB1639, Kemp, memoir, p.91; IWM PP 6993 Littlewood, M,. diary, 27 May, 1918; THM Seaforths 81-2, Cooper, memoir, pp.111, 112; LC GS 1635, Turing, memoir; Fraser, 'War Diary 1915,' p.137; Cavendish, *An Reisimeid Chataich*, p.258; Beattie, *48th Highlanders*, pp.265-266, 279, 293-294; LC GS 1153 Murray, Maj. C.M., Diary, 14-16 October, 1917, 19, 21 March, 1918, & 'Report on the part taken by the S.A. Field Ambulance in the operations during the recent battle from 21st March, 1918' (contained within Diary); IWM Books Reid, 'Shoulder to Shoulder,' p.214; THM Camerons 92-35, Welsh, memoir, p.67; IWM Books Cooper, 'Domi Militaeque,' p.196; Wauchope, *Black Watch*, vol.2, p.312; LC Transcripts, Anton, C.S., transcript of Tape 364, interview with Liddle 1976; Cluness, *Doing his bit*, p.56; Malcolm, *Argyllshire Highlanders*, p.48; LC GS 1761 Wilson, memoir pp.98-99.

was caught unawares during the initial bombardment on the night of 12/13 July, when billeted in the cellar of a convent at Ypres. The entire company was affected. Within seven days one officer and 36 other ranks of the company were dead, and Captain Rowan hovered between life and death for weeks. Eventually he recovered but had to relinquish his commission in September, 1918.[119] Soon afterwards, the Liverpool Scottish were caught badly when in trenches in front of Wieltje, on the nights of 21 to 24 July, when the enemy launched sustained bombardments with mustard-gas shells. In four days, largely due to gas shelling, their fighting strength was reduced by four officers and 141 other ranks.[120] In October-November 1917, in the vicinity of Dumbarton Lakes and Gheluvelt, the 4/5th Black Watch found that gas shells were being used by the enemy in large quantities, and the losses from these, and other causes, were many. After one tour in the front area the 4/5th sent back 200 casualties suffering from gas, and, in addition, nearly the whole Battalion seemed affected by it.[121]

On 3 March 1918, in the trenches near Passchendaele, B and C Companies of 2nd Argylls were heavily shelled at night with mustard gas, through which 3 officers and 35 men were gassed and had to be sent to England.[122] A day or two prior to the German offensive in March, 1918, 1st London Scottish "had over 100 casualties from mustard gas in the support line."[123] Major G.A. Smith, serving with 5th Gordons recorded that a gas bombardment on the night of 26/27 April, 1918, resulted in 75 men being sent to hospital. The next day a further 25 men followed.[124] In 15th Division, 6th Camerons, 5th Gordons and 9th Gordons were particularly hard hit during the operations between 21 July and 3 August, 1918,[125] when both 44th Brigade HQ and 5th Gordons, for example, were caught out by gas sprinkled in the cellars in which they took shelter. "Oh! He's a filthy low down cad is a German," wrote William Kemp, in 5th Gordons.[126] On 24 August, 1918, while attacking German positions on the Scarpe, 6th Gordons came under attack by mustard gas. "In two days more than 100 men had to be sent down suffering from this latest form of poison. The injuries were rarely severe, but even slight cases had to be sent away for a fortnight's treatment."[127] Finally, in the period 9-12 September, 1918, the 42nd Battalion C.E.F. (Royal Highlanders of Canada) were in the line opposite Sauchy-Cauchy. During this time:

---

119 Macleod, *6th Camerons*, pp.74-75; THM Camerons 02 111, Notes on Rowan by Leszczuk. See also on this incident: IWM 4370, Christison, memoir, pp.62-63; LC GS 0262 Campbell, letters to fiancée, 13, 14, 22 July, 1917. Christison's account is quite different from Macleod's. For other accounts of this attack from 15th Division, see: GHM PB1639, Kemp, memoir, p.91; IWM 15460 Chandler, 'Report of the gas shell bombardment of Ypres, night of 12/13th July, 1917', Copy of Third Army No. G.10/203 dated 23/7/17; IWM 6993 Littlewood, memoir, pp.28-29, diary, 13-20 July, 1917.
120 McGilchrist, *Liverpool Scottish*, p.117. See also: LC GS 1579, Taylor, 'Reminiscences', p.12; 'Further Reminiscences', pp.3, 5, 6.
121 Wauchope, *Black Watch*, vol.2, p.88.
122 Cavendish, *An Reisimeid Chataich*, p. 261.
123 LC GS 0360, Coppard, memoir. See also: LC WF Recollections, S18, Sloan, memoir; IWM 1659, Scammell, letters to mother, 26, 31 March, 6, 8, 25 April, 1918.
124 GHM PB234 Smith, Maj. G.A., diaries, 27, 28, 29 April 1918.
125 Apart from sources cited for 5th Gordons, see also: Macleod, *6th Camerons*, p.110; GHM PB1892.3.30 *15th (Scottish) Division, Narrative of Operations from 15.7.18 to 7.8.18*, Appendices II & III; GHM PB123 Mulligan, Pte John, diary, 3-4 August, 1918.
126 GHM PB1639, Kemp, memoir, Vol.2, pp.49-50. See also: GHM PB102, Geddes, Godfrey Power, diary, 1 August, 1918; GHM PB3758 Shirreffs, James Dunn, diary, 3 August, 1918.
127 Mackenzie, *Sixth Gordons*, p.172.

The Battalion position was heavily shelled one very still night with mustard gas shells. Box respirators were immediately adjusted and there were no casualties during the night. Next day, however, while the men were sleeping in the bottom of rudimentary trenches occupied there, the gas which had settled into the damp ground was diffused by the hot sun with the result that some fifty men were very badly gassed and had to be evacuated.[128]

These are just a few of the more dramatic examples of Highland troops suffering significant casualties from mustard gas. But was the kilt a contributory factor? Intuitively one would think so, but that great defender of the kilt, Norman Macleod, would disagree. He argued that,

it was generally the parts of the body where the skin was tender that got burnt. The skin of the legs having got hardened by exposure to the weather, was generally able to withstand the effects of gas in the same way as the hands and the face. Again, most of the cases of burning were caused by men sitting down on the ground which was saturated with gas. The kilt being thick, the gases could not easily penetrate it, and no doubt its swinging in the air, when the men got up, helped dispel them. In fact, the men did not suffer much from the effects of burning unless the shell burst close enough to sprinkle them with the liquid.[129]

Douglas Wimberley is more cautious, but lends some support:

Some medical authorities now argued that the bare thighs of the Highlanders led to unnecessary casualties; others stated that the 7 yards thickness round the middle of the Jocks' bodies, which the kilt provided, was a better protection against mustard gas than were trousers. It kept out the gas from burning the skin for some seconds longer, and the contaminated kilt could be so much more quickly discarded, thus preventing such bad burns. Anyhow, while the argument went on, right up to victory in 1918, the kilt remained as our battle dress.[130]

Steel and Hart wryly observe on Macleod's comments how Highland officers "were well used to turning every wartime eventuality into yet one more testament to the efficacy of the kilt." Instead they describe mustard gas as a serious threat to kilted units, but they do not produce the evidence to contradict his claims.[131] There is, in fact, undoubtedly some truth in what Macleod says. Some of the worst blistering was caused by liquid mustard sprinkled onto, or seeping into, clothing. It would be retained in the clothing and then evaporate against the skin. Since the kilt was thicker then trousers, especially at the back, theoretically it would possibly provide better protection, and Wimberley's additional observation on how quickly it could be discarded is certainly correct. On the other hand, sitting on the ground in a kilt could leave at least part of the legs or worse directly in contact with contaminated ground. But what does the evidence indicate?

---

128 Topp, *42nd Battalion*, p.261.
129 Craig-Brown, *Historical Records*, Vol.4, pp.327-328. See also: Macleod, *6th Camerons*, pp.74-75, and his comments in Mackay, *The Romantic Story*, Appendix.
130 IWM 430, Wimberley, 'The Kilt in Modern War.'
131 See Steel, Nigel & Hart, Peter, *Passchendaele* (London: Cassell, 2001), p.79.

A report was prepared on the mustard gas cases admitted to No. 16 General Hospital B.E.F. between 24 and 27 July, 1917. All were gassed during the night of the 21st and morning of the 22nd, and almost all came from the same sector (91 Field Ambulance). The following effects on the skin were observed, the extent depending on the severity of the case:

> A cutaneous erythemia, blistering and early desquamation, involving especially the eyelids, face and neck, scrotum, buttocks, armpits and thighs; in other words the parts either most exposed or moist. The thighs were involved chiefly in those cases wearing kilts.[132]

The historian of the Liverpool Scottish noted that the gas "attacked the skin – especially the softer parts of it – and caused painful sores. In these circumstances the kilt is not an ideal garment."[133] Harry Taylor, in the same battalion noted that the gas "affected the skin, and this played havoc with kilted regiments who were singularly vulnerable, for obvious reasons."[134] Likewise, the historian of 4th Seaforths notes that the gas "was a powerful irritant, raising huge blisters on the skin, and causing cuts and abrasions to fester." "The kilt was a distinct disadvantage where mustard gas was concerned as some knew to their cost. They couldn't sit down for days. They daren't. It was not lethal but most inconvenient."[135] After the battle of Menin Road in September, 1917, 7th Seaforths, "had to pass through mustard gas after being relieved, a slow progress for an hour in pitch dark, unable to sit down as ground much barraged."[136] A sergeant in 15th Battalion C.E.F. (48th Highlanders) explained that "mustard gas is especially hard on Highlanders, as a hurried leap into a mustard gas filled shell-hole might, and often did, result in serious and excruciatingly painful burns under the kilt, even though none were swallowed."[137] Philip Christison observed how in 6th Camerons (Macleod's battalion, be it noted), "heat generated gas out of the men's clothing and some got gassed even with all precautions."[138] Finally, Sergeant H.E. May, of the Gordon Highlanders, witnessed the effect of a mustard gas attack on a working party on the night of 24/25 May, 1918; "flesh inflamed and almost raw where the mustard variety of gas had burnt it – a serious disadvantage to a kilt." In the morning,

> In the garden at the billet lying about the grass were close on a hundred men, denuded of their clothing, who lay about and writhed in veriest agony. The worst gas cases. With the passing of a few hours blisters were raised by the mustard gas. One man had a blister that reached from his neck to the bottom of his spine and extended the whole width of his back.[139]

---

132 NLS MS 20234, Haldane, Dr J.S., Correspondence, 'Note on gassed cases admiied to 16 General Hospital July 24th, 25th, 27th 1917 by Major George W. Norris & Captain E.B. Krumbhaer (M.O.R.C., U S A), No. 16 General Hospital, B.E.F., n.d., c. 31 July 1917.
133 McGilchrist, *The Liverpool Scottish*, p.117.
134 LC GS 1579, Taylor, 'Reminiscences', p.12; 'Further Reminiscences', pp.3, 5, 6.
135 Haldane, *4th Seaforths*, p.225; IWM Books Haldane, '4th Seaforths', p.108.
136 *Lieut-Colonel Robert Horn*, p.82.
137 Beattie, *48th Highlanders*, pp.265-266.
138 IWM 4370, Christison, memoir, p.63.
139 May, 'In a Highland Regiment,' pp.205-206.

The most important evidence, however, regarding the kilt and mustard gas is provided by the accounts of burns to individual soldiers. There are a number of accounts by soldiers affected by the gas which do not mention burns to the legs or groin.[140] This does not mean that they did not occur, for soldiers might be reticent about damage to the groin area. Fortunately, there do exist a number of accounts by burns victims. Philip Christison, for example, was evidently splashed by mustard during a bombardment. "One shell landed in my trench almost beside me and did not burst – just a sort of plop. I felt a burning sensation just above my right knee. (I still have the scar)"[141] Captain R.E. Badenoch, serving with 4/5th Black Watch, who also came under gas bombardment, wrote that, "I am glad to say the worst I got was gas blisters on my leg."[142] James Sloan came under gas bombardment with 1st London Scottish. He was blinded and taken to hospital at Boulogne. When he got his sight back,

> There was still a lot of discomfort round the crotch where all my skin had been burned off but after a few weeks I was well enough to be sent to a convalescent camp near Rouen… My burnt 'privates' took a long time to return to normal.

When he finally returned to his battalion in the latter part of 1918, the gas had kept him out of the front line for at least six months.[143]

Private Douglas, serving with 8th Black Watch, describes in detail his experience with mustard gas in 1918. On 27 May, he and his pal, Albert Smith, were detached as observers. Between the 27th and 30th, they observed enemy shelling in the vicinity of their battalion's support trench, which they had to visit to collect rations, noticing a distinct smell of gas. On the morning of the 30th, at Heifer Farm, both men experienced soreness in their legs, "above the knees, and especially round our privates." At the end of the day, they reported to the M.O. "After inspecting the affected parts, which looked as if they had been scalded, he instructed the Corporal to bathe the parts affected, which was mostly on and around our privates, also instructed him to give us some sort of powder … As we left the Aid Post, we both had the feeling that the Medical Officer had not much idea what was wrong with us. We understood later that we were the first two 'Mustard Gas Cases' that had come before him." Douglas then reported to Battalion HQ, delivered his report, and also informed the battalion Major of the discomfort they were experiencing. "The Major then asked me to lift my kilt up and show him the affected parts. As this was more or less an order, I could not do anything else but obey … as Albert Smith and I were the first two "Mustard Gas Cases" in the Battalion, his curiosity had got the better of him."

The two soldiers continued on duty, but the discomfort became increasingly worse. On 1 June, however, the battalion went out of the line to a camp at Hondeghem. Here Douglas had the good fortune to meet an RAMC corporal attached to a nearby RFC Balloon Section, who took it on himself to look after him. Each evening the corporal bathed the affected parts and

---

140 See: IWM 8592 Macgregor, letters to wife, 16 November, 1 December, 1917, 21 April to 18 May, 1918, passim; 27 May, 17 June, 29, 31 October, 1918; IWM 1659, Scammell, letters to mother, 26, 31 March, 6, 8, 25 April, 1918; ASHM N-E11 Bowie, diary; BWA Hay, memoir, pp.230-234.
141 IWM 4370, Christison, memoir, pp.62-63.
142 BWA Badenoch, memoirs, p.14.
143 LC WF Recollections, S18, Sloan, memoir.

dusted them with boracic powder, so he "felt much easier between the legs than otherwise I might have done." However, the condition grew worse and finally, on 8 June both men were marked for hospital. Although not sent further back than Calais, Douglas only finally rejoined his battalion on 8 July. It had taken 9 days from first feeling the discomfort to being sent down the line, and a further month before he was able to rejoin the battalion. In reality the effect of the Gas was to render him ineffective for 40 days.[144]

William Kemp, was gassed in early August, 1918, with 5th Gordons. Temporarily blinded, he was evacuated to Rouen, from where he was discharged to Scottish Base Depot on 23 August. He spent only a weekend there before rejoining the battalion at the Quarter Master's stores at Bracquemont on 27 August. But that was not the end of the matter.

> Since being gassed my blood had got into a very poor state and I had several boils on my skin in places where the gas had raised blisters. I had not thought much of them, but one near the top of the inside of my legs was getting particularly bad and during my first day at Bracquemont as it became so sore, I spent the day in bed instead of going up to the trenches. The following day as it was no better I went to get it dressed at a Field Ambulance. When the doctor saw it he told me it was not a boil but an abscess and that I should have to go straight off to hospital again to have an operation on it.

Again, Kemp was not sent further back than Le Touquet, finally returning to his battalion on 16 September. Altogether, the effects of the gas had removed him from the line for seven weeks.[145]

Finally, Douglas Wilson, in 5th Camerons, noted in June, 1918 that, thanks to much crawling in long grass and crops sprayed with mustard gas, his legs, knees and thighs were irritable and showed signs of blistering. Somewhat to his surprise, he received permission from the C.O. to discard his kilt pro tem for breeches. "The Jock was prone to blistering of knees and thighs from gas burns. Was there ever a means of hitting one's foe below the belt so loathsome as this?"[146]

There is enough evidence here to demonstrate that the kilt did indeed leave Highland troops vulnerable to mustard gas. In these circumstances some battalions, at least, did go so far as to issue drawers for additional protection. This was the case in the 1st London Scottish, at least in 1918. When Horace Manton of that battalion was asked what was worn under the kilt, he confirmed that nothing at all was worn in England, but that men were given 'bloomers' in France because of mustard gas, "so it didn't go onto the private parts. If it came onto your private parts it'd be a bit painful, wouldn't it?"[147] James Sloan confirms that the battalion "had all been issued with anti-gas impregnated pants" before they came under mustard gas bombardment prior to the German March offensive, but no-one wore them "because they were louse playgrounds."[148] Drawers also seem to have been issued to the two kilted battalions in 33rd Division, 2nd Argylls and the Glasgow Highlanders. Graham Hutchison, serving with the Machine Gun Corps in 33rd Division, recalls the introduction of mustard gas:

---

144 IWM 4586 Douglas, memoir, pp.540-698, passim.
145 GHM PB1639, Kemp, memoir, Vol.2, pp.49-51, Vol.3, pp.53-56.
146 LC GS 1761 Wilson, memoir, p.47.
147 IWM 9756 Manton, interview.
148 LC WF Recollections, S18, Sloan, memoir.

At first this new horror was difficult to cope with. Not only did it choke the lungs, but it inflicted, also, severe burns upon the flesh. The two kilted Battalions in the Division, the 93rd Highlanders and the 9th H.L.I., were the first to be submitted to shelling with mustard gas. Those afflicted suffered awful agonies. A conference was called at Divisional Headquarters to decide as to the best means of dealing with this new gas, and for providing effective measures against it. It was agreed that the Highlanders must be forthwith equipped with long cotton drawers. Highland officers were asked to submit proposals as to what form these drawers should take; colour, number of buttons, and the details required with such exactitude by an Ordnance Service which can only think in terms of "Drawers, cotton, pink, legs long, buttons four, Highland Regiments for the use of." All the latent genius of "Q" was employed in the production of these pants; and the Highland Regiments could be observed later in the line, safely attired in drawers, presenting an appearance of standard lamps, their kilts resembling the shades.[149]

Captain J.C. Dunn, Medical Officer of 2nd Royal Welch Fusiliers, was in the same division, and confirms this, writing of August, 1917, "Meanwhile, our kilted regiments wearing full-length grey woollen drawers, for the protection of bare parts, beat any burlesque of the garb of old Gaul ever seen on the stage."[150] Douglas Wilson, in 5th Camerons, records somewhat ambiguously that, presumably in his battalion, which had problems with mustard gas in June, 1918, "a compromise was arrived at by issuing long hose-tops that could be drawn up over the knees, with the partial abandonment of the true Highlander's sans culotte habit."[151] Finally, in the South African Scottish, around the end of July, 1917, according to Arthur Betteridge;

> We were told of a new type of Gas the Germans were using. This filthy new gas attacked the eyeballs and testicles especially. We were then issued with trousers to be worn in the trenches or whenever we were preparing for an attack. Kilts remained with our kitbags on these occasions.[152]

However, it is not clear how long this measure remained in force, for Betteridge only remained with the battalion until early September, 1917. Overall, there is no evidence that the issue of drawers or trousers in response to mustard gas was mandated across the Army. Decisions in the kilted battalions appear to have been made on a local basis and only five battalions have been more or less reliably identified in which the practice occurred.

Deception

Kilts were an instant giveaway to enemy Intelligence regarding the units they were facing, and the arrival or disappearance of kilts was, of course, an advertisement to the Germans that a

---

149 Hutchison, *Warrior*, pp.195-6.
150 Dunn, Capt J.C., *The War the Infantry Knew 1914-1919*, (London: Abacus, 1994), p.375 (first published 1938).
151 LC GS 1761 Wilson, memoir, p.47.
152 LC GS 0132 Betteridge, memoir, p.107.

change of unit had taken place in the line. When, in February, 1918, 51st Highland Division changed its location, and 6th Black Watch relieved the West Yorkshires of 6th Division, "we were ordered to wear our greatcoats constantly for the first few days, not because of bad weather, for the weather was fair and mild, but to prevent enemy observers noticing that a relief had taken place."[153] Norman Beaton recalls that when 7th Gordons occupied a different set of trenches near Laventie in July, 1915, the Germans "enquired of the Irish [Connaught Rangers] how long the kilties (meaning us) had been in beside them? But they got no answer."[154] Not only was this useful intelligence but it could also have more immediate repercussions. When, in June 1916, 2nd Gordons relieved an English battalion in the trenches opposite Mametz, the relieving party unwisely took a short cut over the top rather than go through the communications trench. The Germans, seeing kilts, then knew that a relief was taking place and immediately shelled both front line and communication trenches, which were still full of men making their way up to their positions, causing heavy casualties.[155]

Knowing the usefulness of unit identification to the Germans, the higher command on occasion required Highland troops to go into trousers for deception. This occurred in 51st Highland Division before the Somme, in order to disguise the fact that the division had increased its frontage when other troops were withdrawn from the line preparatory to the Somme battle.[156] It is not clear how long this situation lasted, but probably until the division was relieved in this sector, which was on 13 July, 1916. It is evident that the rare privilege of wearing English uniforms did not meet with universal approval.[157] Similar efforts at deception were made before the Cambrai offensive, to disguise the assembly of 51st Highland Division. Private W.G. Cameron, serving with 7th Black Watch, records that before the Cambrai offensive, when the battalion lay just behind Havrincourt Wood, their orders were "that no kilties had to be seen in the district in case of it getting to the enemy's ears."[158]

We have seen that kilts might be abandoned for raids because of the danger to bare knees, but this might also be done to prevent identification. Private Albert Hay was serving with 1st Black Watch in 1918. He records that for a raid they undertook on 8 July, they, "were issued with khaki shorts and one identification disc in place of the two normally carried. This disc had a number only and did not carry particulars of Religion, Regiment, name and number as on the ordinary two discs – one grey and the other brown."[159] Clearly this was all done to reduce the chance of identification, as for protection of the knees when crawling over barbed wire on raids, shorts can have had little advantage over the kilt.

There were nevertheless occasions when the kilt could provide useful identification to one's own side. On 29 December, 1916, for example, Lieutenant Robert Mackay of 11th Argylls noted that, "Farquharson and I were nearly shot by one of our own Lewis Gun men while taking

---

153 IWM Books Cooper, 'Domi Militaeque,' p.205.
154 GHM Beaton, memoir, p.44.
155 GHM PB375, Pailthorpe, memoir, p.7.
156 Bewsher, *Fifty First*, p.65.
157 Maclean, John, *On Active Service with the Argyll and Sutherland Highlanders in Belgium and France*, (Edinburgh: Scottish Chronicle Press, n.d.), Vol.1, pp.68-69; Malcolm, *Argyllshire Highlanders*, p.33; Sutherland, *Fifth Seaforth Highlanders*, p.69; Mackenzie, *Sixth Gordons*, pp.90-91.
158 LC GS 0257, Cameron, memoir. See also: Wauchope, *Black Watch*, vol.2, p.295; GHM PB1892.3.18 McDonald, 'Uncle Harper's Duds,' p.110.
159 BWA Hay, memoir, pp.134/136.

a walk in No Man's Land. (We had gone out without warning ALL our front line men.) By chance the gunner got a glimpse of my bare knees and kilt, and recognised we were not Huns."[160]

It seems that on at least one or two occasions in 1915, German troops did disguise themselves as Highlanders for deception. Captain Boyle, adjutant of 1st Argylls, recorded that during a German attack on May 9, 1915, Germans "were seen wearing kilts, khaki trousers and even French uniform – indeed an officer of the K.S.L.I. shot a Highlander."[161] Some support for this comes from Ian Hamilton, an officer with 1st Gordons. On 16 June, 1915, while a P.O.W. at Burg bei Magdeburg, he recorded that, from a newly arrived prisoner, he learned that during the German gas attack at Ypres, when they attacked the British after they had won back the trenches lost by the French, "The first two of these attacks the G's were all dressed up as Highlanders", with kilts apparently taken from British prisoners.[162] Similarly, it is reported that during the battle of Loos, 11th Argylls were holding a position on Hill 70, when they thought they saw reinforcements, who turned out to be Germans wearing captured kilts over top boots and trousers.[163]

Some lesser practicalities

Kilts were generally found to be uncomfortable to sleep in. In his dugout in March, 1915, Lieutenant Douglas Gillespie, in 2nd Argylls, put on trousers to sleep: "One can't lie down in a kilt without waking up to find it round the neck."[164] Nevertheless, unlike trousers, the kilt could conveniently be used as a blanket when removed. Sometimes it was used as an over-blanket.[165] More often, it was used to sleep on.[166]

The kilt at least did have an advantage over trousers when it came to natural functions. Around February, 1917, shortly after he had joined the South African Scottish in France, J.E.P Levyns was taken to see the latrine in the front-line trench.

> While there Byrne told me that the Scottish regiments in their kilts had enormous advantages over the trousered troops, because if, when engaged in their natural functions, they heard anything coming, they could get up and run, whereas the poor devil in trousers had to get the things up before he could get moving![167]

---

160 IWM 11144 Mackay, diary, 29 December, 1916. For other examples, see: Craig-Brown, *Historical Records*, Vol.3, p.43; ASHM N-E8, Campbell, George, typescript memoir, 1935; LC, POW 056 Millar, memoir.
161 LC GS 0177 Boyle, diary, 9 May, 1915.
162 GHM PB1498 Hamilton, diary 16 June, 1915.
163 ASHM N-E11 Bowie, diary.
164 Gillespie, *Letters from Flanders*, pp.27, 113, letters 1 March, 24 April, 1915.
165 Lyon, *In kilt and khaki*, p.159; Aiken, *Courage Past*, pp.35-36, citing recollection of T.M.G. Robertson, late 9th H.L.I; IWM 12043 Collins, interview.
166 Albert Hay, quoted in Young, *Forgotten Scottish Voices*, p.202; Dinesen, *Merry Hell*, p.176; Rule, *Students*, p.174; IWM 430 Wimberley, memoir, Pt 2, p.29; GHM PB1706/2 Robertson, diary, 4 July, 1916; IWM Books Cooper, 'Domi Militaeque,' pp.128-129, 155-156; IWM 4586 Douglas, memoir, pp.906-907.
167 Levyns, *The Disciplines of War*, pp.62-63.

Or as Tom Walker, from 7th Argylls, put it, "you couldn't be caught with your pants down!"[168] In August 1918, Thomas Dinesen, suffering from an upset stomach, found that "the kilt does come in handy sometimes!"[169] As Arthur Wrench explained, the accepted cure-all for stomach ache was the Number 9 pill, "so that you are ready to rush into 'rear action' in a hurry. Then is the moment one might appreciate the convenience of the kilt."[170]

In battle

In the heat of battle, the romance of the kilt met the reality of war. The battlefield revealed the stark contrast between the noble image of the Highland soldier and the squalid business of killing. The images are now horrific, shocking, undignified, but above all sad.[171] During Third Ypres, Private Wullie Murison, in 6th Gordons, saw a young soldier who "had been shot at such close range that his body had been severed in half. His head and shoulders were lying in the trench but the remainder of his body from kilt to feet appeared to stagger several more yards."[172] In the darkness after Aubers Ridge, Lieutenant Lynden-Bell in 1st Seaforths "had a look around at the ground we had just been on and I found the head of my Sergeant and a bit further on I found his 2 legs still wearing his kilt."[173] Arthur Wrench, in 4th Seaforths, witnessed the Arras battlefield the day after the battle began.

> Fritz of course has got all his artillery back into action and is pounding his old position to blazes. The carnage is terrible and it is all like one huge charnel house. The dead are lying everywhere mercilessly butchered and there isn't a single person in all the world who can be held to blame. One young fellow of the Seaforths is stretched out as if he had just been lain down to rest. Another's head is completely battered in with the butt of a rifle. One other has his helmet broken and embedded in his skull, and in another place a Seaforth and a German are lying dead together with their fingers locked around each others' throat. Dead are also down in the shell holes in positions too awful to mention. Some are only visible beneath the water and sometimes a pair of heels can be seen projecting from others. It is all so sickening and if the folks away behind the lines could only see this, surely there would be no more war. But this is not war. It is only licensed murder.[174]

---

168 Walker, *Tom Walker Remembers*, p.5.
169 Dinesen, *Merry Hell*, p.229.
170 IWM 3834 Wrench, diary, p.238.
171 Apart from the examples cited below, see: GHM PB2984, Strachan, memoir; Andrews, *Haunting Years*, p.54; NLS MS 944-947, Ramage, diary, 16 May, 2 June, 1915; Rule, *Students*, p.215; Thomas Williamson quoted by Young, *Forgotten Scottish Voices*, p.136; IWM 16335, Racine, memoir, p.65; IWM 430 Wimberley, memoir, p.34; BWA Cumming, undated letter; Burns, *Once a Cameron Highlander*, p.88; IWM 3834 Wrench, diary, p.72; IWM 2528 Bradbury, memoir, p.19; Fred Hollingsworth quoted in Nicholls, *Cheerful Sacrifice*, pp.96-97; IWM Books Cooper, 'Domi Militaeque,' p.148; Private McLellan, quoted by Lloyd, *London Scottish*, p.122; Cluness, *Doing his bit*, p.51; BWA Badenoch, memoir, p.18; THM 2013-072 (S) Braes, diary, 20 January, 1916; LC GS 1761 Wilson, memoir, p.81.
172 GHM PB3712, Murison, memoir.
173 LC GS 0993 Lynden-Bell, transcript of interview.
174 IWM 3834 Wrench, diary, pp.105-106, 10 April, 1917.

224   Those Bloody Kilts

The romance of war: dead Highland soldier. (Author's collection)

There was little dignity for kilted solders in death.[175] Lieutenant Norman Collins, of 6th Seaforth Highlanders, recalls how, during the attack on Y Ravine at Beaumont-Hammel on 13 November 1916, "I went out and saw men dropping right and left, I've a vision of a Gordon Highlander pitching forward with his rifle onto his hands and knees, stone dead, his kilt raised showing his backside."[176] After the battle, on the15th, Frank Brooke, a stretcher-bearer with the same battalion, 4th Seaforths, found that, in Y ravine, "One Jock lay on the slope of a shell-hole, his kilt blown up on his chest exposing his body and his limbs, red and pulped. It was horrible. Thousands of men had passed him and yet no one had the thought to lower his kilt. I left my place in our file and pulled it down."[177] Similarly, after the battle of Arras, in April, 1917, Leslie Cooper recalled that,

> The South Africans had captured the ground on which we worked. Many of their dead were lying where they had fallen … Among the attacking South Africans were the 4th Batt (Scottish). Some of the dead were face down, some on their backs, but in almost all cases the kilt had been thrown forward leaving their nakedness for all to see. Without ceremony, but with a touch of reverence, those who were close by had pulled down the kilt. It is strange what men will do at times such as these![178]

---

175 Apart from the examples cited below, see: GHM PB 2183, Watson, memoir, p.14; Bird, *Ghosts*, p.58; Rule, *Students*, pp.71-72; ASHM N-E2, Todd, memoirs.
176 Van Emden and Humphries, *Veterans*, p.102.
177 IWM Books Brooke, 'Wait for it', p.142.
178 THM Seaforths 81-2, Cooper, memoir, pp.62-63.

The Kilt: The Hazards of War 225

More romance. Another dead Highlander, from the Tynecot visitor centre. (Photograph, author)

Michael Longley, in his poem 'Wounds' recalls a memory of his father, of the padre of the London Scottish re-arranging the kilts of dead soldiers for the sake of decency and dignity.

> Here are two pictures from my father's head -
> ...
> Next comes the London Scottish padre
> Resettling kilts with his swagger-stick,
> With a stylish backhand and a prayer.
> Over a landscape of dead buttocks
> My father followed him for fifty years.[179]

Conclusions

When all the evidence is examined, it is clear that, despite its defenders, the kilt was not a practical garment for modern warfare. In the previous chapter we demonstrated the overall impracticality of the kilt when faced by the elements. In addition, we have now seen how the kilt harboured lice; it made men vulnerable to mosquitoes or other biting insects, and hence

---

179 Longley, *Collected Poems*, 'Wounds.' His father, Richard Longley, joined the London Scottish aged 17 in 1914. He won the Military Cross, and by the time he was 20 had risen to command a company.

malaria; it caught easily on the barbed wire, endangering lives; it encouraged cuts from barbed wire and other abrasives like rough vegetation; the cuts acquired through these means and by chafing quickly turned septic in the insanitary conditions in the trenches; it made men vulnerable to mustard gas; finally, from an intelligence point of view it facilitated unit identification by the enemy. The evident disadvantages of the kilt could scarcely be better highlighted by the number of occasions on which it was replaced or supplemented by trousers, shorts or improvised garments made of sandbags.

The impracticality of the kilt did not go unnoticed in the Army staffs. Astonishingly, as Colonel Nicholson, on the staff of 51st Highland Division, reveals, their commander, General Harper, made an unsuccessful attempt to abolish the kilt, at least in the trenches. "The General had sound views where sentiment should begin and end. He entirely agreed with the wish of the division to abolish the kilt. It was in fact inconceivable that in such a war a kilt should be worn." He outlines several of the disadvantages we have considered and goes on, "We were the most Highland Division in the Army, yet only three hundred of our 20,000 had ever worn a kilt before the war, and those three hundred were mostly gillies. Whenever possible the men wore trousers instead – when for instance they were on road control or detached."

> We put the case forward and said that the whole division wanted trousers. G.H.Q. and Third Army were against us, replying that we were the only Highlanders who would consent to part with our kilts; but though Third Army threw cold water on our suggestion, G.H.Q. consented to forward it to the War Office. The War Office flatly refused to look at the proposal. So we accumulated some four hundred pairs of trousers per battalion as trench stores. I am not one to throw cold water on sentiment, but you can get nearly as much sentiment out of a hackle in the side of your bonnet with a little imagination … For a long time a great many of our men had made for themselves breeches of oat-sacks or sandbags, or else wore only the apron.[180]

It seems most likely that this approach to abolish the kilt was made during or after the winter of 1915/16.[181] It would certainly have had some support from below. At the age of 83, William Robertson, who had served with 1st Seaforths, wrote, "the kilt is not the dress for the trenches."[182] David Hood, who served in 2nd Argylls felt, "A kilt was the most awful thing, the most ridiculous thing ever I came across for warfare."[183] Robert Burns, who served with 7th Camerons, put it succinctly: "It wasn't suitable to warfare."[184]

C.S.M. Jim Murray, a pre-war Regular, also served with 1st Seaforths, and felt as early as September, 1915, that the kilt should be done away with at the front: "The nights are getting terrible cold now & this is only September & it is hard to say what I'll need for the winter … I hear we are getting long boots this winter … I wish they would complete it & discard the

---

180 Nicholson, Col. W.M., *Behind the Lines*, (London: Jonathan Cape, 1939), pp.145-146.
181 Nicholson left 51st Highland Division for 17th Division in June, 1916, while Harper did not take over the command of the Division until September, 1915. As the Division did not arrive in France until May, 1915, it would have had no experience of severe conditions before the winter of 1915/16.
182 IWM 11334, Robertson, memoir, p.7.
183 IWM 10786, Hood, interview.
184 LC Tape 963, Burns interview.

macnab as it is both cold & a proper breeding ground for lice."[185] Lieutenant Guy Macgregor, serving with 6th Argylls, remarked critically of the kilt in January, 1918, "I wish the people who are enthusiastic about the garments – the Colonels and Majors – had to wear the thing. That wd stop it in a week. But as long as it is only subalterns & privates who have to endure the thing it's likely to last as long as stupidity – & that's immortal."[186] He was blunter still in September: "I have on my kilt. I dislike the kilt intensely. The orders for it to be worn are only given by those who never wear it themselves & like to have round them men whose costume is a badge of inferiority. I have to wear it today because I am battalion orderly officer."[187]

On the other hand, Private Cooper, who served in both 6th Black Watch and 12th Argylls, felt pride outweighed the drawbacks: "I don't believe there is much chance of the kilt being done away with as a dress out here. In spite of the discomforts of it there is a good deal of sentiment and prejudice which would rise in arms against any such change. I, for one, am not sorry I wear a kilt, and am proud of it too! I am sure we would all feel our dignity outraged if we were ordered to do away with our kilts."[188] And later: "I assure you there is no more pitiable spectacle than a Highland Battalion coming out of action, especially if the weather has been wet … Still, I should be aggrieved to see the kilt disappear from the army … Some of our men would do anything to avoid wearing the kilt. I cannot understand them. I am proud of my kilt, proud to have worn the tartan of so gallant a regiment."[189] Likewise, James Fraser, who served in 'U' Company in 4th Gordons, pointed out the disadvantages of the kilt but stated that nevertheless, "we would not have given up the kilt for anything or anybody."[190]

So opinions differ. Clearly, if there was a case to be made for the kilt, it was not on the grounds of practicality, but on the grounds of 'esprit de corps'. The central question is really not, "Was the kilt impractical?" – it was – but "Was the impracticality of the kilt outweighed by its advantages to 'esprit de corps'?" In seeking to defend the practicality of the kilt, Macleod and his supporters, no doubt principally motivated by 'esprit de corps' are on untenable ground and miss the point. Wimberley, by contrast, is much more moderate, and bases his defence on 'esprit de corps'. Was he right? We will leave this discussion to our final conclusions.

---

185 IWM 15118 PP Murray, James Mossman, letter to wife Jeanie, 11 September, 1915.
186 IWM 8592 Macgregor, letters to wife, 6 January, 1918.
187 Ibid., letter to wife, 12 September, 1918.
188 IWM Books Cooper, 'Domi Militaeque,' p.175.
189 Ibid., p.349.
190 Fraser, 'War Diary, 1915', p.44.

8

The Pipes

> What is the piper playing, that battles in my blood?
> Winds in it, waves in it, waters at the flood.
> Sadness in it, madness in it, weeping mists and rain.
> What is the piper playing that beats within my brain?[1]

> A fine lot of men marching up and down playing the pipes is top-hole.[2]

As we have seen in reviewing the Highland regiments on the eve of war, in 1914, the bagpipes were fundamental to the life of a Highland regiment, where they permeated every aspect of life. The pipes controlled the daily routine of the regiment with duty pipe calls. They entertained the officers at formal mess dinners. They were used on the march, for parades and inspections, and for recruiting. They were used for competitions and for entertainments, and they were played at funerals. Last, but not least, they were used in battle, with the most celebrated instance being the winning of the Victoria Cross by Piper Findlater of the Gordons in 1897 on the heights of Dargai. As one of the icons of Scottishness, the pipes emphasised Scottish identity, while, through the use of particular pipe tunes, they stressed regimental identity too. Their officers played a considerable part in retaining, encouraging and preserving pipe music. Everywhere that Highland regiments were formed, the pipes were deemed essential to their existence, so that the practice of maintaining pipe-bands was duplicated with expatriate fervour in the Highland regiments raised elsewhere in the Empire, notably amongst the many Canadian militia regiments and in the Transvaal Scottish and the Cape Town Highlanders in South Africa. This chapter considers how the pipes went on to be used in the war. It addresses also what the soldiers really thought of them and their impact on morale.

Immediately after the war, Douglas Haig had little doubt about the contribution of the pipes:

> The Pipers of Scotland may well be proud of the part they have played in this war. In the heat of battle, by the lonely grave, and during the long hours of waiting, they have called to us to show ourselves worthy of the land to which we belong. Many have fallen in the fight for liberty, but their memories remain.[3]

---

1 From the poem *The Pipes: Onset*, by Joseph Lee.
2 IWM 2854 Bates, letters of 2 & 23 May 1916.
3 Foreword to Seton & Grant, *The Pipes of War*, 1920.

In this chapter, this assessment is put to the test. The standard work on the pipes in the Great War, in which Haig's tribute appears, was published by Seton and Grant as long ago as 1920.[4] This work, while not entirely omitting the other uses of the pipes, gives greatest prominence to their use in battle. This is perhaps natural but, for a balanced view, it is necessary also to look at their significant use both in training and behind the lines. Furthermore, while apparently using impeccable sources, the authors cite them only sketchily, so we must look for corroboration in letters, diaries and memoirs. Amongst these, we are fortunate in possessing several particularly useful sources; a published account by Ian Mackay Scobie, Pipe President of 1st Seaforths, an IWM interview with Harry Ditcham, a drummer with the 2nd Argylls, and the diary of Dan Macleod, Pipe Major with 4/5th Black Watch.[5]

Constitution and maintenance of pipe-bands

As we have seen, when the war broke out, a large number of new battalions were raised more or less from scratch; the 2nd and 3rd line Territorials, Kitchener's Army and battalions raised in Canada and South Africa specifically for overseas service. No respectable Highland battalion could be without its pipe-band, and strenuous efforts were made to ensure that all of these new battalions were appropriately equipped. The 10th Seaforths, for example, a Kitchener battalion, were raised at the end of October 1914. In January, 1915, Colonel J.A Stewart Mackenzie (afterwards Lord Seaforth) presented the battalion with a handsome set of pipes, pipes and drums were purchased out of private funds, and in April, 1915, the people of Inverness arranged a concert in aid of the band fund.[6]

In the Canadian Expeditionary Force, those new CEF battalions which were more or less directly formed from pre-existing Militia battalions inherited their pipe-bands. Such were the 15th Battalion CEF, formed from the 48th Highlanders of Canada, and 13th Battalion CEF, formed from the 5th Royal Highlanders of Canada.[7] Other Dominion battalions had to raise their pipe-bands afresh, but all did so.[8] The exigencies of war might also require existing pipe-bands to be reconstructed. Thus the 1/4th Camerons lost their pipe-major, John Macdonald, "the foremost of modern pipers", shortly after they arrived at Bedford, when he was declared unfit. They also lost two of the best pipers in the band, Gray and Chisholm, who were appointed to be pipe-majors respectively of battalions of the H.L.I. and the Gordon Highlanders.[9]

---

4   Seton & Grant *The Pipes of War*. Instances of the pipes in action in the War are also cited by Malcolm, *The Piper*. More recent, but very brief, treatment is provided by West, 'Scottish Military Music,' pp.659-660 and Murray, *Music*, pp.290-293.
5   Mackay Scobie, *Pipers*; IWM 374 Ditcham, interview; IWM 16387 Macleod, diary.
6   Addison-Smith, *10th Seaforth Highlanders*, pp.16, 19, 23. On obtaining pipes for other battalions see Craig Barr, *Home Service*, p.33; McEwen, *Fifth Camerons*, pp.7-8; Macleod, *6th Camerons*, p.4; Craig-Brown, *Historical Records*, Vol.3, p.465, Vol.4, pp.273-4; LC GS 1008 Macdonald, letter, 30 August 1915; Aiken, *Courage Past*, 1971, p.6
7   Beattie, *48th Highlanders*, pp.25, 49; Fetherstonhaugh, *13th Battalion*, p.17.
8   See Urquhart, *Canadian Scottish*, p.22; Topp, *42nd Battalion*, pp.21-22; Craig-Brown, *Historical Records*, p.25; McEvoy & Finlay, *Seaforth Highlanders of Canada*, p.60; Fetherstonhaugh, *13th Battalion*, p.176; Hayes, *Eighty-Fifth*, p.115; Bruce, Turnbull & Chisholm, *Historical Records*, pp.23, 37-39; Juta, *Transvaal Scottish*, pp.85, 126; Orpen, *Cape Town Highlanders*, pp.89-90.
9   Craig-Brown, *Historical Records*, Vol.3, p.423.

Given that all Highland battalions took care to be properly provided with pipers, Seton and Grant describe how nevertheless their numbers were reduced on mobilisation in 1914:

> When a regiment is mobilised it at once loses most of its pipers. Whatever the strength of the band may have been in peace time, only the "sergeant piper" [Pipe Major] … and five "full" pipers are normally retained as such. The remainder, while acting as pipers when opportunity offers, – and designated accordingly – serve in the ranks.[10]

The initial policy regarding active service overseas appears to have been always to take the pipers but possibly to leave the drums behind. Once deployed, it was also often found necessary to make use of both full and acting pipers in some purely military capacity, for example as bombers, orderlies, stretcher-bearers or even Lewis gunners. In this alternative capacity many pipers won recognition for outstanding bravery. These achievements are outside the remit of this discussion, but they deserve acknowledgement here.

With casualties amongst the pipers and a lack of drums in the early months of the war, pipe-bands might temporarily disappear. As the war progressed, however, a remarkable feature of the Highland regiments was the way that their pipe-bands were gradually re-constituted, until they became the accepted rule behind the lines. In the 2nd Argylls, for example, on the outbreak of war, Harry Ditcham was a drummer. Interviewed by the I.W.M. in 1974, he confirmed the wartime role of the pipers outlined above. According to him, the bandsmen became stretcher bearers, the drummers went to their platoons as buglers, while the pipers, who consisted of the Pipe-Major and five other pipers, went to war as pipers, each allocated to a company, i.e. to H.Q. Company and Companies A-D. Despite this, the battalion took their drums with them to France in 1914, only to lose them with the baggage wagons in the great retreat after Mons. Jimmy Dixon, an A.S.C. driver attached to the battalion, recalls throwing the drums off a wagon into a ditch to make way for sacks of bread. Moreover, the loss of three pipers killed, three wounded and three prisoners-of-war during 1914 so disorganised the pipe band that the remaining pipers were re-employed in other roles. Nevertheless, determined efforts were made to restart the pipe and drum band, and new pipers, drummers and new drums were obtained in October 1915. Major Hyslop noted on 29 October that, "We have … restarted the Pipe Band as we have managed to get drums to replace the ones that we lost in 1914 and this will be a great asset when out of the trenches." This is confirmed by Harry Ditcham, who, as a drummer, was initially deployed as a bugler with his platoon. Sent to the rear during the great retreat, he was subsequently used, along with the other surviving drummer/buglers, as a runner, until the pipe-band was reconstituted and he resumed his activities as a drummer.[11]

Another example is provided by 1st Camerons. After they disembarked at Le Havre on 14 August 1914, they marched "with drums and pipes" to a rest camp at Greville near Harfleur. However, during the retreat from Mons, the pipes and drums were sent to the base, and the pipers and drummers employed on other duties. After determined efforts, Major Ernest Craig-Brown managed to reconstitute five pipers by January, 1915. This was not good enough, though, for Craig-Brown. Much later, as C.O., he made strenuous efforts to build up a full band of pipes

---

10   Seton & Grant, *The Pipes of War*, p.35.
11   IWM 374 Ditcham interview; IWM 11047 Dixon, James, ASC, Interview 1989; Cavendish, *An Reisimeid Chataich*, pp.252, 364, 378; ASHM N-E2 Hyslop diary.

and drums. On 14 May,1916, he could proudly record, "our first attempt at drums since the beginning of the war in August 1914," and on 7 June, wrote that "the 1st Battn pipes & drums are now in being and are the talk of this billeting area."[12]

In 4th Black Watch, Dan Macleod was a pre-war Territorial piper. He mobilised with the battalion and disembarked in France with them on 25 February 1915. From that time until after the battle of Loos, he was principally employed either on working parties or as a stretcher-bearer, in which capacity he acted in the Battle of Loos. He records a few band practices before Loos, which continued in October, jointly with the 2nd Battalion. Only on 18 November 1915 does he record, "Paraded as pipers". He was himself made Acting Pipe Major, then Battalion Sergeant Piper in January 1916. But throughout this period and into March 1916, the pipers' stretcher-bearer duties continued. It was not until 8 March 1916 that he was able to record, "Off the Stretcher Bearers". Then, at last, after taking over the pipes on the amalgamation of 1/4th and 1/5th Black Watch a few days later, the playing of Retreat and Tattoo became a regular occurrence. More was to come, though, and on 6 May 1916, he managed to get a loan of drums from the 1st Hertfordshires. Drum practice followed, and on 22 May 1916, we find the first mention of a Drum Major in his diary. Then, on 1 June 1916, the band played retreat with drums, an event so notable that all the officers turned out to watch. By 2 February 1917, he had got the band made up to a complement of 12 pipers and seven drummers. Finally, after the Armistice, he made up the pipers to a total of 16 plus himself. This did not mean, however, that the pipers were absolved from other duties. Throughout the whole period, according to the requirements of the moment, we find them not only piping, but also acting as guides, runners, stretcher bearers, and guards, undertaking training in bombing, musketry and the Lewis gun, and employed on miscellaneous tasks, including digging, carrying parties, cleaning billets and roads, moving Lewis Gun barrows and even burying a horse.[13]

The challenge of maintaining pipe-bands might be even greater in distant lands like Mesopotamia, where 1st Seaforths made valiant efforts to keep their pipes going, at one point successfully having emergency pipe-bags made up from harness leather furnished by the Supply and transport Corps. Until after arriving in Palestine in 1918, the battalion had no drums, and the pipes played solo, whether on the line of march or in camp. The great heat made their upkeep difficult but, save on one or two occasions, there were usually six to eight sets going.[14] Nothing could better demonstrate the determination of the Highland battalions to keep their pipes going. Clearly, there were perceived advantages to keeping the pipers in being. But what were they, and how were the pipes actually used during the war?

---

12 Craig Brown, *Historical Records*, Vol 3, pp.30, 64 65, 120, IWM 1862, Craig-Brown, letters 3 November, 1914 , 15 and 17 January 1915, Field Message Books, Craig-Brown to Messrs Holt & Co., 30 September 1914 and note to Sgt A Ferguson, 7 December 1914, Regimental Diary 15, 17, 19 January 1915 and 14 May, 1916, and letters to Col Mackintosh, 29 April and 7 June, 1916.
13 IWM 16387, Macleod, diary, passim.
14 Mackay Scobie, *Pipers*, p.44. The pipers of the 2nd London Scottish also experienced challenges in keeping their pipes going in Salonika and Palestine. See Malcolm, *The Piper*, pp.198-99.

The pipes in battle

The popular image of the piper at war is of him piping troops into battle. The piper's memorial at Longueval on the Somme depicts a piper going over the top. It was a powerful image for the newspapers, and even in recollection it remained powerful in the minds of some soldiers. In an interview in 1976, Henry Mabbutt, who served with 2nd Camerons on the Western Front, was asked if, when they went over the top, they had the pipes. He replied:

> Oh yes. Always the pipes. Yes, yes. If the platoons were spread out, and probably we were going over on a quarter of a mile front you'd have three pipers, one on each flank and one in the centre. But of course he didn't lead. He was immediately behind you. But a lot of them got killed.[15]

By contrast, Lieutenant Douglas Wilson of 5th Camerons, wrote scathingly of inaccurate reporting by Philip Gibbs of his battalion's attack at Meteren in July 1918.

The pipers' memorial at Longueval. (Photograph, author)

> We learned with astonishment that 'The Highlanders attacked to the martial strains of their pipe-band.'… Well, well! Pipers at this stage of the war were irreplaceable and were never allowed in the line or within some miles of it … All ranks received these tidings with mixed feelings – anger, irritation, contempt. These ink blobs made us feel as foolish as children playing hop-scotch in a class-room when they should have been at their lessons.[16]

Which then is the correct picture: Harry Mabbutt's recollections in 1976 or Douglas Wilson's caustic comments? Seton and Grant certainly lay strong emphasis on the role of the pipers in playing their companies into battle. They do however acknowledge that the practice was neither consistent nor universal. Given the initial diminution of the pipers' wartime role, they cite no examples from 1914, and state that the first example of pipers playing, or trying to play their companies into action was within the 1st Black Watch at Cuinchy on 25 January 1915. They cite numerous subsequent examples, but state that by the later stages of the war, in 1917 to 1918, "on

---

15 IWM 860 Mabbott, interview.
16 LC GS 1761 Wilson, memoir, p.87.

the whole it was being found increasingly difficult to renew the depleted ranks of the pipe bands, and most regiments were simply driven to keeping their pipers out of action as far as possible except on special occasions."[17] They do however, state that the practice picked up again in the more open warfare of the hundred days from August 1918.

A simple statistical analysis of the examples they provide helps to flesh out the picture. In presenting the records of the pipers during the war, they list 52 "Highland" battalions. Of these, they cite instances of the pipes played in battle against 30 battalions, i.e. 58 percent of battalions. But they also record that, in the case of 22 of the listed battalions (i.e. 42 percent of battalions) the use of pipers in action was either limited or disallowed, including 15, or 50 percent of those battalions which permitted their use on some occasion. In other words, in the case of 37 out of the 52 battalions listed (71 percent), either no use of the pipes in battle is cited, or some restriction on their use is specifically mentioned. The authors also list 46 instances of specific battalions being piped into battle on specific occasions, several of these being in the same battle, most notably Loos in September, 1915, where instances are claimed for 13 separate battalions.[18] Of these instances, 39 out of 46 (85 percent) occurred in 1915-16 and only eight (15 percent) in 1917-18. Not only that, but of the instances in 1916, all but 2 occurred before the end of July, such that 80 percent of the instances cited for the whole war actually occurred before the end of July 1916, and only 20 percent thereafter. Further, of the 10 instances recorded after July 1916, five actually occurred in a single battalion, the 16th Battalion C.E.F. (Canadian Scottish), to which interesting phenomenon we will return.

The conclusions drawn from Seton and Grant's evidence should however be used with care. In compiling their book, very shortly after the war, the authors made use of potentially impeccable sources; "correspondence with commanding officers, pipe presidents and pipe majors of many units in the Imperial armies".[19] Unfortunately they do not cite precise sources in support of individual instances, there are some errors in the information they present, and it is both incomplete and inconsistent. We need to look, therefore, to independent sources for corroboration. When we do so, we find that there is abundant evidence that the pipes were indeed used in action. Mackay Scobie relates that during the fighting in 1914 and up to May 1915, the 1st Seaforths lost several piper casualties. Some of these were employed as pipers, others as bearers or in the ranks. At Neuve Chapelle, the companies were played into action, and Piper Pratt was killed whilst playing.[20] When the inexperienced battalions of Kitchener's Army went into action at Loos on 25 September 1915, they took a number of pipers with them. 53-year old Pipe Major House of 10th Gordons insisted on going into action.[21] Philip Christison, of 6th Camerons and Robert Burns of 7th Battalion both heard pipers in action at Loos.[22]

In respect of such actions, David Murray refers, somewhat critically, to what he calls the "Findlater/Dargai syndrome", suggesting that pipers were attempting to copy the action of Piper Findlater in winning the Victoria Cross at Dargai. "Estimable as his action was, Findlater

---

17   Seton & Grant, *The Pipes of War*, p.30.
18   Instances are also cited in Part 2, "Records of the Pipers", in Malcolm, *The Piper*. For the most part these duplicate the examples quoted by Seton & Grant, which may well have been his source for much of his information on the Great War. He does cite a few additional examples, but these do not alter the argument.
19   Seton & Grant, *The Pipes of War*, p.vii.
20   Mackay Scobie, *Pipers*, p.40.
21   GHM PB507, Wallace, memoir. He was the C.O. concerned.
22   IWM 4370 Christison, memoir, p.36; Burns, *Once a Cameron Highlander*, pp.68-69.

was to motivate a host of would-be imitators, many of whom were to die emulating his example in the hope of winning the coveted award."[23] Notwithstanding the courageous actions of these men, he has a point. Nevertheless, the use of pipes in battle continued even after Loos. When 9th Division attacked the village of Longueval on 14 July 1916, Lieutenant Anderson, of 7th Seaforths, relates that "I took my coy into the village with a Piper playing at my side."[24] Similarly, Captain Neil Weir of 10th Argylls states that, in the attack on Longueval on 14 July 1916, "When my Company got disorganised when moving on the objective I got Wilson, the piper, to play the Regimental March, which he did in grand style, thus reassembling the Company."[25] And Herbert Sotheby, who also served in the 10th Argylls confirms that Longueval was captured "with the pipers playing the "Regimental March" and the "Charge"[26]

The pipes were also carried into action by the Canadian Scottish during their attack on Regina Trench on 8 October 1916. Here Piper Jimmy Richardson advanced with No.4 Company in the leading wave. He was instructed not to play until ordered to do so by his company commander. When the company reached the enemy wire they were held up and their commander shot dead. At this point Piper Richardson asked his C.S.M. if he should play. He was told to go ahead, and according to witnesses played up and down in front of the wire for fully ten minutes. His C.S.M. meanwhile got what men he could together, got through the wire and started clearing the trench. Piper Richardson was only 18 years old. He had not originally been detailed for the attack. He had asked to be paraded before the C.O. and there pleaded to be allowed to go into action so earnestly that his Colonel granted his wish. He was killed a few hours after he performed his gallant deed, which earned him a posthumous Victoria Cross.[27]

There are examples of pipes being used in battle also in campaigns further overseas. When 1st Seaforths took part in the abortive attack on the Turkish trenches at Sheikh S'aad in Mesopotamia, on 7 January, 1916, at a critical moment in the fighting, Acting Pipe-Major Neil McKechnie and Pipers Alex and Colin McKay struck up the Regimental charge, "Cabar Feidh", and continued to play for some time. McKechnie and Alex McKay were both wounded. In this and other actions in Mesopotamia, the pipers of 1st Seaforths either played their companies into battle, or did excellent work in bringing up ammunition.[28] When Lieutenant Malcolm Thorburn of 2nd Black Watch took part in the abortive attempt to relieve Kut on 21 January 1916, he was wounded in the Turkish trenches, but "I came to with the pipes playing beside me, and I knew we had the trench!"[29] On the Salonika front, when, on the night of 13/14 August 1916, C Coy, 1st Argylls, took part in an attack on Homondos, to take an enemy machine-gun post, "the piper played the charge".[30]

Thus we find evidence from independent sources to corroborate several of the instances cited by Seton and Grant, and even to provide new ones. But there is also evidence to support the restrictions placed on the use of pipers in battle. We have already heard Douglas Wilson's

---

23 Murray, *Music*, pp.289-292.
24 IWM 7668 Escombe, letter from Lieut. C.B. Anderson, dated 13 or 23 July, 1916.
25 Saul, *Mud and Bodies*, p.67, Account by Lt Neil Weir.
26 Sotheby, *10th Argylls*, p.21.
27 Urquhart, *Canadian Scottish*, pp.180-182.
28 Mackay Scobie, *Pipers*, pp.40, 43.
29 IWM 511 Thorburn, letter 28 January 1916.
30 LC GS 1026 Maclean, memoir, p.30, and transcript of interview.

caustic explanation of the realities as far as the 5th Camerons were concerned. Similarly, on 9 May 1915, when 1st Camerons attacked at Aubers Ridge:

> This attack marked one great break with the tradition of the 79th in that the pipers were not with the assaulting force, as it was deemed advisable, in the conditions of the campaign, to keep them behind the line so that they would be available to play to the battalion on the march and when in billets.[31]

In the 2nd Argylls, significant casualties amongst the pipers, together with the loss of their drums in 1914, caused the pipe band to be disbanded and the remaining pipers were used as orderlies, stretcher-bearers, and ammunition and ration carriers. After the pipe band was reconstituted in October 1915, the pipers "occasionally played the battalion into action", but "latterly accompanied the battalion from billets as far as the trench area."[32] Likewise in the 11th Argylls, Lieutenant Robert Lindsay Mackay recalls that the battalion lost nearly all their pipers in the Battle of Loos in September 1915. "Thereafter, pipers, being irreplaceable, were never sent into battle again, or allowed near the front line in trench warfare."[33]

The diary of Dan Macleod, Pipe Major of the 4th then 4/5th Black Watch provides an interesting perspective. In the early part of the war, in his battalion, the pipers were used as stretcher-bearers and it was in that capacity that he served, as a Corporal Piper at Loos, winning the Military Medal for bringing in his mortally wounded C.O. under fire. By the time that the battalion went into action at Beaumont-Hamel, however, on 3 September, 1916, as we have seen, the pipe-band had been reconstituted in the battalion, and a piper was allocated to each company for the attack. Miraculously, all survived. But when the battalion went into action again at Beaumont-Hamel on 13 November, the pipers' role was to provide rum and tea to the battalion as they went up, then to take up ammunition, bombs and water to the new front line. Likewise, when the battalion went into action at Pilkem ridge on 31 July 1917, the pipers' role was to take up rations to the front line, and at Cambrai, on 20 November, 14 of the band went up to act as stretcher-bearers. Finally, faced with the German offensive in 1918, the band were first employed drawing bombs for the battalion, then as stretcher-bearers. It does appear from the diary that the sole occasion on which the battalion pipers accompanied companies into action was during their initial attack on Beaumont-Hamel in September 1916.[34]

All in all, the evidence from independent sources tends to support the picture presented by Seton and Grant. Once pipers had been reconstituted in their battalions after the early months of the war, they did pipe their companies into battle on a number of occasions in the offensives of 1915 and in the earlier part of the Somme offensive. After the end of July 1916, their use in battle became increasingly infrequent. The truth was that for pipers to pipe troops into battle exposed them to terrible risk, and casualties would soon become so heavy that the battalion would be left without any effective pipers for their many other duties. They were therefore generally kept out of the fighting in order to reduce casualties or used in other necessary support roles. It is evident, however, that there was no overarching policy on the matter. The use of the

---

31   Craig-Brown, *Historical Records*, Vol.3, p.151.
32   Cavendish, *An Reisimeid Chataich*, p.364
33   IWM 11144, Mackay, commentary on his own diary, written in 1972.
34   IWM 16387, Macleod, diary, passim.

pipes might depend very much on the whim of the Commanding Officer, which brings us to the remarkable case of the Canadian Scottish.

Lieutenant Colonel C.W. Peck took command of the Canadian Scottish on 3 November 1916, after, it will be noticed, the action of the battalion in which Piper Jimmy Richardson won his V.C. He was a strident advocate of the use of the pipes in action. Despite encountering substantial criticism,[35] he put his views into action. When the battalion went into action, five pipers accompanied it, one for each company and the Colonel's piper. Canadian Scottish pipers went into the assault at Vimy Ridge on 9 April 1917, at Hill 70 on 15 August 1917 and in the Luce Valley on 8 August 1918, when Piper Paul mounted one of the tanks, named "Dominion" and played the troops on the right flank into action with "The Blue Bonnets over the Border".[36] Objections were raised that the pipes could not be heard over the barrage, but Colonel Peck insisted, probably correctly, that this was a temporary phenomenon. Others objected that the conspicuous nature of the pipers would lead to unnecessary loss of life, but Peck argued that officers, machine gunners and runners were equally conspicuous and the danger went with the role. After the death of Piper Richardson, several more of the pipers were killed and six wounded before the end of the war, all but two of these casualties being incurred while the pipers were leading the advance in battle. The benefit was the effect on the men's morale. The regimental historian endorses Peck's decision unequivocally:

> To the Commanding officer who had the courage to redeem this ecstasy of the ancient glory of the Celt, from the slough where it had been cast by members of that race, traitors to their birthright, who had the vision to link it to a great purpose, every Highlander should pay honour.[37]

In reality, these "traitors to their birthright" were the C.O.'s of distinguished Highland regiments, equally concerned with the lives and morale of their men, who had come to a different conclusion.

It is clear from numerous accounts that in fact, apart from the documented instances of pipers playing their companies into action, the principal use of the pipes as far as fighting was concerned was limited to piping the companies going up to the trenches or to battle to a relatively safe point behind the front, and then collecting them there when they returned. In the 4th Gordons, for example, Captain R.L. McKinnon recalls coming out of the trenches for the first time early in 1915, when "about a mile out from camp we found the pipers waiting for us, and one of them attaching himself to my platoon, marched at our head and played us back."[38] Robert Dawson wrote to his mother on 5 April 1915 that, "usually the pipers meet us and play us back…The pipers also play us to the trenches at least part of the way, – it is very cheering."[39] And George Leys describes marching back to billets on the night of 18/19 September 1915, after his first spell in the trenches with the same battalion., when "the pipers came to play us back the latter half of the way."[40]

---

35   Urquhart, *Canadian Scottish*, p.198.
36   Ibid., pp.215, 231, 233-235,273; Fetherstonhaugh, *13th Battalion*, pp.195-6.
37   Urquhart, *Canadian Scottish*, pp.198-200.
38   GHM PB583, McKinnon, memoir.
39   GHM PB1937, Dawson, letter to mother 5 April 1915.
40   IWM 11125 PP Leys, C.G, manuscript memoir.

During the Battle of the Somme, a piper of the 7th Seaforth Highlanders pipes men back from the front after the attack on Longueval, 14 July 1916. (IWM Q4012)

There are innumerable other examples of this practice, which appears to have been fairly universally observed.[41] It is evident, then, that, although the highest calling of the piper may have been to play his company into battle, the principal use of the pipes during the war was not in battle. Rather they were used both in training and behind the lines, essentially to boost morale, and we will now turn to these uses.

Behind the lines and in training

Behind the lines and in training, the pipes were used in many different ways. They were played to accompany marches, parades and inspections: they were played at funerals and in acts of

---

41 See for example: GHM, PB3712, Murison, memoir; LC GS 1436 Scott, 2Lt. J.G., letter 25 January 1915; IWM 1862 Craig-Brown, Regimental Diary, 15 April, 1915; GHM PB1700/2, Robertson, diary of the Somme Jul-Sep 1916, IWM 4586 Douglas, memoir, pp.613-614; LC GS 1/61 Wilson, memoir, p.84; McEvoy & Finlay, *Seaforth Highlanders of Canada*, p.113; IWM 43 Dunton, interview; GHM PB1892.3.18, McDonald, 'Uncle Harper's Duds,'p.86; GHM PB242, Stansfield, extract in notebook from letter of 25 Feb 1915; Rule, *Students*, pp.69-70; Sommers, Cecil [Norman Cecil Sommers Down], *Temporary Heroes*, (London: John Lane, 1917), p.35; IWM 11739 Sangster, letter 21 September, 1915; Beattie, *48th Highlanders*, p.168, Aiken, *Courage Past*, p.50; GHM PB1639, Kemp, memoir, p.73; GHM PB2183, Watson, memoir, p.13; Fetherstonhaugh, *13th Battalion*, p.186; THM C92-35, Welsh, memoirs, pp.83-84; IWM 2528 Bradbury, memoir, p.37.

remembrance, at officers' mess functions, and at Retreat, Tattoo, concerts, entertainments and sports days. They were even used on some occasions to regulate the day behind the lines, just as though the war was simply an unpleasant distraction from routine. Indeed, perhaps the most remarkable feature of their use was the attempt to continue or emulate peace-time practice in war, fulfilling two of the principal functions of military music; "to regulate the military day in camp and garrison; and 'to excite cheerfulness and alacrity in the soldier.'"[42]

Thus the pipes continued to be used in training to regulate the day. Individual pipers would play set regimental tunes, often amusingly appropriate, to indicate duties during the day.[43] Recruits generally found themselves awakened to the old Jacobite tune, 'Hey Johnnie Cope, are ye Wakin' yet?' When the newly enlisted John Cooper arrived for training at 3/4th Black Watch at North Camp, Ripon, in May 1916, he found that the next morning he was roused by 'Johnnie Cope'. 'Brose and Butter' was used for playing at meal-times, while 'Donald Blue' was 'Lights Out'.[44] At tea-time, in Jock McLeod's training battalion, 3rd Camerons, they would play 'Hey, Jock, are ye glad ye 'listed'., and at 'Lights out' it would be, 'Johnny, lie doon on your wee pickle straw. It's no very big & it's no very braw!'[45]

This routine extended to life behind the lines.[46] In his diary, Dan Macleod lists the duty pipe calls which were used in 4/5th Black Watch.[47] When John Cooper passed through base camp at Etaples in December 1916, before being drafted to 6th Black Watch, he noted that 'Lights Out' was signified by a piper playing 'Donald Blue', and reveille by 'Johnnie Cope'.[48] In early 1917, Lauchlan Maclean Watt, serving as chaplain to an unspecified battalion of the Black Watch, noted the pipers' routine in a French village where the battalion was briefly billeted: 'Hey, Johnnie Cope' at reveille, 'O gie my love brose and butter' at meal times, and 'Donald Gorm' at Lights Out.[49]

Customs were maintained also in far-flung territories; in Mesopotamia,[50] for example, and Salonika. In 1st Garrison Battalion Seaforth Highlanders in Salonika, Captain Wyllie recorded in January, 1917, "Time to change for dinner evidently as a piper has taken up his stand outside my tent and is playing the 'Bonawe Highlanders' for all he is worth."[51]

Another peace-time tradition kept up, not only in training battalions, but also behind the lines, was the playing of pipes in the officers' mess. Douglas Wimberley records guest nights in the Officers' Mess in 3rd Camerons at Invergordon:

---

42 Murray, *Music*, p.1.
43 See, in addition to the examples quoted: GHM PB1937 Dawson, undated letter; IWM 4440 Croft, interview; IWM 3608, Anderson, memoir; Lyon, *In Kilt and Khaki*, p.111; Davies, *The Compassionate War*, pp.8-9; GHM PB2183, Watson, memoir, p.2; THM S89-26, Crask, letter 13 June 1916; IWM Books Brooke, 'Wait for it,'p.18; IWM 3460 Macmillan, letter from Pte Sandy Macmillan, n.d.
44 IWM Books Cooper, 'Domi Militaeque,' pp.11, 21.
45 IWM 5821 Semple, letters from Pte Jock McLeod, 8 July & 15 August, 1915.
46 Apart from refs below, see IWM 5525 Steven, letter 22 June 1915; Rule, *Students*, p.185; GHM PB375, Pailthorpe, memoir, p.6; IWM 1862 Craig-Brown, Regimental Diary, 28 January, 1915 and letter 23 October, 1916; IWM 2294 Fraser, J., letter 20 August, 1916; IWM 2854 Bates, letter 20 March 1917; THM Camerons 92-35 Welsh, memoirs, pp.57, 70.
47 IWM 16387, Macleod, diary, 17 November 1915, 21 May 1917.
48 IWM Books Cooper, 'Domi Militaeque,'p.82.
49 Watt, *In France and Flanders*, pp.158-159.
50 Webster, *Mesopotamia 1916-1917*, letter to Joey 20 March 1917.
51 IWM 7508 Wyllie, diary, 21 January 1917, & see also 14 January, 1917 and 31 January 1918.

The Guest Nights seemed to me to be very, very long. After the pipers had played Marches, Strathspeys and reels, we would have a long pibroch from the Pipe major, and when that was over and the Pipe Major had had his dram, and given the Gaelic Toast, as often or not before we were allowed to get up from the table, the Mackintosh would order a second pibroch of his own choosing to be played. In time I learnt to understand and indeed appreciate pibroch playing, but that came years later, and in Invergordon days the classical music of the pipes was totally unfamiliar to me; they just seemed to be a medley of sound, unconscionably protracted.[52]

Behind the lines in France, Dan Macleod of 4/5th Black Watch records playing for the officers mess a dozen times, twice playing pibroch, and noting with satisfaction that, on one of these occasions, he "waltzed with a countess's daughter."[53] Elsewhere, the pipes are found entertaining the officers in Salonika, Mesopotamia, Varna, Eski-Chehir in occupied Turkey and in occupied Germany after the Armistice. On 24 January 1918, while 1st Garrison Bn Seaforth Highlanders was in reserve by the Struma River,

> It was amusing last night when the piper was playing for dinner to hear Mann whom I sent out to ask the piper to play certain tunes, rush out of the door in a great hurry in case he forgot the names before he got as far as the piper. Mann being an Englishman was quite mystified at the names and I believe that he thought at first I was 'pulling his leg'.[54]

Some individual officers even kept their own sets of pipes and took them on campaign. Such a man was Captain Billie Mackay, in 4th Camerons,[55] In 1st Seaforths in Mesopotamia, there were a number of officers who played the pipes, among whom were Lieutenants. D. Cameron, N.T. Macleod, and Captain Nicolson, R.A.M.C., all excellent performers, as well as Lieutenants Burn and Miller, and Mackay Scobie himself, who was Pipe President. A number of the officers had practice chanters.[56] The office of Pipe President, occupied in peace-time by one of the

---

52 IWM 430 Wimberley, memoir, Vol.1, pp.20-21. For other examples in training battalions, see Saul, *Mud and Bodies*, p.12, citing N.A.C. Weir; IWM 3460 Macmillan, letter from Pte Sandy Macmillan, 4 December 1917.
53 IWM 16387, Macleod, diary, passim. For other examples see THM Camerons 90-120, Mackay, letter to mother 30 October 1915; Urquhart, *Canadian Scottish*, p.48; THM Camerons 94-8, Mackay, 'Tell Them of Us,' letters from Ian Mackay 11 April 1915, 8 August 1915; Gillespie, *Letters from Flanders*, p.232, letter 11 July 1915; Malcolm, *Argyllshire Highlanders*, pp.24-25; IWM 1862 Craig-Brown, Regimental Diary, 21 June, 1916; IWM 1713 PP Laurie, Maj. Gen. Sir John, 'Ts account of action of 1st July, 1916; GHM PB493, Pearson, 'The 10th and 8/10th Battalions,' p.8; Topp, *42nd Battalion*, p.101; Fetherstonhaugh, *13th Battalion*, p.152; IWM 2854 Bates, letters 28 November 1916, 18 January & 16 March 1917; IWM 13511 Macgregor, letter of 17 August, 1917; Beattie, *48th Highlanders*, p.263; GHM PB1639 Kemp, memoir, p.42.
54 IWM 7508 Wyllie, diary, 25 January 1918. For other far flung examples see LC GS 0731 Hay-Young, letter 21 May 1916, LC GS 0456 Dick, diary; IWM 7508 Wyllie, diary, 30 September 1916, 26 January 1917, 25 October, 26 December 1917, 26 December 1918, 27 April 1919; LC SAL 059 Shipton, diary, 3 August 1918; ASHM N-E10 Gairdner, letter 19 June 1919.
55 THM Camerons 94-8, Mackay, 'Tell Them of Us,' letter from Wm Mackay 11 April 1915; see also letters from Ian Mackay of same date and 16 April 1915.
56 Mackay Scobie, *Pipers*, p.44. See also Macleod, *6th Camerons*, p.8; LC GS 1436 Scott, letter 31 January 1915; ASHM N-E8 Munro, letters 13, 26/27 and 29 June 1915.

battalion officers, was indeed seemingly maintained during the war. In 1st Camerons, once the pipes had been received back in the battalion in January, 1915, and pipers delegated to take charge of them, Major Craig-Brown "appointed Matheson (A & SH) acting pipe president to see to them. He is a musical fellow, a Glasgow medical student in times of peace." At about the end of July 1916, Neil Weir was made Pipe and Band President of 10th Argylls, while the 1st Seaforths maintained the position of Pipe President even in Mesopotamia, where the duty fell to Mackay Scobie, who, to our good fortune, wrote a book about his experiences.[57]

Another tradition maintained during the war was the pipers' send-off to well-loved officers. When Lieutenant-Colonel Ernest Craig-Brown finally left his beloved "79th" at the end of January, 1917, "We had a great & inspiring send off from the 79th. They lined both sides of the road & I was marched down the middle by the pipes playing 'Happy we've been a'thegether' and the band playing 'Auld Lang Syne.' I had much handshaking to do." [58]

Tradition was also maintained while on campaign by the composition of pipe-tunes to celebrate notable events.[59] Shortly after the battle of Neuve Chapelle, the Pipe Major of 4th Camerons composed a march called 'The 4th Camerons at Neuve Chapelle', which he played to the officers at dinner in April 1915.[60] In 6th Camerons, the Pipe President was Philip Christison, who played the pipes himself, although, as he himself confessed, not to a high standard. At Vacqueriette, on 25 May, 1917, "Pipe Major Macmillan presented me with a copy of a Strathspey he had composed in my honour and called 'Captain Christison'". This was no doubt in honour of his role in the Capture of Monchy-le-Preux on 11 April, where he had earned a bar to his Military Cross.[61] On the Salonika front, pipers of 81st Infantry Brigade composed a number of tunes during the war:

The Macedonian Battlefield by Pipe-Major John Steele, 2nd Camerons
The Balkan Hills by LCpl Piper James Gillon, 2nd Camerons
The Camerons' Farewell to Salonika, by LCpl Piper James Gillon, 2nd Camerons
The 81st Brigade crossing the Struma by Pipe-Major Ross, 1st Argylls[62]

In Mesopotamia, Captain Mackay Scobie, Pipe President of the battalion, composed 'The 1st Seaforth Highlanders entry into Baghdad, 1917'.[63] This did not entirely win the approval of Second Lieutenant John Webster, who wrote, "One of our majors has written a new pipe march, 'The advance on Bagdad'. It's quite a good lively tune, but I think rather a crib on another like it."[64]

57 IWM 1862 Craig-Brown, letter 15 January, 1915; David, *Mud and Bodies*, p.72, account by Lt Neil Weir; Mackay Scobie, *Pipers*, passim.
58 IWM 1862 Craig-Brown, letter of 1 February, 1917. See also Webster, *Mesopotamia 1916-1917*, letter to mother, 1 January 1917.
59 For additional examples see Malcolm, *The Piper*, pp.43-44.
60 THM Camerons 94-8, Mackay, 'Tell Them of Us,' letter from Ian Mackay 11 April 1915.
61 IWM 4370 Christison, memoir, p.60.
62 Craig-Brown, *Historical Records*, Vol.3, pp.383-386.
63 Mackay Scobie, *Pipers*, p.51.
64 Webster, *Mesopotamia 1916-1917*, letter to Rua of 1 April 1917. See also: Malcolm, *Argyllshire Highlanders*, p.26; IWM 16387 Macleod, diary, 3 July, 10 August 1916.

The glamour of the kilt: superb illustration by Harry Payne from a set of postcards depicting the Gordon Highlanders, published by Tucks shortly before the war. Such uniform sets were collected by boys and both reflected and contributed to the popularity of the Army, the Empire and the Highland regiments. (Author's collection)

The Highland soldier as Imperial icon. In a popular illustration of 1914 by Lawson Wood, Britain's defiance of the German invasion of Belgium is characterised by a soldier of the Black Watch. From a contemporary postcard published by Dobson, Molle & Co. (Author's collection)

Bronze low-relief at the South African memorial, Delville Wood, shows a soldier of the South African Scottish leaving the wood. (Photograph author)

Swank. 'The Cock o' the North': illustration by Reg Maurice on a contemporary postcard by the Regent Publishing Co. (Author's collection)

Ascending the outdoor stairs on trams and buses was a risky business when wearing the kilt. A cartoon by D. Tempest on a postcard published by Bamforth & Co. (Copyright Bamforth & Co.)

The hazards of winter: a classic contemporary postcard by Donald McGill published by the Inter Art Co. (Author's collection)

The idealised image of the piper at war. Piper Laidlaw of the K.O.S.B. winning the Victoria Cross at Loos, an illustration by E.F. Skinner, providing the frontispiece to Volume 4 of *The War Illustrated*.

NAUGHTY NETTA'S KNITTING KNICKERS FOR THE SEAT OF WAR.
Chacun doit se rendre utile.

Comforts from home. Perhaps not the most appropriate gift for Highland soldiers and likely to be thrown into No Man's Land once lice-infested. A contemporary comic postcard by the Inter-Art Co. (Author's collection)

Support from home. Many soldiers maintained frequent communication with family, friends and sweethearts at home through an excellent postal service. A sentimental contemporary postcard by Tuck's. (Author's collection)

Identity. Scottish pride. A contemporary postcard published by J. Salmon.
(Copyright J. Salmon Ltd, England)

Image of the bayonet-toting Highland soldier. A contemporary postcard of the Seaforth Highlanders by Ernest Ibbetson, published by Gale & Polden. (Author's collection)

Popular image. 'The charge at St Quentin 1914.' The stirrup charge that never was. Imaginary repetition of the legendary feat at Waterloo, painted by Harry Payne for a contemporary postcard published by Tuck's. (Author's collection)

To see ourselves as others see us. A Highland soldier personifies Britain in this unflattering Italian postcard, produced no doubt before Italy joined the war on the side of France, Britain and Russia. (Author's collection)

To see ourselves as others see us. A contemporary German postcard in the Kriegs Erinnerungs Karte series demonstrates German satisfaction at taking Highland soldiers prisoner. (author's collection)

Corporal Pollock of 5th Camerons wins the Victoria Cross at Loos. A contemporary advertising card by Walker, Harrison & Garthwaites Ltd. (Author's collection)

War Memorial, Dornoch. Many men from Dornoch served and fell in 5th Seaforth Highlanders. (Photograph, author)

Pipe band playing to resting troops after the capture of Longueval on 14 July 1916. (IWM Q4001)

The pipes and drums would also regularly play 'Retreat' in the evening, both in training and on campaign.[65] At Tain, in August 1914, Private Robert Dawson in 4th Gordons noted that "Every evening either the brass band or pipe bands play for an hour or two". After the battalion moved to Bedford, he noted that at Retreat, "the pipe band marches slowly up and down the street playing some fine music." "I'm coming to think that there is nothing like the pipes now."[66] Behind the lines, Pipe Major Macleod records the playing of Retreat and Tattoo in 4/5th Black Watch on innumerable occasions[67], and this was general practice. After George Leys' draft had joined the 4th Gordons in France on 10 September 1915, in the evening, "the playing of the 'Retreat' was deservedly popular, and one felt that here, miles from home, was a bit of auld Scotland, and church parade itself did not do more to unite the individual to his neighbour than did this old regimental custom."[68] Retreat was played everywhere that Highland troops were present; in Salonika[69], in Mesopotamia[70], and at Solingen in occupied Germany, where the 51st Gordons were based for a time from the end of June 1919.[71] Even on board the S.S. Andania, carrying the 5th Argylls to Alexandria in June 1915, "The pipe band plays on deck from 6 to 7 each evening."[72]

The pipes were also of course the essential accompaniment to marching. We have already seen how they were used to accompany troops marching to and from the trenches. They were used on countless other occasions to accompany marching troops; on route marches in training or behind the lines; in long marches behind the lines to shift location, and on local marches to the ranges or to the baths.

In training, and to keep troops fit behind the lines, they would be used on route marches. Hal Kerridge, who served in both the London Scottish and 1st Gordons had a high opinion of the moral effect of the pipes during his early training with the London Scottish:

65   Individual refs are too numerous to cite here. The examples quoted are typical.
66   GHM PB1937 Dawson, undated letter & letters of 20 September and 18 October 1914.
67   IWM 16387 Macleod, diary, passim.
68   IWM 11125 Leys, memoir.
69   IWM 6873 Hendry, memoir.
70   Mackay Scobie, *Pipers*, p.44.
71   Anon, *The 51st Battalion*, pp.33-35.
72   ASHM NE 5 Main, letter 5 June 1915.

> Well, they were the things that kept you going on the march … we'd probably done twenty miles with a pack on your back, and we'd finish up in Richmond Park dead beat and just about crippled and as we got into the gates of Richmond Park the band would start up and [you could see] shoulders up immediately, and we'd finish like that as a group were just going out.[73]

The pipes accompanied their battalions on the numerous long marches behind the lines as they shifted from one sector to another. On these marches the pipe-band would sometimes march at the head of the battalion, when the companies might take turns at marching behind the band[74]. On other occasions the pipes would be split between companies or platoons, such that each could march behind its own piper/s.[75] Sometimes pipers of another battalion might assist.[76]

The pipes were heard everywhere that the regiments marched, not only in France and Flanders but in Mesopotamia, Salonika, Constantinople, Egypt and Palestine. A few examples will suffice. At the end of July 1916, at the end of a gruelling march to the Somme, Captain William Kemp recalled how 8/10th Gordons:

> marched into billets, past General Marshall, our Brigade Commander, with heads up and kilts swinging for were not the pipes playing our own March Past "HIELAND LADDIE"? One can march to pipes as to no other instrument and it was on occasions like this march into Barly that we had some extra pride in the "land of our sires", the "land of the mountain and the flood" that we had all come out to fight for and if necessary to die for.[77]

More romantically, towards the end of October 1918 in the Balkans, 1st Argylls

> Marched through the Cresna pass to Krupnic. In the Pass, with sheer rock sides, were the river, a small gauge railway and a good road. A single piper led the battalion and the echo up and down the pass was terrific, the piping sounded marvellous.[78]

The pipes were particularly used to send battalions and also new drafts on their way to the Front. Favourite tunes were "Happy have we been all th' gither" and "Will ye no come back again."[79] Drafts might even be piped to the station from the camp at Etaples.[80] On arrival at their own battalions, they would often be met by a piper and piped in.[81] There were send-offs too for demobilisation. When a big party of 1st Garrison Battalion Seaforth Highlanders left for home from

---

73 IWM 18836 Kerridge interview.
74 GHM PB2183, Watson, memoir, p.11; IWM 4586 Douglas, memoir, pp.435, 453, 468, 478.
75 Beattie, *48th Highlanders*, pp.262, 264, 381; IWM 4586 Douglas, memoir, p.82.
76 IWM 1862 Craig-Brown, letter of 5 July, 1916. See also Craig-Brown, *Historical Records*, Vol. 3, pp.185, 228; Anderson, *1st Argylls*, p.43; Topp, *42nd Battalion*, p.92.
77 GHM PB 1639 Kemp, memoir, p.33.
78 LC GS 1026 Maclean, typescript written up from diary after war, p.48.
79 See for example *The 11th Battalion Gordon Highlanders*, 1916, p.20.
80 IWM Books Cooper, 'Domi Militaeque,' p.86.
81 Hutchison, *Warrior*, p.45; Gillespie, *Letters from Flanders*, letter 26 February 1915; IWM 11125, Leys, memoir; IWM Books Brooke, 'Wait for it,' p.181; GHM PB2788/1 Emslie, diary; IWM 15347 PP King, Capt H., typescript recollections, p.36.

Pipers of 2nd Black Watch pipe the battalion into Beirut, 10 October 1918. (IWM Q12407)

Eski-Chehir in occupied Turkey in June, 1919, "Five gharries drove past with a piper playing hard in each of them more or less drunk. They returned at 2.30 this morning, still playing, at least one of them, the others having long since collapsed."[82]

The pipes were sure to announce the arrival of Scottish battalions at their various destinations across the world. When the 48th Highlanders of Canada eventually crossed the Atlantic and arrived in Plymouth in October 1914, their pipers played 'The Cock o' the North' on their transport, the 'Megantic'.[83] When the troop ship carrying the Canadian Scottish anchored off St Nazaire on 14th February 1915, after a stormy passage from England, "the full Pipe Band assembled on the upper deck and played marches and reels," while the next day, the C.O. deliberately paraded his battalion through the town headed by the pipes.[84] In December 1917, 6th Argylls arrived at Brescia in Italy in the wake of the disastrous Italian defeat at Caporetto. When the pipers started up, and " 'The Campbells are Coming' sent its martial echoes reverberating over that sea of broon faces lit with glittering eyes, even the sullen-looking groups of war-weary soldiers woke up to a new enthusiasm."[85] When S.S. Andania, carrying 5th Argylls, arrived off

---

82 IWM 7508 Wyllie, diary, 29 June 1919.
83 Beattie, *48th Highlanders*, pp.18, 20, 25.
84 Urquhart, *Canadian Scottish*, p.42; Zuehlke, Mark, *Brave Battalion* (Mississauga, Ontario: Wiley, 2008), p.28. See also on arrival in France; IWM 10819 Brittan, diary; GHM PB583, McKinnon, memoir, p.4; Burns, *Once a Cameron Highlander*, p.49.
85 Maclean, *On Active Service*, Vol.2, p.68.

Gibraltar in early June 1915, "the Pipe Band formed up on deck and gave a vigorous rendering of 'The 79th Farewell to Gibraltar'".[86] When the Garrison Battalion of the Gordon Highlanders was carried to India in early 1917, the pipe band announced their arrival at Freetown, in Sierra Leone, and at Cape Town and Durban in South Africa.[87] On 9 December 1917, the pipes of 2nd London Scottish played the battalion into Jerusalem.[88] The most triumphal march, however, for those who had the privilege, was that across the German border or the march across the Rhine at Cologne during the occupation. Invariably this was accompanied by the full pipe-band, the most popular tune being 'Blue Bonnets over the Border'.[89]

Children, however, could burst the bubble of pomp. In November 1914, when 6th Gordons disembarked at le Havre:

> When the troopship drew up at the quay, among the first to step ashore was the Pipe Major. He at once began to tune up, and soon attracted the attention of the natives, to whom the kilt and the bagpipes were still strange. Great amusement was caused among the men who lined the rail of the "Cornishman" when a small French child, some eight years of age, mistaking the Pipe Major for a wandering minstrel, cane shyly up and offered him a copper.[90]

The pipes would also be turned out for parades and inspections, both at home in training and behind the lines overseas. Perhaps the most notorious of these was Lord Kitchener's inspection of the New Army with the French Minister of War in freezing conditions in early 1915. On this occasion, as the visitors approached the 5th Camerons,

> Lord Kitchener was heard to remark to his companion that "this was Lochiel's battalion"; and then, as if in further proof, asked the colonel to play "The March of the Cameron Men." Lochiel having given the necessary order, there then arose a most strange and dismal noise from the rear, which lasted while the two great men, accompanied by the colonel and the adjutant, carried out a rapid inspection of the ranks. What it was that the pipers played that day was never known, not even by themselves; for the cold had so numbed their fingers that they could not play a note.[91]

The pipes would play too at funerals. This was particularly true of officers, whose bodies were generally retrieved from the battlefield often at great risk. The most frequently played tunes were 'Flowers of the Forest', a lament for the Scottish dead at Flodden, 'Lochaber no more', and 'Land o' the Leal' (Land of the Loyal).[92] Captain Youngson, Quartermaster of 5th Gordons, remembered a burial in the battalion in early 1916 in the area of Neuville St Vaast:

---

86   ASHM N-E5 Main, letter 8 June 1915; LC GALL 066 Nicol, letter 7 June 1915.
87   GHM PB2459 Williams, diary of voyage. See also GHM PB3112, Blinco, diary.
88   Malcolm, *The Piper*, p.199.
89   Urquhart, *Canadian Scottish*, p.327, Beattie, *48th Highlanders*, pp.398-399; Fetherstonhaugh, *13th Battalion*, pp.308, 310, McEwen, *Fifth Camerons*, p.107; Craig-Brown, *Historical Records*, Vol.3, p.281; IWM 4586 Douglas, memoir, pp.1171, 1180-81.
90   Mackenzie, *Sixth Gordons*. p.8.
91   Craig-Brown, *Historical Records*, Vol.4, p.59. There are numerous other examples.
92   There are many examples, too numerous to cite here.

One night in particular stands out. We brought down three of the lads. It was a beautiful moonlit night. There was the sound of neither rifle nor gun – all was silent, but soon we heard the wail of the bagpipes – "The Flowers o' the Forest" – sounding over the tree-clad hillside as the pipe major came to pay the last honour to his comrades. The last rites were performed quietly and reverently, and our hearts turned to those who, in a few days in Buchan homes, would be mourning.[93]

Similarly the pipes would play in acts of remembrance. On 20 December, 1916, representative parties of the 1st Black Watch and 1st Camerons attended the dedication of a St Andrew's Cross erected on the eastern edge of High Wood in memory of the members of the two Highland battalions who fell in the neighbourhood. 'Lochaber no More' was played by Sergeant-Piper R. Smith, the Black Watch, and Lance-Corporal Piper J. Macleod, Cameron Highlanders, whilst those taking part in the ceremony stood at the salute.[94] On 17 February 1918, the South African Brigade took part in a memorial service at Delville Wood, where a tall wooden cross was erected in memory of those who had fallen there. A lament on the pipes, composed by Pipe-Major Sandy Grieve of the South African Scottish, preceded the drumhead service.[95]

More pleasantly, the pipes were used for entertainments and concerts of all kinds, both at home, where they might play a particular role in fund-raising, and behind the lines. These were primarily of course to entertain the troops[96]. But they were particularly used to build good relations with allies. Retreat, band practice and special concerts were common sources of entertainment for French villagers.[97] Otherwise the pipes would play to entertain visiting French generals at Divisional HQ,[98] Early in the war, while staying at Arques, 4th Seaforths' battalion headquarters was opposite those of a French Cavalry Corps. On 25 November 1914, a joint concert was held with the French, a 'Fontaine Musicale franco-Britannique'. The Seaforths' pipers danced a foursome reel, the Highland Fling and the Sword dance.[99] On 19 October, 1917, when the 1st Camerons played a game of football against the 19th Belgian Regiment, the pipes and drums played alternately with the Belgian band during the match.[100] In March 1918, the pipe band of the 6th Argylls, who were then deployed in Italy, was sent with the pipers of another battalion to "give some entertainment to the Romans," and performed to great effect in the village of Frascati.[101] They would also play at Army HQ,[102] and for V.I.P.'s such as Prince Arthur of Connaught[103]

---

93   GHM PB1892.3.1, Youngson, memoir, pp.20-21. For other moving examples, see: IWM 5525 Steven, letter 12 May 1915; ASHM N-E8, Munro, letter from H. Reid, Chaplain 1/8th ASH; THM, Camerons 91-46 Brownlie, John, letter to his mother, 12 February, 1918.
94   Craig-Brown, *Historical Records*, Vol.3, pp.218-219.
95   Orpen, *Cape Town Highlanders*, pp.89-90.
96   Sommers, *Temporary Heroes*, pp.72-73; Mackenzie, *Sixth Gordons*, p.64; IWM 2854 Bates, letters of 2 & 23 May 1916: GHM PB2549, Leathem, Dr W.H., Chaplain to 1st Gordons, transcript of diary.
97   Saul, *Mud and Bodies*, p.61, letter from Lt Neil Weir, 20 June 1916; Hayes, *Eighty Fifth*, p.228; IWM 114 Allen, letter of 9 August 1915; Craig-Brown, *Historical Records*, Vol.3, p.279.
98   Craig-Brown, *Historical Records*, Vol.3, p.223, Macleod, *6th Camerons*, p.55.
99   IWM 12311 Mason-Macfarlane, memoir by David Mason-Macfarlane, p.24.
100 Craig-Brown, *Historical Records*, Vol.3, pp.232-3.
101 IWM 8592, Macgregor, letters dated 20 & 28 March 1918.
102 Urquhart, *Canadian Scottish*, pp.220-221; Craig-Brown, *Historical Records*, Vol.3, p.250.
103 Urquhart, *Canadian Scottish*, pp.220-221.

and the Commander-in-Chief.[104] The 12th Argylls took part in a most prestigious improvised concert while they were in the Balkans at the conclusion of the Salonika campaign. "The Queen of Roumania had Scottish connections and insisted our pipe band play at the Palace in Bucharest."[105]

Pipers would play in hospitals to cheer up the wounded. On Christmas Day 1916, Jock Macleod was in hospital in Malta, recovering from malaria, jaundice and veld-sores. "In the afternoon there was a concert in the hospital…the pipe major of the 2nd Camerons, who was wounded in the back in our little battle, turned up, and played. His was the most popular turn of the evening."[106] On 26 January 1918, the C.O., Lieutenant Johnston, Billy the Goat, and the pipe band of the Canadian Scottish, with an astonishing 42 pipers and drummers, all set out on a four-day visit to Paris, during which they gave concerts at the British Embassy Church, the Army and Navy League Club, other soldier clubs and the Canadian Hospital at St Cloud.[107] And on 18 July 1918, while staying at Mogneville, the officers and pipers of the 5th Gordons visited a nearby chateau which was being run as a French hospital. The pipers "gave great pleasure to the nurses and wounded "Poilus" by piping and dancing on the lawn for an hour or two.[108]

The pipes would also appear on special occasions. They would play often at Christmas[109] but particularly of course at New Year.[110] On other occasions they might play to celebrate the liberation of French or Belgian villages.[111] Finally, they came out to celebrate the Armistice. On the evening of 10 November, 1918, Arthur Wrench wrote in his diary:

> And now it is night. I don't know how to say what I feel like saying. It is quite impossible. Probably long after this is over I will be better able to express all these emotions that possess every one of us for meantime I think we are all mad. At least there is absolute madness in what's happening outside. It is officially announced that an armistice has been signed to take effect at eleven o' clock tomorrow when hostilities will cease … And so what a racket. The Argylls band are out in force and even here we can hear them play. These drums are being beat as they never were beat before. I never dreamed the skins could stand such 'wallopping' nor the pipes to sound so wild and grand. What a great and glorious feeling it is. The war is over and we have won.[112]

---

104 McEvoy & Finlay, *Seaforth Highlanders of Canada*, p.60.
105 LC GS 0456 Dick, memoir, p.63. Queen Mary of Rumania was the daughter of Alfred, Duke of Edinburgh and grand-daughter of Queen Victoria. The King and Queen of Italy also had the 2nd Gordons and 6th Argylls play to them by special request: see Malcolm, *The Piper*, p.38.
106 LC GS 1027 Macleod, letter 27 December 1916.
107 Urquhart, *Canadian Scottish*, p.246.
108 GHM PB1639 Kemp, memoir, Vol.2, p.42.
109 IWM 1697 PP Chater, A.D.; IWM 13511, Macgregor, letter of 26 December, 1915; Fetherstonhaugh, *13th Battalion*, pp.311-312; Hayes, *Eighty Fifth*, p.229; McKinnel, *Diary*, Christmas Day 1914
110 Mackenzie, *6th Gordons*, pp.80, 187; IWM 3834 Wrench, diary, 1 January 1919; IWM Books Reid, 'Shoulder to Shoulder,' p.170; Urquhart, *Canadian Scottish*, pp.116, 329; Maclean, *On Active Service*, Vol.2, p.73; GHM PB1639 Kemp, memoir, Vol.2, p.8; IWM 7508 Wyllie, diary, 5 January 1918; McEvoy & Finlay, *Seaforth Highlanders of Canada*, pp.88, 178; Urquhart, *Canadian Scottish*, p.243; Fetherstonhaugh, *13th Battalion*, pp.311-312; LC GS 0456 Dick, diary; ASHM N-E11 Bowie, diary; IWM 3834 Wrench, diary 31 December 1916.
111 Fetherstonhaugh, *13th Battalion*, p.305; Urquhart, *Canadian Scottish*, p.325.
112 IWM 3834 Wrench, diary, 10 November 1918. See also: IWM 4576 PP Yarnall, G.S., diary, 11 November 1918; Beattie, *48th Highlanders*, pp.262, 264: Urquhart, *Canadian Scottish*, p.324: ASHM

The pipes also played at football matches, at battalion, brigade and divisional sports days and at horse shows, both in training[113] and behind the lines,[114] and even at Highland gatherings. After the Armistice, there were even piping and dancing competitions organised amongst the battalions left in France and Belgium.[115] Famously, the Highland Division held a Highland Games at Bedford in April 1915, at which piping competitions took place.[116] The most spectacular manifestation was on 6 July, 1918, when the 3rd Canadian Infantry Brigade held a Highland Gathering at Tincques. Both 15th Scottish and 51st Highland Divisions were in the neighbourhood and were invited to participate, and there was a pipe band competition with 26 bands competing. In this competition, the Canadian pipe bands proved generally inferior in both piping and drumming to the pipe bands of the old Highland regiments from Scotland (even though the winning Scottish bands were Territorials, the Regulars not being present). The 6th Gordons won 1st prize and were selected to go to Paris for the procession on 14 July. Perhaps the most remarkable aspect of the event was when, in the afternoon, all the bands were massed and 284 pipers and 164 drummers played Retreat together. "At the head of the centre column, bursting with pride, and keeping in time to the fraction of a second, marched "Flora Macdonald", the 13th Battalion goat."[117]

Perhaps the strangest use of the pipes occurred in practising attacks. Prior to the battle of Arras, in 51st Highland Division the attack was practised twice daily, "with the pipers spread out in front, and playing to represent a barrage."[118] In July, 1917, before Third Ypres,

> The imitation attacks were always preceded by a human barrage, composed of the pipe band complete with pipes, drums and bugles, oddments of the transport, and signallers equipped with flags. This motley party produced the creeping barrage, and the efforts of pipers and drummers who frantically emulated the scream and burst respectively of shells (which all had heard) were worthy of the cause. We often wondered, but did not dare to ask, what our musical genius, Pipe-Major Milton, thought of it all.[119]

This last unusual use of the pipes was, of course, specific to the war, but virtually all other uses simply reflected an attempt to emulate peace-time practice, both in training and behind the lines. Thus in war, as in peace, the pipes permeated every aspect of the life of the Regiment.

    N-E11 Bowie, diary; Topp, *42nd Battalion*, pp.293, 294; *The 51st Battalion*, p.13.
113 GHM PB1937 Dawson, letter to mother, 25 June 1915.
114 IWM 2854 Bates, letters 2 & 10 June, 1 October 1916; IWM 3460 Macmillan, letter from Pte Sandy Macmillan, 19 May 1917; GHM PB2183 Watson, memoir, p.18; GHM PB1639 Kemp, memoir, p.84. See also LC GS 1625 Turing, memoir; Craig-Brown, *Historical Records*, Vol 4, p.325; IWM 430 Wimberley, memoir, Vol.1, p.84; Topp, *42nd Battalion*, p.195; McEvoy & Finlay, *Seaforth Highlanders of Canada*, p.103; Beattie, *48th Highlanders*, p..310; Fetherstonhaugh, *13th Battalion*, p.242.
115 IWM 8592 Macgregor, letters 25, 26 January, 2, 3 February, 1919.
116 GHM PB2370 *Bedfordshire Times and Independent* 9th April 1915.
117 Beattie, *48th Highlanders*, p.311, Macleod, *6th Camerons*, pp.105-106; IWM 11144 Mackay, diary 6 July, 1918; Mackenzie, *Sixth Gordons*, p.162; Craig-Brown, *Historical Records*, Vol.4, p.25; Fetherstonhaugh, *13th Battalion*, p.243; Hayes, p.115; McEvoy & Finlay, *Seaforth Highlanders of Canada.*, pp.104-5; Urquhart, *Canadian Scottish*, pp.264-265; GHM PB1892.3.1, Youngson, memoir, p.43; IWM 16387 Macleod, diary, 6 July 1918.
118 GHM PB1892.3.18 McDonald, 'Uncle Harper's Duds,'p.76.
119 Peel & Macdonald, *The Great War*, p.38.

They were not simply a 'bolt-on' added to Highland regiments to give them that little bit extra. Instead, at every stage of a soldier's career they reminded him of who he was and what he represented. They reinforced his identity at every opportunity, which in turn was central to esprit de corps. They did so in two ways; national and regimental. They were of course uniquely Scottish. They identified the Scottish soldier as different and were consequently a source of national pride. Alongside this they helped identify the soldier not just as a member of a Scottish regiment, but through the application of custom, of an individual Scottish regiment. By reinforcing identity, they were central to building esprit de corps. It is no wonder therefore that, as we have seen, after an initial hiatus, pipe-bands were reconstituted behind the lines, and no wonder also that after early losses, most battalions should seek to keep their pipers safely out of the action. But alongside this careful cultivation of identity, what did the men really think of the pipes? And what conclusions should we draw about their effect on morale?

Morale

John Cooper, who saw service in the 3/4th and 6th Black Watch, wrote:

> Some affected to hate the pipes, and probably a few did actually dislike their music, but I think most men had an affection for the simple, stirring or plaintive tunes. I certainly loved the pipes, and no small part of the charm of some days in my army career is associated with tunes used upon notable occasions.[120]

This is probably accurate. Amongst the letters, diaries and memoirs left by solders of the Highland regiments there are many appreciative comments and few criticisms. Even non-Highlanders., like Captain Bates, who joined 8th Black Watch as M.O., or Private Dennis, a Yorkshireman drafted into 11th Camerons, came to appreciate the pipes.[121]

There were dissenters. Graham Seton Hutchison, an Argylls officer, recalled hearing retreat beaten on successive evenings by the bands of the 1st Queen's and 2nd Worcestershires and the pipes of the Glasgow Highlanders.

> With the inhabitants … I think the 9th H.L.I. were preferred … But for me, the disciplined precision of the drums and fifes, showing so high an efficiency, won the first claim to esteem and affection, and this despite an inherent allegiance to the pipes.[122]

Pipers could also require a degree of tolerance. As Jock McLeod reported of the 3rd Camerons in 1915:

> The Pipers are always men from 'ta Hielants' & they're a queer lot, too. We'd one in our Hut, & if he woke up in the night instead of having a smoke he'd have a tune on the Pipes!

---

120 IWM Books Cooper, 'Domi Militaeque,' p.21.
121 IWM 2854 Bates, letter 28 June 1917; IWM 6926, Dennis, memoir, p.291.
122 Hutchison, *Warrior*, pp.179-180.

He never required any persuasion to play! It gets hold like a bad habit. We're a wonderful crowd![123]

To the poetically inclined, the pipes could conjure evocative images of past glory. The Seaforths soldier-poet, E.A. Mackintosh, imagined the ghost of a MacCrimmon piper leading the 4th Camerons off to war from Bedford in 1915:

> And there in front of the men were marching
> With feet that made no mark,
> The grey old ghosts of the ancient fighters
> Come back again from the dark;
> And in front of them all MacCrimmon piping
> A weary tune and sore,
> "On the gathering day, for ever and ever,
> MacCrimmon comes no more."[124]

I.G. Andrew, who trained as a private with the 6th Camerons in the Bramshott area in the winter of 1914/1915 recalls:

> I know of nothing that so stirs the blood as to step out on the hard high-way on a keen, frosty morning, with a thousand other good fellows, to the skirl of the piper ahead … I am not an undiluted admirer of the pipes but there are, I think, two settings in which they are incomparable. One is on the march – there is nothing so infinitely rousing and heart-stirring, at least to a Scot, as the inspiring skirl of a full pipe-band. The other is a solitary piper in the evening, heard across a Highland loch.[125]

A lance-corporal who served with 1st Seaforths in the Palestine campaign in 1918, described his feelings as he listened to the pipes playing Retreat at Khan Abdi below snow-covered Mount Lebanon.

> Pipes and Drums! What strange things, they set a man's mind thinking! What jovial madness they set stirring in the blood! I have heard a great orchestra speak in a thunder crash of harmony, but the pipes somehow are different in their appeal; they speak of things primitive and elemental.[126]

More specifically the soldiers record how the pipes lifted their spirits in particular situations; first, for example, when battalions of drafts were piped off to war. When the 4th (Dundee) Territorial Battalion of the Black Watch marched to Tay Bridge Station on 23 February 1915, they were played out by the pipers of the 6th Black Watch, to the strains of 'Hielen' Laddie'

---

123   IWM 5821 Semple, letter from Pte Jock McLeod, 6 August, 1915.
124   Mackintosh, *A Highland Regiment*, 'Cha Till Maccruimein. Departure of the 4th Camerons.'
125   LC WF Recollections, A9, Andrew, memoir. See also THM Camerons 96 52, Laidlaw, 'Grandpa's War,' letter from Douglas Laidlaw 30 June 1916.
126   Mackay Scobie, *Pipers*, pp.48-49, quoting 'The Log of a Lance-Jack', by William Fraser.

and 'Happy we've been – a thegither'. As Linton Andrews recalled, "Our blood tingled with the sense of drama, our hearts swelled with pride."[127] Lieutenant S.C. Russell, ordered to conduct a draft of men from 3rd Camerons to France one Sunday in March 1915, recognised what this rousing send-off meant to the men and expressed his frustration when they had to march to the station in silence, owing to the protest of the local Free Church Minister.[128]

But the magic might not work the second time round. Frank Brooke had marched off from camp at Ripon to the sound of the pipes in a draft of Seaforths in early summer 1916. Later, after being wounded at the front, he left Ripon again, in June 1917, in a draft of 240.

> We received a tremendous send-off. The C.O. Depot led us to the station and we were played 'out' by the full band of pipers and drummers......We were not bucked. We cursed as we quickly put out cigarettes and pipes at the command, "March to ATTENTION!"
> "Happy we've been altogether …" skirled the pipers once again.
> "That bloody tune puts years on me", said Harry, as we resumed the 'March at Ease'.
> "It gave me a thrill last time", I replied.
> "Aye, lad, but there's a lot of water passed under Leeds Bridge since then" – bitterly.
> "… Yes, and some good pals gone west", I said.[129]

The pipes were also appreciated when they met the weary soldiers coming out of the trenches to pipe them back to billets or dugouts. H.S. Taylor, who served in the ranks of the Liverpool Scottish, recorded his own feelings about the pipes in 1978, when he was 81.

> Many people, I know, do not care for pipe music, but I can assure you that they might think differently could they only see the effect on a bunch of dead-weary, fed-up soldiers staggering out of the trenches, loaded with the usual impedimenta of heavy gear, rifles, packs, equipment, plus a sand-bag containing various treasures, edible and otherwise. For myself, I experienced an uplift of both body and spirit, never to be forgotten, even after sixty-one years.[130]

His feelings are broadly reflected by other soldiers' accounts,[131] although even the pipes could not overcome utter exhaustion. As Norman Down of 4th Gordons, wrote of a march out of the trenches in April 1915, "… no pipes that ever played could guard against that feeling of utter and complete weariness which overcomes you as you plod hopelessly along, half dead and half asleep."[132] Similarly, Alexander Rule, also with 4th Gordons, wrote of a march back from the trenches in Sanctuary Wood around July, 1915, "With our brains thoroughly befogged by the weariness induced by a continued lack of sleep, we scarcely knew whether the pipes were playing

---

127 Wauchope, *Black Watch*, vol.2, p.5; Andrews, *Autobiography*, p.85. See also for such feelings of pride GHM PB1937 Dawson, letter to mother 19 February 1915; IWM 4474 Johnston, memoir, p.2.
128 THM Camerons 97-22 Russell, memoirs, p.188.
129 IWM Books Brooke, 'Wait for it,' pp.18, 211.
130 IWM 4755 PP Taylor, H.S., typescript memoir.
131 Sommers, *Temporary Heroes*, p.35; IWM 11125 Leys, memoir; IWM 11739, Sangster, letter, 21 September, 1915; Beattie, *48th Highlanders*, p.259; IWM Books Brooke, 'Wait for it,', p.262.
132 Sommers, *Temporary Heroes*, p.35.

or not."[133] Nevertheless, as they marched back into billets at the end of the march out, when the pipes struck up again generally shoulders would go back and pride in regiment would cut in once more. When the 8/10th Gordons marched back into Arras on 12 April 1917, after three days' fighting,

> each company's pipers halting and standing aside at the entrance to the Grande Place struck up, as usual, "Hielan' Laddie" as the companies marched past into the square where the billets were. The men were dog-tired, 'done to the world', and covered with mud from head to foot, yet, without a single word of command, when they heard the pipers strike up the 'March Past' every man, sloping his rifle, marched into the square with head erect and kilts and arms swinging, lots of them with tears in their eyes thinking of their own chums, or perhaps even brothers, whom they had seen killed during the last few days fighting. It was touching and magnificent; they were human beings who mourned the loss of chums but they were soldiers and Scotchmen also, proud of what the army had accomplished since dawn on April 9th and above all, proud of being "Gordon Highlanders." It was a sight to stir the blood.[134]

There are fewer commentaries on the moral effect of the pipes as the soldiers were piped into the trenches or towards the battlefield. It was their uplifting effect on the march out which has attracted most attention.

Many soldiers recall how long marches, either route marches or moves behind the lines, were made easier by the music of the pipes.[135] Bernard Blaser notes how the intermittent music of the pipes provided a stimulus during long marches with 2nd London Scottish in Palestine. When the pipes burst forth,

> The effect is wonderful. Your back, and the back of your neighbour, in fact everyone's back, immediately straightens; shoulders are squared, and the step again goes with a swing as though each man is anxious to convey to his fellow sufferers that he is not at all tired, but, on the contrary, quite fresh. In ten minutes the unwelcome double beat of the drums is heard, one more round, and the music stops. The rhythm of the step again falls to pieces, backs begin to droop, heads drop lower, and chins rest on chests in the struggle with the strain on endurance.[136]

Many accounts record how backs would straighten and the men march at attention as they were piped in on completion of the march.[137] Nevertheless, Lieutenant Cecil Harper in the 10th

---

133 Rule, *Students*, p.162.
134 GHM PB1639 Kemp, memoir, p.73. See also GHM PB2183 Watson, memoir, pp.13, 17; THM Camerons 92-35 Welsh, memoir, pp.83-84.
135 See IWM 3460 Macmillan, diary, 29 May 1915, and letter from Pte Sandy Macmillan, 1 June 1917; Fraser, *Doctor Jimmy*, p.51, Rule, *Students*, p.37; Lyon, *In kilt and khaki*, pp.45-48; IWM Books Cooper, 'Domi Militaeque,' pp.32-33; GHM PB1700/2, Robertson, diary; Maclean, *On Active Service*, Vol.1, p.74; GHM PB375 Pailthorpe, memoir, p.30; Watt, *In France and Flanders*, pp.115-116.
136 Blaser, *Kilts across the Jordan*, p.236.
137 IWM 430 Wimberley, memoir, Vol.1, p.30; IWM 3834 Wrench, diary, afternote to 26 November 1916; Malcolm, *Argyllshire Highlanders*, p.22; IWM Books Cooper, 'Domi Militaeque,' p.114.

Gordons records how on a long 20-mile march in France to Hazebrouk on a very hot day in July 1915, "The pipes kept us in good heart, but I still associate the tune Black Bear with heat and thirst, and aching legs, whenever I hear it.[138]

Many soldiers recorded their appreciation of the pipes playing Retreat in the evening.[139] Indeed, it is Retreat, rather than the more formal entertainments laid on for them, which attracts most appreciation in soldiers' accounts.[140] "I'm coming to think that there is nothing like the pipes now," wrote Robert Dawson, in training with 4th Gordons at Bedford.[141] In July, 1915, while behind the lines in billets in France, Douglas Gillespie of the Argylls recorded:

> Sometimes … the pipers march up and down the village street in the evening, playing for all they are worth; last night it was 'The Barren Rocks of Aden', which is a familiar tune at home, but seems to mean much more when you hear it out in France, perhaps because it was written for Scotsmen far from Scotland.[142]

Even the duty pipe-calls, carefully maintained behind the lines, could provide comfort and reassurance. Sir John Turing remembers the effect of the pipes when resting after fighting with 8th Seaforths in the closing stages of the war:

> We were resting in a partly destroyed village but sleeping in army huts. I shall always remember waking up to reveille played on the pipes, followed by the infinitely beautiful and haunting air, played in slow-march time, "Believe me if all those endearing young charms". It was wonderfully soothing to the nerves. We might have been back at Cromarty or Fort George.[143]

In this respect, in considering military music more generally, David Murray stresses the moral effects of established routine, which he feels, "reminded everyone that whatever things may have been like 'up there', the regiment and the battalion would go on in its time-honoured and inimitable fashion, whatever happened.[144]

But sentiment did not always prevail. In July 1917, an increasingly disillusioned Frank Brooke found himself detached from his battalion, behind the lines at a Corps Reinforcement Camp near Lederzeele.

> The pipe-bands in our division [51st] (with the exception of our immediate brigade's) all rolled in and made things livelier still by playing 'Retreat' every night. Some more of my

---

138 IWM 7593 Harper, memoir.
139 GHM PB1706/2 Robertson, diary; Craig-Brown, *Historical Records*, Vol.3, p.263; IWM 5821 Semple, letter from Pte Jock McLeod, 9 September, 1915; IWM Books Cooper, 'Domi Militaeque,' p.21; IWM 7408 Lorimer, p.112, letter to his mother dated 26 September, 1916; LC GS 0262 Campbell, diary, 25 May, 1917.
140 For positive comments on other entertainments see GHM PB1892.3.18 McDonald, 'Uncle Harper's Duds,' p.86; Burns, *Once a Cameron Highlander*, p.160.
141 GHM PB 1937 Dawson, undated letter & letters of 20 September and 18 October 1914.
142 Gillespie, *Letters from Flanders*, p.232, letter of 11 July 1915.
143 LC GS 1635 Turing, memoir.
144 Murray, *Music*, p.226.

boyhood's dreams materialised – now it was too late – and it was with a blasé air that I watched the Seaforths, the Gordons, the Black Watch, and the Argylls.[145]

The haunting sounds of a lament played at funerals or in acts of remembrance could also be deeply affecting. Lauchlan Maclean Watt was serving as chaplain at a hospital behind the lines in 1916. When a young Highland soldier died there,

> We got the pipe-major of a famous Highland regiment to come over; and when the brave dust was lowered, while a little group of bronzed and kilted men stood round the grave, he played the old wail of the sorrow of our people, 'Lochaber no more'. I heard it last when I stood in the rain beside my mother's grave; and there can be nothing more deeply moving for the Highland heart. The sigh of the waves along Hebridean shores called to me there, among the graves in France.[146]

The pipes undoubtedly had plenty of swank, and as a result, Highland soldiers might feel a certain superiority with their pipes compared with the instruments normally carried by other regiments, especially the English. John Cooper recalls how, when marching to Drucat on 16 January 1917, "This day ... we passed an English regiment "going up" and it was amusing to hear how our band completely muffled not only their tooting fifes but even their brass band!"[147] And in August 1915, Second Lieutenant Gillespie of 4th Argylls reported, "The English regiments are jealous and make rude remarks about the pipes, but a mouth organ is a miserable instrument compared with them."[148]

Unsurprisingly, with this advantage, and cocky attitude, the pipes were not universally loved outside the Highland regiments. In February 1918 at Arras, there was an unfortunate incident between some officers of the Guards and those of the 8/10th Gordons, who, prior to returning to the line, had arranged a jolly dinner with singing, dancing and piping at the officers' club.

> The pipe music did not appeal to the English blood of the "Guardees" and one of them wrote in the suggestion book the night after our dinner that "Large dinner parties such as were held last night should not be allowed in this club and that on no account should pipe music ever be permitted in a gentleman's club." ... When this was seen it rather tickled our fellows and Leith wrote below the Guardee's suggestion that "Old Women in bloomers should not interfere with the time honoured customs of the glorious Highland regiments who are winning this war." To this the Guards could only write the feeble reply "Rot" but several English officers added remarks in appreciation of the pipes and condemnation of the Guards and there the matter rested with full points, I think, to the pipe music.[149]

In fact, even English soldiers could find encouragement and inspiration in the music of the pipes. Alexander Rule, in 4th Gordons, describes marching back to billets in early March, 1915,

---

145 IWM Books Brooke, 'Wait for it,' p.228.
146 Watt, *In France and Flanders*, p.2. For other examples, see Blaser, *Kilts across the Jordan*, p.242; IWM 6873 Hendry, memoir; IWM 11144, Mackay, commentary on his own diary, written in 1972.
147 IWM Books Cooper, 'Domi Militaeque,' p.117.
148 Gillespie, *Letters from Flanders*, pp.89, 256-257, letters of 6 April & 1 August 1915.
149 GHM PB1639 Kemp, Vol.2, pp.11-12.

after his Company's first spell in the trenches, where they had been introduced to trench life by the experienced soldiers of the Suffolk Regiment.

> After two days in reserve we marched back to La Clytte and were met half-way by our regimental pipers, to the great joy of our English comrades. I realised then for the first time the almost magical effect of stirring march tunes on tired troops; drooping heads were thrown back and dragging feet were lifted into a swinging stride. Even the Sassenach blood of the Suffolks was stirred, and they voted the bagpipes the king of music for the march.[150]

Similarly, when Private Frier of 20th Bn London Regiment marched up to the trenches in June 1915:

> As we were marching up, in the dark of course, we passed the Black Watch coming out for a rest, every man tired but bucked up by their beautiful bagpipes which were playing in front. I have heard some sort of bagpipes on our gramophone, but this was a treat. Passing these big highlanders in the middle of the night with their bagpipes in full song, it quite cheered us up as well.[151]

The pipes might not just inspire the members of a Regiment. Wyllie records that it was the pipes of the 1st Argylls which first brought British troops to Constantinople. "An English lady who had been in Constantinople during the war gave me an account of all they went through, and of how she first heard the Pipes of the Argyles as they marched through and as she told me she burst into tears."[152]

It might be thought nevertheless, that, as, for the most part, the pipers spent their time behind the lines and did not experience the danger of the trenches or the assault, there might be some resentment directed against them, given the contempt in which most front-line soldiers held those with cushy jobs behind the lines. Jim Foulis, an officer with the 5th Camerons, wryly wrote from behind the lines to his young niece Nancy that, "The bagpipes are playing some fine tunes. They do not play when we are in the trenches so they play a lot when we are back in camp."[153] Harry Ditcham, as we have seen, served as a drummer in the pipe-band of the 2nd Argylls after it re-formed in October 1915. Asked whether the pipe band helped to cheer the troops up, he replied, "Well, this is a problem. I couldn't answer really. I suppose to a degree it did, but in a way we were rather envied at not having to go into the front-line trenches."[154]

Some indication of this feeling is provided in the memoirs of the disillusioned Frank Brooke, a stretcher-bearer with 4th Seaforths. He observes that, the day before going into action on 20 September 1917:

> We were treated, after tea, to a selection of barbaric, heart-searching, clan fighting tunes by the pipers and drummers. Whether anybody felt more 'bucked' about the attack thereby I do not know. But they blew, and banged, and marched up and down in time-honoured

---

150 Rule, *Students*, pp.69-70.
151 IWM 13042 PP Frier, G.D., letter to mother June 1915.
152 IWM 7508 Wyllie, diary, 2 April 1919.
153 IWM 3563 Foulis, Capt J.B., undated letter.
154 IWM 374, Ditcham, interview.

> fashion, and put their hearts into it and gave of their best. Their audience would have done a much better 'best' if they could have changed places. The band wasn't going into action … We moved off at 10.00 in pitch darkness, the band informing everybody that "The Campbells are Comin'", and then departing to their beds.[155]

But more sympathy was shown by Private James Campbell of 6th Camerons, His pal Willie McNeil from Row was piping in a Royal Scots band. "And as bands do not do trench work nowadays he is pretty cushy. And he deserves to be for he has done his bit in the trenches as a stretcher bearer the whole of our first year out."[156]

However, as these are the only suggestions of criticism found amongst hundreds of letters, diaries and personal accounts, it does not seem that envy of the pipers' cushy existence was at all widespread. Rather there seems to have been genuine gratitude for the music of the pipes in the many roles assigned to them.

In fact, from the many appreciative comments we have recorded above, it is evident that the pipes had an extremely beneficial effect on morale. Undoubtedly, part of the reason was the stirring quality of the music itself and its direct appeal to the spirit, as we have seen, for example, when returning from the trenches tired beyond measure, in moments of relaxation listening to Retreat or in moments of sadness at funerals. But alongside the direct emotional impact of the music itself was the impact of its associations. Partly these associations were individual and private, for example thoughts of home triggered by the reassuring sound of the familiar. Partly they were collective and perhaps subconscious, the reinforcement of national and regimental identity. As we have stressed above, this was central to the role of the pipes as they permeated every aspect of the life of the Regiment, and, at every stage of a soldier's career, reminded him of who he was and what he represented. It is indeed quite difficult to disentangle these separate threads from general statements of appreciation. What was the real emotional basis of the soldiers' response to the pipes? Was it the wild, thrilling or mournful music itself, or was it the pride which went with its associations? Perhaps the best evidence of the sheer emotional power of the music is provided by the soldiers of the Suffolks and the London regiment who found themselves heartened and inspired by the music of their comrades-in-arms from Scotland. We have probably quoted sufficient examples to demonstrate that in fact these two strands, the music and its associations, were inseparable. What is certain is that by stressing identity, and through the sheer emotional impact of the music, the pipes were fundamental to both esprit de corps and morale generally. Charles Malcolm sums this up rather well:

> To the soldier fighting his country's battles on foreign soil the appeal is vivid and direct. The breath of the piper can call forth tears or laughter, it can inspire contempt of danger, arouse the pride of race, and evoke readiness for self-sacrifice. Who that has heard it can ever forget the sound of the pipes at a soldier's funeral?[157]

We will return to this question later when we bring together the various threads of this study and seek to identify how they affected the morale of the Highland soldier.

---

155 IWM Books Brooke, 'Wait for it,' pp.246-7.
156 LC GS 0262 Campbell, diary, 28th March 1917.
157 Malcolm, *The Piper*, p.36.

9

Discipline

'Wot 'orrible murder 'ave these blokes up there committed?'[1]

In this chapter we start to address discipline, by addressing crime and punishment. It is of course acknowledged that a well-disciplined battalion can exercise self-discipline, without any need for the charge sheet. Discipline and punishment are not the same thing. Much discipline was down not to the strict exercise of punishment, but to the extent to which men accepted their military socialisation during training, and to the relationship between men and their N.C,O,'s and officers, which we address separately in the next chapter. We have indeed noted in Chapter One a suggestion that discipline in the Highland regiments was based less on draconian enforcement and more on the mutual respect which existed between officers and men. What was the reality? How much 'crime' was there? What were the common offences and how were they punished? And to what extent was there a special attitude towards discipline in the Highland regiments? To investigate this issue, we are fortunate in possessing several sources which record disciplinary offences and their punishments. Part 2 Orders survive for 1/8th Argylls, virtually complete from October 1914 until the end of 1916, and these record all courts martial and C.O.'s punishments worthy of record in orders, giving an excellent picture of the administration of discipline in this, one of the most highland of battalions.[2] Part 2 Orders also survive for 1st Black Watch for 1918.[3] These orders do not record minor offences but do record courts martial. At the top end of the scale, Corns and Hughes-Wilson[4] record all soldiers executed during the war by regiment, and it is possible to extract from this source details of all Highland soldiers so punished. In addition there is a wide range of supplementary material gathered from individuals relating both to individual crimes and punishments and to the general way in which discipline was exercised in the battalions. We will look first of all at the Courts Martial in general terms, before considering particular offences and their punishments. We will then consider more general statements about the way in which offences were punished or managed, and offer some initial conclusions, before plunging into the next chapter on the operation of the unit hierarchy.

---

1   IWM 11334 Robertson, memoir, p.4.
2   ASHM 1/8th Battalion Argyll & Sutherland Highlanders Part 2 Orders, 1914-1916.
3   BWA Part 2 Orders, 1st Battalion Black Watch, 1918.
4   Corns, Cathryn & Hughes-Wilson, John, *Blindfold and Alone* (London: Cassell, 2005), pp.484-503.

Discipline 257

At the highest level, we find that 12 Highland soldiers (including one Canadian) were executed during the war, of whom one, James Adamson of 7th Camerons, was shot for cowardice (out of only 18) and one, Francis Murray, of 9th Gordons (attached R.E.) was shot for murder (out of 35). The remaining 10 victims were all shot for desertion.[5] The number of Highlanders shot seems proportionately neither extravagantly high or low.

In 1/8th Argylls, the court martial cases may be broken down between those recorded at Bedford, to the end of April, 1915, and those recorded in France and Flanders from May, 1915, to the end of 1916. While at Bedford, two courts martial, neither for particularly serious offences, are recorded; first, for failure to appear on parade, and, second, for drunkenness. The sentences were fines and detention. Between the battalion's deployment to France in May, 1915, and the end of 1916, when the record ends, 10 courts martial are recorded. Interestingly three of these cases involved offences at the base at Etaples, where they were tried; one for breaking out of camp and drunkenness; a second for absence without leave, and a third for feigning disease. In all cases Field Punishment No.1 was imposed. The seven cases which occurred within the battalion vary in nature and include some very serious offences. Private McPherson was found guilty of sleeping while on sentry in the trenches; Private Powell was tried for "misbehaving before the enemy in such a manner as to show cowardice"; Private Fowler for stealing money, the property of a comrade; Private McMillan, for failing to appear on parade and for drunkenness; Private Macgregor, for failing to appear on parade and disobeying an order to march to the trenches. The remaining two cases involved drunkenness and simply resulted in Senior N.C.O.'s losing their rank. The sentences for most cases though were stern, and varied from six month's imprisonment to death, but most sentences (including the death penalty) were commuted by Brigade and/or suspended by the Army. The only long prison sentence not commuted or suspended was that for theft.

Part 2 Orders for 1st Black Watch for 1918 record 32 courts martial, that is to say about five times as many per annum in this Regular battalion in 1918 as for the Territorial Argylls in 1915-1916. Elsewhere, we find at least 16 Field General Courts Martial taking place in 11th Argylls, a New Army battalion, between August and November, 1917, including 12 in just three days between 13 and 15 August, 1917, so the Black Watch total may not have been untypical.[6] Of the 33 charges in 1st Black Watch incurring punishment, 13 (39 percent) relate to Absence Without Leave, five each (15 percent each) to disobeying lawful orders, drunkenness and neglect, and five (15 percent) to the rest, of which the most serious was desertion. Punishments again varied from loss of rank to Field Punishment No.1 (F.P. No.1), to imprisonment with hard labour (IHL) up to five years' penal servitude, sometimes commuted and/or suspended.

Of course, below the level of court martial, Commanding Officers and Company Officers had the power to award punishments, and most punishments occurred at this lower level. Fortunately, in Part 2 Orders for 1/8th Argylls, we have a record of all such lower level punishments deemed appropriate to be recorded by the C.O. While at Bedford, 60 such lower level disciplinary offences are recorded, of which 'absence' provides the most significant proportion (57 percent) and drunkenness (18 percent) the only other significant contributor. Subsequently, Table 9.1 shows the breakdown of 333 sub court martial crimes recorded in Part 2 Orders when

---

5 Ibid., pp.484-503
6 IWM 11144 MacKay, transcript diary, 13-15 August, 24 October, 23, 28 November, 1917, pp.35-36, 45, 46.

overseas in 1915-1916.[7] The highest category is 'Absence' (35 percent), followed by drunkenness (19 percent), non-compliance with orders and/or insolence (14 percent), loss of kit or rations (eight percent), possessing a dirty rifle (six percent) and neglect of duty (four percent).

Table 9.1 Non court-martial offences recorded in Part II Orders 1/8th Argyll & Sutherland Highlanders May 1915 to December 1916

Offence	Cases	%
Absence	116	35
Drunkenness	64	19
Non-compliance with Order/Insolence	48	14
Losing items	25	8
Dirty rifle	21	6
Neglect of duty	12	4
Remainder	47	14
Total	333	100

Absence

If we now look at individual crimes and punishments, we may start with 'absence,' the principal disciplinary offence recorded in the sources above. The most serious form of absence was desertion. We have already noted that ten Highland soldiers were shot during the war for desertion, and several death penalties are recorded as carried out in the sources.[8] Others were 'fortunate' to receive lesser sentences including both a year and six months' imprisonment.[9] Part 2 Orders for 1st Black Watch record that Private McCabe was found guilty in January 1919 of desertion, between 2nd January, 1916 and 20th March, 1918, and was sentenced to five years penal servitude, commuted to two years Imprisonment with Hard Labour (I.H.L.). A list of appropriate punishments recorded by Captain Thomas Young in 3/6th Black Watch in 1915-1916 (Table 9.2)[10] notes 70 days detention minimum for desertion and 142 days detention for deserting if under orders for a draft.

Individual deserters are recorded from a range of different battalions; Regular, Territorial and New Army.[11] A number of these cases occurred at home,[12] notably a Seaforth who tried

---

7   Note: Some of these punishments were awarded by external bodies (e.g. Depot at Etaples). Punishments have only been recorded when the nature of the crime is stated. Sometimes more than one offence is punished at the same time.
8   BWA Stewart, diary, 14, 15 February, 1916, 27 July, 1917; BWA Badenoch, memoir; IWM 1862 Craig-Brown, diary, 7 March, 1915.
9   THM Seaforths 89-122 Paterson, memoir.
10 BWA Young, Captain Thomas, field message book.
11 THM Seaforths 81-2 Cooper, memoir, pp.170, 172; THM Seaforths 89-122 Paterson, memoir; THM 2013-072 (S) Braes, memoir, pp.6, 8; BWA Stewart, diary, 14, 15 February, 1916, 27 July, 1917; BWA Badenoch, memoir; IWM Books, Cooper, 'Domi Miitaeque', pp.321-322; IWM 1862 Craig-Brown, diary, 7 March, 1915; LC GS 1203 Oldham, diary, 2 October, 1918; GHM PB3309 Pelham Burn, letter to mother 26 November, 1914.
12 THM Seaforths 89-122 Paterson, memoir.

swimming from Ardersier to the Black Isle but drowned in the attempt.[13] Others occurred in transit on draft, sometimes by escaping from trains.[14] The most remarkable case is related by John Cooper, who served with 12th Argylls in Constantinople in 1919.

> Serious crime was not common during our stay. Only one case of desertion came under my notice. One evening another man and I were on our way back to barracks, and were just getting out of the crowd where the street widens at Taxim, when a ragged figure stepped up and muttered, 'Give me a fag, Jock.' We started back, and then the speaker said, 'It's all right, I'm an Argyll.' We looked at him, and he was indeed in a pitiable state. He was clothed in rags, and had not a single piastre. My friend gave him a cigarette, and we hurried away. We agreed to say nothing unless we were questioned, knowing well that the poor wretch would be compelled to give himself up very shortly, if he were not caught. In a few days he was arrested, and lodged in our guard-room. It appears that he had 'married' some woman and gone to live with her people, who, when they found that his desertion meant the failure of his financial resources, turned him adrift. He got a term of imprisonment, of course.[15]

Table 9.2 Appropriate punishments listed by Captain Thomas Young, 3/6th Black Watch, Ripon, 1915-1916 (Source: BWA)

Crime	Recommended punishment
Absence	2 days pay for every day absent
Trans. Enlist (i.e. enlisting in another corps despite already serving)	Goes back to original corps If tried gets 42 days detention
Desertion	70 days detention minimum
Absence (habitual absence)	56 days detention
Absence when under orders for draft	112 days detention
Refusing to obey orders. Must be tried (Ct Martial)	56 days detention
Deserting if under orders for draft	142 days detention
Allowing a prisoner to escape	42 days detention
Escaping	56 days detention
Striking N.C.O.	112 days detention
Drunk when for draft (kept here)	56 days detention

The lesser charge of 'absence without leave' might also incur a court martial. In 1/8th Argylls, we find one case at Etaples for absence without leave, for which the sentence was 28 days F.P. No.1 and loss of six days' pay, i.e. for the time of absence, which was a common procedure. As we have seen, in 1st Black Watch in 1918, 13 court martial charges recorded (39 percent of the total) related to this crime, which was punished severely, generally by F.P. No.1, sentences

---

13   THM 2013-072 (S) Braes, memoir, p.6.
14   THM Seaforths 81-2 Cooper, memoir, pp.170, 172; THM 2013-072 (S) Braes, memoir, p.8; GHM PB3309 Pelham Burn, letter to mother 26 November, 1914.
15   IWM Books, Cooper, 'Domi Militaeque', pp.321-322.

varying from 28 days to 90 days. In four cases I.H.L. was imposed, with terms from four months to two years, but in two of these cases these latter sentences were commuted to F.P. No.1, in one case suspended, and in one case the term reduced from nine months to three. In two other cases, the sentence was simply to reduce the guilty party from corporal to private. Stiff sentences were also handed out in 1st Argylls. Thus in June, 1915, Private Ross was convicted of absence and disobedience of orders, and was sentenced to three years' penal servitude, commuted to two years, one with hard labour, while Private Candey was convicted of absence and sentenced to one year's imprisonment, commuted to 84 days F.P. No. 1.[16]

At the lower level, below that of court martial, at Bedford in 1/8th Argylls, 34 cases of absence are recorded. In every case, the culprit lost pay equivalent to the days absent, but in all but two cases, involving detention for seven and four days, there was no other penalty. It seems that these absences may have been tacitly condoned, possibly because of difficulties with transport to the remoter parts of Argyllshire. In any case, only nine of the absences were for more than three days, and 21 were for one or two days only. In the large number of cases recorded in the battalion in France in 1915-1916, 'Absence' covers a multitude of sins and may be broken down into sub-categories, i.e. absence from parade or roll-call (45 percent), absence from a working party or other specific duty (25 percent), absence after leave (16 percent), absence from billets or camp (seven percent), and others, largely unspecified (nine percent). It is clear that absence from parade or roll-call covers a multitude of circumstances, and the punishments consequently vary, normally loss of pay or Field Punishment No.2. But on six occasions F.P. No.1 was inflicted. Four of these cases occurred at the Infantry Depot at Etaples, but the two heaviest penalties were inflicted within the battalion; in one case, 28 days F.P. No.1 and loss of three days pay, in the other 21 days F.P. No.1. The punishments would nevertheless depend on circumstances. By contrast, absence from a working party or other specific duty was nearly always treated severely, and in over half of all cases F.P.No.1 was awarded. The heaviest penalty, of 28 days F.P. No.1, was awarded once, for "absence from roll call and leaving working party without permission," but 21 days F.P. No.1 were awarded in seven other cases. The bulk of these cases occurred in September, 1916, when a total of 231 days of F.P.No.1 was awarded for this offence in just one month. Absence from billets or camp was also treated quite seriously, with the worst case being the award of 28 days F.P. No.1 at the Rouen depot. By contrast, returning late from leave was generally treated leniently, with simple deduction of pay for the number of days absent, especially when the absence was one to four days and might have been due to the difficulties of travel to the Highlands. Less frequently F.P. No.2 was awarded, and on one exceptional occasion, 21 days F.P. No.1, together with loss of pay for the 36 days absent. Regrettably no explanation is recorded for the long absence. Interestingly, Captain Young's guidelines for 3/6th Black Watch (Table 9.2) are generally more severe; 2 days pay for every day absent, and 56 days detention for habitual absence.

The sources describe a large number of these lesser crimes of absence. A young inexperienced soldier of the Cameron Highlanders of Canada in Winnipeg deserts his sentry post to visit town for a beer;[17] a group of Londoners in 5th Seaforths at Bedford absent themselves to visit the capital;[18] Frank Brooke, recovered from a wound at Arras in 1917, overstays his embarkation

---

16   LC GS 0177 Boyle, diary, 19, 21 June, 1916.
17   McMillan, *Trench Tea and Sandbags*, p.3.
18   IWM 16335 Racine, memoir, p.21.

leave from Ripon Camp by two days;[19] a soldier of 6th Camerons turns up late from leave having compensated for delays on his homeward journey;[20] Alfred Fennah takes unauthorised leave from 2nd Liverpool Scottish at Ashford to visit his sick mother;[21] a soldier in 43rd Battalion C.E.F. (Cameron Highlanders of Canada) gets "detached" from his unit in France and turns up days later.[22] Private Savage, in 9th Black Watch, was absent on parade about January, 1917. "The Sergt had me up in front of the officer; he gave me 3 hrs extra drill with full pack; had to keep marching as it was freezing cold."[23] In Canada, when orders were received to embark at short notice and embarkation leave denied, large numbers of the Nova Scotia Brigade defied orders and visited their homes to say goodbye, but they all returned.[24] And in the Old Country, many Canadian Highlanders could not resist the temptation to absent themselves from camp to visit their relations prior to their embarkation to the front. Some of these "deserters" even turned up as stowaways on their transports to France, prepared to face the music and equally keen not to miss the chance to do their bit.[25]

Drunkenness

After absence, the next most prevalent misdemeanour was drunkenness. The caricature Scottish drunk was a prevalent image at the time, and Fred Chandler, Medical Officer of 2nd Argylls, felt that drink was a national malady:

> The pity of it is that the one idea of real enjoyment in a Highland regiment is to go and get absolutely blotto on spirits as soon as they have the chance; apart from this they are a good lot but drink is a national madness in Scotland.[26]

On the other hand, Norman Macleod, in his history of 6th Camerons, is adamant in rejecting the claim.

> Out of the thousands of men who passed through the ranks there were not a dozen cases of drunkenness. Even had such a tendency existed, alcohol was prohibited, and could only be supplied to officers' and N.C.O.'s messes on a written note by a Staff Officer. Much talk and publicity have been given to the medicinal rum ration, but those who partook of that ration know just how rare a thing it was. For weeks on end rum was never seen, even in the line. It would only be procured on the production of a medical certificate that conditions were such as to render it necessary.[27]

---

19 IWM Books Brooke, 'Wait for it', p.210.
20 LC GS 0252 Campbell, J., diary, 16, 17 June, 1916
21 Fennah, *Retaliation*, pp.67-68.
22 McMillan, *Trench Tea and Sandbags*, p.17.
23 LC Middlebrook Somme 1918, Savage, letter, 1976.
24 Hunt, *Nova Scotia's Part*, pp.139-141.
25 Fetherstonhaugh, *13th Battalion*, pp.22, 25-26; Beattie, *48th Highlanders*, pp.28-29.
26 IWM 15460 Chandler, letter to sister Kate, 12 April, 1915.
27 Macleod, *6th Camerons*, p.134.

In reality, he exaggerates the difficulty of obtaining alcohol and there are many contradictory references to drunkenness in eye-witness accounts.[28] Although many men may have been reluctant to get involved – it is claimed that in December, 1914, 75 percent of men in 7th Camerons were teetotal[29] – one doesn't need to sign up to the national caricature to accept that there was a significant disruptive minority.

Serious cases of drunkenness could warrant a court martial. While at Bedford, one man of 1/8th Argylls was court-martialled for drunkenness and fined one pound with 42 days detention. Amongst the same battalion in France in 1915-1916, one man was tried at Etaples for breaking out of camp and drunkenness and sentenced to 42 days F.P. No.1. In the battalion itself, Private McMillan, for failing to appear on parade and for drunkenness, was sentenced to three years' penal servitude, commuted to six months by Brigade and suspended by Army. Another two cases of drunkenness simply resulted in Senior N.C.O.'s losing their rank. In 1stt Black Watch in 1918, drunkenness was dealt with entirely by F.P. No.1, except for one sergeant who was reduced to corporal.

There are many other serious examples in the sources. On 9 October, 1914, in Bedford, Private Arthur Charker of 4th Camerons was stabbed with a bayonet by Private John Fraser during a fight. Both were drunk and were apparently friends. When Private Charker died, Fraser was charged with wilful murder. The case was heard on 16 October and Fraser pleaded guilty to a reduced charge of manslaughter. He was sentenced to 15 months hard labour.[30] When, in the winter of 1916-1917, Sergeant Mackenzie and two pals in 9th Seaforths got drunk on wine they had stolen in Arras, they were court martialled: Mackenzie was reduced to the ranks, and the two others each got twenty days detention.[31] More serious still was drunkenness on duty. In May, 1919, Corporal Jim Shirrefs of the Gordons was caught drunk by the R.S.M., apparently while on guard duty; he was court-martialled and reduced to the ranks.[32] On occasion men would be drunk when required to move up to the trenches.[33] Two soldiers of 13th Battalion C.E.F. were awarded two months F.P. No.1 for this offence.[34] Occasionally, they might even be found drunk in the trenches. An N.C.O. of 13th Battalion C.E.F. was reduced to private for this offence.[35] He was perhaps lucky: in December, 1914, the officer commanding 1/4th Seaforths in France was warned by his general that if any man was found drunk in the trenches, or asleep on duty, he would be shot.[36] Worse still, soldiers might be drunk in battle.[37] During the Great Retreat from Mons, Jimmy Dixon was serving with the Army Service Corps, attached to 2nd

---

28 Apart from the specific sources cited below, see: GHM PB107.1 Grant, diary, 18, 30, 31 August, 1914; THM 2013-072 (S) Braes, memoir, p.11; IWM 16335 Racine, memoir, p.21; IWM 7508 Wyllie, diary, 29 March, 1918; IWM 2528 Bradbury, memoir, p.17; GHM PB2021 Stewart, letter to wife Lil, n.d.
29 Craig-Brown, *Historical Records*, Vol.4, p.274.
30 Watt, *Steel and Tartan*, p.17.
31 THM Seaforths 05-87 Hope, diary, 12 December, 1914.
32 GHM PB3758 Shirrefs, diary, 5,7, 22 May, 1919.
33 ASHM N-E8 Munro, letter 27 June, 1915; ASHM N-E6, MacPhie, diary, 27 March, 25 July, 1918.
34 IWM 10819 Brittan, diary, 4 March, 1915.
35 Ibid., 27 February, 1915.
36 THM Seaforths 05-87 Hope, diary, 21 November, 12, 19 December, 1914.
37 GHM PB375 Pailthorpe, memoir, p.41; LC GS 0993 Lynden-Bell, L.A., typed comments on the battle of Sannaiyat.

Argylls. During the retreat he recalls a Jock riding on a water cart, tied to it, having got drunk on whisky. At a cross-roads a staff major shot him dead and threw him in a ditch. "I cried for his mam and dad. What would they think of him dying like that?"[38] Graham Hutchison noted another unfortunate incident during the battle of Meteren in April, 1918.

> I discovered the estaminet at La Belle Croix Farm on the Hoegenacker Ridge. British soldiers mad with drink. Some inside, and others shouting outside with bottles. They had been filled with funk and now were filled with drink. There was nobody there to make an appeal to their manhood, and, even if there had been, I doubt if any such appeal could have been effective. I drove the men out towards the enemy. Two days later I saw the bottles, empty, and in front of them a large number of twisted corpses. Those were the men I sent out to their death. I can still realise one man in particular, a great kilted Scot. He was crazy with drink, fighting drunk, but with no fight in him. I saw his huge body lurch forward over the hill-top, and then the great torso, huge shoulders and waving arms went limp and he disappeared from view. He was a filthy sight afterwards, the whole body churned with machine-gun bullets, the clotted pools of blood stinking with wine.[39]

At the lower level, below that of court-martial, drunkenness was a common offence. In 1/8th Argylls at Bedford, these lower level crimes were punished by a fine, with or without detention, never more than seven days, although Young's scale of punishments in 3/6th Black Watch called for 56 days detention if drunk when for draft. In France in 1/8th Argylls, drunkenness was a common occurrence. It could occur in billets, in town or when returning from a pass, or when actually on duty; on parade, on the line of march, at headquarters, on guard mounting or in the trenches. The punishment matched the seriousness of the case. Unless this took the form of loss of rank, it invariably involved Field Punishment, usually from seven to 21 days F.P. No.2, often with a fine attached, but in 14 more serious cases (about 20 percent) it involved F.P. No.1, in eight of these cases for 28 days, the most serious cases involving drunkenness in the trenches, on guard duty and in the signals office.

In fact, the sources show that there were several regular occasions, apart from the obvious celebrations, when drunken behaviour was likely. The most frequent was pay day,[40] when men would blow their pay on drink. Other occasions included leaving villages where they had been happily billeted,[41] leaving base for the front,[42] or even after the battle.[43] There is evidence too that drunkenness was encouraged by boredom during demobilisation.[44] Much of the resulting behaviour was harmless, although more abstemious soldiers frequently voice their annoyance

---

38 IWM 11047 Dixon, interview.
39 Hutchison, *Warrior*, pp.242-243.
40 IWM 3449 PP Cordner memoir; LC GS 1549 Strachan, memoir, 13pp; THM Seaforths 89-26 Crask, diary, 23, 30 April, 12 June, 1915; IWM Books, Cooper, 'Domi Militaeque', p.34; THM 4586 Douglas, memoir, pp.506-508; THM Camerons 96-52, Laidlaw, 'Grandpa's War', letter from Thomas Laidlaw to his wife Bertha, n.d., (Aldershot, 1914).
41 IWM 11144 MacKay, diary, 21 June, 1917, p.27; IWM Books, *Lieutenant-Colonel Gavin Laurie Wilson*, p.27.
42 BWA Quekett, memoir, p.12.
43 LC Transcripts Tape 526 McKay, D., interview with Liddle, 1978.
44 IWM 7508 Wyllie, diary, 31 May, 6 June 1919.

at the disruption, noise, mess, arguments and violence.[45] It could also upset the locals.[46] More serious were those occasions when soldiers found liquor stores,[47] stole liquor,[48] or appropriated the rum ration.[49] The punishment would fit the crime. In February, 1916, the Gordon R.T.O. orderly at Bethune and two members of 1st Glasgow Highlanders enjoyed a riotous night on a case of whisky found in the officers' kit waggon. The first-named received 28 days and the two others 21 days F.P. No.1.[50] As we have seen, the most serious cases would go to court-martial.

Just occasionally, drunkenness could be comic. Philip Christison records a visit of the Corps Commander, Lieutenant-General Sir Aylmer Hunter Weston, known as "Hunter-Bunter," to the lines of 6th Camerons.

> He was a poseur. One day on going round our line he came upon a figure on a stretcher covered entirely by a blanket and attended by two stretcher-bearers. He sprang to attention, saluted and said "I salute your glorious dead." The blanket was thrown off and the man underneath said, "Whash the old bugger saying?" He had got at the rum and was very drunk and his friends had hoped to conceal the fact.[51]

Drunkenness was not confined to the men. Sadly there are also several examples of drunken officers, to whom drink was more accessible. Generally, these cases were dealt with discreetly, without recourse to the court-martial which might have been invoked for the men. In 7th Black Watch, a Roman Catholic padre is left behind at Bedford because of drunkenness;[52] Territorial Highland officers based at Ripon behave in an unbecoming manner with both drink and women in Harrogate.[53] In 11th Argylls, an officer, a minister before the war, abuses the rum ration;[54] in 5th Camerons in 1918, a junior officer gets drunk in a dugout rather than supervise his working party;[55] in 1st Garrison Battalion Seaforth Highlanders in Salonika, heavy drinking is prevalent amongst the officers and the Quartermaster is regularly drunk;[56] in Mesopotamia, Colonel 'Jack' Stewart, commanding 2nd Black Watch, has to get rid of his Second-in-Command through drink: "I have had to report him; in view of his service he will be invalided and so

---

45 See in particular: IWM 3834 Wrench, diary, 15, 21, 22, 24, 28 December, 1915, 13, 21, 22, 26 February, 22 April, 26, 27 September, 1916.
46 IWM 7593 Harper, memoir, p.14.
47 THM Seaforths S796(R) Cartmell, memoir; THM Seaforths 05-87 Hope, diary, 12 December, 1914; THM Camerons 93-35 Welsh, memoir, p.47; IWM 6702 Low, letter to his wife, Noanie, 25 November, 1914; IWM 3460 Macmillan, diary, 29 February, 1916.
48 THM Seaforths 81-2 Cooper, memoir, pp.41-42; Chambers, *Diaries of World War 1*, p.10; LC WF Recollections, Reece E., typescript memoir, probably written 1970's.
49 LC Several Fronts Recollections, Munro, recollections; LC GS 1579 Taylor, memoir, 'Further Reminiscences', p.6; IWM 10819 Brittan, diary, 8 March, 1915; ASHM N-E11 Bowie, 'diary' (memoir) [describing events after Loos].
50 IWM 3460 Macmillan, diary, 29 February, 1916.
51 IWM 4370 Christison, memoir, p.53. This story may be too good to be true. An alternative version is provided by: GHM PB1892.3.18 McDonald, 'Uncle Harper's Duds.'
52 IWM 114 Allen, letter to wife, 1 May, 1915.
53 IWM 12643 Ferrie, letters to mother, 7, 13 February, 1916.
54 ASHM N-E11 Bowie, 'diary' (memoir) 3 January, 1917.
55 LC GS 1761 Wilson, memoir, pp.116-117.
56 IWM 7508 Wyllie, diary, 17, 19 October, 30 November, 1916, 13 February, 16 July, 5 August, 1917.

escape a F. Gen. Court Martial; I'm sorry, but it HAD to be done, he's a d----d good soldier too (when sober)."[57] Such behaviour was most harmful in front of the men, in whom it inspired instant disrespect.[58] Arthur Wrench provides one example, from August, 1916, at Armentieres:

> Two lieutenants of the 5th Seaforths had to be conducted to the Gordon H.Q. at 2 p.m. and one of them was particularly well 'oiled' and blethered to me all the way in no very creditable way for an officer. He was more eager to be guided to an estaminet than up the line and started looking into so many different deserted houses. He also promised me a drink if I would show him where he could get it ... It was all I could do, with the other officer's help, to get on with the job, and the other was a younger officer and not willing to go against the desires of his senior. The damned fools.[59]

Disobedience

Disobeying lawful orders was generally dealt with severely by court martial. In 1/8th Argylls in France, Private Macgregor, for failing to appear on parade and disobeying an order to march to the trenches, was sentenced to two years I.H.L., commuted to one year by Brigade and suspended by Army. In 1st Black Watch in 1918, three cases out of five were dealt with by I.H.L. At least one of these sentences, for one year's imprisonment, was implemented; one was reduced to 90 days F.P. No.1. Apart from I.H.L. the other sentences were reduction of a sergeant to the ranks, and 60 days F.P. No.1. Young's guidelines in 3/6th Black Watch insist that a man must be tried by court martial for refusing to obey orders, with the recommended punishment 56 days detention.

Table 9.3 Punishments for disobedience, insubordination and violence towards superior officers recorded in miscellaneous sources

Crime	Battalion	Punishment
Assaulting N.C.O.	1/6th Argylls	1 year IHL suspended (Jul 15)
Speaking back to officer	11th Argylls	90 days F.P. No.1 (Sep 17)
Disobeying a command	9th Argylls	1 year IHL, commuted to 2 months F.P. No.1 (Dec 15)
Striking a sergeant	4th Gordons	40 days detention (Dec 14)
Disobeying an order	7th Black Watch	1 year IHL (Nov 17)
Attempting to strike a sergeant	1st Garr. Bn. S.Hrs.	5 years penal servitude (Jun 17)
Insubordination to N.C.O.	1st Glasgow Hrs	42 days F.P. No.1 (Nov 14)
Insubordination to N.C.O.	1st Glasgow Hrs	56 days F.P. No.1 (Nov 14)

57 BWA Stewart, letters to wife, 20 February, 11 April, 1918.
58 IWM 3834 Wrench, diary, 23 August, 1916, 4 July, 1918; ASHM N-E.11 Bowie, 'diary' (memoir) 3 January, 1917; IWM 4586 Douglas, memoir, pp.719, 724-725.
59 IWM 3834 Wrench, diary, 23 August, 1916.

The punishments for disobedience mentioned in miscellaneous sources[60] are summarised at Table 9.3. None of them relate to regular battalions, most to Territorials, but punishments are broadly in the same order as those awarded in 1st Black Watch.

In 1/8th Argylls in France in 1915-1916, there were a significant number of lesser cases, which almost invariably involved Field Punishment, mostly F.P. No.2, of seven to 21 days. Sometimes a fine or reversion of rank was awarded instead. In more serious cases, about a quarter, F.P. No.1 would be awarded, generally of seven to 14 days.

Neglect

Neglect of duty varied in seriousness and could often go to court martial. By far the most serious charge was sleeping while on sentry.[61] In 1/8th Argylls in France, Private McPherson was found guilty of sleeping while on sentry in the trenches on 30 October, 1915. He was sentenced to death, but the sentence was commuted to two years' I.H.L. by the Brigade Commander, then suspended by the Army Commander. Robert Johnston was on sentry duty in 9th Royal Scots in the summer of 1915, and recognised how easily exhausted men could be found asleep while standing at their post.

> I remember Aylmer Maxwell, my platoon commander in August, 1915 … He was visiting sentries early one morning and I was on duty in the platoon front. I was standing on the firestep, with my chin resting on my hands, looking out over No Man's Land. From far away, I heard his voice say, 'Sergeant Johnston,, are you asleep?' With a great effort, I managed after a pause to reply, 'No, sir, I think there is a Boche at the wire.' But this gave me a fright and I never again rested my head on my hands when on the firestep.

He notes that about this time, their Divisional commander, General Milne, knowing of the increase in the number of men charged with being asleep at their posts while on sentry, shocked the Division by an order that the death penalty would be imposed in any further case of this nature. Within a few weeks about 20 men of the Camerons and Argylls were sentenced to death. The measure had the desired effect. The sentences were read out to all units on three successive parades with excellent results. No further cases occurred. The sentences themselves were not confirmed by the General but were suspended.[62]

The approach to these offences varied considerably. In July 1915, in 1/6th Argylls, two men were each awarded 56 days, F.P. No.1 and one man was sentenced to nine months hard labour (three months commuted).[63] In the same month in 1/4th Black Watch, Alex Thomson "had to

---

60 ASHM War Diary 1/6th Battalion; IWM 4586 Douglas, memoir, pp.91-92; Forrester and Crawford, *War Diary 9th Argylls*; LC GS 0434 Dawson, diary, 31 December, 1914; GHM PB234 Smith, diary, 30 November, 1917; IWM 7508 Wyllie, diary,19 June, 1917; IWM 3460 Macmillan, diary, 19 November 1914.
61 Apart from the references cited below, see also Gillespie, *Letters from Flanders*, pp.175-176, 204, letters home, 31 May, 21 June, 1915; Webster, *Mesopotamia 1916-1917*, p.86, letter to mother, 12 February, 1917; BWA Stewart, diary, 13 August, 1915.
62 LC Transcripts, Johnston, memoir.
63 ASHM War Diary 1/6th Battalion.

put one of the sentries under arrest for sleeping on his post though it did seem a bit rough on the youngster as we had been working night and day" The Colonel, "not wishing to make it a court martial case – which would have been truly serious for the prisoner – dealt very leniently with him."[64] In 1/6th Black Watch, one soldier who persistently fell asleep on sentry was dealt with gently, being found another job by the sergeant before he got himself or his comrades into trouble.[65] And in Salonika in 1917, Private Diack, 2nd London Scottish, was caught asleep whilst on outpost duty and sentenced by the C.O. to 21 days .[66] By contrast, in July, 1916, Private McAteer, 1st Argylls, was court-martialled, found guilty of sleeping on his post, and sentenced to death, although this was commuted to five years' penal servitude, this sentence also commuted.[67]

Other cases of 'neglect' might lead to courts martial. Five are recorded in 1st Black Watch in 1918, including accidentally wounding a comrade with a Lewis Gun, and allowing a number of men to have their equipment off in the front system. These were all dealt with by F.P. No.1 or by reduction in rank.

At a lower level, in 1/8th Argylls, neglect of duty was punished in a similar way, according to the seriousness of the charge, with F.P. No.1 awarded on three occasions in France in 1915-1916, notably for neglect of duty when on guard and when acting as observation sentry. Loss of rations or kit by contrast was invariably punished by fines, with eight days' pay deducted for loss of iron rations, and various amounts of days' pay for loss of kit, the highest recorded being 10 days' pay for the loss of a kilt! Elsewhere, we see the loss of iron rations being dealt with simply by a caution in 8th Black Watch.[68] Possession of dirty rifles was also punished by stoppages of pay, in 1/8th Argylls, most frequently for seven days. Amongst other lesser misdemeanours, seven days F.P. No.2 were awarded for "failing to salute the Captain of the King's Guard at Buckingham Palace," while Private John Laing of 1st Black Watch received in September, 1914, "6 days confined to camp for smoking in the trenches."[69]

A number of cases of poor weapon handling in 1/8th Argylls appear to have been dealt with without court martial, all being punished by F.P. No.2. It is strange that these cases did not go to court martial, given that one involved shooting a comrade, and another involved a soldier wounding himself in the hand with a Very pistol. A string of such weapon handling accidents is recorded in other sources, including two serious wounds inflicted on comrades and one fatality, when a customs officer at Dundee docks was accidentally killed by a soldier of 2/9th Royal Scots.[70]

Avoiding censorship

There are several cases of convictions for avoiding censorship. In 9th Seaforths, the provost sergeant was court martialled and reduced to the ranks for forging the signature of the padre to

---

64   BWA Thompson, narrative, Vol.2, pp.44-45, 49.
65   IWM Books, Cooper, 'Domi Militacque' pp.322-324.
66   LC GS 0875 Julium, F., manuscript diary, 13, 15 January, 1917.
67   LC GS 0177 Boyle, diary, 21 July, 1 August, 1916.
68   IWM 4586 Douglas, memoir, p.397.
69   BWA Laing, Pte John, diary, 20 September, 1914.
70   IWM 10819 Brittan, diary, 5,7 March, 1915; GHM PB507 Wallace, diary 17 August, 1915; LC GS 0252 Campbell, diary, 3 January, 1917; IWM 3608 Anderson, manuscript memoir.

avoid censorship, although he had not given military information and the letter contained only words of love.[71] At the lower level in 1/8th Argylls, Private Jarvie was sentenced to 28 days F.P. No.1 for attempting to post a letter which had been irregularly censored, while Acting Corporal Milne reverted to private "for signing a certificate on a green envelope to the effect that the contents of the envelope referred to nothing but family and private matters, well knowing that the contents of the said envelope were not as described in the said envelope,"

Looting

Looting was a serious problem. Although Norman Macleod claims that, as far as 6th Camerons were concerned, "Cases of looting were unheard of, and not one was recorded in the battalion,"[72] this is flatly contradicted by Lieutenant Douglas Wilson, in the same battalion, who wrote at Thieushouk in July, 1918,

> There are regulations against helping oneself, but I turn a blind eye on what goes on (within reason) on the theory that what isn't taken will go to waste anyhow. A little of what you fancy is a somewhat shaky doctrine perhaps too easily bolstered up by facile excuses. I really have no pricks of conscience over the few luxuries of diet the lads (myself among them) manage to secure.[73]

And later he recalls looting the abandoned ruins of Caestre.[74] There are numerous other cases.[75] For example, on 4 December, 1914, 6th Gordons were billeted at Hazlebrook.

> Some of the officers were in a house evacuated by Germans who left a lot of jewelry and all sorts of stuff. A lot of souvenirs were taken. The C.S. and another got in in the evening and landed back with their pockets full. They gave away a lot of the things – I got a jolly nice case with a cigar and cigarette holders.[76]

Again, Norman Beaton, in 1/7th Gordons notes that, while in billets at Houplines, in September, 1916, "A few of us went away souveniring through the empty houses. All the gas metres that had not been burst open before we burst open, and collected quite a lot of money, which we kept of course for our own use as it belonged to nobody then."[77] Clearly Norman Macleod's view is somewhat roseate. Looting and damage to billets could cause ill-feeling with the locals, and the

---

71   THM Seaforths 81-2 Cooper, memoir, pp.47-48.
72   Macleod, *6th Camerons*, p.134.
73   LC GS 1761 Wilson, memoir, p.61.
74   Ibid., pp.93-94.
75   In addition to those cited below see Cluness, *Doing his bit,* p.43; IWM 7508 Wyllie, diary, 22, 26 November, 1916; IWM 4586 Douglas, memoir, pp.1183-1186, 1244; THM Camerons 93-35 Welsh, memoir, pp.40, 117-118; Royal Scots Museum, Beatson, diary, 3 November, 1915; IWM 2528 Bradbury, memoir, p.73; ASHM N-E1 Dalziel, diary, 26 December, 1914; *France 1916-1917-1918*, p.11.
76   LC GS 1422 Sanders, diary, 6 December, 1914.
77   GHM uncatalogued Beaton, memoir, p.141.

latter, in particular, had to be paid for.[78] Perhaps it was normal practice to turn a blind eye to looting, and that may be why it does not figure in our Part 2 Orders for either 1/8th Argylls or 1st Black Watch.

Theft

With regard to theft of army property, a few instances are recorded.[79] Much more common was the procedure of 'finding' kit to replace kit one had lost oneself. Robert Greig, who served in 2nd Seaforths, describes the problem rather well:

> It frequently happened that the soldier lost some part of his kit. When that happened, unless he lost it 'under shell fire,' the renewal was entered in his paybook for reduction of his pay. That being the case, it naturally followed that the men objected to paying for things lost, especially when they were not always in a position to keep a strict eye on their property. So they would go to their platoon sergeant or some one likely to know these things, and enquire as to what they lost, and invariably they got the answer – 'You know what you do: find it' – which being interpreted meant replace the article at the expense of someone else's kit. And if the man was too honest to do that, he had to pay for the article, and probably found that, for his honesty, someone had 'won' something from his kit, which generally had the effect of curing his honesty![80]

A blind eye was not always turned to theft. In 1/8th Argylls, Private Fowler was sentenced in France to six months imprisonment for stealing money, the property of a comrade, and this was the only long prison sentence awarded by court martial in the period which was not commuted or suspended. At the lower level, three cases of stealing from a comrade are recorded, one of which, stealing socks, was punished by 21 days Field Punishment.

S.I.W. and scrimshanking

Self-inflicted wounds (S.I.W.) were not unknown in the Highland regiments. We find reports of such in Regular, Territorial and New Army battalions[81] (1/6th Argylls, 11th Argylls, 1/4th Black Watch, 1/8th Black Watch, 1st Camerons, 1st Liverpool Scottish). Just to give one example, John Bowie, in 11th Argylls, records that on 17 September, 1915, in France, "An old time soldier with plenty to say and diddle recruits for booze could not stick this life and shot

---

78   Gillespie, *Letters from Flanders*, p.57, letter home 18 March, 1915; GHM PB107.1 Grant, 12 May, 1915.
79   Fraser, *Doctor Jimmy*, p.58; IWM 7508 Wyllie, diary, 16 November, 1918.
80   Chinese, *Doing his bit*, p.43. See also: LC GS 0418 Dane, diary, 9 September, 1915; THM 2013-072 (S) Braes, memoir, pp.5-6; IWM Books, Cooper, 'Domi Militaeque', p.18.
81   ASHM War Diary 1/6th Battalion, casualty return, 18 August, 1918; IWM 4586 Douglas, memoir, pp.415-416, 898-900, 1244-1245; IWM 5525 Steven, letter home, 5 July, 1915; THM Camerons 82-72 Sorel-Cameron, Maj. G.C.M., memoir, 'My Personal Experience in the German War 1914-15'; LC GS 1579 Taylor, memoir, p.9.

himself through the wrist. This is after doing 21 years' service of fighting in India, Africa & Egypt. He was sentenced (after being cured) to lose pension, & discharged as an undesirable character.[82] We do not know how the frequency of S.I.W.'s in Highland battalions compares with that in others, but the fact that the practice occurred is in itself an indication of the fallibility and normalcy of the Highland soldier. Suicides also occurred. In May, 1919, Captain Wyllie in occupied Turkey comments on the number of attempted suicides in his battalion, 1st Garrison Battalion Seaforth Highlanders.

> Lt McFarlane's servant attempted to shoot himself last night with his rifle but was prevented by the Mess Corporal who happened to see him in time. There have always been a large percentage of men in the Salonika Army who have been charged with this offence and it is believed that the climatic conditions have had a good deal to do with it.[83]

And in July he recorded that, "One of the men in the Transport attempted to cut his throat last night. He made a deep gash on each side of the throat with a razor but failed to do any serious damage. The doctor was sent for and put in eight stitches."[84]

Allied to the S.I.W. and a further indication of normalcy was the practice of feigning sickness in order to evade duty, in army parlance "scrimshanking." This was quite common,[85] although J.C. Cunningham, serving with 1st Argylls, observes that "the only time I ever heard of men openly talking of malingering" was when the rats assumed terrifying proportions in the Somme sector in 1915."[86] Captain Alex Scott in 7th Argylls sums up the problem rather well:

> The M.O … has more to do with the smooth running of the battalion machinery than almost anyone. It is he who steps in between the genuine sick man and the company officer, whose unending problem is how to keep his working parties up to strength. And it is the M.O. who, with open connivance of the Adjutant, makes life uncomfortable for the scrim-shanker. In every regiment there are some men who scrim-shank (malinger) only on special occasions, but there are also a few professionals who have nothing to learn in the art. Between these and the M.O. there is constant war … the trouble when we are actually in the firing-line is that men often become seriously ill before they complain at all. But in billets, the rumour that a heavy fatigue is impending produces at once a crop of mysterious aches and coughs.[87]

---

82 ASHM N-E11 Bowie, 'diary' (memoir).
83 IWM 7508 Wyllie, diary, 9 May, 1919.
84 Ibid., 14 July, 1919.
85 In addition to the sources cited below, see also: Craig Barr, *Home Service*, p.275; IWM 11144 PP MacKay, diary, 3 August, 1917, p.33; GHM PB1892.3.18 McDonald, 'Uncle Harper's Duds', p.9; GHM PB1892.3.1 Youngson, memoir, p.6; IWM 14335 Marr, memoir, pp.23-24; LC GS 1023 Maclaren, I, letter to mother, 30 September, 1916; IWM 2854 Bates, letters to fiancée 2 September 1916, 27 February 1917; IWM 1862 Craig-Brown, diary, 11 January, 1915; Fennah, *Retaliation*, p.131; IWM 3834 Wrench, diary, 16 May 1917.
86 LC GS 0409 Cunningham, notes by him, written 1976.
87 One of the Jocks (Capt Alex Scott), *Odd Shots*, pp.138-141.

Expedients used to claim sickness were imaginative: a man pours undiluted creosol into his boots so that it might inflame a scratch on his ankle;[88] another ties his putties tight round his legs to simulate varicose veins;[89] a soldier with a sore hand attempts to give himself blood-poisoning by inserting a penny inside the bandage.[90] Some were rather less well-calculated. Captain Bates, M.O. with the 1/8th Black Watch, reports:

> I had a rather tough nut to deal with yesterday. He turned up with the sick and complained of pain round the shoulder and collar bone. Didn't know how it came on – no accident, no blow, just came on "suddenly" during the last month (!) He said first that his collar bone "gave" and later that it "cracked". The dialogue ran somewhat as follows:
> Yours truly: "So your collar bone 'gives' and 'cracks'?
> The Warrior: "Yes, doctor, it both 'gives' and 'cracks' "
> Y.T.: "Quite sure it doesn't ever 'crack' and 'give'?"
> T.W.: "No sir, never 'cracks' and 'gives' but 'gives' and 'cracks' "(!)
> Y.T.: "Well, you won't die of it and that's the sort of ailment you'd better keep to yourself."
>
> I don't think we'll see *him* again. He was enlisted under compulsion and had the air of a scrimshanker from tip to toe which I am just beginning to learn. There are very few of them in this battalion, I'm glad to say.[91]

Such scrimshanking could lead to court martial. One soldier of 1/8th Argylls was court-martialled at Etaples for feigning disease and was sentenced to 14 days F.P. No.1. Another soldier in the battalion received the same sentence without court martial for reporting sick without sufficient cause. One by-product of scrimshanking was that men who were genuinely sick might be disbelieved,[92] or that they might hold back from reporting sick so as not to be accused of scrimshanking themselves.[93] In early January, 1917, for example, Andrew Gilmour moved up to the support line with 14th Argylls.

> It was my turn to stage P.U.O. – I collapsed under the additional weight of a pick and shovel. There was nothing unknown really, coffee from shell hole water made me violently ill; but my reception when I finally staggered to our M.O.'s dugout was underserved – 'So it was the sight of a job of work that made you feel faint?' 'I suggest you take my temperature before you insult me further,' I hissed. He did so and gave me a chit to present at the Casualty Clearing Station.[94]

---

88 Gillespie, *Letters from Flanders*, p.127, letter home, 2 May, 1915.
89 ASHM N-E11 Bowie, 'diary' (memoir).
90 THM Camerons 93-35 Welsh, p.109.
91 IWM 2854 Bates, letter to fiancée 20 September 1916.
92 IWM Books Brooke, 'Wait for it', pp.312-313.
93 GHM PB375 Pailthorpe, memoir, p.33.
94 LC GS 0627 Gilmour, 'The Other Enemy', *The Beam*, September, 1982, pp.34-35.

Cowardice

It has already been noted that, out of only 18 men shot for cowardice during the war, one, James Adamson of 7th Camerons, was a Highland soldier.[95] He was found guilty of, "When on active service misbehaving before the enemy in such a manner as to show cowardice in that he in the trenches on 28th July 1917 having previously been warned, refused to and did not take part in a raid on the enemy's trenches at 7 p.m. on the date aforesaid, for fear of his personal safety." There were other more fortunate cases. In 1/8th Argylls, Private Powell was tried for "misbehaving before the enemy in such a manner as to show cowardice in that he in the field on 13th Nov. 1916 when in the front-line assembly trench when ordered to proceed over the parapet with his battalion to attack the German lines did not do so through fear for his personal safety." This was clearly at Beaumont-Hamel. He was sentenced to fifteen years penal servitude, a sentence confirmed by Brigade with a recommendation that it should be suspended. We will return to this question in our chapter on Courage and Failure.

Gambling

Gambling was another fairly common vice. In 1st Seaforths, on board ship, en route to France from India in 1914,

> Being now on active service, Field Punishment No.1 was introduced and half-a-dozen Crown and Anchor devotees captured 'tween decks by the Provost Sergeant and his Policeman, were awarded seven days. At sea, with no waggon or gun wheels readily available, the anchor cable ranked on the fo'c'sle was resorted to for the one hour after 'retreat' tie-up. The Bosun enquired of me as I chatted with a comrade on the for'ard well-deck, 'Wot 'orrible murder 'ave these blokes up there committed?'[96]

John Cooper trained with 3/4th Black Watch at Ripon in 1916, and notes the prevalence of gambling:

> The gamblers got busy too on pay-nights. I have seen men sit up half the night, with a candle under a bucket, playing 'Nap' or 'Banker' until most of them had lost all their pay. Gambling was forbidden, but much of it went on. Any N.C.O. could stop it if he thought fit, or dared, but few of the juniors would do so, although the sergeants did. There was also another gambling game, 'Crown and Anchor' played with the assistance of dice, at which much money changed hands. The man who had a 'Crown and Anchor' set could make money fast, but of course it went fast on drink or other riotous living. The one game of this nature which was tolerated was 'House', because it was played only for very small stakes, and was really more in the nature of a sweepstake than anything else.[97]

---

95 Corns & Hughes-Wilson, *Blindfold and Alone*, pp.208-211.
96 IWM 11334 Robertson, memoir, p.4.
97 IWM Books, Cooper, 'Domi Militaeque', p.34.

Prostitution

Prostitution and its consequences were also common, although I have no evidence that this was a greater or lesser problem in Highland regiments than in others. Alex Moffat was with 1st London Scottish at Villeneuve St Georges on L.O.C. duties in October, 1914. About 35 to 40 years later he met one of his old comrades, called Ballard.

> 'Oh,' I said, 'I remember. all those years ago at Villeneuve St Georges, you were then 16 years of age and nicknamed Baby Ballard, very shortly to be sent home as under-age.' He replied, 'You are quite right … I remember well asking you along with three others to take us (as you spoke good French) to a red light house. This you agreed to do stipulating that there was to be 'no funny business.' I also remember that on being seated there with Madame drinking coffee and the girls being paraded you eventually said to us, 'Come on chaps, out you come. I told you there was to be no funny business' and I can still remember the look of consternation on Madame's face as we marched out.'[98]

In mid-April, 1916, the South African Scottish embarked at Alexandria for France. "There was one regrettable incident, when one of our fellows jumped over the side because he was afraid of reporting he had V.D. which would be reported to his wife if he went to hospital."[99]

Mutiny

Whingeing of course was the soldier's privilege, and it is not surprising that even some of those who volunteered to serve should re-act against the rigours of the military system and the imposition of military discipline, or the harsh living conditions at the front.[100] This could be a problem if soldiers publicised their grievances to the newspapers,[101] but there was no real danger at the front, unless discontent turned to mutiny. Actual mutiny was rare before the Armistice, although there was apparently some involvement of Highland soldiers in the trouble at Etaples,[102] and there was on occasion behaviour which was mutinous in spirit. John Bowie, in 11th Argylls, records a refusal by the men to accept lousy blankets, at Basingstoke, in February, 1915.[103] Philip Christison relates a visit to his battalion, 6th Camerons, after they had suffered heavy losses at the beginning of the Third Battle of Ypres:

> On Saturday 4th August General Gough, who was in command of the 5th Army, inspected our remnant. He remained mounted and said: "Well done, you did your best, I deplore your losses. I am sure you will all want to avenge their deaths so I am making you up with a large

---

98 LC GS 1124 Moffat, Alex, typescript diary, addendum.
99 LC GS 0132 Betteridge, memoir, vol.1, p.22.
100 See for example, THM Seaforths 89-26 Crask, letter to mother 1 July, 1915; Gilmour, *An Eastern Cadet's Anecdotage*, p.19.
101 ASHM N-E5 Main, letter to wife, Win, 4 August, 1915.
102 IWM 4370 Christison, memoir, p.44.
103 ASHM N-E11 Bowie, 'diary' (memoir).

draft so that you can return and avenge your comrades." A man in the rear shouted angrily: "You're a bloody butcher". He rode off taking no notice, but after that he became known in the 5th Army as "Butcher Gough"[104]

Henry Coates served with 1st London Scottish. He describes mutinous feelings in the last year of the war, though not necessarily in his battalion:

> There were times when out at rest in 1918 we used to go perhaps to the local military cinema to see something like Charlie Chaplin … When the King's photograph appeared at the end of the show you would get rude remarks made, soldiers blowing what in those days were termed raspberries, because we were very near the point when our troops would have mutinied. They were being asked to spend too much blood, being sent back into the line when they'd been wounded perhaps twice or even three times.[105]

After the Armistice, there were several mutinous incidents, relating variously to the perceived unfairness of demobilisation, local breakdowns of administration, resentment of the continued application of petty military discipline, officers' failure to adjust to the changed circumstances and expectations, and a degree of political militancy. Thus, there is discontent and/or incidents recorded in 1/5th Gordons,[106] 1/4th Seaforths,[107] 1st London Scottish,[108] 16th Battalion C.E.F. (Canadian Scottish),[109] and the Machine Gun Battalion of 51st Highland Division.[110] Discontent among 3rd Black Watch at Haddington[111] spread to Constantinople,[112] when a number of discontented men were sent from the Black Watch to join 12th Argylls there in 1919. Most seriously, at least one Canadian Highlander was involved in the explosive situation at the Canadians' demobilisation camp near Rhyl, where five men were killed in a mutiny. Roy Henley of 42nd Battalion C.E.F. was court-martialled, found guilty and given three years. He was sent to Parkhurst where he spent three months before he was released and sent home to Canada.[113]

Other misdemeanours

Alongside the more significant offences, there were of course a string of minor offences including failing to look after horses properly (through ignorance), lending out a battalion bicycle, smiling

---

104 IWM 4370 Christison, memoir, p.65.
105 IWM 9833 Coates, interview.
106 GHM PB1639 Kemp, memoir, Vol 3, pp.86-88.
107 LC GS 0895 King, memoir; IWM 3834 Wrench, diary, 7, 27, 30 December, 1918, 2, 3, 6, 7, 8, 20, 31 January, 4, 6, 7 February, 1919.
108 LC WF Recollections, S18, Sloan, memoir.
109 Urquhart, *Canadian Scottish*, pp.326, 330.
110 IWM 2528 Bradbury, memoir, p.88.
111 IWM Books Cooper, 'Domi Militaeque', pp.287, 290-292, 295-297.
112 IWM 7508 Wyllie, diary, 21, 23 September, 1919; IWM Books, Cooper, 'Domi Militaeque', pp.310-311, 334, 339-340, 348-349.
113 LC Transcripts, Tape 850, Henley, interview.

on parade, and poor personal hygiene.[114] Colonel 'Jack' Stewart had charge of a large draft en route to Mesopotamia to join 2nd Black Watch.

> I have however one loathsome individual, a B.W. man who is rather 'off his onion' and absolutely declined to wash. His idiosyncrasy did not become known until he was in a verminous condition, but since then he has been confined to a cell, clothed in blue hospital kit, and has been compulsorily scrubbed by two hefty Highlanders daily, so I hope to land him clean and 'a man and a brother.'[115]

More amusing, though not for the men, are punishments in 1/8th Argylls for "committing a nuisance" in the camp lines (seven days F.P. No.1) and urinating in a communications trench (seven days F.P.No.2).

General points

Perhaps the most remarkable feature of the disciplinary record in Part 2 Orders for 1/8th Argylls and 1st Black Watch is the number of days Field Punishment No.1 awarded. In 1/8th Argylls, this was 984 days in the 605 days the battalion was in France from 7 May, 1915 to 31 December, 1916. In other words, at any one time there were on average either one or two men of the battalion undergoing F.P. No.1. This is perhaps not what one would expect from this most highland of Territorial battalions. Rather than indicating an informal approach to discipline based on mutual respect, it demonstrates that, however informally officers and N.C.O.'s chose to behave towards the men, the informality was backed up by stern discipline when necessary. In 1st Black Watch in 1918,[116] the total number of days F.P.No.1 awarded in courts martial alone was 1,067, such that, even without lower level-punishments, on average at any one time three soldiers of the battalion were undergoing F.P. No.1, twice the number in 1/8th Argylls in 1915-1916. This suggests that the exercise of discipline was even sterner in 1st Black Watch than 1/8th Argylls. But we can only speculate on the reason. Did this reflect the difference between Regular and Territorial discipline, or did it reflect the difference between a battalion composed largely of conscripts in 1918 and one composed of volunteers in 1915-1916? We do not know.

But how was F.P. No.1 actually administered? It is not certain to what extent the full humiliating penalty of being tied up to a wheel or post for an hour a day was actually imposed. As we have seen, it was certainly used in 1st Seaforths, on board ship, en route to France from India in 1914.[117] It was also applied in 13th Battalion C.E.F., where two men sentenced to F.P.No.1 for drunkenness in February, 1915, are described as tied to carts.[118] And it was being applied in 1/5th Gordons, a Territorial battalion, in December, 1918, when, in the restless period following

---

114 See for example: IWM 14340 McArthur, diary, 26 June, 1915; IWM 3449 Cordner C., memoir, GHM PB107.1 Grant, diary, 13 May, 10 June, 1915; LC GS 0875 Julian, diary, 21 April, 1917; IWM 16387 Mcleod, diary, 6, 7 July, 1916; BWA Gordon, resume of letter home, 20 May, 1916.
115 BWA Stewart, letter to wife, 1 March, 1917.
116 BWA Part 2 Orders, 1st Battalion Black Watch, 1918.
117 IWM 11334 Robertson, memoir, p.4.
118 IWM 10819 PP Brittan, diary, 25 February, 1915.

the Armistice, Corporal James Shirrefs noted, "Mutiny in the Battalion tonight. The men … released a prisoner who was strapped [to] posts doing No.1 punishment. The Officers could do nothing with them and they were successful in keeping the man out of arrest."[119]

But to a certain extent, F.P. No.1 was the gentle option. It is clear that many sentences of imprisonment were commuted to F.P. No.1 so that the soldier concerned could not use his sentence to evade his duty to serve in the trenches. About June, 1918, Lieutenant Leslie Cooper, serving in 7th Seaforths, was detailed as a member of a court martial of a private of the 9th Battalion.

> We found him guilty and passing sentence stipulated that it must be served in the line. About this time some men deliberately got a court martial in the hopes that they would get a long sentence which would be served at the base. I heard later that the man made a nuisance of himself. Every time he was warned for a working party he took his boots off and the regimental police had a job getting them on again.[120]

Likewise, Private Douglas recalled that, when 11th Argylls were relieved from the trenches in the Arras sector in September, 1917, "As soon as we arrived at Blangy Park Camp, an escort was waiting for a private in our Platoon called Walker, who was doing 90 days Field Punishment. Walker had been doing his turn in the trenches along with the rest of us, and as soon as he came out of the trenches, he was again put under arrest and put back into the Batt. Guard Tent along with the other battalion prisoners."[121]

Another harsh punishment was deprivation of rank. Compared with imprisonment and F.P. No.1, this may seem a relatively mild punishment, but, quite apart from the humiliation, the consequences for Senior N.C.O.'s were considerable. On 25 November, 1915, Colour Sergeant Guthrie in 1/6th Black Watch observed that "Q.M.S. Miller & Dr Mjr Macneill are up for a Court Martial, for being Drunk and absent from quarters."[122] Then on 6 December he reported:

> The two men who were court martialled, one of whom was the Acting Q.M.S. whose job I have got, have both been reduced to the ranks and sent back to duty with the Company as ordinary privates: hard on them, but still harder on their poor wives & bairns at home who will be reduced from Sergts' Separation Allowance to that of ordinary privates. Punishments for drunkenness are heavy whilst on active service.[123]

The process was also humiliating. Daniel McFarlane describes the procedure applied in 7th Camerons while on the march from France to Belgium after the Armistice.

> One morning the band failed to turn up and all the Battalion was drawn up awaiting them. When they eventually appeared they were anything but soldierly. They were unkempt, unwashed and unshaven. it was obvious that all the band had been on the skite the night

---

119 GHM PB3758 Shirrefs, diary, 9 December, 1918.
120 THM Seaforths 81-2 Cooper, memoir, p.181.
121 IWM 4586 Douglas, memoir, pp.91-92.
122 BWA Guthrie, letter to his wife Crissie, 25 November, 1915.
123 BWA Guthrie, letter to his wife Crissie, 6 December, 1915.

before. The drum major was obviously not sober and was marching at the head of the band with glazed eyes and unsteady gait. In due course, they appeared on a charge of the orderly room and received punishment. One of which I can recall was the public humiliation of the Drum Major when he was reduced to Corporal. This was a serious business for him, as he was a regular soldier of many years service, including India. He had been out in 1914 … In the presence of the Battalion he had to remove his glengarry which revealed his age, then his stripes as Drum Major were stripped from his sleeve He seemed to have finished his war on a wrong note.[124]

John Forbes Knowles witnessed the punishment of a Senior N.C.O. of 1/4th Gordons at Bedford in December, 1914:

When we got back to Bedford we were lined up on either side of Dynefor Road to witness the punishment of a court martial. It was quite dark except for the street lamps. I could not see the face of the prisoner clearly, but he seemed a matured man – sergeant Stewart was the name read out in the indictment. He was accused of beating a private with his fists on the ribs and back. Captain Lyon, junior Major, read out the charge and the decision of the court martial, which was reduction to the ranks. The Sergeant Major cut off his stripes, while the Sergeant of Police marched him up and made him eyes right the Colonel as he was marched back. It was not a pleasant scene to have a share in. One cannot help pitying the culprit, though the punishment was just. I am sure most of the men felt as I did, and there would have been a bit of a row had the punishment been for any other offence such as insubordination.[125]

In 1/8th Argylls, the Pipe Major from 1915 was Willie Laurie, a Ballachulish man.

It was 'somewhere in France,' and a sergeant from Ballachulish was reduced to the ranks by a Court Martial, the sentence being duly carried out in front of the Battalion on parade. When the ceremony was over, the C.O. gave the command to march off in column of route, and Willie Laurie turned to the band and said: 'Don't play.' The whole Battalion marched silently out of the field and on to the hard road – and then Willie gave his second order. Turning round as he marched, he ordered; 'Gie them "A man's a man for a' that".' Which they did. It was Willie's tribute to his unfortunate neighbour.[126]

Some soldiers have commented on the overall nature of discipline in their battalions. Their views give a little weight to the notion of variance between Regulars, Territorial and New Army battalions. Private James McGregor Marshall was a wartime volunteer to the Black Watch who was drafted to the 2nd (Regular) Battalion in 1915. "The discipline was very severe," he wrote, "but it learned us some things we knew nothing of in civil life – clean living, religious

---

124 THM Camerons 89-17 McFarlane, memoir.
125 GHM PB1699 Anon., 'As We Go up the Line to Death,' p.23, extract from diary of John Forbes Knowles, 21 December, 1914.
126 Malcolm, *Argyllshire Highlanders*, pp.143-144.

prestige, for all were Presbyterians, duty, & loyalty to Scotland, to be spick & span on parade."[127] Nevertheless, there are several recorded instances of a soft touch being applied in the administration of discipline in Regular battalions. Graham Hutchison, an officer with 2nd Argylls, noted the relatively compassionate way in which drunkenness was handled in the battalion in France in 1914:

> Our warriors out of Glasgow… unused to the customs of Continental Europe, learned some bitter lessons. But we dealt with them in kindly fashion, even when wild intoxication sent them reeling to their barns or when they missed parading for the trenches. Sympathy, tolerance, and some knowledge of the frailty of human nature were needed in those days. The charge for failure to parade was that of 'desertion upon active service in that he failed to appear at the appointed place …' The punishment – death. But though men sometimes faced the tribunal of a Court Martial on such a charge, we know that, however willing the spirit, the flesh was weak when soaked with the wines of Flanders.[128]

By contrast, John Cooper served in a Territorial battalion, 1/6th Black Watch. He wrote:

> One might have thought discipline lax. The truth is it was very real though not apparent to the casual observer. Crime, i.e. army crime, was rare, because no one could benefit himself by deserting from the only place where he could reckon on finding his bread and water sure. Petty crime was not often punished, although N.C.O.'s and officers reproved sharply those who did not keep themselves and their goods in order. Even serious things were sometimes not even reported, for the penalties were severe, and no N.C.O. or officer cared to get any of his own men into serious trouble if it could be avoided.[129]

Elsewhere he expands on this theme.

> In France officers did not care to 'crime' men unless for very serious offences, and because the penalties after a court-martial were very heavy, even for slight offences, many went unpunished, or only lightly punished, by our own officers. Military law is proverbially, amongst civilians, a byword for harshness; but really it is not so, owing to the spirit of fairness in which it is worked. … I must say very few officers I ever had any dealings with appeared to enjoy dealing out punishment, and most were lenient. It was a saying amongst us that a court-martial was the fairest trial a man could get. That is not saying, of course, that the sentence inflicted was always fair in our opinion. I never saw a court-martial actually in progress, but men who had taken part as accused, witnesses or escorts at such trials, always maintained that the accused got the benefit of any doubt, and that the evidence admitted had to be clear and any contradiction between witnesses went far towards acquittal, even though several points might appear fairly conclusively proved.[130]

---

127 BWA Marshall, 'Reminiscences.'
128 Hutchison, *Warrior*, p.57.
129 IWM Books, Cooper, 'Domi Militaeque', p.91.
130 Ibid., pp.322-324.

Claud Low, responsible for conducting a draft of London Scottish men to 1st Battalion in France in November, 1914, however, attributed the good behaviour of these early volunteers to their middle-class background.

> Our men were crowded up to an extent probably never experienced by any of them previously, but they did not seem to mind & were all cheerful & happy. Already I feel proud of these fellows; their discipline is good & the drafts from other Regiments on board are in my opinion considerably less efficient in that respect … it makes all the difference in the world when men find themselves huddled together for long periods with comrades who have been brought up in decent homes; they cannot behave otherwise than like gentlemen & their habits leave practically nothing to be desired.[131]

Norman Macleod gives a very upbeat picture of the discipline in 6th Camerons, a New Army battalion:

> Front-line infantry soldiers can only speak of front-line infantry troops, and so far as these men were concerned allegations of drunkenness and loose living are scandalously untrue. These men about whom so much has been written were not sordid mercenaries out for rapine and loot. They were volunteers in the truest sense of that word, young men inspired with a great sense of duty, and ready to sacrifice very life in duty's cause.[132]

According to the regimental history, amongst the new recruits to 7th Camerons in December, 1914, "Crime or petty offences were practically unknown."[133] It appears that amongst these keen Kitchener volunteers there was less need to wield the disciplinary stick:

> Looking back, it appears extraordinary how willingly and uncomplainingly the men had borne the crowding and many discomforts and hard work. For a time seventy hours a week had been the programme of training. Volunteers in the truest sense of the word, they cheerfully and uncomplainingly for a shilling a day endured a state of affairs which would have produced something more than discontent in pre-war days. Crime, even the usual minor military offences, was practically unknown. They had no time for it, they were so keen and terribly in earnest to learn the profession of arms. It was no uncommon sight to see men in their huts, after a strenuous day's training, studying drill books and discussing military problems … These men were not conscripts. Patriotism and 'esprit de corps' alone influenced them, and they submitted themselves willingly and unquestioningly to rigorous discipline and hard training solely in order to serve their country. Herein lies the secret of success. It was sometimes difficult to regular officers to understand this spirit.[134]

Likewise, when, in September, 1915, Captain J.B. Lorimer, serving with the 8th (Reserve) Battalion Cameron Highlanders, attended a banquet given by the Royal Burgh of Tain, "the

---

131 IWM 6702 Low, letter to his wife, Noanie, 24 November, 1914.
132 Macleod, *6th Camerons*, p.134.
133 Craig-Brown, *Historical Records*, Vol.4, p.274.
134 Ibid., Vol.4, p.278.

Burgh seemed very pleased with us and seemed struck with the fact that during the 4 months we have been here not a single police case involving a soldier had appeared in the Burgh Courts."[135]

There were certainly examples of compassion and leniency shown by officers in all types of battalions. While conducting a draft from base camp to 1st Black Watch, Lionel Sotheby noted:

> My sergeant, McWilliams, has just brought me a crime made out against 3 of my men, who got into the train this afternoon & were accused of pocketing a bottle of wine. I am sorry for the men as to be confined in a train for 48 hours is no joke, and I am prepared to be lenient, as we are at the end of the journey. If we were going to have another long stop like this, I should make an example of them, to stop it recurring again, but as we shall be at the front in the morning & I know what it is for a man to start badly with a crime against him, I will let them off. I told McWilliams that & he was pleased. I shall give them a good lecture in the morning, however. I am taking full responsibility for tearing up the crime, but I am prepared & do not mind what anybody may say, as I think I have done right.[136]

At Bailleul in November, 1914, the Commanding Officer of 1st Glasgow Highlanders, a Territorial battalion, tried Private Baillie for being drunk in charge of the waggon bearing the officers' baggage, and let him off on the understanding that he would turn teetotal for the rest of his life![137] Another instance of understanding in the same battalion is recorded by Norman Macmillan, in 1st Glasgow Highlanders, when in the trenches he deserted his post to find out if two men from another post, who had gone out to reconnoitre, had actually returned.

> I was going round to my post again, having barely been away a minute when I heard Sergeant Mackinnon's voice. 'Private Macmillan, why are you away from your post?' I called back the reason just as I entered our trench again. Suddenly I discovered that Major Bock and Captain Menzies were in the trench. Major Bock understood the situation but pointed out to me (more in sorrow than in anger, I thought) how serious my infringement was, even tho' made with good intentions, and that men had got two years for as simple a mistake before. However, he was very decent about it in not taking my name or particulars.[138]

More examples come from other Territorial battalions. In December, 1918, after the armistice, Corporal James Shirrefs, in 1/5th Gordons, was brought up before the Commanding Officer for the crime of giving a junior N.C.O. a "shaking up", but got off with a severe reprimand, his Company officer having spoken up strongly on his behalf.[139] Another case of compassionate treatment is recorded by Sam McDonald in his history of 51st Highland Division:

> One day in the Orderly room, a C.O. had brought before him a man who had just come out from home with the drafts. This man was charged with seriously assaulting an officer. It appeared that whenever he had arrived in France an Orderly Officer who inspected the

---

135 IWM 7408 Lorimer, letters to mother 21 September, 1915.
136 LC GS 1507 Sotheby, diary, 27 January, 1915.
137 IWM 3460 Macmillan, diary, 25 November 1914.
138 IWM 3460 Macmillan, diary, 22 March, 1915.
139 GHM PB3758 Shirrefs, diary, 5-9 December, 1918.

draft found fault with this man because of the dirty condition of his clothes. The man explained that he was not to blame, as on the boat his clothes had been almost destroyed. The officer had said 'Go and tell that to the Marines.' The man replied quietly, 'It is true, sir,' upon which the Officer coming up close to him shouted angrily, 'Don't answer me back,' and at the same time flicked the man on the legs with a stick. This was too much for the man, who then trounced the Officer soundly. In presence of that Officer's C.O. the man admitted what he had done, and expressed regret. He was then sent to his own C.O. to be dealt with. This was really a case for a Court Martial but the latter had a quality for understanding men, and knowing how to deal with them.

The C.O. established that the man had been a bank clerk in Burnmouth before the war, but had got into trouble with drink and had been sent to the Argentine by his parents. He was George Deans, known previously to the C.O. as Buzzer, the son of the late Minister of the parish. He had returned from the Argentine to join up. The C.O. let him off with a caution, saying,

'I believe from what I know of you, that there is something fine in you. I am to trust you and give you your chance. I know I should send you up for Court Martial, but instead I am to let you off. Now go, and do the best you can to make good, and let the home folks be proud of you.' 'Thank you, Sir, I will try my hardest,' was the response.

The fellow subsequently became a most efficient N.C.O., got a commission, and ended the war with a D.S.O. and an M.C.[140]

Douglas Wilson, Lewis Gun Officer with 5th Camerons, a Kitchener battalion, records an instance of turning a blind eye in May, 1918.

Early one morning ... passing quietly through the long grass of the orchard I came across a young Jock surreptitiously milking a cow behind a hedge. Intent on his work he did not hear me and I made no sound, waiting until the mess-tin was brimming. The operation over, he straightened up, slapped the flank of the source of supply, turned, and confronted me. His palsy was such that the tin all but slipped from his fingers. I hurriedly steadied it. 'Do you know what the unforgiveable sin is, my lad?' He didn't, and the cow with a fine unconcern for obstructions switched its indulgent fly-whisk and moved placidly away. 'Well, it's the sin of being found out. Don't let it occur again. And it's the long jump for you if one drop of that milk is spilt. Now beat it. You haven't seen me this morning, have you? Understand?' Exit. This soldier later appeared at company orderly room expressing the desire to become a Lewis Gunner.[141]

The Canadians were arguably a case apart. An N.C.O. of the 13th Battalion C.E.F. wrote:

Discipline in ours. This is varied. It is not good compared with the regulars, but it is quite good all the same, and I have never yet heard of a man refusing to obey an officer's order. The Canadians as a whole have a frightful name all over the country for bad discipline, but that

---

140 GHM PB1892.3.18 McDonald, 'Uncle Harper's Duds', pp.86-89.
141 LC GS 1761 Wilson, memoir, p.21.

is earned by not saluting when on leave. But after all these things are not the important part of discipline. What is important is to get orders obeyed and that is done very well indeed.[142]

In his history of 16th Battalion C.E.F. (Canadian Scottish), Colonel Urquhart offers a fascinating appraisal of the soldiers of the battalion. They were characterised, he felt, by independence and individualism, including a fair sprinkling of high-spirited contrary spirits, intolerant of leader's faults and errors. Thus there came to be a certain freedom in disciplinary arrangements, what he describes as "the discipline of general consent."

> It is the end that matters, in this case the willingness of men to fight on, and die fighting. The rigid and domineering type of discipline could never have secured those results in the Canadians. They were self-reliant men, fighting for a cause; they, therefore, expected to be treated as men, and that basis of relationship established they were prepared to act their part without fear of consequences.[143]

Conclusions

Reviewing the application of coercive discipline within the Highland regiments as a whole, we see that, while discipline was often exercised with a human face, underpinning the humanity was a rigorous code of punishment which was routinely applied across the various battalions. Highland soldiers were not exempt from the extreme penalty, but below that we see also the imposition of stiff sentences of imprisonment when appropriate, as well as the liberal use of Field Punishment No.1, with some evidence that the humiliating spectacle of being tied to a post or wagon wheel was enforced, at least in some battalions. There is little evidence that Highland soldiers were somehow subject to a gentler code of discipline than their other Army colleagues, based on mutual respect. The underlying backbone of coercive Army discipline was there to be applied when necessary and was unhesitatingly used. There is some evidence to suggest that discipline may have been more relaxed in Territorial battalions than in the Regulars. There is also some evidence that the volunteers of 1914 and 1915 did not really need the big stick to be wielded for as volunteers they were doing a job they had willingly chosen to do. There is also ample evidence to show that officers, including Regular officers, would administer formal discipline with compassion, ensuring, for example, that a completely exhausted man on sentry duty did not potentially face the death penalty for falling asleep. This is not however sufficient to suggest a code of discipline grounded primarily in mutual respect. The iron rod of coercive discipline was always there, available to be used when necessary in serious cases and to set an example. As we have acknowledged in the introduction, however, the threat of harsh punishments was only one way in which discipline could be maintained. Much depended on self-discipline, and on the relations between officers, N.C.O.'s and men. In the next chapter we will look at how these relationships worked, and hopefully throw more light on the forces which bound a unit together as an effective disciplined force.

---

142 quoted in Fetherstonhaugh, *13th Battalion*, p.22.
143 Urquhart, *Canadian Scottish*, pp.331-345.

10

Hierarchy

> "I am proud of every man in my platoon. I know them all & stick up for them, & I fairly smile with delight when I see some little sign that they like me."[1]

The previous chapter examined the coercive exercise of discipline and concluded that this was a fundamental part of the exercise of discipline in the Highland regiments. Such coercion was, however, only one side of the picture. Discipline was not only maintained through the strict application of rules, but also through the relations which existed between the ranks. This chapter is devoted to examining the way relationships between ranks operated in the Highland regiments, and particularly any evidence for that mutual respect and informality across rank divides which is sometimes said to characterise them.

At the head of the battalion pyramid was the Commanding Officer. More than anyone else, he set the tone of the battalion. He needed to provide regimental pride, authority, advice, encouragement and backbone. It was an awesome responsibility. Colonel 'Jack' Stewart took over command of 2nd Black Watch in Mesopotamia in April, 1917, but he could still harbour secret doubts about his command in August: "sometimes I get panic stricken and think that things are all awry, but I'm getting over that feeling."[2] The C.O. was potentially the loneliest man in the battalion. At times, the only person in whom he could confide might be his wife at home. Stewart touched on the loneliness of command in a letter to his wife:

> The best of writing to you is … second that although a good deal of what I write may appear, and probably is, frivolous, it takes me away from 'shop.' Out here I am more or less alone as there is and of course must always be, a fairly well-defined line between C.O. and the 'rest', so forgive any frivol old girl. I have to keep 'the children' happy and contented, and some frivol occasionally is good not only for them but for me too.[3]

This loneliness might be compounded for Regular or ex-Regular officers by the social changes consequent on the expansion of the officer corps. Colonel Stewart was pleased to have some of

---

1 IWM 8592 Macgregor, letter to wife Dulcie, 9 March, 1918.
2 BWA Stewart, letter to wife, 5 August, 1917.
3 Ibid., letter to wife, 17 October, 1917.

his old friends near him when he re-joined his battalion in August, 1918, "for nice as the 'children' are, they have different ideas etc and one is apt to feel rather lonely sometimes."[4]

Leadership styles might vary between informal and strictly disciplinarian, but the ideal style would combine strong direction and efficiency with humanity. Considering first the relationship between C.O.'s and their officers, it is quite clear that on occasion, this relationship failed. When it did so, one might discover not an officers' mess held together by mutual esteem and common purpose, but a dysfunctional grouping held together principally by army discipline.

Such a situation appears to have arisen in 9th Black Watch, where 'Jack' Stewart, then a major and second-in-command, was, between July and October, 1915, very critical of the snappily strict and condemnatory attitude of his C.O., Colonel Lloyd.[5] Even his adjutant asked to resign his post. Eventually, in November, 1915, Colonel Lloyd was sent home ill, and the problem, if there truly was one, disappeared with him.

In December, 1915, Major C.W.E. Gordon, a regular Black Watch officer, arrived to take on the role of second-in-command of 8th Gordons. His Commanding Officer was Greenhill Gardyne. Gordon was not impressed.[6] "He is no good whatever & knows nothing about the game as it is played now. He is quite frank about it & he has told me, he has lost his nerve, & also knows nothing of trench war & he certainly does not."[7] Perhaps unsurprisingly, on 1 March, 1916, Gordon was ordered to take over command from Gardyne, who was sent home on account of ill health, Gordon having evidently engineered the move himself. Another case is provided by 8th Black Watch, where the Medical Officer, Johnathan Bates, having appreciated the style of his two former C.O.'s, was very critical of the social demeanour of their successor, Colonel Anstruther. He described him at dinner "totally monopolising the conversation of 10 full grown men! And all about himself – what he had seen, what he had done, etc, etc, in a very loud voice! All the members of the British aristocracy he had met when on leave, and so on."[8] A third example comes from 5th Camerons. Having joined this battalion at the front in April, 1918, Lieutenant Douglas Wilson found the C.O., Colonel J. Inglis, ('Jingles' to all but himself), stand-offish and off-hand in decision-making, with corresponding impact on the spirit of the officers' mess. When Major Kennie Cameron took over command in the absence of 'Jingles' on leave, just prior to the battle of Meteren, there was a lightening of mood.[9]

This of course indicates that in other cases the relationship between the C.O. and his officers worked very well. Lieutenant Ken Gauldie, in 8th Black Watch, wrote to his father, idolising his C.O., the Colonel Gordon we have already met, after the battle for Longueval in July, 1916.

> There is one man in our battalion whom every man almost worships – Colonel Gordon …
> I nearly wept when a rumour came through that he had been killed, but, thank goodness it was untrue. We should have been a flock of lost sheep without him. I have never seen

---

4   Ibid., letter to wife, 21 August, 1918.
5   BWA Stewart, diary, 12, 13, 18, 20 July, 21, 30 August, 1 September, 1915. On this relationship see also Stewart's letters to his wife, 17, 18, 19, 30 July, 5, 6, 8, 16, 17, 19, 22, 30 August, 1, 5, 12, 23 September, 4 October, 1915.
6   See BWA Gordon, 'diary', 11, 21-22 December, 1915, 22 January, 18 February, 1, 5, 11, 21, 26 March 1916.
7   BWA Gordon, 'diary,' 11 December, 1915.
8   IWM 2854 Bates, letter to fiancée, 14 July, 1917. See also letters of 21 May, 22 June, 29 July, 1917.
9   LC GS 1761 Wilson, memoir, pp.9, 20, 28-29, 39, 56A-57, 70.

anything like his equal for getting the best out of everyone; everyone seems to want to do his best for him.[10]

His view was shared by the M.O., Johnathan Bates, when Colonel Gordon moved on in September, 1916: "I am really most awfully sorry he has gone. A fine soldier, a delightful man – and he has been so good to me. I shall miss him very much indeed."[11]

The C.O.'s job was not made easier by the rapid turnover of junior officers during the war. Colonel Hugh Allen, commanding 7th Black Watch, lamented in May, 1916, that, "Really I don't know half my officers by name now; they come up in batches & disappear into their companies and one never has a chance of getting to know them."[12] Nevertheless, good C.O.'s showed great concern for the officers under their command; 'Jack' Stewart for example, while commanding 9th Black Watch, urging his wife to write to the father of an officer killed in action, inviting his young padre to visit his wife in London, and later, while commanding the 2nd Battalion, visiting wounded officers in Cairo and Alexandria.[13] He consistently refers to his officers as his 'children' and it is evident that he sees himself as father of the battalion.[14] As such, of course, a C.O. would feel genuine grief at the loss of his family.[15] Colonel Gordon, commanding 8th Black Watch, had to write 14 letters to the next of kin of officers of the battalion killed on the Somme in July, 1916.[16] Then on 7 August, he felt severely the loss of an excellent officer in a bombing accident: "He was such a nice fellow & knew his job. It's a very great blow to me."[17]

Yet at the same time a C.O. would need to act sternly and decisively when necessary if standards were to be maintained. Colonel Gordon was not impressed by the standard of his officers when he took over 8th Black Watch. He soon set an example.

> [5 March, 1916] I had a great job tonight in trying to get an old communication trench cleared for a drain to get away a large body of water. The Coy commander, a perfect fool of a man, could only help by standing at one end with a torch, saying it was a big job. I will pass him a little job tomorrow by removing him from command of his coy. [which he did] It was snowing like the Devil all the time, but we managed to get the thing going right enough.[18]

Captain Wyllie draws attention to the necessity of disciplinary intervention by the C.O. faced with a failure of officers' standards, including drunkenness, in 1st Garrison Battalion Seaforth Highlanders in Salonika.[19] And John Bowie records an extraordinary public reprimand for the officers of 11th Argylls in February, 1917, when they appeared on a surprise parade late,

---

10 BWA Gauldie, Lt K., letter to father, 22 July, 1916.
11 IWM 2854 Bates, letter to fiancée, 22 September, 1916. See also his amusing anecdote of his encounter with the Colonel on his own arrival in the battalion, in letter to fiancée, 17 May, 1916.
12 IWM 114 Allen, letter to wife, 30 May, 1916.
13 BWA Stewart, letters to wife, 8, 21 February, 1916, 23 July, 1918.
14 Ibid., letters to wife, 21 February, 1916, 17 October, 1917, 23 July, 1918.
15 See for example Ibid., letter to wife, 17 May, 1916.
16 BWA Gordon, 'diary', 27 July, 1916.
17 Ibid., 7 August, 1916.
18 Ibid., 5 March, 1916. See also 3 and 16 March, 1916.
19 IWM 7508 Wyllie, diary, 6, 9, 16 February, 1917.

unshaven and with dirty buttons and dirty faces, suggesting that there was a serious problem with their attitude.[20] Such drastic public humiliation was rare. More frequent no doubt was the friendly but firm advice administered, for example, by Ernest Craig-Brown, first as second-in-command, then as C.O. of 1st Camerons, who recognised the essential inexperience of most wartime officers.[21] On 16 August, 1916, he wrote privately to B Company Commander, Macbean:

> You must get more value out of your platoon commanders … don't allow the trench to become a toom for rubbish. Keep them clean & tidy & insist that the men are Cameron Highlanders first & foremost & that they, as such, must set a good example to all the regiments. All this can be accomplished only by intelligent & organised supervision by OFFICERS who must hold the N.C.O.'s responsible that orders are thoroughly carried out.[22]

Overall the Commanding Officer had a tough job to maintain the spirits and standards of his officers, to balance sternness with avuncular advice, and formality with familiarity. As we have seen, while some did extraordinarily well, not all were able to achieve the best balance. In the final analysis, they too were ordinary men thrust into extraordinary situations, and did the best they could.

The Commanding Officer's influence of course extended not just to the officers but to the whole of the battalion, where he could very much set the tone for discipline and efficiency. Lieutenant Bryant Cumming served in 2nd Black Watch. On the move to embark for Mesopotamia in November, 1915, he notes;

> We are with the 1st Seaforths and by Jove the difference in discipline is marked. At one station they left 89 men and 4 officers behind. They from the C.O. downward considered it hugely funny. I should not care to be near Wauchope if that happened with us.[23]

'Jack' Stewart was immensely proud to take over command of 2nd Black Watch in Mesopotamia in April, 1917. Somehow he communicated this pride to his men, with evident benefit to morale. At one concert party he made a speech to the men about 'little things that count.' "Could have heard a pin drop when I told them how pleased and how proud I was to command the Bn and THEN they started cheering."[24] Yet he was happy to acknowledge the amount his battalion's reputation owed to its men. "When generals etc come and say pretty things it's apt to make one think that all is due to oneself, but believe me I try and curb all that sort of thing; it's NOT me one bit, it's the officers , N.C,O.'s and MEN."[25]

---

20   ASHM N-E11 Bowie, 'diary,' 28 February, 1917.
21   IWM 1862 Craig-Brown, E., diary, 11 January, 1915. See also order from him to O.C.'s Coys & other officers, 17 January, 1915, order from him to O.C. Coys, 4 March, 1915, order from him to all officers, 27 March, 1915, letters to Capt Chrichton, 4 January, 1915, to Capt Trotter, 4 January, 1915, diary, 26 June, 1916, recording a German trench raid, and reports by him on the incident to 1st Bde, 27, 30 June, 1916.
22   IWM 1862 Craig-Brown, E., letter to Macbean 16 August, 1916.
23   BWA Cumming, letter to parents, n.d., November, 1915.
24   BWA Stewart, letter to wife, 10 July, 1917.
25   Ibid., letter to wife, 21 November, 1917.

The C.O. of 14th Argylls, who was not permitted to go overseas with his battalion, cried like a youngster when he saw the men off at Southampton in May, 1916,[26] illustrating the strong attachment that a commanding officer might feel for his men. In turn, the men would respect a Colonel who clearly had the interest of the battalion at heart. John Cooper, in training at Ripon with 3/4th Black Watch, regretted the departure of his Colonel, when the Territorial 3rd line training battalions were amalgamated. "He was as fine a gentleman as anyone ever had for an officer … and all his actions were kind, gentle, dignified, and we knew we had a good man at the head of affairs."[27] The death of a C.O. in action could evoke genuine grief across the battalion. Alex Thomson, in 1/4th Black Watch, recalls the burial of his Colonel after the battle of Loos; "everyone present (all that remained of the battalion) was deeply moved."[28]

A good C.O., like Colonel C.W.E. Gordon, commanding 8th Gordons in March, 1916, could feel sorry for the men enduring harsher conditions than himself. "I am sorry for the men. I think they are wonderful people. I came back to a dry change & a dry room. They went back to a wet dug-out & no change whatever."[29] When, in the bitter winter of January, 1917, an Argyll battalion in 51st Highland Division reached their desolate winter quarters at Bonelle Huts, the Colonel flatly refused to accept them and acquired billets in Le Crotoy, a small fishing town which had not been intended for billets.[30] There was respect for the C.O. who shared danger in the trenches. During the battle of Aubers Ridge on 9 May, 1915, Alex Thomson, in 1/4th Black Watch met the Colonel while advancing into a forward trench. "The Colonel was pale, but spoke a few cheery words to every man who passed him and I am sure we all appreciated them."[31] And respect too for the C.O. who was prepared to 'rough it' and share the hardships of his men. Private Douglas, in 8th Black Watch, was impressed by the fact that, after the Armistice, on the march into Germany, Colonel French "had more or less walked along with us all the way since leaving Harlebeke in Belgium."[32] He was less complimentary about French's predecessor, Colonel Hadow, who always rode when the battalion was on the march and always wore his bonnet while the men were obliged to march in steel helmets.[33]

This concern would be expressed in other ways too. C.O.'s would personally comfort the wounded. On 22 September, 1915, Colonel Wallace, commanding 10th Gordons, wrote to his daughter; "One young machine gun man was shot through the lungs this morning, and I saw him after he had been given first aid; his name is Grant and I shook hands with him. He gave me his left and apologised for doing so, poor fellow. His right was strapped to his side and there is shrapnel in his lungs, & he is dying."[34] A C.O. might take a more lenient approach to the sick than his Medical Officer, recognising that a man was not scrimshanking;[35] he might arrange for his wife to visit wounded soldiers of the battalion in hospital at home;[36] ask his wife to provide

---

26   LC Tape 630/647 Macdonald, interview.
27   IWM Books Cooper, 'Domi Militaeque', p.57.
28   BWA Thompson, narrative, vol.2, p.92. See also: IWM 43 Dunton, interview.
29   BWA Gordon, 'diary', 5, 7 March, 1916.
30   [Gregory] *France 1916-1917-1918*, p.10.
31   BWA Thompson, narrative, 9 May, 1915.
32   IWM 4586 Douglas, memoir, pp.1181-1182.
33   Ibid., pp.453-455.
34   GHM PB507 Wallace, letter to daughter, 22 September, 1915, and note dated 23 September, 1915.
35   LC AIR 258A Recollections, Murray, memoir.
36   BWA Stewart, letter to wife, 2 May, 1916.

assistance to the wife of a wounded soldier;[37] or even, at the parent's request, himself keep an eye on the progress of men from a more genteel background, who had enlisted in the ranks.[38] After the Armistice the young commander of 1/8th Argylls took up the Education Scheme which was just then being started, and interviewed personally practically every man in the Battalion to advise them of the courses that would most benefit them.[39]

Commanding Officers would also play an important role in the organisation of comforts for the men, generally working through their wives, whose role might be even more pivotal in the organisation of comforts at home, working together with other officers' wives. This was very much the regimental family in action. Thus we find Colonels 'Jack' Stewart in 2nd Black Watch,[40] Ernest Craig-Brown in 1st Camerons,[41] and Hugh Allen in 7th Black Watch all receiving comforts for their battalions through their wives. The correspondence of Colonel Allen is particularly rich in this respect, with his wife ultimately taking over a Central Comforts Fund, which rumbled along in a delightful combination of earnest endeavour and petty jealousies.[42] The comforts provided included anti-vermin shirts, cigarettes, tobacco, pencils, electric lamps, candles, books, papers and magazines, plum pudding and dried fruits. Colonel Allen was particularly pleased to arrange a supply of footballs and football shirts and shorts.[43] He also obtained trench periscopes[44] and even baths for the men,[45] both rather damning indictments of government supply.

This concern was noted and appreciated by the men. Private Douglas, in 8th Black Watch, was impressed how his Colonel, French, seemed genuinely upset on being told by a runner that six men of the battalion had been killed.[46] Harold Judd, who served in 2nd London Scottish in Palestine and France appreciated how their C.O., Colonel Ogilby, would routinely distribute cigarettes to the men on guard duty.[47] Personal recognition, a little informality and even an avuncular chat would be noticed and appreciated. When Alexander Braes, a soldier in 8th Seaforths, rejoined the battalion from leave in December, 1915, "The C.O. who had taken us over at Loos had been badly wounded in that battle and now he was back with his men. He gave me a very warm handshake, one that gave me the feeling that I would go through Hell with this man."[48] Gordon Crask, in training with the Seaforths at Fort George, records how when a draft was about to leave the Fort for the front, the Colonel shook hands with all the draft and wished them luck.[49] Arthur Wrench, attached to Brigade Headquarters, found himself alone with Colonel Scott of 1/5th Seaforths, after going with him to inspect a working party, and

37 Ibid., letter to wife, 12 November, 1918.
38 IWM 114 Allen, letters to wife, 2, 3, 8, 10, 14 July, 8 August, 1915.
39 IWM Misc 15017 Wilson, biography, p.34.
40 BWA Stewart, letter to wife, 7 August, 1917, 17, 29 October, 1917, 29 January, 1918.
41 IWM 1862 Craig-Brown, letters home, 10, 15 December, 1916, to mother, 20 January, 1917.
42 IWM 114 Allen, letters to wife, 1, 7, 9, 15, 16, 18, 19, 24, 25, 30 May, 4, 14, 25 June, 16, 18, 22, 23, 24, 25, 28 October, 3, 6, 8, 9, 13, 17, 22, 26, 28, 29 November, 13, 16 December, 1915, 3, 7, 11, 22, 23, 25 January, 4, 5, 13, 20 February, 8, 18, 20, 23 March, 21 April, 19, 30 June, 10, 11 July, 1916.
43 Ibid., letters to wife, 18, 23 October, 1915, 22 January, 1916.
44 Ibid., letters to wife, 4, 13, 14, 20 June, 1915.
45 Ibid., letters to wife, 17, 22, 23, 26 October, c.15, 17 November, 3, 6, 7 December, 1915, 29 February, 1916.
46 IWM 4586 Douglas, memoir, pp.1020-1021.
47 LC Several Fronts Recollections, transcript of Tape 1545, Judd, interview.
48 THM 2013-072 (S) Braes, memoir, p.40.
49 THM Seaforths 89-26 Crask, diary, 23, 30 April, 12 June, 1915.

was impressed by his unstuffy openness and informality.[50] John Cooper was impressed by the attitude of Sir Robert Moncrieffe, commander of the amalgamated Black Watch Territorial training battalion at Ripon., when he spotted, among the group of 'returned' men waiting outside the doctor's hut, a man whom he had known in France. He immediately called the man out and talked with him for a little. [51]

Equally, a lack of concern would create the opposite effect. When John Cooper was finally demobilised from 12th Argylls in Constantinople on 3 October, 1919, he was not impressed that the Colonel never even said 'Good-bye.' to his demobilised draft. Indeed, respect for the Colonel was not universal. Albert Strachan, in 6th Gordons felt that the C.O. who had replaced their own Colonel McLean by Summer 1915, "was a nasty bit of stuff – always finding fault."[52] And things evidently reached a sad state in 11th Argylls, where Lieutenant Robert MacKay records how, towards the end of November, 1917, genuine contempt for their C.O., Major Duncan, had apparently set in amongst the ranks:

> By this time, the morale of our Bn had reached such a 'low' that in the Bn H.Q. dugout, where only a canvas screen separated officers from men, our cook, mess waiter and servants were singing out loudly the most foul obscenities about the 'C.O.' These choruses were known and sung throughout the whole unit. Officers and men shared the same feelings.[53]

From the Commanding Officer, we turn next to consider relations between the other officers and their N.C.O.'s. This relationship, of course, was vital to the successful operation of the battalion, key roles being played especially in the guidance of young officers by experienced platoon sergeants, Company Sergeant Majors and sometimes the Regimental Sergeant Major. There are many acknowledgements of the importance of this relationship,[54] both by officers and Senior N.C.O.'s. Cecil Harper, for example, was granted a commission in 10th Gordons. He writes of his training:

> To me the most memorable was our Company Sergeant Major Morrison. As a reservist, he had fought in the Regiment in two previous campaigns. Immediately prior to mobilisation he had been a ticket-inspector on the city tramways in Aberdeen. He loved the regiment and anything in it. He possessed the rare art of coaching young subalterns in their job without exhibiting any lack of respect. He always saved our face before the ranks … He watched over us like sons and was always ready with vigilant eye and quiet suggestion.[55]

Lieutenant John Turing records how his Company Sergeant Major in 8th Seaforths tactfully advised him that in an excess of zeal he was overworking his platoon, and made practical

---

50   IWM 3834 Wrench, diary, 18 May, 1918.
51   IWM Books Cooper, 'Domi Miitaeque', p.69.
52   GHM. PB2984, Strachan, memoir.
53   IWM 11144 MacKay, diary, 26 November, afternote, 1972, p.46.
54   Apart from refs cited below, see: LC GS 1516 Stables, letter describing his experiences, 5 February, 1979; LC GS 1367 Robertson, memoir, p.47; IWM 6702 Low, letter to his wife, Noanie, 15 September, 1915; IWM 7593 Harper, memoir, p.16.
55   IWM 7593 Harper, memoir, p.11.

suggestions with which he fell in.[56] Peter Stewart, an old soldier who had come over from India to join the effort and was posted to 8th Gordons, wrote in July, 1915, that as C.S.M. with young officers he had great responsibility. "They depend on me a great deal and I hope I shall never disappoint them."[57]

This is not to suggest that N.C.O.'s did not on occasion need the drive and direction of officers to keep them up to the mark. We have already observed how Ernest Craig-Brown in 1st Camerons had to advise his inexperienced officers to supervise their N.C.O.'s in order to get the most out of them. Sometimes, officers were just not up to the job, like the subaltern in 5th Camerons who preferred to get drunk in a dugout rather than supervise his working party.[58] At other times they had to step in to make demotions and promotions in order to get their platoons working.[59] The quality of a company or platoon would depend very much on the quality of its individual officers and N.C.O.'s, but also on the individual men themselves, who sometimes could provide drive and leadership from below.[60]

In general, officers respected their Senior N.C.O.'s,[61] and could demonstrate practical concern, for example by providing a reference for a discharged sergeant,[62] or arranging an appointment at base for a run-down Colour Sergeant.[63] The loss of a Senior N.C.O. in action frequently gave rise to expressions of grief and genuine affection by his officers.[64] Such respect, concern and affection could be reciprocal.[65] William Kemp, in 8/10th Gordons, was especially proud when he heard that his company N.C.O.'s had rather unconventionally signed a letter to the C.O. recommending him for a decoration for his actions on 28 March, 1918, during the German offensive.[66] (He was indeed awarded the M.C.) Captain Gibb of 7th Camerons records the attention of a senior N.C.O. when he stumbled home after the desperate fighting at Arras on 28 March, 1918. He was greeted by his signalling sergeant "like a man returned from the dead," was filled with rum and looked after by "a wee signaller, Pte Coney, who wrapped me in his coat and ordered me to 'Haud yer tongue, sir, an' get to sleep.'"[67] The relationship would be strengthened by shared dinners,[68] sports[69] and even high jinx,[70] all helping to create 'esprit de

---

56   LC GS 1635 Turing, memoir.
57   GHM PB2021 Stewart, letters to wife Lil, 11 July, 7 September, 1915.
58   LC GS 1761 Wilson, memoir, pp.116-117.
59   IWM 430 Wimberley, memoir, vol.1, p.31; LC GS 1761 Wilson, memoir, p.83.
60   Douglas Wilson provides a neat summary. See LC GS 1761 Wilson, p.30. See also his example of Corporal Gardiner at pp.68-68A.
61   LC GS 1549 Strachan, memoir.
62   GHM PB91 Flockhart, Sgt George, letter to him from Capt James E. Adamson, 22 February, 1916.
63   BWA Guthrie, letter to his wife Crissie, 14 July, 1915.
64   GHM PB242 Stansfield, letter (extract) 23 October, 1914; IWM 5525 Steven, letter home, 12 May, 1915; THM Camerons 94-99 Stewart-Murray, Capt Lord James, letter to father, 24 September, 1914; IWM 6702 Low, letter to his wife, Noanie, 16 June, 1916.
65   Apart from examples cited, see also: David, *Mud and Bodies*, p.126, letter to Weir from Q.M.S. J. Brodie, 3 August, 1918.
66   GHM PB1639 Kemp, memoir, Vol 2, p.31.
67   THM Camerons 90-62 Gibb, Capt E.J.C., typescript memoir, 'The German attack at Arras, March, 1918.'
68   GHM PB1639 Kemp, memoir, p.63; IWM 4576 Yarnall, diary, 1 February, 1917.
69   GHM PB242 Stansfield, letters (extracts) 6 March, 26 May, 1915.
70   Ibid., letter 16 December, 1914.

corps'. In this sense one can talk of a regimental family. Peter Stewart, the old soldier we have already met in 8th Gordons, let the C.O. have sight of a photo of his little son Ian in military uniform. "Colonel Wright saw his photo and was delighted. He said he looked a well drilled and set up lad. He wanted to know if Ian was going to be the next of the family in the Regiment."[71]

As far as the relationship with their men was concerned, several officers reflect on the burden of responsibility they felt.[72] Not all felt they were up to it, like Bob Nicol, an old pal of Arthur Wrench, who had been commissioned from the ranks, and was then transferred from a labour battalion to an infantry battalion, the 7th Seaforths.[73] Whatever their level of self-confidence, officers needed to win the respect of their men, and to do so, ideally, they needed to get to know them.[74] This was not always easy, given the rapid turnaround of personnel during the summer offensives on the Western Front.[75] It was aided somewhat by the process of censoring letters, although this itself could be resented as intrusive.[76] Douglas Gillespie, in 2nd Argylls, certainly found the process difficult.[77]

Officers in Regular battalions might know their men well and vice versa. Private John Laing, a veteran soldier in 1st Black Watch, noted on 29 September, 1914, "Just had some officers from home to make up the strength. We have no less than 5 now, Captain West in charge, and a good sort he is. I went through the South African War with him as he was in charge of our M.I."[78] Officers in Territorial battalions, recruited locally before the war, might know their men well,[79] and a certain informality prevailed.[80] James Racine, a wartime recruit to 5th Seaforths at Bedford, noted in October, 1914 that,

> Our lieutenant was a very nice fellow who had been with the battalion for seventeen years and had risen from the ranks; he talked and smoked with the men and was most popular. The senior officers and the battalion sergeant major were very different (being from the regular army) and were officious; they regarded us as only amateur soldiers.[81]

But as, with casualties and drafts, battalions became more polyglot and new officers were posted in, the task became harder.

Sometimes, even outside the Territorial battalions, officers and men might meet who were known to each other in civilian life. Lieutenant Angus Macnaghten, posted to 1st Black Watch, found that: "Rather curious I have a Sergt McGregor in my Coy whose brother used to be a

---

71 GHM PB2021 Stewart, letter to wife Lil, n.d. [1915].
72 IWM 2854 Bates, letter to fiancée, 2 February, 1917; IWM 6702 Low, letter to his father or mother, 25 December, 1914.
73 IWM 3834 Wrench, diary, 17 September, 1917.
74 Gillespie, *Letters from Flanders*, p.38, letter home 7 March, 1915; LC Several fronts Recollections Kingsley, memoir; LC GS 1367 Robertson, memoir, p.34.
75 GHM PB375 Pailthorpe, memoir, p.68.
76 THM Seaforths 81-2 Cooper, memoir, pp 46-47; IWM 6702 Low, letter to his wife, Noanie, 11 December, 1914.
77 Gillespie, *Letters from Flanders*, letter home 16 September, 1915.
78 BWA Laing, diary, 29 September, 1914.
79 GHM PB1892.3.18 McDonald, 'Uncle Harper's Duds', pp.11-12.
80 See for example, GHM. PB2924 Strachan, memoir.
81 IWM 16335 PP Racine, memoir, p.12.

shepherd in Monachyle, & once pulled in a tug of war team for me."[82] Scott Ferguson joined 1/4th Seaforths as a newly commissioned subaltern in January, 1918, and enjoyed meeting fellows in the ranks from his home town of Forfar.[83] In these cases, the previous association reinforced bonds. This was not the case with Private William Couston in 7th Black Watch, who wrote home in December, 1916:

> You mention that Harold Inch is home on leave. Well mum I ran across him *several* times after the last 'affair', but he did not recognise me. Lt Inch & Harold Inch of school-days are very different persons you know. It wd never do for Lt I to talk to Pte W.J.C. Oh, no, that was always his style.[84]

Not all officers made the same investment of time in getting to know their men. William Kemp, a platoon commander in 8/10th Gordons, was a keen advocate of the process:

> Some officers, especially very young and new ones, did not always fully realise their responsibilities and duties as an officer, and, while quite brave in the trenches, did not take nearly the interest in their platoons that the men expected and needed. I made it a practice as long as I had a platoon to spend some little time each day with my fellows at their billet to find out all their complaints and troubles and if they had any grievances tried to get them put right.[85]

Of course, officers could also win respect through their bravery.[86] Men would congratulate an officer receiving a decoration when they thought it was well deserved.[87] After the battle of Meteren in July, 1918, Lieutenant Douglas Wilson in 5th Camerons records that "a small parcel was handed to me by a Lance-Corporal. It was a bundle of Boche cheroots and cigars from the men of 'Don' Company who had been under my immediate command. Just a token, which touched me more than I can say."[88] It helped too if officers were prepared to get stuck in and assist with hard menial work when the chips were down. Guy Macgregor was a subaltern in 1/6th Argylls and successfully worked hard to win the respect of his men, when his platoon took over a rather difficult and tiresome job.

> I have enjoyed for the first time the intoxicating emotion of comradeship between myself & the men. I am proud of every man in my platoon. I know them all & stick up for them, & I fairly smile with delight when I see some little sign that they like me. I tell you it's a difficult prize to win – the trust & affection of your men.[89]

---

82 IWM 3696 Macnaghten, letter to wife, 30 September, 1914.
83 LC GS 0552 Ferguson, letters to his mother, 21 February, 13, 15 May, 1918.
84 BWA Couston, letter to mother 5 December, 1916.
85 GHM PB1639 Kemp, memoir, p.43.
86 See also for example: LC GS 1761 Wilson, memoir, pp.80-81; ASHM N-E11 Bowie, 'diary'; IWM 4474 Johnston, memoir; IWM 11144 MacKay, diary, 6 August, 1917, and afternote, 1972, 23 September, 1918, pp.35, 76.
87 GHM PB18 Boustead, letter from Willie Woolmore, 28 May, 1917.
88 LC GS 1761 Wilson, memoir, p.76.
89 IWM 8592 Macgregor, letter to wife Dulcie, 9 March, 1918.

Later, when he was serving with the battalion in France, he was delighted to tell his wife that he was now held in high esteem by the men.[90] Private Jack Mackenzie, in 5th Camerons, wrote to his wife Minnie, in July, 1915, "We are all so proud of our officers, they were a treat. It is fine to be under men like them, the chaps would go anywhere with them. Our two just went at it with the rest of it, digging & filling sand bags and filling them up, and passing jokes the whole time."[91]

Nevertheless, an interest in one's men was vital to understanding and motivating them to fight and 'stick it.'

> An understanding platoon officer was of course in a position to smooth out difficulties, and the Jocks were quick to respond to the interest he displayed in their well-being provided it was genuine and not officious. He could make too much contact or too little; he lost face with familiarity but gained immeasurably if he had a capacity for exchanging a joke; if he was standoffish or unapproachable he got nowhere.[92]

Some officers did enjoy socialising with the men. William Kemp, an officer in 8/10th Gordons, wrote how, in the trenches, before the raid on the Butte de Warlencourt,

> I spent a very pleasant three days with Sgt Spence, Simmie my servant, a good and faithful one, and Moore, or 'Baldy' as everyone called him. Moore … was an extremely good fellow; his stories of his two little kiddies at home kept us remarkably cheery. Altogether we were a very cheery quartette.[93]

Lieutenant Jim Dale, recently commissioned in 2nd Liverpool Scottish, enjoyed the company of the men. "I find them pleasant fellows & like sitting with them at night & yarning in the trenches.[94] Old Etonian Lionel Sotheby, a subaltern in 1st Black Watch, wrote that, despite the heavy officer casualties at Aubers Ridge on 9th May, 1915, "I have no wish to be anything than a second Lieut, out here – one is part of the men themselves then, and that is what I like."[95] Archie Ross, of 1st Camerons, was never seen anywhere without his fiddle, which he used to play in the trenches to cheer up his platoon."[96] Lieutenant Russell of Aden, Cameron Highlanders, not untypically, claimed a unique camaraderie in the Highland regiments. Responsible for conducting a draft to 2nd Camerons in March, 1915,

> We were joined by a large draft from the 3rd Black Watch, stationed at Nigg, who were destined for their first battalion. The Senior Officer in charge was a Major Wauchope, afterwards a general of much distinction. When we arrived at Perth, the door of the carriage was flung open, and two somewhat inebriated Jocks of the Black Watch put their

---

90 Ibid., letter to wife Dulcie, 23 October, 1918
91 IWM 926 PP Mackenzie, letters to wife, 3, 6, 14 July, 1915. See also Fennah, *Retaliation*, pp.59-60.
92 LC GS 1761 Wilson, memoir, p.30.
93 GHM PB1639 Kemp, memoir, p.59.
94 IWM 12157 PP Dale, Lt J.L., letter to Aunt Edie, 31 May, 1917.
95 LC GS 1507 Sotheby, letter to unknown, 15 May, 1915.
96 THM Camerons 97 22 Russell, memoirs, p.183.

heads round the door, and shook Major Wauchope warmly by the hand, and greeted him as an old comrade. They had served under him in peacetime. An example of the friendly camaraderie that has always existed in the Highland Regiments, which has never been fully understood or appreciated by the English.[97]

And Douglas Wilson, Lewis Gun Officer in 5th Camerons, dealt with the situation with humour when he found himself being impersonated by one of his men.[98] Such informality was appreciated. Arthur Wrench, of 1/4th Seaforths, but serving at Brigade H.Q., writes favourably of the Brigade Major, in August, 1916, who was happy to share a joke with him when after a tiring cycle ride he declined a tot of whisky. "He is a real, genuine sort of man, and I always have had a good word for him; only wish there were a lot more officers like him in the army."[99]

Officers in fact frequently demonstrated much consideration for their men. They would be expected to put the welfare of their men before their own and were respected when they did so.[100] Thus we find them assisting with leave arrangements in compassionate cases,[101] or arranging through home to lend money to a sergeant going on leave who is owed pay.[102] When, after the German offensive in March, 1918, home leave for drafts from the 5th Argylls Reserve Training Battalion at Ripon was cancelled, Ripon was inundated with families from all over the country, finding it almost impossible to get either food or accommodation after their long journeys, so the officers arranged to feed a lot of them here and let them into the lines (contrary to all regulations).[103] Officers assist with 'finding' blankets for their men in winter conditions;[104] in emergencies they may purchase food or clothing for their men out of their own pockets;[105] an officer in 1/4th Black Watch gives a wounded man his Burberry;[106] in 8th Black Watch the Medical Officer arranges base jobs for men who are worn out and unfit for duty in the trenches;[107] Noel Chavasse, M.O. to 1st Liverpool Scottish, starts a special 'Sanitary Squad' for "fellows who were a little run down, but not actually bad enough to be on the sick-list;"[108] and an officer at Boulogne greets warmly soldiers who had previously served under him.[109]

These acts of consideration were appreciated by the men. Thus Private Douglas in 8th Black Watch is impressed when during battle in September, 1918, his platoon officer, Lieutenant Yule, provides him with an extra tot of rum for his nerves, and when he gives his own sandwich to a hungry soldier.[110] He was also impressed when, on a long march behind the lines, his company commander relaxed the rule for wearing steel helmets, and marched with the men, rather than

---

97   THM Camerons 97-22 Russell, memoirs, pp.188-189.
98   LC GS 1761 Wilson, memoir, pp.111-112.
99   IWM 3834 Wrench, diary, 3 August, 1916.
100 GHM uncatalogued Beaton, memoir, p.83.
101 BWA Duke, A.W., letter to mother 31 October, 1915.
102 Campbell, *Letters,* p.53, letter home, 21 July, 1915.
103 ASHM N-E5 Main, letter to wife, Win, 31 March, 1918.
104 IWM 8592 Macgregor, letter to wife Dulcie, 19 April, 1918.
105 BWA Thompson, narrative, 27 February, 14 March, 1915.
106 IWM 5525 Steven, letter home 17 May, 1915.
107 IWM 2854 Bates, letter to fiancée, 29 August, 26 September, 1916.
108 Jackson, 'Captain Noel Godfrey Chavasse.'
109 IWM Books Cooper, 'Domi Militaeque', p.81.
110 IWM 4586 Douglas, memoir, pp.1021-1022.

rode, and when his platoon commander on the same march exchanged his half empty pack for the full pack and equipment of a struggling soldier.[111] He also admired another young platoon officer who took the trouble personally to inspect his men's feet, although he maintained he was the only platoon officer to so, the others depending on their N.C.O.'s.[112] Norman Macmillan was favourably impressed by the actions of his own company officer when he rescued them from the job of loading stores at Southampton in November, 1914, en route to France with 1st Glasgow Highlanders.[113]

And of course, officers had to deal with casualties. Norman Beaton records the compassion of the officers in 1/7th Gordons when his brother was killed on the night of 5/6 July, 1916, and how they dealt sensitively with the situation:

> There were tears in his officer's eyes when he was telling me, as he was a great favourite, both with the officers and men. I didn't know what to do that day after that, and worried about my other brother as I had not seen him, when he came along to where I was with his kit. His officer had sent him out of the trenches to be at the burial. My officer came along and sympathised with us and told me to take my kit also and go out.[114]

Many officers considered it a duty to look beyond themselves and arrange comforts for their men. This kindness may have gone beyond their formal regimental responsibilities but was entirely consistent both with their officer training and their inherited sense of *noblesse oblige*. Indeed, it may well have been expected within the Regiment. Wives, families and friends were enlisted to send additional comforts such as cigarettes and socks to the men, whose own wives and families may have been less able to support them. These comforts would be paid for by, not by the Army, but by the officers, their families or their social circle. In this way the duty of care and the maintenance of privilege sat relatively comfortably together in the social milieu of the time. The range of comforts provided was extraordinary.[115] They included clothing; gloves and mittens, socks, mufflers, balaclava helmets, shirts, cardigans, semmits (vests), as well as towels and handkerchiefs. In 10th Gordons in 1914, officers were even asked to arrange for the supply of khaki hose-tops for the men before these could be provided by government.[116] So much clothing was provided, indeed, that on some occasions, particularly when a move was expected, officers had to write home to turn off the supply.[117] Other comforts provided included cigarettes, pipes and tobacco, and all sorts of sweet foods including chocolate, Edinburgh rock, sweets, toffee, cakes, as well as tinned coffee. More practical gifts included writing paper and candles, while other gifts catered to the men's entertainment, including footballs, books and reading material, mouth organs, penny whistles and playing cards. Rather late in the day, Colonel Arthur Grant, commanding 5th Gordons at Bedford, records that on 6 March, 1915 he "went to Gamages in

---

111 Ibid., pp.478-479, 485-489.
112 Ibid., pp.463-464.
113 IWM 3460 Macmillan, diary, 4 November 1914.
114 GHM uncatalogued Beaton, memoir, pp.122-124.
115 There are too many individual references in the sources to cite here.
116 IWM 7593 Harper, memoir, p.12.
117 GHM PB3309 Pelham Burn, letters to parents and sister, 5, 10, 20, December, 1914; BWA Duke, letter to mother 28 December, 1914; IWM 3696 Macnaghten, letters to wife, 9, 15 October, 1914; IWM 1862 Craig-Brown, E., letters to home, 3, 25 November, 1914.

Holborn & bought a small billiard table & a lot of other games for the use of the men. I ought to have had all these things long ago."[118] In 1915, Henry Pelham Burn also made efforts through home, at his own expense, to obtain nine trench periscopes for 6th Gordons,[119] and sniper rifles for 1st Gordons,[120] noting that, "It seems rather absurd that one should have to get all these things for oneself but the authorities either are too bound-up in red tape or else do not take sufficient interest in one's requirements." The gifts were highly appreciated by the men.[121]

Apart from providing comforts, officers' wives might also be enlisted to visit the men's wives at home, to share their burden of worry, and to comfort those who had lost loved ones at the front. Lieutenant Sidney Steven, a pre-war Territorial officer in 1/4th Black Watch, wrote home on 18 March, 1915, after Neuve Chapelle:

> Just a short note to ask you if you would kindly visit John Howie, 50 Ferry Road. He is the father of one of my chaps killed in action on the 10th. He went missing and I got a note tonight to say that he was found dead by the 1st Seaforths when they were clearing up their field of battle and he was buried by them on the 11th. Howie was an excellent fellow and one whom I always respected and looked to for an example of a good soldier. He never caused any trouble and was always on parades.[122]

Guy Macgregor, a subaltern with 1/6th Argylls even encouraged one of his men to visit his mother at home while on leave in February/March, 1918.[123]

Several officers record their huge respect, even love, for the men under their command steadfastly going about their duty.[124] William Kemp had huge affection for the volunteer soldier: "He is the finest hero and gentleman on the face of the earth. I love him. I have seen him in my own command and there I learnt to love him; he is almost without equal on this earth."[125] Likewise, Grant Fleming won the D.S.O. when serving as a subaltern with 1st Gordons. He modestly put his achievement down to the men he commanded. "They were the real heroes. They did the actual fighting. They won me the D.S.O. I merely led them and shepherded them and got all the kudos. They got most of the kicks."[126]

Sometimes officers' attitudes could be ambivalent, a combination of condescension and admiration, expressed by the aristocratic Ivar Campbell, attached to 1st Seaforths, after a demonstration attack in support of the Loos offensive.

---

118 GHM PB107.1 Grant, diary, 6 March, 1915.
119 GHM PB3309 Pelham Burn, letters to parents, 15, 22, 26 February, 8 March, 1915.
120 GHM PB3309 Pelham Burn, letters to parents, 25 June, 1, 2, 7 July, 8, 22, 31 August, 1915.
121 See for example ASHM N-E11 Macleod, letters to mother, 8 December, 1915, 10 and 11 February, 1916.
122 IWM 5525 Steven, letter home 18 March, 1915. See also: ASHM N-E5 Main, letter to wife, Win, 7 August, 15 September, 1915.
123 IWM 8592 Macgregor, letter to wife Dulcie, 15 March, 1918.
124 Apart from examples below, see also: ASHM N-E5 Main, letter to wife, Win, 5 July, 1915; IWM 7668 Escombe, letter to him from 'Andy' Anderson, 21 June, 1916; IWM 6702 Low, letter to his wife, Noanie, 18 June, 1916.
125 GHM PB1639 Kemp, memoir, p.39.
126 IWM 15345 Fleming, memoir, pp.36-37.

Sometimes, back in billets, I hate the men – their petty crimes, their continued bad language with no variety of expression, their stubborn moods. But in a difficult time they show up splendidly. Laughing in mud, joking in water – I'd 'demonstrate' into Hell with some of them and not care.[127]

Unsurprisingly, the death of their men could affect officers deeply.[128] One of the saddest tasks of platoon and company officers was to write letters of condolence to the next of kin of men who had died or been killed in action.[129] They would also deal with enquiries from relations of those both dead and missing.[130] Captain Wyllie, in 1st Garrison Battalion Seaforth Highlanders, anticipated this interest. When he had a man of his company buried at Constanza, and another at Varna, he was able to take photographs of the graves to send home to their people.[131] The writing of letters of condolence was not a pleasant job,[132] and a young subaltern might feel he lacked the experience necessary to write to the middle-aged wife of a sergeant with a family.[133] Some of the letters appear a little formulaic, and the hard truth is sometimes concealed. Most men "died instantly", without agony, and when a man had perhaps been obliterated by a shell, this is disguised.[134] Nevertheless, in most cases the letters incorporate human touches which betray real emotion, and cut to the heart even today. Hugh Bartholomew, an officer in 14th Argylls, wrote to the mother of Lance Corporal Moir, who was killed on 18 May, 1917.

> This news must come as a terrible blow to you, Mrs Moir, for I have known your son for some time, and feel certain that he must have been greatly loved at home. The life out here is one of the best tests of a man. Your son was always a cheerful, willing, and clean soldier – one of the best I had in my company. Many a time when I felt my spirits low, I have gone round the line and I have seen your son and others, cheerful, never grousing, but sticking it and putting up with the many hardships which they meet with here, and I have

---

127 Campbell, *Letters*, pp.77-78, letter home, 27 September, 1915.
128 As well as examples below, see: ASHM N-E8 Munro, letter to sister Effie, 13 June, 1915; Bartholomew, *George Hugh Frederick Bartholomew*, p.65, diary entry; GHM PB1639 Kemp, memoir, p.38; THM Seaforths 81-180 Murray, letter to sister Alex, 19 May, 1915; LC GS 0298 Chavasse family, letter from Noel Chavasse to Miss Madeleine Twemlow, 5 June, 1915; IWM 8592 Macgregor, letter to wife Dulcie, 22 October, 1918.
129 ASHM N-E7 Doig, Mrs, letter of condolence from Capt J.M. Scott, 20 May, 1915; THM Seaforths 84-65 Vickery, Cpl James, letter to his mother from Lieutenant I.G. Clark, n.d.; THM Seaforths 91-27 McIntosh, letter to his wife from Lt D.B. Mellis-Smith, 26 November, 1916; LC GS 1023 Maclaren, letter from Lt Col Wylie to his parents, 17 November, 1916; BWA MacGregor, Sgt Gordon, letter to his father from Col A.G. Wauchope, 9 December, 1916; THM C80-15 Chase, Pte Edwin Henry, extract from Croydon newspaper, 30 March, 1915; THM Camerons 97-25 Reid, Pte Harold Wilson, letter to his mother from Capt M Beaton, 16 June, 1915; IWM 1953 PP Ross, J.A., letter from Lt J M Reid to Mrs Ross (mother), 27 August, 1918.
130 ASHM N-E11, Macleod, letters to mother, 8 December, 1915, 10 and 11 February, 1916.
131 IWM 7508 Wyllie, diary, 23 December, 1918.
132 THM Camerons 94-8 Mackay, 'Tell Them of Us', letter from Ian Mackay to mother, n.d. (1915).
133 LC GS 0552 Ferguson, letter to his mother, 26 April, 1918; THM Seaforths 81-2 Cooper, memoir, pp.68-69.
134 See for example LC GS 1761 Wilson, p.84.

been cheered up again by their example. He was a fine soldier and would have become a fine man.[135]

With such feelings, officers could feel hard the moment they were posted away from their platoons or companies.[136] It was this respect and affection for the men of the battalion too which led D.W. Pailthorpe, Medical Officer to 2nd Gordons, to resist the opportunity to seek a safer posting:

> Amongst the Jocks I had now seen more unselfishness for their own lives and tenderness in dealing with the desperate hurts of others, more readiness to help each other in the face of danger and to share whatever slight alleviation of their lot might occur, more steady faithfulness and loyalty to their leaders, more dour courage when there was little room for anything but despair than can ever possibly be recorded … The Jocks with whom I laboured and whom I loved had themselves no choice. Far harder was life for them and for the 'duty' men far more dangerous – they had to continue until killed or wounded. I knew that they had never let me down and never would. Therefore I remained.[137]

The love and respect felt by officers towards their men was generally reciprocated when deserved. There are many expressions of respect and affection in the sources.[138] Officers took secret delight when affectionate nicknames, applause at concerts or overheard comments made them realise they were popular.[139]

Soldiers could feel deeply the loss of their officers.[140] Private Stewart, a reservist recalled to the colours in August, 1914, to join 2nd Seaforths, noted in his diary on 30 November, 1914, "Mr Hepburn killed by sniper. Awfully sorry for him, so young."[141] Special efforts would be made by volunteers to retrieve their officer's body from the battlefield.[142] The touching appreciation of the family for the volunteers who retrieved the body of Captain Duncan Macbean (2nd Gordons) in 1915 survives in the Gordons' archives.[143] Perhaps most touching of all are the letters of condolence written by ordinary soldiers to the loved ones of officers killed in action.[144] Corporal Thomson wrote of Captain Macbean;

---

135 Bartholomew, *George Hugh Frederick Bartholomew*, pp.65-66, letter from Bartholomew to Mrs Moir, 19 May, 1917.
136 GHM PB1639 Kemp, typescript memoir, p.35; GHM PB18 Boustead, letter to mother, 8 March, 1917; IWM 18455 Turnbull, letters to mother, father and sister, Sylvia, 21, 26 September, 1914.
137 GHM PB375 Pailthorpe, memoir, pp.61-62.
138 See for example: IWM 4440 Croft, interview; GHM PB1639 Kemp, memoir, Vol 2, p.20; IWM Books Brooke, 'Wait for it', p.115.
139 GHM PB1639 Kemp, memoir, Vol.2, pp.11, 15; THM Seaforths 89-26 Crask, letters to mother, 9 and c.13 November, 1915; GHM PB375 Pailthorpe, memoir, p.29.
140 LC GS 0252 Campbell, diary, 30 November, 1917.
141 THM Seaforths 84-117 Stewart, Pte J., diary, 30 November, 1914.
142 LC GS 0890 Kershaw, letter from Capt Thomas Taylor to 2Lt Kershaw's father, 2 October, 1915.
143 GHM PB149 Macbean, Lt D.G.F., letters to Mrs Penniman Eddy from his father, Mr Forbes Macbean, 6 July, from Pte Francis Forsyth, 26 July and from Cpl W. Thomson, 26 July, 1915; PB242 Stansfield, letter from Mr Forbes Macbean, 24 June, 1915.
144 Apart from examples cited, see BWA Couston, letters to mother 29 April, 25 May, 1917.

Hierarchy 299

> This war has taken toll of hundreds of brave men, but none braver than *Our* D Coy Captain Macbean. He never knew what fear was, and the harder the 'scrapping' the better he liked it. As it was, he could have saved his life, but he thought of his men first. I can't tell you how sorry D Co. was to lose him, because we would have followed him anywhere. Any German prisoners we take --- --- We will remember our Captain.[145]

When Sir John Fowler, adjutant of 4th Seaforths was killed on 22 June, 1915, a Dingwall boy wrote home to his parents, "We felt as if we had lost a brother."[146]

Some officers failed to engage or treated their men with appalling insensitivity. Private Douglas, in 8th Black Watch, was not impressed by one platoon commander: "The only time he spoke to us was when giving an order, and when in the line, we very rarely saw him."[147] Harry Strachan joined 7th Gordons at Banchory in August 1914, after two of his elder brothers had been mobilised with the same battalion. They went to Bedford for training. "On December 19th, the O.C. Company, an unfeeling man, got we three brothers together and said simply, 'Your Mother is dead. I'll try to arrange for your getting home for 3 days.' That was all. We knew that the 11th child was imminent and both died."[148] Arthur Wrench, in 1/4th Seaforths, criticised a march in the blazing sun in August, 1916, as a result of which he heard eleven men had died. On a subsequent train journey, some officers' kit was lost. "Enquiries and special runs are afoot at once as to the loss of this kit and it seems to be of much more importance than the loss of eleven men on that previous march."[149]

Indeed, there was sometimes a contempt for officers in general. John Bowie in 11th Argylls writes of the contempt felt for some officers towards the end of 1917.

> Commissions were given to every kind of soldier at this time, anyone who wished to become an officer he had no bother .. Without fear of contradiction, if you knew of the biggest fat head in the company he was the one to apply for a commission and get it. Many were beginning to come to the B.E.F. and they were only a 'laughing stock' to the troops. The men had absolutely no faith in their leaders. All they were able for was to hide in dug-outs and when requiring to do their needs their servants carried it out.[150]

In 8th Black Watch, in 1918, Private Douglas felt that there was only one officer who took a personal interest in his men. Most of the others "left their men solely in charge of their Platoon N.C.O.'s when clear of parades etc. They either thought the men preferred to be left to themselves, or it was not good for discipline to get too familiar with the men under them."[151] More generally this disrespect was directed towards individual officers, and sadly there are many examples.[152] Neil Hendry, for example, serving in 2nd London Scottish in Palestine, notes that

---

145 GHM PB149 Macbean, letter to Mrs Penniman Eddy from Cpl W. Thomson, 26 July, 1915.
146 Fowler, *Captain Sir John Fowler, Bart*, pp.7, 8
147 IWM 4586 Douglas, memoir, p.853.
148 LC GS 1549 Strachan, memoir.
149 IWM 3834 Wrench, diary, 9, 11 August, 1916.
150 ASHM N-E11 Bowie, 'diary.'
151 IWM 4586 Douglas, memoir, pp.464-466.
152 GHM PB1726 Fettes, diary, 13 April, 1915; THM 2013-072 (S) Braes, memoir, p.26; LC GS 0771 Hirsch, diary, 12 September, 1916; LC Transcripts, Tape 850, Henley, interview.

when the battalion went into action in November, 1917. "Looking back, we suddenly saw the Adjutant's horse go down, and very nearly a shout of joy went up as he was far from being a liked man."[153] This contempt could be based on perceived incompetence,[154] the avoidance of danger,[155] an obsession with bull,[156] petty orders,[157] unnecessarily harsh punishments,[158] over-working the men,[159] nepotism[160] and even the assumption of ruthless posturing.[161]

What made the men's blood boil above all was the perception of dual standards. In Salonika, in 12th Argylls, officers use scarce transport to carry bottles of whisky, when the men are hungry and short of rations;[162] in 11th Argylls, officers exploit tired men to fetch their whisky, take more than their fair share of the rum ration, appropriate more than their fair share of the rations, and expropriate the men's coke ration for their own comfort;[163] in 1st Black Watch, the officers use the men to collect straw for their own dugouts, but not for the men;[164] in 1st Glasgow Highlanders the officers attempt to use the men, tired out after a route march, in a mock attack simply for the benefit of their French civilian acquaintances.[165] Occasionally, however, the men would have the last laugh. Philip Christison relates a delightful tale of one General receiving his come-uppance:

> Major Gen. Egerton, Inspector of Infantry, was a well-known disciplinarian. One day he was going round my Company of 6th Camerons and there was a miserable little Glasgow man in the ranks who was a bit "soft". All day this man was just behind the rest in all he did and the General screamed at him each time. Finally Private Duffy failed to get up and rush forward with his section. The General galloped up to him as he struggled to overtake his section and let out a volley of abuse. Private Duffy turned round and said, "Och, awa! And no bother us, ye've been bothering us a' day." The General was struck speechless and nearly fell from his horse.[166]

Inevitably, in the social milieu of the time, some officers were inclined to take a condescending view of the men under their command. Captain Don Main, in 1/5th Argylls, on board S.S.

---

153 IWM 6873 Hendry, memoir.
154 LC GS 1549 Strachan, memoir.
155 LC GS 0252 Campbell, diary, 7 September, 1917.
156 IWM 4586 Douglas, memoir, p.80; GHM PB2644 Anderson, letter to brother-in-law, George Bruce, 30 November, 1914; BWA, Junks, diary, 14 August, 8 September, 1916; IWM Books Cooper, 'Domi Militaeque', pp.61-62.
157 IWM 3460 Macmillan, diary, 2 November 1914.
158 IWM 4586 Douglas, memoir, pp.455-456; IWM 13263 Bryden, W.N., typescript transcript of his daughter's and grand-daughter's memories of his service.
159 GHM uncatalogued Beaton, memoir, pp.99, 142-143; LC GS 0627 Gilmour, Andrew, 'The Other Enemy', *The Beam*, September, 1982, pp.34-35.
160 GHM PB2644 Anderson, letter to brother-in-law, George Bruce, 30 November, 1914.
161 IWM Books Brooke, 'Wait for it', pp.298-299.
162 ASHM N-E12.Fisher, 'The 12th Battalion,' p.16.
163 ASHM N-E11 Bowie, 'diary.' For unfair allocation of rations, see also for 1/4th Black Watch, Andrews, *Autobiography*, pp.98-99.
164 BWA Laing, diary, 7 April, 1915.
165 IWM 3460 Macmillan, diary, 28 May, 1915.
166 IWM 4370 Christison, memoir, p.30.

Andania, steaming towards Egypt in June, 1915, wrote, "Men are very trying at times and often need looking after like little children."[167] Intelligent soldiers in the ranks would resent this condescension. R. Denham, a medical student at Aberdeen University, enlisted in 4th Gordons in 1916, aged 19:

> What I disliked most about my army life was the fact that we never seemed to be regarded as anything approaching normal intelligent human beings and seldom received any information regarding what was going on around us. We all did just what we were told with as much grace as we could muster.[168]

John Bowie in 11th Argylls records a case of a good fighting soldier's outstanding achievement in manning a Lewis Gun during the German 1918 offensive being overlooked for a medal allegedly because he was considered to be "of the 'Hooligan' class."[169] After the Armistice, Arthur Wrench was invited to take on the role of officers' mess waiter, the incumbent having been demobilised, but contemptuously refused. "Imagine me waiting table to that little rat? He was never better off in his life before and will no doubt have to brush his own boots again when he gets back to 'civvy' life."[170]

Otherwise, given the number of promotions made from the ranks, especially from those battalions formed early in the war with a large intake from the professional classes, it was inevitable that old pals, who served together as recruits, would sometimes encounter each other across the rank divide. This could be potentially awkward. In some cases, officers deliberately maintained distance, in a manner that could be quite humiliating. Arthur Wrench in 1/4th Seaforths records an encounter with a former colleague in the ranks, since commissioned.

> Was cycling back from the batt. when I saw three of our second lieutenants coming along. One was a fellow who was a full private with me at Fort George and this is his first time out. The others looked pretty raw too. But I felt I wanted to dismount and speak to him a minute although he only gave me a dirty look which nearly froze me stiff. After all, is an officer so damned superior that it forbids a recognition between old pals? So to Hell with him.[171]

In rather more cases, the encounters were handled sensitively.[172] John Cooper trained with the Black Watch at Ripon in 1916. Having been drafted to 1/6th Black Watch in France, in December, 1916,

---

167 ASHM N-E5 Main, letter to wife, Win, 12 June, 1915. See also LC CO 066 Murray, Albert Victor, letter from 2Lt K.J. Campbell, 23 March, 1915.
168 LC WF Recollections D8 Denham, memoir.
169 ASHM N-E11 Bowie, 'diary.'
170 IWM 3834 Wrench, diary, 31 January, 1919.
171 IWM 3834 Wrench, diary, 15 May, 1917.
172 Apart from references cited below, see: IWM 3460 Macmillan, letter from Alex Macmillan to mother, 9 September, 1916; IWM Books Cooper, 'Domi Militaeque', pp.31, 62; IWM 4586 Douglas, memoir, pp.1287, 1293-1294; LC WF Recollections A9 Andrew, memoir.

> Judge my surprise to see Lt Clark, whom I had known at Ripon, and 2nd Lt George M. Steel, who had also been at Ripon, and beside whom I had often sat in the Morgan Academy! Of course, we were on parade – but what heartless militarist will condemn us, if I so far forgot decorum as to smile broadly, and George, instead of peering into the mechanism of my rifle, smiled too, and said, 'Hullo, John! I'll see you later.' As things turned out, it was some days before we could have a conversation.[173]

Alex Macmillan served in the ranks of 11th Argylls, before himself attending officers' training, after being wounded at the front in 1917. He did not forget his former pals in the ranks who had helped him, writing to his mother; "Could you bake two cakes please. I want to send two parcels to France for Xmas, to 2 of the best pals I can ever have, Willie Needham … & Gordon Farries, who took me to the dressing station after I was buried."[174]

A special relationship existed between officers and their servants. Although not all servants were a success,[175] many officers record their dependence on and appreciation of their servants.[176] This relationship could become quite friendly and intimate.[177] Officers shared the tribulations of their servants,[178] and demonstrated their concern in practical ways, for example, allowing their servant to share a small dugout in the trenches,[179] or by invoking the help of wives and mothers at home. One asks his mother to send tobacco and comforts to his servant, wounded in hospital;[180] another asks his wife to visit his wounded servant in hospital;[181] one officer's wife visits the wife or mother of his servant, just to offer support;[182] another asks his mother to visit his servant's wife to give her a parcel to send to him.[183] The affection between officer and servant could be very strong. Graham Hutchison, an officer in 2nd Argylls, pays a tribute to his servant, Peter, shot by a sniper in March, 1915, which is astonishing in its intensity. Peter was an orphan. Gathered from the streets of Glasgow, he was sent to a school on the outskirts of the city. There he acquired a sound education, and shone like a star as a piper and dancer. In due course he joined the regiment. "At war, Peter became my batman, a faithful servant, a friend and counsellor, an ever-present companion to give me confidence in the darkness of a dangerous night, and good cheer." When Peter was killed next to Hutchison in the trenches on 2nd March, 1915;

> I held his hands a moment as a soul winged its way from that horror. Then I covered him; there was nothing man could do. Little Peter had bidden me fare well … Peter was

---

173 IWM Books Cooper, 'Domi Militaeque', p.87.
174 IWM 3460 Macmillan, letter from Alex Macmillan to mother, 4 December, 1917.
175 IWM 6702 Low, letter to his wife, Noanie, 11 December, 1914.
176 IWM 15460 PP Chandler, letter to sister Kate, 12 April, 1915; LC GS 0890 Kershaw, letter dated 19 July, 1915; One of the Jocks (Scott), *Odd Shots*, pp.55, 58; IWM 18455 Turnbull, letter to sister Sylvia, 7 January, 1916; LC GS 1761 Wilson, memoir, pp.22, 98; THM Camerons 94-8 Mackay, 'Tell Them of Us,' letters from Ian Mackay to mother, 16, 19 April, 1915.
177 GHM PB1892.3.1 Youngson, memoir, p.19; IWM Books Cooper, 'Domi Militaeque', p.194.
178 IWM 8592 Macgregor, letter to wife Dulcie, 15 January, 1919.
179 GHM uncatalogued Beaton, memoir, p.87.
180 Mackenzie, *Diary and Letters*, p.43, letter to mother, 22 October, 1914.
181 IWM 6702 Low, letter to his wife, Noanie, 15 March, 1915.
182 ASHM N-E5 Main, letter to wife, Win, 4 August, 1915.
183 Webster, *Mesopotamia 1916-1917*, p.11, letter to mother, 16 October, 1916.

incomparable – the friend in need, the friend of perfection. I knew him as one incapable of fear, of stainless honour, sincere, modest, unselfish, his mind a veritable garden of flowers in which were blooms of matchless purity and fragrance, its paths overhung everywhere with the red roses of sacrifice.[184]

Such feelings could be reciprocated. In August, 1916, Private William McLaren, servant to Lieutenant Charles Macgregor wrote to his officer's wife after Macgregor had been wounded:

I have been with Mr Macgregor since he joined my Battalion on the 8th Oct last and this has upset me very much as I was very much attached to him and he was always so nice and kind to me, and we never had an angry word all the time. He was very much liked by our Colonel, Captain, Brother Officers & men and his loss is much regretted … Hoping to hear good news soon of my Officer from Mr Macgregor Senr & yourself.[185]

Servants could express genuine sorrow on being parted from their officers,[186] and would write letters of condolence to their officer's loved ones in the event of his death.[187] Captain Alan Shewan was killed at Martinpuich on 15 September, 1916 while serving with 11th Argylls. In a letter of condolence, his soldier servant wrote a short poem;

He was a master true & Kind,
Beloved by one & all,
The memories he has left behind
Kind actions oft recall[188]

We have already considered the relationship between N.C.O.'s and their officers. It remains to consider that between N.C.O.'s and their men, a subject which has been far less studied. The senior N.C.O in the battalion was of course, the Regimental Sergeant Major. Arguably his role was just as important as the Commanding Officer in maintaining the spirit and ethos of the battalion. Pailthorpe, M.O. of 2nd Gordons, spoke with great respect of their R.S.M., Robert Fleming:

He was a great disciplinarian whose word was absolute law and he was entirely fair. I complained once to him … that I had lost several stretcher-bearers returned to duty to their companies owing to their having given trouble when out of the line and in billets near the drummers and pipers who were under the charge of the Drum Major. The Sergeant Major gave me his views which I can't repeat and at that moment the Drum Major was seen in the

---

184 Hutchison, *Warrior*, pp.66-72.
185 GHM PB161 Macgregor Charles Lewis, letter from Pte William McLaren, his servant, to Mrs C.L. Macgregor, 29 August, 1916.
186 GHM uncatalogued Beaton, memoir, p.179; IWM 233 McKechnie, letter from servant Ferguson to McKechnie, no date.
187 ASHM N-E7 Forbes, Alexander Bruce, letter of condolence from his servant, William Gemmell, to his mother, 4 November, 1918.
188 IWM 6444 Shewan, extract from letter of condolence from his servant.

distance. The Sergeant Major bellowed for him and he came up at the double and stood to attention – a V.C. and a fine soldier but not quite the man that Fleming was. I moved off as I heard the beginning of the exhortation which was extremely forcible. I had no more trouble with my stretcher bearers wherever they might be billeted.[189]

About June, 1918, Major Pailthorpe asked R.S.M. Fleming why he messed alone with the Regimental Quarter Master Sergeant. Fleming replied, "If I messed with our present Company Sergeant Majors, Sir, they'd be calling me Bob after 48 hours!"[190]

In practice, though, while the R.S.M. might set the tone, the day to day running of platoons and companies depended very much on their own N.C.O.'s, whose role, as we have already discussed in considering officer-N.C.O. relations, was vital. Lieutenant Wilson, who served in 5th Camerons in 1918, made astute observations on this role:

If trench life had its periods of tension, anxiety or pure drudgery, when things were quiet and movement by day impossible, boredom and slackness were easily bred and difficult to counter. When men had nothing to occupy them for any length of time petty troubles were apt to flare up, and they could spread like a contagion. It was here that the good N.C.O. with the knack of handling his platoon or section was invaluable. He could snuff out or tamp down argumentation before it developed into quarrelling; he knew the personalities in the mixed grill of the ranks, and his success lay in his compounding common sense, humour and reasonable latitude with firmness of touch when required.[191]

Styles varied. Some distance from the men was desirable, but was not universally applied.[192] Some rough and ready justice might be administered (rather than putting men on charges) and could be accepted if fair.[193] Senior N.C.O's, like officers, could grow attached to their men[194] and the best would look after them like a father, trying gently, for example, to break the news of a soldier's father's death.[195] D. Dick in 14th Argylls recalls how, in the appalling conditions after the Somme, a thoughtful sergeant prepared a tin of Maconochie and a mug of tea for some of his exhausted men.[196]

Like their officers too, N.C.O.'s could feel the burden of responsibility. George Stables was haunted by a mistake he made when, in October, 1918, as a platoon sergeant in 6/7th Gordons, he took out on patrol a man who was sweating on leave who was killed.[197] Another mistake affected Private Donald McKay in 5th Camerons who, in July, 1916, found that he was not relieved after being put on guard duty at Delville Wood for half an hour by his sergeant. Abandoned and found, he finally arrived back in the battalion after a spell at Etaples. When

---

189 GHM PB375 Pailthorpe, memoir, p.40. For another anecdote, see pp.68-69.
190 GHM PB375 Pailthorpe, memoir, p.75.
191 LC GS 1761 Wilson, memoir, p.30. See also: GHM PB1639 Kemp, memoir, p.43.
192 IWM Books Cooper, 'Domi Militaeque', p.31; IWM Books Brooke, 'Wait for it', pp.163-164.
193 LC GS 1026 Maclean, memoir, p.8.
194 GHM PB2021 Stewart, letter to wife Lil, 25 July, 10 August, 1915; LC GS 1203 Oldham, diary, 15 April, 1917.
195 LC GS 1422 Sanders, diary, 24 November, 1914.
196 LC GS 0456 Dick, memoir, p.45.
197 LC GS 1516 Stables, letter describing his experiences, 5 February, 1979.

he turned up, "the sergeant that saw me, he started to cry when he saw me. 'Well, McKay, I thought I would never see you again. That night I sent you on guard,' he said, 'we got the order to retire and I forgot all about you.' 'Oh,' I said, 'I am still alive anyway.'"[198]

Many soldiers record their appreciation of their Senior N.C.O.'s.[199] They might respect the R.S.M., even if they did not fully appreciate his gentle manner,[200] while their own S.N.C.O. might appear as a father figure,[201] even if their avuncular welcome to barracks might not be replicated by their welcome to the drill square.[202] John Cooper, in training at Ripon with the Black Watch, indeed felt that his company was held together by the Sergeant Major:

> If we had not had a real good fellow for a Sergeant Major, I fear 'A' Company would have had a bad time. 'Jock' Wilkie was an old regular, and one of the best. He tolerated no nonsense, but he was, I am sure, the one who kept peace, and saved a deal of trouble to us from the two commanders we had.[203]

I.G. Andrew was recruited into the Glasgow University company of 6th Camerons in 1914. He had enormous respect for the experienced reservist N.C.O.'s put over them, and provides delightful cameos of them.[204] As in the case with their officers, kindness and consideration would be noted. Private Douglas noted how, in the support trenches near Arras in November, 1917, Sergeant Grey was sharing a dug-out with a prisoner who was released from detention to serve in the line when the battalion went up. He was impressed that, when the sergeant received a parcel from home, he was kind enough to give Walker a meat sandwich out of it.[205] Frank Brooke expresses appreciation that, when he with another companion became separated and delayed returning from a fatigue party, his Company Sergeant Major came to look for them in person, rather than detail the job to a subordinate.[206]

Unsurprisingly, soldiers would write letters of condolence to the loved ones of their N.C.O.'s, just as they would for officers. Private Tom Ritchie was wounded in an attack on 16 June, 1915, in which his sergeant, Alex McCallum, was killed. On 25 July, 1915, he wrote to his sergeant's father from Wrest Park hospital:

> He was a gallant lad and a splendid soldier under fire; what more can one want of his sons in a time like this? I trust you do not grieve too much. There is always one who looks on while men quarrel like ants and Honours brave men in a righteous cause. Alex was one of those men.[207]

---

198 LC Transcripts Tape 526 McKay, interview.
199 IWM 4440 Croft, interview, 1979; IWM 4586 Douglas, memoir, pp.397-398; Fennah, *Retaliation*, p 74; IWM 3460 Macmillan, diary, 22 March, 1915.
200 IWM 4586 Douglas, memoir, pp.320-321.
201 GHM. PB2984 Strachan, memoir.
202 IWM 14335 Man, memoir, p.12.
203 IWM Books Cooper, 'Domi Militaeque', p.62.
204 LC WF Recollections A9 Andrew, memoir. On Willie Watt, see also: Anon, *Souvenir Booklet 6th Camerons*, pp.39-40, tribute by 'W.D.R.'
205 IWM 4586 Douglas, memoir, p.158.
206 IWM Books Brooke, 'Wait for it', p.169.
207 IWM 2940 PP Ritchie, T.K., letter to Mr D McCallum, 25 July, 1915.

It is nevertheless clear from the sources that some N.C.O.'s were not popular or struggled to win respect and authority.[208] In some cases this was down to abuse of their position. Thus, we find a corporal in 11th Argylls accused of taking an unfair share of rations and blankets.[209] And in November, 1914, Sergeant Spence Sanders in 6th Gordons in France noted, "Having trouble with the men – they say we keep too much jam for the sergts mess – so we do as well."[210] N.C.O.'s are accused of shirking on working parties;[211] of ordering privates to clean up their own billets;[212] of with-holding green envelopes;[213] of expropriating gambling money;[214] and of victimisation.[215] While training with 2nd Liverpool Scottish in England, Corporal Alfred Fennah was damning of the R.S.M. and the "minions" who supported him.[216] He even records an attempted assault on the R.S.M. which back-fired.[217] Fennah's personal approach to his own rank as corporal appears to have been avuncular and familiar rather than disciplinarian, and it was this approach which probably lay behind his poor relationship with his company commander and the R.S.M.[218]

Ultimately, Fennah's approach to discipline appears to have been out of kilter with that in the battalion, and he was sent away from the battalion in France to a base job, to the great regret of his platoon sergeant.[219] The same independence of spirit probably lay behind some of Private Norman Macmillan's criticism of his N.C.O.'s in 1st Glasgow Highlanders. As he writes in September, 1915, "[Sergeant] McGlashen in Penny's presence inferred that he was not over-pleased to have me back again owing to my (to him) unpleasant habit of giving him advice when I thought his ideas lacking in all they might be."[220]

It is evident that there are many instances of harmonious relations across the Highland battalions, between C.O., officers, N.C.O.'s and men; good relations that undoubtedly contributed to morale and 'esprit de corps.' The care shown for their charges by C.O.'s, officers and N.C.O.'s is sometimes very impressive indeed. It is equally evident that sometimes these relationships broke down, to the point of dysfunction. There are some examples of C.O.'s held in contempt, and even more of officers and N.C.O.'s. Constant change did not ease the situation. The notion of a 'band of brothers,' held together by mutual respect rather than by coercive discipline is too idealistic to stand up to rigorous enquiry. There certainly was a great deal of mutual respect, and a great deal of discipline was certainly maintained quietly in this way through soft power. But in the final analysis, one sees ordinary men thrust into extraordinary situations, coping as best they could. Some were up to it and rose magnificently to the occasion; others were not. So,

---

208 IWM 4586 Douglas, memoir, pp.114-115; THM Seaforths 81-180 Murray, letter to sister Alex, 24 April, 1915; BWA Guthrie, letters to his wife Crissie, 24 September, 15 October, 1915.
209 IWM 4586 Douglas, memoir, pp.114-115, 147-148.
210 LC GS 1422 Sanders, diary, 24 November, 1914.
211 IWM 3460 Macmillan, diary, 4 February, 1915.
212 Ibid., 20 August, 1915.
213 Ibid., 19 June, 1915.
214 LC Several Fronts Recollections, Munro, Recollections.
215 IWM 4586 Douglas, memoir, pp.329-332.
216 Fennah, *Retaliation*, p.81.
217 Ibid., p.102.
218 Ibid., p.113.
219 Ibid., pp.138-139.
220 IWM 3460 Macmillan, diary, 30 September, 1915. For an example of this rather fractious attitude, see his diary, 10 November, 1915.

the soft power of human relationships always had available as back-up if necessary the hard rod of coercive discipline. Furthermore, the good working relationships identified between C.O.'s. officers and men will not strike anyone who has served in the British Army as remotely unique. They were the bread and butter of regimental life, as were their successes and failures. The principal conclusion about relationships between ranks in the Highland regiments is not their uniqueness; it is their normalcy.

11

Comradeship

> In those days [neither] fury nor fear, let slip
> Tho' it were by Hell, the delight could strip
> From youth's war-vanquishing comradeship.[1]

It is perhaps a truism to state that the awfulness of war may nevertheless engender the finest feelings of brotherhood. This was certainly felt by many of those who served in the Highland regiments. Major A.G. Wade for example even thought that the feeling of comradeship engendered during wartime was compensation when compared with the degradation of peacetime unemployment.

> The fact remains that war produces – or perhaps I should say brings to the surface – some of the finest feelings and emotions of which men are capable. Such things as tolerance, bravery, devotion, and, above all, the truest and finest of all comradeships … Then a man's reputation did not rest on his social position, or what his father or grandfather had done. He went through on his face value – his value as a soldier and a comrade … Peace has, so far, failed to produce anything resembling this state of things![2]

Linton Andrews, who served in 1/4th Black Watch, truly valued this comradeship:

> Even if I sometimes hated to be a soldier, I was now glad to have been one. Soldiering had imbued me with immense, lasting sympathy for the under-dog, for the millions of patient obscure workers. 'Love the brotherhood' now had a wider, deeper meaning for me than it had when I saw the words daily displayed at Christ's Hospital [where he had been at school].[3]

Likewise, Hugh Boustead, writing of the South African Scottish before the Somme:

---

1 Macleod, John, Dunning, *Macedonian Measures*, (Cambridge University Press, 1919), p.8, poem 'Gomonic.'
2 Wade, *Counterspy*, pp.66-67.
3 Andrews, *Autobiography*, p.101.

I suppose that if we had been individuals confronting alone the agony of the Somme, we should have run away; but we were tied inextricably to one another by our training and our shared experience. No other endurance except great danger at sea or on the mountains could bring about the same link of comradeship. We were bound to one another, men on the same rope.[4]

This comradeship was a vital quality. In a sketch intended for publication in the newspapers, Captain Alex Scott of 1/7th Argylls draws attention, ahead of his time, to the link between this comradeship and the will to fight.

> When his trench is being heavily shelled, a man may divide his time between abusing the Kaiser, and telling himself what a fool he was ever to leave home; but he sits tight because his neighbours are sitting tight. When ordered to advance under the fire of machine guns and their devilish inventions, he keeps on the move because the rest of the platoon are on the move too.[5]

N.C.O.s and Men

Many Highland soldiers[6] record the happy state of comradeship which existed in their units. In June, 1915, for example, Norman Macmillan wrote of his group of friends in the Glasgow Highlanders:

> Our little six has now grown to eight by the inclusion of two others from No.3 Section. We all get on very well together. It makes it very much nicer to know that you have some fellows that you can count on to back you up thro' thick & thin. And this is what our eight would do, seven of them for any one who needed their help in anything.[7]

Likewise, Ian Andrew, a member of the Glasgow University Company of 6th Camerons, at night in his hut at Bramshott Camp, felt a sense of "a noble fellowship dedicated to a great purpose, that gripped my heart and moved me almost to tears."[8]

N.C.O.'s and men, and indeed officers, shared many of the attributes of comradeship, but there were differences. Unlike the junior ranks, Senior N.C.O.s might create messes, which helped to create and maintain bonds between themselves. David McMillan, who was a Company Sergeant Major in 43rd Battalion C.E.F. (Cameron Highlanders of Canada) notes that in his company, "No matter where we were, no matter what the conditions (except if we were in the

---

4   Boustead, *The Wind of Morning*, p.31. For similar Canadian views, see Beattie, *48th Highlanders*, p.191, and Urquhart, *Canadian Scottish*, p.337.
5   One of the Jocks (Scott), *Odd Shots*, p.13.
6   Apart from specific refs cited below, see: Chambers, *Diaries of World war 1*, pp.41-43; IWM 13262 Bryden, R.E.C., letter to father, 1 April, 1916; Fennah, *Retaliation*, p.81; Anon, *9th Royal Scots (T.F.) B Company on Active Service, from a Private's Diary February-May 1915* (Edinburgh: 9th Royal Scots, 1916), pp.38-40; Mitchell, *Off Parade*, poems, 'Off Parade', p.7, and 'Rambles', p.12.
7   IWM 3460 Macmillan, letter to mother, 25 June, 1915.
8   LC WF Recollections A9, Andrew, memoir.

front line) we always had a sergeants' Mess of sorts and we made a point of living with some semblance of decency and never 'pigging it.'"[9] Similarly, Captain Sutherland notes how in 5th Seaforths, at Henencourt in September, 1915, "The sergeants of 'B' Company resolved to form a Sergeants' Mess, for which they hired a room in a village farm. So successful was the venture that the opening ceremony took place with great eclat four nights in succession."[10]

Otherwise, senior N.C.O.s might fall victim to the same careerism and professional jealousy which, as we shall see, was quite common amongst the officers. John Bowie, in 11th Argylls, notes how, when a new C.Q.M.S. was appointed, he aroused the jealousy of the others who conspired to bring him down by engineering a charge of 'Wilful damage to Government property.' He was able to defend himself and was honourably acquitted by the Colonel.[11] Similarly, the letters of Alick Guthrie, a Senior N.C.O. in 1/6th Black Watch, and a pre-war Territorial, contain frequent references to the S.N.C.O.'s' promotion pyramid. In December, 1915, then Acting R.Q.M.S., he wrote:

> I have heard that Sergeant Gray is coming out to us shortly to take up the Regt. Sergt Major's job. My! Won't he be a big man? I am glad he won't be able to lord it over me. It was always a sore point with him that I held a senior rank to him, and he would have been my senior had I still been Coy S.M.[12]

In most other respects, however, the N.C.O.s appear to have shared the experience of the men with regard to comradeship.

The way in which the ordinary soldiers coped was generally by chumming up with a small group of pals,[13] who would stick by one another, share effort, pool resources, and give mutual support, like Norman Macmilllan's group of eight. Ian Andrew described the process:

> Before long it was noticeable how we all tended to fall into inseparable groups of threes or fours. Four was a particularly good number, because by getting together when the platoon fell in we could be sure of sticking together during the long route marches which were a regular feature of our training. I have always thought I was singularly lucky in our quartet, but then so I suppose did every other gang of close associates … We four became inseparable. We marched together, drilled together, ate together and at night slept next to each other wherever we might be – tent, hut, billet or under the open air of heaven.[14]

How necessary this was is illustrated by the case of one of these men. Donald Thomson was a musician, a gifted pianist.

---

9 McMillan, *Trench Tea and Sandbags*, p.11.
10 Sutherland, *War Diary*, p.39.
11 ASHM N-E11 Bowie, diary, fol 25 December, 1917.
12 BWA Guthrie, letter to wife Crissie, 8 December, 1915. See also his letters of 21 June, 1915, 23, 28 January, 7 March,1916.
13 Apart from refs cited, see: THM Seaforths 81-180, Murray, letter to sister Alex, 15 January, 1915; THM Seaforths 89-122 Paterson, memoir; THM 2013-072 (S) Braes, memoir, p.4; THM Seaforths 89-26 Crask, letters to parents, 25, 26 April, 25 May, 4? June, 1915.
14 LC WF Recollections A9, Andrew, memoir.

Comrades. Men of 9th Royal Scots. (Author's collection)

> Vague and dreamy ... he drifted sadly about, never quite able to attune himself to the rigours and coarseness of Army life ... Poor Donald was not really cut out for soldiering, either from the point of view of temperament or physique, yet he stuck it out with remarkable spirit and refused to take the easier way out of applying for a commission. All three of us did our best to shield him from the worst rigours of soldiering.[15]

The importance of this support might be recognised by battalions. When Private Anderson's draft joined 1/9th Royal Scots at the front in about April, 1916, "Those friends who wish to remain together are sent so far as is possible to the same platoon, and five of us who had been together since Dundee are lucky enough to be posted to 'No.9' platoon."[16]

Not everyone found it easy to fit in and find friends. Willie Macmillan, for example, struggled to make friends in 7th Seaforths, complaining in July, 1915, that his comrades did not offer him any bread in the trenches:

> altho' I always share anything extra I have, no one offered me a bit ... This platoon is made up of 2 cliques; men from Wick, & men from Lancashire, with a few men from Glasgow & Edinburgh to complete it. I'm sorry to have to admit that after 10 months I can't bring myself to like either the Wick or the Lancashire men.[17]

---

15 LC WF Recollections A9, Andrew, memoir
16 IWM 3608 Anderson, memoir.
17 IWM 3460 Macmillan, letter from Willie Macmillan to mother, 21 July, 1915.

It appears that he had been effectively deserted by the pal he joined up with, who had left to join the Royal Engineers. "I made a big error in not going with a more proven pal."[18]

One initial barrier to friendships was the gulf between the coarseness of the more disreputable uneducated 'working-class' recruits and the more refined manners of the more educated recruits, many of whom were 'middle-class' and who provide a disproportionate amount of our written testimony. As Arthur Wrench wrote of his early training with the Seaforths at Fort George in 1915, "Taken on the whole it was an interesting and novel introduction to the human side of man's nature where refinement and vulgarity, and education and ignorance co-abided."[19] Many recruits express their shock and disgust at the coarseness of their fellows,[20] not least, new Derby recruit Herbert Junks, who joined 3/4th Black Watch at Ripon on 31 July, 1916. "The language at meal times is disgusting, each man seems to vie with his neighbour as to who can use the most and foulest language. I think I shall never be able to stick it."[21] Pay night, as already noted when considering discipline, was a time for drunkenness and excess.[22] The use of prostitutes and general sexual licence appalled others.[23] Peter McGregor, who had joined 14th Argylls, a married man with children, and a most tolerant observer, wrote to his wife from Ernsettle camp.

> Some of the chaps come in awfully 'fu'. Then they talk quite openly about what they do with the Plymouth ladies – how they enjoy it – and so forth – how much it costs.
>
> You should hear how the chaps talk about the girls here, and what they do to them – one told me two of them had tea in a house near here kept by two widows. After tea they turned out to be – guess what? – another chap told me they had a girl in a field – Two of them – think of it![24]

When, after hospitalisation, Private Douglas, formerly of 11th Argylls, returned to the Argylls training battalion at Ripon camp, he found himself in doubtful company in his hut, which was dominated by three members of the 'Redskins,' a Glasgow gang.[25]

Otherwise, there was contempt for those men who failed to display the selflessness expected by their more idealistic critics. Private Charles Fettes was not impressed by the men of 1/4th Gordons, when coming out of the trenches for the first time in March, 1915: "Nothing but groans and yells of dissatisfaction were heard from our lot … Selfishness seems to be a minus quantity amongst these other fellows. I am absolutely disgusted with the way our fellows carry on."[26] And George Ramage, a teacher in civilian life, drafted to 1st Gordons in April, 1915,

---

18 Ibid., letter from Willie Macmillan to mother, 8 September, 1915.
19 IWM 3834 Wrench, diary, introduction.
20 Apart from the refs cited, see: IWM Books Cooper, 'Domi Militaeque,' pp.18-19, 338, 350; Andrews, *Autobiography*, p.82; IWM 3460 Macmillan, letter from Alex (Sandy) Macmillan to mother, postmark 15 December, 1915; IWM Books Brooke, 'Wait for it,' pp.84-85; LC GS 1027 Macleod, letter to mother, 15 September, 1914.
21 BWA Junks, diary, 1, 5 August, 1916.
22 IWM Books Cooper, 'Domi Militaeque,' p.350.
23 See also: IWM Books Cooper, 'Domi Militaeque,' pp.18-19; Andrews, *Autobiography*, p.82; IWM 3834 Wrench, diary, 13 December, 1915.
24 IWM 21092 McGregor, letter to wife Jen, 14 July, 27 August, 1915.
25 IWM 4586 Douglas, memoir, pp.293-295.
26 GHM PB1726 Fettes, diary, 6 March, 1915.

found similar faults in his regular battalion. On 4 May, he records men falling over in the mud on the way to deliver coke and rations to the firing-line.

> Another man falls with a curse and as I stop to help him I slip on a greasy knoll & fall flat ingloriously on my back beside him. I laughed at my collapse but he was damned sullen at his – thought he was to vent his annoyance on me who had stopped to help him. These damned working-class grousers don't see any humour in anything … falls, curses, grumbles every moment, never a joke or cheery remark – damn them – and these are the Gay Gordons … they have no proper spirit about them these men.[27]

In the Glasgow Highlanders, there was a significant difference in background between the two elements which made up the battalion which went to France; the men of the original battalion, "from lowlier families" and the 400 recruits from the 2nd line battalion who were drafted in at the last minute to make up numbers, "from good family homes." Norman Macmillan was one of the 400. In the retrospective preface to his diary, he notes the division in relatively moderate terms,[28] but, in a diary entry made just a year after the event, he is acerbic about the attitude of the original 1st Battalion men to the 400.

> And to those who might have helped us we turned in vain. The first Batt. men, to whose detriment we had been landed, spared us not an idle thought. We were fair game. We were on the roster. Now their turn had come. They returned us deliberate evil for an evil whose original in us was abstract, undreamt of by us. We believed in the honesty of man. We thought that all were sportsmen. We were basely deceived. Our very food, vile tho' it was, was pilfered. We were domineered, disdained, subjected to abuse. We were bottom dog.[29]

Faced with such a social difference, for some the solution was to find friendship with kindred souls. Alexander Braes, for example, who had volunteered for service with the Seaforth Highlanders, arrived at Fort George on 8 September, 1914. There he met a pal, Jimmie Collins, who "seemed as anxious for my company as I was for his." But Jimmie was sent to Aldershot that same day.

> It was with regret that I waved my hand to Collins, as he marched out. Now that he was gone I had to make the best of it on my own. I had never been used to mixing with crowds of men, excepting twice when I had stayed at the Co-operative Camp at Rothesay; but then it was with my friends (who were gentlemen in every respect and whom I had carefully selected) but now I was amongst a crowd of strangers who were dirty and starving, through no fault of their own.[30]

Gordon Crask, a public-school man from Bradford who had enlisted in the Seaforth Highlanders in April, 1915, managed to team up with others of similar background at Dingwall. "I have

---

27 NLS MS945 Ramage, diary, 4 May, 1915. See also entries for 27 April, 7, 22, 23 May.
28 IWM 3460 Macmillan, diary, Preface.
29 Ibid., 17 January, 1916.
30 THM 2013-072 (S) Braes, memoir, p.4.

found a very nice fellow called Burnham who was educated at Dulwich School – he has introduced me to all the public-school men here. There are about ten of us, so we shall have a nice time together." Later, at Fort George, he teamed up with a group of seven other Bradford fellows and an old school friend.[31] When Linton Andrews, a journalist, first joined his local Territorial battalion of the Black Watch in Dundee in August, 1914, he found the situation initially intolerable, but things improved vastly when some of his office colleagues joined, and together they created a group called 'the Fighter Writers,' which included the poet, Joe Lee.[32]

Some doubtful characters might find themselves threatened with expulsion from a group. One such was Joe Rice, in a group with William Paterson in 3/5th Seaforths in Summer, 1915, in Tent No.11.

> Much as we liked Joe (for he was ever willing to oblige) he had one failure, to which I think every old soldier like Joe is more or less addicted. He loved the bottle better than his wife and family, and many a night we threatened to 'split partnership' and throw him out, leaving him to the tender mercies of the hooligans in No.10 tent. They were a motley crowd of Belfast men of the worst type, who were continually in trouble. But one couldn't help liking Joe despite all his faults, and he continued with us for many months as batman and storekeeper.[33]

Those who did not find themselves in a like-minded group might find occasional consolation in meeting others of similar background. George Ramage was delighted to find 4th Gordons alongside 1st Battalion in April, 1915. "Met Forbes, Allerdyce, Knox of Aberdeen University. Very glad indeed to have educated, unprejudiced men to talk to at last."[34] Others might take consolation from the fact that, with their education, they might still be tacitly respected as mentors by the less educated members of their platoon, as John Cooper found when he was retained for service in the East with 12th Argylls after the Armistice.[35]

Some men never fully accepted the social world of the army. George Ramage was unable to become selfishly streetwise:

> In evening we were sent to an old excellently constructed large disused headquarters dugout to break it up for its beams & planks. Worked loyally like a nigger under a corporal till the C.O … ordered that no more wood was to be brought up, so got no wood for my dugout. Other workers had sneaked away against orders with enough wood for their dugouts while I worked on loyally under the corporal. I had expected that the wood would be divided amongst the dugouts. My reward for honesty & obedience was that I had no cover while the selfish had abundance. Honesty is not the best policy.[36]

---

31 THM Seaforths 89-26 Crask, letter to mother, 25, 26 April, 25 May, 4? June, 1915.
32 Andrews, *Autobiography*, pp.82-84. see also: IWM Books Cooper, 'Domi Militaeque,' pp.18-19; Burrows, Rob, *Fighter Writer* (Derby: Breedon Books, 2004).
33 THM Seaforths 89-122 Paterson, memoir.
34 NLS MS944 Ramage, diary, 14 April, 1915.
35 IWM Books Cooper, 'Domi Militaeque,' p.338.
36 NLS MS945 Ramage, diary, 28 May, 1915.

By contrast, Frank Brooke, who joined 1/4th Seaforths about July, 1916, claims that "eventually I became as foul-mouthed and as easily addicted to 'scrounging' (i.e. thieving) as the rest. I saw cleanly-minded boys deteriorate rapidly, but it was impossible to avoid becoming so brutalised."[37] He claims to have witnessed an incident which deeply disturbed him.

> My attention was attracted to a group of kilties highly delighted at something in their midst. I strolled over to find a Belgian girl, barely six years of age, wearing a balmoral bonnet, from which escaped pretty flaxen hair, mouthing the foulest obscenities that ever disgraced my mother tongue, coupling with them atrocious gesturings and posturing after lifting her ragged frock to expose her dirty nakedness.[38]

Despite the friendships he did make, he came to hate "the forced intimate companionship of loose-talking, foul, animal-like brutes (in the main)."[39]

More common, however, was an acceptance of the situation, and a realisation that fine qualities might lurk beneath rough exteriors. One who recognised this was the placid Peter McGregor. Amongst other kindnesses, on return from leave, he wrote, "decent chaps are there to help and sympathise over your coming back and feeling homesick" In the end, he declined the possibility of a commission in order to stay with his pals. "It's best all round to be surrounded by your pals in moments such as we have come through."[40] Even George Ramage could acknowledge instances of fine comradeship in the trenches, notably when he was shot through the hand in a trench in June, 1915.

> The 4 bombers at my post were all very kind. Was somewhat helpless & my slightest request was attended to at once with great kindness & sympathy. They put on my puttees properly, tied sling, opened pack, lit cigs, filled pipe, gave me tea & part of their rations, for I had had none for more than a day ... I had some candles in my pack. With these they made a fire for the tea, the finest I ever got in the trenches ... They dug a rest for me at my direction. They gave me souvenirs of German, French & English ammunition, prepared my haversack for me to take with me. Good chaps all.[41]

Men came to be valued for what they were inside, not for their rough exterior. William Fraser Mitchell of 4th Seaforths recognised the issue sympathetically in his poem, 'The man who swears.'

> 'He's an awful chap to swear!' –
> But there's this to say for that:
> You get at him, right there,
> And you get it off him, pat!
> …

---

37 IWM Books Brooke, 'Wait for it,' pp.84-85.
38 Ibid., p.92.
39 Ibid., p.206.
40 IWM 21092 McGregor, letter to wife Jen, 17 October, 19 December, 1915, 21 June, 1916.
41 NLS MS945 Ramage, diary, 18 June, 1915. see also entries for 8, 9 May, 1915.

> I do not hold by swearing,
> But I'd rather have his kind,
> Than the chap whose timely bearing
> Sets his sail to every wind.[42]

The result was, in some cases, to transform understanding and values.[43] Linton Andrews reflected;

> I must have been class-proud and priggish in those early days of the war. So many of the recruits struck me as sensual and dishonest. Now they were my comrades, faithful and true. Had I changed or had they? Probably all of us. Soldiering must have revolutionized some of our moral and social values. There was no doubting my comrades' military virtues. In action they would fight to the death. Out of the line they were friendly, sympathetic human beings again. In battle a man would run frightful risks to help a wounded comrade to safety … Now, especially in danger, I had a strong sense of brotherhood, or at least togetherness, with my fellows. I think almost all of us in the Black Watch had this feeling.[44]

And James Campbell, in 6th Camerons, wrote after Loos;

> Since the big weekend [Loos] I respect and like men I previously detested and have lost all respect for other decent chaps. And all because they turned up trumps or didn't when the pinch came. When we were hard pressed I'd have licked the boots of any man who would carry ammunition and keep the gun in action. And lo, on the Sunday morning, a man I had never drawn well with, came with a case of ammunition and we worked the gun together all day.[45]

Of course, particular individuals had a disproportionate part to play in establishing the spirit of individual groups, a fact well noted by several observers. Lieutenant Cecil Harper in 10th Gordons noted that:

> Our company was fortunate in having a little group of five or six Durham miners from West Hartlepool, who had been together in a male choir in former days. Anywhere, and in any circumstances … they would get together and sing beautifully in harmony. They came to be known throughout the Highland brigade as 'I Company choir'… They contributed greatly to morale; and they knew this and would start without any prompting.[46]

In No. 11 Platoon, 1/6th Argylls, it was John Donnelly who ensured fairness:

---

42 Mitchell, *Off Parade and other Verses*, p.10.
43 Apart from refs cited, see: LC WF Recollections A9, Andrew, memoir; IWM 3460 Macmillan, letters from Alex (Sandy) Macmillan to mother, 20 (postmark), 25 December, and to pal James, 26 December, 1915; IWM 14321 Small, letter to Miss Ethel Shaw, postmark 7 March, 1915.
44 Andrews, *Autobiography*, p.94..
45 LC GS 0262 Campbell, diary, 22 October, 1915.
46 IWM 7593 Harper, memoir, p.18. See also: Andrews, *Autobiography*, p.94.

A big man of powerful physique – big in mind as in body … He is the acknowledged 'father' of the platoon; he is, by virtue of his sense of justice and fairness, the arbiter in any differences that may arise; he is invariably called upon to distribute the platoon rations when the orderlies of the day bring them along … Is there some hesitancy on the part of any newcomers to claim what is their due in anything, John is there and breaks the ice for them. Is a distribution of anything taking place and an absent one likely to be forgotten, John is the first to remember him.[47]

And in the South African Scottish, Hugh Boustead recalls the astonishing comradeship shown by a young American soldier called Veitch, during the Senussi campaign.

The first thing that struck me on that march was the extraordinary selflessness of his behaviour. If any man was limping or absolutely whacked, he would immediately take his rifle from him without a word and carry it himself. He would share his rations, and he would share his last drop of water with a comrade. Never had I seen anyone who bore the marks of utter selflessness more unconcernedly and more naturally.[48]

But if it took dominant individuals to set the tone, there are innumerable instances of kind consideration recorded by Highland soldiers. Joining a new battalion, for example, could be a daunting experience, as Charles Cordner found to his cost when from 15th Argylls he was drafted to 2nd Battalion on 1 July, 1916. He found himself one morning laid out by a blow to the chin, having had the audacity to immerse his shaving brush in a pail without permission, and in addition before an old soldier.[49] Contrast this with the friendly welcome and assistance provided by the veteran Archie Miller to John Cooper when he joined 1/6th Black Watch in December, 1916,[50] or the friendly help given by Sammy Moore to Sandy Macmillan, when he joined 13th Argylls at Catterick in December, 1915, simply because he too came from Cambuslang.[51] Even the unfortunate Private Cordner clearly soon won some comrades. At the end of seven days' C.B., received for smiling on parade, he was notified to appear for Guard next day. His colleagues joined in to help him scrub his equipment and burnish bayonet and scabbard, so well that he obtained the coveted award for being the best turned out soldier on guard.[52] Private Welsh notes that in January, 1917, still weak from a recent illness, he was required to undertake a march of 25 kilometres. "I was not just in a fit state to walk that distance, but my fellow S.B.'s were a practical lot who would never desert a mate, so they saw that I would have nothing to carry but my haversack and belt."[53] When Frank Brooke was training at Ripon with the Seaforths Territorial training battalion, he realised that weekend passes were no use to the Scots, so on two weekends he took a Scots bugler-boy back home with him to his family in Leeds for a break.[54]

---

47   Maclean, *On Active Service* Vol 1, p.31.
48   Boustead, *The Wind of Morning*, p.27.
49   IWM 3449 Cordner, memoir.
50   IWM Books Cooper, 'Domi Militaeque,' pp.88-89.
51   IWM 3460 Macmillan, letter from Alex (Sandy) Macmillan to mother, postmark 25 December, 1915. See also: IWM 3608 Anderson, memoir.
52   IWM 3449 Cordner, memoir.
53   THM Camerons 93-35 Welsh, memoirs, p.16.
54   THM Seaforths 98-11 Brooke, Frank, memoir, pp.6-7.

There are numerous other instances, some of course under fire and at risk to life. Soldiers of 2nd Seaforths behave without any sign of selfishness towards each other when under gas attack on 6 May, 1915;[55] men rescue a wounded comrade from No Man's Land under fire;[56] a dying Seaforth thinks to give up his last cigarette to his pal.[57] An unusual case was that of Private Alex Drummond, who became something of a hero in the Black Watch, when, in an American hospital in France, he saved the life of the man lying next to him, who urgently needed a blood transfusion to live. Private Drummond offered to donate his own blood at considerable danger to himself. The soldier's life was saved, and fortunately Private Drummond pulled through too.[58]

Comradeship was also demonstrated in the sharing of comforts received from home amongst groups of pals,[59] generally food and cigarettes, but also books and magazines. When men, temporarily or permanently, left their sections on leave, on a course, or to a new post, it was normal for their parcels to be shared amongst their group of comrades.[60] Of course, not everyone entered into the spirit of things, and some rarely or ever received parcels themselves. Private Douglas, from Walker-on-Tyne, who joined the 5th reserve battalion of the Argylls at Ripon in April, 1917, found it difficult to chum up with the men in his hut.

> When receiving a parcel from home, I always used to share the contents with the chaps who slept nearest to me in the hut, but soon found that very rarely they shared any of their parcels with me, their cronies from the same part of Scotland where they belonged were asked to participate in the contents. This show of 'Clannishness' did not pass unnoticed by me.[61]

Much later, in August, 1918, when serving in 8th Black Watch (but then as an observer with brigade HQ), he received a parcel of 'eats' from home.

> These eats, according to my usual practice, I divided amongst the other observers … Some of the chaps were very decent with any eats they had received in their parcels, sharing them

---

55 LC Several Fronts Recollections, Kingsley, memoir.
56 IWM 6702 Low, letter to wife Noanie, 25 December, 1914.
57 Cluness, *Doing his bit*, pp.23-25.
58 BWA Drummond, newspaper cutting from *People's Journal*, February, 1917, and poem by R.N. Marshall, 6th Black Watch, 3/18.
59 BWA Couston, letter to mother, 1 August, 1916, 19 March, 1917; BWA Guthrie, letter from R. Ferguson to Guthrie's wife Crissie, 18 July, 1915; IWM 16335 Racine, memoirs, p.48; THM Camerons 93-35 Welsh, memoirs, p.14; IWM Books Cooper, memoir, 'Domi Militaeque,' pp.17, 134; ASHM N-E8 Jordan, letter to mother, 3 December, 1917; ASHM N-E6 O'Connor, Pte Daniel, letter to wife, 12 May, 1915; ASHM N-E8 Kelly, Archie, letter to brother Robert, 5 September, 1914. See also letter to mother, 6 September, 1914; IWM 3460 Macmillan, letter from Alex (Sandy) Macmillan to mother, n.d. [January, 1916], and to 'Bus' at home, 20 January, 1916, letter from Norman Macmillan to Bessie, 22 November, 1914, to mother, 11 December, 1914, 15 February, 31 March, 15, 22 May, 1915; IWM 13262 Bryden, letter to father, 7 April, 1916; Stothers, *Somewhere in France*, pp. 50-51, 62; IWM 21092 McGregor, letter to wife Jen, 16, 22 June, 14 July, 5, 9 September, 2 October, 1915.
60 BWA Guthrie, letter from R. Ferguson to Guthrie's wife Crissie, 18 July, 1915; LC GS 1008 Macdonald, letter to father, 31 December, 1916; GHM uncatalogued Beaton, memoir, p.181; IWM 3460 Macmillan, letter to mother, 14 March, 1915; IWM 21092 McGregor, letter to Nell, 2 July, 1915.
61 IWM 4586 Douglas, memoir, pp.15-16.

out with their particular pals. But others were just the reverse, and of course there were the unfortunate ones who hardly if ever received a parcel form home … I always felt sorry for those chaps, because they must have felt it pretty badly at times.[62]

Robert Dawson, in U Company of 4th Gordons showed consideration to a fellow in his company in such a position, writing to his mother, "there is one fellow who … gets very few parcels … He would no doubt [be] glad to receive any little thing, but of course, don't give away my name."[63]

When all shared, pals could occasionally enjoy a feast. On 11 May, 1915, Norman Macmillan in the Glasgow Highlanders recorded in his diary:

> Last night we had a jolly good tea, and this morning a jolly good breakfast, for last night in the post, Teddy Cotesworth got two parcels, Willie Weir one, and Penny one. We had tea, oatcake and sardines for tea, oatcake and ham for breakfast, soda, syrup, treacle, potatoes, and oatmeal scones, butter, marmalade jelly, cake, etc. And sitting out in the open with the things spread out on a sheet it was for all the world like a picnic.[64]

Such comradeship might extend also to prisoners of war. Private Alick Raeper of 1st Gordons was taken prisoner on 26 August, 1914. In March, 1915 he wrote to his mother from Sennelager:

> Well I've a chum here who has not had a parcel or anything since December … Well my chum says that he'd be very glad if you could send him out a shirt, a pair of drawers and a pair of socks and gloves. I think you had better send him two pairs of socks as he'll need them. You might also put in some tobacco or cigarettes as he smokes both pipe and cigarettes. Also put in a few little tasty bits if you have room for them. He's been a very good chum to me so it's the least I can do.[65]

Comradeship came to the fore when pals were wounded or killed. Wives or family of soldiers at the front would visit or write to the families at home of soldiers wounded[66] or killed in action,[67] to offer some support or consolation. Soldiers in hospital at home would be visited not only by their own family and friends but by the family and friends of their pals at the front.[68] This might be particularly appreciated by Canadians with no accessible family in the old country. Private Arrol Brown, in 73rd Battalion C.E.F. (Royal Highlanders of Canada) wrote to his cousin Nesta in Cardiff in April, 1917, as follows:

---

62 Ibid., pp.908-909.
63 GHM PB1937 Dawson, letter to mother, 25 June, 1915.
64 IWM 3460 Macmillan, diary, 11 May, 1915.
65 NLS Acc.7660 Raeper, Pte A., letter to mother, 14 March, 1915.
66 BWA Guthrie, letter to him from Margaret Ferguson, 17 September, 1915.
67 IWM 21092 McGregor, letters to wife Jen, 13, 24 August, 1916.
68 LC GS 1008 Macdonald, diary, January-February, 1917, passim; IWM 13263 Bryden, letter to unknown recipient, n.d. (October, 1916?).

> One of our fellows who was in our Coy Machine Gun Section was wounded and sent to a hospital near where you are and I would consider it a favour if you could look him up as I am sure he has no friends on your side of the water.[69]

In one touching case, Private Darricot, a stretcher-bearer of 1st Camerons, wrote to Private Calder after he brought him in after Aubers Ridge:

> Having seen your name in the paper where you are I drop you these few lines hoping you are getting on alright and will soon be better. I also hope you never need to come back to the war again for I think you have had enough of it like myself … see and don't forget to write back and let me know how you are getting on. Goodbye for the time.[70]

And of course, men would write letters of sympathy or support to the wives or family of their pals who had been wounded,[71] letters of condolence for those who had died,[72] and sometimes letters of explanation and sympathy in response to enquiries from the bereaved, desperate to hear the circumstances of their loved one's death.[73] When Peter McGregor in 14th Argylls was killed, his pal (and his wife's brother-in-law) Charlie Holroyd, wrote to his wife, Jen.

> It is a sad sad loss and my whole heart goes out to you in sympathy … I never had a brother and especially since being out here Pete was that and more to me. His good humour, cheery word and ready joke never failed us and often when we have been 'dead to the world' a word from him would buck us up and we would carry on … Give my love to Margaret and Bobby, to you my whole heart goes out in sympathy. Would that I could do more.[74]

In addition to belonging to a small circle of pals, many soldiers had particular pals with whom they lived closely, knocked about together, and with whom they were on intimate terms; in army parlance, their half-section.[75] These close pals provided another degree of support. In 1/7th Black Watch, William Cameron and his pal Billy Munn were known as 'the two brothers';[76] in 43rd Battalion C.E.F. (Cameron Highlanders of Canada), David McMillan and his pal Tom Rae, both senior N.C.O.s, were known as the 'Gold Dust twins.'[77] In 1/4th Seaforths, Frank Brooke, a Yorkshireman, teamed up with another Yorkshire lad called Tommy Smith after Tommy's own best pal had been knocked out on a fatigue party. "It was ecstasy having Tommy

---

69 IWM 11310 PP Prichard, Miss N., letter to her from Pte Arrol Brown, 1 April, 1917.
70 THM Camerons 85-9 Calder, Pte J., letter to him from Pte B. Darricot, 23 May, 1915.
71 BWA Guthrie, letter to him from Margaret Ferguson, 17 September, 1915.
72 THM Seaforths 84-65 Vickery, letter to his mother from Cpl A.C. Telfer, 6 October, 1917; IWM 15118 Murray, J.M, letter to widow Jeanie Murray from CQMS W.S. McKenzie, 10 June, 1916; THM C80-15 Chase, letter to his widow from Pte George Hampton, 15 March, 1915; LC GS 0262 Campbell, diary, 20 September, 1916.
73 GHM PB2815 McWilliam, letter to his father from Pte James Harper, 9 March, 1918; BWA, Couston, letter to mother, 26 August, 1917.
74 IWM 21092 McGregor, letter to his wife Jen from Charlie Holroyd, 15 September, 1916.
75 Apart from refs cited below, see: IWM 3608 Anderson, memoir.
76 LC GS 0257 Cameron, memoir.
77 McMillan, *Trench Tea and Sandbags*, pp.6-7.

as a constant companion. His cheerful and everlasting grin, and flow of homely Huddersfield dialect, took most of the bitterness from my gloomy thoughts."[78]

J.E.P Levyns joined the South African Scottish in 1916, aged 18, and was sent to the brigade's base at Potchefstroom. He deliberately looked for someone to act as his half-section. He struck up a friendship with a man called Bresler, but later found an even closer friendship with Keith Gordon Young. "Young and I each had soft hearts, and we were each just nineteen years of age. [In fact, Young was just sixteen.] In our off-duty hours we got into the habit of spending the time in each other's company, discussing the world in which we found ourselves and planning the world and society as we should like to see it when the war was over."[79] It was not unusual for best pals to pool blankets and sleep together for warmth.[80] James Campbell in 6th Camerons records in March, 1916: "At night the boys came down from the trenches in a blizzard and they were soaked through. Johnnie Hay stripped to the skin and slept with me." Then, in September, after marching out of the trenches in torrents of rain, "After tea, Johnnie and I got everything off and got inside our blanket."[81]

The down-side of such close comradeship was that separation and loss could be devastating. When close pals were lost, through leave, courses, postings, wounds or death, soldiers could feel extremely lonely. Private William Couston in 1/7th Black Watch, missed first his pal Bob Carswell, who had been hospitalised home, and then another pal, Broome, with a lacerated knee. "I feel so lonely at times – so many of my chums gone," he lamented. "There is practically none in this crowd of whom I can make a companion."[82] In July, 1918, Private Douglas's pal in 8th Black Watch, Ross, was killed. As his best pal Albert Smith was absent gassed, "I was rather cut up about it, because … Ross was the only chap other than Albert Smith I had any real desire to chum up with."[83] In 1/4th Black Watch, Linton Andrews' good friend and co-writer, Nick (John Beveridge Nicholson), was killed by a German sniper on 15 July, 1915. "To Joe [Lee] and to myself, who had been Nick's closest comrades for almost a year, this was a heart-breaking loss. The war seemed different from then onwards."[84] When Frank Brooke was told that his close pal Tommy had been killed during an attack on 20 September, 1917, he went to pieces. His other pals gave him three mugs of rum and put him to bed. After that, "I lived in solitude as far as possible, and preferred it. After losing Tommy it was impossible to chum with another fellow for 'keeps'… I wanted, only, to be alone."[85] After Levyns had teamed up with his pals Young and Bresler, as we have seen, in his draft for the South African Scottish, the draft moved by train to the railhead and marched via Duisans to join the battalion. However, when they reached the battalion at Arras, Young was posted to A Company, but Levyns to B.

78   IWM Books Brooke, 'Wait for it,' pp.119-120, 226.
79   Levyns, *The Disciplines of War*, pp.32, 38, 40-41.
80   IWM 4586 Douglas, memoir, p.325; Levyns, *The Disciplines of War*, p.66; IWM 3460 Macmillan, diary, 5 March, 1916; Anon, *9th Royal Scots (T.F.) B Company*, p.35; THM Seaforths 89-122 Paterson, memoir.
81   LC GS 0262 Campbell, diary, 24 March, 18 September.
82   BWA, Couston, letters to mother, 25 May, 15 June, 16 July, 3, 12, 26 August, 1917.
83   IWM 4586 Douglas, memoir, pp.711, 772.
84   Andrews, *Autobiography*, pp.89-90.
85   IWM Books Brooke, 'Wait for it,' pp.263-264, 271, 293-294, 307.

I tried to protest to the officer who had brought us up from Duisans, saying that we had been told at Bordon that care would be taken to see that half-sections were not separated. He replied that Young and I should have reported at Duisans that we were half-sections. There was nothing he could do now, but I could get the matter put right when the regiment came out of the line, in a few weeks' time. With that I had to be content. At least, I still had Bresler beside me, which I like to think was a comfort to him as well as to me, for he had not made many friends.

When, shortly afterwards, the company went into the firing line, Bresler was posted to an Observation Post at the end of a sap. "When he disappeared, I felt as lonely and unhappy as I had the previous night when Young and I were parted." Later the same day, Bresler was killed in the O.P., shot through the head by a sniper. "I was numb with horror and grief. I could not put it out of my mind." Then in March, 1917, Levyns was hospitalised to England, with trench fever. While in the South African Hospital in Richmond Park, he heard news of the death of Young at Arras, which led him to lose his Christian faith.[86]

In some cases the loss was not of a pal but of a brother. Brothers William and Cecil Bryden both joined the London Scottish and served with 1st Battalion in France. When Cecil was killed on the first day of the Somme, William "had terrible guilt feelings about the fact that he had encouraged Cecil to join up in the first place." A year later, William was still affected by the loss: "July 1st is a day I cannot forget, how hateful it seems."[87] When James Campbell's brother Peter, in his own battalion, 6th Camerons, died of gas poisoning suffered at Loos, he was mortified by the loss: "During all our lives Peter and I were together and we were not like ordinary brothers. I cared more for him than anyone else on earth and to think of him is agony. And yet I can think of nothing else."[88]

Such was the strength of comradeship, which could last until death. Captain H.B. Todd recalled the action of one wounded soldier of 2nd Argylls after the battle of Loos, who stayed with his dying chum on the field until the end, three days later. "I knew he would like me to be with him at the last." Only then did he crawl back to his own lines where he died later as his own wounds had turned gangrenous through lack of attention.[89]

One factor which militated against the development of strong comradeship was the constant change inflicted on all battalions through casualties and the reception of new drafts. In some respects, this posed a risk to esprit de corps.[90] There could be tension between the original members of the battalion and the incomers. As we have seen, this was certainly displayed in the Glasgow Highlanders, in the attitude of the 1st Battalion men towards the 400 2nd Battalion men who joined them at the last minute.[91] It was also witnessed in the 48th Highlanders of Canada (who constituted 15th Battalion, C.E.F.), in the attitude of the 'old timers' to the

---

86   Levyns, *The Disciplines of War*, pp.45-47, 53-56, 60-62, 79.
87   IWM 13263 Bryden, letter to unknown recipient, 4 July, 1917, and memories of his reminiscences by his daughter Mary Lawton, written 2003.
88   LC GS 0262 Campbell, diary, 11 October, 1915 to 6 November, 1915, passim.
89   ASHM N-E2 Todd, memoir.
90   See for example LC GS 0030 Anderson, Brig. R.C.B., transcript of Tapes 338 and 382, interview with Liddle, 1976.
91   IWM 3460 Macmillan, diary, Preface and entry for 17 January, 1916.

new draftees, although the new men, with their cheerful optimism, could actually help to lift morale.[92] Similarly, when Captain Claud Low joined 1st London Scottish in France at the end of November, 1914, he observed;

> I am very pleased to see a number of my old friends here. They are not as happy as formerly and look tired out, but we are all fresh men in the draft from London & can cheer them up a bit. The next fight will be delivered with all the old vigour & perhaps we will help them to win fresh laurels & not live upon theirs.

And again, "These fellows from home have put new life in the regiment who were much shaken over the recent fighting."[93]

Whatever the case, it is certain that constant change made social groupings fragile and transient, and casualties were by no means the only cause. As Linton Andrews observed, "Very few friends in the ranks can have soldiered together all through the First World War. Casualties, secondings, courses of instruction, commissions, changes of rank, did much to separate friends."[94] Norman Macmillan, for example, was a victim of such fragility. In June, 1915, he had celebrated his group of comrades in the Glasgow Highlanders. By September he had himself left them to become a brigade bomber.

> Klovborg … has been appointed a 'Baltic Interpreter'… So he is away. This leaves only Penny in the platoon out of the eight we had in June. Curious how we have become separated, more especially as it was not by the wish of any of us. Just sheer fate! Nothing else. And Penny will soon get his commission, so I am not particularly sorry to be out of the platoon myself since practically all my special friends are away.

Perhaps unsurprisingly, it was not long after this that Macmillan started thinking seriously of a commission.[95]

Soldiers had to cope with this constant disruption and change. The bonds within groups were however strong. Soldiers did not want to be separated from their pals. When Harry Taylor, in 1st Liverpool Scottish, was recommended by the M.O. in July, 1917, for a base job, he successfully appealed to his platoon commander to have the order rescinded so that he could stay with his friends for a forthcoming attack.[96] Sergeant George Stables notes how, after being sent on a course in 1918, he was transferred to a different company. "Since I came out to France I was always with C Coy; knew all the men and N.C.O.s. I may say that I was not very pleased about it, but had to be doing with it. D Coy was strange to me."[97] Willie Paterson had made a good group of friends in 3/5th Seaforths, but when the third line Territorial battalions of the Seaforths were amalgamated, and Paterson was sent on a musketry course to become an

---

92 Beattie, *48th Highlanders*, pp.83-84, 91, 150, 160.
93 IWM 6702 Low, letter to Aunt Bella, 29 November, to wife Noanie, 29 November, 1914.
94 Andrews, *Autobiography*, pp.89-90.
95 IWM 3460 Macmillan, letter to mother, 10 September, 1915, to Bessie, 20 November, 1915. See also his diary, 21 July, 1915.
96 LC GS 1579 Taylor, Reminiscences, p.12.
97 LC GS 1516 Stables, letter describing his service, 5 February, 1979.

instructor, he was "separated from my friends and comrades," and "longed to get out to France, there to make a new start."[98] Alfred Fennah served in 1st Liverpool Scottish. Having developed a septic hand and arm in early 1915, he was put in an ambulance for hospital. "Just as it was starting to move off, some of my own special chums came crowding to the back of the van, and I think of the whole lot I was the most upset, feeling very glum and despondent on being compelled to leave them."[99]

Men who were hospitalised or on leave might yearn to be back with their comrades-in-arms. When James Sloan was given home leave in 1918, after being in France for over a year, "reality was not there; reality was back with my mates in the platoon, and it was with no reluctance that I got aboard the boat that took me to Le Havre."[100] Jock Macleod, hospitalised in Malta in 1916, and away from his battalion, 2nd Camerons, in Salonika, similarly expressed his desire to be back with his comrades, in his poem, 'Farewell to Macedonia.'[101]

> Would I were back with them, the strong and daring
> My patient men, my friends who laughed in Hell,
> New ills they suffer that I am not sharing –
> I am in comfort, they before Roupel.[102]

However, when men did return from absence, they might find that their old circle of friends had been broken. Private Thomas Alexander was wounded fighting with 8th Seaforths at Loos. When, after recovery, he re-joined his old platoon in France, there was not one of his old comrades left.[103] When, after the Armistice, Private Douglas returned to his platoon in 8th Black Watch, having been detached to Brigade HQ since July, he found that, "Apart from Albert Smith, Craighead, and one or two others, they were all strangers to me."[104] To some, though, even when there had been substantial changes, simply to be back with the platoon was sufficient. Having fallen sick in June, 1917, John Cooper did not re-join his old platoon in 1/6th Black Watch until January, 1918, but despite many changes, he felt at home. "You cannot imagine how much at home I felt in that small company after seven months' wandering around at the base. Only those who experienced it can know the real affection for the platoon and those in it that existed there."[105]

Many soldiers however would feel it badly when circles were broken. They would miss their pals badly when they had to go away for any reason.[106] When 11th Argylls lost many casualties at Arras on 23 April, 1917, John Bowie felt the loss of old comrades: "It is with great regret most

---

98 THM Seaforths 89-122 Paterson, memoir.
99 Fennah, *Retaliation*, pp.61, 64.
100 LC WF Recollections S18 Sloan, memoir.
101 See also the poems by A.E. Mackintosh, 'From Home, To the Men who fell at Beaumont Hamel,' 'From Home, Cambridge' and 'To Sylvia' in Campbell & Green, *Can't shoot a man with a cold*, pp.164, 170-171, 179, 186.
102 LC GS 1027 Macleod, item 233A.
103 THM Seaforths 02-138 Alexander, diary, May, 1916.
104 IWM 4586 Douglas, memoir, p.1115.
105 IWM Books Cooper, 'Domi Militaeque,' p.191.
106 See for example: LC GS 0262 Campbell, diary, 15 October, 1916; BWA Guthrie, letter to wife Crissie, 15 October, 1915.

of the men who answered the call early in the war that fell, leaving strange faces amongst us and it is hard to find a good pal blending with your character."[107] After Loos, William Chambers, serving in 7th Camerons, wrote: "The strain of this last two weeks has almost been too much. I am weary of this senseless killing, I feel so much alone now all my good pals have gone. I seem to be fated to go on and on till the end of time."[108] Pete Small, in 5th Gordons, wrote after Arras, "I have lost every pal I had, including a particular pal who had been with me all through."[109] Faced with a breakdown of the old comradeship which sustained them, men felt discontented,[110] and, as we have seen for Norman Macmillan, for some it was a spur to change. Ian Andrew was a Glasgow University student who joined the ranks of 6th Camerons. After being wounded at Loos, he decided to apply for a commission:

> I realised that for me the 6th Camerons had ceased to exist after the Battle of Loos. It would be more than I could bear to return to a battalion where few of the original B Company still lingered on, the time had come to make a clean break with the past.[111]

Of course, the men had not only to deal with the absence of their comrades, but also with their mutilation and death. Arthur Betteridge, who served in the South African Scottish, felt that the death of close friends was not allowed to linger.

> The shock of losing one's closest friends in battle was never allowed to last. Constant proximity of other tried and trusted pals in all conditions at the front, relieved the tension. … death and mutilation were daily occurrences finally accepted … – in fact the quick death or severe wounds of men you knew well came to be regarded as inevitable occurrences … Even the heavy loss of colleagues was accepted philosophically.[112]

Lieutenant Douglas Wilson of 5th Camerons distinguished between the group reaction and that of the individual:

> The loss of a close comrade sometimes knocked a man off balance, mentally and physically. This could be but a passing phase with a gradual return to efficiency, though it could lead to continued deterioration, a change in disposition and permanent disability as a fighting soldier. But the group reaction was usually fatalistic. Men would say, 'He's bought it – too bad.' The war had to go on, and the sense of loss sooner rather than later was swamped by the affairs of the present. In the down to earth existence even the immediate past tended to become strangely remote, quite quickly.[113]

---

107 ASHM N-E11 Bowie, diary, 23 April 1917.
108 Chambers, *Diaries of World war 1*, p.37.
109 IWM 14321 Small, letter to Miss Ethel Shaw, 1 July, 1917.
110 IWM Books Cooper, 'Domi Militaeque,' p.328.
111 LC WF Recollections A9, Andrew, memoir
112 LC GS 0132 Betteridge, memoir, appendix compiled posthumously, pp.236-237.
113 LC GS 1761 Wilson, memoir, p.65.

It is quite evident that Wilson is right. Many individual soldiers, however well they managed to cope, were badly hit by the loss of comrades.[114] As Archie Tweddle, of 1/4th Seaforths wrote in June, 1915:

> A party of 6 of the mortar gun section were in the trench when 2 heavy shells came over, killing one man – a good pal of mine, & wounding 3 terribly badly … We soldiers are supposed to get used to that sort of thing, but alas, for me it is quite impossible.[115]

Men wrote simple poems to commemorate their fallen pals,[116] while Alan Mackintosh, soldier-poet of 5th Seaforths, felt that it would be better to die in battle with one's friends than survive when they were killed.[117] After the battle of Arras, 7th Camerons were involved in burying the dead.

> We managed to collect sixty-four bodies of Camerons, which we buried in one grave … In order to save space, the majority of the men were buried lying on their side. A touching feature was the fact that someone had taken each man's arm and put it round the body lying next to it. From the top of the trench one could imagine that the men were sleeping, embraced in each other's arms, more especially as they were buried in their kilts just as they had fought, no blankets or other covering being available. Altogether it was a most moving scene.[118]

The diary of William Chambers, a wartime volunteer drafted to 1st Camerons, records an anonymous poem, entitled La Bassee Dec., 1915:

> So pass round the vin rouge again Mac
> Here's luck in the wine that is red,
> Let us drink to the boys who got 'Blighties.'
> Drink deep to the pals who are dead.[119]

Officers

Like the men, many Highland officers record the happy state of comradeship which existed in their units.[120] In the case of the officers the practical unit in which comradeship was formed was

---

114 THM Camerons C03-87 Tudhope, Pte J., letter about battle of Loos written from hospital [1915]; THM Seaforths 81-180 Murray, letter to sister Kate, 12 May, 1915; THM Seaforths 96-36 Tweddle, letter home 13 May, 1915; LC GS 0262 Campbell, diary, 16, 17, 20 September, 1916; IWM 21092 McGregor, letters to wife Jen, 18 April, 13 August, 1916.
115 THM Seaforths 96-36 Tweddle, letter home 20 June, 1915.
116 See: THM Seaforths 86-182 Innes, Cpl Arthur, memorial poem to him; THM Seaforths 92-15 Frame, LCpl E., memorial Song to him.
117 Mackintosh, *A Highland regiment*, p.37, poem 'Before the Summer' (1916).
118 Craig-Brown, *Historical Records,* Vol.4, p.315.
119 Chambers, *Diaries of World war 1*, p.25.
120 Apart from specific refs cited below, see: LC GS 0731 Hay-Young, letter to sister Margaret, 9 April, 1917; LC GS 1026 Maclean, memoir, p.7; ASHM N-E2 Hyslop, diary, 9 August, 1914; ASHM

Comrades. Captain Hyslop DSO and Hutchinson, 2nd Argylls, in cellar of farmhouse that formed part of frontline, Christmas Day 1914. (IWM HU128734)

the mess. The frequent practice was to mess by companies, it being often impractical behind the lines to institute a full battalion mess. While this arrangement encouraged a strong esprit de corps between company officers, at the same time it worked against the fuller integration of junior and senior officers across the battalion. It was nevertheless generally appreciated by the junior officers, who preferred the informality of the company mess to the stuffier formality of the battalion mess.[121] In the latter case, however, much would depend on the attitude of the C.O. or the senior officers. When Lieutenant Neil Weir joined 10th Argylls at Aldershot, he felt that, "Our Mess life was a happy one. Everyone felt at home, as the Colonel was never ashamed to sit by the youngest subaltern during meals."[122] On the other hand, Johnathan Bates, M.O. to 8th Black Watch complained in March, 1917, that their Second-in-Command, Major Anstruther "is an awfully nice chap but takes life far too seriously. I know that if I took the war as seriously

---

N-F.5 Main, letter to his wife Win, 21 March, 1918; IWM 12643 Ferrie, letter to brother Allan, 12 September, 1915; LC GS 0552 Ferguson, letter to mother, 21 May, 1918; IWM 3460 Macmillan, letter from Alex (Sandy) Macmillan to mother, 6 June, 1918; GHM PB1639 Kemp, memoir, p.43; LC GS 1003 Macdermott, Lord, typescript recollections; IWM 2854 PP Bates, letter to fiancée, 11 July, 1916. See also his letters of 8, 9, 23 May, 1916

121 LC GS 1367 Robertson, memoir, p.37; IWM 114 Allen, letter to wife, 1 January, 1916; LC GS 0588 Fraser, J.A., letter to father, 21 July, 1917; GHM PB1639 Kemp, memoir, vol.2, pp.10, 62.
122 David, *Mud and Bodies*, p.10, extract from Weir's diary.

as he does, I'd go dotty in a fortnight."[123] Indeed, a certain stuffy formality, especially amongst officers of the old school, was an occupational hazard for young subalterns.[124]

It was not unusual for junior officers to receive a rather stand-offish welcome to their new battalion.[125] Other officers however record the kindliness of their welcome.[126] It might nevertheless take a little while to gain real acceptance.[127] Lieutenant Robert Mackay had reported to 11th Argylls on 13 September, 1916. Only in August, 1917, after performing bravely in battle,

> I was aware at the time, somehow, that the attitude of the older majors and captains towards me had changed, and they had now accepted me as one of themselves, an original, proved member of the battalion, and not an untried interloper. Their speech lost a curious harsh element or tolerance, and was replaced by a still more unexpected understanding.[128]

Not all messes were harmonious,[129] as not all officers were perfect. In November, 1916, Sir George Abercromby, commanding 8th Black Watch, wrote to the battalion's earlier commander, Lord Sempill, "We have about 45 officers of sorts, 25 B.W., 10 Gordons, 7 Argylls, 2 Camerons, 1 Fife & Forfar Yeoman! What a crowd!! Some are nice, some shits & a few buggers!"[130] When Guy Macgregor, newly commissioned from the London Scottish, attended an officer training course with 2/8th Argylls at Montrose in November, 1915, he was not impressed: "There is no doubt about it, the Officers' mess of the 2/8th A. & S.H. is much more like a reformatory than the abode of self-respecting gentlemen. There's an atmosphere of suspicion, fear, jealousy & watchfulness which I find the most uncomfortable I have ever lived in."[131] There were various explanations for unsettled messes. In some cases, at home, the problem was evidently frustration and boredom, while waiting to be deployed to the front.[132] In other cases, the situation resulted from personality clashes, difficult behaviour or unsatisfactory performance.[133] At Christmas, 1914, for example, Hugh Quekett recorded the departure of one officer from his company with whom he had not got on. "This hardly broke my heart. We were such opposite characters and never really hit it off. His high and mighty attitude as a Barrister looking down on me, a clerk in the city, in his view the lowest form of life, his mincing step, the way he had of picking up a piece of paper between thumb and first finger, were my pet aversions."[134]

---

123 IWM 2854 Bates, letters to fiancée, 4, 6, 28 March, 1917.
124 See for example LC GS 0409 Cunningham, interview 1976.
125 IWM 233 McKechnie, memoir, pp.24-25. see also: IWM 10533 Reid, memoir.
126 BWA Quekett, memoir, p.11; LC Several Fronts Recollections, Kingsley, memoir; GHM PB375 Pailthorpe, memoir, pp.4-6.
127 IWM 3460 Macmillan, letter from Alex (Sandy) Macmillan to mother, 8 July, 1918; IWM 430 Wimberley, memoir, p.20.
128 IWM 11144 MacKay, diary, 6 August, 1917, afternote, 1972.
129 Apart from refs cited below, see IWM 6656 PP Milligan, 2Lt A., letters to mother, 28 February, n.d, (P/mk 8 March), 11 March, to sister Minnie, 28 March, 13 April, 1917.
130 BWA Lord Sempill papers, letter from Sir George Abercromby, 21 November, 1916.
131 IWM 8592 Macgregor, letter to Dulcie Newling, 21 November, 1915.
132 Ibid., letter to Dulcie Newling, 6 March, 3, 10 May, 1 August, 1916.
133 THM Seaforths 05-87 Hope, diary, 21, 22 April, 3 May, 1915; GHM PB1639 Kemp, memoir, p.21; BWA Sempill papers, various minutes June and July, 1915, and letters to him from Sir George Abercromby, 29 June, 1916, 8 October, 1917.
134 BWA Quekett, memoir, p.14.

Sometimes problems resulted from the arrival of dug-outs from home. One such was Major Johnston who came out to 1/6th Seaforths in early 1917 as second-in-command, desperately inexperienced in trench warfare.[135] More damaging was the arrival in 5th Camerons of Captain College, the erstwhile adjutant of 8th Battalion, at the end of April, 1918.

> This was C's first spell of active service though he had been in the Army for over 20 years pre-war, and for the duration to date had seldom or never strayed from the orderly room … It was held that the severity of the combing out process at home must have been unprecedented to have uprooted this veteran … His advent, at all events, was unwelcome to his juniors for very definite reasons. He had a lot of seniority behind him … He had no fighting or even training experience … and it was an injustice to younger officers well-fitted for command that they should be superseded wholly on grounds of seniority.[136]

Captain College succeeded miraculously in keeping himself out of the line for the duration of the war, despite being nominally a company commander.

> Resentment at this fantastic situation was by no means limited to junior officers. At first, other ranks viewed the figurehead as a fat pompous comedian, but gradually the fun went sour on them, comment became caustic and N.C.O.s became particularly bitter.[137]

Another source of dissension was inappropriate behaviour. In 8/10th Gordons one subaltern became victim of an officially prohibited subaltern's court martial, for claiming that he had won the D.C.M., while previously serving in the ranks, but not wearing the ribbon. He was charged with either lying or snobbery. Found guilty of the latter charge he was sentenced to have plum and apple jam rubbed into his head and hair. After that he put up the ribbon, until later it was established that he had not won the medal at all, and he was thrown out of the service.[138] Another case, in 8th Black Watch, was that of Captain Burnet, who was accused by a fellow officer, Captain McClure, in a minute to the C.O., Lord Sempill, of habitually swearing at himself and other officers in front of the men, being on duty under the influence of alcohol, giving unclear orders, and on occasion when in charge of his company, leaving them to meet women. An undated minute, presumably by Sempill, records the opinions of other officers on McClure's minute, to which they give qualified support. Within two days, Burnet had been relieved of his company, and was soon sent down the line sick, apparently genuinely so.[139]

Just as there was a social division within the Other Ranks, so there was in the officers' mess between Regular officers, recruited principally from the gentry, and the Temporary Officers, recruited often from the middle classes. The Temporary Officers, disparagingly referred to as

---

135 IWM 8572 Stewart, letter to mother, 15 March, 1917.
136 LC GS 1761 Wilson, memoir, p.14.
137 Ibid., pp.14, 56.
138 GHM PB1639 Kemp, memoir, p.40.
139 BWA Sempill papers, minute from Capt G.B. McClure to Sempill, 2 August, 1915, undated minute recording officers' opinions of same, letter from Capt Scott M. Burnet to Sempill, 4 August, 1915, letter from le Chirurgien J.A. Cairns Forsyth, 23 June, 1916.

'Temporary Gentlemen,' were the butt of much snobbery.[140] Colonel Hugh Allen, a former regular Indian Army officer commanding 7th Black Watch, found himself on 2 May, 1916, with trench fever in the officers' ward of a Casualty Clearing Station. He did not find the company altogether congenial:

> We have 14 beds in our ward … Most of them are up, & talk all day in various brands of dialect from Orkney to Shoreditch. I think I dislike the temporary gent more when he is ill than at any other time. Did you hear of the notice said to have been put up in the Gunners Mess at Woolwich: 'Temporary Officers are reminded they are expected to behave temporarily like gentlemen.'[141]

Earlier he had commented on the battalion's M.O., Dr Blair, "I suppose he can't help not being a gentleman."[142] When Captain C.W.E. Gordon, a regular officer of the Black Watch, was transferred from being adjutant of 6th South Staffordshire regiment back to 2nd Black Watch in June, 1915, he wrote "It is very nice being back again among gentlemen. I get most awfully tired of the service officer. He is just passable if seen for a fortnight, but to live with him for months he becomes unendurable."[143] Newly commissioned temporary Lieutenant William Kemp, destined for 11th Gordons, a New Army battalion, reported to 3rd Gordons on 1 July, 1915, and found appallingly that, "no officer of the 11th or other New Army battalion was at this time allowed to stay inside the barracks or even to use the Anti-room or mess room except when Orderly Officer. This disgusting ungentlemanly scheme remained in force till September or October, 1915."[144] He goes on to state that Captain Mackenzie, a Regular officer from 2nd Battalion, "once told us that if it hadn't been for the war half of us would never have been given commissions as we were not even gentlemen. I think he forgot that if it hadn't been for the war, half of us would never have wanted them."[145] As the thoughtful Regular officer, Graham Hutchison pointed out, "Many officers of the old Army had yet to have the horizon of their minds lifted to the nobility of a citizen endeavour."[146] Nor was the snobbery confined to the Regular officers. There were even Territorial or Temporary Officers who were sniffy about their companions-in-arms.[147]

But the condescension towards Temporary Officers was not universal, nor were snobbish attitudes necessarily displayed in practice. When newly commissioned temporary Lieutenant D.W. Reid reported to 8th Seaforths at Cromarty, he found,

> In fact, they were a tremendously nice lot of chaps … There was a sprinkling of old regulars called back from retirement but the majority of regulars were chaps who had been out &

---

140 Apart from refs cited below, see also: IWM 114 Allen, letter to wife, 4 August, 1916; ASHM N-E11 Macleod, George, letter to Ellen, 13 February, 1917; David, *Mud and Bodies*, p.10, extract from Weir's diary; ASHM N-E1 Robertson, letters home, 7 March 1915.
141 IWM 114 Allen, letter to wife, 2 May, 1916.
142 Ibid., letter to wife, 23 March, 1916.
143 BWA Gordon, 'diaries', letter home, 18-19 June, 1915.
144 GHM PB1639 Kemp, memoir, p.5.
145 Ibid., p.7.
146 Hutchison, *Warrior*, p.39.
147 BWA Paul, letters to Miss May Merrett, 19 November, 1915, 24 January, 1916, 15 April, 11 August, 1917; IWM 12643 Ferrie, letter to brother Allan, 12 September, 1915.

wounded & so on & a fine lot they were. There was none of the ostracization by regulars of temporary officers of which one met such a lot & which caused such a lot of breast-beating by many temporary officers ... All I remember is what a cheerful, helpful & happy lot they all were.[148]

Graham Hutchison indeed felt that his own horizons were expanded by the more varied background of the temporary officers in his company of 2nd Argylls in November, 1914.[149]

Temporary infantry officers could also take pride in the fact that they, almost universally, were fighting soldiers. When after being wounded, William Kemp passed through Aberdeen, and was ordered back to the front, he remarked, "Drover and I were not as one would expect, sorry to be going back again; we were so heartily tired of the war dodging type of soldier who ruled the roost in Aberdeen that we were only too pleased to be returning to the gentlemen of the 8/10th Gordons."[150]

There was also some tension between Regulars and Territorials. In 1/4th Black Watch, Linton Andrews had great respect for his Colonel, but felt it unfair that, "he preferred to keep decorations for Regulars. 'It's no use giving the M.C. or even the M.M.,' he would say to me, 'to a fellow like you who'll go straight back to your civvy jobs the moment this war finishes. The ribbons will be really useful to regulars.'"[151] And Alistair Milligan, in 1/7th Argylls, was told a story of discrimination regarding medals against Territorial officers in the 2nd Battalion.[152]

Another source of discontent was promotion. Regular officers were keen that their careers should progress, and the same was even true of some Territorial and New Army officers. There are myriad complaints of stalled promotion, supersession and unfairness,[153] especially when officers who had been serving at the front found themselves outranked or even superseded in command by officers sent out from home, Claud Low, in 1st London Scottish, for example, complained in February, 1915:

> Four new officers have arrived from England, none of them below the rank of Captain. No-one quite understands why they have been sent. They have all gone way over the heads of their former officers because they stayed at home & for no other reason. It is a curious situation & presents the greatest difficulty. I don't know what the solution is. The C.O. has

---

148 IWM 10533 Reid, memoir. See also: IWM 5912 PP Elliott, J., manuscript recollections, written 1930s.
149 Hutchison, *Warrior*, pp.51-52.
150 GHM PB1639 Kemp, memoir, vol.2, pp.9, 11.
151 Andrews, *Autobiography*, p.96.
152 IWM 6656 PP Milligan, letter to mother, 11 April, 1917.
153 Apart from specific refs cited, see: LC GS 0731 Hay-Young, letters to father, 10 October, 30 December, 1917, 9 January, 8 February, 1918; ASHM N-E8 Maclachlan, letters from Lt Wilfred Haviland, 14, 18 July, 27 August, 29 December, 1916; ASHM N-E5 Main, letter to his wife Win, 31 July, 1915; LC GS 1761 Wilson, memoir, pp.32A-33, 40; GHM PB1639 Kemp, memoir, p.18; IWM 6702 Low, letters to wife Noanie, 30 November, 27 December, 1914, 18 January, 1915, to Aunt Bella, 8 August, 1915; BWA Sempill papers, letter to him from Sir George Abercromby, 2 March, 1916, letters from J.A. Cox, 28 February, 1916, 4, 19 April, 13, 27 June, n d. (July),1917, 14 February, 1918, 20 January, 1919, from F.Davies (War Office), 29 June, 1917, letter from Lt & QM P Goudy, 30 April, 1918; BWA Quekett, memoir, p.18.

not put any of them in command of a company & they are just odd pieces of seniority, & of course feel very uncomfortable.[154]

"Either I am unfitted to command a Battn or a gross injustice has been done me," complained Major C.W.E Gordon after being appointed second-in-command of 8th Gordons.[155] Newly commissioned Leslie Cooper was posted to 9th Seaforths, a pioneer battalion, where he arrived in November, 1916. There one of the subalterns was Lieutenant Hendry. "My coming was not welcomed by Hendry as he had been in France for a year, in the ranks, and had been given his commission in the field a few days after I had been gazetted at home, and was therefore his senior."[156]

All these disruptive issues were additional to the constant process of change through casualties and postings. H.D. Clark, adjutant of 2nd Argylls when the war broke out, explained how friendships in a pre-war regular battalion flourished when changes were minimal.[157] This no longer applied. Yet despite the disruptions and constant change, there was still much good comradeship amongst the officers. Officers good-naturedly wind up a young gentleman of astonishingly radical political views after dinner;[158] they tease a new officer "about his extreme youth – tell him if he's late to bed, 6.30, he'll be 'peevish in the morning,' and tell him 'he can get down now' after meals, etc."[159] There are good-natured celebrations in 5th Seaforths when on 2 July, 1915, the officers celebrate the birthday of the junior Major, known as 'Faither' to those officers who had fallen under his paternal jurisdiction and sound advice.[160] The officers of 1st Seaforths give a rousing send-off to their doctor from Mesopotamia after two years with the regiment.[161]

Just like the men, the officers shared the comforts they received from home.[162] They were capable too of great compassion. Harry Lauder's son John, serving as a captain in 8th Argylls, was sent to the Duchess of Westminster's Hospital at Le Touquet, suffering from dysentery, fever and a nervous breakdown. After several weeks, he wrote to his father;

> I had a sad experience yesterday … It was the first day I was able to be out of bed, and I went over to a piano in a corner against the wall, sat down, and began playing very softly, more to myself than anything else. One of the nurses came to me, and said a Captain Webster, of the Gordon Highlanders, who lay on a bed in the same ward, wanted to speak

---

154 IWM 6702 Low, Maj. C.J., letter to wife Noanie, 22 February, 1915. See for the resolution, letter to wife Noanie, 14 March, 1915.
155 BWA Gordon, 'diaries', letters home, 7, 14 December, 1915. See also letters home, 21 July, 14 December, 1915, 1 March, 8, 11 April, 1916.
156 THM Seaforths 81-2 Cooper, memoir, p.22.
157 LC GS 0315 Clark, interview.
158 IWM 1862 Craig-Brown, letter home, 21 June, 1916.
159 ASHM N-E1 Robertson, letter home, 10 October, 1915.
160 Sutherland, *War Diary*, pp.29-31.
161 Webster, *Mesopotamia 1916-1917*, p.14, letter to mother, 1 January, 1917.
162 BWA, Macdonald, Coll, letters to wife Mary, 8, 9 January, 1918. see also letter of 12 January, 1918; ASHM N-E2 Hyslop, diary, 21 September, 1914; LC GS 1537 Stewart, W., letter to sister Madge, 24 December, 1917; LC GS 1027 Macleod, letter to mother, n.d., probably 27 February, 1915, to sisters Betty and Molly, 25 February, 1915.

to me. She said that he had asked who was playing, and she had told him Captain Lauder – Harry Lauder's son. 'Oh,' he said, 'I know Harry Lauder very well. Ask Captain Lauder to come over here?' This man had gone through ten operations in less than a week. I thought perhaps my playing had disturbed him, but when I went to his bedside, he grasped my hand, pressed it with what little strength he had left, and thanked me. He asked me if I could play a hymn. He said he would like to hear 'Lead, kindly Light.' So I went back to the piano and played it as softly and as gently as I could. It was his last request. He died an hour later. I was very glad I was able to soothe his last moments a little. I am very glad that I learned the hymn at Sunday School as a boy.[163]

When the opportunity arose, they would visit their friends in hospital,[164] or visit the relatives of those killed in action, as their wives might do at home.[165] Lieutenant Bry Cumming was hospitalised to India, after being wounded with 2nd Black Watch in Mesopotamia on 7 January, 1916. "While in Agra I went and saw one of our Officer's Mother and Father whose son was killed on the 7th, poor lad, and what an ordeal."[166] They would also, of course, write letters of condolence.[167] Captain Boddam-Wetham of 1st Gordons wrote on 13 December, 1914, to the widow of Second Lieutenant Alexander Pirie who had been killed in the trenches the previous day. He had only been commissioned from Sergeant a week previously, having been specially mentioned by Boddam-Wetham himself for gallantry in action at Ypres.

> If I, who have only known him a little, feel his loss so much, how much more can one feel for you to whom he was everything. I cannot say more than that you have our v. deepest sympathy, but you must be proud, very proud, to have been so closely associated with such a gallant soldier and officer, who after all has died fighting well for the country we all love, the people we all love, against a harsh militarism & the greatest army the world has ever seen.[168]

Just like the men, too, comradeship in the officer's mess was enhanced by individual personalities. E.A. Mackintosh fell on the second day of the battle of Cambrai.

> The author of 'A Highland regiment' and 'War the Liberator,' familiarly known as 'Tosh,' poet, litterateur, and hail-fellow-well-met to one and all. His happy smile and cheery personality will long be remembered by us, while his topical songs often cheered us on our way. Of a truly poetic temperament, he laughed away all troubles, and helped to cheer even the most lugubrious members of the battalion by his humour and fun.[169]

---

163 Lauder, *A Minstrel in France*, p.60.
164 LC MES 013 Bonar, Andrew, letter to H.E.R. Widnell, 2 July, 1917.
165 ASHM N-F.5 Main, letters to his wife Win, 17, 31 July, 10, 15 September, 1915.
166 BWA Cumming, letters, 3, 28 March, 1916.
167 LC GS 0890 Kershaw, letter to his father from Capt Thomas Taylor, 2 October, 1915; Bartholomew, *George Hugh Freeland Bartholomew*, pp.73-81; LC GS 1536 Stewart, letters to his mother from Ian Robertson, 14 April, and Capt C.E. Fysh, 16 April, 1917.
168 GHM PB207 Pirie, letter to his widow from Capt C. Boddam-Wetham, 13 December, 1914.
169 Sutherland, *War Diary*, p.143.

Like the men, too, officers had their particular close friends.[170] Jim Cunningham in 1st Argylls wrote home on 6 October, 1914, that he "had a cup of tea ready for Blackie when he woke up. Blackie is Blacklock. You remember he was gazetted the same day that I was. He is a top hole good fellow & we do everything together, make bivouacs together, work for each other & generally act as one." But Blackie was killed on 21 October.

> Poor old fellow ... Algy Blacklock, one of the very best in the world. Though we had not known each other very long, we were the firmest of friends, we did absolutely everything together, even slept together ... I am very fit and well myself. I only grieve for poor Blackie and miss him more than I can say. It was a case of natural friendship which would I know have been life-long. We both made all sorts of plans for after the war, about going to India etc.[171]

Officers could indeed feel great sadness when friends were killed. In May, 1915, Second Lieutenant G.F. Maclean joined 1st Argylls in France from Sandhurst. His Company Commander was Captain Robin Wilson. "During my second tour, one of the company subalterns was killed in No Man's Land ... I learned a side to Robin's character I had not suspected. When we brought Burnley Campbell's body in, Robin leant against the parapet beside him, and the tears were streaming down his cheeks."[172] Likewise, John Hay-Young, in 1st Argylls, was upset when his company was badly cut up on 11 May, 1915; "I miss my subalterns very much: they were all first-rate fellows. Clarke especially was my greatest friend. The night after he was killed I obtained permission to find his body and bury it."[173] Alan Mackintosh wrote of his loneliness after the death of his close friend, in his poem, 'In Memoriam, R.M. Stalker, Missing, September, 1916.'

> The candle's burned out now, old man,
> And the dawn's come grey and cold,
> And I sit by the fire here
> Alone and sad and old.
> Though all the rest come back again,
> You lie in a foreign land,
> And the strongest link of all the chain
> Is broken in my hand.[174]

But however sad the loss, officers could not show emotion for long. L.A. Lynden-Bell, a regular officer, joined 1st Seaforths as a second lieutenant in March, 1915. His brother was killed at 2nd Ypres. Interviewed in 1977, he conceded that his colleagues at the front were good friends and provided support.

---

170 LC GS 1761 Wilson, memoir, p.69 (bis); IWM 10819 PP Brittan, account of how he fell given to his uncle.
171 LC GS 0409 Cunningham, letter to Margot, 6 October, 1914, to mother, 24 October, 1914.
172 LC GS 1026 Maclean, memoir, p.10.
173 LC GS 0731 Hay-Young, letter to father, 16 May, 1915.
174 Mackintosh, *A Highland regiment*, pp.50-52.

But then after all, look at the upbringing we had had all our lives. I mean the whole set up of the British was that you never showed any emotion. However much you disliked school you didn't tell your parents or they would consider you sissy and that was the outlook in the days before 1914. In fact, the outlook most of my life.[175]

The comments of Bryden McKinnell in the Liverpool Scottish lend weight to this assertion. On 28 February, 1915, he visited a fellow officer, Teague, who had been shot in the head a few days before. Shocked and moved by the experience, he nevertheless found that

We hadn't walked for ten minutes before we were laughing and joking and thanking God we were able to do so! For is it not one of the greatest boons which we acquire out here that any sorrow, however great (and which would upset us for a long time at home), is quickly lifted from us.[176]

And Douglas Wilson, who served as a Lieutenant with 5th Camerons in 1918, wrote:

We did not speak much of missing comrades or of the future – not from indifference but just because we were wrapped up in the present. And of course we were most of us young, a state of affairs that, however basic, hardly lent itself to open discussion. Amongst all ranks there were some who, though no older than the rest of us, had long experience of the line and yet retained an unimpaired boyishness of look and conduct. Here and there someone of like age seemed weighed down with years. This last was the exception, and just as well. In the business of living the depressed person was vulnerable, and even if viewed with sympathy made an uncomfortable companion. People tended to shy off from him as if in fear of contagion.[177]

Faced with the loss of their immediate companions, officers could of course feel lonely.[178] They would miss the bonds of comradeship which existed in their old circle, and might have difficulty in adjusting to the new replacement officers around them.[179] After 9th Black Watch had suffered heavy officer casualties at Loos, Major Jack Stewart wrote: "We are now hard at work training our new men; it's dull and in a way sad work training up a new family. I'm afraid the Bn will never seem quite the same to me. Our new officers seem quite a decent lot but I want the old ones back badly."[180]

---

175 LC GS 0993 Lynden-Bell, transcript of Tape 488, interview.
176 McKinnell, Bryden, *Diary*, p.63, 28 February, 1915.
177 LC GS 1761 Wilson, memoir, p.15. See also THM Seaforths 81-2 Cooper, memoir, p.136.
178 BWA, Macdonald, Coll, letter to wife Mary, 4 May, 1918; LC GS 0731 Hay-Young, letter to father, 16 May, 1915.
179 IWM 2854 Bates, letter to fiancée, 7 July, 1917; IWM 5525 PP Steven, letter from Lt Sidney Steven to home 2 August, 1915; LC GS 0731 Hay-Young, letter to sister, Margaret, 2 June, 1915, to father, 16 November, 1916; LC MES 013 Bonar, letter to H.E.R. Widnell, 2 July, 1917; IWM 511 Thorburn, letter to mother, 17 November, 1915.
180 BWA, Stewart, 'diary,' n.d. [September, 1915].

Conclusions

Overall, officers, N.C.O.'s and men shared similar experiences of comradeship; despite social differences, they had the same common human needs. While officers and N.C.O.'s found comradeship amongst their colleagues in their messes (however rudimentary), the men found it in small groups of friends. All might find some comfort in close friendships with particular individuals. Many soldiers, both officers and men, record the warmth of comradeship which existed, characterised by sharing comforts and compassion exercised when pals were wounded or killed. But overall this was not a perfect world. There were tensions introduced by personality clashes and inappropriate behaviour, while amongst both officers and N.C.O.'s there could be a degree of friction occasioned by unsatisfactory performance, the arrival of dug-outs from home, promotion prospects and careerism. Even in the extraordinary circumstances of war, petty grudges in small groups were not uncommon. Officers' messes were in any case largely influenced by the varying conduct of C.O.'s and senior officers. Not all set the best example. There were social tensions too, in particular between the old officer class and the new 'Temporary Gentlemen,' and between 'educated middle-class' and 'uneducated working class' recruits amongst the men, even if shared adversity sometimes resolved these difficulties and led to greater tolerance and understanding. In addition, all ranks had to cope with constant change, due to casualties, postings and drafts, which could prove highly disruptive to the small circles of friends which lay at the heart of comradeship. This was a very transient world. All ranks also had to cope with the loss of friends, and where close intimate pals were involved, this could prove devastating. Officers in particular could not afford to show emotion for too long after sad losses, and all ranks were obliged to move on swiftly from comrades' deaths in order to cope. Apparent callousness could become a coping mechanism. However, the overwhelming sense from the sources is not of callousness but of a sometimes imperfect comradeship which helped to bring out the finest human qualities in war. In this respect there is nothing to indicate that Highland soldiers were unique, either in their qualities or their imperfections. The overall impression in this respect is of the utter normalcy of the Highland soldier. Why would one expect anything else?

12

Lines of Support

We're a happy lot of people, yes we are[1]

Comradeship provided a measure of support at the front. Both officers and men received also support from home, the most practical manifestation of which was the supply of comforts. We have already noted how the sharing of these comforts became in itself a significant contributor to good comradeship, and we have already seen, in considering unit hierarchy, how officers would provide support to their men and their families, not only by providing comforts but also other practical assistance, including for example condolence and hospital visits, with the support of their wives or families at home. These were by no means the only lines of support open to soldiers at the front. In fact, both officers and men received support from family and friends, from regimental associations, from the community and also possibly from religion. It is these other lines of support which we examine in this chapter.

Comforts and practical support

To begin with comforts, these were provided not only by officers, but also from a variety of other sources, including family and friends, regimental 'associations' and members of the wider community, acting either individually or in organised groups.

The range of comforts supplied to the men by family and friends was astonishing, although the nature of the items supplied would depend on their relative means. Items included clothing (shirts, socks, hose-tops, gloves and mitts, balaclavas, scarfs and, less usefully, body-belts), food (basics – such as tea, milk, sugar, bread, butter and pepper – sandwiches, cakes, sweets, biscuits, chocolates, shortbread, puddings, fruit, preserves, cocoa cubes and coffee, sausages, kippers, tinned herrings, salmon, sardines, tinned meat, soup and Oxo cubes), smokes (cigarettes, tobacco, pipes, matches), reading material (newspapers, magazines, bibles), writing pads, wash kit (towel, flannel, sponge, shaving soap, soap cubes), medicines, powders and ointments, various practical items (thermos flask, mouth organ, knife, fork and spoon, handkerchiefs,

---

1   NLS MS944 Ramage, diary, forenote.

electric torch, candles, map, air cushion, film for camera) and, last but not least, money, generally in the form of postal orders.[2]

Private Douglas, a former marine draughtsman in Walker-on-Tyne, serving in 8th Black Watch in 1918, noted that;

> Thanks to mother, Uncle Jim, Uncle Alf, who sent me out 5/– postal orders at regular intervals, I was very rarely short of cash when out of the line. Father too sent me a postal order for 5/– whenever he wrote, but he left most of the letter writing to mother, who wrote nearly every week.[3]

C.S.M. Peter Stewart, in 8th Gordons, was a retired regular Gordon Highlander, living in India, who had felt it his duty to join the colours again, leaving his wife and children behind in India. He was nevertheless kept supplied with comforts by his relatives in England and Scotland.[4] Likewise, some Canadian soldiers received comforts from relatives in the old country. For example, Private Arrol Brown, in 73rd Battalion C.E.F. (Royal Highlanders of Canada) received cakes and cigarettes from his cousin Nesta in Cardiff.[5]

Officers received many of the same comforts as the men,[6] but the luxury of some contributions is astonishing, and illustrates both the social divide between officers and men, as well as

---

2 IWM 3460 Macmillan, letter from Alex (Sandy) Macmillan to mother, 13 March, 1917; letters from Norman Macmillan to mother, Bessie, Nan, passim; THM Seaforths 81-180 Murray, letters to sister Alex, 25, 30 November, 11, 19, 31 December, 1914, 8, 11, 24 January, 7, 25 February, 7, 9 March, 9, 11, 19, 22 April, 13 September, 31 October, 30 November, 6, 11 December, 1915, to sister Kate, 26 November, 8, 13, 24, 30 December, 1914, 7, 14 February, 19 March, 7 April, 26 June, 20 October, 22, 26 November, 3 December, 1915, to brother Joe, 9 January, 1915; THM Seaforths 84-117 Stewart, diary, 17 September, 1914; THM Seaforths 95-125 Sharp, letters to family, 25 July, 23 September, 1915; THM Seaforths 89-26 Crask, diary, 8, 13 May, 1915, letters to parents, 25 April, 4, 6, 7, 11, 12, 15, 17, 18, 28 May, 4? June 1915; LC GS 1422 Sanders, diary, 27, 29 November, 1914, 14 January, 1915; IWM 1659 PP Scammell, letters to mother, December, 1917, to June, 1918, passim; IWM 12968 Thomson, letters to parents from Stewart Thomson, 3, 28 October, 6 November, 1914, 21 November, 6 December, 1915, from Tommy Thomson, 25 October, 1914, from Gordon Thompson, 29 October, 1914; IWM 13262 Bryden, letters to father, 1, 7 April, 24 June, 1916, to mother 4, 12, 18 April, 13, 22 May, 1916, to sister Rhoda, 15, 28 April, 1916, to sister Doris, 8 May, 1916; IWM 13263 Bryden, letters to mother, 14 May, 16 June, 11, 21 October, 1916, 6 January, 26 March, 20 May, 1917; BWA Couston, letters to mother, 1, 10, 25 August, 8 November, 5 December, 1916, 6, 19 March, 29 April, 1917; ASHM N-E12 Mclaren, Cpl John Malcolm, letter to sister Meg, 6 April, 1916; ASHM N-E1 Herbert, letter to wife Nell, 28 May, 1917; THM Seaforths 81-180 Murray, letter to mother, 13 July, 1915. See also his letters to sister Alex, 12 April, 1915, to sister Kate 30 March, 4 April, 1916; IWM 10819 Brittan, diary, 4, 16 March, 10 April, 1915; Stothers, *Somewhere in France*, pp.50-51, 62.
3 IWM 4586 Douglas, memoir, p.447.
4 GHM PB2021 Stewart, letters to wife Lil, 15, 17 July, 12 August, 1915.
5 IWM 11310 Prichard, letter to her from Pte Arrol Brown, 6 February, 1 April, 1917.
6 BWA, Macdonald, Coll, letter to wife Mary, 8 January, 1918; BWA, Duke, letters home, 15, 25 October, 28 November, 1915; BWA Gordon, 'diaries,' letter home, 7 January, 1916; BWA Quekett, memoir, p.14; IWM 3696 Macnaghten, letters to wife, 20 September, 6, 9, 10, 11, 14, 15, 16, 19, 25 October, 1914, and to Col Corrie Walker, 10 October, 1914; IWM 5525 Steven, letter from Lt Sidney Steven to home 26 March, 1915, letter from Lt Harvey Steven to home, 27 September, 1915; ASHM N-E11 Macleod, letter to mother, 8 December, 1915, 11 February, 20 March, 1916; ASHM

the determination of officers to replicate where possible peacetime mess-life behind the lines. Thus, as well as the more mundane items, officers receive whiting, partridge, grouse, pheasant, caviar, oysters, champagne and port, while their practical gifts include field-glasses, lamp, telescope, periscope and compass. Some officers would arrange for the regular supply of a hamper from Fortnum and Mason. Hugh Quekett, for example, in 5th Black Watch, notes that, towards the end of 1914, in his company mess, "We were getting parcels from home, but none of us could compete with Campbell, who had arranged for a weekly parcel from Fortnum and Mason, containing all the expensive goodies." This was Hughie Campbell, a nephew of the late Prime Minister, Campbell Bannerman. Then, "For Christmas, amongst other things, I received a ½ lb barrel of oysters sent by my future father-in-law, a director of Whitstable Oyster Farm."[7] Lieutenant Malcolm Thorburn in 2nd Black Watch wrote happily in June, 1915, "What a blowout we had last night off an F. & M. parcel of Peggy's and how we enjoyed it! … Chicken, Asparagus, Peaches and Cream, Biscuits, Butter and Cheese, with a glass of port at the finish. Not bad for the trenches!"[8] But he wrote indignantly to his mother in October, "Thanks so much for the grouse and parcels, Mother dear. But the grouse were ruined! My word, if your cook was under military discipline, what a telling off she would get! And she deserves it! A perfect disgrace – two fine birds practically ruined and worthless."[9]

In addition to comforts provided by family and friends, a significant amount of comforts were provided through regimental sources. These donations were separate from those obtained on behalf of their men by individual officers, which we have considered elsewhere, although sometimes the distinction is obscure. Generally, these donations were organised by senior figures in the regimental family, or by their wives, arranging and supervising working parties of regimental wives or their friends. At the front, such contributions were not generally sent to individuals, but to battalions or companies, where they were distributed according to circumstance. This support extended also to prisoners-of war, when parcels would more likely be directed to individuals in need. Inevitably, there were some conflicts of responsibility.[10] Numerous such

---

N-E2 Hyslop, diary, 15, 21 September, 1914; IWM 11144 MacKay, diary, 31 December, 1916; IWM 11126 Liddell, letters to parents, 7, 15, 18 October, 4 December, 1914; IWM 15460 Chandler, letters to sister Kate, 29 March, 12 April, 1915; IWM 8592 Macgregor, letter to wife Dulcie, 25 December, 1917; IWM 6656 Milligan, letter to sister Marjorie, 27 February, 1917, to sister Minnie, 21 March, 1917; Bartholomew, *George Hugh Freeland Bartholomew*, p.27, letter home, 25 August, 1916; IWM 6702 Low, letters to Aunt Mary, 5, 18 December, 1914, 20 April, 1915, to wife Noanie, 8, 12 17, 18, 27 December, 1914, 18 January, 4 March, 21 April, 11 May, 18 June, 11, 13 July, 1915, 19 June, 1916, 6 March, 1918, to mother, 20 June, 4 July, 17 October, 19 November, 15 December, 1915, 20 May, 31 August, 1917, 28 February, 14 March, 30 April, 1918, to father, 3 March, 1918; ASHM N-E1 Robertson, letters home, February to November, 1915, passim; IWM 511 Thorburn, letters home, June to November, 1915, passim; LC GS 1027 Macleod, letters home 1914-1918, passim; Webster, *Mesopotamia 1916-1917*, letter to Joey, 5 November, 1916, letters to mother 25 November, (addendum 2 December), 14, 22, 25 December, 1916, 1 (addendum 4), 13 (addendum 19) January, 6 February, 1917 to father 2 December, 1916; Maxwell-Scott, Susan, *Pa's Wartime Letters and This & That*, (privately published, 2010), pp.5, 12.
7 BWA Quekett, memoir, p.14.
8 IWM 511 Thorburn, letter to mother, 4 June, 1915.
9 Ibid., letter to mother, 15 October, 1915.
10 GHM PB227 Sergeant, letters to his mother from Aberdeen & District Prisoners of War Bureau, 7 May, and Blackburn Prisoners of War Help Committee, 13 May, 1918.

contributions are described in the sources, and there is not the space here to list them all.[11] An example is provided by the Cameron Highlanders, who soon set up a Comforts Fund, driven, with good support, by Mr John McLaren, secretary of the Edinburgh Branch of the Regimental Association.

> Every lady connected with the regiment started to do what she could to aid the cause, some collecting subscriptions, others sending goods in kind, or organising arrangements for the provision of warm clothing , socks, mitts, &c. Similar help was rendered by members of different branches of the Association; by friends and well-wishers of the regiment in Edinburgh, Inverness, and elsewhere; by school children in our Territorial district; and by Scotsmen and Scotswomen scattered throughout the Empire. Directly the 1st Battalion left Edinburgh Castle for the Continent, Mrs McLachlan organised the married women left behind into a work party, which met regularly in the schoolroom of Johnston Terrace once a week throughout the whole period of the war to knit warm clothing and socks. This work party, which was reinforced as time went on by wives of reservists and other new-comers to the regiment, was most generously supplied with most of the wool needed by Lady Margaret Cameron of Lochiel.

In all, during the war, the Comforts Fund received, for example, 14,220 pairs of socks, 8,000 pairs of hose-tops and 1,500 pairs of mitts. Initially, the Comforts Fund also provided for prisoners-of-war, but the administrative burden was too onerous, and a separate Prisoners of War Care Committee began work on 1 December, 1916. At 1 March, 1918 the committee was formed largely of the great and good of the regiment, with Lieutenant-General Sir John Spencer Ewart as president, and Cameron of Lochiel, Lady Cameron and Mrs Mackintosh of Mackintosh, for example, as members. The donations were not inconsiderable, with the bulk being provided through the Central Prisoners of War Committee, supplemented by particular donations, for example from the Sergeants' Mess, Depot Cameron Highlanders. Funds were spent principally on foodstuffs, with significant but lesser amounts on bread and biscuits and tobacco.[12]

11   For Black Watch, see: BWA Laing, Pte John, diary, 10 October, 1914; IWM Books Cooper, 'Domi Militaeque,' following p.74, p.76; BWA, Various documents relating to concert parties of the Black Watch; BWA Quekett, memoir, p.19; IWM 4586 Douglas, memoir, p.702; BWA Sempill papers, letters to him from Sir George Abercromby, 2 March, 17 December, 1916. For Argylls, see: IWM 8192 Lawson, letter to sister Bessie, 21 December, 1917; Maclean, *On Active Service*, Vol.2, p.99; Craig Barr, *Home Service*, p.361. For Seaforths, see: IWM 12311 Mason-Macfarlane, typescript memoir, pp.10-11; Addison Smith, *10th Seaforths*, p.24; Webster, *Mesopotamia 1916-1917*, p.14, letter to mother, 30 October, 1916. For the Gordons, see: GHM PB2093 Crauford, letter to mother, 8 January, 1916; GHM PB1865 Neish, Maj. W, typescript, 'Benevolent Funds &c,' Aberdeen, 23 November, 1923; GHM PB227 Sergeant, letters to his mother from Aberdeen & District Prisoners of War Bureau, 7 May, and Blackburn Prisoners of War Help Committee, 13 May, 1918. For Glasgow Highlanders, see: IWM 3460 Macmillan, diary, 8 November, 1914. For 42nd Bn C.E.F. (Royal Highlanders of Canada), see: Topp, *42nd Battalion*, pp.9, 188-189, 313.
12   Craig-Brown, *Historical Records*, Vol.4, pp.473-477; IWM 1862 Craig-Brown, 'Report and Accounts of the Cameron Highlanders Prisoners of War Care Committee for the Quarter ending 28th February, 1918.' See also for Camerons: THM Camerons, 'Letters from Cameron Highlanders Prisoners of war 1916-1919'; THM Camerons 96-51 Letter from R.L. Douglas Hamilton to Cpl W.

Much support also came from the local community outside the strict control of regimental associations, although sometimes it is difficult to judge the extent to which these contributions were truly independent. Support came from villages,[13] towns,[14] counties,[15] churches,[16] schools and universities,[17] local companies,[18] former employers,[19] Highland societies and Scottish associations,[20] newspapers[21] and of course from generous individuals,[22] sometimes passing on the contributions from Flag Days.[23] Such contributions were apparently not always appreciated by the Royal Army Clothing Department, but they were an immense source of comfort to the troops.[24] Again, there is no space to consider these contributions in detail. A few examples will suffice. Sergeant Macpherson of 1st Camerons notes that, after the battle of the Aisne they received a packet of ten cigarettes to each man, "& inside was a small card with a printed message on it, 'The donor of these cigarettes thanks you with all her heart, Scotland for ever.' The card is one of my most cherished souvenirs."[25] In 1915, 1st Camerons received a consign-

Prime, 12 December, 1918; THM Camerons 90-122 Guidance for knitting hosetops for Q.O.C.H., n.d. [probably 1915]; IWM 7408 Lorimer, letter to mothers, 11 June, 13 July, 1915.
13 BWA, Couston, letter to mother, 29 April, 1917.
14 BWA, Guthrie, letters to wife Crissie, 20, 26 December, 1915, 21 January, 1916, letter to him from Mary Crouch, Dunblane, 12 January, 1916; THM Seaforths 81-180 Murray, letter to sister Alex, 24 April, 6 December, 1915, 23 February, 20 March, 1916, to father, 22 May, 1915 (postscript 24 May), to sister Kate, 20 November, 1915; to brother Joe, 9 January, 1916; Peel & Macdonald, *6th Seaforth Highlanders*, p.50; IWM 1862 Craig-Brown, letter home 7 December, 1914, undated draft letter to Lord Provost of Edinburgh; GHM PB1892.3.18 McDonald, 'Uncle Harper's Duds', p.13.
15 Bartholomew, *George Hugh Freeland Bartholomew*, p.40; Peel & Macdonald, *6th Seaforth Highlanders*, p.50; Springer & Humphreys, *Private Beatson's War*, pp.29-30, citing *Scotsman*, 14 November, 1914.
16 IWM 114 Allen, letter to wife, 30 May, 1915; GHM PB1937 Dawson, letter to mother, 31 January, 1915; IWM 3460 Macmillan, diary, 21 December, 1914; IWM 3608 Anderson, memoir.
17 BWA, Guthrie, letter to wife Crissie, 5 July, 1915, letter to him from A. Gale & Co., 15 July, 1915; IWM Books Cooper, 'Domi Militaeque,' p.2; IWM 11144 MacKay, diary, 13 July, 1917; IWM 3460 Macmillan, letter from Willie Macmillan to mother, 6 July, 1915; GHM PB1937 Dawson, letter to mother, 5 April, 1915; LC GS 0434 Dawson, diary, 5 April, 1915; IWM 3608 Anderson, memoir; BWA Couston, letters to mother, 19 March, 29 April, 1917.
18 BWA, Guthrie, letter to wife Crissie, 9 June, 1915; LC GS 1008 Macdonald, letter to father, 8 July, 1916; GHM PB3309 Pelham Burn, letter to father, 10 December, 1914.
19 IWM 4586 Douglas, memoir, p.233; IWM 8592 Macgregor, letter to wife Dulcie, 25 December, 1917.
20 Peel & Macdonald, *6th Seaforth Highlanders*, p.50; IWM 1862 Craig-Brown, draft letter to Stewart Boyle, Chairman, London Inverness-shire Association, 1 December, 1914; BWA Sempill papers, letter to him from Federated Council of Scottish Associations in London, 7 May, 1915.
21 IWM 114 Allen, letter to wife, 16 December, 1915; Bartholomew, *George Hugh Freeland Bartholomew*, p.40; THM Seaforths 96-36 Tweddle, letter home, 27 December, 1914.
22 Bartholomew, *George Hugh Freeland Bartholomew*, p.40; Webster, *Mesopotamia 1916-1917*, p.14, letter to mother, 25 December, 1916; THM Camerons 99-87 Macpherson, diary, 22 September, 1914; IWM 1862 Craig Brown, letter home, 19 January, 1915, letter from Mrs H.V. McKinlay, Edinburgh, to 1st Camerons, 25 March, 1915; GHM PB1937 Dawson, letter to mother, 5 April, 1915. See also LC GS 0434 Dawson, diary, 5 April, 1915; LC GS 1422 Sanders, diary, 29 November, 1914; GHM PB242 Stansfield, letters home, May to September, 1915, passim.
23 GHM PB2021 Stewart, letter to wife Lil, n.d. [1915]; Springer & Humphreys, *Private Beatson's War*, p.30, citing *Scotsman*, 8 June, 1915; NLS MS945 Ramage, diary, 10 May, 1915.
24 Addison-Smith, *10th Seaforths*, p.20.
25 THM Camerons 99-87 Macpherson, diary, 22 September, 1914.

ment of mouth-organs This enabled the battalion to hold a mouth organ competition on 23 April, with prizes for 'Highland or Scots tunes suitable for marching,' and 'Any kind of tune, choice left to the performer.' A stipulation was that, "In all cases the performer must state what he is going to play before he begins"![26] Willie Macmillan in 7th Seaforths received a parcel of chocolate, biscuits and cigarettes from the boys of his old school. He wrote to his mother in July, 1915, "I hope, tho' they all will probably in a few years be trained to fight and ready to take their part if need be, that never again will it be necessary. Training for war is a good thing, actual warfare is horrible."[27] C.S.M. Peter Stewart, in 8th Gordons, was a retired regular Gordon Highlander, living in India, who had nevertheless felt it his duty to join the colours again. He wrote to his wife, Lil, from the front in 1915:

> I am sending you a sprig of white heather which has been worn in my cap in the trenches the last fortnight I was there. I got it sent out from a girl in Scotland, but don't be jealous darling, I have never seen her yet. She is a school girl who helped to subscribe for cigarettes for the soldiers' cigarettes on Empire Day. I had the luck to get hers and wrote thanking her. So she sent me on the heather.[28]

When Private Douglas of 11th Argylls was in hospital in Brighton, at Christmas, 1917, being treated for a septic knee, he received a large parcel from his ship-building draughtsman's office in Walker-on-Tyne, which he had left almost exactly nine months earlier.[29] Finally, when Robert Ashburner of the South African Scottish was in the South African Hospital at Richmond, he found that his bed was endowed by a number of girls in Durban, who called themselves the Bachelor Girls. They sent tobacco, cigars, cigarettes and even beer.[30]

The comforts supplied from home were much appreciated, and often necessary, although on some occasions, they apparently competed wastefully with government issue.[31] Certainly, on occasion the men were receiving more gifts than they could reasonably accommodate. Lieutenant Bryden McKinnell, in 1st Liverpool Scottish, recorded in December, 1914 that "the men won't draw their rations on account of the amount of eating stuff they have received from home."[32] The principal difficulty however was that when the men had to shift location, they simply could not carry more than the bare minimum in their packs, so that excess comforts had to be left behind.[33] Some surplus comforts could nevertheless be put to alternative use. "Socks became excellent rifle covers and holdalls for our various small kit are improvised from the sleeping

---

26 IWM 1862 Craig-Brown, letter home, 23 April, 1915.
27 IWM 3460 Macmillan, letter from Willie Macmillan to mother, 6 July, 1915.
28 GHM PB2021 Stewart, letter to wife Lil, n.d. [1915].
29 IWM 4586 Douglas, memoir, p.233.
30 IWM 24887 Ashburner, interview.
31 IWM 11126 Liddell, letters to parents, 3 October, 23 October, 1914.
32 McKinnell, *Diary*, p.32, 17-19 December, 1914.
33 See for example: BWA, Couston, letter to mother, 1, 4 August, 13 October, 1916, 6 March, 1917; THM Seaforths 81-180 Murray, letters to sister Alex, 25, 30 November, 1914, 27 October, 1915, to sister Kate, 8 December, 1914, 20, 24 January, 1915; IWM 6702 Low, letter to Aunt Mary, 4, 5 December, 1914; THM Seaforths 96-36 Tweddle, letter home 12 December, 1914; LC GS 1422 Sanders, diary, 27 November, 1914.

helmets."[34] Much later in the war, as John Bowie records, about March, 1918, in 11th Argylls, "We had better food than at home and our parcels were nearly all stopped by ourselves."[35]

Support from the community did not just extend to the provision of comforts. There are several testaments to the practical hospitality of the locals, where the training battalions were based, in providing entertainments or recreation facilities. At Tain, a committee of ladies organised a recreation tent for 10th Seaforths;[36] at Invergordon, Lord Seaforth and Mrs Stuart Mackenzie gave a 'bun-fight' to the men of 3rd Camerons;[37] at Inverness, the locals organised 'Welcome Centres' for the men of 7th Camerons. They were "like fathers and mothers to us," wrote Robert Burns.[38] Even the Scouts were mobilised: during the school holidays in 1917, Boy Scout A.M. Campbell worked in the Y.M.C.A. hut at Cambusbarron camp for 8th Camerons.[39] In some cases, the battalions themselves organised thankyou concerts or dinners for the locals, so the goodwill was reciprocal.[40] In most cases, the hospitality was matched by a tremendous send-off to the men, both battalions and drafts, when they left their training locations.[41]

This local support continued after the soldiers had left. Although well-meaning local support could appear as inappropriate hero-worship to some disillusioned soldiers,[42] men on leave would be feted. When Robert Burns returned on leave to his small village of Eaglesham, the children were given the day off school.[43] When Private Thomas Alexander was on leave in May, 1917, after recovering from a wound, he was presented with a gold watch and chain, subscribed for by the people of Holytown, where he lived, for having won the Military Medal.[44] Former employers would write letters of condolence to bereaved relatives.[45] When Captain Sir John Fowler, serving with 1/4th Seaforths, was killed in the trenches on 22 June, 1915, exceptionally his body was brought home for burial at Inverbroom, from where he ran his large estate. A regular officer in 2nd Seaforths, since 1913 he had been adjutant of the 4th (Territorial) battalion, with which he went to the front. No fewer than eleven boys from his own property accompanied him to the front. On his return, his remains in the hearse were accompanied by Mr McHardy, head stalker of the estate; the pall bearers were the heads of departments on the estate. The funeral involved not only many military representatives, but also significant local

34 IWM 3608 Anderson, memoir.
35 ASHM N-E11 Bowie, diary, March, 1918.
36 Addison Smith, *10th Seaforths*, p.11.
37 LC GS 1027 Macleod, letter to mother, 24 January, 1915.
38 Burns, *Once a Cameron Highlander*, pp.25-27. See also: Craig-Brown, *Historical Records*, Vol.3, p.415, Vol.4, p.273.
39 LC DF 148 Campbell, memoir.
40 Addison Smith, *10th Battalion Seaforths*, pp.31-32; IWM 8592 Macgregor, letter to Dulcie Newling, 27 February, 1916.
41 Andrews, *Autobiography of a Journalist*, p.85; IWM 132 Paterson, memoir, pp.19-20; IWM 2294 Fraser, letter to Gwen Howell, 20 August, 1916; IWM 11255 PP Pennie, W., manuscript memoir, 'An account of my sojourn in France & Germany during the Great War'; Burns, *Once a Cameron Highlander*, pp.25-27; GHM PB1699, 'As We Go Up the Line to Death', p.14, citing diary of John Forbes Knowles, 4 November, 1914; GHM uncatalogued Beaton, memoir, p.13; IWM 3460 Macmillan, diary, 2 November, 1914; IWM 3608 Anderson, memoir.
42 IWM Books Brooke, 'Wait for it,' pp.285-286.
43 Burns, *Once a Cameron Highlander*, pp.94-95.
44 IWM 12392 PP Alexander, Thomas, diary, 10 June, 1916, 2 May, 1917.
45 THM Camerons 00-164, letter from H.M. Office of Works to Mr J. Coutts, 22 May, 1917.

representatives, including the Provost of Dingwall, with a large attendance by local people not only from the estate, but also from Ullapool, the Braemore estate, Lochmelm, Ardchannich, Letters, Coigach and Dundonnell. Both Lochbroom Parish Council and Dingwall Town Council passed motions expressing sympathy to Lady Fowler.[46]

Canadians too might have support from their relatives in the old country. C.S.M. David McMillan in 43rd Battalion C.E.F., was wounded in the attack on Regina Trench on 8 October, 1916. He had his arm amputated at Etaples, and was then sent to Craigleith Hospital in Edinburgh. There he was visited by his mother, from Maxwelltown. Later, when he was shifted to Clarence House near Sheen, he got leave to visit Scotland.

> It was nice to get back to the atmosphere of home for a time, and to see my parents. My sister Jean was still living at Terregles (Dumfries, Scotland) and I must confess that I spent most of my leave there. She and her husband, Harry, were kindness personified, and what pleased me greatly was that I had the use of a saddle horse when I wanted it. Many a pleasant ride I had, and I was happy to get astride a horse again, just to experience the feel of it.[47]

Local people would also visit soldiers in hospital, and entertain them to tea when they were convalescing. In 1917, Robert Burns spent some time in hospital at Invergordon.

> During the stay there we 'poor things' were visited daily by well-wishing ladies whose little gifts and company were greatly appreciated, for this makeshift 'hospital' was lacking in the expected comforts. It would have been almost impossible to accept the many invitations out to tea when we got better.[48]

Boy Scout A.M. Campbell also did his bit by undertaking 14 days duty as a messenger in a Glasgow War Hospital.[49] Private Thomas Alexander, some time convalescent at Ardgowan House, Inverkip, records how Lady Stewart of Inverkip took a genuine interest in his subsequent progress.[50] In 1917, Harry Lauder initiated a fund to be used for giving maimed Scots soldiers a fresh start in life; also to keep those who were paralysed or suffering from shell-shock from cold and lonely institutions by giving them support at home. By the autumn of 1918, the fund had already raised a six-figure sum.[51] Finally, of course, the local people were on hand to give the soldiers a fine welcome home.[52] For the school-children of Eaglesham, when Robert Burns finally came home, it was worth another half-day off school![53] In a remarkable passage, the Canadian David McMillan, who, be it remembered, had lost an arm in the war, waxes lyrical on the supporting role played by the people at home in Great Britain.

---

46 Fowler, *Captain Sir John Fowler, Bart.*, passim.
47 McMillan, *Trench Tea and Sandbags*, p.39.
48 Burns, *Once a Cameron Highlander*, p.142. See also: McMillan, *Trench Tea and Sandbags*, pp.35-36.
49 LC DF 148 Campbell, memoir.
50 THM Seaforths 02-138 Alexander, diary, September, 1917, August, 1918.
51 Lauder, *A Minstrel in France*, pp.308-311.
52 Macleod, *6th Camerons*, p.132; Craig-Brown, *Historical Records*, Vol.3, pp.285-286.
53 Burns, *Once a Cameron Highlander*, p.167.

When we went on leave and were able to divorce ourselves from the environment of the Camp, we came in contact with the civilian population, and we could then better sense the feelings of the people. I got the impression that we were one big family, working in a common cause, each member doing his or her best to reach a common goal – peace with honour! I cannot hope to define this imperceptible bond between civilians and servicemen. It was nothing tangible, but it could perhaps be ascribed to the cheery smile on the faces of the people on the street, in the warm welcome of those kindly folks who invited us into their homes, and in numerous other ways. Never did I hear expressed even an infinitesimal doubt that victory would be ours as I am sure we all felt that right over might would prevail.[54]

Some well-meaning personalities went further, and visited the front.[55] No doubt visits by V.I.P.s were not universally welcome, but one exception was Harry Lauder. His son John was an officer in their local Territorial Battalion, 8th Argylls. After visiting John at Bedford in January, 1915, Harry resolved to organise a recruiting pipe band, which he did, equipping them and paying the bills. While the band toured Britain, Harry toured the country separately, and everywhere he performed he gave speeches urging the young men to enlist. He also visited hospitals.[56] In the winter of 1915/16 he was appearing in a revue at the Shaftesbury Theatre in London, called 'Three Cheers.' On New Year's morning he received a telegram stating that John had been killed in action on 28 December. Harry was devastated and could not face the thought of trying to make an audience laugh, but his friends pleaded with him to go back, and others, who had lost their own sons, wrote to him begging him not to give up making people happy. He was also concerned that 'Three Cheers' would close and that 300 people would be thrown out of work. But the clincher was his belief that John would have wanted him to carry on. So he went back and performed in 'Three Cheers.' The climax was a song, 'The Laddies who Fought and Won,' and he broke down briefly in the line,

> When we all gather round the old fireside
> And the fond mother kisses her son.

He considered retiring after 'Three Cheers,' but was persuaded to continue his efforts, so he made some speeches on food conservation and entertained soldiers in hospitals. He wished to enlist, at the age of 46, but was dissuaded on the grounds that he could best contribute at home.[57] Harry then received letters from soldiers at the front asking him to go over and sing for them. From this was born his famous tour in June, 1917, on which he was accompanied by James Hogge, M.P. for East Edinburgh, and the Reverend George Adam. He gave a large number of concerts to soldiers in hospitals and camps.[58] The tour was a great success.[59]

---

54 McMillan, *Trench Tea and Sandbags*, pp.43-44.
55 GHM PB1892.3.18 McDonald, 'Uncle Harper's Duds', pp.33-34; Aiken, *Courage Past*, p.14.
56 Lauder, *A Minstrel in France*, pp.39-46.
57 Lauder, *A Minstrel in France*, pp.67-109.
58 Ibid., pp108-303, passim.
59 THM Camerons 96-52, Laidlaw, 'Grandpa's War,' letter from Sgt Laidlaw to wife Bertha, 10 June, 1917; NLS Acc.9084, no.37 Macleod, letter to Ellen, 18 June, 1917.

Harry ... sang over a dozen songs and was really 'great.' When he sang 'There's a wee hoos' 'mang the heather,' it was so quiet that you could have heard a pin fall and when in a speech he made at the end, which went straight to our hearts and made us think of Bonnie Scotland and our dear ones at home, many, many of the men, who were a sentimental lot on the whole, had tears in their eyes.[60]

Support did not just come from home. It also came from the townsfolk and villagers in England, on whom the Highland troops were either billeted or stationed in camps nearby. Notably this was the case in Bedford, where the Territorial Highland Division was billeted in 1914-1915, in Hampshire and its margins, where many New Army Highland battalions were billeted in 1915, and in Yorkshire, near Ripon, where the Territorial reserve training battalions came to be based.

The first introduction to English hospitality came as the soldiers were transported south across the border by train. At various stations en route they were fed and watered by lady volunteers, while the locals would cheer them on their way as they passed by.[61] George Ramage was drafted to the front in April, 1915. His train passed through Wolverhampton and Birmingham. "Both sordid towns but their inhabitants cheery & warm hearted. Every man, woman & child within sight of the railway waved something & cheered us as we passed. Such a difference to phlegmatic Scotland."[62] In 1917, after Frank Brooke had been wounded at Arras, he was evacuated to Dover and placed on the train to Chatham. "I almost sobbed when I heard the shrill cheering and prattling of English children waving their 'Good Lucks!"[63]

Support from home. Harry Lauder, in a contemporary fund-raising photograph, dressed as a soldier to perform his wartime song, 'The Laddies who Fought and Won.' Harry's son John was killed during the war while serving in 1/8th Argylls. Harry devoted himself to the war effort, famously visiting the troops at the front in June, 1917. (photographic card, Author's collection)

---

60 GHM PB1639 Kemp, memoir, pp.87-88.
61 IWM 3834 Wrench, diary, Introduction; GHM PB1937 Dawson, letter to mother, n.d. [August, 1914]; GHM PB29.2 Bruce, Maj Robert, diary, 16 August, 1914; IWM 11255 Pennie, memoir, GHM PB3112 Blinco, 'Rough Diary,' p.2.
62 NLS MS944 Ramage, diary, 14 April, 1915.
63 IWM Books Brooke, 'Wait for it,' pp.204-205.

Once they had reached their destinations, there are a few complaints that the locals were seeking to make money out of them. "Our general experience was that the good folk of Liphook could look after the 'saxpence' as well as any Scotsman."[64] But such complaints seem churlish when compared with the innumerable tributes to the friendliness, hospitality and generosity of the local people.[65] Just as in Scotland, the locals laid on facilities and entertainments for their Highland guests and, possibly because the men were so far from home, the tributes are even greater. When B Company, 10th Argylls, were billeted at the village of Itchen Stoke in Hampshire. "No one groused when we came in late and muddy off parade, as we often did and we always found hot meals and baths awaiting us."[66] When 7th Camerons were billeted at Cirencester, the Scottish battalions not finding a place large enough for divine service, the authorities of the Church of England granted leave for 1,200 men to worship according to the Presbyterian manner in the old parish church – a greater spirit of tolerance, as we shall see, than displayed by some chaplains at the front.[67] Captain Youngson of 5th Gordons also notes how at Bedford, the inhabitants "opened their houses and took the troops into their homes and hearts." On route marches, "in the early days, the villagers of Bedfordshire could not do enough for us." "The countryside abounded in fruit, and the thirsty soldiery were regaled with apples, pears and plums as they passed along."[68]

As in Scotland, the local English people gave a great send-off to the Highland soldiers who had been living amongst them.[69] In Basingstoke, Ian Andrew and his pal John Inch had been put up by Mr and Mrs Edgar, a childless couple. "When we left, tears were streaming down good Mrs Edgar's face while Jinch's eyes were suspiciously moist and his high voice abnormally gruff."[70] Indeed, such close relationships were formed that many English townsfolk continued the friendship through letters and the provision of comforts.[71] These were not always appro

---

64 Craig Brown, *Historical Records*, Vol.4, p.275. See also: IWM 12643 Ferrie, letter to mother, 13 February, 1916; IWM 21092 McGregor, letter to wife Jen, 16 January, 1916.
65 IWM 3460 Macmillan, letter from Alex (Sandy) Macmillan to mother, 1 April, 1916; David, *Mud and Bodies*, p.14, letter from Weir to his mother, 6 December, 1914; THM 2013-072 (S) Braes, memoir, p.17; IWM 132 Paterson, memoir, p.25; LC WF Recollections A9, Andrew, memoir; *Souvenir Booklet of the Sixth Cameron Highlanders*, pp.14-15, 17; THM Camerons 02-46 Notes, 'Cameron Highlanders March into Sherborne St John,' compiled by the Sherborne St John History Society, 2002; IWM 6933 Moir, letter to Mrs Bulley, 27 March, 1915; Burns, *Once a Cameron Highlander*, pp.33, 35-36; McEwen, *Fifth Camerons*, p.20; LC GS 1549 Strachan, memoir; GHM PB3279 Matthews, diary, 19 February, 1915; GHM PB1699, 'As We Go Up the Line to Death', p.14, citing diary of John Forbes Knowles, Christmas Day, 1914, 25 January, 1915; GHM PB1937 Dawson, letters to mother, 23 August, 4 October, 1914, 31 January, 19 February, 1915; GHM PB583 McKinnon, memoir, p.1; GHM PB3712 Murison, memoir; GHM PB 107.1 Grant, diary, 10 September, 1914; GHM PB1892.3.18 McDonald, 'Uncle Harper's Duds', pp.8-10; GHM uncatalogued Beaton, memoir, pp.13-15; IWM 7593 Harper, memoir, pp.13-14.
66 David, *Mud and Bodies*, p.14, extract from Weir's diary.
67 Craig-Brown, *Historical Records*, Vol.4, pp.276-277.
68 GHM PB1892.3.1 Youngson, memoir, pp.4-6.
69 GHM PB 107.1 Grant, diary, 2 May, 1915; GHM PB3253 Gray, John, manuscript memoir, written, 1920; GHM uncatalogued Beaton, memoir, pp.13-15.
70 LC WF Recollections A9, Andrew, memoir.
71 THM Seaforths 81-180 Murray, letters to sister Alex, 25, 30 November, 3, 11, 19, 24, 31 December, 1914, 20 January, 20 February, 20 March, 1 May, 6 July, 31 October, 6 December, 1915, 20 March, 10 April, 1916, to sister Kate, 26 November, 8, 19, 24 December, 1914, 16 February, 12 June, 22 August,

priate. Hugh Munro, an officer in 1/8th Argylls, received a letter from a Miss Hipwell of Bedford which "encloses a device of rubber to hold between the teeth during artillery bombardment! Well-meaning but ludicrous!"[72] Willie Macmillan received letters from the friends he made at Alton in Hampshire when serving with 7th Seaforths.[73] The attentive nature of this support is apparent from a considerate letter written by a Blanche Hayward in Alton to Willie's mother on 13 June, 1916. She had received a letter from Willie dated May from Amara hospital in Mesopotamia, to say that he had been wounded in action with 1st Battalion in April. She goes on:

> I hope by now the wound is healing, though it would be a blessing I think if he had not to go near any fighting again. Please excuse hurried writing, but I wanted to relieve your mind in case you had not heard. We are only too pleased to do anything we can to cheer up the heroes who are away from all their dear ones.[74]

A measure of the strength of the relationships established was that a number of Highland soldiers spent part of their valuable leave visiting their new friends in Bedford and elsewhere.[75]

A final element of this support within England was that those Highland soldiers hospitalised in England received well-meaning visits from the local people just as in Scotland.[76] Charles Cordner, for example, of 2nd Argylls, wounded near Zonnebeke Wood in September, 1917, found himself in hospital at Chichester. During his stay he had one visitor who came about twice a week with a few biscuits and played a game or two of draughts each visit. "He was in his eighties, and told me he had been in the Navy, and in his younger days had sailed before the mast with the famous Sir Charles Beresford."[77] After Ian Andrew was wounded at Loos, he was sent to Haxby Road Auxiliary Hospital in York, originally planned as a hostel or community centre for Rowntree's Chocolate Factory. While there, he enjoyed the hospitality of the Rowntree family. "I shall have to consume a vast amount of Rowntree's chocolates before I repay that debt!"[78] Robert Burns was sent to convalesce at Bedale, in a large house which was given to the Red Cross by a Mr Gray, a shipbuilder of Hartlepool. There he was entertained by whist

    10, 30 October, 22, 26 November, 1915, 30 March, 1916, to father 22 May, 1915 (postscript 24 May); THM Seaforths 87-141 Heriz-Smith, extracts from 'Noon Star'; 87-125 Heriz-Smith, letters; *Souvenir Booklet of the Sixth Cameron Highlanders*, pp.15, 17; McEwen, *Fifth Camerons*, p.20; Craig-Brown, *Historical Records*, Vol.4, pp.276-277; IWM 19680 White, letter from 2Lt J. Ledingham, 21 November, 1918, letters from 2Lt James Gray, 22 September, 1918, and from his widow, Edith Gray, 17 November, 22 December, 1918, letters to her from Pte D.C. Skinner, 16 September, 1916, 25 February, 1917.

72 ASHM N-E8 Munro, letter to unknown recipient, 28 May, 1915.
73 IWM 3460 Macmillan, letter from Willie Macmillan to mother, 4 August, 1915.
74 IWM 3460 Macmillan, letter from Blanche Hayward, Alton to Willie Macmillan's mother, 13 June, 1916.
75 Burns, *Once a Cameron Highlander*, pp.35-36; Craig-Brown, *Historical Records*, Vol.4, pp.276-277; GHM PB1937 Dawson, letter to mother, 29 July, 1915. see also: LC GS 0434 Dawson, diary, 27 July, 1915.
76 Apart from refs cited, see IWM Books Brooke, 'Wait for it,' pp.204-205.
77 IWM 3449 Cordner, memoir.
78 LC WF Recollections A9, Andrew, memoir.

drives, concerts, tea parties, motor runs, and even sleigh-rides in the snow, pulled by the Gray family's two Shetland ponies, 'Dot' and 'Carrie.'[79]

Support came also from expatriate Scots. Highland soldiers passing through Durban, for example, which was a regular stop on the route to India, were feted by the local Scots community. Private George Brown, sailing with a draft ultimately to join 2nd Black Watch in Mesopotamia, notes that, "One family from the Isle of Lewis took 3 or 4 of us to their home where we had another tea! They promised to write home for us in case our letters were censored."[80] Private Drummond also sailing with a draft to join 2nd Black Watch, "had an invitation through a friend to a gentleman's house about four miles out of Durban. He belonged to Kirkcaldy but had been in Durban for over twenty years. We were entertained in a first class manner and it just reminded me of being at home."[81] And as the ship carrying 1st Garrison Battalion Gordon Highlanders pulled out of Durban harbour on 22 February, 1917, en route to India, "A young lady probably connected with a Girl Guides Brigade signalled with flags as we left the water way (Scotland for ever)"[82] Occasionally soldiers would meet and be feted by Scotswomen living in France.[83] Parcels were even received from Hong Kong[84] and the British Legation in Peking,[85] although these may not necessarily have been from Scots. One definite Scottish expatriate supporter was Mr Robert Bone, Superintendent of the Egyptian Coastguard Services, a Port Glasgow man.[86] When 5th Argylls passed through Alexandria in June, 1915, he invited a lot of the Port Glasgow lads to meet him, and provided tea for some of the officers. When he heard of the casualties in the battalion from Gallipoli being brought to Alexandria, he visited the Port Glasgow and Greenock boys in the hospitals with his children, providing cakes, scones, biscuits, custards and cigarettes. He also arranged for the regular supply of the Greenock Telegraph from home.

Letters from home

Alongside parcels, soldiers also received letters from home. The postal service, at least to France and Flanders, was excellent. Consequently, the soldiers did not just live in their own military world. Many of them were receiving regular letters from home, and were living in two worlds; the world of war, and the world of home. In this respect they differed from the folk at home, who could not really comprehend the awfulness of war, because they had never experienced it. The men, by contrast, were, in principle, only temporarily detached from their world at home, to which they could relate entirely. So, while their loved ones at home lived in one world, the soldiers, who received regular letters from home, lived in two. Letters were the means by which

---

79 Burns, *Once a Cameron Highlander*, pp.135-138.
80 BWA Brown, memoir, p.35.
81 BWA Drummond, memoir.
82 GHM PB3112 Blanco, 'Rough Diary,' pp.34-39.
83 IWM 3460 Macmillan, diary, 4 March, 1916; GHM PB1706/2 Robertson, diary, 2 August, 1916.
84 IWM 6444 Shewan, letter to Uncle Bob, Hong Kong, 14 November, 1915.
85 THM C80-13 Postcards from Bandsman Rossor and Pte Elder to Peking, 26 March, 1915
86 ASHM N-E5 Main, letters to his wife Win, 1, 8, 22 June, 10, 15 September, 1915; ASHM N-E5 Bone, Robert, Alexandria, letter to Auntie Janet, 16 July, 1915, and extract from Greenock Telegraph [?] April, 1916.

this strange situation was maintained, and their delivery became of the utmost importance. Colonel Stansfield of 2nd Gordons commented, almost certainly correctly, in July, 1915, "The new soldier is much more dependent on his mail, than the old regular was."[87] Bernard Blaser, who served with 2nd London Scottish in Palestine, had no doubt about its importance.

> A mail, however small and however long overdue, always marks a red-letter day, especially when you are in the heart of a strange land and have nothing but your own optimism to make life worth living. On the arrival of the mail the news travelled round like the wind, and everyone was filled with eager expectation ... To those of us who received these links with home, the letters acted for some days as a stimulant, and provided food for thought and sweet recollections.[88]

This was especially so for the married soldiers, as Robert Burns, who served with 7th Camerons, observed when interviewed in 1996.

> Well, we single fellows, just in our teens, we were alright. But it was heart-breaking to know that some of your comrades were young lads about 21 or 22, married some having children, and all you could get out of them, 'Wonder how my wife's getting on; wonder how the bairns are getting on.'... it was a heartbreak to hear those married men talk about their wives. It was a heartbreak.[89]

The sad fact for historians is that, although thousands of letters written by soldiers from the front have survived, because they were lovingly kept at home, very few letters written to the soldiers survive, as they were unable to keep them. In most cases, all we can do to understand the letters the men received is to draw inferences from their replies. A few letters from home though do survive, to enhance our understanding. On the positive side, they brought love from home.

Support from family. A long-serving soldier of the Seaforth Highlanders with his family. Would he still be there for them at the end of the war? (Author's collection)

87 GHM PB242 Stansfield, letter home, 27 July, 1915.
88 Blaser, *Kilts across the Jordan*, pp.218-219.
89 LC Tape 1316 Burns, interview. See also: IWM 12678 Burns, transcription of interview.

Gordon Crask, for example, who was from Bradford, and arrived at Dingwall to join the Seaforth Highlanders in April, 1915, was heartened by thoughts of home and his sweetheart, Mabel; "Had ever such a nice little letter from Mabel. She does buck me up. I only wish that she was here. I should get well in no time."[90] Other letters offered support and encouragement. Some letters survive, for example, from Willie Macmillan's mother to him, when he was serving in 7th Seaforths at Aldershot. "You are one of 'the thin red line of 'eroes,' & you must never say die, but peg on & stick in." "You know what the Apostle Paul says about 'enduring hardship as a good soldier of Jesus Christ.' It seems to be the lot of a soldier to endure & it is those that 'endure to the end' that win the prize."[91] Second Lieutenant Lionel Sotheby, an Old Etonian, attached to 1st Black Watch, received a letter from E. Lyttelton, Eton Master, in March, 1915, which advised him: "You have a noble standard of officer's duty yet before you & I don't think you will let yourself lower it."[92] By contrast, Private William Couston, a school-teacher in civilian life, received letters from the children of his old village schools through 1917 and 1918: "It is very good of them to be so mindful of me."[93] Other letters stirred thoughts of the beauties of home. John Cooper wrote home on 8 October, 1917.

> I received your letter of 3rd October this morning and in spite of the fact that it has, as you say, no news to speak of, it is none the less welcome and interesting because it contains the graphic and literary account of a ramble on Tents Muir. Such descriptions of the natural scene of the homeland are very precious and refreshing to the exile – they are like a bit of dear old 'Blighty' suddenly let into France and for the moment taking one out of France and all it means to us soldiers; such a tale brings a breeze from the hills of home into our lives; and after all it is just for the home that we are here and it is the thought of home and the folks there that add a sweetness to our lives, that prevent us from becoming hard and sullen.[94]

Still other letters brought news of the family at home. Some touching letters do survive from Jen McGregor to her husband, Peter, serving at the front with 14th Argylls, giving news of their two children, Margaret and Bob.[95]

> [1 September] Margaret and I walked home looking into every shop window all the way down! She is such a nice wee chum to go out with. I just love going out with them now they are so big and understanding. When I was bathing Bob tonight he said, 'I just *wish* I had a tail.' I said, 'Why?' 'To wag when I feel happy!' He is getting to be a fine tall laddie, so clean and nice in spite of small sins. I adore him sometimes … I am longing for you to come and give me a hug … I am longing for another letter from you. I hope there will be one soon. I am always thinking about you. You are continually in my thoughts and I love

---

90 THM Seaforth 89 26 Crask, diary, 24, 25 April, 8, 10 May, 1915.
91 IWM 3460 Macmillan, letters from Mrs Macmillan (mother) to Willie Macmillan, 10 November, 8 December, 1914.
92 LC GS 1507 Sotheby, letter from E. Lyttelton, 4 March, 1915.
93 BWA, Couston, letters to mother, 15 June, 17 September, 1 October, 1917, 2 February, 1918.
94 IWM Books Cooper, 'Domi Militaeque,' pp.172-173.
95 IWM 21092 McGregor, letters to him from wife Jen, 31 August, 1, 7, 13, 16 September, 1916.

you more than I ever did before. At least I think I do, but I always love you so much I don't see how I can love you any more.

[16 September] Margaret said tonight she adored me & no matter however much I scolded her it made no difference in her love. She is always very loving at night when I tuck her into bed. They both are particularly loving at that time. They always put up a little prayer for Daddy to be kept safe and come home to them all right.

But Daddy had already been killed in action, on 13 September, 1916.

If such mail could be a comfort to those that received it, the lack of mail could be crushing to those who did not, as Bernard Blaser observed.

> For the unfortunates who did not, disappointment and despondency was all *they* got from the mail. I have known men not to receive a letter for months on end, owing to the continual loss of mails at sea or other causes, and they have become so depressed and miserable that they were entirely indifferent as to whether they survived the war or not. They felt absolutely forgotten, and the total absence of any possibility of leave home, coupled with the uncertainty of how long they were to be 'buried alive,' often caused them to sink into such a deplorable state of apathy and neglect of their personal cleanliness that in time they fell sick and had to go to hospital. There the change of environment and decent food generally restored their health and nursed them back to a normal state of mind.[96]

Unsurprisingly, 'Lonely Soldiers' columns appeared in some newspapers inviting members of the public to write to the lonely, but the system was open to abuse, sometimes of a rather amusing kind.[97] Genuine letters from well-wishers to the genuinely lonely however undoubtedly did some good.[98] Lieutenant A.M Clement in 1/6th Argylls, appears to have been receiving little or no mail, and was very gratified to receive parcels and letters from members of the Friends of Whitecraigs Golf Club between July and September, 1915. He wrote:

> I shall be pleased to hear from you or any other member of the Club who cares to share a few moments and drop me a line because out here there is nothing a soldier likes better than to get a letter no matter from whom, because we then see that although we have a rough time the folks at home have not altogether forgotten us. If any person would write me a note now and again I would be very pleased to get them, if you would be so kind as to give my address to any who wish it.[99]

Miss Sybil Smith, who, as we have seen, befriended soldiers of 6th Seaforths in the Highland Division when they were billeted with her in Bedford in 1914-1915, also appears to have written to soldiers she had not met, as a soldier's friend. Private J, McDonald of 1st Argylls touchingly

---

96 Blaser, *Kilts across the Jordan*, pp.218-219.
97 LC GS 1761 Wilson, memoir, pp.64-65; LC GS 1026 Maclean, memoir, p.12
98 Apart from refs cited below, see: THM Seaforths 07-42 Rowell, Miss, transcripts of letters sent to her from Dmr MacKenzie and Pte Thomson.
99 ASHM N-E6 Clement, Lt A.M., letter to Mr Gowans, Whitecraigs Golf Club, 19 July, 1915. see also letters of 29 August and 10 September, 1915.

replied to her; "I was very pleased when I received your parcel of sweets and 'smokies,' and your letter inviting me to write and say how I'm getting along. I have only one person to write to and it is not very often that the mail brings me anything."[100] Lance Corporal Low, of 9th Gordons, received letters and comforts from his 'little friend,' a seven-year old girl, Mary, who lived with her parents and brother Robbie in Tebay, Westmoreland. The correspondence is very touching.

> I received the parcel you so kindly sent me, but Oh little friend, it made me feel so much, that I was very nearly wishing that I hadn't written you, and yet it made me glad, for I haven't had any letters from my people for over a month, and the parcel and the letter you sent me has cheered me up ever so much ... Will you tell your little brother that I enjoyed the Chocolate and Cigarettes very much and your mother's cake, why little friend it was one of the finest cakes I ever tasted.[101]

In some respects, however, mail was a double-edged sword, for it could bring bad news as well as good. Major Jack Stewart, in 9th Black Watch, noted the reaction of his C.O., Colonel Lloyd, when he received a wire in August, 1915.

> At lunch T. got a wire and very abruptly left the room. I could see that something was wrong but didn't like to go after him, but when he came back, about an hour afterwards, he told me that his only brother had been killed in the Dardanelles. Poor old boy, I *am* sorry for him, his brother was a Major in the R. Welsh Fus., the Bn we relieved at Chiseldon.[102]

Private Albert Hay, in 1st Black Watch noted the loss of one man by suicide in May, 1918.

> We lost one of our men – Private R.S. Clark, No.14411 – on the 7th of May by his own hand. He had received a letter, written on blue note-paper, on the previous day, and after reading it we noticed that he seemed depressed, but he told no one of his trouble and it came as a shock to us when we found that he was missing, and later found him a little way along the trench with a wound in the head, and his rifle discharged.[103]

Alfred Fennah was detached from his battalion, 1st Liverpool Scottish, to the depot in France, when he heard of the death of his younger brother on 3 June, 1917. "This period was a very sad and grief-stricken one for me. I felt it was the end of everything. At home, the few remaining members of the family (Mother and two Sisters) were prostrate with grief."[104] These cases illustrate the extent to which soldiers of all classes were living in two parallel worlds. Fennah himself wisely realised the implication of this for dealing with individuals.

---

100 THM Seaforths 87-125 Heriz-Smith, letter to Sybil Smith from Pte J. McDonald, 3 March, 1915. See also letter to her from Bandsman Owen Gentles, 13 March, 1915.
101 LC GS 0981 Low, letter to Mary, 31 August [1917].
102 BWA, Stewart, letter home, 14 August, 1915.
103 BWA, Hay, memoir, p.112.
104 Fennah, *Retaliation*, pp.145-146.

> Companionship was most necessary as we, the rankers, always had, more or less, difficulties to contend with: if we missed them in army life, then they continually cropped up in connection with home affairs … when on parade and in charge of men, I always tried to remember that things were not always so bright and cheerful as they seemed by their outward appearance.[105]

A sense of betrayal

If the soldiers at the front received touching support in letters, parcels, visits and other kindnesses from the people at home, they were also conscious of perceived dishonesty or disloyalty, which by contrast engendered bitterness. Arthur Wrench wrote contemptuously about untruths in the newspapers.

> Tonight newspapers reach us containing the accounts of the Glasgow and Edinburgh provosts' experiences 'IN THE TRENCHES.'[According to Wrench they got no closer than three miles to the front line.] My God, they should be shot. They tell the folks at home we are spoiled and get more than we can eat, and advise them not to send us so much food stuff. Also that we are all well and happy. Well, we are happy just because it is our will to be so, as otherwise this awful life would soon drive us all crazy. After all, we are human beings, and WE are not just out here on a visit. So we say to hell with you, and wish you were IN the trenches one night when a mine is being put up. Then perhaps they would understand what it is to be HAPPY.[106]

Private Patrick Jordan, a Roman Catholic from Donegal, serving with 1/8th Argylls, wrote to his mother in October, 1917, "I hear there's some trouble just ready to break out over there in Ireland again. It's bad that."[107] On another occasion, he wrote about some rioting,

> It is a blooming disgrace. The people out here if you would hear them about them, they think you're as bad if you're Irish at all. It looks very bad in such a big war going on at present. It's out here they should be. That would put the fear of God in a few of them. Irishmen out doing their bit well and them quarrelling at home.[108]

S. Bradbury trained at home with the Camerons but served at the front with 5th Seaforths. His memoir includes a bitter poem by Richard Hyman about strikers at home, entitled 'My Brother on the Clyde,' which concludes:

> I've picked the old gun up again, my bit of iron too
> I'm just a common soldier, so I'll have to see it through,
> But if they lets us down at home and if he reads I died,

---

105 Ibid. p.69.
106 IWM 3834 Wrench, diary, p.28, 20 May, 1916.
107 ASHM N-E8 Jordan, letter to mother, October, 1917.
108 ASHM N-E8 Jordan, letter to mother, date illegible, 1917?

> Will he know he helped to kill me, my Brother on the Clyde.[109]

There was also some contempt for non-fighting battalions. Willie Macmillan, recuperating from a wound suffered in Mesopotamia with 1st Seaforths, at the Infantry Depot in Poona in India, in September, 1916, records a tragic altercation there.

> The 2/4 Wilts Territorials have been in Poona for two years doing garrison duty, and there is no love lost between them and the remnants of fighting battalions which find their way here. Anyhow, an altercation arose, and the result was the death of private W. O'Brien of the Seaforths, who was down from Mesopotamia on furlough. He had the D.C.M. too. Isn't it disgraceful that a man who has been through the heaviest fighting in France and Mesopotamia, should ultimately become the victim of a canteen brawl, with men of a battalion that hasn't done any fighting in the war and isn't likely to?[110]

Arguably, however, the greatest contempt was felt for those civilians who failed to volunteer (prior to conscription), for pacifists and for war profiteers. Brian Brooke, a colonial official in British East Africa, who came home to serve as an officer in the Gordon Highlanders, wrote contemptuously of those who did not volunteer, in his poem 'Coward.'

> 'Poor wretched, frightened little churls, who fear to do your share,
> But hang around to flirt with girls, and drink, and smoke, and swear.
> I tell you those who fight in France are not so brave as you;
> They simply chose to take their chance, as many men can do,
> They merely stride the open grave, and simple death they face,
> But which of them, like you, could brave dishonour and disgrace?
> ...
> When war is done and all is through, let Britain bear in mind
> The courage of the dauntless few who dared to stay behind.[111]

And E.A. Mackintosh, the Highland poet within 5th Seaforths, in his poem 'Recruiting,' castigates the hypocrites at home:

> Fat civilians wishing they
> 'Could go out and fight the Hun.'
> Can't you see them thanking God
> That they're over forty-one?[112]

---

109 IWM 2528 Bradbury, S., memoir, p.97. See also: THM Seaforths 81-180 Murray, letter to sister Alex, 17 January, 1916.
110 IWM 3460 Macmillan, letter from Willie Macmillan to mother, 11 September, 1916.
111 Brooke, *Poems*, pp.174-177.
112 Campbell & Green, *Can't shoot a man with a cold*, pp.139-140.

Captain Claud Low, in 1st London Scottish, wrote home from the front in December, 1914, "I shall find it hard to forgive any young fellow after this war if he has not got his medal for landing in France."[113] A little later, he remarked,

> We all received with joy the news that 3 seaport towns in England have been bombarded, & in censoring the letters of my coy I find they all rejoice. It will wake old England up, for indeed there are many thousands of so-called patriots singing Rule Britannia who have never done a hand's turn for their country.[114]

Jock Macleod, in 2nd Camerons, in April, 1915, condemned the Cambridge pacifists at home: "The only thing that we can hope for now is that a Zeppelin will drop a bomb on to their houses, and give them a minute taste of what it is like here."[115] Norman Beaton, serving in 1/7th Gordons, and hospitalised from the front, was allowed out of his hospital at Govan at the end of December, 1916. "I was surprised and disappointed when I got into the city and saw the amount of young fellows still in civilian clothes. When in France, we were led to believe that every available man was in France fighting, or in England training. But that was only bluff to cheer us up out there."[116] And Captain Sutherland of 5th Seaforths wrote after their defensive action against the German offensive of March, 1918:

> When I looked on our survivors the sixth day coming slowly back, footsore and weary, with dazed eyes – dazed from what they had come through, and from utter weariness of body and mind – when I saw our lads of 19 and 20, after putting in a most gallant fight, dropping by the roadside, utterly exhausted and done, and thought of some at home who think of nothing but how much money they can make out of this accursed war, I am tempted to ask if it is worth our fighting for such skunks who seem to have neither patriotism nor self-respect as long as their precious skins are safe.[117]

Support from Religion

One source of support, much more prominent then than a hundred years later, was Christian faith. The principal vehicle for this support was the regimental padre or chaplain. The ability and quality of these men varied considerably. As Lieutenant John Fraser in 7th Gordons wrote in August, 1917, "Our Presbyterian padre who lives with the 5th Gordons is not very popular. The C. of E. man lives with us & he is a much greater favourite. The Presbyterian padre is a conceited little pup from Greenock."[118] No doubt the great majority tried to exercise their duty as conscientiously as possible, and they did provide some practical helpful support. They would

---

113 IWM 6702 Low, letter to wife Noanie, 15 December, 1914.
114 IWM 6702 Low, letter to wife Noanie, 18 December, 1914. See also letter to Aunt Mary of same date.
115 LC GS 1027 Macleod, letter to father, 27 April, 1915.
116 GHM uncatalogued, Beaton, memoir, pp.193-194.
117 Sutherland, *War Diary*, p.158.
118 LC GS 0588 Fraser, letter to father, 11 August, 1917.

Support from religion. The Scottish Churches Hut at Montreuil depicted on a contemporary postcard. (Author's collection)

routinely write letters of condolence to the next of kin. Fred Langlands, for example, chaplain to 2nd Argylls, wrote to the father of Lieutenant G.E. Smith, killed in action at Loos.

> Try hard and let a feeling of pride and thankfulness mingle with and soften your sorrow, pride that a son of yours in the service of his country was faithful unto death – that indeed he gave his life like a crusader of old in a just and sacred cause.[119]

Coll Macdonald, chaplain to 8th Black Watch, spent much time answering enquiries from relatives about the dead, missing and wounded, a task which required great care and tact and was the source of some distress.[120] "I have a very warm side to the West Highland lads and when any of them is wounded or killed I feel it very keenly."[121] He received enquiries too through his wife Mary, and enlisted her support in writing to relatives.[122] When he finally stepped down from his duties at the front, he wrote, "On my way home I must wait at least one day in London to see men in Hospital and the relatives of one or two who had fallen."[123]

There is little criticism of the padres for this practical work. The same is not true of their formal religious services. Colonel Hugh Allen, commanding 1/7th Black Watch wrote of attending a "dismal" Church of England service on 26 June, 1916.[124] When 1/7th Gordons received a new

---

119 ASHM N-E2 Smith, Lt G.E., letter from Fred Langlands, Bn Chaplain, 2nd Argylls to Mr Smith, 4 October, 1915.
120 BWA Macdonald, Coll, letter to wife Mary 14 June, 1917. See also his letters of 5, 6, 7, 9, 16, 28 November, 7 December, 1917, 30 March, 9 April, 1918.
121 BWA Macdonald, Coll, letter to wife Mary, 1 October, 1917.
122 Ibid., letter to wife Mary, 9 November, 1917.
123 Ibid., letter to wife Mary, 10 May, 1918.
124 IWM 114 Allen, letter to wife, 26 June, 1916.

padre in November, 1917, he was "terribly U.F. and prosy" and preached for "far too long."[125] By contrast, Lieutenant William Paterson, a model Presbyterian, who joined 1/6th Seaforths in 1917, felt that religious services brought officers and men together:

> We have a simple little service regularly, and I believe the 'congregation' come nearer to the true faith than that of any church in all England or Scotland. Officers and men alike look forward to this service. It brings them closer together, and while in progress we are all equal. The same words appeal to officer and man alike.[126]

And in August, 1917, Private William Couston was impressed by a sermon in the Scottish Churches Tent by a Dr Kelman.

> His sermon was indeed a treat … He struck a very personal note when he spoke about the great loneliness of army life. I have mentioned it often enough to you I'm sure … It was extremely practical & worth remembering … He gripped the men from the start … Kelman is the sort of man we need in France. He can do more good than half a dozen other parsons put together – if you only heard what we get sometimes for a sermon![127]

Arguably, however, the key duty of the padre was to engage with the men and provide spiritual and moral support to the individual soldier. Robbie Macmillan was posted as chaplain to 2nd Camerons in November, 1915, and received some solid advice from the Commanding Officer.

> My predecessor was mentioned in the last list of despatches, & the C.O., one of the best men that ever stepped, told me that he deliberately puts down the great part of the success of this regiment to my predecessor's influence on the men. Yet he had no parade services for the first 3 solid months & practically his only opportunity was getting to know the men by moving in and out among them & sharing their life & going through a very hot time with them. He had some very narrow shaves. Well, that must be my work too. I had had some magnificent parade services … but there will be little of that in future … But after what the C.O. told me about my predecessor, it seems that the most effective way is the way of small things & then if a big attack comes on, I may be able to prove my influence with the men when they get wounded.[128]

This was easier said than done. Captain Bates, M.O. to 8th Black Watch wrote of the new padre who had joined the battalion in June, 1917, presumably Coll Macdonald: "The [new] padre is sitting on his bed opposite writing hard. He is really a dear old boy – but too old, I think. He finds it hard to understand the natural roughness of the men, which in itself, is rather lovable, I think."[129] Donald McLeod, a Presbyterian chaplain serving both 1st Black Watch and 1st

---

125   LC GS 0588 Fraser, letter to father, 5 November, 1917.
126   IWM 132 Paterson, memoir, p.50.
127   BWA Couston, letter to mother, 19 August, 1917.
128   NLS Acc.11627/86 Macmillan, Rev. R.A.C., letter to J.W. Buchan, 19 January, 1916.
129   IWM 2854 Bates, letter to fiancée, 30 June, 1917.

Camerons, expressed reservations about his own ability to engage with the men,[130] and Robbie Macmillan, although understanding the need to engage, was wracked with self-doubt:[131] "You know how unfitted I am in making up to men I don't know." As well as being unprepared for the necessary engagement with the men, padres could also lose respect by being narrow-mindedly sectarian,[132] a trait admittedly shared by some of the men they served.[133] They could also be somewhat prudish. Dr W.H. Leathem, sometime chaplain to 1st Gordons in France, was offended by the number of racy French postcards he found on display. "La vue Parisienne," he declared, "is a pestilence throughout the officers of the Army."[134]

In these circumstances it is unsurprising that some men should take a cynical view of padres. The diary of William Chambers, serving with 1st Camerons, contains a scathing poem about them.

> Oh ain't he a splendid fellow
> So stalwart so brave and so tight
> Just fancy, he's been to the trenches
> And sat in a dugout all night.
> He'll go home and lecture the people
> Of the boys who are bearing the brunt
> He'll shout it from pulpit and steeple
> Of how he went up to the front.
> He'll tell them of spiritual comfort
> Given to the soldiers so glum
> And even attempts with teetotal support
> To deny us our issue of rum.
> But in the line the Boys will grin
> And get on with the good old war
> While wondering sometimes in their hearts
> 'What are these Padres for?'[135]

There was, however, respect when padres took a genuine interest in the men,[136] or when they visited them in the trenches. Colour Sergeant Alick Guthrie, in 1/6th Black Watch, wrote in July, 1915; "We had a visit [in the trenches] from the Padre yesterday & he spent all the afternoon among the men. He has got more pluck than – no names – some you would expect to see it in."[137] Coll Macdonald, chaplain to 8th Black Watch, visited the men in the trenches on 9 August, 1917. "They stared in astonishment at me. Their looks clearly said – can a sane

---

130 NLS Acc.9084, no.7, McLeod, Donald, letter to sister Nan, 29 June, 1917.
131 NLS Acc.11627/86 Macmillan, Rev. R.A C, letters to J.W. Buchan, 23 November, 1915, 19 January, 1916.
132 GHM PB1639 Kemp, memoir, vol.2, p.47; GHM PB2549 Leathem, diary, 21 October, 1916.
133 IWM 8192 Lawson, letter to sister Bessie, 13 May, 1917.
134 GHM PB2549 Leathem, diary, 4-7, 9 September, 1916.
135 Chambers, *Diaries of World war 1*, p.42.
136 IWM 3460 Macmillan, letter to mother, 3 September, 1915.
137 BWA Guthrie, letters to his wife Crissie, 20 June, 14 July, 1915.

man visit these trenches who is not obliged to do so!"[138] Equally they may have been surprised to see a chaplain in the trenches at all. Even more respect was felt for those padres who went forward with the men into battle. Such were, for example, John Kellie, padre of 6th Camerons, killed on the opening day of Third Ypres,[139] and Father MacNeill, Roman Catholic padre of 5th Camerons, badly gassed and wounded on 12 October, 1917, in the same battle.[140] At the furthest extreme, as we have already noted, were those churchmen who, condemning the exemption of clergymen from the Military Service Acts, enlisted as fighting soldiers, as eventually did Robbie Macmillan, paying the ultimate price at Arras on 11 April, 1917.[141]

It would be a mistake however to equate support from faith with support from the padre. Whatever the effectiveness of the padres, many Highland soldiers, in a different world to ours, went to war with a deep Christian faith. There are many examples.[142] In September, 1915, Major Jack Stewart, in 9th Black Watch, wrote in his diary:

> I have found Joshua 1 just *the* greatest chapter in the Bible that I have ever read, verse 9 especially has carried me through not only the anxious times in the trenches but the less anxious but still more humanly annoying times when T. [his C.O.] has been, well, not at his best.[143]
>
> [Joshua 1.9 "Have not I commanded thee? Be strong and of good courage; be not afraid, neither be thou dismayed: for the Lord thy God is with thee whithersoever thou goest."]

Norman Macmillan in the Glasgow Highlanders wrote to his mother in December, 1914; "The Bible arrived safely & has been much appreciated by others as well as by myself. One chap, a sailor-man I am very friendly with, Phil Wood by name, finds himself without one for the first time in five years, during which time he has been at sea."[144] In a 'last letter' to his parents written just before the battle of Cambrai, at which he was killed, Willie Paterson offered comfort to them through his certainty of an afterlife: "Think of me as having gone forth into a purer & more peaceful world, where I will meet you all some day."[145] And religious comfort is offered too in letters by soldiers to their pals' bereaved relatives: "It was God's will to take your son, and I hope he will bring peace to the world soon."[146] Private Douglas in 8th Black Watch noted in April, 1918:

> Amongst the draft from Edinburgh was one who had been in the Salvation Army … every night before lying down to sleep he used to kneel and say his prayers. None of the chaps

---

138 BWA Macdonald, Coll, letter to wife Mary, 9 August, 1917.
139 Macleod, *6th Camerons*, p.82.
140 McEwen, *Fifth Camerons*, p.95.
141 NLS Acc.11627/87 Macmillan, Rev. R.A.C., miscellaneous papers.
142 Apart from those cited, see ASHM N-E8 Jordan, letters to mother, 21 January, 3 December, 1917; BWA, Guthrie, letter to wife Crissie, 20 June, 1915; Macleod, *Poems*, p.16, poem 'Before the Battle'; LC GS 0360 Coppard, memoir, p.20.
143 BWA, Stewart, diary, n.d. [September, 1915].
144 IWM 3460 Macmillan, letter to mother, 3 December, 1914.
145 THM Seaforths 89-122 Paterson, letter to parents, 16 November, 1917.
146 GHM PB2815 McWilliam, letter to his father from Pte James Harper, 9 March, 1918.

round about, who like me could not help but see him praying, passed any remarks to him. I think like me they rather admired him, and so left him to it.[147]

By contrast, other soldiers took a somewhat cynical view of religion, expressed in a song recorded at the front of a diary kept by Lance Corporal Ramage, a draftee to 1st Gordons in April, 1915:

> We're a happy lot of people, yes we are
> We're a happy lot of people, yes we are
> For our sins are all forgiven
> And we're on our way to heaven
> We're a happy lot of people, yes we are[148]

Willie Macmillan, in 7th Seaforths, wrote, perhaps sadly, to his mother in July, 1915; "I think every man in the coy has, or had, a testament, or at least a gospel of St John. I have seen a good many of them being used for fuel, as also the hymn books supplied by the Church of Scotland. Of course, when there is no other paper what can they do?"[149] Others, confronted by the awfulness of war, found religion irrelevant or lost their faith completely. Frank Brooke noticed, "the absence of anything truly meant by 'religion,' the mockery of both sides believing in, and exhorting, the same 'all-powerful being.'"[150] William Chambers, in 1st Camerons, wrote, "I can get no comfort in prayer or the occasional religious administrations we get from the Padres. The only comfort is to get away from this senseless slaughter and seek forgetfulness in pleasure and relaxation in the peaceful fields while resting away behind the lines."[151] While J.E.P Levyns was in the South African Hospital in Richmond Park, he heard news that his close pal, Keith Young, had been killed at Arras.

> The bitterness of my grief turned all my doubts to conviction. This world of suffering and hate was no creation of an omnipotent God of Love, but the chance product of innumerable laws of physics and chemistry operating over unimaginable gulfs of time. Goodness, love and beauty were illusions created by the mind of man to preserve his sanity on a planet where the implacable forces of nature made life live on life and survival depended on brute strength and cunning.[152]

Such disillusionment did not go unchallenged.[153] George Macleod, in 11th Argylls, wrote in July, 1917:

> I have heard it said that a man comes out of this war with a very real religion, or no religion at all. That is a very common saying here, nowadays – personally, I think that any man who

---

147 IWM 4586 Douglas, memoir, p.340.
148 NLS MS944 Ramage, diary, forenote.
149 IWM 3460 Macmillan, letter from Willie Macmillan to mother, 6 July, 1915.
150 IWM Books Brooke, 'Wait for it,' p.206.
151 Chambers, *Diaries of World War 1*, p.41.
152 Levyns, *The Disciplines of War*, p79.
153 See also Macleod, *Macedonian Measures*, p.7, poem 'Mount Olympus.'

sees this war must come out with a very real religion or cut his throat! I can't see how it's bearable to the 'no religion at all' class. It's quite bearable to the former class.[154]

And some solace in his faith was at least found by Private John Macadam of 1/4th Camerons, as he lay mortally wounded on the battlefield of Festubert in May, 1915:

Dear father,
It is now at least four days since I was wounded and I am in the same spot. The pain is not as bad at present and I feel that I am very near death. I am too weak to shout for stretcher-bearers any more. They are too far away to hear me and I am cut off from our lines by ditches. I wish I could see you all before I die, but 'God's Will be done.' I think I am the last of the Camerons in the field alive. The rest have all died or else reached safety. I am quickly getting weak, so Goodbye, father, Goodbye all.
　Your dying son,
　John
　Pray for me.[155]

Conclusions

In this chapter we have demonstrated the many ways in which soldiers, both officers and men, received support from outside their immediate battalion. We have shown the importance of the supply of comforts from family and friends, from regimental associations and from the community. We have seen how the practical support of the local community, whether in Scotland or England, could continue after the soldiers left for the front, for example in the form of letters, gifts or hospital visits. We have also noted support from expatriate Scots and visitors to the front, most notably Harry Lauder. When support was not forthcoming, however, from strikers, pacifists, or 'shirkers' there was a corresponding sense of betrayal. We have noted the importance of letters from home and observed that while the two worlds of home and the trenches were utterly different, the truly remarkable postal service could keep soldiers in touch with their families. Thus, while families at home could never experience life in the trenches, and could only truly inhabit their own world, the soldiers themselves could, through familiarity with home and frequency of letters, be living in both worlds simultaneously. Finally, we have seen how, in a world very different from ours, despite the failure of some chaplains to engage, and despite the theological problem of suffering and some related disillusionment, simple Christian faith continued to sustain many soldiers through the war.

154　NLS Acc.9084, no.37 Macleod, G.F., letter to mother, 25 July, 1915.
155　THM Camerons 85-91 Macadam, John, letter to father from battlefield of Festubert, May, 1915.

13

Identity

'I joined the Gordon Highlanders and not the British Army.'[1]

We have already addressed the question of identity in several contexts, most importantly of course in relation to the kilt and the pipes, but also, for example in the problems encountered when drafting men from one regiment into another, in particular to a non-kilted corps. Identity clearly mattered in the Highland regiments, and was potentially a vital contributor to esprit de corps. As such, it really requires a chapter to itself, to explore its meaning, while at the same time bringing together some of the strands we have identified earlier in the study. Identity, indeed, is not a simple one-dimensional issue. There were several layers of identity; identity as a Scot, as a Highland soldier, as a member of a Regiment, and, within the Regiment, of a battalion. We will need to carefully disentangle these different elements. Related to the question of identity are self-image, perception by others and reputation. These elements, potentially more contentious, will be addressed in the next chapter.

We may start by considering regimental and battalion identity. The two are not the same. As we have seen, each Highland regiment had several battalions. It was the regiment which was the repository of tradition; the battalion was merely the functional unit in which that tradition was put to good use. As such, of course, a battalion might develop its own identity and pride, while a regiment's traditions might be enhanced by the performance of its separate battalions. But battalion identity was never entirely separate from regimental identity, just as, at the higher level, regimental identity was never entirely separate from membership of the British or Imperial Army. The Territorial battalions were all subsumed under the regimental system, and Lord Kitchener was wise to create his New Army as additional battalions of existing regiments, thus ensuring at a stroke that every new recruit to a Highland battalion had at least a hundred years of regimental lore behind him. In Canada, by contrast, as we have seen, Sam Hughes put such heritage at risk when he ignored the old Militia regiments in creating the Canadian Expeditionary Force. There was moreover an advantage to the separation of the abstract idea of the regiment from its tangible expression, the battalion. While a battalion could be rendered temporarily ineffective in a single engagement, the regiment would always live on. Oddly, it is Harry Lauder who provides the perfect summary of the importance of this continuity. "The men

---

1 GHM PB375 Pailthorpe, memoir, p.37.

who compose a regiment may be wiped out, but the regiment survives. It is an organisation, an entity, a creature with a soul as well as a body. And the Germans have not discovered a way yet of killing the soul!"[2]

Regimental identity was expressed in various tangible ways; by uniform, particularly the kilt, by the pipes and by songs. It was also expressed in less tangible ways through the inheritance of history and tradition. We will concentrate first on the tangible elements, of which the first was simply the name. The London Scottish were keen to drop their sub-title, '14th County of London' and be simply addressed as the London Scottish Regiment,[3] emphasising their separateness, but were unsuccessful in this aspiration. David McMillan notes that he joined the Cameron Highlanders of Canada, or as it was officially known, the 43rd Battalion C.E.F., at Winnipeg in December, 1914. "I think we were all proud to be known as 'The Camerons.' Never did the O.C. or any of the troops refer to us as the 43rd Battalion, although we could not prevent others from doing so."[4]

Turning next to the uniform, regarding the kilt, it was specifically the tartan which applied to regimental identity, and we have already commented in an earlier chapter on the pride of the men in their regimental tartan as well as in the kilt per se. We have also noticed the resistance to the introduction of khaki kilts, as well as the 'battle of the tartans' in 16th Battalion C.E.F. (Canadian Scottish). Suffice to add that the kilt could also support specific battalion identity, as some Territorial battalions were themselves proud to be distinguished by unusual 'non-regimental' tartans: thus, 5th Seaforths wore the Sutherland tartan rather than the Mackenzie tartan worn by the rest of the regiment, while the Glasgow Highlanders (9th H.L.I.) wore Black Watch tartan rather than the Mackenzie tartan also worn by the rest of the Highland Light Infantry, including the other kilted battalion, the 6th. In any case, the tartan itself could be used to summon up fighting spirit. As the Glasgow Highlanders moved forward on 9th May, 1915, "a party of Black Watch passed, and a hoarse injunction, 'Remember the Tartan, lads!' was probably of more value to those who heard it than much talk about the 'offensive spirit' on the part of the higher command."[5] In September, 1919, John Cooper, who had served in 1/6th Black Watch, but was transferred to 12th Argylls in Constantinople, after the Armistice, wrote:

> So long as I live, I shall never see the Black Watch tartan without feelings of pride and joy that I was once a member of that splendid regiment. I have known the Regiment in the peace of home service, and amidst the din, the horror, the exacting duties of war; and I don't think you could find a more splendid set of men anywhere than composed the 6th Black Watch while I knew it.[6]

The kilt, of course, was not the only distinctive feature of the Highland uniform. When, in September, 1915, Douglas Wimberley, then a young Cameron officer, attended a musketry course at Strensall Camp near York, he insisted on wearing his tartan trews, according to regimental standing orders, rather than the khaki trousers expected by the staff.[7] After serving as

---

2   Lauder, *A Minstrel in France*, pp.217-218.
3   IWM 6702 Low, letter to wife Noanie, 17 December, 1914.
4   McMillan, *Trench Tea and Sandbags*, p.3.
5   IWM Books Reid 'Shoulder to Shoulder,' p.54.
6   IWM Books Cooper, 'Domi Militaeque', p.349.
7   IWM 430 Wimberley, memoir, p.23.

Machine Gun Officer with 1st Camerons, he was transferred to the Machine Gun Corps, but remained a Highlander at heart. Given command of a company, he maintained a piper, and when, by great good fortune, in July, 1917, his company was attached to 51st Highland Division, he managed to replace their flat caps with balmorals![8] When John Cooper, in the Black Watch, was taken prisoner during the German offensive of March, 1918, he confiscated the red hackle from a balmoral being worn by a Seaforth prisoner, for his own use.[9] Private Billy Millar, also taken prisoner then, risked his life by striking a German soldier who tried to cut off his Seaforth shoulder strap.[10] Both John Cooper and Private Jock McLeod of 5th Camerons, hospitalised at home, determinedly retained their bonnets in the face of lady visitors.[11] After the war, Private Douglas, who served in both the Argylls and the Black Watch, records that he kept his balmoral bonnet, with its 'Black Watch Red Hackle' for years, and still possessed his Argylls Glengarry.[12]

Members of the Black Watch were proud of their unique distinction, the Red Hackle, proudly displaying it at a London theatre, for example.[13] But the hackle itself was the cause of some friction within the regiment, for initially its use was confined to men of the Regular battalions, in itself a source of some battalion pride.[14] Major Jack Stewart, serving in 9th Black Watch, a Kitchener battalion, was informed to his annoyance that Colonel C.E. Stewart, commanding 1st Battalion, "does not want any other B.W. Bns to wear the red hackle, which is perfectly absurd, as we are all one Regiment." The problem was resolved however, and the first 500 hackles arrived at 9th Battalion in September, 1915.[15] 8th Battalion received theirs in October.[16] Apparently the honour was not accorded to Territorial battalions until May, 1916, when 7th Battalion received theirs.[17] The Canadian Black Watch battalions followed suit, 13th Battalion C.E.F. receiving their hackles in November, 1916, and 42nd Battalion in November, 1917.[18]

In fact, the whole ensemble of Highland uniform promoted pride. Second Lieutenant Phil Paul, in 11th Black Watch, wrote from Aldershot in December, 1915.

> When next I arrive in London to see you I shall be gorgeous to a degree beyond belief. Swank!!! That's where the pride of regiment comes in, you know, and it's a very real thing, that same pride. To feel that you as a soldier in a certain mob have a definite tradition to uphold means a lot. The Highland Brigades have always done well and I can only hope that when I go out there I'll be able to help carry on the tradition.[19]

8   Ibid., pp.57-60, 68, 69, 104.
9   IWM Books Cooper, 'Domi Militaeque', p.224.
10 LC POW 056 Millar, memoir.
11 IWM 5821 Semple, letter from Pte Jock McLeod, 12 April, 1916; IWM Books Cooper, 'Domi Militaeque,' p.159.
12 IWM 4586 Douglas, memoir, p.1474.
13 LC GS 1367 Robertson, memoir, p.5.
14 BWA Marshall, reminiscences.
15 BWA Stewart, diary, 22, 25 July, 6 September, 1915, letter to wife, 24 July, 1915; Wauchope, *Black Watch*, Vol.3, pp.118-119.
16 BWA Sempill Papers, letter from Lt & Q.M. P. Goudy to Sempill, 13 October, 1915. See also letter from J.S.S. Ewing to Sempill, 12 October, 1915.
17 Wauchope, *Black Watch*, Vol 2, pp.10, 260. See also. Andrews, *Autobiography*, p.92.
18 Fetherstonhaugh, *13th Battalion*, p.147; Topp, *42nd Battalion*, p.176.
19 BWA Paul, letter to Miss May Merrett, 1 December, 1915.

When Lieutenant Grant Fleming of 1st Gordons was appointed to be Town Major at the village of Cannetmont early in 1917, his C.O. told him, "'Remember you are a Gordon. Wear spats and swank about as if you were God Almighty.' The theology is a bit cock-eyed (it is the only occasion on which I have heard it suggested that God wears spats), but the advice was sound."

Outsiders coming into a battalion would, of course, be expected to conform. In a draft passage omitted from his published history of 4th Seaforths, Haldane notes that when the C.O., Colonel Stewart, was killed on 23 May, 1916, he was succeeded by Lieutenant-Colonel Unthank, who came from 10th Durham Light Infantry.

> Colonel Unthank … came to the battalion as a Sassenach and as one who was proud of the fact. In the eyes of the battalion it was not a recommendation and a persistency in wearing a 'cheese cutter' was rather galling to regimental pride. But the battalion had found its man. Colonel Unthank took to the glengarry which was worn by all the officers and became proud of the battalion.[20]

Indeed, he continued to command the battalion successfully through into 1918, while Noel Chavasse, V.C., Medical Officer to the 1st Liverpool Scottish, always donned the regimental Glengarry and badge instead of his regulation R.A.M.C. hat.[21] The same tact was not always shown in reverse. When Major C.W.E. Gordon, a regular Black Watch officer was posted to 8th Gordons, initially as second-in-command, he continued to wear his own uniform and Black watch Glengarry."[22] Indeed, it does not appear to have been unusual for Highland officers to continue to wear their own uniforms after transfer to different Highland regiments.[23]

We have already dealt at length with the pipes and noted the use of regimental pipe-tunes and pipe-calls. All contributed to identity, down to company level, and there is no need to repeat the discussion here. Alongside the pipes there were also a variety of songs, generally sung on the march, which might be adopted informally by the men.[24] To give the flavour, we will quote the ditty sung by George Ramage when he left Rouen station with a draft of Gordons in April, 1915, to join their battalion;

> We are the Gordon swells boys
> We are the Gordon swells
> Down in King Street there we stand
> Singing Alexander's Ragtime Band
> You ought to see my home in Dixie
> Under the yum yum tree

---

20 IWM Books, Haldane, M.M., '4th Seaforths,' draft. See also IWM Books, Brooke, 'Wait for it,' p.108.
21 Jackson, 'Captain Noel Godfrey Chavasse.'
22 BWA Gordon, 'diary', 11 March, 1916. See also: IWM 430 Wimberley, memoir, p..41.
23 See for example IWM 8503 Byrom, memoir, p.27. See also: IWM 19860 White, letter from Alastair Macdougall, 2 February, 1918.
24 See for 8th Argylls, ASHM N-E8 McGuinness, notebook, & Malcolm, *Argyllshire Highlanders*, p.19; for 1/6th Argylls, Maclean, *On Active Service*, Vol.2, p.93; for 6th and 7th Camerons, Mackenzie, *Sixth Gordons* p.64 and THM Camerons C572 Panton, letter to brother Tom, 29 September, 1915; for 6th Gordons, GHM PB1253 Wood, Charles Hutchieson, autograph album.

For we're going on a holiday to Germanie
On the good ship Robert E. Lee[25]

The New Army Camerons battalions, 5th, 6th and 7th, shared an extraordinary chant, popular, effective and completely unintelligible, which went like this:

Sa la sa va
Sa la sa va
Corabella, Corabella
Chin-chin-chingo
Camerons y-gorra
Camerons y-gorra
Y-gorra, y-gorra, y-go-o-o-ra

The song originated in Glasgow University, 'Varsity' taking the place of 'Camerons' in the original version. Tradition had it that it was really a sort of Maori war-cry brought to Glasgow by a New Zealand student.[26]

Turning now to the less tangible elements of identity, some efforts were made during training to inculcate regimental history and tradition. Both Hal Kerridge and James Sloan were heavily indoctrinated in the traditions of the London Scottish. "In its most exaggerated form this resulted in a firm conviction that the British Army consisted of the London Scottish, the Guards Brigade and a lot of other regiments that helped to make the numbers up but did not count for a great deal."[27] This indoctrination extended also to the Canadians, the Royal Highlanders of Canada, for example, providing their men with an introductory booklet to the regiment.[28]

However, at the front, the obvious impediment to regimental or battalion esprit de corps was, as we have seen, the constant change and renewal of personnel. As early as February, 1915, Captain Claud Low, in 1st London Scottish, expressed concern that with large new drafts, "we will almost certainly lose our identity & our character. You will understand that we have certain habits, customs, faults, or whatever they may be called & whether they are good or bad we don't want to lose them."[29] Consequently, additional efforts were made at the front to inculcate regimental pride. Colonel John (Johnnie) Stansfield, commanding 2nd Gordons, for example, made determined efforts in 1915 to inculcate an awareness of the old 92nd amongst new recruits.[30] Colonel Jack Stewart, having fairly recently taken over command of 2nd Black Watch in Mesopotamia, delivered lectures to new recruits in May, 1917, on Regimental history.[31] When Private Dennis was drafted to 11th Camerons in June, 1918, after the disbandment of his own

---

25 NLS MS 944 Ramage, diary, 17 April, 1915.
26 LC WF Recollections A9 Andrew, memoir. See also: Burns, *Once a Cameron Highlander*, pp.48-49; McEwen, *Fifth Camerons*, pp.13-14.
27 LC WF Recollections S18 Sloan, memoir. And see IWM12678 Kerridge, interview. For Black Watch see BWA Jack, diary, 9 May, 1917.
28 Anon, *The Royal Highlanders of Canada, allied with the Black Watch (Royal Highlanders)* (London: Hugh Rees Ltd., 1918).
29 IWM 6702 Low, letter to wife Noanie, 24 February, 1915.
30 GHM PB242 Stansfield, letter to Uncle Jack, 30 June, 1915, letter home (extract), 10 September, 1915.
31 BWA Stewart, letter to wife, 23 May, 1917.

battalion, 21st Battalion, King's Royal Rifle Corps, he felt "I was no longer in the finest regiment of the British Army – no longer a rifleman." But on Sundays in July or August, the new draftees were given some instruction in the traditions of their new regiment, including uniform, dancing and the pipes.[32] When 5th Gordons were stationed at Nivelles after the Armistice, they took the opportunity to visit the field of Waterloo and had dinner there.[33] Such instruction might not be universally well received, particularly if delivered after the Armistice, when the men simply wanted to get home.[34]

Territorial and New Army soldiers in particular were conscious of the onus on them to maintain their regiment's standards and reputation. On 23 September, 1915, just prior to the supporting attack at Bellewaarde, young Lieutenant Jack Sangster in 1/4th Gordons, a Territorial battalion, wrote home: "I trust that at whatever cost the traditions of the Gordon Highlanders will be upheld. We are to be near by our own 1st Batt., the Regular Batt., and I hope we won't disgrace them."[35] Private John Cooper, who trained with 3/4th Black Watch in 1916, a Territorial training battalion, felt then that "On us now depended the continuance of the splendid record of the regiment, and proud most of us were to belong to it, and to have the opportunity of sharing its fame, perhaps of increasing it."[36] There was corresponding pride and satisfaction when standards were maintained. After 8th Black Watch had been in action at Longueval in July, 1916, their C.O., Colonel Gordon, wrote: "Whatever we gave or got, the 8th B.W. very worthily upheld the traditions of this Regt. No troops could have fought better, & their feat on the evening of the 18th was perfectly magnificent."[37]

General Officers and Commanding Officers would sometimes appeal to men for greater or continued endeavours by appealing to their regimental tradition.[38] Perhaps the most remarkable example of invoking regimental tradition came at the depot in France in 1915. There, Alexander Maclean, chaplain to Scottish troops, found amongst a draft for 1st Gordons a piper, whose great-grandfather had been a piper in the regiment at Waterloo, where "he stood within the square and played the ancient challenge-march, 'Cogadh no Sith', as the French cuirassiers hurled themselves upon the immovable ranks in vain." The Colonel then arranged for the padre to tell the men about the incident, before he called them to attention while the piper played his tune to them in memory of the men of Waterloo. This was duly done. When the padre arrived at the station to see off the draft, he found they had chalked all over the carriages in huge letters 'The Waterloo Draft.'"[39] Such appeals to tradition were not always so well received. On 12 May, 1915, 1st Gordons paraded before a General who gave them a pep talk before their move. "'Same old bloody muck,' murmured the old soldiers in the ranks."[40]

---

32 IWM 6926 Dennis, memoir, pp.259, 272.
33 GHM PB179 Marr, diary, 18 January, 1919.
34 See GHM PB375.8 Shirreffs, diary, 5 June, 1919.
35 IWM 11739 Sangster, letter home, 23 September, 1915.
36 IWM Books Cooper, 'Domi Militaeque', p.26.
37 BWA Gordon, 'diary', 20 July, 1916. See also for 9th Black Watch after Loos, BWA Lloyd, Lt Col T.O., typescript 'Address by Lt.-Col. T.O. Lloyd commanding 9th Bn The Black Watch on 2-10-15.'
38 See for example: IWM 1862 Craig-Brown, diary, 25 February, 1915; LC GS 1507 Sotheby, diary, 25 February, 1915; NLS MS 20249 Haldane, diary, 23 February, 1916; Maclean, Rev. Alexander Miller, *With the Gordons at Ypres*, (Paisley: Alexander Gardner,1916), p.57.
39 Maclean, *With the Gordons at Ypres*, pp.22-24.
40 NLS MS 944 Ramage, diary, 12 May, 1915.

Many soldiers express simple pride in their regiment or battalion, or both. Linton Andrews, who served in 1/4th Black Watch, wrote,

> Though English by birth, I was thoroughly imbued with the Black Watch spirit. It would have broken my heart to be transferred to another regiment. This never happened, although I was destined for many changes. I rejoiced in the courage, the humours, the strong characters of my comrades.[41]

Soldiers record their pride when they consider their battalion to have out-performed others, even off the battlefield, for example in endurance while marching, in smartness, or is sport.[42]

Many others record pride in the achievements of their particular regiment or battalion on the battlefield, for example those of the 10th Gordons, 1st Camerons and the Service battalions of the Camerons at Loos,[43] 2nd Black Watch at Hanna in Mesopotamia, 1916,[44] 6th Camerons at Arras,[45] 1/7th Gordons at Cambrai,[46] 1/4th Seaforths during the German 1918 offensive,[47] and 2nd Argylls throughout the war.[48] Officers were concerned that their battalion's achievements should be properly recognised. For example, Colonel Lord Sempill was dissatisfied with the recognition given to 8th Black Watch for their part in the attack on the Hohenzollern Redoubt during the battle of Loos and fought hard to remedy the situation.[49]

There was of course some disillusionment. When the war-weary Frank Brooke was at Ripon camp, having been wounded for a second time at Cambrai, serving with 1/4th Seaforths, he visited his brother.

> He was for the 'Front.' He talked of nothing else but how grand it seemed. He couldn't understand why I shouldn't be proud to have been 'in the thick of it' with such a 'posh' regiment as the Seaforth Highlanders ... To have been at Beaumont Hamel, and Vimy Ridge, and Messines, and Cambrai.[50]

---

41 Andrews, *Autobiography*, p.95. See also: IWM 6702 Low, letter to wife Noanie, 26 November, 1914, letter to Aunt Mary, 30 November, 1914; LC GS 1027 Macleod, letter to mother, 3 February (= 3 March?), 2 April, 1916; BWA Stewart, letters to wife, 3, 19 May, 1917, 1 February, 14 October, 12 November, 1918; IWM 430 Wimberley, memoir, p.26; : IWM Books Brooke, 'Wait for it,' pp.30, 86-87; NLS Acc.11627/86 letters from Rev. R.A.C. Macmillan to J.W. Buchan, 7, 23 November, 1915; NLS Acc.8802 no.4 Sellar, diary, 28 February, 1915; GHM PB375 Pailthorpe, memoir, p.47.
42 IWM 4370 Christison, memoir, pp.31, 34; IWM 5821 Semple, Letters to her from Pte Jock McLeod, 8, 26 July, 6 August, 1915.
43 GHM PB507 Wallace, letter to daughter, 29 September, 1915; Chambers, *Diaries of World War 1*, p.39; IWM 7408 Lorimer, letter to mother, 15 November, 1915.
44 BWA Cumming, letter home, n.d., c. February, 1916.
45 Macleod, *6th Camerons*, p.67.
46 LC GS 0588 Fraser, letter to father, 23 November, 1917.
47 LC GS 0552 Ferguson, letter to mother, 15 April, 1918.
48 ASHM N-E2 MacMillan, background notes, written 1976.
49 BWA Sempill Papers, letters from Sempill to Brig.-Gen Ritchie, 19, 24 January, 1916, letters from Ritchie to Sempill, 1 November, 1915, 2 February, 1916, letter from Sempill to Lord Beresford, 8 July, 1917, letter from Beresford to Sempill, 12 July, 1917, letter from Sempill to Sir F. Davies, 13 March, 1917, letter from Davies to Sempill, 15 March, 1917. see also Lt.-Col. Gordon Duff to Sempill, 3 February, 1916, letter from J.S.S. Ewing to Sempill, 20 February, 1916.
50 IWM Books Brooke, 'Wait for it,' p.293.

Another dissonant voice was Guy Macgregor, regarding his feelings for his own battalion, 1/6th Argylls, after it made a name for itself in 51st Highland Division.

> If I cared a rap about military glory it might interest me. But I'm like Wolfe, the lad who won Canada for us: as he sailed down the St Lawrence to the attack he recited Gray's Elegy & said 'I would rather be the writer of that poem than take Quebec tonight.' Sound judge.[51]

Popular poetry extolled the virtues of famous regiments, like the poems 'The Gay Gordons' and 'Jock McGraw, The Tale of a Gay Gordon,' both written by John Mitchell and published in Aberdeen,[52] although these are more indicative of the pride of the local community in their regiment than that of the soldiers themselves. Other poems in honour of their regiments or battalions were however composed by ordinary soldiers, like Donald Robertson, 'the Kildary Bard,' who wrote 'My heart's wi' the Seaforths.'[53] Such soldiers' poems were not always to Burns' standard. In the autograph book of Charles Hutchieson Wood is a poem signed by himself, dated 7 April, 1915, when he was serving in 2/6th Gordons at home, in which he extols the valour of the Gordons at Neuve Chapelle, at which he was not present;

> The order came, Charge! Gordons charge!
> Fix bayonets all! Advance!
> For honour, country and King George
> We'll drive them out of France.[54]

Particular achievements on the battlefield during the war were leant on to reinforce esprit de corps. On 30 January, 1918, 8/10th Gordons had a special battalion parade to commemorate the anniversary of their famous raid on the Butte de Warlencourt, while the whole theatre was taken over for the battalion that night to see the show 'Robinson Crusoe.'[55]

Regimental identity was of course particularly strong amongst those who had made the regiment their life, some of whom were simply following a long tradition of army service. "I joined the Gordon Highlanders and not the British Army," Major Turnbull, acting C.O. of 2nd Gordons, informed his M.O., Captain Pailthorpe.[56] After Colonel Johnnie Stansfield was mortally wounded at Loos on 25 September, 1915, he sent a message from hospital, "Well done, dear old 92nd." He died three days later.[57] In June, 1916, C.S.M. Brown of 2nd Gordons was mortally wounded by shell-fire. In his last moments, "He roused himself once more and said

---

51 IWM 8592 Macgregor, letter to wife Dulcie, 29 October, 1918.
52 GHM PB2025 McCurragh, Pte T., postcard published by the Bon Accord Press in Aberdeen, containing a poem by John Mitchell, entitled 'The Gay Gordons, posted 5 November, 1914; GHM PB2554/2 Mitchell, John, *Jock McGraw, The Tale of a Gay Gordon*, Wm Smith & Sons, Aberdeen, 1916.
53 Robertson, Donald, *Some Poems by the Kildary Bard*, (Kildary, 1918).
54 GHM PB1253 Wood, autograph album. See also: LC GS 1843 Bradford, David, poem by E.C.Melville, 1915; GHM PB2416/12 Young, Pte John, unattributed poem, 'The Charge of the Gordons'; THM C79-110 Hogg, Sgt J., untitled manuscript poem.
55 GHM PB1639 Kemp, memoir, Vol.2, p.11.
56 GHM PB375, Pailthorpe, memoir, p.37.
57 GHM PB242 Stansfield, note in notebook.

'Goodbye Gordons – I've had a grand time with ye.' Not a word about any relation, only his regiment – ten minutes later and within about forty minutes of his being hit he had parted from his regiment for ever."[58]

This sense of identity with the regiment, as we have seen in previous chapters, when considering the support offered from home to the men at the front, extended to wives and families. Former regular Gordon Highlander Peter Stewart, who had returned to Britain from India to re-join his regiment, and had been posted to 8th Gordons as C.S.M., wrote to his wife, "Buck up old girl and be a Gordon, for you surely know by this time that once a Gordon always a Gordon."[59] Loyalty to the old regiment would outlast separation. Colonel Jack Stewart, commanding 2nd Black Watch in Palestine noted in February, 1918; "Yesterday a Sgt who used to belong to the 42nd and who is now in the Flying Corps came to see me and 'for a present' brought me a beautiful stick made from the propeller of a Hun plane, with a ferrule made from the Hun bullet; a regular Bond St stick. Rather touching of him, I thought."[60]

Officers and men might be reluctant to be posted or drafted away from their battalions. Here the distinction between regimental and battalion loyalty is significant. Both officers and men might dislike changing their regimental identity by transferring to other corps, but leaving a battalion, even for a battalion of the same regiment, meant also potentially leaving one's friends, and, as we have already seen, the ties of comradeship were important for both officers and men. This loyalty was all the stronger at critical times. Thus, we find that, in some cases, men, like Linton Andrews in 1/4th Black Watch, were reluctant to take commissions, if that meant transferring from their battalion.[61] I.A. Andrew, in the Glasgow University Company of 6th Camerons stopped his application for a commission when deployment to France was imminent as "I did not wish to be separated from my battalion on the eve of action."[62] Otherwise he might have shared the fate of his pal, John Inch, who was in tears as he had to part from the battalion to take up a commission in the Argylls on the very eve of the battle of Loos, the first big trial for the battalion.[63] Jock Macleod, Machine Gun Officer in 2nd Camerons in Salonika, feared that his men were to be transferred bodily into the Machine Gun Corps. "They are threatening to put my men into flat caps and English breeks. They will break their spirit, if they do." Fortunately, the problem was resolved by finding volunteers.[64]

Officers might vigorously resist postings elsewhere, even when these meant much 'cushier' postings behind the lines, or even promotion.[65] John Turing served as a junior officer in 8th Seaforths. After recovery from a wound suffered at Third Ypres, he reported back to the 3rd Battalion at Cromarty. There he was offered and declined a company in 51st Division because he

---

58   GHM PB375, Pailthorpe, memoir, p.7.
59   GHM PB2021 Stewart, letter to wife Lil, 2 July, 1915.
60   BWA Stewart, letter to wife, 1 February, 1918. And see: GHM PB2459 Williams, diary.
61   Andrews, *Autobiography*, p.93.
62   LC WF Recollections A9 Andrew, memoir.
63   Ibid.
64   LC GS 1027 Macleod, letters to mother, 16 March, 14 May, 1916.
65   Apart from refs cited below, see: IWM 11144 MacKay, diary, 12, 16, 17, 19 February, 1918, and afternote, 1972; IWM 15460 Chandler, letter to Marjorie Raimes, 9 May, 1915; GHM PB375, Pailthorpe, memoir, p.32; LC GS 1551 Strang, letter to brother Willie, 20 March, 1916; Bartholomew, *George Hugh Freeland Bartholomew*, letter home, 9 February, 1917.

preferred to return to his platoon in the 8th Battalion. "I have never regretted that decision."[66] In July, 1916, Keith McDermott, in 1st Seaforths, declined a job on the staff in Mesopotamia as D.A.G. in order to return to his battalion. "I didn't join the regiment to sit in an office with a red hat on."[67] Lieutenant Ian Grant, in 2nd Camerons, found himself at Divisional Headquarters in January, 1915, recovering from shock. There he was offered a headquarters job. "It was rather a chance from a personal point of view as one meets all the swells etc. But I have come back to my platoon and these filthy trenches and shells and feel I've done right."[68]

Perhaps the most remarkable examples of battalion loyalty were provided by those soldiers who insisted on remaining on duty after being wounded, fearing that, if they went to hospital, they might subsequently be drafted to another battalion. After 2nd Gordons had attacked Bullecourt on 7 May, 1917, Pailthorpe "found there were many men slightly wounded chiefly with small bits of high explosive who had said nothing about these wounds as they feared to be sent on – not to the UK but to the base alone and then back to some strange battalion."[69] In July, 1918, in 14th Black Watch, eight men in 'B' Company, lightly wounded by the same shell, asked to remain on duty for the same reason.[70] And in about September, 1918, John Bowie, in 11th Argylls, received a dose of mustard gas, which affected his throat and made him temporarily blind. "A good many went to hospital, but I wanted to stay for a few days and get cured with my own regiment, because, should I go to hospital, I might go to another regiment when better, and did not like [to be] amongst new men, when I had pals here."[71]

When officers and men were obliged to leave their battalions, for better or for worse, their attachment was shown by their sadness.[72] In 1st Garrison Battalion Seaforth Highlanders in Salonika, when in April, 1918 an officer's servant left for Britain with malaria, "he nearly broke down and did not want to leave the regiment. He had been out here for three years."[73] Then in June, 1919, when demobilisation was in progress from occupied Turkey, the Regimental Sergeant Major wept when the time came to leave the Regiment.[74] Captain Pailthorpe, M.O. to 2nd Gordons, was inconsolable when he was posted away from his beloved battalion in July, 1918. "One loves once in the Army, and wholeheartedly, but one never truly loves again. I had been ready enough to die with the Regiment and cared nothing for anything outside it."[75]

One hazard, to which reference has already been made, was the danger of being posted to a different regiment or battalion either from home, or from base depot or one of the holding battalions which existed behind the lines at various times. This hazard applied to both officers

---

66 LC GS 1635 Turing, memoir.
67 MacDermott, *Robert Keith McDermott*, pp.18-19, letter home, 23 July, 1916.
68 THM Camerons 02-58 Grant, letter to Aunt Vi, 27 January, 1915.
69 GHM PB375, Pailthorpe, memoir, p.44.
70 Ogilvie, *The Fife and Forfar Yeomanry*, p.123.
71 ASHM-E11 Bowie, diary, September, 1918.
72 Apart from refs cited see: THM 2013-072 (S) Braes, memoir, p.22; IWM 2854 Bates, letters to his fiancée, 13, 14 May, 1917; LC GS 0177 Boyle, diary, 7 November, 1915; BWA Stewart, letter to wife, 21 June, 1916; IWM 18455 Turnbull, letter to mother, father & Sylvia, 28 May, 1916; *Lieut.-Colonel Robert Horn*, p.91; IWM 6702 Low, letter to wife Noanie, 4 March, 1915; ASHM N-E2 Hyslop, diary, 8 November, 1915, 25, 30 January, 29 February, 1916; THM Camerons 90-120 Mackay, letter to mother, 30 October, 1915.
73 IWM 7508 Wyllie, diary, 26 April, 1918.
74 Ibid., 29 June, 1919.
75 GHM PB375, Pailthorpe, memoir, p.77.

and men, and indeed the mere fear of it happening was unsettling and corrosive.[76] Ivar Campbell was an officer of 3rd Argylls. In May, 1915, he noted, "Many of our officers have had to go to other regiments; cursing and swearing as they go." Having arrived at the base at Rouen, he was posted to 1st Seaforths. "I'm cursing my luck," he wrote.[77] S. Bradbury enlisted into 3/4th Camerons in April, 1916. Drafted to France in December, in January he was told he now belonged to the 2nd Entrenching Battalion, with which he served in Flanders. On 19 March, 1917, he was informed that the battalion was to be broken up and the men transferred to line regiments. "We were given two or three Regiments to choose from (all Scottish) and I chose the 5th Gordons and received a new number and a Gordon cap badge with colours but in the afternoon, several of us were told that there were too many in that Regiment and so we were posted to the 5th Seaforths." Thus in less than a year since joining up, Bradbury had been a Cameron, a Gordon and a Seaforth![78]

Soldiers might go to extraordinary lengths to avoid being drafted to another regiment or battalion. Private Andrew Gilmour, serving with 14th Argylls, remembered a newcomer who joined the battalion in the winter of 1916/1917. In 1914, he had enlisted in the 11th Argylls and had been severely wounded at Loos. Once recovered, he found himself in a draft to the Black Watch and deserted. When they had gone, he gave himself up and was sentenced to one month's imprisonment at Aldershot. After that he was sent straight off to France, this time to the 14th Argylls, which pleased him mightily. "'The Black Watch are a fine regiment, nae doot; but I'm an Argyll, man, I'm an Argyll.'"[79] Another well-meaning deserter was Private Macmillan in 1st Argylls, known as 'Black Jock.' He was a regular soldier who had come over with the battalion from India. Lightly wounded by a shell, a month later, he returned to the battalion. But then the battalion found he had been posted as a deserter. He had simply walked out of the Convalescent Depot without permission. "Once you are in one of them," he explained, "they may post you to any battalion, so I just walked out and came up to the battalion."[80]

Those who became detached from their battalion might long to get back and do all they could to do so.[81] L.A. Linden-Bell, for example, newly commissioned as a regular officer in 1914, served with 1st Seaforths. After being hospitalised in Mesopotamia with sand-fly fever, he was seconded to work at General Headquarters in Baghdad, despite protesting that he wanted to return to his regiment. After an open-air life he found the work in Baghdad

> not only deadly boring but unhealthy. In spite of living with two splendid people I wrote to our adjutant imploring him to get me back. he tried without effect. Finally I decided to get

---

76 See for example: IWM 14335 Marr, memoir, p.95; LC WF Recollections S18 Sloan, memoir; Maclean, *On Active Service*, Vol.1, p.16; LC Transcripts Tape 526 McKay, interview; LC GS 1537 Stewart, letters to mother, 18 August to 30 October, 1917, passim; GHM PB1639 Kemp, memoir, Vol.2, p.9; GHM PB283 Watson, memoirs, p.10.
77 Campbell, *Letters*, pp.8-11, letters home, 26 May, n.d, 2 June, 1915.
78 IWM 2528 Bradbury, memoir, pp.14-16.
79 LC GS 0627 Gilmour, 'The Other Enemy', *The Beam*, September, 1982, pp.34-35.
80 LC GS 1026 Maclean, diary, p.9.
81 Apart from Lynden-Bell, see: THM Seaforths 81-180 Murray, letters to sister Alex, 20 February, 3 March, 1915; Topp, *42nd Battalion*, p.81; IWM 7408 Lorimer, letters to mother, 2, 7, 16 January, 3 February, 1917, letter to Uncle Will, 18 February, 1917; LC GS 1027 Macleod, letters to sister Betty, 14 February, 1 March, 1917, to mother 21 March, 5, 16 April, 30 May, 9 June, 1917.

a chill & be readmitted to hospital and went up onto the roof at night and upset a bath of cold water over me and let it dry on me. I got double pneumonia and nearly died … I record this to confirm that … much as I dreaded the fighting I missed my friends so much and was so upset by changing from being an important person to a nobody that I pined to go back.[82]

There was great satisfaction when officers and men were posted back to their own regiments or battalions. "Shall be glad to get back again," wrote H. McArthur, a signaller with 1/8th Argylls, "as out here, a soldier's home is his regiment."[83] When Major Johnnie Stansfield rejoined 2nd Gordons in May, 1915, after recovery from wounds, and assumed command, he wrote, "I love them and want nothing more than the old 92nd."[84] Captain C.W.E. Gordon, a Regular Black Watch officer, was delighted to be transferred from his post of adjutant of the 6th South Staffs, a Territorial battalion, back to 2nd Black Watch. "The difference in being with men (I mean Private Soldiers) one knows, & who belong to one's own Regt, & working with men one has no interest in really, is enormous."[85] There was sadness when battalions which had built up a strong 'esprit de corps' during the war were demobilised. In January, 1919, in Italy, Pailthorpe, now detached to a Field Ambulance, went over to his old battalion to say goodbye. "The 2nd Bn. The Gordon Highlanders was about to die. Somewhere at home the Battalion would be resurrected but it would never be the same again."[86]

Regimental or battalion loyalty was by no means absolute. Alongside those who resented separation were others who either deliberately sought transfers or willingly acquiesced in their necessity. There were many reasons for seeking to leave one's own battalion; to get to the front, to take or regularise a commission, to further promotion, to escape unhappy situations, to pursue technical interests or adventure, and to escape life in the trenches.

One perfectly honourable reason for seeking a transfer was to escape from a training or reserve battalion to get overseas to the front. To this end, H.P. Samson tried but failed to transfer to the Royal Engineers;[87] D.W Reid successfully volunteered for service with trench mortars;[88] Others transferred to the Machine Gun Corps, like Gordon Crask,[89] and Willie Ferrie, who felt that the exchange of uniform was a pity, "but it is of no consequence in comparison with the advantages of the change."[90]

Another reason for leaving was to take a commission, in which case a soldier would normally be commissioned in another battalion, and quite possibly in a different regiment, the choice of which might depend on recommendation through personal connections.[91] Ian Andrew, who was

---

82 LC GS 0993 Lynden-Bell, memoir, 'The Effect on the Emotions', probably written c.1977.
83 IWM 14340 McArthur, diary, 28 August, 1915.
84 GHM PB242 Stansfield, letter home (extract), 24 May, 1915, letter to Uncle Jack & Aunt Lila, 29 May, 1915.
85 BWA Gordon, diary (actually resume of letters), 16, 25 June, 1915. See also 15, 14 (or 16) April, 1916.
86 GHM PB375, Pailthorpe, memoir, p.32.
87 LC DF 148 Recollections Samson.
88 IWM 10533 Reid, memoir.
89 THM Seaforths 89-26 Crask, letters September, 1915 to September, 1916, passim, but see especially letters to mother, postmark 14 April, postmarks 4, 6 May, 11 May, 1916.
90 IWM 12643 Ferrie, letters to mother, 13, 20 February, to brother Allan, 20 February, 1916.
91 See for example, BWA Quekett, memoir, p.10; IWM 3460 Macmillan, letter from Alex (Sandy) Macmillan to mother, 17 January, 1918.

a member of the Glasgow University company of 6th Camerons, made his decision after he was wounded at Loos. "I realised that for me the 6th Camerons had ceased to exist after the Battle of Loos. It would be more than I could bear to return to a battalion where few of the original B Company still lingered on, the time had come to make a clean break with the past." Through connections he found a home in the Scottish Rifles.[92] J.K. Stanford, who had enlisted in the London Scottish in November, 1914, was advised to apply for a commission when at Dorking with 2nd Battalion, about March, 1915. "I had no hesitation in shedding what I always felt was a 'bogus regional connection' and putting my name down for the Suffolk Regiment."[93] The somewhat disillusioned J.E.P. Levyns, of the South African Scottish, applied for a commission while recuperating from trench fever in England in 1917. His principal desire appears to have been to avoid trench service in the ranks. "I was determined not to go back to the B.E.F. as a private if I could possibly avoid it!" Eventually he was permitted to join the Royal Flying Corps.[94]

Another reason for leaving a battalion was to regularise a commission, in which case it was quite common to seek a position in the Indian Army, like Captain G.S. Mackay, serving then with 1st Garrison Battalion Seaforth Highlanders in Salonika.[95]

Sometimes officers sought to change regiments to further promotion. Lieutenant Russell, in 1st Camerons, felt about March, 1918 that his promotion prospects in the battalion were blighted. As a result he obtained a transfer to the Scots Guards, but it did not have the desired result.[96] Captain John Hay-Young, in 1st Argylls in Salonika, was in February, 1917, appointed to be second-in-command of another regiment. "I am very sorry indeed to leave the regiment but the job gives me promotion, & there is always a chance of getting command."[97] Otherwise promotion beyond battalion C.O. brought with it a necessary parting, and understandable mixed feelings. Colonel Standish Crauford wrote in November, 1916, "Sorry as I am to leave the regiment in which I have served whenever wounds permitted during '14, '15 and '16, it is a great source of pride to command a Brigade."[98]

Others sought staff jobs to escape from battalions where they were not happy. One such was Lieutenant McKechnie. Transferred against his will from 1/6th Argylls to 11th Battalion, where he was heavily overworked, he managed through divisional contacts to secure a job behind the lines as an Assistant Provost Marshal.[99] Another discontented officer was E.A.S Oldham. After he lost his company in 1/5th Seaforths to new officers posted to the battalion from home, he secured a post in 3rd Army School as an Instructor.[100]

Others sought posts in the technical arms, particularly the Machine Gun Corps and the Royal Flying Corps. In some cases, these transfers were based on interest or experience. Thus, Donald Clappen, who transferred from the London Scottish to take a commission in the R.F.C in October, 1915, had been an aviation instructor at Hendon before the war.[101]

92   LC WF Recollections A9 Andrew, memoir.
93   IWM 10529 Stanford, memoir, p.24.
94   Levyns, *The Disciplines of War*, pp.84-87.
95   IWM 12688 MacKay, letter to mother, 4 June, 1917.
96   THM Camerons 97-22 Russell, memoirs, pp.241-242, 246-247, 249.
97   LC GS 0731 Hay-Young, letter to mother, 19 February, 1917.
98   GHM PB2093 Crauford, letter to mother, 21 November, 1916.
99   IWM 233 McKechnie, memoir, pp.24, 44-49.
100 LC GS 1203 Oldham, diary, 11 January, 1917 to 23 March, 1918, passim.
101 IWM 9 Recording Clappen, Donald W., IWM interview, 1973.

W. MacKenzie successfully transferred from 9th Black Watch to the Special Company, R.E. (the poison gas corps), partly following his scientific interest.[102] Hugh Monaghan joined the 79th battalion C.E.F. in 1915, but after his arrival in Britain shortly effected his transfer to the Royal Flying Corps, which appealed to him much more. "There was action, excitement, novelty and independence."[103] At the end of August, 1915, Duncan Bell-Irving, a Gordons officer, but attached to 2nd Camerons, was allowed to transfer to the Royal Flying Corps. His company commander told him, "You're a Gordon? … Well, th' Commanding Officer says you're not one of us, you may volunteer for this Flying Corps, if you're so minded. He'll not let a Cameron go!"[104] Jock Macleod, a machine gun specialist in the Camerons eventually transferrred to the M.G.C. in 1918.[105]

Others made the move, like some of those who took staff appointments, to escape an unhappy situation in their battalion. Lieutenant Douglas Wilson was in 1918 Lewis Gun Officer in 5th Camerons, but was so frustrated by being messed about by his C.O. that he ultimately transferred to the M.G.C.[106] In the case of Norman Macmillan, his departure from the Glasgow Highlanders to take a commission in the R.F.C. was facilitated by the departure of most of his old pals from his platoon.[107]

It is nevertheless true that part of the attraction of the R.F.C. in particular was to escape the life of an infantryman in the trenches, as is acknowledged by Macmillan. "I have already done twelve months as private & I would not look forward to another twelve months under similar conditions." Donald Clappen had also had enough. "For the first time in my life I found I was covered with lice in my kilt and it was then that really made me think that trench warfare was not for me." Such thoughts were probably also instrumental in the decision of his fellow South African Scot, Arthur Betteridge, to apply for the R.F.C.[108] Mackenzie, by contrast, saw the likely alternative to transfer to the Special Company, R.E. as a commission in the Black Watch. "As the average life span of a Second Lieutenant was about 3 months, I didn't fancy it."

Finally, on some occasions officers were content with unforeseen postings to other regiments or battalions. Leslie Cooper, who served in 9th Seaforths, a pioneer battalion, was posted from the depot to 7th Battalion, a fighting battalion, about April, 1918, when he returned to France after recovering from a wound. He successfully resisted all attempts by 9th Battalion to recall him as "I felt I would rather be with a fighting battalion than return to the work the 9th did."[109] R.W.F. Johnston had joined 9th Royal Scots, a Territorial battalion, in 1910, and joined them at the front in May, 1915, where he served as platoon sergeant. However, after leave, when he was at Etaples, he was mistakenly recorded as belonging to 1st Royal Scots and drafted to join them. He noticed the error "with pleasure," and was accepted by them, as his father had been in

---

102 LC WF Recollections, MacKenzie, memoir.
103 Monaghan, Lt. Hugh B., *The Big Bombers of World War 1*, (Burlington, Ontario: Ray Gentle Communications Ltd., n.d. c.1976), p.34.
104 O'Kiely, *Gentleman Air Ace*, pp.54-55.
105 LC GS 1027 Macleod, letter to mother, 25 February, 17 March, 30 May, 14 October 1918, to father, 5 July, 1918.
106 LC GS 1761 Wilson, memoir, pp.59, 102.
107 IWM 3460 Macmillan, letters to sister Bessie, 17, 31 October, 20 November, 2 December, 1915, 12 February, 1916, diary, 7 March, 1916.
108 LC GS 0132 Betteridge, memoir, pp.105-106.
109 THM Seaforths 81-2 Cooper, memoir, p.179.

the regiment.[110] In December, 1915, Henry Pelham Burn, an officer of 1st Gordons, took over command of 10th Argylls. He does not appear to have been dismayed at the move. "They are a splendid capital lot & a good lot of men." "I have an excellent lot of young officers here." But in March, 1916, he was told he was to transfer to command 8th Battalion of his own regiment, the Gordons. "I am very annoyed about it as this Battalion is first class & we all get on very well. The authorities think that it is necessary for the C.O.'s to belong to same Regiment as they command, but nowadays with new armies etc., it is not at all necessary."[111]

A strong sense of regimental identity was also displayed when battalions of the same regiment found themselves in the same vicinity behind the lines. Meetings wold occur between officers and men, sometimes between whole battalions,[112] football matches would be arranged,[113] and battalions might turn out to cheer or turn out their pipe bands for fellow battalions passing through their billets.[114] As an example, Lieutenant Robert MacKay, in 11th Argylls, notes slightly subversively arranging a meeting between 10th and 11th Argylls in March, 1917.[115] Similarly, but much less subversively, at the end of May, 1915, there was a historic meeting between the two Regular battalions of the Argylls, when 1st Battalion found itself the left-hand battalion of 27th Division, with 2nd Battalion alongside as the right-hand battalion of their own division. The parent regiments of these battalions, the 91st and the 93rd, had never wished for their amalgamation in the first place, and this was the first time since that event in 1881 that the two battalions had met. Fortunately there was no battle royal. On 10 June, 1915, the officers had a splendid lunch party together, and all the Regular Officers of both battalions were photographed together.[116] Regimental unity was expressed in other ways too, by letters of condolence or messages of congratulation from other battalions.[117]

Canadian Highland battalions took the opportunity to cement relations with their parent Scottish regiments, and to seek advice on regimental custom. After 13th Battalion C.E.F. (Royal Highlanders of Canada) arrived on Salisbury Plain in October, 1914, they very soon sent emissaries to Regimental Headquarters at Perth and established contact also with 9th Black Watch at Aldershot.[118] In April, 1918, when 72nd Battalion C.E.F. (Seaforth Highlanders of Canada) were at Wakefield Camp, just north of Arras, they exchanged visits with 2nd Seaforths. More reciprocal visits took place in May, when the 72nd were at Auchel, and at their battalion

---

110 IWM 4474 Johnston, memoir, pp.39-41; IWM 13586 Johnston, interview.
111 GHM PB3309 Pelham Burn, letters to mother, 13, 29 December, 1915, 14, 19 March, 25 April, 16 July, 1916.
112 BWA Stewart, diary, 21, 22 July, 1915; GHM PB1639 Kemp, memoir, p.3; IWM 1862 Craig-Brown, diary, 21, 23 June, 1915.
113 IWM 3460 Macmillan, letter from Alex (Sandy) Macmillan to Tony, 6 July, 1917.
114 LC GS 1203 Oldham, diary, 25 July, 1916; IWM 12311 Mason-Macfarlane, memoir by David Mason-Macfarlane, p.29; Craig-Brown, *Historical Records*, Vol.3, p.438; IWM 3460 Macmillan, diary, 24 November, 1914; IWM Books Reid, 'Shoulder to Shoulder,' p 18; Fetherstonhaugh, *13th Battalion*, p.143.
115 IWM 11144, MacKay, diary, 3 March, 1917. See also: IWM 3460 Macmillan, letters from Alex (Sandy) Macmillan to mother, 24 February, 12 March, 1917.
116 LC GS 0409 Cunningham, notes written by himself, 1976; ASHM N-E2 Hyslop, diary, 31 May, 1915: Anderson, *1st Argylls*, pp.43-44.
117 GHM PB107 Grant, diary, 17 March, 1915; BWA Stewart, letter to wife, 3 October, 1915.
118 Fetherstonhaugh, *13th Battalion*, pp.20-21, 24, 56-57.

sports there on 8 June, the pipe band of 2nd Seaforths was present.[119] 1st Camerons and the 79th Cameron Highlanders of Canada exchanged visits in November, 1917[120] Such feelings went two ways. When Frank Brooke's draft of Seaforths marched to the docks at Folkestone in 1916, "Our fellows saw a Canadian Seaforth among the crowd and cheered hysterically. I felt touched."[121]

Against such strong regimental identity, must be set cases of inter-battalion disputes within the same regiments. Some might be at a high level. There was outrage, for example, at command level, in both 1st and 7th Camerons at an ultimately unsuccessful proposal by Lochiel that, since the 4th (Territorial) Battalion of the Camerons had been disbanded, the 7th (Service) Battalion should be re-designated the 4th.[122] At a lower level, there was a running dispute between 5th and 6th Gordons, which seems to have been based on precedence, and which culminated in fisticuffs at Bedford in the 'battle of Coventry' shortly after Hogmanay, 1914.[123] Such misdirected martial ardour may not have been good for regimental harmony, but was at least an indication of strong esprit de corps at the battalion level.

The classic stories of battalion defamation however relate to the cheese and the wire, concerning 1/7th and 1/5th Gordons respectively. Captain Youngson, in 1/5th Gordons, notes that it was in 1915 that the incidents took place.

> The ration party of a sister battalion [1/7th] was on the way to the line when, so the story goes, a cheese fell off the limber. It started to roll, and the movement startled some of the party, one of whom [the Q.M., allegedly] loosed off a revolver shot. The story got about, and when any other troops met that battalion, they were met by the chorus, 'Fa [who] shot the cheese?' This was countered with 'Fa stole the barbed wire?' – another story. One of our working parties had been up wiring and, with the approach of day, stopped work. As they would be returning next night to continue operations, they left the wire they had not used, as they did not wish to have to carry it back and up again the following night. The Bosche, however, stole a march on them, and when they went up there was no wire!![124]

Strong regimental identity went hand-in-glove with a degree of inter-regimental rivalry. There are many examples,[125] but two will have to do. William Darling, a new recruit to 9th Black Watch in Aldershot in Autumn, 1914, was summoned to assist in suppressing a disturbance in

---

119 McEvoy & Finlay, *Seaforth Highlanders of Canada*, pp.94-95, 103.
120 Craig-Brown, *Historical Records*, Vol.3, p.233.
121 IWM Books Brooke, 'Wait for it,' p.47.
122 NLS Acc,9084, No.7, McLeod, letters to sister Nan, 1, 24 June, 1017.
123 GHM PB3712 Murison, memoir; GHM PB107.1 Grant, diary, 3 January, 1915; GHM PB1892.3.1 Youngson, memoir, '1914-1919,' p.7; Nicholson, *Behind the Lines*, p.43.
124 GHM PB1892.3.1 Youngson, memoir, pp.16-17. See also: LC GS 1549 Strachan, memoir; GHM PB1892.3.18 McDonald, 'Uncle Harper's Duds,' p.19; GHM uncatalogued Beaton, memoir, pp.75-76
125 IWM Books Cooper, 'Domi Militaeque', p.50; IWM 4586 Douglas, memoir, pp.1255-1256; THM Seaforths 81-180 Murray, letters to mother, 18 June, 1915; LC GS 1761 Wilson, memoir, pp.28-29, 43; IWM 1862 Craig-Brown, diary, 6 July, 1916; IWM 11923 PP Sutherland, J., letter to father, c. October, 1915; McEwen, *Fifth Camerons*, p.7; Macleod, *6th Camerons*, p.91; Craig-Brown, *Historical Records*, Vol.4, p.333; GHM uncatalogued Beaton, memoir, pp.72-75, 87; GHM PB283 Watson, memoirs, p.13; IWM 3460 Macmillan, diary, 24 November, 1914; IWM 2528 Bradbury, memoir,

town, where fighting had broken out between Black Watch and Gordons, a Gordon apparently having referred to a broken square, in a jibe at the Black Watch's misfortune at the battle of Tamai in 1884.

> I think it very moving that these men, who lately owned no allegiance to anyone except the humdrum personal allegiances of everyday life, had somehow accepted the reputation of their recently not even self-chosen regiment as something for which they had a special responsibility, something for which they were prepared, at any rate immediately, to fight, and as events showed something for which when the time came in France and Flanders they were prepared to die.[126]

Duncan Bell-Irving was commissioned into the Gordon Highlanders, but found himself posted to 2nd Camerons, where he had to put up with jibes about the Kaiser's Own Highlanders, because so many of 1st Gordons had surrendered at Le Cateau.[127]

Alongside their regimental and battalion identity, Highland soldiers also took pride in their identity as Scots. As Lieutenant Phil Paul, in 11th Black Watch put it; "Curious thing that Scotsmen are nearly always very Scotch, indeed almost aggressively so. It's just the nature of the beast." "I am proud of Scotland and proud to have been born in Scotland with my part well rooted in the soil of that stern but beautiful country."[128] This pride was shown for example when, after the Armistice, in December, 1918, the King visited the troops of 1/8th Argylls. The men lined both sides of the road and put up crossed flags from the two sides of the road, a Union Flag and the Scottish Royal Standard, so the King had to walk under them.

> The cheers from our side was grand and we gave the King a fine reception when passing down the double line of soldiers. On coming under the two flags he looked up mostly to Scotland's and saluted it. This made cheers much more louder, to recognise our flag. The King knew we were pleased and must have been about deafened by our enthusiasm.[129]

Kilted Canadian soldiers had a rather more complicated identity. In their case, the attachment was not only to Scotland, but to Canada and to Empire. Charles Bannell migrated to Canada where he lived for a number of years on Vancouver Island. He served in the 72nd Battalion C.E.F. and was killed at Passchendaele on 30 October, 1917. In December, 1915, he wrote a poem, 'Song of Empire,' of which this is an extract:

Sons of Britain's mighty Empire
Standing, falling, side by side,

---

pp.50,51; Sutherland, *War Diary*, p 86; IWM 16335 Racine, memoir, pp.70-71; BWA Foreman, memoir, further notes by his son.
126 Darling, *So it looks to me*, pp.128-129. On the Broken Square jibe, see also: Rule, *Students*, pp.184-185.
127 O'Kiely, *Gentleman Air Ace*, p.47, quoting a letter from him to his father, 10 June, 1915. On this insult, see also: IWM 3449 Cordner, memoir; THM Seaforths 81-2 Cooper, memoir, pp.15, 95; Rule, *Students*, pp.184-185.
128 BWA Paul, letters to Miss May Merrett, 5 March, 1916, 6 January, 1918.
129 ASHM-E11 Bowie, diary, 7 December, 1918.

> Now, at last, we all united,
> Brothers now, whate'er betide.
>
> Sons of Britain's mighty Empire!
> Would my tongue could find a name
> That would call us and enthral us
> Each apart and all the same![130]

When the transport carrying 13th Battalion C.E.F. raised anchor at Quebec on 30 September, 1914, "On deck the pipe band burst into the strains of 'Highland Laddie' and 'Scotland the Brave,' while the men, as soon as the pipes were silent, joined in a mighty chorus of 'O Canada' and 'Auld Lang Syne.'"[131]

Some were able to take pride in their more specific Highland identity. As Campbell and Green have demonstrated, Alan Mackintosh, the soldier poet of 5th Seaforths, drew deeply on Highland culture for his poems.[132] In 'Cha Till Maccruimen,' which we have already quoted in considering the pipes, he commemorates the departure of 4th Camerons from Bedford; in 'To a Dead Soldier,' also written at Bedford, he imagines the soul of a dead soldier finding its way back to his homeland according to poetic Highland tradition; and in 'The Undying Race,' written after the battalion was stationed near to Breton troops, he draws on the common history of the Gaels and Bretons as Celts.[133]

There was great pride too in the stunningly beautiful landscape of Scotland. Phil Paul again: "I'd like to show you the Scotland I know and love. Great purple hills and vast lochs, deep narrow arms of the sea ringed in with stern frowning mountains with their heads crowned with mist. Sunrise in a Highland scene is one of the finest things I know."[134] In December, 1915, on the train running north to Glasgow through the Southern Uplands, Norman Macmillan of the Glasgow Highlanders, felt, "this was a country worth fighting for! How different from monotonous mud-flat Flanders! Here was romance breathing from the very hills, the rivers and the glens!"[135] Alan Mackintosh's poem 'Beaumont-Hamel, captured, November 16th, 1916' contains evocative images of the Scottish countryside,[136] while in his poem 'The Highlander,' Jock Macleod, who served in 2nd Camerons, expresses the deep attachment of a Highlander to his homeland, as he imagines the soul of a slain Highland soldier pausing in the Hebrides before journeying to heaven:

> When at length my bullet finds me, and rives the bars of flesh,
> Before I take the tangled roads in quest of Paradise,
> I shall linger in the Hebrides, where ocean-winds blow fresh

---

130 Bannell, Charles Samuel, *His Offering. Poems by Charles Samuel Bannell, Seaforth Highlanders, Canadian Force (Killed in Action, October 30th, 1917)* (Liverpool: J.A. Thompson, n.d.).
131 Fetherstonhaugh, *13th Battalion*, p.16.
132 Campbell & Green, *Can't shoot a man with a cold*, pp.83, 84, 94.
133 Mackintosh, *A Highland Regiment*, pp.16-17, 18-19, 27-28.
134 BWA Paul, letter to Miss May Merrett, 14 December, 1915.
135 IWM 3460 Macmillan, diary, 14 December, 1915.
136 Campbell & Green, *Can't shoot a man with a cold*, pp.162-163, 179.

> Over salt Atlantic leagues from forts of sunless ice.
> ...
> And, Oh! I hope to find in Heaven the joyous scents of Spring
> On birchen woods and bracken braes, when I reach my last abode.[137]

There were of course, exceptions. Lieutenant Guy Macgregor, then in 2/9th Argylls, was of Scottish extraction but normally resident in England. In September, 1916, he wrote to his fiancée,

> Today, just about tea time, I read Gray's 'Elegy' for the thousandth time & loved it more than ever before, & for the first time it sent me longing & longing for little English villages. I never thought when I was in England & longing for Scotland that the day was at hand when I would be in Scotland & longing for England. But here it is. As I read each verse of the introduction, I pictured to myself some different spot in Surrey where I had been happy.[138]

Scottish identity sadly could manifest itself in a dislike for the English. Keith McDermott, a special reserve Seaforths officer, attached to 1st Camerons in December, 1914, noted, "There is a Major here who continually abuses 3 things – English, Barristers, and Oxford men – rather unfortunate; to do him justice, I don't think he knows I'm any of them."[139] (He was all three!) James Racine, himself a southern (Guildford) recruit to 5th Seaforths, noted that at Hogmanay, 1914, "A Scotchman was accused, by another, of being an Englishman. This was taken as an insult and a knife was at once drawn from a hose-top, the attacker was seized and order restored."[140] There was a natural preference not to be posted to an English regiment. Major Hyslop, in 2nd Argylls, observed in October, 1915, "I have been offered an English Battalion in the 28th Division, but prefer to wait for a Scottish one if they will allow me to do so."[141] And in January, 1918, Lieutenant Scott Ferguson, in 1/4th Seaforths, wrote of two of his friends; "It is rotten luck on Brown & Sturrock going into an English regiment, but it can't be helped. They are bound to feel pretty rotten over it."[142] There was also legitimate annoyance at the use of the term 'England' to describe 'Great Britain.' On 9 March, 1915, Ernest Craig-Brown records, rather sarcastically, a special order issued by Haig

> A Special Order was issued by Gen. D. Haig to the 1st Army stating that we are about to engage the enemy under very favourable conditions, & urging us to 'fight like men for the Honour of Old *England*.' Presumably the Scots, Irish & Welsh mercenaries attached to the *English* army are also expected to comply. The order is of today's date.[143]

---

137 Macleod, *Poems*, p.14
138 IWM 8592 Macgregor, letter to fiancée Dulcie Newling, 7 February, 1916.
139 McDermott, *Robert Keith McDermott*, letter home 8 December, 1914.
140 IWM 16335 Racine, memoir, p.20.
141 ASHM N-E2 Hyslop, diary, 18 October, 1915. They did and in November, he was appointed to command 7th Argylls.
142 LC GS 0552 Ferguson, letter to mother, 28 January, 1918.
143 IWM 1862 Craig-Brown, diary, 9 March, 1915. See also: ASHM E11 Bowie, diary, 25 October, 1918; IWM Books, Haldane, '4th Seaforths,' draft.

382 Those Bloody Kilts

Identity. Memorial to 1st Black Watch and 1st Cameron Highlanders erected at High Wood to commemorate their losses September, 1916. From a contemporary postcard, publisher unknown. (Author's collection)

It is interesting to see nevertheless that Lance Corporal Dalziel, a pre-war regular soldier, serving in 1st Argylls, refers to the British soldier collectively as 'the Tommy', accepting this designation for himself and the Highland troops.[144]

Scottish identity was of course reinforced by the creation of the four specifically Scottish divisions described in an earlier chapter, of which 51st Division was specifically Highland, 52nd specifically Lowland, and 9th and 15th Divisions mixed, adding a Scottish divisional identity to that of regiment and battalion. Scottish identity was reinforced too in other ways. When in December, 1916, a memorial was created on the eastern edge of High Wood in memory of the men of 1st Black Watch and 1st Camerons who fell there, it was a wooden St Andrew's Cross which was chosen.[145] Colonel W.N. Nicholson, who served on the Divisional staff of both 51st (Highland Territorial) and 17th (English New Army) Divisions, felt that the strength of Scottish identity favoured esprit de corps in 51st Division: "'Scotland for ever' is still a battle cry. 'St George for Merrie England,' if it ever existed, is now forgot." He felt that the battalions in 51st Division were sustained by their own inherent esprit de corps, while those in 17th Division, while capable of performing extremely well, always needed good leadership to accomplish this.[146]

Scottish and Highland identity was also supported by the symbols and traditions of Scotland. We have already noted at length the pride of soldiers in wearing the kilt. While part of the pride

---

144 ASHM N-E1 Dalziel, diary, 24 February, 1915.
145 Craig-Brown, *Historical Records*, Vol.3, pp.218-219. The wooden cross and base were replaced eight years later by a granite slab.
146 Nicholson, *Behind the Lines*, pp.149, 152.

was based, as we have seen, on regimental identity, and still more might be based, as we shall discuss, on an identity with the Scottish Highlander as representative of a martial race, no doubt much was due to simple pride in national identity. The same is true of the pipes. Probably no other symbols reinforced Scottish identity more than the kilt and the pipes. But there were other traditions which reinforced Scottishness; songs, dancing, Highland games, and the three great national celebrations of Burns Night, St Andrew's Day and Hogmanay.

Scottish songs reinforced identity, but they were by no means the only, or even the major, part of the Highland soldier's repertoire. As we have seen, there were also regimental and battalion songs. Otherwise, as Bob Lawson, in 14th Argylls, noted in October, 1916, "We have a beautiful mixture of psalms, hymns & ragtimes."[147] Songs included popular songs and ragtime,[148] hymns[149] and the familiar soldiers' songs[150] which were often skittish retakes of hymns or popular songs. Student songs were also sung,[151] notably by members of 'U' Company of 4th Gordons. Like the soldiers' songs, these were not always respectable. There were even, amongst some regulars at least, some old marching songs from the Boer War;[152] There were also their own home grown skittish songs,[153] not of a specifically Scottish or regimental nature, such as:

---

147 IWM 8192 Lawson, letter to sister Bessie, 10 October, 1916. See also: Blaser, *Kilts across the Jordan*, p.218.
148 IWM 19680 White, letter from David Skinner, 28 August, 1916; IWM 2854 Bates, letters to his fiancée, 2 May, 15 September, 1916; IWM Books Cooper, 'Domi Militaeque', p.211; IWM 15990 Gunn, letters to brother-in-law, 16 April, 6 November. 1915; IWM 8592 Macgregor, letter to fiancée Dulcie Newling, 27 February, 1916; Gillespie, *Letters from Flanders*, p.118, letter home, 27 April, 1915; One of the Jocks [Scott], *Odd Shots*, pp.45-46; Malcolm, *Argyllshire Highlanders*, p.35; THM Seaforths 89-26 Crask, letters to mother, 9 November, & postmark 13 November, 1915, IWM 43 Dunton, interview; IWM Haldane, '4th Seaforths,' draft; LC GS 1761 Wilson, memoir, pp.61-62, 106-107; LC WF Recollections A9 Andrew, memoir; THM Camerons 89-44 Anderson, memoir, p.12; McEwen, *Fifth Camerons*, pp.13-14; GHM PB242 Stansfield, letter home (extract), 7 January, 1915; IWM Books, Parke, *Memoirs of an 'Old Contemptible'*, pp.47-48; Rule, *Students*, pp.18-19; Sommers, *Temporary Heroes*, pp.72-74; IWM 3460 Macmillan, diary, 25 December, 1914; Lyon, *In kilt and khaki*, pp.3-4, 168-169; Royal Scots Museum, Beatson, diary, 30 May, 1915; McMillan, *Trench Tea and Sandbags*, p.16; Beattie *48th Highlanders*, pp.156-157; Fetherstonhaugh, *13th Battalion*, p.13; Urquhart, *Canadian Scottish*, pp.37-38; NLS Acc. 9084 No.12 Macleod, Rev K.O., letter to sister Nan, 26 November, 1918; NLS Acc.9084 No.37, Macleod, letter to all [at home], 12 October, 1917; NLS MS 944 Ramage, diary, 17 April, 1915; Anon, *The 11th Battalion Gordon Highlanders*, p.8.
149 IWM 3834 Wrench, diary, p.76, 26 November, 1916; Lyon, *In kilt and khaki*, pp.168-169; *9th Royal Scots (T.F.) B Company*, p.37; NLS MS 944 Ramage, diary, 22 May, 1915.
150 Gillespie, *Letters from Flanders*, p.286, letter home, 31 August, 1915, pp.306-307, letter home, 21 September, 1915; One of the Jocks [Scott], *Odd Shots*, pp.45-46; LC GS 1635 Turing, memoir; IWM Books Brooke, 'Wait for it,' pp.88, 233; IWM 3834 Wrench, diary, p.76, 26 November, 1916; IWM Books Haldane, '4th Seaforths,' draft; LC GS 1761 Wilson, memoir, pp.61-62; LC WF Recollections A9 Andrew, memoir; GHM PB1892.3.1 Youngson, memoir, p.24; GHM PB3309 Pelham Burn, letter to mother, 23 February, 1915; Mackenzie, *Sixth Gordons*, pp.37-38; Rule, *Students under Arms*, pp.149, 180; Sommers, *Temporary Heroes*, pp.72-74; IWM 3460 Macmillan, diary, 21 December, 1915; Lyon, *In kilt and khaki*, pp.3-4, 47; Beattie, *48th Highlanders*, pp.31, 101, 156-157, 190, 240, 264; Fetherstonhaugh, *13th Battalion*, p.39; Urquhart, *Canadian Scottish*, pp.37-38; IWM 13511 Macgregor, letter to father, January, 1916; NLS MS 944 Ramage, diary, 28 May, 1915.
151 IWM 8592 Macgregor, letter to fiancée Dulcie Newling, 27 February, 1916; Fraser, *Doctor Jimmy*, p.51.
152 IWM Books Parke, 'Memoirs of an 'Old Contemptible,' pp.47-48.
153 Apart from examples cited, see McEwen, *Fifth Camerons*, pp.13-14; LC GS 1761 Wilson, memoir, p.10; IWM 3460 Macmillan, diary, 25 November, 1914; NLS MS 944 Ramage, diary, 11 May, 1915; Malcolm, *Argyllshire Highlanders*, pp.20-21.

Only last night after tea,
Baron Rothschild said to me
Oh, I wonder what it feels like
To be poor!"[154]

In 51st Highland Division, a great favourite at all battalion concerts was Colonel Rorie who would sing songs of his own composition ... As an encore he would give,

'D—n the Germans, d—n the Huns
D—n the bugger who invented guns.
D—n the Kaiser, d—n the war
Oh what a bally lot of fools we are.'[155]

In 5th Seaforths, as well as his more serious poetry, Lieutenant E.A. (Alan) Mackintosh entertained the troops with his own skittish songs.[156]

While in many respects Highland soldiers shared the repertoire of songs sung by other Tommies, they and their Canadian colleagues also made full use of the Scottish repertoire which both gave them pleasure and reinforced their identity as Scots.[157] They were sung, for example, on a picnic outing from Ripon,[158] in billets in the evening,[159] or in the Officers' mess,[160] One evening in July, 1915, Lieutenant Hugh Munro, of 1/8th Argylls encountered three Gordons singing an old Scots song in the Foret de Nieppe.[161] On Christmas Day, 1915, No.2 Company of 13th Battalion C.E.F. (Royal Highlanders of Canada) could be heard singing 'Loch Lomond' at night.[162] Peter McGregor, in 14th Argylls, training at Aldershot, wrote to his wife Jen in October, 1915, that during a pause in a route march, "some of our platoon behind us began to sing 'Annie Laurie,' 'Maxwellton Braes are Bonny,' and I was never so near tears, and homesick, and Jensick, and family sick, and had the most horrible feelings. I stood there in the midst and wanted to be home."[163] Choirs were even formed.[164]

Favourite Scots songs[165] included 'Auld Lang Syne,' 'Annie Laurie,' 'The Rowan Tree,' 'O' A' the Airts the Wind can Blow,' 'Scotland Yet,' 'My Ain Folk,' Ye banks & braes,' 'Sing us a song

---

154 IWM Books, Brooke, 'Wait for it,' p.105.
155 GHM PB1892.3.18 McDonald, 'Uncle Harper's Duds,' p.35.
156 Campbell & Green, *Can't shoot a man with a cold*, pp.97-98, 134-135; Sutherland, *War Diary*, p.44.
157 Apart from refs cited below, see: IWM 8592 Macgregor, letter to fiancée Dulcie Newling, 27 February, 1916; Bartholomew, *George Hugh Freeland Bartholomew*, p.69. letter home, 13 September, 1917; IWM 3834 Wrench, diary, p.102, 4 April, 1917; McEwen, *Fifth Camerons*, pp.13-14; Fetherstonhaugh, *13th Battalion*, p.13; IWM 21092 McGregor, letters to wife Jen, 18 January, 24 February, 1916.
158 BWA Junks, diary, 19 August, 1916.
159 IWM Books Cooper, 'Domi Militaeque', pp.128, 329.
160 IWM 7508 Wyllie, diary, 5 September, 17, 25 October, 25 December, 1917.
161 IWM 2902 Munro, diary, 24 July, 1915.
162 Fetherstonhaugh, *13th Battalion*, p.75.
163 IWM 21092 McGregor, Peter, letter to wife Jen, 30 October, 1915.
164 IWM 1862 Craig-Brown, letter to him from A. Yeadon, 1 March, 1917.
165 BWA Junks, diary, 19 August, 1916; BWA Duke, letter to mother, 3 April, 1915; Malcolm, *Argyllshire Highlanders*, pp.25, 35; Chambers, *Diaries of World War 1*, p.55; Sommers, *Temporary Heroes*, pp.72-74; IWM 21092 McGregor, letter to wife Jen, 30 October, 1915; IWM Books Cooper, 'Domi

of Bonnie Scotland,' 'The Silver Dee,' 'Scots wha hae,' 'The Skye Boat Song,' 'Loch Lomond,' 'Mary Morrison,' 'Bonnie Mary of Argyle,' 'Hundred Pipers,' 'March of the Cameron Men,' 'Will ye no come back again,' 'The Auld Scotch Songs,' not forgetting 'Tallietoodalum Castle.' They even made up spoof songs based on Scottish classics, like 'Bombing in the gloaming,' noted by John Bowie in 11th Argylls.[166] Some songs were sung in Gaelic,[167] and we have already recorded the famous incident in which Lieutenant Philip Christison encouraged some faltering Camerons at the battle of Loos.

There was of course an overlap between Scottish and music hall songs in those of Harry Lauder, which were popular amongst the troops,[168] including 'The Laddies who fought and won,' 'Just a wee Doch an' Doris,' 'Hey, Donald!' 'The Lass of Tobermory' and 'When the Wedding Bells are Ringing.' When Harry himself visited the troops in June, 1917, he noted that, "Best of all they liked the old love songs, and the old songs of Scotland; tender, crooning melodies, that would help to carry them back, in memory to their hames and, if they had them, to the lassies of their dreams." Among the favourite songs he sang were 'Roamin' in the gloamin' and 'Wee Hoose Among the Heather.'[169]

Scottish identity was also reinforced by observance of the three primary Scottish festivals of Burns' Night, St Andrew's Day, and, most of all, Hogmanay. We find Burns' Night celebrated not only at home,[170] and behind the lines on the Western front,[171] but also in Salonika,[172] and on board H.M.T. Leang Choon with 1st Garrison Battalion Gordon Highlanders, en route for India.[173] Not to be outdone, in 42nd Battalion C.E.F. (Royal Highlanders of Canada), on Christmas Day, 1916, a lecture was given by the Reverend W.A. Cameron on the Life of Burns.[174] Similarly we find St Andrews' Day celebrated, mainly by dinners, at home,[175] behind

    Militaeque', pp.128, 329; THM Seaforths 89-26 Crask, letters to mother, 9 November, & postmark 13 November, 1915; LC GS 1761 Wilson, memoir, pp.106-107; ASHM N-E8 McGuinness, notebook; IWM 7508 Wyllie, diary, 25 December, 1917; Lyon, *In kilt and khaki*, pp.124, 168-169; IWM 2902 Munro, Lt. H.A., diary, 27 July, 1915; McEwen, *Fifth Camerons*, pp 13-14; Anon, *The 11th Battalion Gordon Highlanders*, p.8; IWM 15990 PP Gunn, letters to brother-in-law, 16 April, 6 November. 1915; Gillespie, *Letters from Flanders*, p.118, letter home, 27 April, 1915; LC WF Recollections A9 Andrew, memoir, Fetherstonhaugh, *13th Battalion*, p.75; NLS MS 944 Ramage, diary, 17 April, 1915; IWM 3460 Macmillan, diary, 25 December, 1914, 21 December, 1915; Mackenzie, *Sixth Gordons*, p.64; Burns, *Once a Cameron Highlander*, p.30.
166 ASHM-E11 Bowie, diary, c. March, 1917.
167 IWM Books Cooper, 'Domi Militaeque', p 128; Campbell, *Letters*, pp.8-11, letters home, 26 May, n.d, 2 June, 1915; GHM PB3309 Pelham Burn, letter to mother, 23 February, 1915.
168 IW 11144 MacKay, diary, afternote 1972; IWM 10414 McGregor interview; Malcolm, *Argyllshire Highlanders*, p.35; LC GS 1761 Wilson, memoir, pp.106-107; McEwen, *Fifth Camerons*, pp.13-14; Sommers, *Temporary Heroes*, pp.50-51, 72-74; Sutherland, *War Diary*, p.44.
169 Lauder, *A Minstrel in France*, pp.139, 206, 232, 255, 270.
170 IWM 12643 Ferrie, letter to mother, 25 January, 1916.
171 BWA Guthrie, letter to wife Crissie, 26 January, 1916; IWM Books Cooper, 'Domi Militacque', p.201, IWM 8192 Lawson, letter to sister Bessie, 27 January, 1918; LC GS 0552 Ferguson, letter to mother, 24 January, 1918; IWM 3460 Macmillan, diary, 25 January, 1916; IWM 114 Allen, letter to wife, 25 January, 1916.
172 IWM 7508 PP Wyllie, Capt. A.T., diary, 26 January, 1917, 25 January, 1918.
173 GHM PB3112 Blinco, memoir, p.8.
174 Topp, *42nd Battalion*, p.101.
175 Anon, *The 51st Battalion*, p.41; IWM 21092 McGregor, letter to wife Jen, 30 November, 1915.

386   Those Bloody Kilts

Identity. Men of the Black Watch celebrating New Year's Day in the hutments at Henencourt, 1917. (IWM Q4642)

the lines on the Western Front,[176] at Tripoli in the Levant,[177] at Rous-chouk on the Danube,[178] in Mesopotamia,[179] and in Salonika.[180] We find the Canadians celebrating St Andrew's Day too, both 13th Battalion C.E.F. (Royal Highlanders of Canada)[181] and 15th Battalion C.E.F. (48th Highlanders of Canada).[182] Otherwise, after the Armistice, we find the day celebrated by divisional sports,[183] or an inter-regimental rugby match.[184] In 3rd Camerons, on St Andrew's Day, 1918, a Victory Dance was given in the Sergeants' Mess.[185]

176 BWA MacDonald, Coll, letter to wife Mary, 1 December, 1917; ASHM N-E2 Hyslop, diary, 1 December, 1915; THM Camerons 91-7 Mackay, letter to mother, 2 December, 1915; IWM 1862 Craig-Brown, letters home 1 December, 1914, 1 December, 1916, & diary, 30 November, 1914, 30 November, 1916; Craig-Brown, *Historical Records*, Vol.3, pp.216, 238; GHM PB1639 Kemp, memoir, p.54; ASHM-E11 Bowie, diary, 30 November, 1918.
177 BWA Stewart, letter to wife, 1 December, 1918.
178 LC GS 0456 Dick, typescript memoirs, p.61.
179 LC MES 013 Bonar, letter to H.E.R. Widnell, 2 December, 1917.
180 IWM 7508 Wyllie, diary, 1, 2 December, 1916.
181 Fetherstonhaugh, *13th Battalion*, p.24.
182 Beattie, *48th Highlanders*, pp.31, 282.
183 LC GS 1203 Oldham, diary, 30 November, 1918.
184 Craig-Brown, *Historical Records*, Vol.3, p.278.
185 Ibid., Vol.3, p.397

The occasion most consistently (and riotously) celebrated, however, was Hogmanay. We find this celebrated at home,[186] behind the lines on the Western Front,[187] in Italy,[188] in Salonika,[189] in Mesopotamia,[190] at Tripoli,[191] in P.O.W. camps in Germany,[192] and after the Armistice in France and Belgium,[193] occupied Germany,[194] and on board the liner 'Indarra' en route from Constanza to Constantinople.[195] The kilted Canadian battalions of course celebrated as well.[196] Lieutenant Rory Macgregor, in 5th Camerons, notes that New Year 1916 was celebrated in suitably riotous fashion, in which the officers joined hands to sing 'Auld Lang Syne.' "The custom of joining hands arose, I believe, through it being necessary to hold each other up."[197] English

---

186 IWM 19680 PP White, letter from Donald Macleod, 26 January, 1916; IWM 8503 Byrom, memoir, p.1; Craig-Barr, *Home Service*, p.263; THM 2013-072 (S) Braes, memoir, pp.18-19; IWM 16335 Racine, memoir, pp.20-21; Addison-Smith, *10th Seaforths*, p.11; GHM PB3279 Matthews, James, diary, 31 December, 1914; GHM PB1699 'As we go up the line to death', pp.24-26; GHM PB1937 Dawson, letter to mother, 3 January, 1915; GHM PB107.1 Grant, diary, 1 January, 1915; GHM PB1892.3.18 McDonald, 'Uncle Harper's Duds,' pp.18-19; IWM 21092 McGregor, letter to wife Jen, n.d. [1 January, 1916]; Nicholson, *Behind the Lines*, pp.42-43; GHM PB3253 Gray, memoir.
187 IWM 114 Allen, letters to wife, 30, 31 December, 1915, 1 January, 1916; ASHM N-E1 Dalziel, diary, 31 December, 1914; ASHM N-E2 Hyslop, diary, 31 December, 1914, 1 January, 1915, 1 January, 1916; ASHM-E11 Bowie, diary, 31 December, 1916; IWM 11144 MacKay, diary, 31 December, 1916 to 1 January, 1917; IWM 11126 Liddell, diary, 31 December, 1914, 1 January, 1915; IWM 15460 Chandler, letter to Marjorie Raimes, 1 January, 1915; IWM 8192 Lawson, letter to sister Bessie, 14 January, 1917; Bartholomew, *George Hugh Freeland Bartholomew*, p.45; THM Seaforths S796(R) Cartmell, memoir; THM Seaforths 05-87 Hope, diary, 31 December, 1914 to 2 January, 1915; IWM Books, Brooke, 'Wait for it,' p.162; IWM 3834 Wrench, diary, pp.83-84, 31 December, 1916; IWM 12311 Mason-Macfarlane, memoir by David Mason-Macfarlane, pp.44-45; Peel & Macdonald, *6th Seaforth Highlanders*, p.17; THM Camerons 93-35 Welsh, memoirs, pp.14, 16; IWM 5821 Semple, letter to her from Pte Jock McLeod, 6 January, 1916; Macleod, *6th Camerons*, pp.29, 93; Craig-Brown, *Historical Records*, Vol.3, p.221; GHM PB375, Pailthorpe, memoir, p.38; GHM PB1639 Kemp, memoir, pp.11, 57 and Vol.2, p.8, narrative by Jock Lynn; GHM PB179 Marr, diary, 1 January, 1918; Mackenzie, *Sixth Gordons*, p.80; IWM 1659 Scammell, letter to mother and sister Violet, 4 January, 1918; Fennah, *Retaliation*, p.60; IWM 3460 Macmillan, diary, 31 December, 1915, 1 January, 1916; IWM Books Reid, 'Shoulder to Shoulder,' pp.111, 170, 221; Sutherland, *War Diary*, pp.56-57, 146-147; BWA Sempill Papers, letter from Lt.-Col G. Duff to Sempill, 4 January, 1916, letter from J.S.S. Ewing to Sempill, 22 December, 1915; BWA Laing, diary, 31 December, 1914; LC GS 1124 Moffat, diary, 31 December, 1914; Sotheby, *10th Argylls*, p.39.
188 ASHM N-E6 Gardiner, Capt. Alister, postcard home, 2 January, 1918.
189 IWM 7508 Wyllie, diary, 1 January, 1917, 29 December, 1917, 2, 5 January, 1918; LC GS 1027 Macleod, letter to mother, 6 January, 1916.
190 Webster, *Mesopotamia 1916-1917*, p.58, letter to mother, 1 January, 1917.
191 BWA Stewart, extract from letter of 4 January, 1919.
192 GHM PB1498 Hamilton, diary, 1 January, 1915.
193 ASHM N-E11 Bowie, diary, 31 December, 1918; IWM 3834 Wrench, diary, p.275, 1 January, 1919; Cluness, *Doing his bit*, p.66; IWM 6926 Dennis, memoir, p.291; GHM PB179 Marr, diary, 1 January, 1919; GHM PB3758 Shireffs, diary, 31 December, 1918; IWM 19680 White, letter to her from W. Weir, 31 December, 1918; Mackenzie, *Sixth Gordons*, p.187.
194 IWM 4586 Douglas, memoir, pp.1212-1213; Craig-Brown, *Historical Records*, Vol.3, pp.282-283.
195 IWM 7508 Wyllie, diary, 1 January, 1919.
196 LC GS 0972 Lloyd, A.B., letter to mother, 4 January, 1917; Fetherstonhaugh, *13th Battalion*, p.152, 312; Urquhart, *Canadian Scottish*, pp.116, 243; McEvoy & Finlay, *Seaforth Highlanders of Canada*, p.34.
197 IWM 13511 Macgregor, letter to father, 2 January, 1916.

388   Those Bloody Kilts

(or more sensitive or Teetotal) recruits might not necessarily enjoy the experience. S. Bradbury, a Yorkshire man serving in a draft of Camerons in training at Etaples, recalled his experiences at New Year 1917:

> I think New Year's Eve was one of the worst nights I ever spent. It was a nightmare. Half the fellows in my tent were drunk. Several fights took place and Scotch patriotic songs were sung and shouted until twelve o'clock struck when someone blew a call on a bugle. This seemed to be a sign for everyone to go mad for all raced out and commenced kicking up a most unearthly row, dancing, singing and fighting until about two o'clock in the morning when those who could get back to their tents did so and fell asleep, exhausted with their exertions, the remainder laying out on the sand dead drunk.[198]

He doesn't seem to have entered into the spirit of the occasion.

Another reinforcement of Scottish, and more particularly Highland, identity, was the holding of Highland Games both at home,[199] including in Ireland[200] and behind the lines,[201] even amongst 1st Seaforths in Mesopotamia,[202] 2nd Camerons in Salonika,[203] and 2nd Gordons in Italy.[204] Games were held at battalion, brigade or divisional level, or sometimes between battalions of the same regiment. They might feature competitions in piping and dancing, traditional field events, notably tossing the caber, putting the shot, throwing the hammer, and tug-of-war, and also novelty events, such as pillow fighting, tilting the bucket and wrestling on horseback. Perhaps the greatest event was that organised by the 3rd Canadian Infantry Brigade at Tinques on 6 July, 1918,[205] which we have already noted in relation to the pipes. All Highland units were invited to attend or send representatives, and as the 15th and 51st Divisions were in the neighbourhood there was a considerable gathering. The programme included not only piping, but also dancing competitions as well as wrestling, throwing the hammer, tossing the caber and tug-of-war.

---

198 IWM 2528 Bradbury, memoir, p.6.
199 Burns, *Once a Cameron Highlander*, pp.42, 145; Craig-Brown, *Historical Records*, Vol.3, pp.390, 391. 393; Vol.4, p.278.
200 Craig-Brown, *Historical Records*, Vol.3, p.396.
201 IWM 5525 Steven, letter to home, 30 July, 1915; ASHM War Diary 1/6th Battalion Argylls; IWM 3460 Macmillan, letter from Alex (Sandy) Macmillan to Tony, 19 May, 1917; IWM 8592 Macgregor, letter to wife Dulcie, 14 September, 1917; Maclean, *On Active Service*, Vol.1, p.73; Malcolm, *Argyllshire Highlanders*, p.39; THM Seaforths 89-26 Crask, letter to mother, date obscure, probably 6 June, 1915; *Lieut.-Colonel Robert Horn*, p.73; Craig-Brown, *Historical Records*, Vol.4, p.299; Burns, *Once a Cameron Highlander*, p.122; GHM PB375, Pailthorpe, memoir, pp.6-7; GHM PB1937 Dawson, letter to mother, 25 June, 1915; GHM PB2549 Leathem, diary, 11 October, 1916; Wauchope, *Black Watch*, Vol.2, pp.14, 312; IWM 16387 McLeod, diary, 2 December, 1918.
202 Webster, *Mesopotamia 1916-1917*, pp.21, 23, letters to mother 8, 16 November, 1916.
203 LC GS 1027 Macleod, letter to father, 17 April, 1916.
204 GHM PB1093 Brown, Capt. W.N., Photo album and scrap book, Programme of Events for the gathering of 24 September, 1918.
205 IWM 11144, MacKay, Lt. R.L., diary, 6 July, 1918; Craig-Brown, *Historical Records*, Vol.4, p.25; Fetherstonhaugh, *13th Battalion*, p.243; Urquhart, *Canadian Scottish*, pp.264-265; McEvoy & Finlay, *Seaforth Highlanders of Canada*, pp.104-105.

Identity. Men of the Liverpool Scottish enjoy a tug of war in Games at Tunbridge Wells.
(Author's collection)

Scottish identity was also reinforced by Highland dancing. As we have seen, before the war, Highland dancing was a requirement among both officers and young, nimble bandsmen. In the 16th Battalion C.E.F. (Canadian Scottish), dancing classes for officers were held on the voyage from Canada to England.[206] As with the pipes, however, as battalions suffered casualties amongst pipers and officers, it became necessary to revive dancing and give instruction to new officers and young pipers. Thus, after he had revived the pipes and drums of 1st Camerons. Lieutenant-Colonel Craig-Brown made a determined effort in 1916 to revive a dance-team.[207] In October, he started a dancing class for young officers "as I find a lot of them have no conception of reels or Strathspeys. They all seem keen enough to learn."[208] Dancing classes were being given to all officers in 1/7th Argylls in January and February, 1917.[209]

In his diary, Daniel McLeod, Pipe-Major in 4/5th Black Watch, records starting a dancing class on 5 February, 1917, evidently for the pipers, so that they could perform for the battalion. Thereafter references in his diary to dancing, presumably both practice and performance, are frequent through February to May, 1917. One of his willing dance pupils was Piper Donald Macleod.[210] After May, 1917, apart from two isolated references, there is no dancing in Pipe-Major McLeod's diary until after the Armistice, when practice and performance were evidently

---

206 Urquhart, *Canadian Scottish*, p.24.
207 IWM 1862 Craig-Brown, letter home, 9 June, 1916, & diary of same date; Craig-Brown, *Historical Records*, Vol.3, p.182.
208 IWM 1862 Craig-Brown, letter home, 23 October, 1916, to mother, 13 November, 1916, & diary 23, 30 October, 1916; Craig-Brown, *Historical Records*, Vol.3, p.212.
209 ASHM N-E2 Hyslop, diary, 8 January to 3 February, 1917.
210 IWM 19680 White, letter from Donald Macleod, 3 March, 1917.

taken up again, and on 2 December, 1918, he started dancing classes for the officers.[211] In 3rd Camerons at Ballyvonare Camp in Ireland, waiting for demobilisation after the Armistice, "lessons were also given to those wishing to learn or improve their Highland Dancing technique."[212] Even in prison camp at Burg bei Magdeburg, Lieutenant Ian Hamilton of 1st Gordons noted in January, 1915, "I have … been practising my reel steps a good deal and learning new ones. Davy and I dance every morning before Gym."[213]

Some dancing was done simply for enjoyment, for example at Christmas,[214] or to entertain the locals, either English spectators or visitors at home,[215] or villagers and townsfolk in Belgium or France,[216] or for the entertainment of French or Belgian troops.[217] Generally, dancing was done to the pipes, but some might be to squeeze-bags in billets,[218] or even a fiddle.[219] Dancing took place in the sergeants' mess,[220] and at officers' mess dinners, both at home,[221] and behind the lines,[222] including Salonika,[223] Constanza,[224] and occupied Turkey,[225] when reels or Strathspeys might be danced. This was especially so at St Andrew's Day dinners.[226] Dancing also took place in concerts.[227]. After the Armistice, in France and Belgium, there were formal dances, involving eightsome and foursome reels' and possibly country dances such as 'The Dashing White Sergeant' and 'Strip the Willow.' [228] As we have seen, there were also dancing competitions, which took place during Highland Games.[229]

211 IWM 16387 McLeod, diary, passim.
212 Burns, *Once a Cameron Highlander*, p.160.
213 GHM PB1498 Hamilton, diary, 7 January, 1915.
214 IWM 3460 Macmillan, diary, 25 December, 1914.
215 Craig-Barr, *Home Service*, p.266; Rule, *Students*, pp.10-11, 13, 33.
216 BWA Muir, Cpl J., diary, 31 July, 1915; David, *Mud and Bodies,* p.65; IWM Books Reid, 'Shoulder to Shoulder,' p.361; IWM 612 Gameson, memoirs, p.38.
217 GHM PB1706/2 Robertson, 'Diary' 27 July, 1916; Craig-Brown, *Historical Records*, Vol.3, p.233.
218 GHM PB242 Stansfield, letter home (extract), 13 July, 1915.
219 IWM 3834 Wrench, diary, pp.82-83, 25, 26 December, 1916.
220 BWA Hitchman, diary, 22 February, 2 July, 1915.
221 IWM 8592 Macgregor, letter to fiancée Dulcie Newling, 27 February, 1917.
222 ASHM N-E2 Hyslop, diary, 8 January to 3 February, 1917; THM Camerons 94-8 Mackay, 'Tell Them of Us,' letter from Ian Mackay to mother, 11 April, 1915. See also letter from William Mackay to mother of same date; IWM 1862 Craig-Brown, letter home, 22 October, 1916.
223 IWM 7508 Wyllie, diary, 1, 2 December, 1916, 26 December, 1917.
224 Ibid., 24, 26 December, 1918.
225 Ibid., 27 April, 1919.
226 Ibid., 1, 2 December, 1916; IWM 1862 Craig-Brown, letter home, 1 December, 1916 & diary, 30 November, 1916; Craig-Brown, *Historical Records*, Vol.3, pp.216, 238, 278.
227 BWA Gordon, 'diary,' 5 April, 1916; BWA Guthrie, letter to wife Crissie, 27 August, 1915; IWM Books Cooper, 'Domi Militaeque', fol p.74; IWM 12311 Mason-Macfarlane, memoir by David Mason-Macfarlane, p.29; GHM PB1937 Dawson, letter to mother, 7 March, 1915; Sommers, *Temporary Heroes*, p.73.
228 BWA Duke, letter to mother, 17 January, 1919; IWM 8592 Macgregor, letter to wife Dulcie, 27 January, 1919; LC GS 1635 Turing, memoir; GHM PB1892.3.1 Youngson, memoir, p.49.
229 IWM 8592 Macgregor, letters to wife Dulcie, 2, 3 February, 1919.

Conclusions

It is evident that the Highland soldier had a strong sense of identity, based on Regiment, battalion and Scottishness. Regimental and battalion identity was reinforced by the uniform and the pipes, but also by less tangible regimental history and tradition. There was considerable pride in regiment and battalion, with concern that achievements in battle should be recognised, which we recognise from pre-war experience, and a conscious effort to use these achievements to reinforce esprit de corps. Loyalty was expressed by a reluctance to be posted or drafted away from regiment or battalion, particularly the latter, where comrades were found. There was a generally healthy inter-regimental and inter-battalion rivalry. The building of esprit de corps was, however, compromised by constant change, while regimental and battalion loyalty was not absolute, with both soldiers and officers prepared to leave regiments or battalions in order to get to the front, to take or regularise a commission, to further promotion, to escape unhappy situations, to pursue their technical interest or spirit of adventure and, sometimes, to escape life in the trenches. Alongside regimental and battalion identity was a strong sense of Scottishness, although in the case of expatriate regiments, this could involve a complicated set of loyalties, with Canadians, for example, showing three-way loyalty, to Canada, Scotland and the Empire. This identity was particularly reinforced by the symbols and traditions of Scotland; the kilt, the pipes, St Andrew's cross, the old Scots songs, Highland games, Highland dancing, and the three primary Scottish festivals of Hogmanay, Burns' Night and St Andrew's Day. A minority were able to take pride in a specifically Highland, and sometimes Gaelic-speaking, heritage, while all could glory in the beautiful landscape of Scotland. The formation of four specifically Scottish divisions reinforced this sense of identity. The whole was sometimes accompanied by a certain disdain for the English, usually prejudiced, occasionally absurd, but generally harmless, the reflection of a strong national pride. Together, pride in regiment, battalion and Scottishness provided an exceptional basis for esprit de corps, unlikely to be matched elsewhere in the Army, except perhaps in the Guards.

14

Self-image and Reputation

> "I don't say that any soldier was better than the other and no-one was worse than the other."[1]

In the last chapter we demonstrated the strong sense of identity felt by Highland solders. In this chapter we consider their reputation and self-image, starting with an appreciation of what Highland soldiers thought about themselves, before considering how they were viewed by others and, in particular, how they were viewed by the enemy.

Self-image

Highland soldiers did not have a low opinion of themselves. Indeed, the notion of the Highland Scots as a 'martial race' seems sometimes to underpin their self-image. Coll MacDonald, chaplain to 8th Black Watch, who was a Highlander himself, wrote about the action of the 'true Highlanders' in the battalion at Passchendaele:

> I find our true Highlanders did well on the 12th ... I find that almost all the Gaelic men were killed or wounded. Ossian's lines remain true – they always went forth to the war and seldom returned. It was the same at Loos. The poor Highland lads gave themselves generously, and only a small remnant remains in regiments which were genuinely Highland in 1914 and early 1915. They have a greater pride of race than the Germans themselves, and once engaged they never falter till they fall or reach their objective. If only we had an army of them, all would be well. Much of the elan of the Canadians is due to their strong mixture of Highland blood, and the dash of the French is probably traceable in their Celtic ancestry.[2]

---

1 IWM 12678 Burns, transcription of interview.
2 BWA MacDonald, Coll, letter to wife Mary, 4 November, 1917. See also letter to wife Mary, 14 April, 1918.

Then, regarding the German March offensive, he writes; "Our Highlanders stood as of yore -remember not all who wear the kilt are Highlanders – and few with the Mac to their names remain."[3] And again, "If only we had plenty of kilties the map would read very differently."[4]

In relating the assumed martial superiority of the Highland soldiers to their Celtic blood, Macdonald's comments are blatantly racial. They use manifestly the language of the martial race, and are reflected for example in a poem by George Beattie, written in Mesopotamia in August, 1917, in praise of Sergeant Steele, V.C., which expresses confidence in the power of Scottish blood:

> You may sing of the prowess of Beowulf
> When Saxon and fiend-dragon met,
> But the boys in their kilts and their khaki
> Have the blood of the best in them yet[5]

A similar assumption of martial prowess is made by Major Norman McQueen in the foreword to the history of 10th Argylls, in which he claims that the men "were possessed of the love of battle for its own sake which is the heritage of the true Scotsman through the ages."[6] Here the connotation is not racial, but one of heritage. The distinction is real but arguably fine in terms of self-belief. Again the view is reflected in a poem by E.A. Mackintosh, 'A Creed' in which he draws on his Highland heritage to help define his purpose in the war;[7]

> This is the right of my race, the heritage won by my fathers,
> Theirs by the years of fighting, theirs by the price they paid,
> Making a son like them, careless of hell or heaven,
> A man that can look in the face of the gods and be not afraid.

Similarly, in his poem, 'Scotland the Brave,' Donald Robertson, 'The Kildary Bard,' depicts Scottish soldiers as the inheritors of the (not specifically Highland) traditions of Bruce and Wallace.[8] At the battle of Loos, in 5th Camerons, Sandy Morrison, a true Gael, is said to have taken his Highland heritage to heart and "elected that day to carry an axe instead of the ordinary rifle and bayonet. His dead body was found afterwards with the axe beside it, and around lay the bodies of three of the enemy bearing on them the wounds which he had dealt them with that terrible weapon."[9] Likewise, Private Jack Gunn, in 1/8th Argylls appears to identify with the image of the battle-loving Highland soldier, when he wrote to his pal from Bedford in April, 1915; "One thing I know. If we got within a few hundred yards of the Germans there's no officer in the world would stop us from a bayonet charge. We sure are a wild crowd."[10] Cameron

---

3   Ibid., letter to wife Mary, 30 March, 1918.
4   Ibid., letter to wife Mary, 18 April, 1918.
5   IWM 17561 PP Steele, Thomas, V.C., poem by Geo A Beattie, 'Sergeant Steele V.C.', 10 August, 1917.
6   Sotheby, *10th Argylls*, pp.xvii-xviii, foreword by Maj. Norman McQueen.
7   Mackintosh, *A Highland Regiment*, p.43.
8   Robertson, *Kildary Bard*.
9   McEwen, *Fifth Camerons*, p.47.
10 IWM 15990 Gunn, letters to brother-in-law, 16 April, 19 September, 1915.

Image. Soldiers of 8th Black Watch practice a bayonet attack at Bordon Camp, 1915. (IWM Q53939)

of Lochiel, commanding 5th Camerons, made use of the same self-image, when he addressed his companies on the eve of the battle of Loos, "reminding them that as in the old days there were few troops in Europe who could boast of having stood up to a Highland charge, so it was for them to prove on the morrow to the Germans that they, in these latter days, had not fallen in any way short of the fighting spirit of their ancestors."[11] By that time, having seen some service at the front, Jack Gunn took a less romantic view. "Pray God, we never make a charge, that is all I say, as it is too much like a sudden death for me. You don't charge men in these days – you charge machine guns, firing 600 rounds a minute."[12]

Given the inheritance of such views, it is perhaps unsurprising that Highland soldiers had a fine conceit of themselves. Lieutenant Bryden McKinnell, in the Liverpool Scottish, already had an elevated view of the status of his battalion when he wrote in his diary on 4 November, 1914, "If the London Scottish and if we ourselves get into it shortly, which we all hope (and everyone here thinks we will), the result I think will do more for recruiting in Britain than anything else."[13] George Ramage observed that when 1st Gordons marched through Vlamertinghe on 13 June, 1915, "Indians and English Tommies billeted there turned out to greet us. The English have a high opinion of the Jocks as fighters evidently."[14] Howard Panton of 6th Camerons wrote, "It was our Brigade that took Loos and Hill 70 and our Division which held it. All Scotch and proud of it."[15] Jock McLeod in 5th Camerons could write in January, 1916, "Fritz only funks two things – kilties and Canadians!"[16] In July, 1917, Dave Skinner, in 4/5th Black Watch wrote to Mrs White, a friend he had made while stationed in Yorkshire, from 39th Divisional Reinforcement Camp, where he observed the variety of tartans:

> Being Scotch myself, it's hardly for me to say so, but it would do your heart good to see them. Old Scotia's Sons, bronzed and strong, full of life & vigour and daft on Football. Their morale is very high. They talk of the Aleman disdainfully and any probable attacking

---

11   McEwen, *Fifth Camerons*, p.46.
12   IWM 15990 PP Gunn, letters to brother-in-law, 16 April, 19 September, 1915.
13   McKinnell, *Diary*, p.3, 4 November, 1914.
14   NLS MS 944 Ramage, diary, 13 June, 1915.
15   IWM 11241 Panton, letter to brother Tom, 29 September, 1915.
16   IWM 5821 Semple, letter from Pte Jock McLeod, 23 April, 1916.

doesn't seem to worry them one whit. I'd back the pick of them against Caesar's Champions of Old far less the present-day Huns.

But perhaps then remembering he was writing to Yorkshire, he added, "but don't let's forget the lads of the Rose. They're all good lads & true and guid luck tae them and all of us."[17] Robert Dawson in 1/4th Gordons wrote to his mother in September, 1917: "Of course, there's no one to come up to the Scotch, I have found that out here and we have a splendid opportunity of educating ourselves in that respect for we have representatives of all countries here. There are no doubt some fine Englishman but give me the Scotsman every time."[18] A poem written in May, 1918, states proudly,

> When a' the bitter fechtin's done,
> An tales o' hoo the war was won
> Are written clear on history's page,
> An handed doon frae age tae age
> What is the name that nane daur mock?
> Jock.[19]

Amidst the bombast, there are occasional flashes of realism. Major Ernest Craig-Brown, second-in-command of 1st Camerons, felt that the Germans had got the better of them at Nonne-Boschen on 11 November, 1914. "To be quite candid the Germans got the better of us on the 11th & the Scot Gds, Camerons & B. Watch did not come out of the ordeal as creditably as we would wish." In an account of the action, in which the battalion was taken by surprise by a German attack, he describes his company, "hurriedly scrambling out of their trenches both in the firing line & in the support & following the Scots Guards in a confused & undisciplined crowd. I shouted to them to turn & open fire, but I might just as well have shouted to the winds."[20]

Perhaps the greatest hyperbolae surrounded the reputation of 51st Highland Division. Jim Elliott, who served in 9th Royal Scots, wrote in the 1930's that when his battalion joined 51st Division (on 1st March, 1916) it was "even then called the 1st Division of Storm troops."[21] This is nonsense. 51st Division did not really begin to make its reputation until Beaumont-Hamel on 13 November, 1916. In that battle, although it did not take its final objectives, the Division showed great resolution, and following earlier disappointments on the Somme, at last had an achievement of which it could feel proud. Captain Youngson, in 5th Gordons, records a poem written after Beaumont-Hamel;

> When the war was declared, the Chief o' the Huns
> thocht he'd march across France wi' his men and his guns.

---

17 IWM 19680 White, letter from David Skinner, 12 July, 1917.
18 GHM PB1937 Dawson, letter to mother, 23 September, 1917.
19 GHM PB1253 Wood, autograph album.
20 IWM 1862 Craig-Brown, letter home 14 November, 1914, and account of the action at Nonne-Boschen, written 2 November, 1915.
21 IWM 5912 PP Elliott, transcript of letter written 1930's.

> But he made in his plans an unlucky omission.
> He didna' tak' coont o' the Hielan' Division.[22]

Arthur Wrench of 1/4th Seaforths took a legitimate pride in the achievement, but his dismissal of the role of other troops is less than generous. "What we would all like to know is where are all those British troops about that we read so much about in the papers?" In fact, 63rd Royal Naval Division, for example, were operating on the right flank of 51st Division, with equal or greater success at Beaucourt. However, for Wrench, Beaumont-Hamel was "the key position to the whole of the Somme," and "we are wondering what the papers will have to say about it this time in praise of the division."[23] The battle was undoubtedly a watershed in self-perception. John Gammell was Brigade Signalling Officer in 153rd Brigade, 51st (Highland) Division. Interviewed many years later by his son-in-law, he observed that, by the time of the German offensive of 1918, "we were 'Haig's darlings.' you see ... Because before Beaumont Hamel in 1916, on the Somme, we were 'Harper's Duds,' no good. But after Beaumont Hamel we became 'Haig's Darlings'.... At Beaumont Hamel ... we made our name as a fighting division."[24] Likewise, when Frank Brooke re-joined his battalion, 1/4th Seaforths, in mid-1917, after recovering from a wound, he found that the division (51st Highland) had changed.

> The division was favoured of the Heid Yins, Beaumont Hamel and Vimy Ridge had established a reputation – we were 'next to the Guards on the Kaiser's Black List,' we were now 'Harper's devils' or 'Hun-destroyers,' a play upon our initials 51st Highland Division. Anything less devilish or destructable than most of my comrades was never seen. Nevertheless 'we' were a 'proud division.'... We were now 'storm troops,' and must expect many moves and stunts ... we were attackers, and in future, sudden deaths and ghastly wounds would be our portion.[25]

But to what extent was this feeling simply self-image? There seems no doubt that the relative success of 51st Division at Beaumont-Hamel was exploited by its commanders to build morale in a division which had not enjoyed success earlier on the Somme. Thus, a holiday with sports and celebratory dinners was decreed in the division on the first anniversary of the battle.[26] Rightly or wrongly, the reputation of the division, amongst Highland soldiers anyway, soared. Only two months after the battle, Hugh Boustead (in 9th Division) stated in January, 1917, that "it is the finest division in the British Army at the present time,"[27] while according to Coll Macdonald (also in 9th Division), writing after Cambrai, 51st Division was "the finest Division in the British Army."[28] Whether or not these accolades were justified, hard times still lay ahead. On 23 March, 1918, in 154rd Brigade Headquarters, Arthur Wrench noted huge losses in 51st

---

22 GHM PB1892.3.1 Youngson, memoir, pp.26-27.
23 IWM 3834 Wrench, diary, pp.73-74, 18, 19 November, 1916.
24 LC Transcripts Gammell, transcript of conversation between John Richard Gammell, aged 90, and his son-in-law Michael Wilson.
25 IWM Books Brooke, 'Wait for it,' pp.217-218.
26 IWM 3834 Wrench, diary, p.167, 13 November, 1917; Peel & Macdonald, *6thSeaforth Highlanders*, p.52; GHM PB583 McKinnon, memoir, pp.79-80; GHM PB234 Smith, diary, 13 November, 1917.
27 GHM PB18 Boustead, letter to mother, 5 January, 1917.
28 BWA MacDonald, Coll, letter to wife Mary, 29 November, 1917.

Division during the German offensive. "The Germans have not yet broken our line tho', and it might seem that the Highland Division is hanging on, as it were, to the very last shreds of its reputation."[29]

It is unsurprising that soldiers who were so sensitive about their reputation should find themselves at odds with the press. On occasion this was simply because of the ridiculous exaggerations in the newspapers. We have already seen, for example, Douglas Wilson's scathing comments on inaccurate reporting by Philip Gibbs of his battalion's attack at Meteren in July 1918. There are other examples. Despite his earlier bombast, Bryden McKinnell of the Liverpool Scottish found the men of the London Scottish to be amused by the exaggerated depictions of their actions in the papers.[30] And Captain Claud Low, in 1st London Scottish, showed remarkable understanding when he wrote in December, 1914;

> Illustrated papers continue to show brilliant pictures of this Regiment & now that I am here it is possible to understand the feelings of resentment which not only other regiments have but the London Scottish have against all this advertisement. It is bad for us, for although we have lost between 500 & 600, other Regiments have lost considerably more & done magnificent work.[31]

Similarly, in March, 1915, George Murray, in 1/4th Seaforths, was amused by the tendency of the *Ross-shire Journal* to exaggerate the role of his own battalion. "To read it, you would think that the 4th Seaforths were holding the whole line themselves, & we have many a laugh over it."[32] And two days later, he complained, "I see that the North Country papers are nothing else but 4th Seaforths & 4th Camerons. There is no word about the Regular Battalions who did practically all the work."[33] Douglas Gillespie, in 2nd Argylls, writing in May, 1915, was likewise highly critical of the newspapers.

> I have just been looking at a full-page photo in an illustrated weekly, with stirring title, 'How three encountered fifty and prevailed,' and a footnote describing their gallant deeds in detail. The dauntless three belong to this regiment, but we were a little puzzled, because we have never been at la Bassee, where their exploit took place. A closer inspection showed that the trees were in full leaf, and that the men were wearing spats and hose-tops, which we have long since abandoned for general use. Finally, someone recognised the sergeant as our shoemaker sergeant, and his companions as two men from our second-line transport. They are usually at least three miles from the trenches, and the whole story is a lie from beginning to end, without a shadow of truth in it. It makes one distrust all newspapers more than ever, to catch them out like that. The photo must have been taken somewhere on the retreat last year.[34]

---

29 IWM 3834 Wrench, diary, p.184, 23 March, 1918.
30 McKinnell, *Diary*, p.11, 20 November, 1914.
31 IWM 6702 Low, letter to wife Noanie, 15 December, 1914.
32 THM Seaforths 81-180 Murray, letters to sister Kate, 7 March, 1915.
33 Ibid., letters to sister Alex, 9 March, 1915.
34 Gillespie, *Letters from Flanders*, p.147, letter home, 12 May, 1915.

Such modesty is refreshing. Much more frequent were complaints that the newspapers were failing to give appropriate (or perhaps more than appropriate) credit to the Highland troops. William Newton joined the Gordon Highlanders aged about 15, even though he was not Scottish and was born in Torquay.

> On one occasion there was a picture paper called the 'Daily Graphic' which came out … and right at the centre of this particular paper was a picture of the London Fusiliers making a bayonet charge at Neuve Chapelle. However, they said. 'Have a look at this picture.' I had a look at it … 'It doesn't show the Scotsmen keeping the Germans heads down.'[35]

John Bowie, in 11th Argylls, was scathing about the newspaper coverage of Loos. "The papers arrived a few days after; never mentioning the Scots and headed – HOW THE GUARDS TOOK HILL 70."[36] Johnnie Wood, an officer with 10th Gordons, who was present at Loos, resented the plaudits given to other divisions, while "the people who did take and hold Loos and Hill 70 are scarcely heard of. It was the 44th Brigade of the 15th Divn which took both and not another soul had a hand in it."[37] A little earlier he had written, "Some of the accounts of Loos are awful piffle … I saw in an illustrated paper some sketches etc. of the taking of Loos and there was not a kilt in the lot."[38] There was particular resentment in 6th Camerons against "that blighter Beach Thomas," a reporter for the 'Daily Mail,' for attributing the capture of Monchy-le-Preux (during the battle of Arras) to English troops and claiming "the Scotch troops get too much credit for their work." "He's a bloomin' twister, that man."[39] In fact, on this occasion the credit was shared. Beach Thomas however became something of a bete noir amongst Highland troops.[40]

There was resentment when the press lauded the achievements of Welsh, English, Irish or even Portuguese troops, rather than the Scottish troops involved, and a feeling that this was unfairly done to help sustain morale.[41] Henry Pelham Burn, commanding 152nd Brigade in 51st Division wrote to his mother shortly after the start of Third Ypres:

> I see that all the correspondents are talking about Welshmen & Englishmen in their accounts of the battle but it was the 51st Highland Division that did best. It is always the indifferent & bad troops that get all the kudos to build them up & little mention is made of those that consistently do well. The Welshmen this time did well enough though – sandwiched in between Guards & Highlanders.[42]

---

35   IWM 24855 Newton, interview.
36   ASHM-E11 Bowie, diary.
37   NLS, Acc.12729, Wood, letter to brother Willie, 9 November, 1915.
38   Ibid., letter to brother Willie, 16 October, 1915.
39   LC GS 0262 Campbell, diary, 17 April, 1917; IWM 4370 Christison, memoir, p.52.
40   BWA MacDonald, Coll, letter to wife Mary, 22 September, 1917; IWM 3834 Wrench, diary, p.239, 9 September, 1918.
41   IWM 430 Wimberley, memoir, p.40; David, *Mud and Bodies,* p.102; Sutherland, *War Diary,* p.165.
42   GHM PB3309 Pelham Burn, letter to mother, 3 August, 1917.

It is a moot point whether this resentment was born of genuine discrimination in the press, or derived from an inherent assumption amongst the Highland troops that they should routinely deserve the bulk of the praise. At times there was probably an element of both.

Another side of Scottish identity was the frequent, though not universal, tendency to show disdain for English soldiers. Some of this may have been merited, if the English battalions or divisions supporting or flanking the Highland battalions failed to prove sufficiently resilient; on other occasions the English may have been useful scapegoats. Either way, the rapid descent into nationalistic scorn, a strong counterpart of Scottish pride, is not the most endearing feature of Scottish identity. Soldiers of 14th Argylls, for example, were critical of the standard of the English battalions with which they had to train at home.[43] "I saw a squad of Surreys," wrote Peter McGregor. "My word, they did look like Bill Sykes, and loafers and street-corner hawkers. Each man capable of anything in the way of low crime." There was some disdain for the intelligence of the English recruits. John Cooper of the Black Watch found himself in the autumn of 1917 detached assisting in trench training at Etaples. "For stupidity," he wrote, "some of these English recruits would be hard to beat."[44] Jock Macleod, an officer of 2nd Camerons, temporarily employed as Machine Gun Instructor at the base in Salonika, noted that, "The majority of my class for M.G. Instruction are Englishmen who have joined the Army in the last year. They are very 'slow in the uptak',' in comparison with the Scotsmen who formed my M.G. Section in the 2nd Camerons."[45] Highland soldiers might also feel that the English battalions sometimes could not match them for smartness. When John Cooper was part of the 12th Argylls in Constantinople in 1919, he claimed, "Altogether we were the tidiest soldiers in the city: some of the English battalions permitted their men to run about in a fashion which would not have been tolerated with us."[46]

Much more serious was a tendency to accuse English troops of letting the Highland troops down. This was especially so at Loos,[47] where "these damned English Regts lost all we had gained and after taking part of it again a second time for them they lost it again."[48] During Third Ypres, John Bowie claims that 11th Argylls were let down on their left flank by the Border Regiment.[49] In March, 1918, John Cooper of 1/6th Black Watch was taken prisoner when his position was over-run during the German offensive. "The general impression amongst us was that we had been badly let down by the 6th Division which was on our left. The enemy over-ran the 6th Division, and then came in on our left."[50] 5th Camerons felt during the same offensive that they had been let down by the "Twenty-Worst" Division on their flank.[51] Sergeant Dugald MacIntyre also complained in 1918 about English battalions retiring on the flank of

---

43   IWM 8192 Lawson, letter to sister Bessie, postmark 4 March, 1916; IWM 21092 McGregor, letter to wife Jen, 2 October, 1915, 6. 10, 16, 30 January, 6 May, 1916.
44   IWM Books Cooper, 'Domi Militaeque', p.177.
45   LC GS 1027 Macleod, letter to mother, 27 March, 1917.
46   IWM Books Cooper, 'Domi Militaeque', p.308.
47   ASHM-E11 Bowie, diary; LC WF Recollections A9 Andrew, I.G., memoir; IWM 11241 Panton, letter to brother Tom, 29 September, 1915; IWM 11923 Sutherland, letter to father, c. October, 1915.
48   BWA Sempill Papers, letter from J S S Ewing to Sempill, 1 October, 1915.
49   ASHM-E11 Bowie, diary, 31 July, 2 August, 1917.
50   IWM Books Cooper, 'Domi Militaeque', p.223.
51   LC GS 1761 Wilson, memoir, pp.11-11A.

2nd Argylls.[52] Major Charles Murray, serving with the South African Field Ambulance is likewise scathing about the performance of English troops during the German offensive:[53]

> This battle has shown, what I have always feared, but never yet liked to express, and that is that English troops have no longer any real gut. Never have Scottish or Colonial troops given in like the English, and I feel very little reliance can ever be placed in them again. All through the war it is the Scottish first and latterly the colonial troops that have done all the fighting. Our failures in every case have been due to the cowardice of the English troops. Our Press have lauded up their failures and condoned their lack of patriotism and courage by fulsome praise of paltry incidents, and feeble excuses.

It appears that the Germans even tried to exploit anti-English sentiment amongst the soldiers of 51st Division. On 20th May, 1916, "the Germans floated over a number of red paper balloons and attached to them were papers printed in English and containing accounts of the Irish rebellion; they also said that the English were making the Scotch and Irish do all the fighting while they looked on."[54] At least as far as the Scots were concerned, they had miscalculated.

For even Highland soldiers could sometimes appreciate the efforts of their English comrades. 1/4th Gordons joined 8th Brigade in 3rd Division in February, 1915. Captain McKinnon recorded: "The 8th Brigade consisted of the 1st Gordons, 2nd Royal Scots, 2nd Suffolks and 4th Middlesex, and a fine lot they were. We soon became excellent friends with them, and they were at all times most helpful and good to us." In July, at Brandhoek, they found themselves next to the 4th Middlesex.

> Our men were always very friendly with them, one of the chief bonds of friendship at this time being the mysterious games of 'Crown and Anchor' and 'House.' I am afraid that our fellows lost a good deal when they started these games, though I know in later days that they could hold their own with anyone. Still it passed the time pleasantly.[55]

James Anderson, Alexander Rule and Norman Down, all of 1/4th Gordons, record the friendly introduction to the trenches provided by 2nd Suffolks,[56] while Cecil Harper notes the same courtesy provided to 10th Gordons by the men of 7th Londons.[57] Ian Andrew was wounded with 6th Camerons at Loos.

> As my wounds were being attended to in a dressing-station at Philosophe, I heard the sound of a regimental band approaching and limped to the door. Up the street came a battalion of the Grenadier Guards, marching as no other troops in the world could march,

---

52 ASHM N-E11 MacIntyre, Sgt Dugald, undated letter (1918) extracted from Black, Nancy, *From a Hollow on the Hill* (1999).
53 LC GS 1153 Murray, diary, 24, 25, 29 March, 10, 12, 16 April, 2 May, 1918.
54 ASHM N-E2 Hyslop, diary, 20 May, 1916.
55 GHM PB583 McKinnon, memoir, p.27.
56 GHM PB2644 Anderson, letter to father, n.d.; Rule, *Students under Arms*, p.64; Sommers, *Temporary Heroes*, p.23.
57 IWM 7593 Harper, memoir, p.29.

immaculately turned out, the finished product of years of training and centuries of military tradition. With a sigh of mingled admiration and relief, I re-entered the dressing station, still in my tattered shirt. I felt I could leave the situation to them – there was no fear of the German counter-attack breaking through now.[58]

Indeed, an extraordinary rejoinder to nationalistic hubris is provided by Graham Hutchison, a pre-war regular officer of the Argylls:

> Of the first thirty-three Divisions, all but five were essentially English. In reading accounts of battle, especially in the contemporary press of the period, one is inclined to form the view that the Highland, Welch and Irish soldiers were dominant in these armies. But this was not so. English soldiers, patient, well disciplined, stubborn in defence, courageous in attack, fought and won the battles on the Western Front. The Scots, Irish, and Welch, Australians, Canadians, and the glorious South African Brigade contributed their part. Nevertheless, in terms of battle tactics, and in numbers of men, the trumpetings in the Press were out of all proportion to the weight of those not English in the scales.[59]

And none of the point-scoring mattered to Donald Robertson, the Kildary Bard, as he expresses clearly in his poem, 'Scotch or English?'

> Scotch or English, does it matter?
> Aren't we brothers, one and all?
> Serving 'neath the same old banner,
> Joining hands to stand or fall.
>
> Scotch or English, we're together,
> Joy or sorrow, come what may.
> We're united, we are brothers,
> Linked together in the fray
>
> Scotch or English, we are brothers,
> Joining hands to win or die.[60]

Perhaps on this topic, we should leave the last word to Robert Burns, who served in 7th Camerons. Interviewed in 1998, he said, "I was just an ordinary soldier, and we did as we were told. I don't say that any soldier was better than the other and no-one was worse than the other. In uniform out there everyone was a hero in my opinion."[61]

Whatever the truth of the matter, there was a real perception in the Highland battalions that they were used disproportionately in the fighting, for the toughest jobs.[62] This belief was no

---

58 LC WF Recollections A9 Andrew, memoir.
59 Hutchison, *Warrior*, p.92.
60 Robertson, *Kildary Bard*.
61 IWM 12678 Burns, transcription of interview.
62 IWM 860 Mabbott, interview; IWM 18836 Kerridge, interview.

doubt to some extent engendered by their own belief in their own worth, but it also contributed to that pride, and was something of a counterpart to disdain for the English.

Astonishingly, this perception was in vogue as early as January, 1915, when Lieutenant Lionel Sotheby, attached to the Black Watch, met a fellow of the Seaforths at base camp, who told him "it was as good as signing your death warrant" to join the Highland regiments, "as they were practically in all the worst fighting & were always used for reinforcements."[63] It can hardly have been true so early, and this statement underlines the element of auto-suggestion in the perception. It is seen again in April, 1915, when George Ramage noted at the base camp at Rouen, "Soldiers here tell me that the Gordons are the fighting regiment, always in the thick of the slaughter."[64] And again in May, 1915, when Gordon Crask, with 3/4th Seaforths, wrote to his mother from Dingwall, "The Scotch regiments are collecting D.C.M.'s and D.S.O.'s as a habit, and seem to be in the thick of everything."[65] And it is seen once more in February, 1916. At that date 1st London Scottish were transferred from the 1st Division to the 56th (London Territorial) Division. Interviewed in 1988, Stewart Jordan felt that, in making the move "we became the senior regiment, well, we became what we called the Black Watch of the 56th Division. We were the only Scottish one in it, you see, and I think we had some of the rough bits to do. We were the Scottish of the 56th Division."[66] At about the same time, Peter McGregor, in training with 14th Argylls at Witley Camp, wrote, "We all know pretty well what we will get to do when we go to the front; the worst work, the most dangerous I mean. If you notice the Highlanders get all the work; are put in at every point to stiffen the English chaps."[67] A little later, in April, 1916, Jock McLeod of 5th Camerons, could write: "Will seems to be enjoying the Army life A1 *as yet*! … At least he wasn't fool enough to join a Highland Regt! The short cut to sudden death!"[68] It seems likely that the perception, probably initially self-generated, had been reinforced by the disproportionate use of Highland troops at Loos. By 1917, the year of Arras, Passchendaele and Cambrai, there was a clear perception amongst Highland troops that they were being deliberately used as 'storm-troops,' or to be sent in to plug the gap in dangerous situations.[69] William Kemp felt that this was also true of 15th Division during the 1918 German offensive.[70]

The assertion that Highland battalions were used disproportionately as 'storm troops' has been accepted by, for example Campbell and Green.[71] We will not be making any attempt here to validate or disprove the assertion, for such comparative work lies outside the scope of

63 LC GS 1507 Sotheby, diary, 6 January, 1915.
64 NLS MS 944 Ramage, diary, 16 April, 1915.
65 THM Seaforths 89-26 Crask, letter to mother, 18 May, 1915.
66 IWM 10391 Jordan, interview.
67 IWM 21092 McGregor, letter to wife Jen, 16 January, 1916.
68 IWM 5821 Semple, Letter from Pte Jock McLeod, 23 April, 1916 .
69 BWA MacDonald, Coll, letters to wife Mary, 17 June, 24 September, 1917; THM Camerons 97-22 Russell, memoirs, pp.175-275, pp.224-225; IWM 13593 PP Jolly, W., letter to mother, 19 April, 1917; Macleod, *6th Camerons*, p.86; Craig-Brown, *Historical Records*, Vol.4, p.318; LC GS 0588 Fraser, letter to father, 21 July, 1917; LC Middlebrook Somme 1918 Crowder, W.H., manuscript memoir, written 1976; GHM PB1937 Dawson, letter to mother, 23 September, 1917; GHM PB3309 Pelham Burn, letter to mother, 4 March, 1918.
70 GHM PB1639 Kemp, memoir, Vol.2, p.32.
71 Campbell & Green, *Can't shoot a man with a cold*, p.14.

this study. What is important here is to recognise the common belief that it was true, and the sustenance this gave to the self-image and pride of the Highland soldier.

To see ourselves as others see us

Self-praise is one thing; praise from others is another. In this respect the Highlanders seem to have been well enough regarded. 1/6th Gordons, for example, were singled out for praise by their brigade and divisional commanders after Neuve Chapelle, largely because of their determined gallantry as a Territorial battalion, the Terriers as a whole still being largely unproven in battle, despite their arrival in theatre from November, 1914. Sir John French added his plaudits when he visited the Brigade on 20 April, 1915.[72] Likewise, French spoke to 6th Camerons after Loos, and was generous with his praise, especially as they were fresh to soldiering as New Army soldiers.[73] Before the German offensive in 1918, 15th Division held the critical ground covering Arras. After the Germans had been held, the Corps Commander, Sir Charles Fergusson, sent a message to Major-General Reed, V.C., commanding the division: "I knew you could be relied on to stick it out. Well done! There are fresh troops in support of you now, but I want the honour of holding Arras to be yours alone."[74] The Highlanders were convinced too that they especially were loved by the Canadians. Such at least was the opinion of Arthur Wrench and Lieutenant Scott Ferguson, both in 1/4th Seaforths, and Jock McLeod in 5th Camerons.[75] Captain Pailthorpe felt also that the Gordons had the respect of the Australians. On their march out after their abortive attack next to High Wood on 20 July,

> Just after dawn we passed through a camp occupied by Australian troops. I suppose the Battalion looked pretty haggard and tired. The Australians poured out of their bivouacs to look at the Jocks and stood respectfully to attention as the Battalion went through. I thought this unrehearsed compliment on their part just after reveille by men not over lavish with ceremonial was indeed testimony to the Gordons.[76]

15th Division won admiration from the French for their action at Buzancy on 28 July, 1918, when they were detached to assist the French Army with operations on the Marne.[77] There, they were relieved by the French 17th Division under General Gassoins, who wrote to Major-General Reed, V.C., commanding 15th Division as follows:

---

72 Mackenzie, *Sixth Gordons*, pp.50-51, 56-57.
73 IWM 6933 Moir, letter from unidentified soldier about the battle of Loos, September, 1915; IWM 11241 Panton, letter to brother Tom, 29 September, 1915.
74 Macleod, *6th Camerons*, p.102.
75 LC GS 0552 Ferguson, letter to mother, 8 May, 1918; IWM 3834 Wrench, diary, pp.265-266, 13 November, 1918; IWM 5821 Semple, letter from Pte Jock McLeod, 24 January, 1916.
76 GHM PB375, Pailthorpe, memoir, p.22.
77 Stewart & Buchan, *Fifteenth Division*, pp.256-259; Macleod, *6th Camerons*, pp.112-115; Buchanan-Smith, 'The Gordon Highlanders Loos and Buzancy', pp.12-13; ASHM-E11 Bowie, diary, 8 August, 1918.

> I found at Buzancy the traces, still fresh, of the exploits of your Scottish soldiers, and the officers of my staff were able to see clearly what hard fighting you had had to gain possession of the village, and above all, of the park. Wishing to leave on the spot some lasting tribute to the bravery of your Scottish soldiers, I entrusted to one of my officers the task of erecting there, with the material at hand, a small monument emblematic of the homage and admiration of my divisions for yours, and on which are inscribed thistles and roses and, beneath, the words:
>
> 'Here the noble thistle of Scotland will
> flourish forever among the roses of France.'
>
> This monument was erected on the highest point of the plateau where we found the body of the Scottish soldier who had advanced the furthest on 28 July.

Much later, on 26 January, 1919, 45th Brigade of 15th Division took part in the victory parade in Brussels.

> As the massed pipers of the Scottish Division approached the saluting base, a roar of cheering broke from the half-frozen onlookers. In a place of honour, opposite His Majesty the King of the Belgians, stood a small group of French officers, and as the pipers approached, one heard cries of 'Les Ecossais'; and a few seconds later, clear above the cheers of the crowd, came a shout from the French officers, 'The Highlanders, la Division de Buzancy!'[78]

Perhaps the greatest tribute paid was from General Maxse, who in 1917 sent 51st Highland Division an extraordinary message, which does indeed suggest that it was well-viewed by the High Command;

> What has struck me most is the thoroughness of the organisation within the Division, and the fact that all usual war problems have been thought out beforehand, discussed in detail, and are embodied in simple doctrines well known to all ranks. The result is the Division always fights with gallantry, and can be depended on to carry out any reasonable task which may be allotted to it in any battle. For this reason, I venture to place it among the three best fighting Divisions I have met in France during the past three years.[79]

What is interesting about this message is that it does not rest on intangible elements of esprit de corps or morale, or on the character of the Highland soldier, but on the Division's organisation for war. None of the elements he singles out for praise are potentially unique to a Highland division.

There is some suggestion that the reputation of the Highland soldier may have led them to be used on occasion to maintain discipline. Shortly after disembarking at Salonika with 2nd Camerons, Jock Macleod reported:

---

78 Stewart & Buchan, *Fifteenth Division*, pp.280-281; Macleod, *6th Camerons*, pp.127-128.
79 GHM PB1892.3.18 McDonald, 'Uncle Harper's Duds,' p.105.

> This Battalion was chosen from the whole of the Salonika force for the purpose of providing guards for all the British governmental depots in the town. The O.C. Base asked for the best-disciplined, smartest, and most alert battalion. They chose us. The reasons they had to have so good a battalion was first to impress the Greeks; second because whenever the British put up a sentry post the Greeks put up a drinking booth and there was much trouble with all previous guards. It is some compliment to be chosen but it is very hard work.[80]

Then, after the Armistice, 2nd Argylls were sent to Le Havre, and the Glasgow Highlanders were sent to Rouxmesnil Camp on the outskirts of Dieppe in case of mutiny among restless soldiers awaiting demobilisation. The Argylls had to break up a 'Crown and Anchor' school at Le Havre. Otherwise, neither battalion needed to get involved in what might have been very unpleasant duties.[81]

We have seen that the Highland soldier was not short of self-esteem, but while much of his reputation may have been self-generated, he did succeed in winning serious plaudits from both his allies and the higher command. However, the reputation of a soldier rests most solidly on the opinion of his enemies. What did the Germans really think of the Highlanders? Was there a genuine fear? or was German fear simply imagined; another feature of the Highlander's penchant for nationalistic hubris? Here it must be admitted that the real answer to this question does not lie in the accounts by the Highlanders themselves, which form the bedrock of this study, but in the German archives, which have not been examined by this writer. Consequently, any investigation of the question here must be unbalanced, limited in scope and cautious in reaching conclusions.

There are of course a number of statements by Highland soldiers which express their belief that the Germans were afraid of them, without providing any supporting evidence. For example, Andrew Anderson, a pre-war regular N.C.O. who served with 1st Camerons at the front, between August, 1914 and being wounded at Gheluvelt on 29 October, 1914, felt that "The kilt is a real morale … breaker as far as the enemy is concerned. The Highlanders proved in this war, as their forefathers did before them, to be dour, skilful fighters. They put the fear of death into many a German when on patrol or when charging over the top with bayonets fixed."[82] And Peter McGregor, in training at Witley Camp with 14th Argylls, wrote in January, 1916; "the Huns don't like the Highlanders. In fact, they fly whenever they see the kilts, and finish them off. They never take a Scottie prisoner. They finish him off."[83]

Anderson does however support his statement by claiming that this fear was why the Germans called the Highlanders "Ladies from Hell."[84] There are a number of references to this alleged German term, although its origin is uncertain, and it did not of course necessarily denote fear; it might equally have been intended to express ridicule. It does seem though that it was genuinely used by some Germans. Thus, in May, 1915, Captain Claud Low, in 1st London Scottish, wrote, "The French Company I relieved captured a German scout in the corn before our arrival

---

80 LC GS 1027 Macleod, letter to mother, 21 December, 1915.
81 LC GS 0030 Anderson, transcript of interview. See also IWM 5251 Anderson, interview. See also IWM 10414 McGregor, interview; IWM Books Reid, 'Shoulder to Shoulder,' p.363.
82 THM Camerons 89-44 Anderson, memoir, p.25.
83 IWM 21092 McGregor, letter to wife Jen, 2 January, 1916. See also: GHM PB3253 Gray, papers.
84 THM Camerons 89-44 Anderson, memoir, p.25.

& found on him a picture of abuse relating to ourselves. We were described as 'WOMEN OF HELL.'"[85] If this is hard evidence for German use of the term, we still do not know either how widely it was used, or whether it denoted fear, ridicule or some other emotion. The term was, however, a gift for British propagandists, and we find various outpourings along the lines of a poem by Bernard Shadwell, entitled 'The Ladies fra' Hell,' which includes the lines;

> There are ladies on earth and in heaven as well,
> But the Germans must dance with the 'Ladies from Hell.'[86]

There is some evidence that the Germans disliked Highland troops. For example, according to John Bowie, in 1/8th Argylls, when 15th Division paraded in Brussels on 26 January, 1919, the Belgians told them that while under occupation, "the Germans always talked about enemy troops they never liked, the 'Scottish' above all. When a Scotchman went about Brussels as a prisoner of war, there was never a dourer or more harshly treated man."[87] This is third-hand information, but probably based on some modicum of fact.

Instances of alleged German respect, dislike or fear are reported from early in the war. Andrew Young was captured with 1st Gordons at Le Cateau in 1914. Afterwards, in a group of prisoners about 80 strong, at the town of Vervick, "We were marched round the town and paraded before the people, as the ferocious Schottlanders (Scotsmen), defeated in battle and now held in captivity. At the town's Green we were marched round in a circle about six times. Meanwhile a camera was clicking, and no doubt when the film reached Germany, we would show up about 500 strong."[88] This incident appears to demonstrate, if not fear or dislike, at least an awareness of the Highlanders' martial reputation, and therefore the propaganda value to be gained by exhibiting Highland prisoners. In August, 1915, Douglas Gillespie of 2nd Argylls wrote that, in their last trenches, the Germans "wanted to know if we were the Black Watch; they are very frightened of the Black Watch, since one memorable night last winter when the Black Watch chased a lot of them through a village and slew them with picks and spades."[89] This is interesting, but a search of the Black Watch history finds no such memorable incident recorded. Again, according to an unidentified soldier of 6th Camerons, at Loos, "A German General was captured in that lot, and he told our officers when he was taken in that, if they took away the Kilties and the Guards Regiments, they would wipe the earth with us."[90] If this is true, it indicates at least some respect for the Highlanders' fighting abilities. Much later, Thomas Lyon records an incident during a raid by the Glasgow Highlanders on 27 June 1916:

> One of our men was preparing to throw a bomb into a dug-out when, in the glare of his electric torch, he saw a middle-aged German, bearded of face and bald of head, laboriously climbing the stairs. The Highlander waited. When he had almost reached the level of the

---

85   IWM 6702 Low, letter to wife Noanie, 18 May, 1915.
86   GHM PB2366 Shadwell, Bernard, typescript poem, 'The Ladies fra' Hell.' See also Lauder, *A Minstrel in France*, pp.112-113.
87   ASHM-E11 Bowie, diary, January, 1919.
88   GHM PB1755 Young, 'Memoirs of Captivity.'
89   Gillespie, *Letters from Flanders*, pp.284-285, letter home, 29 August, 1915.
90   IWM 6933 Moir, letter from unidentified soldier about the battle of Loos, 1 October, 1915.

trench the German's unsuspecting eyes suddenly lit on the kilt of his enemy. A look of incredulous bewilderment overspread his features – a look that changed to one of horror and fear as his eyes travelled slowly upward and over the khaki tunic. His jaw dropped, a gasp that was almost a sob escaped his lips, and he fell on his knees and whined and babbled for mercy.[91]

Lyon was writing for wartime publication, so his account may be elaborated, but it does indicate a fear of merciless execution which we will need to consider.

The most convincing evidence of German fear of Highland troops, against which much of the other evidence appears circumstantial, is however provided by a document which was circulated around 51st Highland Division by Major Bewsher, Intelligence Officer of the Division (and later Divisional historian).[92]

> The War Office has, I hear, just come into possession of a document of extraordinary interest, some day a thrilling story may be told of how and where it was secured. The document is one recently prepared by the Germans' Headquarters' Staff and placed in the hands of the divisional commanders in the field for their guidance. It is a list of British Divisions in their order of 'Furchtbarkeit' which may be translated 'Much to be fearedness.'
>
> 'Furchtbarkeit' is frightfulness, but not 'Schrecklichkeit' the frightfulness as practised in Belgium and elsewhere. In this historic list, pride of place is given to the following, i.e.:-
>
> 1. Fifty-first Division
> 2. Fifty-ninth Division (reformed)
> 3. Guards Division
>
> (Signed) F.W. BEWSHER, Major
> for Lieut-Colonel, General Staff
> 51st (Highland) Division
> 25th February, 1918

This news was of course a great morale booster to the officers and men of the Highland Division, as no doubt it was intended to be.[93] But what did it really mean? And what was the context? In what sense were these divisions to be feared? Was it because they were most likely to be used in an offensive? Was it because they were the most effective in battle? Or was it because they were the most ruthless in battle? Without the context and the original papers we do not know, but there is at least some evidence that it may have been the last.

According to Hal Kerridge, who served in both the Gordons and the London Scottish, the Scots had a reputation in the German army for not taking prisoners. As a result, they were surprised when

---

91 Lyon, *More Adventures*, pp.117-118.
92 IWM 2528 Bradbury, memoir, p.94.
93 BWA MacDonald, Coll, letter to wife Mary, 21 June, 6 October, 1917; ASHM N-E2 Hyslop, diary, 5 May, 1917; IWM 3834 Wrench, diary, p.155, 20 September, 1917; LC GS 0588 Fraser, letter to brother Gordon, 5 August, 1917; Mackenzie, *Sixth Gordons*, p.132.

they were taken prisoner and treated well.[94] There is good evidence to back up this assertion. On 23 October, 1917, Ian Mackay, now acting C.O. of 6th Camerons, noted that the battalion captured a German who stumbled into their trenches. "He wore a very worried look when he saw that his captors were in the kilt and he implored them not to torture him. He certainly was trembling all over when he was up before me."[95] On 28 September, 1918, Private Douglas of 8th Black Watch saw prisoners coming in from the battlefield, "They apparently were not too happy at having been captured by kilted troops, and not sure of what kind of treatment would be handed out to them."[96] Then on 1 October, he saw three German prisoners who had been brought in by the Black Watch: "If any of our kilted troops had occasion to pass near to them, the Germans obviously looked none too happy."[97] On 28 October, 1918, Arthur Wrench wrote that the Seaforths had taken over a hundred prisoners. "What scared looking creatures they are with eyes almost popping out of their heads. Perhaps they think they are going to be put up against the wall or something as I hear they are taught to expect this 'mercy' from the 'women from Hell' if they are taken prisoner.[98] Similarly, on 5 November, 1918, the Glasgow Highlanders captured two German prisoners.

> The officer … appeared to have grave doubts about how we dealt with prisoners – the Germans, he said, treated them well – and he seemed to think that his unfortunate groom was in special danger of being murdered. Considering that he had lived in England he might have known better, but perhaps it was the kilt that put the fear of death on him.[99]

There is even evidence that this fear had by 1917 communicated itself, possibly through German-inspired newspaper reports, or even German instruction, to Bulgarian troops on the Salonika front[100] and Turkish troops in Palestine. Neil Hendry notes that when his battalion, 2nd London Scottish, over-ran a Turkish position in Palestine on 31 October, 1917, they found only killed and wounded on the enemy position. "According to a doctor we captured, the men had flown along the trenches to be taken prisoner by the trousered regiment, as they did not want to be captured by the skirted devils as they called us. They were given to understand we took no prisoners." A few days later, in another attack, Hendry was wounded. While making his way back to the doctor,

> I saw some Turkish prisoners here which (in fun) I ran at with my bayonet. They were instantly down on their knees with arms up shouting: merci! merci! This brought forth a great shout from our chaps, as I must have looked a villainous bloody being, with all this grime of weeks, and blood.[101]

It is unlikely he would have appreciated the joke if the boot had been on the other foot.

94 LC Tapes 1618/1619 Kerridge, interview.
95 THM Camerons 94-8 Mackay, 'Tell Them of Us; Ian and William Mackay, 4th Bn QOCH, Letters from the trenches 1914-1918', typescript, letter from Ian Mackay to mother, 23 October, 1917.
96 IWM 4586 Private Papers, Douglas J.A. manuscript memoir, pp.1003-1004.
97 Ibid., p.1025.
98 IWM 3834 Wrench, diary, p.258, 28 October, 1918.
99 IWM Books Reid, 'Shoulder to Shoulder,' p.346.
100 IWM 7508 Wyllie, diary, 29 May, 1917.
101 IWM 6873 Hendry, memoir.

Conclusions

In this chapter we have examined the Highlanders' self-image and reputation. We have seen how they generally held a very high opinion of themselves, rooted in notions of the martial race, which was not always born out in practice. They had an expectation that their exploits would be given prominence in the press, an assumption that they were used disproportionately in difficult fighting, and a tendency to show disdain for English soldiers. This inflated self-image was not always born out in reality, and occasionally one finds voices of moderation and realism. They did win some plaudits from some dispassionate observers, and it is possible that their fierce reputation encouraged their use on occasion to keep discipline. There is little evidence to show that the Germans were particularly frightened of Highland troops, although the significance of their assessment of 51st Highland Division needs examination and re-appraisal in context. There is however sufficient evidence to suggest that the fear of mistreatment by kilted soldiers was a genuine concern amongst German soldiers and may even have been officially encouraged. We will consider the whole question of ruthlessness, the use of the bayonet, the taking of prisoners and the killing of prisoners by Highland soldiers in the next chapter on ferocity and compassion.

15

Ferocity and Compassion

> There's nothing I read with more pleasure than the Air Force news about tons of bombs dropped on German cities.[1]

In this chapter we examine the conflicting qualities of ferocity and compassion in relation to the Highland soldier, A popular image of the Highlander was that of the ferocious bayonet-toting soldier. To what extent was this grounded in reality? We will address first the attitude of the Highland soldier towards the enemy, including both hatred and the recognition of common humanity. In particular we will address his perception of the enemy's behaviour on the battlefield. We will then consider the conduct of the Highland soldier himself on the battlefield, looking at ruthlessness and the treatment of prisoners, as well as the exercise of compassion and even 'live and let live.' There are some difficult areas to address here, but in all cases we have tried to establish the truth of behaviours through the evidence only.

Attitudes

There is abundant evidence regarding the attitude of Highland soldiers to the enemy, but it needs to be addressed with care. For one thing, attitudes varied widely between individuals. There was no universal package of attitudes held uniformly across the many battalions. Moreover, the attitudes of some individuals clearly changed as the war progressed and their experience grew. Many letters may report rumour or hearsay as fact, or exaggerate stories for shock or effect. Furthermore, some apparently 'genuine' letters or accounts may actually have been written deliberately for publication in newspapers, and may exaggerate or even invent examples of German barbarism or malpractice for propaganda purposes. For example, in the Argylls Museum at Stirling is an interesting "history" of the 2nd Battalion in the World War, written by Private Stewart McGregor-Craig. It seems to have been compiled as a piece of propaganda, as it contains several fanciful references to German atrocities:

---

1 IWM 8592 Macgregor, letter to wife, 8 November, 1918.

[February 3] The Huns have wrought terrible destruction. We bury all the dead women and children. They are lying all over the place some with bayonet wounds and some who have been shot. Others hanging from tree tops where they have been hanged. And all the sights are enough to sicken. One woman had her breast cut off. Arms and legs, some hands cut off. Oh, it is enough to break a man's heart, the sights we see.[2]

Nevertheless, using the sources critically, it is possible and reasonable to identify certain commonly expressed attitudes which clearly had wide resonance.

It is true that hatred of the Germans amongst the soldiers was widespread and sustained throughout the war.[3] There was anger at the Germans for (in the popular perception) starting such a dreadful war, and for the destruction that the war brought. There was contempt for German militarism and lust for power[4], and outrage at the perceived barbaric methods they used to achieve their ends[5], which offended the prevalent notion of fair-play and sportsmanship[6]. There was an earnest desire to "get at" the Germans;[7] a desire for revenge, to teach the Germans a lesson, to see the war through until the total defeat of Germany, and to see the Germans suffer in their own country as they made others to suffer[8]. At Aldershot, training with 5th Camerons in October, 1914, Jim Foulis wrote to his young niece Nancy in Scotland.

By the way you must tell mummy not to let Willie get too fat in case he might burst, and then there would be a dreadful explosion. Tell mummy if Willie is going to explode to be sure to send him to Germany first for then the explosion might kill a lot of those very very bad Germans ... It was very wicked of those bad Germans to shoot Uncle Willie, so I hope to get near them soon and shoot a great lot of them just the way Uncle Teddy shoots the bunnies.[9]

Even just before the Armistice, on 8 November, 1918, Lieutenant Guy Macgregor, in 6th Argylls, could write to his wife, Dulcie, who was engaged in war work:

---

2   ASHM N-E2 McGregor-Craig, Private S., typescript copy of manuscript 'History of 2nd Argyll & Sutherland Highlanders in World War' [from 9 August, 1914 to 15 October, 1915]. See also IWM 16841 Harrison, letter to daughter Ellen, 24 July, 1916.
3   For general expressions of hatred, other than those cited elsewhere, see: THM Camerons 02-58 Grant, letter to Aunt Molly, 16 October, 1914; BWA Stewart, letter to wife 5 May, 1916.
4   Gillespie, *Letters from Flanders*, p.78, letter 29 March, 1915; Wheatley, *Echoes from Hell* (Hitchin: Dodman Press, 1982), letter from Wallie Martin to Mrs Dorothy Hay Bonnay, 12 May, 1915; BWA Stewart, letter to wife, 1 September, 1915.
5   Gillespie, *Letters from Flanders*, p.140, letter, 10 May, 1915; GHM PB3309 Pelham Burn, letter to mother, 18 May, 1915; THM Seaforths 81-180, Murray, letter to brother Joe, 15 September, 1916; LC GS 1761 Wilson, memoir, p.12.
6   IWM 14269 Private Papers, Couper, letter to mother, 23 May, 1915; BWA Stewart, letter to wife 14 June, 1917; LC GS 1535 Stewart, Tape 359, interview. For a rare recognition of decent German sportsmanship, see Bryden McKinnell's comments on the *Emden* in McKinnell, *Diary*, p.5.
7   LC GALL 066 Nicol, letter to mother, 12 May 1915; LC GS 0890 Kershaw, letter home, 30 June 1915; GHM PB2021 Stewart, letter to wife, 11 July, 1915.
8   Gillespie, *Letters from Flanders*, p.306, letter, 19 September, 1915.
9   IWM 3563 Foulis, letters to niece, Nancy Lilburn, n.d and 4 October, 1914.

> I want to hear of your big aeroplanes getting busy. I like to think of you busy with these carburettors. There's nothing I read with more pleasure than the Air Force news about tons of bombs dropped on German cities.[10]

The anger against causing the war is well expressed by Captain Frederick Chandler, shortly to take up a position as Medical Officer to 2nd Argylls: "God, how I hate the Germans! Not for the stupid reasons one reads in the papers, but simply because they caused this war."[11] Simple exposure to the destruction of war and the sufferings of the civilian population reinforced the resentment. C.S.M. Peter Stewart in 8th Gordons wrote to his wife about July, 1915:

> It makes one's heart bleed for the little ones, and many a time I have cried quietly to myself and taken a new resolution that I would help to my utmost to pay back the swine for their inhumanity. I have been in a town darling, 'Armentieres' … full of helpless women and children and the Germans have been throwing shells all over it. I saw a bright little lad about the same as my Ian hit across the face with a piece of shrapnel shell and lay bleeding almost at my feet. I took the little lad to hospital and thank God he got over it … Do you wonder love if we swear there will be no quarter when our opportunity comes. I may not be spared … but should I go you may all console yourself with the fact that my life was given in as just a cause as ever life was given in.[12]

Anger, resentment and hatred were kept alive by the continuous way in which the Germans, from their initial invasion of Belgium, pushed or breached the limits of acceptable 'civilised' warfare. We have already met Ross Husband, a Scottish minister, who joined up outraged by German abuses in Belgium. Major Standish Crawford, in 2nd Gordons, felt of the Germans that, "They have been such brutes when in the ascendancy in Belgium, I am afraid we have little pity to spare for their terrible losses. Besides which it is only by decimation that the German military system can be broken for good."[13] As late as 23 February, 1915, First Corps bulletin was publicising to the British Army German atrocities at Tamines in Belgium, demonstrating that six months after the event, atrocity stories were still being used by the Army staff to stiffen resolve.[14] The trail of destruction and the plight of civilian refugees in the early mobile war further inflamed passions.[15] Captain Cland Low, in 1st London Scottish, wrote bitterly from Pradelles, "I am in the house of a priest. The poor chap was shot by the Germans when in occupation of this village a short time ago. They shot him because he could not or would not give up the key of his church." And a little later he remarked on the deserted houses in the village, with

---

10 IWM 8592 Macgregor, letter to wife, 8 November, 1918.
11 IWM 15460 Chandler, letter to Marjorie Raimes, 26 November, 1914. See also: IWM 3460 Macmillan, letter from Willie Macmillan to mother, 22 October, 1915.
12 GHM PB2021 Stewart, letter to wife, n.d. (July, 1915). See also: GHM PB1639 Kemp, memoir, pp.28, 39; THM 2013-072 (S) Braes, diary, p.27, 7 September 1915; IWM 132 Paterson, memoir, p.35; GHM PB1892.3.18 McDonald, 'Uncle Harper's Duds', pp.138-139.
13 GHM PB2093 Crawford, letter to mother, 27 October, 1914.
14 LC GS1507 Sotheby, diary, 23 February, 1915. The incident was real. 269 civilians were killed in a mass execution. See Horne, John & Kramer, Alan, *German Atrocities 1914, A History of Denial*, (Newhaven & London: Yale University Press, 2001), pp.36-38.
15 ASHM N-E2 Hyslop, diary, vol 1, pp.49, 54, 65-66, 69.

bullet holes in them, "I am sorry for the French to have their homes smashed up in this way; they have done nothing to call for such punishment. What satisfaction it gives me to assist in righting the wrong!".[16]

The use of poison gas by the Germans, begun on 22 April, 1915, reinforced hatred and bred the desire for revenge[17]. "These Germans are filthy swine for using asphyxiating gas which is against all the rules of war. Nothing is too bad for the brutes," wrote Harry Pelham Burn, of 1st Gordons.[18] "The Germans are dirty dogs to use gas. I hope we manage to find something similar only worse. Nothing is bad enough for them," wrote Captain Charlie Couper, in 4th Black Watch.[19] Alex Gillespie, in 2nd Argylls, noted the feeling aroused in his men: "They were keen to win before, but they are ten times keener now, and even the faint hearts who said they were 'fed up with the war' see now what they are fighting against."[20] Captain Frederick Chandler, M.O. to 2nd Argylls visited a clearing station full of gas casualties and was appalled by what he saw. "From that moment I hated the Germans. I still hate them, and years hence … I shall remember what I saw on May 4th, 1915"[21] The subsequent use of gas throughout the war continued to arouse strong feelings. On 12 October, 1916, Lieutenant Robert Mackay of 11th Argylls recorded a gas shell attack. "Made one wild. Don't want to take prisoners after this."[22] Arthur Wrench, in 4th Seaforths, noted the awful success of a reciprocal British gas attack in June, 1918. Having witnessed German gas attacks, "I hardly feel that any one of us have the least pity."[23]

Hatred continued to be reinforced through 1915. The sad sight of Ypres in flames in May left an impression, although the main accounts seem to be exaggerated with a view to publication or propaganda.[24] Even the story of the crucified Canadian had resonance. Jock McLeod, in 5th Camerons, who believed the story, reported on 10 August, 1916, by then safely in Britain, that some of the boys of the battalion "say they found two Gordons crucified in some trees when they went over" at the Somme.[25] If these stories were fanciful, there was nothing unreal about

---

16   IWM 6702 Low, letter to Aunt Mary, 30 November, 4 December, 1914. See also: IWM 1862 Craig-Brown, letter dated 7 January, 1915; LC GS1507 Sotheby, diary, 26 February, 1915.
17   Apart from specific refs cited see also: BWA Thomson, narrative; LC GS 1027 Macleod, letter to mother, 5 May, 1915; THM Seaforths 81-180, Murray, letter to sister Kate, 28 April, 1915; GHM PB107.1 Grant, diary, 29 April, 1915; GHM PB2021 Stewart, letter to wife, 4 June, 1915; GHM PB583 McKinnon, memoir, p.24; THM Seaforths 07-42, Rowell, letter from Dmr R. Mackenzie, 2 October, 1916; THM Camerons 97-22 Russell, memoirs, p.199.
18   GHM PB3309 Pelham Burn, letters to parents, 22, 30 April, 4, 6, 18 May, 1915.
19   IWM 14269 Couper, letter to mother, 26 April, 1915.
20   Gillespie, *Letters from Flanders*, pp.146-147, letter, 11 May, 1915. See also pp.115-116, letter, 25 April, 1915, p.129, letter, 3 May, 1915, p.149, letter, 13 May, 1915. For a similar transformation in 9th Royal Scots see *9th Royal Scots (T.F.) B Company*, pp.66-67.
21   Chandler, 'Winter and Spring in Flanders 1914-1915', p.8. See also IWM 15460 Chandler, letter to Marjorie Raimes, 9 May, 1915. That Chandler's outrage was genuine, and not blown up for propaganda purposes for the article, is confirmed by Gillespie, *Letters from Flanders*, p.136, letter, 6 May, 1915.
22   IWM 11144 Mackay, diary, 12 October, 1916.
23   IWM 3834 Wrench, diary, 10 June, 1918.
24   GHM PB1726 Fettes, diary, 'Impressions on visiting Ypres', n.d.; *9th Royal Scots (T.F.) B Company*, p.75; NLS MS 846 Ramage, diary, 13 June, 1915.
25   IWM 5821 Semple, Letters from Jock McLeod, 24 January, 10 August, 1916.

the sinking of the *Lusitania*, or false about the reaction to it[26]. Lieutenant Alex Gillespie in 2nd Argylls wrote; "How pleased the Germans will be that they have sunk the *Lusitania*! … It's no use protesting against them now, except with the bayonet."[27] And Harry Pelham Burn, already disgusted by the German use of gas, wrote: "That sinking of the Lusitania is appalling, the worst thing they have done yet & now nothing is too bad for them."[28] The *flammenwerfer* was also introduced in 1915. "There is nothing too bad for the Huns not to adopt," wrote Colour-Sergeant Alick Guthrie, 6th Black Watch.[29] And Alex Gillespie commented, "They won't stop the war with all these infamous weapons, but they will make their name loathed for evermore."[30]

More outrage was stirred by aerial bombing, partly of the troops themselves[31], but also of Britain, especially London, by Zeppelins[32] and then Gotha bombers[33]. Opinions differed on the desirability of reprisals.[34] Major Bates, Medical Officer to 8th Black Watch, wrote on 15 June, 1917, to his fiancée in the London area: "They really are the limit … To see wounded men is bad enough – but women and children – horrible. I see that one bomb dropped in a school – poor kiddies."[35]

The ongoing U-boat war continued to outrage the soldiers, especially when nurses or hospital ships were among the victims.[36] The Hospital Ship *Britannic*, sister ship of the *Titanic*, was sunk by a mine laid by a German U-boat on 21 November, 1916, though fortunately most of those on board were rescued. Jock Macleod wrote from Hamran Military Hospital in Malta, "It is quite in keeping with the normal Hun war policy to go for Hospital Ships. It is really quite strange that they have respected them for so long."[37] When *SS Aragon*, a legitimate target, was torpedoed on 30 December, 1917, with the loss of 610 lives, Ronal Brown in 5th Argylls believed that nurses were among the dead. "I don't think I would save many crews of U Boats," he wrote.[38] For the Canadian Highlanders, the greatest outrage was the sinking of the Hospital Ship *Llandovery Castle*, torpedoed on 27 June, 1918, with the loss of 234 Canadian doctors,

---

26 Apart from specific refs cited, see also: THM Seaforths 89-26, Crask, diary, 9 May, 1915, in which he refers to the Lusitania as the Titanic; postcard to parents, 11 May, 1915; NLS MS 845 Ramage, diary, 11 May, 1915.
27 Gillespie, *Letters from Flanders*, p.138, letter, 9 May, 1915.
28 GHM PB3309 Pelham Burn, letter to Ella, 11 May, 1915.
29 BWA Guthrie, letter to wife Cissie, 4 August, 1915.
30 Gillespie, *Letters from Flanders*, p.257, letter, 1 August, 1915.
31 LC GS 1027 Macleod, letters to father, 3 March, & mother, 5 March, 1917.
32 BWA Guthrie, letter to wife Cissie, 4 January, 1916.
33 BWA Macdonald, Coll, letter to wife Mary, 13 June, 1917; IWM 8192 Lawson, letters to 'Tom' (brother?), 31 July, 1917, to sister Bessie, 30 November, 1917, 13 March, 1918; BWA Stewart, letter to wife 11 September, 1917. For a soldier's condemnation of the reprisals against German civilians in London, see: IWM 8592 Macgregor, letter to wife, 10 September, 1917. The raid would have been the Gotha raid of 4 September, 1917.
34 LC GS 1027 Macleod, letters to father, 3 March, & mother, 5 March, 1917; IWM 8192 Lawson, letters to 'Tom' (brother?), 31 July, 1917, to sister Bessie, 30 November, 1917, 13 March, 1918; BWA Stewart, letters to wife 11 September, 1917, 21 November, 1917.
35 IWM 2854 Bates, letter to fiancée,15 June, 1917. This is a reference to the German Gotha raid on London on 13 June, 1917, which included the bombing of Upper North Street School in Poplar which killed 18 children.
36 Apart from specific sources cited, see: IWM 7508 Wyllie, diary, 8 February, 1917.
37 LC GS 1027 Macleod, letter to father, 24 November, 1916.
38 ASHM N-E5 Brown, letter to parents, 5 January, 1918.

nurses and patients. In the early morning of 28 July, 1918, 150 men of the Canadian Scottish launched the '*Llandovery Castle* Raid' on the German lines, as a deliberate reprisal.[39]

Yet more outrage was caused by the wasteland left by the Germans when they made their strategic withdrawal to the Hindenburg Line in March, 1917.[40] "After the bestial wreckage of the retreat we are in no mood to take prisoners" wrote Guy MacGregor, an Argyll officer.[41] "Oh! How I'd love to be in a party mining Berlin and wrecking the whole of the damned Bosche country," wrote Bob Lawson, in 14th Argylls.[42] "In sure brutality no nation can vie with the Germans,"[43] wrote Coll Macdonald, chaplain to 8th Black Watch.

Finally, the plight of the villagers and refugees caught up in the mobile warfare of the German retreat, and their tales of suffering under German occupation, aroused the ire of the Highland soldiers once again[44]. Captain George Macleod, in 8th Argylls, wrote:

> The Bosche are shelling *with Gas* All the villages, they know, are thickly populated with refugees; so that today 3 cart loads of Civilians – gassed – arrived. Can you imagine the sight? Wee Babies ... [sic]However I am not going to describe it. Suffice to say, it's the worst I have seen in nearly three years of Active Service, and daily you see sights that literally make you *cry*.[45]

At Hauchlin, after a heavy gas bombardment, the chaplain of 7th Argylls buried 17 women and girls in the same grave. "The 'Jocks' went back to their final battles in good heart, and with grim resolve."[46] At St Roch, a suburb of Cambrai, Arthur Wrench felt, "When I see these emaciated looking boys and hear what they have had to suffer I think that the Germans can hardly claim to be human beings at all."[47]

Clearly, there was much contempt for German actions and clearly this instilled in some men a desire for ruthless retribution. But this was only one side of the coin. There was at the same time considerable admiration for German prowess in war.[48] "There is no doubt about it,"

---

39 Fetherstonhaugh, *13th Battalion*, pp.245-246; McEvoy &Finlay, *Seaforth Highlanders of Canada*, p.110.
40 Apart from specific refs cited see: THM Camerons 93-35 Welsh, memoirs, pp.32, 36; NLS Acc.9084 No.7 McLeod, letter to sister Nan, Good Friday (postmark / April) 1917; IWM 2854 Bates, letter to fiancée, 25 July, 1917; THM Seaforths 89-122 Paterson, memoir; THM Camerons 94-8 Mackay, 'Tell Them of Us', letter from Ian Mackay to mother, 12 August, 1917.
41 IWM 8592 Macgregor, letter to wife, 15 April, 1917.
42 IWM 8192 Lawson, letters to sister Bessie, 1 July, & to 'Tom' (brother?), 31 July, 1917.
43 BWA Macdonald, Coll, letter to wife, 27 July, 1917. See also letter to wife, 2 July, 1917.
44 Apart from specific refs cited below, see: LC GS 1761 Wilson, memoir, p.93; IWM 8592 Macgregor, letter to wife, 14 October, 1918; IWM 3834 Wrench, diary, 21, 27 October, 1918; Hayes, *Eighty-Fifth*, pp.179, 186; Sotheby, *10th Argylls*, pp.110-113; NLS Acc.9084 No.12 Macleod, letter to sister Nan, 12 November, 1918; IWM 11144 Mackay, diary, 1918; IWM 8592 Macgregor, letter to wife, 1 November, 1918.
45 NLS Acc.9084 No.37 Macleod, letter home, 24 October, 1918.
46 Morrison, *7th Battalion The Great War*, p 50.
47 IWM 3834 Wrench, diary, 31 October, 1918.
48 See: GHM PB3309 Pelham Burn, letter to mother, 26 February, 1915; LC GS 1027 Macleod, letter to mother, 28 April, 1915; NLS MS 845 Ramage, diary, 26 May, 1915; GHM PB2021 Stewart, letter to wife, 30 July, 1915; BWA Stewart, letter to wife 19 October, 1915; GHM PB3309 Pelham Burn, letters to mother, 12 July, 1916, 27 March, 1918; IWM 7668 Escombe, letter from 2Lt C.B.

wrote Captain Charlie Couper, "the Germans are very brave, absolute rotters with their gas etc, but still good fighters."[49] Such attitudes could often co-exist somewhat awkwardly with utter contempt for German methods. They might even, occasionally, if rarely, induce some pessimism about the eventual outcome of the war.[50] Much rarer, but especially characteristic of those who had actually lived in Germany for a time, was an appreciation of German culture and the notion of a fine people led astray.[51] Ross Husband, the Scottish minister who joined the Black Watch as an infantry officer in 1916, had studied theology in Germany before the war at Marburg and Heidelberg, and had no hatred for the German people. A sermon he delivered on 'Love your enemies' is very touching:

> It would be well if in these heated days we occasionally remind ourselves of what Germany has been in the past, of her contribution to religion, philosophy, literature and music … the Germany that produced Luther and Goethe, Bach and Beethoven … It is a sorrow to us that the Germans should have embarked on mad political ventures; it is our hope that they may some day return to their old ways – to their right mind..[52]

Some writers, generally writing after the event[53], have denied that there was hatred for the Germans amongst the fighting men, but this view is simply untenable in the face of the evidence above. Frank Brooke, who served in 4th Seaforths, states, "We had no enmity, individually, with the Germans. The 'hate', on both sides, was inspired by blood-lust and battle-heat instilled by instructors."[54] No doubt this was partly true, but it ignores the anger demonstrated above. Graham Hutchison, some time officer with 2nd Argylls, wrote in his memoirs that, by other ranks, the enemy were usually referred to, not as the Hun or the Bosch, but by the affectionate term "Gerry."[55] This is not supported by the sources, where the term "Gerry" is rarely seen, where "Bosch" and "Hun" are widely used, if not simply "Germans" or occasionally the affectionate term, "Fritz". Interviewed in 1991, Norman Collins, who served as a Seaforth officer, denied feeling hatred for the Germans: "No, we had friendly feelings … We were under the same conditions as the Germans … We didn't feel any real animosity towards them because they didn't commit any atrocities as far as we knew."[56] This testimony, long after the event, is simply not supported by the evidence.

What Collins's statement does suggest, however, is that, alongside the hatred for Germans, was a recognition that individual German soldiers, like our own, were caught up in a game not of their making and were subject to the same suffering; a powerful recognition of common

---

    Anderson, 13 (possibly 23) July, 1916; IWM 12043 Collins, interview; GHM PB1706/2 Robertson, 'Diary,' 11 September, 1916; NLS Acc.9084 No.37 Macleod, letter to 'All' (at home), 25 October, 1917.
49 IWM 14269 Couper, letter to Tom Couper, 16 May, 1915.
50 LC GS1507 Sotheby, diary, 17 January, 1915; GHM PB3309 Pelham Burn, letter to mother, 18 May, 1916.
51 See also: LC GS1507 Sotheby, diary, 17 January, 1915.
52 Ross, *A Scottish Minister and Soldier*, pp.45-46.
53 See, for example, Wade, *Counterspy*, pp.161-163.
54 IWM Books Brooke, 'Wait for it', p.160.
55 Hutchison, *Warrior*, p.53.
56 IWM 12043 Collins, interview.

humanity, potentially in conflict with feelings of hatred. Hal Kerridge, a Londoner drafted into 1st Gordons, who had had his hair cut by a German when he was a child, stated, "As a nation, we would fight the Germans ... but if you reckon individually ... you find they're ordinary human beings ... They didn't like the war any more than we did. They didn't want to kill you any more then you wanted to kill them. But they had to fight for their country."[57] Captain Frederick Chandler, M.O. to 2nd Argylls, records how on Christmas morning, 1914, he had a German soldier properly buried. "'Rest in peace, poor Fritz,' thought I; 'it is not you or your like that have caused all this; there is not a private soldier in any of the combatant armies who would not make peace tomorrow.'"[58] The soldier-poet, Alan Mackintosh recognises in 'Snow in France' a common humanity in describing Scottish and Saxon soldiers watching across No Man's Land.[59] During the battle of Arras, Frank Brooke in 4th Seaforths was wounded on the left thigh by a shell fragment and was looked after and assisted off the battlefield by a captured German stretcher-bearer. When they finally found him a stretcher, "The German S.B. was watching and I impulsively gripped his hand. 'Merci!' 'La guerre no bloody bon', he replied. 'No bloody bon,' I agreed." His experiences led Brooke down a socialist path: "It was despicable that such men should be set at each others' throats to make profits for bloated hogs called 'business-men.'"[60]

It is clear that feelings of common humanity co-existed with feelings of hatred, and to claim that either was exclusive is not supported by the evidence. The overall view towards the enemy was ambivalent, not only within groups but within individuals. The resolution of this moral dilemma was the recognition of the need to kill the individual enemy in order to destroy the system and leadership; the need to confront a people led astray. "By God," wrote Lieutenant Guy Macgregor, two days after the Armistice, "there's been more criminal folly & pride in the leading of that people than of any people in the world great or small, ancient or modern."[61] There was a desire amongst many to see the job through to the end, to avoid a compromise peace and to ensure the Germans were punished for their actions.[62] In December, 1916, Jock Macleod of 2nd Camerons, in hospital in Malta, sent his father an epigram entitled "To the Pacifists".

> Unmoral moralists, who paint
> The Guilty German as a saint,
> Your peace would bring (as well you know)
> A bloodier war with that foul foe
> Fouler; your peace would render vain
> The blood we spend, the tears, the pain[63]

---

57 LC Tapes 1618/1619 Kerridge, interview.
58 Chandler, 'Winter in Flanders 1914-15', pp.4-5. See also: IWM 15460 Chandler, letter to sister Katie, 29 March, 1915.
59 Campbell & Green, *Can't shoot a man with a cold*, p.100 (from *A Highland Regiment*, p.31).
60 IWM Books Brooke, 'Wait for it', pp.160, 199-201.
61 IWM 8592 Macgregor, letter to wife, 13 November, 1918.
62 IWM 6702 Low, letter to wife, 17 July, 1915, to mother, 13 November, 1918; Royal Scots Museum, Beatson, diary, 12 August, 1915; Sutherland, *War Diary*, p.158; IWM 2854 Bates, letter to fiancée, 7 September, 1916; GHM PR2093 Crawford, letter to father, 16 August, 1916; LC GS 1761 Wilson, memoir, pp.75-76; GHM PB1639 Kemp, memoir, p.57.
63 LC GS 1027 Macleod, letter to father, 23 December, 1916.

The Highland soldier, then, carried on to the battlefield a complex range of feelings towards the enemy; a hatred of his methods and what he stood for, some admiration of his military prowess, a recognition of his common humanity, but a determination to see things through to the end. But how did the Highland soldier actually behave on the battlefield? Before addressing this question, it is necessary to address one potential source of hatred so far unexamined; his own perception of enemy behaviour on the battlefield.

There are countless complaints in the sources about German malpractice on the battlefield; behaviour that was either unsporting or contrary to the accepted rules of warfare. Whether these complaints were justified or not is largely immaterial. What mattered was that they were believed and spread. The Germans were accused on occasion of killing the wounded.[64] The accusations were certainly taken to heart. Colour-Sergeant Alick Guthrie of 6th Black Watch wrote on 23 May, 1915, "From what I have seen and heard already I would rather blow my brains out than fall wounded into their hands."[65] Duncan Mackenzie, in 4th Camerons, was wounded at Festubert. "What was ringing in my ears was what I had previously been told that the enemy bayoneted the wounded."[66] Similarly, Hal Kerridge, who served in 1st Gordons, was wounded in the back by shrapnel during an attack in 1918. Interviewed in 1998, he recalled that he started to crawl back to his own lines, as if the enemy should retake the area, he might be finished off rather than taken prisoner.[67] The Germans were also accused of sniping at, or even throwing bombs at, the wounded lying on the battlefield,[68] although presumably in many cases they hardly knew whether their targets were wounded or not. True or false, this left an impression. After being told of one episode at Neuve Chapelle, Lionel Sotheby recorded "one intense desire to kill, kill, kill the Germans in front."[69]

Perhaps the most burning accusation levelled at the Germans was their shooting at stretcher-bearers or those tending the wounded[70]. This also left an impression. "The Germans are swine", wrote Captain Bryden McKinnell in the Liverpool Scottish.[71] "These Huns are only fit to be killed," wrote Major Cland Low, 1st London Scottish, "They are not good society for civilised people. It would never occur to any decent minded Christian to shoot a man on a stretcher or a stretcher bearer who is unarmed & wears a brassard."[72] On 1 August, 1917, Lieutenant Robert Mackay of 11th Argylls was occupied with a stretcher-party searching for wounded.

64　Mackenzie, *Diary and Letters*, diary, 26 August, 1914; McKinnell, *Diary*, pp.30-31; Gillespie, *Letters from Flanders*, pp.113-115, letter, 24 April, 1915; GHM uncatalogued Beaton, memoir, p.39; Craig-Brown, *Historical Records*, Vol.3, p. 48. See also: IWM 1862 Craig-Brown, letter dated 29 September, 1914; THM Camerons 99-87, Macpherson, diary, 14 September, 1914.
65　BWA Guthrie, letter home 23 May, 1915.
66　THM Camerons 94-8 Mackay, 'Tell Them of Us', letter from Duncan Mackenzie to William Mackay, 15 March, 1973.
67　LC Tapes 1618/1619 Kerridge, interview.
68　Apart from specific refs cited, see: Chambers, *Diaries of World War 1*, p.23; GHM PB107.1 Grant, diary, 28 May, 1915; ASHM N-E11 Bowie, diary, 14 August, 1916; LC GS1507 Sotheby, letters to mother, 11 May, 1915 & to brother Nigel, 1 June, 1915.
69　LC GS1507 Sotheby, diary, 13 March, 1915, and letter to unknown recipient, 16 March, 1915.
70　THM Seaforths 87-125, Heriz-Smith, letter from Bandsman Owen Gentles, 13 March, 1915; BWA Guthrie, letter home 23 May, 1915; Chambers, *Diaries of World War 1*, p.23; IWM Books Brooke, 'Wait for it', pp.198-199; LC GS 0132 Betteridge, memoir, Vol.1, p.237; Gillespie, *Letters from Flanders*, pp.113-115, letter, 24 April, 1915.
71　McKinnell, *Diary*, pp.30-31.
72　IWM 6702 Low, letter to mother, 21 April, 1918.

Found at last, when no other of our men could be seen, a demented wounded Boche. Felt like leaving the blighter, but could not. Got him on a stretcher. But men objected. Took an end of the stretcher myself. Then Boche turned a machine gun on us as our little party with the wounded Boche stumbled down the Roulers railway line. So much for civilised warfare! I fear that no prisoners will be taken by any of my men in the next show.[73]

Allied to this were alleged abuses of the Red Cross badge. When 10th Argylls attacked on 12 October, 1917, during the battle of Passchendaele, "Red Cross parties of the enemy were ... seen dumping ammunition boxes in the shell-holes."[74] And Private Albert Hay in 1st Black Watch observed that on 19 September, 1918,

During the close fighting Lieutenant Baxter captured a trench filled with Germans, every one of whom wore the Red Cross badge. These men had been firing until the moment their trench was captured, when one of them threw something into a dugout. It proved to be a machine-gun, which was still hot when found.[75]

Perhaps more significant still for battlefield actions was alleged German duplicity during or after the act of surrender. The Germans were accused of pretending to surrender and opening fire on the party sent to receive them.[76] Otherwise, from Neuve Chapelle to Arras, they were accused of opening fire or throwing bombs after surrendering.[77] At Arras, for example, Germans who had surrendered and who were making their own way to the British lines unescorted, were accused up picking up rifles, dropping down into shell-holes and shooting in the back the advancing soldiers of 14th Argylls.[78]

The Germans were also accused of doctoring ammunition, to produce soft-nosed bullets which caused terrible wounds, either by reversing the bullets or by tampering with the nose. Four accounts of this practice have been found. Three relate to 1915,[79] but there is one from the Somme.[80] Albert Strachan, who served in 6th Gordons until taken prisoner at Loos wrote in his memoirs: "At Festubert was the only time I saw a German beaten ... One German wounded was found with 6 of his cartridges which he had interfered with. He didn't half get a beating."[81]

Other alleged German malpractices included the shelling of a church turned into a hospital during the battle of Le Cateau,[82] the assumed deliberate shelling of a burial party during

---

73 IWM 11144 Mackay, diary, 1 August, 1917.
74 Sotheby, *10th Argylls*, pp.67-68.
75 BWA Hay, memoir, pp.172-174.
76 Craig-Brown, *Historical Records*, Vol.3, p.45; Fetherstonhaugh, *13th Battalion*, p.61.
77 IWM 2854 Bates, letter to fiancée, 4 July, 1916; Wauchope, *Black Watch*, Vol.1, pp.178-179 & p.179, note 1. See also: IWM 14269 Couper, letter to mother, 21 March, 1915; Gillespie, *Letters from Flanders*, pp.113-115, letter, 24 April, 1915; THM Camerons 81-203 MacKay, letter to father, 21 May, 1915.
78 LC Transcripts, Tape 619, McCrow, interview.
79 IWM 16335 Racine, memoir, p.36; GHM PB3309 Pelham Burn, letters to mother, 18 May, & to Henry, 23 May, 1915.
80 IWM 15085 PP McDonald, Lce-Sgt George, diary, 17 July, 1916.
81 GHM PB2984 Strachan, memoir.
82 ASHM N-E2 Hyslop, diary, vol 1, p.36.

Hate. The Germans shell a church being used as a hospital on the retreat from Mons, according to an illustration by F. Matania, which appeared in *The Sphere* and is reproduced here on a contemporary French postcard by l'Atelier d'Art photographique. (Author's collection)

Passchendaele,[83] poisoning water in streams,[84] the use of Cameron prisoners as human shields,[85] German callousness to their own wounded,[86] and even the extraordinary story of soldiers of 1st Black Watch at Aubers Ridge, captured, stripped naked, released and used for target practice.[87] This last story was told to Harry Lauder by his son, John, and features in Harry's book, *A Minstrel in France*, still being used to arouse passions in 1918. If some of these stories were fanciful, credence inspired by the real instances of the Germans pushing the limits of acceptable warfare, they nevertheless reinforced the image and left a deep impression.[88]

There was another side to this though, and in fairness, there were also some touching examples recorded of "fair play" by the Germans. In the Liverpool Scottish, both Captains Bryden

---

83 BWA Macdonald, Coll, letter to wife, 21 August, 1917.
84 Gillespie, *Letters from Flanders*, p.155, letter, 18 May, 1915.
85 Craig-Brown, *Historical Records*, Vol.3, p.92.
86 IWM 6444 Shewan, letter to Uncle Bob, 22 August, 1916.
87 Lauder, *A Minstrel in France,* pp.248-249. This extraordinary story does not appear in the Black Watch regimental history, as it surely would if it were considered to be true. It was not however, invented for Harry's book,; It was very likely related to him by his son as he states, as it was current at the time. See for the rumour: Chambers, *Diaries of World War 1*, p.23; and for the likely explanation, LC GS1507 Sotheby, letter to mother, 11 May, 1915.
88 GHM PB107.1 Grant, diary, 13 May, 1915; THM Seaforths 97-4, McDonald, Sgt Thomas, 'First World War Diary' doggerel verse.

McKinnell and Noel Chavasse, their M.O., recorded separate examples of the Germans withholding fire on stretcher-bearers,[89] and the regimental history of the 42nd Battalion C.E.F. (Royal Highlanders of Canada) records similar forbearance by an enemy airman while strafing the troops with his machine-gun.[90] The Canadian regimental histories record two instances of German officers proposing local ceasefires to enable the collection of the dead and succour of the wounded, both in 1917, one at the height of the Passchendaele offensive.[91] When the Canadian Scottish advanced on 17 August, 1918, during the battle of Amiens, the battalion "went forward across the ground its patrols had fought over on August 16th. There were found some of its casualties of that date, bandaged and speaking well of the treatment they had received at the hands of their opponents."[92] Finally, Private William Couston, in 7th Black Watch, found himself in October, 1917, in a part of the country which the Germans had rapidly evacuated earlier that year. He noted their scorched earth policy, but wrote that,

> I came across a German cemetery in which three English soldiers are buried. Fritz has given them a decent burial & erected a nice cross over each grave ... It makes one think a little more kindly of the Huns in seeing such respect paid to our dead. It will be a great relief to some poor body to know where their men rest.[93]

Such examples reinforced the notion of common humanity.

It did not always require atrocities or malpractice, real or imagined, to inspire hatred. The experience of coming under shell-fire, and the loss of one's own pals, a normal and necessary condition of warfare, could do the same.[94]

Behaviour

This, then, was the background of hatred and humanity within which the Highland soldier went into battle. Perhaps unsurprisingly, on the battlefield it is evident that he frequently behaved utterly ruthlessly and on occasion with brutality. At Loos, many prisoners were taken, but there was much killing. John Bowie, in 11th Argylls records how at Loos his Pipe Major captured a live German in a building and dropped him from the second storey to land on his skull.[95]

Many Germans took refuge in the cellars of the houses. There followed a prototype mopping up operation, in which "the bombers were having the time of their lives ... If the Germans would not come out, in went a bomb."[96] This was fair enough, but there was evidently also much

---

89 McKinnell, *Diary*, p.27; IWM Books Chavasse, Capt Noel, Various papers, letter, 28 September, 1915.
90 Topp, *42nd Battalion*, pp.171-172.
91 McEvoy & Finlay, *Seaforth Highlanders of Canada*, p.42; Topp, *42nd Battalion*, pp.171-172.
92 Urquhart, *Canadian Scottish*, p.283
93 BWA Couston, letter to mother, 1 October, 1917.
94 LC GS 0262 Campbell, diary, 6 August, 1915; GHM uncatalogued Beaton, memoir, p.170; IWM 5821 Semple, letter from Jock McLeod, 18 March, 1916; GHM PB2021 Stewart, letter to wife, 15 August, 1915.
95 ASHM N-E11 Bowie, diary, 25 September, 1915.
96 NLS Acc. 12729, Wood, letter to brother Willie, 29 September, 1915.

gratuitous killing of those enemy soldiers who did emerge from the cellars. Alexander Braes in the ranks of 8th Seaforths, wrote that "the work of clearing the cellars was very easy at first. We stood outside the entrance and shouted on them to come up and as they came up into the open so we ran our bayonets through them."[97] Private David Wood was present with 7th Camerons. He wrote:

> Two Kilties caught a German who shouted for mercy & said he was a Christian. The fellows said, 'Alright, you'll be an angel tomorrow', and bayoneted him. Other 2 caught 2 officers & 4 men who were asking for mercy; they. 'By ---- you'll get mercy this time,' & bayoneted the lot. After finishing them off they went through their pockets. It was terrible.[98]

Howard Panton was also in 7th Camerons . He and his colleagues had a German officer in a cellar surrender to them.

> We came across three of our lads who had discovered some Huns in a cellar hiding. One lad was fair mad and wanted to bayonet each one as he came up the stair. We held him back for a little but the fourth Hun was a huge chap and as he came up his brains were scattered along the wall by a shot from this chap. The others we eventually disposed of. I could tell you hundreds of such incidents but they are all too gruesome.[99]

There was a somewhat disturbing pride amongst members of the Highland battalions when reporting taking so few prisoners at Loos.[100]

The ruthless process of clearing the cellars at Loos was applied to enemy dug-outs through the Somme and afterwards. William Chambers, in 1st Camerons, observed on 10 July, 1916:

> We now follow up our barrage so closely … that the enemy are often still in their shelters when we reach their trench, and our job is then to roll Mills bombs and Stoke[s] Mortar [bombs] down the openings, and thus destroy the occupants like rats in a trap. A bloody business indeed, but only too necessary from our point of view.[101]

The implication here is that no warning or opportunity to surrender was given. Sometimes this might depend on the individual. Revenge for perceived previous malpractice might be a motive. Near Bazentin-le-Petit on 14 July, 1916, Captain Pailethorpe, M.O. to 2nd Gordons, recalls a C.S.M. ruthlessly bombing some over-run German dug-outs. :

> When he returned he said, 'I suppose you think that's rotten, Sir?' I made no remark, waiting for him to speak. He said, 'If you had been with the battalion (he meant then the 1st Battalion) at K6 where the Germans kept pitching bombs at our wounded on the wire, you'd feel the same – I swore then I'd never give any of them any mercy after that.'

---

97 THM 2013-072 (S) Braes, diary, pp.30-31, 25 September 1915.
98 THM Camerons 01-148 Wood, Pte David, letter to sister Julia, n.d.
99 IWM 11241 Panton, letter to brother Tom, 29 September, 1915.
100 BWA Stewart, letter to wife 1 October, 1915; BWA Cumming, undated letter, presumably to parents.
101 Chambers, *Diaries of World War 1*, p.57.

Ruthlessness. Battle of the Scarpe. Patrol of 6th Seaforth Highlanders demonstrate firing into a dug-out in a deserted German trench to dislodge any remaining Germans, 29 August, 1918. (IWM Q7013)

Similar tactics were used to clear out deep dug-outs at Beaumont-Hamel,[102] at Arras,[103] and at Cambrai. Little mercy can have been shown at Cambrai towards the dead Germans Douglas Wimberley found in a dug-out on the second day of the battle. "At the entrance there were three dead bayoneted Germans in their stockinged feet who were but partly clad – they could not have known of the attack till the first Jocks were almost on top of them."[104] The process continued until the end of the war. In late October, 1918, Philip Christison was Second-in-Command of 6th Seaforths. As they advanced they found small parties of the enemy who had taken refuge in cellars and deep dug-outs. "Some would not surrender so a mortar-bomb was exploded in the entrance; but mostly they were only too glad to give up."[105]

For all this ruthlessness, mercy could be shown when mopping up, even in the worst of circumstances, for example at Passchendaele by some Canadian Scottish soldiers,[106] or by Archie Munro in 2nd Gordons after crossing the river Piave;

---

102 GHM uncatalogued Beaton, memoir, p.156; Sutherland, *War Diary*, p.84 ; IWM 7508 Wyllie, diary, 4 October, 1917.
103 IWM 15345 Fleming, memoir, p.30. See also for Arras: IWM 11144 Mackay, diary, 9 April, 1917.
104 IWM 430 Wimberley, memoirs, Vol.1, p.89.
105 IWM 4730 Christison, memoir, p.73.
106 Urquhart, *Canadian Scottish*, p.233.

> Inspecting a dug-out with a sergeant, they found one with an Austrian soldier at the foot of the steps. The sergeant said, 'Let him have it!' but Archie aimed at the bottom step and fired. The Austrian put his hands up and shouted to his mates to come out, and about ten emerged, with their hands above their heads.[107]

There is no doubt that this ruthless method of trench clearance was effective, and the threat of it was intimidating. Douglas Wimberley was following up 51st Highland Division on the first day of the Cambrai battle:

> In front of the tanks could be seen running figures – some of our friends, the Boche, who preferred trusting to their legs and a wound from a tank Lewis Gun in the open rather than waiting in their dug-out for a Mills Bomb from the Jocks.[108]

Raids were also notable for ruthless practice,[109] and here the principal driver was time. Unless the objective of the raid was actually to take prisoners for identification purposes, there was no time to deal with them. Dug-outs were bombed in the same manner as for trench clearance. Notable successes were a daylight raid by 10th Argylls on 6 January, 1917, when an estimated 100 Germans were killed,[110] and the famous raid by 8/10th Gordons on the Butte de Warlencourt on the 29th when it is estimated that 150 Germans were burnt alive, being trapped in blazing dug-outs. "Who said roast pork?" wrote William Kemp, "It was a most fitting death for Huns."[111] But mercy could be shown. On a raid made by the Canadian Scottish on the Hill 70 front on 13 February, 1918, the raiders ruthlessly threw mobile-charges down dug-outs. One of the leaders wrote:

> Returned back along the line and were putting our last mobile charges down a dug-out. We pulled aside the hangings and there sitting on the steps were two Huns, youngsters; badly scared and apparently wounded. As they were wounded we left them, but the corporal didn't like the idea of letting them be an excuse for not putting the mobile charge down, but I chased him along to the next dug-out.[112]

Machine-gunners who kept firing until the last minute could expect little mercy.[113] Writing about the assault of 31 July, 1917, S. Bradbury in 5th Seaforths states:

> On reaching his third line we encountered a few snipers and machine gunners but these were soon 'napooed' by short sharp rushes till we reached them and then of course it was

---

107 LC Several Fronts Recollections, Munro, Recollections.
108 IWM 430 Wimberley, memoirs, Vol.1, p.88.
109 Apart from examples cited below, see: IWM Books Reid, 'Shoulder to Shoulder,' p.175; Sotheby, *10th Argylls*, p.92; Peel & Macdonald, *6th Seaforth Highlanders*, p.28; ASHM N-E11 Bowie, diary, 17/28 June, 1916; ASHM N-E12 Fisher, Colin, 'The 12th Battalion,' p.20.
110 Sotheby, *10th Argylls*, p.41.
111 GHM PB1639 Kemp, memoir, p.62.
112 Urquhart, *Canadian Scottish*, p.250, quoting an unidentified officer.
113 Apart from examples cited below see also: LC GS 1761 Wilson, memoir, pp.72-73; IWM Book Brooke, 'Wait for it', p.309; Macleod, *6th Camerons*, p.64; Blaser, *Kilts across the Jordan*, p.92.

'hands up' and a cry for mercy which they got; I don't think! Fritz's next line had many machine gun emplacements and the guns rattled away until they saw that the game was up, then they caved in and received the same treatment as their comrades in front.[114]

Sniping of course was a particularly ruthless game. Archie Tweddle, in 4th Seaforths, wrote on 28 February, 1915;

> There is a glorious fascination in taking a real deliberate aim at a single German & pulling the trigger. I am afraid all the civilization that I ever had has left me & I have become a murderer – however I am afraid that is my duty.[115]

Where enemy duplicity or malpractice was directly experienced on the battlefield, retribution could be swift.[116] Arthur Betteridge, for example, recalls that when the South African Scottish recaptured a portion of Delville Wood

> it was found two of our badly wounded men who could not be evacuated had been killed by Prussians bayoneting them. This news flashed through to the men still alive and fighting, who were very bitter. No Germans were taken prisoner by our chaps in the few days following this sorry, inhuman act.[117]

Otherwise, revenge could be sworn or taken for heavy losses sustained in an attack, for previous losses, or for the killing of a popular officer.[118] On 26 October, 1918, for example, the Glasgow Highlanders took the village of Englefontaine. Prisoners were taken and many Germans killed. "The recent losses that they had suffered did not perhaps tend to make the Highlanders more merciful." "After the action a Worcestershire officer told the C.O. that he had asked a Glasgow Highlander N.C.O. how many prisoners he had taken and got the reply, 'Prisoners? None, my ammunition's not done yet!'"[119] In his poem, "Three Battles to the 51st Division", the soldier-poet E.A. Mackintosh of 5th Seaforths exulted in the killing at Beaumont-Hamel, as revenge for the slaughter at High Wood in July:

114　IWM 2528 Bradbury, memoir, p.36.
115　THM Seaforths 96-36, Tweddle, notebook, letter of 28 February, 1915. See also: Chambers, *Diaries of World War 1*, pp.67-68.
116　Apart from examples cited, see also: LC GS 1761 Wilson, memoir, pp.72-73; GHM PB1892.3.18 McDonald, 'Uncle Harper's Duds', p.145; ASHM N-E11 Bowie, diary, 9 April, 1917; THM Camerons 02-40 Johnston, background notes; GHM PB 580 D.C.B., 'The attack June 1918 at La Bassee Canal as remembered by Charles Cran'; LC GS1507 Sotheby, diary, 13 March, 1915; ASHM N-E8-5. Un-attributed typescript account, 'At Beaumont-Hamel with the 8th Argylls, Nov. 13th, 1916'; Sutherland, *War Diary*, p.102.
117　LC GS 0132 Betteridge, memoir, Vol.1, p.45.
118　Apart from examples cited, see: Blaser, *Kilts across the Jordan*, p.112; THM Seaforths 81-180, Murray, letter to sister Alex, 15 May, 1915; IWM 5525 Steven, letter from Lt. Harvey Steven to home, 6 October, 1915; ASHM N-E11 Bowie, diary, 25 September, 1915; Sotheby, *10th Argylls*, p.49; Cavendish, *An Reisimeid Chataich*, p.258.
119　IWM Books, Reid, 'Shoulder to Shoulder,' pp.333-334.

> Ghosts of the heroes
> That died in the Wood
> Looked on the killing
> And saw it was good.[120]

And sometimes there appears to have been merciless killing for no particular identified reason.[121] Frank Brooke was at Arras, as a stretcher-bearer with 4th Seaforths. Moving up behind the assault, he met Sergeant John Campbell and asked him, "Have you any prisoners?" "No", he replied, "What for wad we tak' prisoners? They're a' deid!"[122] Finally, Lauchlan Maclean Watt, who served as a chaplain with both the Gordon Highlanders and the Black Watch, relates the following "amusing" story, which illustrates how lightly the merciless killing of Germans might be viewed even within the church:

> It is told of Jock that, on another occasion, when a German held up his hands after a good deal of dirty work with them, and said, 'Mercy, Englishman! I'll go to England with you,' Jock replied grimly and coolly, 'Maybe, but ye see that's no exactly whaur I'm gawn to send ye.'[123]

In fairness, there were also examples of restraint and attempts made by officers to contain the killing.[124] At Loos, while searching a deep dugout with two companions, John Bowie came across a wounded German:

> One of the other couple made to rush his bayonet through him and the German tore his shirt open, showing a fine crucifix on his chest, sticking it out, inviting the bayonet to finish his misery. The chap immediately withdrew exclaiming 'NAW'. The look of the crucifix is enough on a Roman Catholic.[125]

Clearly, despite such restraint, there was a considerable amount of merciless killing on the battlefield, frequently with no quarter given. After 1st Black Watch launched a raid on the night of 3 July, 1917, near the town of Nieuport, their chaplain, Donald McLeod, noted that the men could be "frightful savages when they get loose." "Legalised murder is the true name for a lot that goes on in war: and the strange fact is the joy men take in killing other men."[126]

But to what extent were the soldiers simply acting under orders? There is conflicting evidence on this topic. Duncan Mackenzie, who served in 4th Camerons at Neuve Chapelle, in March, 1915, claimed long after the event that, "on assembling outside the trench on the night of

---

120 Campbell & Green, *Can't shoot a man with a cold*, pp.167-169 (from *War the Liberator*). See also Sutherland, *War Diary*, p.81.
121 See for example: IWM 15175 White, memoir; IWM 13511 Macgregor, account of the actions at Longueval and Delville Wood, written July, 1916.
122 IWM Books Brooke, 'Wait for it', pp.194-195.
123 Watt, *In France and Flanders*, p.179.
124 LC GS 0158 Bolton, memoir, 'Reactions to First World War'; LC Transcripts, Tape 603, Rose-Miller, interview.
125 ASHM N-E11 Bowie, diary, 25 September, 1915.
126 NLS Acc.9084 No.7 McLeod, letter to sister Nan, 5 July, 1917.

the 10th of March, the instruction was passed along before we set out to take the village:- 'NO FIRING, NO PRISONERS, BOMBS and BAYONETS ONLY.'"[127] I have found no corroborative evidence for this, and Private Monty Goodban, in the same battalion, records the taking of about 300 prisoners in the same battle, after their white flags were respected.[128] Private George Ramage, in 1st Gordons, recorded in his diary that one of his platoon officers in 1915, Lieutenant Thom, "told us he would not mind if we took no prisoners."[129] This is probably true, and seems to constitute "passive permission" from a specific individual rather than a direct order. Unfortunately the context is unknown. There is more evidence from Loos. Private David Wood in 7th Camerons states that, "Orders were take no prisoners but they gave up in such large numbers that you couldn't help it.[130] Private Frank Collier, in 2nd Argylls, records that "We got their 1st and 2nd lines very quickly, taking no prisoners, which order we received beforehand."[131] Jim Sutherland in 1st Camerons made the same claim;

> Before we had left our own trenches, we got orders to 'take no prisoners', so when we got into the German first line, they were packed in their dug-outs, but a couple of hand bombs did the trick!!! It was cold-blooded murder but at that time we were seeing red and past all state of saneness. There were hundreds of them putting up their hands and crying for mercy, but it was no use; they were all done in!![132]

Given the ruthlessness and lack of mercy we have already recorded at Loos, it does seem possible that some soldiers at least were acting under orders. During the battle of the Somme, on 15 July, 1916, the Glasgow Highlanders moved into High Wood, where "it had been suggested that no prisoners should be taken," although humanity prevailed and some were.[133]

On 12 April, 1917, Lieutenant Oldham of 5th Seaforths, stated that the battalion did very well in the battle of Arras, "and very few prisoners were taken! I had told them not to worry about them."[134] And on 15 April, Harry Pelham Burn, now commanding 152nd Brigade in 51st Highland Division, wrote of their performance "I prefer dead Bosch to prisoners … & I am glad to say that this Division is not as fond of taking prisoners as some."[135]

On 25 August, 1917, Private Douglas, in 11th Argylls, was briefed about a forthcoming operation to take a German pillbox, in which the commander of the storming party, Captain Cameron, ordered that no prisoners had to be taken.[136] There seems to be no reason to doubt that this is accurate. In his diary for 19 September, 1917, Arthur Wrench of 4th Seaforths, then a brigade runner, notes that, "At the R.S. saw Col. Rowbotham's 'orders' written up outside the

---

127 THM Camerons 94-8 Mackay, 'Tell Them of Us,' letter from Duncan Mackenzie to William Mackay, 15 March, 1973.
128 IWM 12205 PP Goodban, Pte M.S., diary, 11 March, 1915.
129 NLS MS 844 Ramage, diary, 20 April, 1915. Note that although Ramage's comment appears under the date of 20 April, 1915, the exact timing of Thom's remark is uncertain.
130 THM Camerons 01-148 Wood, letter to sister Julia, n.d.
131 ASHM NE-2 Collier, journal.
132 IWM 11923 PP Sutherland, J., letter to father, c. October, 1915.
133 Aiken, *Courage Past*, pp.56, 58.
134 LC GS 1203, Oldham, diary, 12 April, 1917.
135 GHM PB3309 Pelham Burn, letter to mother, 15 April, 1917.
136 IWM 4586 Douglas, memoir, pp.63-65.

orderly room. It was with reference to the attack on Poelcapelle tomorrow morning and ended with 'NO PRISONERS' [crossed out], which with the line scored through meant 'do as you please.'"[137] Nevertheless, many prisoners were actually taken during the attack. Finally, in the Gordons archives there is an unattributed record of an address by Colonel Wolfe Murray to 1st Gordons on the eve of the battle at La Bassee Canal, which took place on 14/15 June, 1918.

> Officers, N.C.O.'s and Men: Tomorrow at 3 a.m. you go 'over the top.' My advice to you is take no prisoners. Kill all the Boches. If you don't, they will eat part of your rations and their spawn will live and fight us again 20 to 25 years from now. I wish you good fighting and good luck.[138]

I have no independent validation of this account. It does however appear that there was at the very least some official acquiescence in the use of the bayonet on potential prisoners, and at worst orders to do so, albeit such orders were rarely written down. By contrast, Sergeant Charles Forman of 8th Black Watch states that, before they went into action on 20 September, 1917, "strict orders were given that prisoners *must be taken*, [author's italics] as the Germans the rumour [sic] that the Jocks don't take prisoners."[139] This extraordinary statement, if true, would suggest that higher command felt the issue was real and becoming noticeable, and wished to stamp it out either for reasons of ethics or image.

Killing the enemy at the point of surrender is one thing; killing prisoners after they have been taken is another. There are, sadly, a number of examples of this practice. The ruthlessness at Loos has already been described. Alexander Braes served in the ranks of 8th Seaforths there. He records;

> One batch of Germans whom the Black Watch had rounded up were placed against a wall and one of our machine-guns did the rest. Another batch were being marched back when one of their number took a rifle from one of our wounded and shot him dead. That was sufficient. The whole bunch of about forty were put into a trench and the guards threw several bombs amongst them.[140]

Howard Panton was also at Loos in 7th Camerons. He and his colleagues had a German officer in a cellar surrender to them: "the German we did not know what to do with so we sent him on in front and as he got a few yards away I shot him.[141] When R.S.M. Neilson of 1st Gordons, nicknamed 'Scraggs' was killed by a sniper during an action on 1 March, 1916, Corporal Harry Robertson had mixed feelings: "I wasn't so sorry for him. I saw him shoot 2 prisoners that morning about 7.0 a.m. I told him what I thought of him – he told me to go to hell. Guess he went first anyway."[142] Norman Collins, in 4th Seaforths, recalled that at Beaumont-Hamel:

---

137 IWM 3834 Wrench, diary, 19 September, 1917.
138 GHM PB 580 D.C.B.
139 BWA Forman, memoir.
140 THM 2013-072 (S) Braes, diary, pp.30-31, 25 September 1915.
141 IWM 11241 Panton, letter to brother Tom, 29 September, 1915.
142 GHM PB1706/2 Robertson, 'Diary', additional notes written in Rouen in 1918.

I did hear one or two stories of German prisoners being killed on the way back. And I know one particular one, I'm not going to say too much about it, but we didn't think it right and I was told afterwards that that man had lost two brothers and he was a bit demented himself.[143]

During the attack on the la Bassee Canal in June, 1918, Private Charlie Cran and his colleagues took 10 prisoners at a German pill-box:

So now the problem was there was only eight of us. We couldn't spare any men to take them back as we still had another line of fortifications to take. They would have ganged up on one Gordon and have killed him, so we told them to vamoose back to our lines … We kept watching them. Suddenly they decided to make a break for it back to their own lines. We went down on one knee. No order was given and we poured rapid fire into them until every one of them was dead.[144]

On other occasions, German prisoners only survived through the intervention of Highland officers. Johnnie Wood, for example, an officer in 10th Gordons, did well to preserve a large batch of over 200 prisoners at Loos from the men, who wanted to finish them off.[145] Likewise, Neil Weir, an officer with 10th Argylls, helped to stop the killing of about 50 prisoners by some overenthusiastic men of the Black Watch and Seaforths during the assault on Longueval on 14th July, 1916.[146] Lieutenant Richard Watson was in action with 8/10th Gordons at Arras on 22 April. At one stage, "I was just in time to see some Boche prisoners being shelled by their own guns. I wanted to scupper some of them, but Vickers, M.O. of the Black Watch, wanted them for stretcher bearing, and they were saved."[147] Lieutenant John Turing went into action with 8th Seaforths in Third Ypres on 31 July, 1917. He was in the second wave and his job was to "mop up".

My attention was suddenly directed to a nearby shell-hole. Out of it came two scared Bosches, holding up their hands and 'Kamerading' as the 'Jocks' called it. I saw my corporal clubbing one of them with a rifle and shouted to him to stop it at once. My platoon sergeant helped me to call him off. Poor Urquhart, the corporal, had just had his brother killed by the Bosches in another attack, and his highland blood was boiling with bitterness and rage against them, and he was determined to revenge his brother's death. But we could not allow butchery.[148]

In some cases escorts might be required to save prisoners from vengeance, as John Bowie, in 11th Argylls, recalls of a sniper captured during the Somme.[149] On occasion prisoners might

---

143 IWM 12043 Collins, interview.
144 GHM PB 580 D.C.B., 'The attack June 1918 at La Bassee Canal as remembered by Charles Cran.'
145 NLS Acc. 12729, Wood, letter to brother Willie, 29 September, 1915.
146 David, *Mud and Bodies*, p.66.
147 GHM PB2183 Watson, memoirs, p.14.
148 LC GS 1635 Turing, memoir. For other examples, see: ASHM N-E8.5. Anon, 'At Beaumont-Hamel'; LC GS 1761 Wilson, memoir, p.77.
149 ASHM N-E11 Bowie, diary, 14 August, 1916.

be killed simply because the job of escorting them back to the rear might be too dangerous. Graham Hutchison recalls:

> On one occasion, during the minor operations to the east of High Wood in August, 1916, I witnessed a Highland sergeant in charge of three prisoners, following a shallow communication trench under heavy shell fire, hesitate, then dispatch his prisoners with a rifle and return to the front line.[150]

During Passchendaele, Roy Henley, in 42nd Battalion C.E.F., was in a daylight raiding party which managed to capture three German prisoners, but was then cut off. Knowing that they would have difficulty getting the prisoners back, the corporal pushed the three prisoners into a shell-hole and tossed a grenade in after them.[151]

Prisoners might also be given short shrift if they proved awkward. John Bowie records an incident on 15 September, 1916, during an attack on the Somme, when a party of Germans were taken prisoner while sheltering in a dugout. The officer proved awkward and insulting, so the escort "shot him dead without any hesitation and the remainder got afraid and were marched back peacefully."[152] Bradbury in 5th Seaforths recalls how at Arras, he advised a young Argyll in charge of a party of obstinate German prisoners to "get rid of" the leading troublemaker.[153]

There might also be a refusal by individual soldiers to help wounded German prisoners. William Chambers in 1st Camerons described how, on a very dark night, he and his pal Paddy McGuire picked up a stretcher containing a wounded German without knowing it. "As soon as P. McG discovered the fact he refused to carry it any further while there were men of our own lying back at the dump waiting to be carried away."[154]

In fact, the whole process of surrendering was fraught with risk. Private Thomas Alexander of 8th Seaforths records that on 10 August, 1916, during the battles of the Somme, "Jerries came running out of Martinpuich towards us, as prisoners, but men opened fire and the artillery started, so they had to go back again."[155] Sergeant Charles Forman in 8th Black Watch describes how, as they were advancing on 20 September, 1917, they came up against a pill-box, with three or four Germans standing on top with their hands up to surrender, one of whom was instantly unthinkingly shot by one of his men.[156] Wounded in an attack in October, 1918, Charles Forman recalls, "I saw 2 German prisoners. I beckoned them over to me, and they were only too glad to help. They were safe with me. If they had been roaming about long on their own they might have been picked off with a bullet."[157] It appears that on occasion, as we have already seen, German soldiers used Red Cross armlets to increase their chances of survival when positions were over-run or when taken prisoner.[158]

---

150 Hutchison, *Warrior*, p.184.
151 LC Transcripts, Tape 850, Henley, interview.
152 ASHM N-E11 Bowie, diary, 15 September, 1916.
153 IWM 2528 Bradbury, memoir, p.19.
154 Chambers, *Diaries of World War 1*, pp.65-66.
155 IWM 12392 Alexander, diary, 10 August, 1916.
156 BWA Forman, memoir.
157 Ibid. See also BWA Hay, memoir, p.190.
158 IWM 4586 Douglas, memoir, pp.412-414; BWA Hay, memoir, pp.172-174.

Lucky man. South African Scottish troops carrying a wounded German on a stretcher during the Battle of the Menin Road Ridge, 21 September 1917. (IWM Q2869)

German prisoners were frequently pressed into use to carry the wounded.[159] Whatever the ethics of this practice, it did at least help to ensure their survival, assuming they were not killed by shelling from their own side. By contrast, Douglas Wimberley's exploitation of frightened German prisoners to help construct machine-gun positions during the battle of Cambrai was a clear breach of the rules of warfare.[160]

Unsurprisingly, perhaps, German prisoners were often frightened and fearful of their fate.[161] Douglas Wimberley was able to push his enslaved prisoners to prodigies of labour as, "I fancy that they had seen a few of their comrades bayoneted or shot a few minutes previously."[162] This was often put down to the fear of the kilt by their captors. We have considered this point at length in the previous chapter, and indeed it is just possible that the Germans had been told to expect ruthless treatment from kilted troops, given the ruthlessness we have described above, But in fact, the killing or serious mistreatment of prisoners was rare. What was more common was the reluctance to take prisoners in the first place.

One way that German prisoners hoped to survive was by offering "souvenirs" to their captors.[163] Such souvenirs included military items such as forage caps, field-glasses or iron crosses, but also included valuables, such as watches, in a process which on occasion was little

---

159 Chambers, *Diaries of World War 1*, p.57.
160 IWM 430 Wimberley, memoirs, Vol.1, p.88.
161 Apart from specific examples cited, see: ASHM N-E2 Hyslop, diary, vol 2, p.23; Craig-Brown, *Historical Records*, Vol.3, p.72.
162 IWM 430 Wimberley, memoirs, Vol.1, p.88.
163 Peel & Macdonald, *6th Seaforth Highlanders*, p.32; IWM 3460 Macmillan, Sandy (Alex) Macmillan to mother, 30 April, 1917; IWM Books Brooke, 'Wait for it', pp.195-196; IWM 2528 Bradbury,

The fortunate ones. Troops of 51st Highland Division with German prisoners during the battle of Cambrai 20 November, 1917. (IWM Q6276)

more than enforced looting. Often the surrender of "souvenirs" was expected and effectively carried out under threat of reprisal. As we have seen, Douglas Wimberley, for one, saw nothing wrong with this procedure."[164]

Despite Wimberley's assertion, prisoners were often treated more generously. Indeed, in the early stages of the war[165] and again during the final advance in 1918,[166] considerable effort was expended in protecting German prisoners from French civilians. There was also sometimes a reassuring recognition of common humanity in the treatment of prisoners. Captain Johnnie Wood, for example, noted that 15th Division took a significant number of prisoners on 15 September, 1916, during the taking of Martinpuich.

> The average Jock is often reported as being very fierce and bloodthirsty in battle, but these Germans could not have fallen into kinder hands. Everybody seemed ready and eager to share his water bottle with any German, and do everything possible for them, and the

---

memoir, p.21; IWM 4586 Douglas, memoir, pp.412-414; GHM PB 580 D.C.B., 'The attack June 1918 at La Bassee Canal as remembered by Charles Cran.'
164 IWM 430 Wimberley, memoirs, Vol.1, p.67.
165 THM Camerons 99-87 Macpherson, diary, 24 August, 1914; Craig-Brown, *Historical Records*, Vol.3, pp.31, 35; IWM 18455 Turnbull, letter to mother, dad and Sylvia, 15 September, 1914; LC GS 1124, Moffat, diary, 19 September, 1914; IWM 12007 Wilson, memoir, pp.32-33; ASHM N-E11 Bowie, diary, 18 September, 1915.
166 ASHM N-E11 Bowie, diary; Urquhart, *Canadian Scottish*, p.319.

Colonel whom we entertained thanked us profusely for the way we were treating and attending to the men, many of whom were wounded and a good few seriously.[167]

And long after the event, interviewed in 1998, Robert Burns, who served in 7th Camerons, stated, "The men who were taken prisoner, they were just human beings, the same as us. Our regiment didn't kill any prisoners; we weren't like that. I don't say others did it, but we treated them all as human beings."[168]

Indeed alongside the ferocity, to which much attention has been devoted, there was compassion, which extended also to the wounded. Captain D.W. Pailthorpe, M.O. to 2nd Gordons, records removing German wounded from dug-outs on 2 July, 1916. "They seem grateful – poor devils for the fact that we were carrying them into the care of the British instead of being left to die in these smashed up dug-outs.[169] John Bowie of 11th Argylls records that on 24 September, 1918, B Coy made a raid and only took one German whom they had pity on

> He received a stomach wound but not dangerous. On finding himself on a stretcher for hospital and being carried by British he could hardly realise he was a prisoner. Finally he commenced to cry like a kiddy, although he looked young. On examining his Pay Book he was only 15 years old.[170]

When Private Douglas of 11th Argylls, was transferred from a hospital train to a hospital ship at Calais, he was upset that "the orderlies at the stairway did not take the same amount of care when handling the stretchers with the German wounded. This I thought was not quite playing the game."[171] Norman Collins was present at Beaumont-Hamel with 4th Seaforths:

> I remember a German, a young German prisoner ... hopping, coming in with a piece of wood ... acting as a crutch ... And I wasn't popular because I had him put on to a stretcher and taken back with the British wounded behind the lines ... but he was a young fellow, he didn't look more than eighteen, he was badly wounded and he couldn't walk except hop with this crutch ... and I suppose I felt sorry for him [172]

Sergeant Sid Wood, serving in an unspecified battalion of the Seaforths, took part in the attack on 31 July, 1917:

> As soon as dawn broke, out came the Germans from their trenches, white flag in hand, saying 'Kamerad'. Poor devils, our shellfire had driven them half insane. Many of them were wounded. I asked one for a souvenir. He understood me, and turned round and showed me the back of his thigh. There was a tear in it about 6" long and his trousers were

---

167 NLS Acc. 12729, Wood, letter to brother Willie, 22 September, 1916.
168 IWM 12678 Burns, transcriptions of interviews.
169 GHM PB375 Pailthorpe, memoir, p.15.
170 ASHM N-E11 Bowie, diary, 24 September, 1918.
171 IWM 4586 Douglas, memoir, pp.212-213.
172 IWM 12043 Collins, interview.

saturated in blood. 'What a souvenir' – I directed him to the nearest dressing station and turned away with a lump in my throat.[173]

Compassion towards the enemy wounded might extend also to their stretcher-bearers. John Bowie, in 11th Argylls, records an incident during the battle of the Somme, when, after catching the Germans counter-attacking, they let their stretcher-bearers pick up the wounded: "The bearers saluted towards our lines when their task was ended in us paying respect to their Red Cross work."[174]

Even snipers could feel sorry for their victims. Private J. Macdonald, in 1st Argylls, wrote to his female pen pal in Bedford on 3 March, 1915, noting that he had sniped a German. "I feel a bit sorry for that poor Devil (He's a soldier the same as myself and perhaps a better man) but he should not have been so careless."[175]

As the war drew to a close, and the enemy were obviously beaten, the mood might lighten. Captain Wille Brown, in 2nd Gordons, noted that after the crossing of the Piave, "the Austrians were absolutely beaten now and surrendered, white faced, hands up, from every hole and corner. You couldn't kill them; they were such miserable sights."[176] He described how a chase after a sniper ended in laughter and mercy when both pursued and pursuer had to stop to take breath. Then when they took the Austrian headquarters, the prisoners emerged, "with a dozen small boys in uniform, cadets up for experience and instruction. The sight of these frightened youngsters dispelled the last vestiges of savagery raised by the snipers."[177]

There was feeling too for the Germans in defeat. Harold Judd, who served with 2nd London Scottish, recalled when interviewed in 1997, that, after the Armistice;

> The saddest sight I ever saw was the defeated army, marching back to their country. They had to take their equipment to bits and put it at the side of the road, laid down their arms … and then these poor devils, well, they were almost crying, the day they went back. And there wasn't a man in the London Scottish had a cigarette or a bit of tobacco when they went, because we gave it to them.[178]

Alongside the ferocity of war, there was recognition of common humanity. In May, 1918, Lieutenant Guy Macgregor, in 6th Argylls, wrote to his wife: "I hope you are feeling better now about the fighting on the Western Front. No woman of any decency could think about it without a sinking of the heart. Whether it is English boys or Scotch boys or German boys who are being slaughtered in heaps, it's a pity, & for every one there is a broken heart or two at home."[179] Arthur Wrench, in 4th Seaforths, watched German prisoners being brought in on 31 July, 1917, the opening day of the Passchendaele offensive. "Poor devils. Who can blame them for being scared? It was pitiful to

---

173 THM Seaforths 01-25 Wood, Sgt Sidney V, DCM, letter to wife Flo, 6 August, 1917.
174 ASHM N-E11 Bowie, diary, 28 August, 1916.
175 THM Seaforths 87-125, Heriz-Smith, letter from Pte J. McDonald, 3 March, 1915 [assumed 1915, year not stated on original]. See also Alan Mackintosh's poem, 'No Man's Land,' in Campbell & Green, *Can't shoot a man with a cold*, p.100 (from *A Highland Regiment*, p.29).
176 GHM PB1889 Brown, letter, 17 December, 1918.
177 GHM PB1889 Brown, typescript memoir, 'The 20th Brigade on the River Piave, October, 1918.'
178 LC Several Fronts Recollections, Judd, interview. See also IWM 3834 Wrench, diary, 21 October, 1918; IWM Books Reid, 'Shoulder to Shoulder,' p.348.
179 IWM 8592 Macgregor, letter to wife, 3 May, 1918. See also his later letter, 25 August, 1918.

see them and to know that they were all human beings like ourselves sent into this fury of war for God knows what or whom."[180] Douglas Wilson, in 5th Camerons, observed German prisoners after an action at Meteren on 19 July, 1918. "One or two of our own youngsters were hobbling back, wounded like their captives; I noticed a young Bavarian with his arm round the neck of an equally young Jock who was making heavy weather of walking uphill – both were smiling."[181] Little could show better this feeling of common humanity than the actions of Captain Cland Low. On 11 July, 1915, he wrote to his wife, stating that on the 9th the body of a dead German, August Kleeb of Infanterie Regiment Nr.113 was discovered in an empty ruined house, and he had collected particulars, including those of next of kin, Marie Mosen of Herbolzheim (Breisgau)

> I could not write but I suggest that you send a note to this lady & say that your husband fighting in France found the body & buried it decently; after the war if she writes to you, you will inform her of the spot. He was evidently killed in December last. It might mean a lot to someone.[182]

Such recognition of common humanity did not require a rejection of the war. Rather there was, as we have already recognised, the feeling of a people led astray. As Guy Macgregor put it, "The German people were led astray, led astray as simple people may be, by trusting in the brains of clever people & ignoring the admonitions of their own hearts."[183]

The best known example of shared humanity was, of course, the Christmas Truce of 1914. This has been well-described elsewhere.[184] Several Highland battalions were involved; 2nd Argylls,[185] 2nd Seaforths[186] and 2nd and 6th Gordons.[187] In 6th Gordons, it effectively lasted well into the New Year. Yet Captain Bryden McKinnell in the Liverpool Scottish was nevertheless happy to record:

> Luckily the troops holding our immediate line of trenches just waited until the Germans got out of the trenches, then they let them have it, rapid fire; it stopped any of this 'scratch my back and I'll scratch yours' sort of nonsense.[188]

---

180 IWM 3834 Wrench, diary, 31 July, 1917.
181 LC GS 1761 Wilson, memoir, p.73. For similar accounts of fraternisation amongst the wounded, see: IWM Books Cooper, 'Domi Militaeque,' p.158; LC Tape 921, Stuart, interview; IWM 3834 Wrench, diary, 13 November, 1916.
182 IWM 6702 Low, letter to wife, 11 July, 1915.
183 IWM 8592 Macgregor, letter to wife, 4 October, 1918.
184 See: Brown, Malcolm & Seaton, Shirley, *Christmas Truce*, (London: Pan Books, 2001); Weintraub, Stanley, *Silent Night*, (London: Simon & Schuster, 2001); Thermaenius, Pehr, *The Christmas Match* (London: Uniform Press, 2014)..
185 LC GS 1535 Stewart, Tape 359, interview; ASHM NE-2 Collier, journal, Christmas Day, 1914; ASHM N-F.2 Hyslop, diary, vol 1, pp.94-96; IWM 11126 Liddell, diary, 24 & 25 December, 1914. See also his letters to his mother, 25 December, 1914 & to his friend, Flum, 29 December, 1914; IWM 15460 Chandler, letter to sister Alethea, 24 & 25 December, 1914. See also letter to Marjorie Raimes, 1 January, 1915
186 Mackenzie, *Diary and Letters*, p.63, diary, Christmas Day, 1914.
187 LC WF Recollections G5, Gillespie, typescript record of interview; LC GS 0828, Imlah, A., letter to father, 28 December, 1914, reproduced in the *Banffshire Journal*, 5 January, 1915; LC GS 1422 Sanders, diary, 25 December, 1914, to 10 January, 1915.
188 McKinnell, *Diary*, p.42.

More remarkable, and less well known, were the instances of "live and let live" which occurred at other times throughout the war. The image of the aggressive bayonet-toting Highland soldier would appear to preclude such activity. This was far from the case and a number of instances are recorded. Sometimes these were just short truces for mutual convenience. Thus, in December 1916, 7th Argylls were holding the line in front of the village of Pys, in the vicinity of Courcelette, where conditions were atrocious for both sides. "So difficult was it on both sides to carry down wounded or to bury dead, that the Red Cross Flag was scrupulously respected. German infantry and Argylls could have been seen there at dawn every day almost side by side, burying their dead in No Man's Land, and shivering in the December sleet."[189] Indeed the common war against the elements is a common theme in such arrangements. A long truce, lasting several days, until eventually stopped by orders from above, was enjoyed between 2nd Argylls and the Saxon regiment opposite in early 1915, in order to construct breastworks when both sets of trenches became waterlogged.[190] When 6th Argylls were involved in mud-clearing in the winter of 1916/17, they heard German working parties doing the same job, and both sides left each other alone to get on with it.[191] Such activity was not confined to the Western Front. For 1st Seaforths in the trenches in Mesopotamia in the summer of 1916, faced with locust-plagues, "Life became so intolerable that quite a definite sympathy arose between ourselves and the Turks, so much as to say – 'There is quite enough to fight without fighting one another.'"[192]

Sometimes "live and let live" might apply to the mutual avoidance of danger. Daniel McFarlane in 8th Seaforths remarked that in December, 1915, with both sides engaged in nerve-racking patrols, they agreed to "a mutual policy of live and let live."[193] One night in February, 1917, Private Welsh met a sentry who had observed a German patrol lost in the mist, looking for a gap in the wire. "'Why did you not shoot them?' 'No me! I did not come out here to murder some poor devils lost in the mist, so I told them to go further to the right and try and crawl through under it.'"[194]

On at least three occasions, relatively peaceful co-existence lasted for weeks. Jim Cunningham, then machine-gun officer with 1st Argylls, wrote of the trenches the battalion occupied in the Armentieres area in June, 1915:

> I'm told nobody ever thinks of firing except a little at night just to satisfy the Generals. The only time people fire is when the Germans are digging. We sometimes fire as we see the shovel come over the top of the trench. Then they signal a hit or a miss as the case may be. You hear this is the place where at Xmas they had a six weeks truce.[195]

Similarly, Captain John Hay-Young, wrote, "After what we have been accustomed to, it is just peace not war … The Germans … are most peaceful and rarely fire, and you never hear a gun!

---

189 Morrison, *7th Battalion The Great War*, pp.22-24. See also: Topp, *42nd Battalion*, p.95.
190 Chandler, 'Winter and Spring in Flanders 1914-1915', pp.3, 5. See also: LC GS 1535 Stewart, Tape 359, interview; Hutchison, *Warrior*, pp.61-62; THM Camerons 93-35 Welsh, memoirs, p.11.
191 Maclean, *On Active Service*, Vol.2, p.15.
192 LC Several Fronts Recollections, Kingsley, memoir.
193 THM Camerons 89-17, McFarlane, memoir.
194 THM Camerons 93-35 Welsh, memoirs, pp.24-25.
195 LC GS 0409 Cunningham, letter to mother 10 June, 1915.

It is a farce. Long may it last!!"[196] Cunningham observes also how, later in 1915, in the Somme sector, there were two huge craters on the battalion's front. "We occupied the outside of half the lip and the Germans occupied the outside lip of the other half. At the Craters themselves it was a case of live and let live."[197] Frederick Jackson served in the Liverpool Scottish. He recalled towards the end of November, 1915, in the St Eloi area, an extraordinary unofficial truce with the enemy, which lasted for three weeks. On one occasion, "Sergeant Fergusson went over to the German crater one night for cognac and cigars with these Saxons and met an old schoolfriend in the German Army, who had been at school with him at, I think, Liverpool University College."[198]

There were, however, some less happy experiences.[199] Attempts by men of 16th Battalion C.E.F. (Canadian Scottish) to fraternise at Christmas, 1915, were cut short by a burst of machine-gun fire.[200] James Racine with 5th Seaforths records that, in August, 1915 in the front line at La Boiselle;

> Only fifteen yards separated the enemy trench from our own. It had been comparatively quiet and the Germans and [our] men had exchanged souvenirs by simply tossing them from one trench to the other. One day, however, one of [our] men shouted out, 'I'm sending over a present, Fritz.' Instead of throwing a souvenir, he threw a live bomb. From that time onwards, the place was a little hell to occupy.[201]

Conclusions

It is evident that hatred of the Germans was widespread amongst Highland soldiers and was fuelled by continuous perceived German breaches of the norms of 'civilised' warfare, real acts, which underpinned the exaggerated propaganda, and which continued until the Armistice. There was some respect for the Germans as soldiers, and also as a people, with a recognition of common humanity. But the latter-day denial that hatred existed is simply not supported by the evidence. Overall, feelings were ambivalent, with a common notion being that of a people led astray by their leaders. Passions were further aroused by both unsupported allegations and eye-witness evidence of German mal-practice on the battlefield, although examples of enemy fair-play were also noted. The awful experience of shell-fire and the loss of one's pals also contributed to hatred. On the battlefield, Highland soldiers could display dreadful ruthlessness, at times brutality. This was evident at Loos, but also subsequently throughout the war in clearing dug-outs and on raids. There is evidence not only of liberal use of the bayonet at the point of surrender, but also of the killing of prisoners. It is possible that the Germans did feel some fear of kilted troops because of a reputation for mistreatment or not taking prisoners, and there is no

---

196 LC GS 0731 Hay-Young, letters to father, 31 May, 15 June, 1915.
197 LC GS 0409 Cunningham, notes written 1976. See also: LC GS 1026 Maclean, diary, p.15.
198 Jackson, 'Captain Noel Godfrey Chavasse.'
199 Apart from references below, see THM S796(R) Cartmell, memoir; IWM 16335 Racine, memoir, p.52.
200 Urquhart, *Canadian Scottish*, pp.114-115.
201 IWM 16335 Racine, memoir, p.55.

doubt that some Highland troops revelled in their reputation for fierceness. At the same time, there were some notable examples of restraint, and some prisoners were treated generously, with a recognition of common humanity. Such a feeling was most famously displayed during the Christmas Truce, but also, and much less commonly known, in several instances of a deliberate policy of 'live and let live.'

16

Courage and Failure

> Nobody in my opinion could possibly be in the trenches or be under shell fire and not be frightened. I can't imagine it."[1]

In this chapter we investigate the fallibility of the Highland soldier. There is no shortage of sources which stress the courage of the Highland soldier, but few, if any, which address the other side of the coin. There is a need to redress the balance. This is not to deny, of course, the many incidents of courageous, even heroic, behaviour by Highland soldiers on the battlefield, or the many other ways in which quiet courage and determination were shown. We spend less time on these exploits simply because they are well known, even taken for granted. By contrast, the fallibility of the Highland soldier has received little attention, and this chapter seeks to redress the balance. We will look first at fear, for arguably there can be no courage without fear. We will then look at 'shell shock', or rather nervous disintegration after sudden trauma, and nervous breakdown over time. We will also of necessity look at the question of cowardice, and personal strategies for the avoidance of danger. In examining all these elements we will nevertheless see examples of great courage shine through. The chapter will conclude with what is hoped will be a balanced view of the courage and fallibility of the Highland soldier.

But to set our discussion of fallibility in context, let us look first at two unspectacular incidents which, leaving aside the V.C.'s, remind us of the courage with which we more traditionally associate the Highland regiments.[2] The first story is related by Captain Pailthorpe, who took up the position of Medical Officer with 2nd Gordons shortly before the Somme.

> On the morning of June 30th the bombing Sergeant approached me. 'May I speak to you, sir?' 'Yes, what is it?' 'It's about Private Wright, sir – you've marked him unfit – he thinks his arm is alright now and as he has been training for the Gaff [July 1] he'll feel disappointed if you stop him going in with the rest'. Wright was a young bomber aged 19 whom I had thought – owing to his youthful appearance and an abscess that he had under his arm – to have kept … out of the attack, but his arm was now actually sound and as he wanted to go I said 'Yes'. There was a formal sick parade at 3 p.m. at which only two men

---

1 IWM 12043 Collins, interview.
2 For other inspirational examples, see: GHM PB1639, Kemp, memoir, p.18; GHM PB507 Wallace, memoir; GHM PB375 Pailthorpe, memoir, pp.40, 57.

appeared – ... only two men and yet most of the men knew just what they might encounter on the morrow. They knew too their own traditions. It would be no fault of theirs if July 1st was a failure. I felt if I had to go into this sort of thing it was at least great to be with them – great with no little responsibility. I did not wonder that Colonel Gordon felt proud of his battalion.

Private Wright was killed in the attack, shot through the abdomen. "I wrote to Wright's family and had a letter back. He was, of course, the only son."[3]

A second example is related by C.S.M. Peter Stewart in 8th Gordons, who wrote proudly to his wife about the behaviour of his men after shelling in August 1915:

Some of my poor lads have suffered this morning. One lad I shall remember as long as God spares me; he has a heart like a lion. When the war broke out he was in America. He came home to Scotland and enlisted in the regiment. The poor lad this morning caught the full effects of a shell. His left hand was blown off and he was wounded in about six other places (neither of them slight). He was bandaged up as well as could be done in the trenches and had to lie waiting for the doctor. His thoughts were all for the others. When I went to him he was singing 'It's a long way to Tipperary'. He looked up to me and said, 'How did the other[s] get on?' Although the others were gone to their last roll call I told a white lie and said, 'Oh, they're all right, how are you doing now?' He replied, 'I'm doing grand, are you all right yourself [Sergeant] Major?' Poor old chap, he was a good lad and I think his heart will pull him through.

Another lad who I am afraid I will never see in the field again only seemed to worry because he did not know how he would manage to sleep on a soft bed again. A lad who had his foot blown off said that leg had always been a trouble to him. First he broke it, then he had rheumatics in it, and now it was bad again. He has had three brothers killed in the war. I am sure, love, their pluck could not be beat by any soldiers that ever lived and they are not the superior class we heard about, just the same old working lads who have made the Army what it is and will keep it there.[4]

Recognising such courage, we may turn now to look at fallibility, and will start by exploring the question of fear. Interviewed in 1976, Brigadier I.M. Stewart, a pre-war regular officer with 2nd Argylls, asked if he had felt apprehensive when coming under shell-fire for the first time at Le Cateau, denied that men were frightened

No, I don't think one had, anybody had, any apprehension. One looked upon war as part of your ultimate purpose, you see. The men weren't frightened. Naturally one didn't like it but one just had to remember the extremely high emotional idealistic condition we were in. You see, Britain at that time was at the end of a romantic period. Kipling was our poet and Land of Hope and Glory was our song.[5]

3   GHM PB375 Pailthorpe, pp.9-10, 15,16.
4   GHM PB2021 Stewart, letters to wife, 7, 12 August, 1915.
5   LC GS 1535 Stewart, interview.

Courage and Failure 441

Memorial to Sergeant John Meikle, V.C., outside Dingwall railway station, erected by his railway comrades. Meikle was a railway clerk at Nitshill station before he enlisted. He was killed in action on 20 July, 1918. (Photograph, author)

Others strongly disagree. Interviewed the same year, Brigadier R.C.B. Anderson, who served as a junior officer with 9th Argylls during the war, stated, "It is nonsense to say that people are not frightened because you are. There is no doubt about that but one managed to conquer it. That is the only thing to do."[6] Norman Collins, who served as a subaltern in 6th Seaforths, felt, "You're always frightened. Nobody in my opinion could possibly be in the trenches or be under shell fire and not be frightened. I can't imagine it."[7] It is indeed conceivable that professional soldiers, in the first months of the war, took fear in their stride, and there are soldiers who state, on occasion at least, that they felt no fear.[8] But most accounts demonstrate that, unless somehow suppressed, fear was almost universal and omnipresent at critical times.[9] Fear was common to all ranks, officers and men, even to Commanding Officers. Colonel Wallace, commanding 10th Gordons, had his baptism of fire at Vermelles on 28 July 1915:

> I was distinctly frightened and when after a little we emerged from our shelter to the open again, I am afraid that my glasses were directed more to ascertaining the neighbourhood of friendly cover than to the operations of digging which I had often seen before and which did not present any novelty to me, which the shells did.[10]

There was also in all ranks the fear of giving in to fear, or of being seen to be afraid. When J.E.P. Levyns joined the South African Scottish in 1916, "I had one great fear: that when the test of battle came, I would prove to be a coward. I was the least pugnacious of men and had been horribly afraid of being hurt in the few fights I had had at school, fights in which I had always been the loser!"[11] A.E. Mackintosh, war-poet of the Seaforths, who took a harsh view of failed nerves, in his poem 'Death,' prayed that he would not be seen if he were to break down himself:

> Oh, God of battles, I pray you send
> No word of pity – no help no friend,
> That if my spirit break at the end
> None may be there to see.[12]

True courage was really the ability to overcome such fear. William Kemp put it rather well when he wrote; "I always considered that the truest form of courage was not that of the fellow who ignored shells at all times, but that of the lad who, naturally very windy, was able, because he knew it was his job and had to be done, [to carry] through any task no matter how dangerous."[13] As Robert Burns, insisted in 1996, "Every man that went over the top was a brave man."[14] The issue was particularly pertinent to officers, who could not afford to show their fear in a position

---

6   LC GS 003 Anderson, interview.
7   IWM 12043 Collins, interview.
8   LC GS 0257 Cameron, memoir.
9   See, for example: LC GS 1026 Maclean, diary, p.54; IWM 24887 Ashburner, interview.
10 GHM PB507, Wallace, diary, 28 July 1915. See also: GHM PB2093 Craufurd, letter to father, 14 October, to mother, 15 October, 1916.
11 Levyns, *The Disciplines of War*, pp.27-28. See also LC Transcripts Wilson, interview.
12 Campbell & Green, *Can't shoot a man with a cold*, p.192.
13 GHM PB1639 Kemp, memoir, Vol.2, pp.44-45.
14 LC Tape 1316 Burns, interview.

of responsibility.[15] In this respect they were not always successful,[16] and risked contempt from the ranks. Arthur Wrench, for example was not overly impressed by a demonstrably nervous officer of 7th Gordons in September, 1918. "Windy creatures like him make me sick, especially when they are vested with such responsibility. It makes me wonder what in all the world men of his type are given a commission for. They are just a lot of irresponsible fools."[17] Yet old hands in the ranks could be remarkably sympathetic to young officers. Newly commissioned Lieutenant Cowan joined 2nd Argylls at the front in October, 1915. As he took his platoon up to the trenches for the first time, they came under shrapnel fire. "I was in a hell of a funk; funk over myself and funk that I should show it to the other people. I thought I'd done rather well actually, and a little voice said by my side, 'We all feel like that the first time.'" This was his platoon sergeant![18]

Certain categories of men may have been more or less susceptible to nerves. Some, like Hugh Boustead,[19] felt that the officer's need to concentrate his attention on his command responsibilities made him less susceptible to dwelling on fear. Otherwise, there is some evidence that married or engaged men were more susceptible to nerves, as they had more to lose. Captain Wyllie, in 1st Garrison Battalion Seaforth Highlanders on the Salonika front, noted,

> The subaltern I have got with me here, 2/Lt Mann, was perfectly all right and a jolly good sub till he became engaged to a girl at the Base and now his nerves are not quite what they used to be, not from the fact of his being engaged but solely because he begins to hope that he will get out of the show alive as he has now got something more than himself to live for.[20]

Otherwise, those returning to the front after recovery from sickness or wounds might also be more susceptible to nerves. At least Private Douglas thought so.

> From my own observation, although not in every case, men who had been out before, being wounded during the 1915, 1916 & 1917 Battles, and had been discharged from Hospitals and returned to their Units, on returning again to a combat unit in France, were, due to their previous experience of being wounded, inclined to be windy when in the line, and it was all credit to them that they carried on day after day, in spite of their fears.[21]

---

15 LC CO 066 Murray, letter to him from 2Lt Kenneth Campbell, 23 March, 1915; LC GS 003 Anderson, interview; IWM 15175 White, 'General Remarks on War'; GHM PB2183 Watson, memoir, p.6; GHM PB1639 Kemp, memoir, p.74 and 'Narrative of the Fighting at Arras 9th/11th April' by Lieut. J.W.T. Leith, M.C.
16 See, for example, IWM 4586 Douglas, memoir, pp.374-375; THM Camerons 93-35 Welsh, memoirs, p.69; LC GS 1761 Wilson, memoir, p.76.
17 IWM 3834 Wrench, diary, 3 September 1918.
18 LC Tapes 636/653 Cowan, interview. And see: IWM 12043 Collins, interview.
19 Boustead, *The Wind of Morning*, p.37. See also: GHM PB375 Pailthorpe, memoir, p.62.
20 IWM 7508 Wyllie, diary, 1 December, 1917; BWA MacDonald, Coll, letter to wife Mary 15 January, 1918 [original incorrectly dated 1917]. See also: IWM 4586 Douglas, memoir, pp.88-89.
21 IWM 4586 Douglas, memoir, p.863. See also: THM Seaforths 81-2 Cooper, memoir, pp.80-81, 83, 97.

Fear was at its starkest in specific situations; for example, on first hearing the sound of the guns,[22] going into the line for the first time,[23] taking up rations,[24] when under heavy shell-fire,[25] under aerial bombardment,[26] when making one's way to and from the trenches,[27] on patrol,[28] on raids,[29] waiting to go over the top,[30] under gas attack,[31] or in battle.[32] Victor Silvester was only 16 or 17 when he first went up the line with 1/7th Argylls.

> The first time I went up the line we were going up a communications trench and there was light shelling going on and one of the shells landed in the communication trench ... probably about 20 yards ahead of me ... it landed at the soldier's feet and it blew one of his legs off below the knee, the other one above the knee and all his body and that ... was covered with shrapnel. We got him into a stretcher and he was taken away but died on the way. I can't tell you what that did to one and the only thing ... one was more afraid of letting anyone else know that one was frightened and one daren't show it. I suppose if you had been there on your own ... I can't say what you would have got up to ... run away ... but, ... everybody being there ... and the other soldiers and everyone ... and the drilling that you'd had ... the training, it made you stick it out.[33]

Lieutenant Robert White described the last moments before 1st London Scottish went over the top at Gommecourt on 1 July, 1916:

---

22 David, *Mud and Bodies*, p.22, diary extract; GHM uncatalogued Beaton, memoir, pp.18-21.
23 LC GS 0771 Hirsch, interview; GHM uncatalogued Beaton, memoir, pp.18-21.
24 LC GS 0993 Lynden-Bell, 'The Effect on the Emotions.'
25 LC GS 1761 Wilson, memoir, p.58; IWM 4586 Douglas, memoir, pp.352-353, 710-711, 713-714; LC GS 0262 Campbell, diary, 12 November, 1915; THM Camerons 96-52 Laidlaw, 'Grandpa's War,' letters from him to his wife Bertha, 1, 15, 16, 25 July, 1916; IWM 3608 Anderson, memoir; Levyns, *The Disciplines of War*, pp.69-70; IWM 14269 Couper, letter to mother 12 March, 1915; IWM 4586 Douglas, 'Khaki Apron,' pp.374-375; LC CO 066 Murray, letter to him from 2Lt Kenneth Campbell, 23 March, 1915; LC GS 0731 Hay-Young, letter to father, 16 May, 1915; David, *Mud and Bodies*, p.35; LC GS 0552 Ferguson, letters to mother, 21, 23 February, 1918; THM Seaforths 02-23 Dixon, 2Lt H.E.O., letter to Col. Macfarlane, 6 April, 1917; IWM 15175 White, 'General Remarks on War'; IWM 511 Thorburn, letter to mother, 11 June, 7 August, 1915; IWM Books Cooper, 'Domi Militaeque,' p.193; Campbell, *Letters*, letter of 27 September, 1915, pp.77-78; IWM 21092 McGregor, letters to wife Jen, 15, 17, 21 June, 6 August, 1916, to sister-in-law, Lydia, 30 June, 1916.
26 BWA MacDonald, Coll, letter to wife Mary, 30 September, 1 October, 22 December, 1917; LC GS 0552 Ferguson, letter to mother, 29 January, 19 February, 1918; GHM PB1639 Kemp, memoir, Vol.2, pp.44-45.
27 LC GS 1761 Wilson, memoir, p.69; THM Camerons 93-35 Welsh, memoirs, p.69; GHM PB1639 Kemp, memoir, pp.38,80.
28 THM Camerons 89-17 McFarlane, memoir; GHM PB1706/2 Robertson, recollections.
29 IWM 15175 White, 'General Remarks on War.'
30 LC GS 1625 Turing, memoir; GHM PB1639 Kemp, memoir, p.60; GHM PB2183 Watson, memoir, p.20.
31 LC GS 1625 Turing, memoir.
32 IWM 4586 Douglas, memoir, pp.419-420.
33 LC GS 1470 Silvester, interview.

> About 7 a.m. the bombardment commenced, giving one that sinking feeling of the heart akin to seasickness. Word came down one man fainted. Went to see him & found that he was one of the 7 men who had been posted to my platoon out of the draft. I felt sorry for them, for it must have been some shock to encounter such earth convulsions so soon. Gave him some of the Cocoa [prepared for himself by his batman] & warmed him up a bit. Nearer 7.25 gave order to fix bayonets. Very tense moments, every nerve in the body seemed to be quivering. [Then they were off.] I mounted the steps & immediately forgot my fears.[34]

L.A. Lynden Bell served as an officer with 1st Seaforths on the Western Front and later in Mesopotamia. Detained in Baghdad by sand-fly fever, he was interviewed by a member of G.H.Q. who wanted two officers for a job in the military secretary's office for a few weeks. "I told him I wanted to rejoin my regiment and then went to my tent and prayed & prayed that I would be spared another battle."[35]

Fear could be magnified when a soldier was left on his own. Private Douglas records how, on 20 October, 1918, he was on observation duties on his own in a farm building which came under shell-fire:

> I started to lose my grip on myself and became terror stricken, and more so when a salvo dropped so close, as if they had landed just at the other side of the wall I was sheltering behind, the dreaded thought uppermost in my mind that I might get a shell all to myself. The heavy shelling gradually eased and with it I again slowly regained my grip of myself, the feeling of terror had passed. Was not sorry when Lce/Cpl appeared in the door-way … to know my 2 hours spell was up.[36]

One way of dealing with fear was fatalism. David McMillan, who served in the 43rd Battalion C.E.F. (Cameron Highlanders of Canada) wrote about the necessary attitude of the combat soldier:

> If he can become fatalistic, and establish in his mind that the shell which does not carry his number is not likely to harm him, he may not worry too much. The shell which has his number is the one which will probably get him and if he is fortunate in being a true fatalist, he will accept this.[37]

But fatalism might also be accompanied by dangerous superstition. Sergeant George Stables, in 6th Gordons, recalls an action on 14 October, 1918, when a Corporal Henry was wounded in the head. "I went over to bandage him and found out that he had no bandages in his tunic. I took out my own first aid bandages and bandaged his head. He wouldn't take first aid bandages

---

34 IWM 1517/5 White, memoir, 'Gommecourt, 1916.'
35 LC GS 0993 Lynden-Bell, 'The Effect on the Emotions.'
36 IWM 4586 Douglas, memoir, pp.1067-1068. See also: GHM PB1706/2 Roberston, diary, 18 July, 1916; GHM uncatalogued Beaton, memoir, p 119; THM Camerons 93-35 Welsh, memoirs, pp.88-89.
37 McMillan, *Trench Tea and Sandbags*, p.16. See also: IWM 5525 Steven, letter home 1 July, 1915.

with him in action. If he did he thought he would get wounded. I came across several cases like him."[38]

There was also, of course, as we have already seen in the case of young Victor Sylvester, the powerful force of military indoctrination and obedience to orders. Arthur Betteridge of the South African Scottish observed after the war.

> Death and mutilation were daily occurrences finally accepted. One rarely discussed with friends and comrades the ugly features … Only subconsciously did one occasionally think the same fate may soon happen to you. It was not a question of bravery. We were kept busy with the normal regimental chores; no matter what orders were given, they were automatically carried out – no questions asked.[39]

And there was the rum issue. Although this could be abused, a small dose of rum prior to an attack was almost universally regarded by those at the front as a useful tonic for nerves, despite opposition by the tee-total lobby. Lieutenant John Turing was waiting to go over the top with 8th Seaforths on 31 July, 1917.

> Thank God, here came the rum issue. Everyone had a tot and spirits rose a little and a few whispered jokes were exchanged. Those narrow-minded cranks at Headquarters who refused rum to troops going 'over the top' could never have experienced this long drawn out waiting in chilling mist. We were chilled to the bone and vitality was low at this hour, and we were naturally a bag of nerves. A tot of rum was wonderfully warming both to body and spirit.[40]

There is no shame in fear, and it is surely not contentious to acknowledge that most Highland soldiers were afraid. What is more difficult is to address those occasions when nerves failed. Here we may make a distinction between breakdown following sudden trauma ('shell shock'), and breakdown or deterioration over a period of sustained stress.

It is the sudden trauma cases which find their way into the record as 'shell shock' cases. It is quite evident from soldiers' accounts that there was a steady trickle of such casualties in the Highland regiments throughout the war, and this is confirmed by some surviving battalion casualty returns, even if these tend to be incomplete and inconsistent.[41] In his diary, for example, Colonel Craig-Brown, commanding 1st Camerons, records a continuous trickle of officer casualties from shell-shock during the Somme battle in August 1916:

> 17 August: 2Lt Hetherington (A & SH) suffering from shell shock [Sent to hospital]

---

38 LC GS 1516 Stables, letter to Liddle, 5 February, 1979. See also: LC GS 1549 Strachan, memoir.
39 LC GS 0132 Betteridge, memoir, p.236. See also: LC Tapes 1618/1619 Kerridge, interview; IWM 10117 Bartholomew, interview.
40 LC GS 1625 Turing, memoir. See also: LC GS 1761 Wilson, memoir, p.70; IWM 3460 Macmillan, diary, 18 October, 1915; Nicholson, *Behind the Lines*, p.291; IWM 4586 Douglas, memoir, p.341; IWM 3834 Wrench, diary, 12 November 1916.
41 See, for example, ASHM War Diary 1/6th Argylls, casualty returns October, 1915 to September, 1916.

28 August: 2Lt R.M. White (A & SH) sent down with shell shock. [He had only joined the previous day.]

29 August: 2Lts Bateman and Thomson sent down with shell shock at 7 p.m. [Thomson had only joined on the 27th.][42]

Shell shock affected both officers and men fairly indiscriminately, and casualties occurred both in the main battles and in the quieter periods between. It was a fact of life. As Hal Kerridge, who served with 1st Gordons between 1916 and 1918, put it, "Some people got shell shock … like some people got trench-foot."[43] The nature of the trauma is often not indicated,[44] but there appear to have been three main triggers, sometimes acting in conjunction; heavy shelling, perhaps with a very close detonation, being buried alive as the result of an explosion, and the death of a close friend or colleague.

There are numerous accounts in the sources of trauma from shelling in the Highland regiments.[45] Not all the victims exhibited the same symptoms, which varied from nervous breakdown, to collapse, to involuntary shaking, to apparent madness. The intensity of the trauma varied from case to case. Consequently, we should not assume that all were hospitalised to home for special treatment. Some will have recovered fairly quickly and returned to duty after a rest, perhaps not moving back beyond the battalion transport lines. Others will have become totally ineffective and mentally scarred for life. We only have room here for a few examples to illustrate the nature of the trauma.

'John' Horn, a pre-war regular, was acting C.O. of 1st Seaforths at Aubers Ridge on 9 May, 1915, where the battalion suffered devastating casualties. "One man, quite a level headed orderly of mine, went clean off his head and put his arms round my neck and sang."[46] Lieutenant Hugh Munro, of 8th Argylls, recorded in May 1915, "Artillery bombardments have made two men funny … Man in my platoon is getting strange and was found in his billet one night with a loaded rifle; swears he hears spies at night and wakens up whole platoon at night."[47] Returning wounded from the battlefield of Loos on 25 September, 1915, Jim Sutherland of 1st Camerons

---

42 IWM 1862 Craig-Brown, diary.
43 LC Tapes 1618/1619 Kerridge, interview.
44 ASHM N-E8 Maclachlan, letter to him from Wilfred Haviland, 15 November, 1916; GHM PB18 Boustead, letter from him, 18 July 1916; IWM 11144 MacKay, diary, 9 April, 1917; IWM 11637 Leppan, transcribed diary.
45 Apart from refs cited, see: ASHM N-E8 Campbell, memoir; IWM 6444 Shewan, AB152 entries, 19 August, 1916; Fetherstonhaugh, *13th Battalion*, p.90; IWM 2902 Munro, diary, 19 June 1915; IWM 16387 McLeod, diary, 8 October, 1915; IWM 4586 Douglas, memoir, pp.542, 739; IWM 14340 McArthur, diary, 12 June, 1915; LC GS 1625 Turing, memoir; THM Seaforths S796 Cartmell, memoir, THM Camerons 02-58 Grant, letters to father, 16 January, to Aunt Violet, 19 January, 1915; LC GS 0298 Chavasse, letter to Miss Madeleine Twemlow, 5 June, 1915; McKinnell, *Diary*, p.50, entry for 18 January, 1915; IWM 3460 Macmillan, diary, 9 July, 1915; Beattie, *48th Highlanders*, pp.123, 139, 165, 269; Zuehlke, *Brave Battalion*, p.127, IWM 21092 McGregor, letter to wife Jen, 13 August, 1916; THM Seaforths 97-4 McDonald, diary; IWM 612 Gameson, memoir, p.24; LC GS 0177 Boyle, diary, 21 April, 1915; LC GS 0132 Betteridge, memoir, p.47; LC GS 1422 Sanders, diary, 24 December, 1914, 15 January, 1915; IWM 12007 PP Wilson, memoir, p.44; GHM PB1706/2 Robertson, diary, 24 July 1916
46 *Lieut.-Colonel Robert Horn*, p.54.
47 IWM 2902 Munro, diary, 11 May 1915.

found "chaps running about stark-mad."[48] When 2nd Seaforths were shelled in the trenches on 20 June, 1916, "we had no casualties barring one man who went off his head! Apparently, he always went mad with fear under shell fire."[49] John Cartmell, serving in the ranks of 2nd Seaforths, notes that prior to the attack on 1 July, 1916, there was an intense bombardment of the enemy. "The noise was terrific, and a man in No.6 Platoon lost his senses and had to be taken away half an hour after our arrival in Mount Joy. There were several 18 pdr Q.F. batteries in the open about 30 yds from the trench."[50] Returning from a mission as a runner at Delville Wood on 18 July, 1916, Corporal Harry Robertson of 1st Gordons "nearly got stuck by one of our own fellows. He seems off his head – cursing and swearing he was – and he certainly looked a bit "off". Shell shock."[51] Captain Pailthorpe, M.O. of 2nd Gordons, records how, at the Butte, in October 1917, "A young Gordon sergeant, who was the only survivor of 6 men from another shell burst, was brought to me unwounded – he had no idea where he was and was trembling from head to foot."[52] Tom Chamberlain, serving in 5th Camerons came under heavy shell-fire during the German offensive of 1918. Two men in his section were killed and he was wounded. He was surprised to see another man, a private, for whom he had great respect, sitting on all fours weeping, unable to take the strain any more. "It left a deep impression on me."[53] In August, 1918, the Germans shelled the billets of 1st Camerons. Two men got shell shock as the shell caught the corner of the room where they were sleeping. "Two squirming twitching black objects can be detected over by what was once a window." Both were stretchered to the M.O.[54]

Lieutenant R.E. Badenoch received his commission in 1915, trained at Ripon and joined 1/7th Black Watch at the front in August, 1916. When the battalion was in the Hebuterne sector in early October, 1916, there was a lieutenant who had been at Ripon at the same time as Badenoch.

> He was a good athlete, big and powerful, played for the football team, was a bit of a boxer and was the life and soul of the Officers Mess. He went to France on a later draft than me and I thought he would be a regular fire eater and a good leader. He was posted to our Coy but on the contrary he was useless in the trenches. If there was any gun fire, he shook like an aspen leaf and could scarcely speak. The upshot was he was given a job behind the lines as 'Town Major' and so far as I know was never back in action.[55]

Burial alive was a fairly common occurrence, when trenches or dugouts were blown in, and was also often generally accompanied by the close explosion of a shell or a mine. This was clearly traumatic for those affected. The War Diary of 1/6th Argylls records, for example, that on 8 October, 1915, an enemy bombardment of their trenches at Thiepval caused severe damage with several dugouts completely blown-in and men buried. Four men were killed and

---

48   IWM 11923 PP Sutherland, undated letter.
49   THM Laurie, diary, 20 June, 1916.
50   THM Seaforths S796 Cartmell, memoir.
51   GHM PB1706/2 Robertson, diary, 18 July 1916.
52   GHM PB375 Pailthorpe, memoir, p.54.
53   LC GS 0280 Chamberlain, interview.
54   THM Camerons 93-35 Welsh, memoirs, p.134.
55   BWA Badenoch, memoir.

several wounded, but 15 men were sent to hospital suffering from shock. Further cases of shock occurred as the result of an enemy mine detonation on 26 March, 1916, which buried many men and killed five outright.[56] There are many other references in the sources.[57] Private D McKay in 1/4th Seaforths described how he was buried by a shell on the Somme in September, 1916.

> I was walking along the top of a trench going for water when it happened but lucky again some of my mates spotted me and came and dug me out but I was in quite a state and was sent down the line and land[ed] back in England. After treatment and leave, back to Ripon to be made ready for France again, I arrived back in the regiment in Jan., 1917.[58]

Signaller H.N. Bradley was shelled in a trench at Poelcappelle, with his fellow signallers LCpls Morrell and Mackie, on the night of 11/12 October, 1917, while waiting to go over the top in the morning.

> One shell burst on the parapet above us. Poor Mackie's nerves were shattered and he fled up the trench. Two other fellows near L/Cpl Morrell and myself were completely buried. I got a spade and dug like fury to get them out. Morrell's nerves were pretty well gone and at first he was pretty helpless. 'For Heaven's sake give me a hand,' I cried. 'No harm will come to us – this is a work of providence.' Shells were bursting all around us, but I felt quite secure somehow. My words served to cheer Morrell, and he set to work with a will. We managed to get at their faces first by good fortune. Then it took us about a quarter of an hour to free them. They were unconscious, but we chafed them and they soon came round. Their nerves were completely gone. The stretcher-bearers were called for and these two were carried away, and the Officer also told Mackie to go down the line, as he was shaking like a leaf. That left just two signallers to go over in the morning.[59]

Another cause of nervous breakdown was the death close by of a close friend or colleague.[60] We have already touched on this when discussing comradeship. Again there are several examples in the sources. Captain Claud Low in 1st London Scottish described how his colleague Captain Stebbing was badly shaken at Aubers Ridge on 9 May, 1915, and fainted when one of his subalterns was killed beside him by a shell. "S. has however recovered ... although not in great form." But a month later, he had gone back to hospital, as his eyesight was damaged, but probably also through nerves.[61] Lieutenant Johnnie Wood, in 10th Gordons, describes how

---

56 ASHM War Diary 1/6th Argylls
57 BWA MacDonald, Coll, letter to wife Mary, 19 January, 1918; BWA Forman, memoir; ASHM N-E8 Munro, letter to sister Effie, 13 June, 1915; LC GS 0895 King, memoir, pp.72-73; THM Seaforths S796 Cartmell, memoir; IWM 3460 Macmillan, diary, 29 November, 1915; LC GS 0418 Dane, diary, 9 October, 1915; Topp, *42nd Battalion*, pp.159-160
58 LC Middlebrook Somme 1918 MacKay, D., letter to Liddle, 13 June, 1976.
59 LC Western Front Recollections B28 Bradley, H.N., 'Signaller H.N. Bradley's Experiences at Poelcappelle 10th to 14th October, 1917,' written 13 November, 1917, after being admitted to Leith Hospital, Scotland.
60 Apart from refs cited, see: GHM PR1639 Kemp, memoir, pp.74-75; LC GS 003 Anderson, transcript of interview.
61 IWM 6702 Low, letters to wife Noanie, 11 May, 18 June, 1915.

their trenches came under bombardment in November, 1915. "Up the trench I went and met a Machine Gunner coming running down in a terrible state of nerves and crying like anything. I asked him what was up and he said all his chums on the gun had been killed."[62] At the battle of Mont Sorrel in June, 1916, Lieutenant 'Barney' McCoy of the Canadian Scottish was killed by a shell. When informed, Lieutenant 'Pete' Osler, "Barney's special chum, stood by himself for a little while dazed, and then, seeming to grasp what had happened, completely broke down."[63] Captain Pailthorpe, M.O. of 2nd Gordons records how, prior to the battalion's attack on Ginchy on 5 September, 1916

> K, an officer, came to me and said he would not go over the top – he was shivering from shell shock or nerves but I produced a thermometer … and registered him as having a temperature of 99 degrees – I told him he'd better lie in the trench. Unless the men thought he was ill there could be trouble – he had been a gallant enough fellow up till July 20th when a young orderly to whom he was attached had a large bit of shell in his chest and K. had to watch him die in pain for 2 hours without being able to help unless he shot him – after this he was not the same.

After the battle, the M.O. told the C.O. about K. "and suggested a long course somewhere, when we got out, was the only thing for him."[64]

The effects of such traumatic experiences could last for a long time, till well beyond the end of the war, and could re-surface when both officers and men were sent back to the front prematurely, either from a short rest behind the lines, or from more drastic hospitalisation to home.[65] Audrey Prior recalls how her brother Charles, an officer in 9th Argylls was saved by good fortune from some of the worst fighting on the Somme.

> He was travelling in a train on his way back to France after a short leave and in the carriage opposite him was sitting a General. Evidently he had noticed Charles' reaction at the sudden roar as the train passed another going in the opposite direction at speed. When the clamour was over, the General leaned across and spoke to Charles, saying, 'Young man, you are not fit to go back to the trenches. You are suffering from shell shock.' Thereupon he wrote out a chit and gave it to Charles. On showing it to the Authorities he was granted extended leave which almost certainly saved his life.[66]

Herbert Junks, training at Ripon with the Black Watch, notes in his diary an incident in August, 1916, when a man suffering from shell-shock quarrelled with some other men and, on the military police being called, drew a bayonet and threatened them. After some trouble he was overpowered and taken to the guardroom.[67] Captain Pailthorpe, M.O. to 2nd Gordons,

---

62 NLS Acc.12729 Wood, letter to brother Willie, 9 November, 1915.
63 Urquhart, *Canadian Scottish*, p.149.
64 GHM PB375 Pailthorpe, p.26.
65 Apart from refs cited, see: LC Tapes 636/653 Cowan, interview; IWM 511 Thorburn, letter to mother, 11 February, 1916; GHM PB375 Pailthorpe, memoir, pp.9-10.
66 LC DF 105 Prior, memoir, pp.2-3.
67 BWA Junks, diary, 26 August, 1916.

recalls an incident in November 1916, when a corporal who had been buried alive was returned to the battalion too early, found he could not stand trench-mortar fire, and had to be sent back down the line again with a note for six months. "Perhaps it was as well that I was still the M.O. and knew him and what he had endured … as otherwise he might have been charged with cowardice."[68]

G.S. MacKay served first with the 1st Camerons on the Western Front, when he was hospitalised at an early stage. Later he served as a captain in the 2nd Battalion, but was attached to the 1st Garrison Battalion Seaforth Highlanders in Salonika, almost certainly due to nervous problems arising from his service on the Western Front. On 18 March 1917, he wrote to his mother that after an aerial bombardment, he shook for two days. "It did seem absurd but I just couldn't help it however much I tried."[69]

Captain Wyllie, serving with the same battalion, records the nervous difficulties experienced by another officer, Lieutenant Cuthbert, some time after a bombing attack at Salonika. Again, it seems likely that, before being posted to the Garrison Battalion, Cuthbert had already experienced trauma on the Western Front. On 5 August, 1917, Wyllie reported that, "The other day one of the Sisters found him weeping bitterly in his bed and on coaxing him she discovered that he was worried about our Airmen whom he was afraid would fall out of their machines." Nevertheless, by 12 September, Cuthbert had been sent back to the battalion, up the line. This was to no avail. By 10 December, he had been sent back down to the base, "as his nerves have made him useless as an officer."[70]

Finally, Lieutenant John Turing recalls how, as a lieutenant in 8th Seaforths, after being wounded himself on 31 July, 1917, he returned to the 3rd Battalion at Cromarty, where he was given command of the Training Company.

> I was a very young twenty-three and, still being shocked from my wound, the responsibility was a strain. One morning when the company had fallen in on parade, I imagined they were going to mutiny! I lost my nerve and went along to the adjutant, Capt Houldsworth, to tell him I could not manage them. He was most kind, came along and stood by me quietly, and pointed out that everything was all right, so I recovered my nerve. I shall always be grateful to him.

He returned to the 8th Battalion about August, 1918. Thereafter he successfully struggled to stay on top of his nerves. When he was finally demobilised in March, 1919, "I was very run down … I used to cover my head with blankets but I could still hear the shriek of 5.9 shells. This trial passed fairly quickly. But, when I went shooting and wounded a rabbit and it squealed, I vowed I would never shoot again, and I never have."[71]

Sudden trauma, with its subsequent complications, was in reality only the most spectacular manifestation of nervous strain in the trenches. Many officers and men were subject to a progressive deterioration of nerves the longer they remained at the front. For many, there was a constant struggle to stay on top of their nerves, and a number failed.

68 GHM PB375 Pailthorpe, memoir, p.29.
69 IWM 12688 MacKay, letter to mother 18 March 1917.
70 IWM 7508 Wyllie, diary, 5 August, 12 September, 25, 30 November, 1, 10 December, 1917.
71 LC GS 1625 Turing, memoir.

A number of sources record this battle with nerves.[72] George Murray, serving in the ranks of 1/4th Seaforths, told his father in May, 1915, that "the nerves are always going. Being in the trenches is not hard work, but the constant mental strain is bound to tell on a chap sooner or later, & even lying in reserve a man has no peace of mind, as nobody knows the moment when their assistance is required."[73] Norman Macmillan, serving in the ranks of the Glasgow Highlanders noted the fears of one of his pals before an attack they made on 14 October, 1915.

> Sandy Riddell was very much troubled over the affair. He said it was impossible to do it. Madness! Murder to send twenty men over to do that. It was a job for nothing less than a double company. He smoked incessantly. When his pipe was empty he immediately refilled it and started afresh. He had no matches and his pipe was continually going out. And every minute he would ask for my matches. And in the short flare-up his face was different: no longer was he the contented looking Sandy of the half-humorous smile. His face was haggard. He looked as he had done when he had jaundice. It was rotten to look at him.[74]

John Bowie in 11th Argylls noted in January, 1917, that his Company Sergeant Major "was not up to much and the sergeants had his work to do as he had the 'wind up' (nerve failure)."[75] Private William Couston went into action with 1/7th Black Watch in May, 1917, when he received a piece of shrapnel in his haversack. He wrote home: "I am in the best of health; only I find my nerves are not just as steady as they were. The longer a fellow is out here, the 'shakier' he becomes. Can you wonder either?"[76] Even such a distinguished soldier as Douglas Wimberley, who commanded a Machine Gun Company in 51st Highland Division, felt that after coming out of the fighting at Third Ypres, "my nerves were worse than they have ever been, before or since."[77]

Clearly, if carrying on while suffering nervous disorder showed admirable spirit, it was not ideal for military efficiency or morale. Lieutenant Douglas Wilson, Lewis Gun officer with 5th Camerons, visited one of his fellow officers in the front-line, in 1918.

> Melville was jittery … Melville gave me the impression of one who was striving hard to maintain control, but was not having much success. He was stale from long service, tired out mentally and physically, indrawn and crochety. He was in a state that did not make for

---

72 Apart from refs cited, see: LC GS 1761 Wilson, memoir, pp.43, 47; IWM 4586 Douglas, memoir, pp.366-367; THM Camerons 96-52 Laidlaw, 'Grandpa's War,' letters from Thomas Laidlaw to his wife Bertha, 1, 15, 16, 25 July, 1916; Campbell, *Letters*, letter of 12 October, 1915, p.83; LC GS 1203 Oldham, diary, 28 March, 1916; GHM PB1639 Kemp, memoir, Vol 3, pp.68, 75; GHM uncatalogued Beaton, memoirs, pp.112-113; BWA MacDonald, Coll, letter to wife Mary 15 January, 1918 [original incorrectly dated 1917]; THM Seaforths 96-36 Tweddle, letter home , 18 May, 1915 (extract); IWM Books Cooper, 'Domi Militaeque,' p.135; GHM PB1706/2 Robertson, diary, 27 July 1916; IWM 8592 Macgregor, letters to wife 22, 25, 31 October, 1, 4, 5, 8, 11, 12, 14, 19, 20 November 1918.
73 THM Seaforths 81-180 Murray, letter to father, 22 May, 1915
74 IWM 3460 Macmillan, diary, 14 October, 1915.
75 ASHM N-E11 Bowie, diary, 3 January, 1917.
76 BWA Couston, letter to mother, 25 May, 1917.
77 IWM 430 Wimberley, memoir, Vol 1, p.80.

good leadership. Had he been offered leave he would have refused it – he didn't want to lose command of his company, and that was to his credit, but was he fit for the command? ... Melville looked to me like cracking anytime.

During the battle of Meteren, in July, 1918, Wilson went forward to retrieve some of his men of 'D' Company from a line now held by Melville's Company. He found him

> wild with excitement, dancing about like a marionette, issuing volleys of orders to which no one was paying the slightest attention, for George Munro had quietly passed it round that the O.C. Company was to be ignored until he (George) said otherwise. Poor Melville. He had a thousand instructions to pour out to me, but when I got busy collecting my men he foamed at the mouth, threatened to place me under arrest and became really obstructive.

Wilson had to threaten to lay him out and place him under arrest in order to get the job done.[78]

One partial antidote to nerves was the suppression of emotion. No doubt, many men felt like Lieutenant Bry Cumming, who joined 2nd Black Watch at the Front about October, 1915. "Can't say I enjoy war shells," he wrote, "make such sickly wounds. I saw a man with both legs broken and I nearly vomited."[79] David McMillan, who served in the 43rd Battalion C.E.F. (Cameron Highlanders of Canada), felt that the fighting soldier "must learn to suppress all emotion, and this applies particularly to those in authority."

> Don't ever think that a front-line soldier is callous, with no feelings or emotion. It is nearer to the truth to say that he has encased himself in a cocoon from which his true feelings will not be allowed to escape. This is how he will preserve his sanity, and enable himself to look upon death with no outward sign of emotion. The emotion is there just the same, bottled up within him but no-one will ever know it if he can help it.[80]

Another antidote was drink. We have already noticed the usefulness of the rum ration for steeling nerves. The problem arose not with the limited ration, but when alcohol was abused. Colonel Nicholson offered some astute observations on drink:

> In such a war nerves were constantly under great strain and it was natural that the majority drank more than in peace, for drink is a drug and a stimulant. In most cases the excess did not matter; all were so fit that they could consume more than normal without ill effect. The danger came with those who required it before a battle. I don't know what disasters, if any, were due to this cause; as a general rule the officers of a unit were much too loyal to let the shortcomings of their seniors get to the ears of commanders. It was a mistaken loyalty, for good men were scarce, and must be saved; no one knew this better than the commanders.[81]

---

78 LC GS 1761 Wilson, memoir, pp.42, 74.
79 BWA Cumming, letter home, n.d. [c. October, 1915].
80 McMillan, *Trench Tea and Sandbags*, p.16. See also LC GS 1761 Wilson, memoir, pp.10-11.
81 Nicholson, *Behind the Lines*, p.291.

Despite the protests of Sam McDonald,[82] there certainly were cases of abuse. During the battle of Meteren, in July, 1918, Lieutenant Douglas Wilson of 5th Camerons found his progress impeded by friendly fire, where a rum-induced drunken N.C.O. was slamming round after round into an empty dilapidated hand-cart.[83]

Sadly, there are more cases in the sources of officer failure, as we have already noted in considering discipline.[84] In 1st Gordons, at Hooge in September 1915, "Monteith was my Coy Capt. He got 'fu' before the charge and was running about like a madman and flourishing his revolver. I can still picture him standing on the parapet shouting 'Come on boys – they can't kill me – the bullet isn't made yet.' He was killed outright 2 minutes later."[85] John Bowie in 11th Argylls, noted in January, 1917, that the officer entrusted with ensuring fair distribution of the rum ration, a minister before the war, "could not go in the trenches amongst his men unless well 'steamed.'"[86] In October 1917, Private Douglas, also of 11th Argylls, was ordered out on a listening patrol under the command of a corporal as apparently "the officer who should have been in charge of the 'Patrol' was the worse for drink."[87] Most tragically, in 1917, Lieutenant Norman Collins was appointed 'Officer's Friend' to an officer in a Highland Regiment awaiting court-martial.

> This officer had taken too much rum when he went over the top and he was incapable of carrying out his duties properly. He was a charming man and I felt very sorry for him … I knew that the least punishment he would get would be to be reduced to the ranks … and sent back to the Regiment as a private. However, in the event, this officer shot himself … before the Court Martial.[88]

This was a tragic way for nervous disintegration to end. More usually, either nervous deterioration would end in collapse or breakdown, or the signs would be recognised in advance, and the person concerned given some rest. There are some clear cases of the former. Captain Charlie Couper of 1/4th Black Watch, for example, wrote on 12 April, 1915, "Just now I have to act as platoon commander of No.13 platoon as, greatly to my surprise, when I got back I found that Gladstone, a great strong chap, he weighed 14 stones, had broken down and gone raving mad. It is very sad."[89] James Racine, serving with 1/5th Seaforths, notes that in October, 1915. "A man who had been with us since we had landed in France shot and killed himself in the dugout. The experiences and conditions had been too much for him and had preyed upon his mind."[90] Colonel Hugh Allen, commanding 7th Black Watch, records the

---

82 GHM PB1892.3.18 McDonald, 'Uncle Harper's Duds.'
83 LC GS 1761 Wilson, memoir, pp.73-74.
84 See particularly IWM 3834 Wrench, diary, 23 August 1916.
85 GHM PB1706/2 Robertson, recollections.
86 ASHM N-E11 Bowie, diary, 3 January, 1917.
87 IWM 4586 Douglas, memoir, pp.141-142.
88 IWM 12043 Collins, interview.
89 IWM 14269 Couper, letter to mother 12 April, 1915 [wrongly dated 12 March], to Tom Couper, 16 May, 1915.
90 IWM 16335 Racine, memoirs, p.68.

breakdown of one of his office staff in April, 1916,[91] while Private Welsh in 1st Camerons records one of his fellow stretcher-bearers collapsing in June, 1917.[92]

In other cases the condition may have been noticed before breakdown occurred or the distinction is unclear from the sources.[93] For example, Lieutenant C.B. Robertson, in 1st Argylls, wrote on 20 March, 1915,

> Poor old Thompson left for England today – his nerves have entirely gone and he has been going through a horrid time for the last three weeks. Any big guns make him jump sky high. I'm awfully sorry for him, I suppose it is an illness just as much as anything else … as a matter of fact it is a good thing he has gone back, he couldn't have stood it any longer and it was perfectly beastly being anywhere near him as he couldn't sit still for five minutes at a time.[94]

As we have seen from some of the examples cited, the condition came increasingly to be accepted as a fact of life, and could be dealt with compassionately. The principal need was for rest, and this was achieved by hospitalisation, by prolonged leave, by temporary 'cushy' postings down the line, or simply by holding nervous cases back at headquarters or the transport lines and giving them temporarily non-fighting roles. Medical Officers might help with special measures, which could help with those both physically and mentally run down. For example, in the St Eloi sector, from 3 April, 1915, Noel Chavasse, M.O. to 1st Liverpool Scottish, started up a 'Sanitary Squad,' comprising men who were a little run down, but not actually bad enough to be on the sick list,[95] while Johnathan Bates, M.O. to 8th Black Watch, set up a small hospital for his battalion in their barracks at Arras.[96]

The pressure on Commanding Officers was immense as, not only had they to cope with the stresses of shell-fire, they had to take on themselves the entire weight of responsibility for the losses suffered by their battalion. The day after the 2nd Gordons had taken heavy casualties on the first day of the Somme, their M.O. records

> I went up to Mametz again and found the Colonel in a dug-out in a sunken road – he looked tired and haggard … He said some pleasant things about the stretcher bearers' work then looked at me and added, 'The Battalion were splendid. I told them it would be a walk over, and look at our losses.' I tried to think of something to say that might be any

---

91 IWM 114 Allen, letter to wife 3 April 1916.
92 THM Camerons 93-35 Welsh, memoirs, p50.
93 Apart from refs cited, see also: BWA Duke, letter to mother, 3 April, 1915; LC GS 0262 Campbell, diary, 13 July, 1916; LC GS 1027 MacLeod, letter to mother, 6 August, 6 October, 1917, to father, 5 October, 1917; IWM 114 Allen, letters to wife 11, 14 July, 9 November 1915, 17 March 1916; Lauder, *A Minstrel in France*, pp.59-63; ASHM N-E11 Macleod, letters to father, 4 October, 1916, to Ellen, 19 October, 1916; ASHM NE-5 Main, letter to wife Win, 26 August, 1915; [Gregory], *France 1916-1917-1918*, pp.17-18; THM Seaforths 81-180 Murray, letter to sister Alex, 17 October, 1915.
94 ASHM N-E1 Robertson, letter home, 20 March, 1915.
95 Jackson, 'Captain Noel Godfrey Chavasse.'
96 IWM 2854 Bates, letter to fiancée 7 November 1916.

consolation but it was hard. The Colonel broke down for a little because he had loved his regiment.[97]

Similarly, Bill Bryden, who served in 1st London Scottish, noted that, after the first day of the Somme, only about 10 percent of the battalion were present to line up and the Colonel was in tears.[98] Sometimes, the C.O. could no longer cope, and at the very least would need a break. Those who were obliged to depart honourably in this way included Colonel Tweedie of 10th Argylls, who went down the line on 28 July, 1916, after being nearly hit by a bomb at Longueval,[99] Sir George Abercromby of 8th Black Watch, who left for the base on 21 May, 1917 due to cumulative strain,[100] and Colonel Murray of 4/5th Black Watch who left after the German offensive of 1918.[101] Sometimes the departure of the C.O. required the M.O.'s intervention, as for Colonel Maitland, commanding 2nd Gordons in Italy in July 1918.[102] A useful first-hand summary of such misfortunes is provided by Colonel Jack Stewart, who found himself obliged to hand over the command of 9th Black Watch in June, 1916, due to nerves. The matter was handled sympathetically. In the event, after a period at home, Stewart was considered fit for more service, and in April, 1917, took over command of 2nd Black Watch in Mesopotamia, where he apparently had no more trouble with nerves. As he wrote, soon after his arrival, "I am all right again now, and the noise of the guns this morning didn't disturb me in the slightest: of course, it's absolutely nothing to what we had in France."[103]

One way of avoiding the hazards and discomforts of the trenches was to avoid service in the line as far as possible. Although such avoidance would of course be the antithesis of the true warrior ethos, there is ample evidence to show that avoidance was practised by some elements in the Highland regiments. One option was to seek a "cushy" posting behind the lines. Commenting on this practice in 1917, Lieutenant William Paterson felt that, as regards junior officers, "Admittedly, there are cases where some of them are lucky in securing what we term 'cushy' jobs behind the lines, but as a general rule even these have served in the line, and by way of a rest are sent behind, and keep their 'cushy' jobs. Luck has favoured such."[104]

We have indeed already acknowledged that a quiet posting behind the lines, or to battalion headquarters, was a perfectly normal compassionate practice for those suffering from nerves. For example, Captain Claud Low, in 1st London Scottish noted on 7 July, 1915, "The C.O. had a memo from the Brigade today asking for the names of officers who were showing signs of strain. This was not for guidance in granting leave, but to perform duties for a period at the base & return again to the fighting line after recuperation."[105] So it was too for the temporary rehabilitation of those worn down by trench complaints such as trench fever, trench feet, or rheumatism. Private William Couston, in 1/7th Black Watch, for example, began to suffer from rheumatic pains in August, 1917. From 12 September he was away from the battalion working

---

97   GHM PB375 Pailthorpe, memoir, p.16. This was Col B.G.R. Gordon.
98   IWM 13263 Bryden, Memories of her father's reminiscences written by Mary Lawton, 2003.
99   David, *Mud and Bodies*, pp.67, 73.
100 IWM 2854 Bates, letter to fiancée 21 May 1917. See also: LC GS 1367 Robertson, memoir.
101 Wauchope, *Black Watch*, Vol.2, p.95.
102 GHM PB375 Pailthorpe, memoir, p.77.
103 BWA Stewart, letters to wife, 21, 24 June, 1916, 15 April, 1917.
104 THM Seaforths 89-122 Paterson, memoir.
105 IWM 6702 Low, letter to wife Noanie, 7 July, 12 September, 1915, n.d. [1915].

in the Scottish Churches Tent until re-joining in February, 1918.[106] Another perfectly legitimate case was Sergeant Alick Guthrie who should not really have been in the war at all. Born in 1864, he was a former Volunteer soldier who had continued his service in the 6th Black Watch, when the Territorial Force had been established in 1908. He was mobilised in 1914, aged 49. It was his Captain who put his name in for a temporary appointment down at the base, as he felt he was looking run down. Guthrie was discharged as a time-expired Territorial on 31 March, 1916.[107] Unsurprisingly then, in a draft of Gordons in 1916, Private James Marr discovered that base jobs were being apportioned fairly to those who deserved them. When he entrained in France for Etaples, a couple of old soldiers in the carriage, on learning that he could write shorthand, informed him that he would easily get a job in the Orderly Room at Etaples and would have a nice 'cushy' job there for the duration of the war. When he took the request to an officer there, he was sadly relieved of his illusions.[108]

But there was scepticism about jobs behind the lines,[109] and some at least was justified. For example, David Skinner, 4/5th Black Watch, had been at the Divisional School in April, 1917, but had rejoined the battalion "He told me that he would certainly have been kept at the Schools but for a few troublesome boils with which he had to report to Hospital and of course, on being discharged, he was sent up here. He also told me that he would have been Orderly Room Sgt if all had gone well."[110] Evidently Skinner would have been perfectly happy to remain unmissed at the School. We have already considered when addressing comradeship, the remarkable case of Captain College, who inexplicably and inexcusably managed to hold the position of company commander in 5th Camerons while discharging none of the frontline duties. Lieutenant Johnnie Wood notes that when his battalion, 10th Gordons, was amalgamated with the 8th Battalion, the remnants of the two battalions went to form an entrenching battalion. "Few of the Captains wanted to go to the new Battalion, preferring to get away to a soft job,"[111] an attitude confirmed by William Kemp.[112] Likewise, Lieutenant Guy Macgregor was perfectly content with his relatively safe posting to 1/6th Argylls, a pioneer battalion, although ultimately acquiescent when in October, 1918, it was transferred to 51st Division to become a fighting battalion.[113]

Others actively sought safer positions.[114] One such officer was Captain John Hay-Young, who had served in 1st Argylls since the start of the war. By October, 1916, he had "had enough of fighting. I would like very much to get a change of air." He actively angled for a Staff job, but instead received a posting to be Second-in-Command of an infantry battalion.[115] Amongst the ranks, George Murray deployed to France with 1/4th Seaforths in November, 1914. Having

---

106 BWA Couston, letters to mother, 17, 22 September, 1 October, 1917, 11, 28 February, 1918.
107 BWA Guthrie, letters to wife Crissie, 14, 16, 20 July, 11, 12, 16 August, 29 October, 6, 9, 11, 22 November, 1, 6, 15 December, 1915, 20 March, 1916. See also the legitimate case of Cpl Harry Robertson at GHM PB1706/2 Robertson, diary, 11 September 1916.
108 IWM 14335 Marr, memoir, pp.19-20, 23.
109 LC GS 0262 Campbell, diary, 30 April, 1916.
110 IWM 19680, White, letter from Donald Macleod, 27 October, 1917.
111 NLS Acc.12872 Wood, letter to brother Willie, 15 May, 1916.
112 GHM PB1639 Kemp, memoir, pp.24,28.
113 IWM 8592 Macgregor, letters to wife 10 April, 1 December, 1917, 2, 4 October, 1918.
114 Apart from refs cited, see also: IWM 8192 Lawson, letter to sister Bessie, 14 January 1917; IWM 233 McKechnie, memoir, pp.48-49; IWM 2854 Bates, letters to fiancée April to July, 1917, passim.
115 LC GS 0731 Hay-Young, letters home 15 October, 1916 to 19 February, 1917, passim.

suffered the winter and lost friends in the battles of Neuve Chapelle and Aubers Ridge, by June, 1915, he was already keen to get out of the infantry and was not alone."[116] He was a qualified engineer. So, while his family at home sought to get him recalled to an engineering job at home., he pursued opportunities to transfer to the Royal Engineers in theatre.[117] In the end neither attempt was successful, but he finally got to leave the infantry when he was wounded in November, 1916, and his leg was amputated just above the knee. More successful was W. Mackenzie, who managed to transfer from 9th Black Watch to Special Company, R.E. (the gas corps).[118] Daniel McFarlane, 7th Camerons, was wounded in the arm in the summer of 1916, before the Somme. He was not sent home, but after hospital in Boulogne was sent to Etaples, and then, not yet judged fit enough for the front line, was sent to join the Army Pay Corps as a clerk, serving at Rouen and Boulogne. He managed to stay there and was only transferred back to his battalion after the German offensive of 1918.[119]

Officers might also seek transfer to a non-infantry unit. This might be one that itself involved considerable risk, like the Machine Gun Corps, the Tank Corps or the Royal Flying Corps. but which, particularly in the case of the R.F.C, might provide the opportunity to escape the life of an infantryman in the trenches, Such transfers might also involve initially extensive courses at home, which would provide a welcome respite.[120]

Others, however, stood firm. Coll Macdonald, who became chaplain to 8th Black Watch in May, 1917, might easily have transferred to a safer position. In the event he had what appears to have been an eight-month posting extended to a full year, and despite his own reservations about his ability to cope, was content to stay on with the battalion for that time.[121] In February 1918, Lieutenant. R.L. MacKay, serving with the 11th Argylls, vigorously resisted an attempt to detain him as an instructor at a Signalling School strongly preferring to rejoin his battalion,[122] while newly commissioned Leslie Cooper was disappointed to be posted to a pioneer battalion, rather than to a fighting battalion."[123] In fact, there were even cases of 'reverse desertion' by some soldiers to ensure they got to a fighting unit at the front. The celebrated Scottish rugby international, W.S. Sutherland, deserted the Lothian and Border Horse and joined 14th Argylls (still at home) in order to get to the front.[124] And Colonel Stansfield, then commanding 2nd Gordons, noted on 5 July 1915, "Yesterday a soldier called Stevenson turned up here. He ran away without leave from the 10th Batt. at Salisbury & came here by bluff to the railway officials, etc. as he wanted to see some fighting without having to wait any more. A good plucked 'un, I think."[125]

---

116 THM Seaforths 81-180 Murray, letter to Alex, 20 October, 1915
117 Ibid., letters to Alex, 9, 20 November,1915, 9 February, 1916, to Kate, 20 November, 1915, 8 February.
118 LC WF Recollections, Mackenzie, memoir.
119 THM Camerons 89-17 McFarlane, memoir.
120 LC GS 0552 Ferguson, letter to mother, 3 February, 1918.
121 BWA MacDonald, Coll, letter to Angus, 26 May, 1917, to wife Mary, 4, 17 June, 7 November, 7 December, 1917, 7, 13 April, 5, 10 May, 1918.
122 IWM 11144 MacKay, diary, 12, 16, 17, 19 February 1918.
123 THM Seaforths 81-2 Cooper, memoir, pp.16-17.
124 LC GS 1008 Macdonald, letter to 'H', n.d. (1915).
125 GHM PB242 Stansfield, letter home, 5 July, 1915.

A second ploy to avoid the trenches was to delay one's return from home after recovery or leave. At the end of 1916, Norman Beaton was hospitalised to Scotland from 7th Gordons with a poisoned finger and boils. Released from hospital in February 1917, after leave he rejoined the T.F. training camp at Ripon, where in April he was placed on a draft for France. However, with a batch of other seasoned veterans he volunteered for the Machine Gun Corps, as "it meant three more months at the least for us in England before we would be sent back to France."[126] By contrast, I.M. Stewart, an officer in 2nd Argylls, wounded at the end of April, 1916, volunteered for the tanks early in 1917 in order to get back into the war. "We were all intensely keen to go back to France, you see; to go back into the war. It was one's job, one's duty."[127] In reality, this is a rather roseate view. Although there was an acceptance of duty, there was frequently dismay at the thought of returning to the trenches, and soldiers could need all their reserves of stoic courage to face the prospect when the time came.[128] Perhaps more representative was the attitude of Lieutenant Bry Cumming. Wounded by shrapnel on 7 January, 1916, while serving with 2nd Black Watch in Mesopotamia, he had been hospitalised to India. When the time came to return to the battalion at the end of March, 1916, he needed to steel himself to the task. Once arrived at Basra, he set out quickly to join his battalion, in time for the next push. "Of course, I could have easily missed it by staying at Basra, only after all we are out here to fight, and I have the greatest contempt for these young swine who linger about at bases sitting on their backsides and call it doing their 'bit.'"[129]

Another ploy was to seek to land a 'cushy' job at home. Some officers and men had landed home defence or training jobs from the outset and were content to keep them. Phil Paul, for example, was commissioned into the Black Watch on 22 June, 1915. From then until 1918, he served continuously in various battalions at home, while continually complaining in his letters to his fiancée (from February, 1918, his wife) about not being posted overseas. It strains the limit of credibility to believe that, had he been determined, he could not have got himself posted to the Western Front. Only on 12 August, 1918, did he finally report for duty with 8th Black Watch. We should not be too harsh; he was killed in action on 1st October.[130] There are scathing comments from fighting soldiers about N.C.O.'s who remained at home at depots and training battalions.[131] As Alfred Fennah put it about some members of 2nd Liverpool Scottish at home;

> There were quite a number of N.C.O.'s and Officers who would have been content to sit down babbling to their Instruction Classes right through the War. In fact, certain N.C.O.'s that I knew were quite willing to pass all their war-time entertaining their squads and singing at concerts. This was the only thing they were proficient in – that and babbling in the mess.[132]

---

126 GHM uncatalogued Beaton, memoir, pp.193-194.
127 LC GS 1535 Stewart, interview.
128 BWA Guthrie, letter to wife Crissie, 19 August, 1915; THM Seaforths 81-2 Cooper, memoir, pp.80-81, 83, 97; THM Seaforths 81-180 Murray, letter to father, 22 May, 1915; IWM 3834 Wrench, diary, 6 December 1917.
129 BWA Cumming, letters home, 25 March, 6 April, 1916.
130 BWA Paul, letters to his fiancée (later wife) May Merritt, passim.
131 Apart from Fennah, see: BWA Forman, memoir; Stothers, *Somewhere in France*, pp.81, 89, letters from J.C. Stothers to brother Steve, 18 September, 3 November, 1917.
132 Fennah, *Retaliation*, p.76.

Of course, as we have seen in the case of the notorious Captain College in 5th Camerons, a significant number of such men were ultimately 'dug out' for service at the Front

Otherwise, 'cushy' jobs at home might be sought by those returning from the front. Private James Marr was wounded in the leg on 22 April, 1917, while serving with the Gordons in France. Hospitalised to Blighty, after convalescence he managed to secure a post as a gas instructor with the training battalion at Ripon. "Possibly this anxiety to escape returning to France might be considered just a little cowardly on my part." He was nevertheless drafted to the front again after the German 1918 offensive.[133] By contrast, W.S Macdonald was a medical student who joined the ranks of 14th Argylls in 1915. He was hospitalised home in early 1917 with trench feet. At Stob Hill Hospital, he was offered a job there until the end of the war, but at that stage he was still trying to get back to his battalion and declined the offer.[134] We must also acknowledge that temporary 'cushy' home postings were quite reasonably used to provide rest at least to officers who were feeling the strain. The benefit of this procedure was recognised by the initially cynical Captain Claud Low, 1st London Scottish, who was sent to hospital at Rouen with trench fever in July, 1915.[135]

Another possible ploy to avoid service on the Western Front was to apply for a posting to another theatre. The remarkably home-bound Lieutenant Paul in the Black Watch did at least unsuccessfully seek a post in Africa. However, there is little evidence of other cases. Temporary officers who applied for regular commissions might be directed to apply to the Indian Army, which would (after 1915) require a posting to other theatres, but this was not necessarily by choice.[136] Captain G.S. MacKay had been attached to 1st Garrison Battalion Seaforth Highlanders in Salonika, while still suffering from nerves brought about by service on the Western Front. He chose to take up an offer of a regular commission in the Indian Army, despite the questioning tone of his mother. "I think you are a wee bit unkind when you say something about the Indian Army being a good way to get out of the job in hand … it will probably mean Mesopotamia. I am just as ready to be killed if I am wanted as anyone if by so doing I am doing any good – of course I much prefer not to be." By 30 October 1917, he was safely at Quetta, joining the 2/89th Punjabis.[137] Otherwise, postings to Mesopotamia, for example, were accepted cheerfully as a stroke of fortune (in ignorance of malaria and typhoid), without being actively sought.[138] And in fact, in 1918, some officers posted to other theatres courageously sought a return to the Western Front, where they felt they could be of more use. The formidable Hugh Boustead, for example, successfully arranged a transfer from his Gurkha battalion in India back to the Western Front. "It was more than I could stand to remain for the rest of the war peacefully on a mountain top in the Himalayas, whilst my friends at home were falling daily at the front."[139]

---

133 IWM 14335 Marr, memoir, pp.90-91, 94.
134 LC Tape 630/647 Macdonald, interview.
135 IWM 6702 Low, letters to wife Noanie, 17 July, 3 September, 1915. See also his letter to Auntie Belle, 18 July, 1915.
136 THM Seaforths 81-2 Cooper, memoir, pp.126, 141, 143.
137 IWM 12688 MacKay, letters to mother, 4 June, 30 October 1917.
138 LC Several Fronts Recollections, Kingsley, memoir. See also: THM Seaforths 89-81 White, letter to mother, 9 November, 1915.
139 Boustead, *The Wind of Morning*, p.45. And see IWM 7508 Wyllie, diary 6 March, 19 May 1918.

However much they might cheerfully or stoically withstand the strain of the trenches, soldiers would however often advise their close relations to endeavour to avoid infantry service on the Western Front.[140]

Commissions offered both perils and opportunities for Highland soldiers seeking to avoid danger. On the one hand, to take a commission in the infantry might be regarded as a passport to an early death, and there are many instances of Highland soldiers declining infantry commissions in order to avoid this.[141] Corporal Harry Robertson in 1st Gordons was offered a commission in the battalion after Delville Wood. "A Lieut. in the 1st Gordons. Good Lord, it means suicide. Live Corpl better than dead Lieut. I told the C.O. He laughed and said nothing."[142] Robert Burns, recuperating with 3rd Camerons in Ireland, was asked to continue as confidential clerk to the C.O. there.

> I said, 'Yes, sir, with pleasure, but I'm waiting for my commission.' 'Oh,' he said, 'You know what's going to happen. When you get your commission, you'll be posted off across the water again and you might never come back, whereas if you remain my confidential clerk, you've every chance of coming out of this alive.' So I said, 'I'd rather come out alive than dead, sir,' So I became his confidential clerk.'[143]

On the other hand, a commission in another corps might offer a way out of the infantry. Corporal Robertson, who we have seen declining a commission in 1st Gordons, subsequently applied (unsuccessfully) for one in the Royal Horse Artillery;[144] Norman Macmillan, serving in the ranks of the Glasgow Highlanders, would have welcomed a commission in the Highland Cyclists! – but ultimately settled for the Royal Flying Corps.[145] Moreover, a commissioning course in Blighty offered the opportunity of a prolonged rest from the Front, which might be supplemented by specialist courses. This was certainly one of Norman Macmillan's objectives in his application. John Bowie noted the phenomenon in 11th Argylls about Autumn 1917.

> Many took this opportunity to get clear of the fighting. It takes six months to make an officer. Many acted the thick head so as he can be retained for another 3 months in a 'backward' examination. Another way was to pretend to be interested in signalling and that gave him another 3 months.[146]

---

140 See BWA Guthrie, letters to wife Crissie, 9 July, 23 October, 1915; Stothers, *Somewhere in France*, pp.89, 107, letters from J.C. Stothers to brother Steve, 3 November, 1917, 19 June, 1918; THM Seaforths 81-180 Murray, letter to brother Joe, 9 January, 1915 [wrongly dated 9 December, 1914], 11 January, 15 September, 1916, to sister Alex, 17 November, 30 December, 1915.
141 Apart from references below, see LC GS 1551 Strang, letter to brother Willie, 26 June, 1915; LC WF Recollections, Mackenzie, memoir; LC Tape 921 Stuart, interview, THM Camerons 89-17 McFarlane, memoir.
142 GHM PB1706/2 Robertson, diary, 20 July, 15 August, 1916.
143 LC Tape 903 Burns, interview.
144 GHM PB1706/2 Robertson, diary, 21 August, 1916.
145 IWM 3460 Macmillan, letters to sister Bessie, 17, 31 October, 20 November, 2 December, 1915, 12 February, 1916.
146 ASHM N-E11 Bowie, diary.

Another way out of the trenches was a 'Blighty' wound. Such wounds of course were randomly dispensed, and cannot be considered an avoidance mechanism. What is significant is the response to them. There are numerous cases recorded in the sources,[147] and many such wounds were received by the soldiers with gratitude to be out of the war, and with a hope that they had seen the last of it. As George Ramage wrote as early as May, 1915, "All newspaper stories of soldiers anxious to get back to the front are absolutely untrue. Everyone wants the war to stop. Many wish for 'Blighty' wounds."[148] Such feelings fell far short of the ideal warrior ethos. For many men, without necessarily losing sight of the need to fight and win, the war had become a torment, an endurance test, and a battle for personal survival. Lieutenant Richard Watson records an incident with 8/10th Gordons during the battle of Arras in 1917:

> Approaching the crest of Orange Hill, I came across a young Cameron with a bloody handkerchief held to his face, sobbing as if his heart would break. I bent over him and gave him a bit of a shake. "I've killed six," he said, "I'm dying." But I made him remove his handkerchief and found that he had a very neat through and through bullet wound in the nose. The shock must have been terrific but there was no danger whatsoever. When I told him so he brightened wonderfully and with a grin and a "so it's a blighty" departed towards the Aid Post.[149]

Other more deliberate ways of evading service in the trenches were scrimshanking (or malingering) and self-inflicted wounds. We have considered both of these practices already in dealing with discipline. Scrimshanking was quite common, but balanced by the tendency for many not to report sick if a major show was in prospect. As we have seen, self-inflicted wounds were fairly common, and suicides not unknown. There is no suggestion here that these practices were more pronounced in Highland regiments than others, but the fact that they occurred is a telling contradiction of the warrior ethos, and a greater indicator of fallibility or normalcy among Highland soldiers.

It remains to consider the question of cowardice. If courage may be defined as the overcoming of fear, then cowardice may be defined as surrender to fear. In this section we consider this most sensitive and contentious situation, when fear led to failure of duty on the field of battle. Here, both officers and men recognised a fine line between nervous disintegration and cowardice. James Racine, serving in the ranks of 1/5th Seaforths, notes

---

147 LC GS 0257 Cameron, memoir; BWA Couston, letter to mother, 5 November, 1916; LC GS 1008 Macdonald, diary, 1 January, 1917, letter from 'Lachie', 27 September, 1917; ASHM NE-10 Petrie, Sgt George Guthrie, manuscript memoir; ASHM N-E8 Ritchie, letter from Pte James Campbell to his parents, 25 November [1917?]; LC Several Fronts Recollections, Kingsley, memoir; LC GS 1625 Turing, memoir; Chambers, *Diaries of World War I*, p.37; THM Camerons 94-8 Mackay, 'Tell Them of Us,' letters from Ian Mackay to mother, 16, 19 April, 1915; NLS MS944-946 Ramage, diary, 1 May, 18 June, 1915; GHM PB1639 Kemp, memoir, p.100; GHM PB2183 Watson, memoir, pp.15,17; LC Tapes 1618/1619 Kerridge, interview; IWM 14269 Couper, letter to Tom Couper, 16 May, 1915; LC GS 0215 Bruce, I.R., letter to sister Maud, 19 December, 1915; GHM PB1706/2 Robertson, diary, 15 July 1916.
148 NLS MS945 Ramage, diary, 11 May, 1915.
149 GHM PB2183 Watson, memoir, p.14.

When out of the line, orders were at times read out by a non-commissioned officer. One item that was always received in silence was the intimation that a certain man of a given regiment has been found guilty of cowardice and that the sentence of death had been duly carried out. We all knew the strain liable to be placed upon a man in the thick of a fight and could imagine the awful feelings that must have driven him to falter. It was a debatable point as to when a man could be accused of cowardice or whether he was simply suffering from broken nerve and not responsible for his actions.[150]

Conversely, even if nerves were recognised compassionately, there might still be a stigma attached. G.P. Rose-Miller served as an officer with 1st Camerons. Asked in 1980 about failure through nerves, he replied;

I know of one case ... of an officer who, having been up the front-line once or twice in attack, about the third or fourth time got the jitters, and they said, 'Alright, you are of no use to us. You are not a leader. Back you go and you will be back down on the staff'... but he was disgraced as far as the Regiment was concerned because he couldn't face the music. He couldn't go over the top again.[151]

Known nervy men might be treated sympathetically and excused accusations of cowardice. David McMillan, who served with 43rd Battalion C.E.F. (Cameron Highlanders of Canada) tells of one N.C.O., in the battalion, Sergeant Davie ... who "should never have been with a fighting unit. Far better had he been working away behind the lines as a non-combatant. He was just not suited for front line duty, and the O.C. never expected it of him." In France, he performed duties at the transport lines and at Regimental H.Q. When the battalion was in the Ypres salient, however, he was ordered to escort a draft of 12 men to Zilliebeck. He led them out, but after coming under shell-fire, he failed to reach his destination and instead brought them back to safety. Brought up before his Company Commander to explain his behaviour, he was lucky to get away with it. "Anyone else would probably have been court-martialled."[152]

Addressing now specific examples of failure, we find a number of instances of failure in the ranks. We have already noted, in considering discipline, the execution for cowardice of James Adamson of 7th Camerons and the court martial of Private Powell of 1/8th Argylls for cowardice at Beaumont-Hamel. In other examples, a man of 1/6th Gordons flees from a section of trench very close to the Germans;[153] in October, 1917, two men of 11th Argylls refuse to go further while on patrol;[154] in May, 1915, an apparently hysterical man of the Black Watch causes alarm amongst 1/8th Argylls, with the false rumour that the Germans had broken through the line and were advancing rapidly.[155] In 2nd Gordons, Captain Pailthorpe, the M.O., records that when, on 3 October 1917, the battalion moved up to the line, one conscript fell out and refused to move.

150 IWM 16335 Racine, memoirs, p.47.
151 LC Tape 603 Rose-Miller, interview.
152 McMillan, *Trench Tea and Sandbags*, pp.17-19.
153 GHM PB2984, Strachan, memoir.
154 IWM 4586 Douglas, memoir, pp.140-147.
155 IWM 2902 Munro, diary, 11 May, 1915.

In the silence anything I said would be heard by the men of the last company. I told the Corporal to hand him over to the nearest Provost Corporal or police though I knew there were none near. I said if I came out of the show I would do my best to get him shot as he refused to take his chance with other men. We moved on. I heard afterwards he escaped from the Corporal, crossed our Divisional area and reported sick at a dressing station belonging to another division. They were far too busy to worry about him and let him go further back. Thus he escaped and somehow managed to get transferred to another Battalion.

A mile further on, he saw two men about to pass him having fallen out and turned back. With threats of the alternative, he exhorted them to take their chance with the other men. They re-joined.[156]

There are rather more unedifying examples of collective panic; in 1/4th Black Watch, in May, 1915. a carrying party drop their burdens and double out of a trench on the false alarm of a gas attack;[157] also in May, 1915, two platoons of 1/7th Gordons are reported to have bolted during one of their initial tours in the trenches;[158] men on working parties abandon their weapons and take cover in a trench when firing breaks out;[159] in summer, 1915, four lads not out of their teens abandon their post on the false report of a German attack;[160] in 1917 in 8th Seaforths, a frightened ration party run down a communications trench to avoid a bombardment;[161] in July, 1915, in the Glasgow Highlanders, a platoon abandons its trench under shell-fire;[162] in June, 1915, men of the 1st Gordons abandon their trenches after a heavy bombardment, on the false rumour that the Germans were attacking;[163] on 27 September, 1915, in 2nd Argylls, men of a newly arrived draft, moving up a communications trench to support an attack, panic and flee back down the trench when they hear the gas alarm, and are only stopped when they encounter the bayonet of the platoon sergeant;[164] there are various accounts of panic during the German offensive of March, 1918.[165] Perhaps the most remarkable account of panic is provided by Major Ernest Craig-Brown, then commanding A Company of 1st Camerons, describing the action at Nonne-Boschen on 11 November 1914, when his battalion was taken by surprise by the Prussian Guards, an episode we have already considered when discussing reputation.[166].

Panic indeed could prove contagious, and it was no doubt for this reason above all others that officers were prepared to use their revolvers on panicky soldiers. Victor Silvester records one instance in the trenches with 1/7th Argylls, when the Germans made a raid, when one man

---

156 GHM PB375 Pailthorpe, memoir, p.51.
157 BWA Thomson, memoir, Vol.2, p.9.
158 GHM PB107.1, Grant, diary, 22, 24, 26 May 1915.
159 Hutchison, *Warrior*, p.55; NLS MS945 Ramage, diary, 20 May, 1915.
160 GHM PB2984, Strachan, memoir.
161 LC GS 1625 Turing, memoir.
162 IWM 3460 Macmillan, diary, 12 July, 1915.
163 NLS MS946 Ramage, diary, 2 June, 1915.
164 ASHM N-E2 Todd, memoir.
165 LC Transcripts &c, Gammell, transcript of conversation; IWM 11144 MacKay, diary, 26 March, 1918.
166 IWM 1862 Craig-Brown, Account of the action at Nonne-Boschen, written 2 November 1915 and letter, 14 November 1914.

Courage and Failure 465

kept on repeating "I think we ought to get out, we ought to get out." An officer was called but failed to persuade him to shut up.

> Well, this officer pulled out his revolver and shot him dead on the spot. Right away it altered everyone's attitude because we [had] started to think we ought to get out. You only have to have someone saying that to you often enough and strongly enough and you thought that's what we must do. Right away when the officer shot this man dead, although it's a most terrible thing when you think of it, it altered the whole morale of the troops who were there. In fact I think if he hadn't done it we should all perhaps have started thinking about getting out.[167]

Turning to the officers themselves, we find a number of cases of failure; an officer breaks down during an attack at Arras and unnecessarily orders a retreat back to the safety of the trenches;[168] an officer fails in his duty to lead a raid;[169] an officer fails in his duty to push forward a post into No Man's Land;[170] an officer openly cowers under enemy shell-fire.;[171] an officer deserts his trench during a bombardment.[172] Daniel McFarlane, serving in 7th Camerons, recalls an incident which occurred when he was in charge of a section on a reconnaissance of the German trenches. When they had gone so far, the officer in overall charge of the mission, attached from the Black Watch, ordered him to complete the mission, while he, the officer, remained in the rear and covered them from possible attack. McFarlane completed the mission, returned successfully to the officer and they returned to report their findings at Headquarters. At that point;

> An officer came into the dugout and, in front of all present, accused our Black Watch officer of cowardice and made me recount how, in the middle of completion of the task, it had been handed over to me. He [the Black Watch officer] made great protest, but it was obvious that the climate of opinion was hostile to him, and the Commanding Officer closed the incident there and then. I never knew what happened to him as he disappeared from the battalion.[173]

According to Zuehlke, in his history of 16th Battalion C.E.F., there was failure at the highest level within the 15th Battalion (48th Highlanders of Canada). Its commander, Colonel John Currie, had little military experience. During Second Ypres he had left the front line on the pretext of rounding up stragglers. He then took shelter at 2nd Canadian Infantry Brigade Headquarters, from which he was ejected. Apparently, he ended up at 2nd Canadian Field Artillery headquarters in a drunken condition. The incident was largely covered up, but Currie was sent back to Canada.[174] It is at the highest level too that regrettably we must consider the

---

167 LC GS 1470 Silvester, transcript of interview. For other threats to shoot panicky soldiers, see LC GS 1625 Turing, memoir, unpaginated, IWM 4586 Douglas, memoir, p.385.
168 ASHM N-E11 Bowie, diary, 23 April, 1917.
169 LC GS 1625 Turing, memoir.
170 GHM PB107.1, Grant, diary, 21, 22, 27 May, 8, 9, 11 June 1915.
171 NLS MS947 Ramage, diary, n.d.
172 NLS MS944, 946, Ramage, diary, n.d. and 2 June, 1915.
173 THM Camerons 89-17 McFarlane, memoir.
174 Zuehlke, *Brave Battalion*, p.93.

surrender of the greater part of 1st Gordons at Le Cateau in August, 1914, which, as we have already seen, earned them the unflattering nickname, 'The Kaiser's Bodyguard.' The surrender occurred when the Gordons, in company with some other troops, were apparently cut off by the German advance. The situation was complicated by the extraordinary fact that the second-in-command, Colonel Gordon V.C., by virtue of being Brevet Colonel had assumed command of the whole body over the head of his C.O., Lieutenant-Colonel Neish, who retained command of the Gordons. Apparently Neish favoured surrender, seeing the situation as hopeless and desiring to save life, while Gordon would have been more inclined to fight on or cut a way out. The courage of their men is not in doubt. Nor, despite an acrimonious law suit, is that of the two officers concerned. It was a question of judgment. It cannot be doubted that, given the critical situation of the retreating B.E.F., any additional disruption or delay to the German advance occasioned by further Gordons' resistance would have been helpful. The surrender was not an instance of cowardice, but it is still a sensitive subject amongst ex-Gordons.[175]

At the beginning of this chapter we set ourselves the task of looking at courage and nerves, and particularly the fallibility of the Highland soldier. We have shown that most Highland soldiers felt afraid. There was no shame in this, for fear in itself was no indicator of cowardice, and most soldiers battled courageously to avoid showing fear, and to avoid surrendering to it. We have identified some striking examples of courage. We have seen also that Highland soldiers were not immune from nervous disintegration after sudden trauma, otherwise known as 'shell shock.' Again, there was no shame in this, for such disintegration was beyond individual control. The gradual erosion of nerve was more problematic, but it came to be accepted that even for those with great inherent courage, nerves could eventually be worn down to the point where some rest was essential to avoid breakdown. Much more reprehensible were the deliberate attempts to avoid service with the infantry in the front line, which we have considered at some length. Even in those cases, the principal motivation may have been self-preservation rather than cowardice, or even a feeling that one had done enough and it was time for others to 'do their bit.' Finally, with regard to cowardice itself, which we have defined as surrender to fear, leading to failure of duty on the field of battle, there were certainly some instances. The Highland soldier was not immune to failure. In none of the areas we have addressed, however, do we suggest that he was unique. In fact, to conclude that the Highland soldier was fallible in this way is simply to stress his normalcy compared with other British soldiers. Highland soldiers did not constitute a martial race apart; they were simply ordinary human beings doing their best to cope in extraordinary circumstances. Writing long after the war, Albert Strachan, who served on the Western Front with 6th Gordons throughout 1915 until captured at Loos, put it rather well.

> Every man did as well as he could – all are not built the same way. Some can stand much more than others. Bravery from my point of view is doing your duty but few have that bravery – whilst awaiting. I was always scared stiff sitting in a trench being shelled and as I have already mentioned was brave carrying a wounded man, very shaky when going back

---

175 Falls, *Life of a Regiment*, pp.6-9; IWM 18455 Turnbull, letters to parents, 20, 21 September, 1914; LC GS 1534 Stewart, miscellaneous papers.

with the empty stretcher. Of course there were a good few who could not manage to discipline themselves. One thing you take for granted, the man who tells you how brave he was was very much afraid. The man who had no fear at any time was a marvel.[176]

---

176 GHM. PB2984 Strachan, memoir.

17

Final Thoughts

"There are worse deaths than leading a platoon of Highlanders into action."[1]

In the previous chapters we have considered various attributes of the Highland soldier, each in isolation. In this concluding chapter we attempt to bring them together. Some of these findings are of cultural significance; others are of more purely military significance. We may distinguish between these two sets of conclusions. In a purely military context, it is evident that most of the characteristics of the Highland soldier we have considered had an impact on morale or may have been consequent on morale, and we will examine our findings in this context. Most of this chapter will consider this issue of morale. Before we address this issue, however, we will address the cultural side.

It is fascinating to see the way in which the kilted regiments from all parts of the empire survived as cultural entities, without necessarily being composed of men from the Highlands. Throughout the war, the British Army's Highland regiments remained predominantly Scottish, albeit with a significant and highly useful input of Englishmen, but, with the exception of a few Territorial battalions, they were not predominantly Highland in composition. At the same time, although lacking full dress, they retained the full panoply of Highland regimental existence; the kilt, the pipes and the traditions, eagerly embraced by the expatriate regiments from Canada and South Africa, as well as south of the border. They had ceased to be Highland in composition but had become cultural entities in their own right. This situation had been reached before the war broke out, perhaps reaching its greatest expression in the formation of so many Highland Militia units in Canada in the 1900's. The process was indeed still ongoing when the war started, with the 50th Militia Regiment (Gordon Highlanders of Canada) being formed only in 1913. No diminution of this phenomenon is apparent during the war; instead, we see its direct continuation in the formation of the South African Scottish. A separate study might look into post-War attitudes.

Nevertheless, when Highland battalions which were composed of genuine Highlanders suffered large casualties, the impact on local communities could be great. There were no 'Pals' battalions' amongst the kilted regiments, although the Glasgow companies of Lochiel's Kitchener battalions of Camerons came close. The battalions most vulnerable to such local

---

1   IWM 7668 Escombe, letter from Lt Anderson to Escombe, 13 July 1916.

'The Jock on the Rock.' 51st Highland Division memorial, Newfoundland Park, Beaumont-Hamel. (Photograph, author)

losses were the true Highland Territorial battalions; the Seaforths, Camerons and 8th Argylls, and in the early battles in 1915, the concentration of casualties in individual communities could be great. While pointing to instances of such casualties, this study has not examined their consequent impact on the local communities, but certainly some commentators felt that the survival of Gaelic itself, already very much on the defensive, was under threat.

Finally, we may note the proliferation of memorials after the war, albeit by no means unique to Highland soldiers, exemplified by the Scottish National War Memorial in Edinburgh Castle, but perhaps reaching its apogee for Highland soldiers in the memorial to 51st Highland Division at Beaumont-Hamel, 'the Jock on the Rock.' This fine statue not only provides a memorial to the Highland dead, but also, erected as it is on the site of the Division's most famous battle, continues the 19th Century tradition of commemorating the achievement of Highland troops in battle. Numerous memorials are scattered throughout the Highlands, including fine statues, for example, at Dingwall, Dornoch and Buckie. In many respects these are in the direct tradition of the South African War, reflecting earlier statues at Alloa and elsewhere, and indicating how much the experience of the Great War reflected that of its much smaller, but still considerable, predecessor.

In a military context, it is evident that most of the characteristics of the Highland soldier we have considered had an impact on morale or may have been consequent on morale. This is true for example of the kilt, both with regard to the pride it engendered as much as to its impracticality in modern war. It is clearly true of the pipes, but it is true too of the less tangible elements we have addressed; the way discipline operated, the relationship between officers, N.C.O.'s and men, comradeship, support from home and religion, identity and reputation. It is also related to ferocity in battle, and to courage and failure. In fact, virtually every element we have addressed has a relationship with morale.

It is equally true that this relationship with morale is fundamental to the significance of the study. For if the attributes of the Highland soldier we have addressed have any military (as opposed to cultural) significance, that significance lies in their relationship with, and impact on, morale. We define morale very briefly as "the will and belief to keep going to victory".[2] The subject is important because morale was critical to the ability of soldiers to cope with the stresses and strains of trench warfare in the Great War. As Watson pithily remarks, "the First World War was, above all, a contest of endurance", while "resilience became the key quality necessary for men and armies to survive and was the determining factor in the long and bloody conflict."[3]

In order to assess the significance of the attributes we have addressed to the overall morale of the Highland soldier, we need to take account not only of those morale factors we have specifically addressed, but also of others on which we have touched only slightly, if at all. For example, we have made little attempt to examine the logistic contributors to morale, by which we mean adequate rations, medical support etc. A model of the Highland soldier's morale built, for example, upon a recognition of national identity, but which ignored the more mundane elements of logistic support, would clearly be invalid. We need instead to relate the experiences of the Highland soldier we have addressed to a holistic model of morale, to help us to set the unique attributes of the Highland soldier in context.

While there have been many different approaches to understanding the nature of morale, and some excellent studies, placing the emphasis variously on psychological, institutional and societal influences,[4] no agreed overarching integrated model has gained currency. The writer has therefore of necessity been obliged to build on this work to construct such a model (Diagram 1). While he takes full responsibility for the defects of the model, he is of course hugely indebted to the thought that has gone before. In the following discussion, we will first of all describe the model, and then relate our findings to its individual elements.

The starting point for the model is the individual. Each man brought to the Army his own individual inherent qualities. These were influenced by his genetic makeup, his upbringing, and of course by the society in which he lived. Each individual then faced the challenge of coping with the strains placed upon him by the war. He was sustained partly by his belief in the cause, and by the opportunities for relaxation out of the line, and he might also evolve what Watson has described as "coping strategies"[5] to survive.

---

2   There have been many attempts to define morale, and a discussion would constitute a paper in itself. See, for example, Baynes, John, *Morale* (London: Leo Cooper, 1987), p.92; Watson, Alexander, *Enduring the Great War* (Cambridge University Press, 2008), pp.140-141; Sheffield, Gary, *Command and Morale* (Barnsley, Praetorian Press, 2014), p.154.
3   Watson, *Enduring the Great War*, pp.1, 22.
4   See in particular Ministry of Defence, *Army Doctrine Publications, Operations* (London: Ministry of Defence, 2010), pp.2.10-2.31, on the Moral Component; Baynes, *Morale*, passim; Holmes, *Tommy*, 2004, Part VI, Heart and Soul, pp.489-612; Sheffield, *Command and Morale*, Chapters 9, 10 and 11; Watson, *Enduring the Great War*, passim: Ferguson, Niall, *The Pity of War* (London, Penguin, 1999) pp.339-366.
5   See discussion below.

Final Thoughts 471

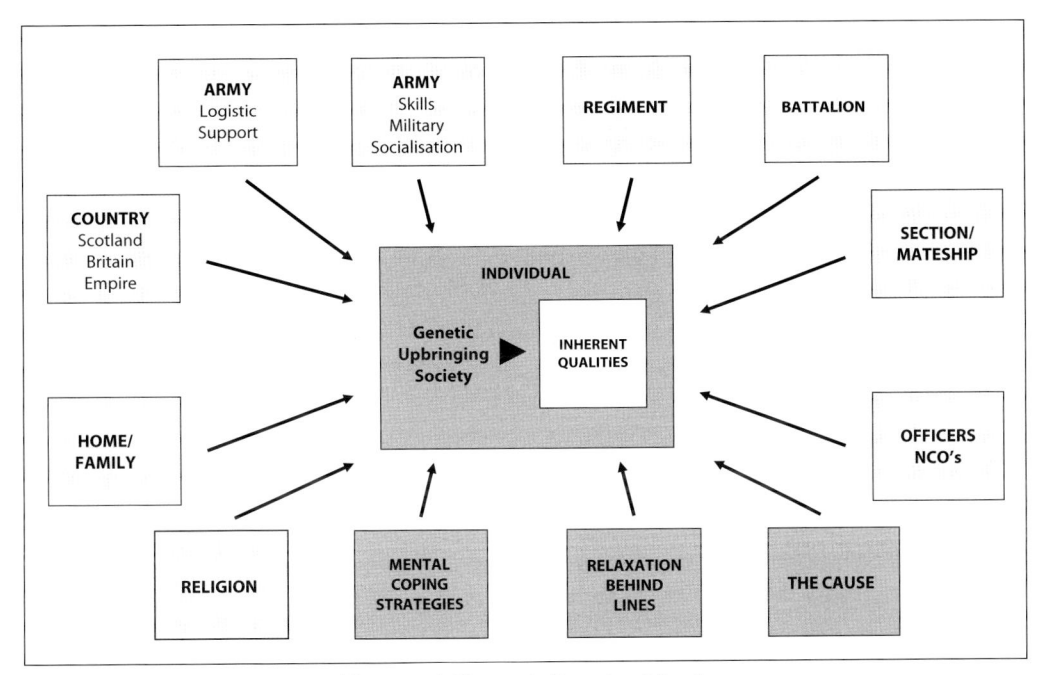

Diagram 1: Factors influencing Morale

But, most importantly, he was not alone. He was helped to cope by his relationship with the groups to which he belonged and the people with whom he had to interface, and these were many and various: the Army, his regiment, his battalion, his infantry company, platoon and section, his officer and NCO's, his closest pals, his country, the folks at home and his God. We may call these relationships "support mechanisms". They might themselves be influenced by societal values imported from peacetime. The model therefore is based on the individual at the centre, coping as best he can with the strains placed on him by war, and responding in his own way to the support mechanisms surrounding him.

These support mechanisms were of course not independent of one another. To a certain extent, their separation is an artificial aid to clarity. For example, the strength to be drawn from the membership of a close-knit infantry section might be hugely limited by a poor NCO; individual relaxation was often spent not on one's own but in the company of comrades from one's section; while listening to the pipes play retreat might be an individual relaxation choice in spare time, but the ceremony was arranged by the battalion. Furthermore, some of these support mechanisms provided similar functions. This is particularly the case with military social groups, which provided both identity and cohesion (two strongly related notions), albeit at different levels. Thus, a soldier might draw strength from his identity as a Scot, as a member of a regiment, as a member of a battalion with a good fighting record, and/or as a member of a close-knit infantry section; all these groups at different levels providing moral cohesion.

Of course, these support mechanisms might fail. The danger then is that they might become damage mechanisms, with a truly negative impact on morale. A soldier who genuinely cannot accept Army discipline will be a square peg in a round hole, and will eventually fall foul of the system. A soldier in a dysfunctional section might find his life is a misery. A soldier might resent the attitude of a supercilious officer. A soldier who loses his best pal may fall to pieces. A soldier confronted by suffering without parallel might lose the solid plank of his religious faith. A soldier outraged by strikes at home might question his belief in the cause. A soldier who is jilted by his sweetheart at home might lose his will to carry on. Each individual's experience would be different, and each would respond in his own way.

If we now try to relate our findings to the model, we may turn first to the individual. The principal personal qualities which serve to promote good morale are loyalty, unselfishness, determination, self-discipline, sense of duty, kindness, courage, respect for others, trust and humour. There is nothing in the study to suggest that any of these characteristics were unique to Highland soldiers. Instead, in examining inter-personal relations, we have found the same mix of human qualities we would expect; group loyalty and individual careerism, self-discipline and looting, compassion and brutality, courage and failure, absolute trust and total lack of confidence, humour and morbidity, with the balance hearteningly in favour of duty and human decency. As we have observed, these qualities were influenced by a man's genetic makeup, his upbringing, and by the society in which he lived. Highland soldiers certainly shared with most of their fellow Britons (although arguably less so, the Canadians) the paternalism-deference exchange which characterised British society in 1914, which, it has been argued pre-disposed soldiers to a ready acceptance of the military system and in particular the relationship with officers.[6] No other exclusive Highland pre-determinants of resilience have been identified, although one might here refer to 'Scottishness,' for a sense of Scottish identity could be considered part of upbringing. We will deal with this later when considering national identity.

It is evidently in 'inherent qualities' that one might expect to find crystallised the romantic attributes of a martial race, and possibly even the joy of war, to which Ferguson refers.[7] We have indeed identified a tendency to use the bayonet brutally in combat, the enjoyment of such action by some soldiers, and a certain pride in their reputation for ferocity. But we have not presented any evidence to suggest that such behaviour was either more or less applicable to Highland soldiers than to others. At the same time, we have shown quite clearly, in examining courage and nerves, that the Highland soldier was fallible. Most Highland soldiers felt afraid, they were not immune from nervous disintegration, they were sometimes eager to avoid service in the front line, and we have observed a few instances of genuine cowardice. In none of these cases do we suggest that he was unique. In fact, to conclude that the Highland soldier was fallible in this way is simply to stress his normalcy compared with other British soldiers. Highland soldiers did not constitute a martial race apart; they were simply ordinary human beings doing their best to cope in extraordinary circumstances.

Each individual then faced the challenge of coping with the strains placed upon him by the war. He was sustained partly by his belief in the cause. There is ample evidence that belief in the righteousness of the cause, and the consequent inevitability of a just victory, sustained many Highland soldiers throughout the war. However cynically we view popular support for the war from the perspective of the 21st Century, we have seen that many soldiers at the time viewed their service as a patriotic duty, which should not be confused with belligerence or jingoism.

---

6 See in particular Watson, *Enduring the War*, pp.3-4, 117-120, Sheffield, *Command and Morale*, pp.176-183.
7 Ferguson, *Pity of War*, pp.357-366.

There was certainly some naivete at the start of the war and a degree of subsequent disillusionment. But much of the disillusionment was identified after the war was over, with the benefit of hindsight. There was a strong reaction to the German invasion of Belgium and to German brutality there, and each subsequent German breach of the conventional "rules of war" brought a similar reaction. Thus, despite some disillusionment, the acceptance of patriotic duty persisted even after the introduction of conscription. There is no reason to believe that these sentiments were unique to the Highland soldier. It was nevertheless a sentiment shared by both sides. As Watson concludes, "Fear of the consequences of an enemy invasion for their countries, and still more for their homes, families and loved ones, meant that for four long and bloody years most Britons and Germans, however scared or reluctant, were nonetheless willing recruits for their national armies."[8]

A further support came from the opportunity to relax behind the lines. Activities included visiting estaminets for food, drink and socialising, football, gambling, reading, concerts, leave, and of course pursuing the fair sex, either local girls or finding sexual release in prostitutes.[9] In many respects, there is no reason to believe that these activities affected Highland troops any differently than others, but some elements of the Highland soldier's experience were unique. While he shared many of his songs with the rest of the army, he had his own individual repertoire of sentimental Scottish songs. Highland games, with traditional sports, dancing and piping, were organised behind the lines. The pipes played Retreat in the evening for all or entertained the officers in the mess. Highland dancing was encouraged and practiced, and both the pipes and dancing featured in concerts. And of course, the Highland soldier enjoyed his three special celebrations of the year; Hogmanay, Burns' Night and St Andrew's Day. Some of these activities were simply informal, like spontaneous sing-songs in the estaminet. Others were deliberately organised by the battalion or company, like the playing of Retreat by the pipe-band, though it was the soldiers' choice to watch and listen. Others still, especially the larger Games and gatherings, were arranged by brigade or division, notably the extraordinary gathering organised by the Canadians at Tinques in 1918. Where the activities were provided or encouraged by company, battalion, brigade or division, they should also be considered as products of those particular Army support mechanisms. The key point here, however, is that a significant amount of recreational activity, whether informal or arranged by the battalion or division, actually promoted and fostered identity, both as a Scot and as a Highland soldier, and, as we shall argue, this was an important contributor to morale.

Finally, the individual soldier might evolve what Watson has described as mental coping strategies.[10] He identifies three, largely sub-conscious strategies: 'adaptation', 'optimism, religion and superstition', and 'positive illusions'. The first strategy, adaptation, involves appropriate risk-assessment strategies, fatalism and humour. The second includes unrealistic optimism, religion and a belief in luck or superstition. The third strategy, 'positive illusions', embraces hopes for an early peace, leave or rest, a focus on short-term rather than cumulative risk, hopes of a blighty wound, "worse-off" comparisons, and, in real danger, avoidance and distraction strategies like cards and music. Watson does a great service in drawing attention to these psycho-

---

8 Watson, *Enduring the War*, p.56.
9 Holmes, *Tommy*, pp.592ff, has a good treatment of such activities.
10 Watson, *Enduring the War*, pp.5-7, 85-107. In this discussion I have preferred to separate out religion as an 'external' support mechanism as it involves the individual in a relationship with God.

logical strategies, which have not previously been explored, but they need to be placed in context alongside the full range of support mechanisms acting on the soldier. With the exception of religion, which is considered separately, we do not claim to have examined these coping strategies in relation to the Highland soldier, for there seems to be no reason why they should apply to him in any way uniquely. There is more work to do here, but it would be surprising if a comparative study were to reveal significant differences between Highland soldiers and others in this respect.

Turning next to the 'external' mechanisms which provided support to the individual soldier, we may start with the Army. The Army provided support in a variety of ways, including pride in its history and traditions, awards and decorations and training in professional competence. But perhaps the most important overall Army (as opposed to Regimental or smaller-group) mechanisms enhancing morale were military socialisation and logistical support.

Military socialisation refers to the process by which Army training and routine inculcated in recruits the Army way of life and way of thinking, all of which was designed to produce better and more effective soldiers. The system actively promoted values which produced and sustained good morale either as a deliberate goal or as a by-product; discipline, patriotism, loyalty, esprit de corps, unselfishness, trust, mutual dependency, knowing where you stand, courage, integrity, self-respect, respect for others, determination, duty, sacrifice, confidence, balanced routines.

If this process was common across the Army, Highland soldiers nevertheless were different in that they trained in the kilt, and they trained to the sound of the pipes. As we have seen, although both were distinct to regiments, which we will consider separately, in terms of tartan or tunes played, both had their appeal beyond the individual regiment in terms of national identity and the reputation and romantic history of the Highland regiments as a whole. The kilt and pipes were central to the cadres in which military socialisation was achieved and contributed to the process by which a strong esprit to corps was built amongst Highland soldiers.

Perhaps the most discussed element of military socialisation has been discipline, partly perhaps because strong military discipline offends civilian susceptibilities. As we have seen, it is true that, when the boundaries of discipline were transgressed, punishments could be harsh, but it would be quite wrong to suggest that the system was based simply on fear of punishment[11]. The training aimed to indoctrinate recruits into the voluntary acceptance of discipline for the general good, and as we have also seen, much could be achieved with a good relationship between officers, N.C.O.'s and men. Generally, those who worked within the rules had little to fear from the system except deserved minor punishments for minor misdemeanours. As Sheffield points out, morale and discipline "although related, are not identical".[12] But there was a strong relationship between morale and the acquiescence in Army discipline. Sure signs of low morale were self-inflicted wounds, shirking, desertion and general indiscipline. In this respect, Highland soldiers on the whole were neither angels nor sinners, and there is little indication that in regard to discipline, the behaviour of Highlanders was significantly better or worse than that of the Army as a whole.

The other major plank provided by the Army was logistical support. By this we mean adequate rations, the right equipment and ammunition to do the job, facilities for rest and getting clean, supply of mail from home, proper casualty evacuation and medical care, and pay. Failure in any

---

11 We should also note the varying approaches to discipline in Regular, Territorial, Kitchener and Dominion battalions: see Sheffield, *Command and Morale*, p.162.
12 Ibid., p.156.

of these areas could have a severe impact on morale. There is no reason to believe that the overall logistical support provided to the Highland soldier was any different to that provided to his colleagues in the Army. In one respect however he did suffer, in that, as we have demonstrated, the kilt was not really suitable for modern warfare. This was potentially damaging to morale, but, as we have discussed at length, the kilt had other undoubted benefits for morale, in terms of pride, self-image, identity and esprit de corps. The key question is whether, in terms of morale, these benefits of the kilt outweighed its impracticality.

At the next level was the Regiment, which was core to the ethos of the British Army and remains so[13]. It was one of the fundamental building blocks of moral cohesion. While in the British Army, soldiers trained and fought in Regular, Territorial and Kitchener battalions, these battalions all belonged to Regiments, and much of their identity and esprit de corps came from the Regiment. As Sheffield states, the British high command believed for morale purposes in a combination of the Regimental system and the paternalism of officers. "These factors were, indeed, to prove vital in the maintenance of morale."[14] Highland soldiers enjoyed this Regimental allegiance as much as any others. They were able to sweep up the history and traditions of their regiment, traditions which might embrace Piper Findlater on the heights of Dargai, or the Black Watch storming the position of Tel el-Kebir. They trained and fought in the uniform of their regiment, expressed in their tartan, their cap-badge, their shoulder-titles, and in minor distinctions of dress like differently arranged hose-flashes, while they marched to pipe-tunes which were specific to their own regiments, all of which reinforced their regimental identity. While the Army provided their identity as Highland soldiers, the regiment provided their identity as Gordon Highlanders or Black Watch. No wonder the Canadians and South Africans sought to create instant regimental tradition or sought allegiance with longer-established regiments in the old country. The Regiment gave a sense of belonging and identity, and, as we have seen, soldiers could be fiercely protective of their regimental allegiance. Loyalty also worked both ways. The regiment itself would extend its duty of care to soldiers' families and might use local connections to provide comforts from home. If a degree of cohesion was provided by the Army itself, far more came from the Regiment. Nevertheless, regimental pride and strong regimental identity was common across all regiments of the British Army. There is little justification for assuming that it was greater in the Highland regiments than others, even though they may have thought so themselves.

By contrast to the Regiment, the battalion, company, platoon and section were the organisms in which our soldiers served and fought. Discipline remained an ever-present regulator, but as Holmes has pointed out, "for most men, almost despite themselves, the carrot of mate-ship weighed heavier than the stick of coercion."[15] It was indeed in these groups that moral cohesion was most important and most relevant. The principal elements of moral cohesion were, to different degrees, shared at each level. These were identity, continuity, common purpose, shared experience (including victory and success), shared values, depths of familiarity, mutual dependency, trust, comradeship, loyalty, a sense of belonging, feeling valued, peer pressure, humour and esprit de corps. As will be apparent, most of these values corresponded to those inculcated through military socialisation during the recruits' early training.

---

13 *Army Doctrine Publication: Operations,* p.2.16.
14 Sheffield, *Command and Morale,* pp.155-156.
15 Holmes, *Tommy,* p.612.

At the lowest level, below that even of the section, were the friendships, sometimes intense, formed between soldiers, in effect "trench households"[16]. Many soldiers formed small groups with whom they would live, eat and knock about together and with whom they would, for example, share presents from home. We have seen this process in operation amongst Highland soldiers. In some cases intense friendships were formed between individuals, which could be a great support but also utterly devastating if one party was killed, and again, we have seen this process in operation. In terms of moral cohesion, the recent consensus has been to identify the smallest groups, at section level or equivalent, as crucial.[17] This is undoubtedly true, and again we have witnessed the importance of such comradeship in operation. This emphasis on small group cohesion, or fighting for one's mates, has even sometimes been placed in opposition to the notion of fighting for a cause or fighting for one's country. In terms of morale however the two concepts are not mutually exclusive. Both elements, the belief in a just cause, and the small-group cohesion which led soldiers to fight for their mates in battle, were effective planks in maintaining morale. Both may be viewed as "support mechanisms" in the sense we have described. Both are still recognised in British Army Doctrine. There need be no conflict between them,[18] and we have recognised both in operation among our Highland soldiers. In examining how comradeship or mate-ship worked amongst our Highland soldiers, we have seen examples of ideal comradeship, but also examples of dysfunctional groups, both amongst officers and men. There seems no reason at all to believe that at this level the experience of the Highland soldier was significantly different from his colleagues in the rest of the Army. If true, this admission is significant, for we have identified comradeship as one of the crucial props of morale.

However, the significance of mate-ship or comradeship at the lower level should not blind us to the importance of support at the higher level. Combat success and reputation were won by the battalion. When a soldier lost the bulk of his section (probably including his best pal) to an enemy shell, it was his platoon, company or battalion which would step in to provide him the support he needed. It was also often the battalion (or even higher-level formations like the brigade and division), which might arrange comforts from home, or which organised much of the recreational activity for the men, such as concerts, football competitions, or beating retreat. We have seen all these processes in action amongst our Highland soldiers. Finally, the inescapable framework in which section-level mate-ship developed was the platoon, company, battalion, Regiment and Army. No level had the monopoly on cohesion. In particular, inspiration and encouragement to the men was not limited to junior officers, however crucial their role, but derived from all levels of the battalion hierarchy, from C.O. down to platoon commander (and indeed to platoon sergeant). It also extended upwards to brigade, division and even Army level. In particular, the battalion C.O., ably assisted by his Adjutant and R.S.M., had a crucial role in setting the standards by which he expected his junior officers and Senior N.C.O.'s to perform. Also at the battalion level, and central to this inspirational role, was the role of the pipe-band, which could provide inspiration and uplift both to tired men on the march and to frightened men going into battle. We have noted examples of these behaviours, frequently inspirational, sometimes less so, throughout our study.

16   Ibid., p.531.
17   See e.g. Watson, *Enduring the Great War*, pp.66-69.
18   *Army Doctrine Publication: Operations,* pp.2.15ff.

Crucial to moral cohesion and to effective leadership was the relationship between officers, N.C.O.'s and men. For most soldiers, this meant essentially their platoon and company officers, their platoon sergeant and corporals and the Company Sergeant Major. In the British Army as a whole, officers traditionally were imbued with the values of paternalism which were still central to the society of the time, and the allied value of noblesse oblige.[19] The care of their men was central. Even when, later in the war, many more officers were either promoted from the ranks or held commissions as "Temporary Gentlemen", they generally took great pains to exercise their duty of care and were trained to do so. Junior officers needed to be brave, competent, firm and fair, clear in direction and provide encouragement. Good officers would ensure their men felt valued and would bring on their potential: they would make provision to relieve boredom, through arranging sports etc.: they would provide extra comforts for their men through their own pockets. They would exercise discipline humanely, for example, by waking an exhausted man sleeping on sentry duty. Because the men had been brought up in the same tradition of paternalism-deference, they generally readily accepted the system and respected their officers as long as they could fill the role. Indeed, hero-worship and devotion to officers was not uncommon. Strong bonds could exist between officers and men. There could of course, be good and bad officers, but, as Sheffield concludes, "The excellence of relations between Other Ranks and regimental officers was a factor of absolutely crucial importance in maintaining the morale of the BEF throughout four gruelling years of attrition on the Western Front."[20] In our examination of battalion hierarchy, we have seen all these positive elements at work in the Highland regiments; we have also seen some sad cases of failure, when officers failed to live up to the standards expected of them, and relations between officers and men were correspondingly poor. There is little or no reason to believe that the relationship between officers and men in the Highland regiments was exceptional. It was another facet of morale in which they shared the common experience of the British soldier.

While there is a considerable literature on the role of the junior officer in the Great War,[21] much less has been written on the role of the NCO. This is a pity, for the NCO was also crucial to morale. Sergeants possibly and corporals certainly were potentially members of the small groups which have been identified as crucial for moral cohesion. Under the supervision of their platoon officer, they played a significant role in discipline and the daily ordering of the soldiers' lives. They also had a duty of care. They were perhaps in a more difficult position than their officers, lacking both the background of paternalism to inform their duty of care, and the reciprocal deference to maintain their authority. This they had to do by virtue of their rank and force of personality alone. Perhaps as a result there were more bad NCO's than bad officers, but this is untested. Certainly their role was crucial. Sheffield comments: "NCO's, who deserve a major study to themselves, co-operated closely with officers to ensure the smooth running of a unit, although the problems of balancing friendship and discipline could be acute. The officer and NCO had to strike a delicate balance between being part of the platoon or company

---

19 It is again important here to note different patterns of behaviour between different parts of the Army, notably between Regular and T.F. officers. See in particular Sheffield, *Command and Morale*, pp.176-177.
20 Sheffield, *Command and Morale*, p.183.
21 See for example, Moore-Bick, Christopher, *Playing the Game* (Solihull, Helion, 2011), and Lewis-Stempel, John, *Six Weeks* (London: Orion Books, 2011).

'team' and being slightly aloof from it. The successful partnership between the officer and NCO, which was in many ways the lynchpin of the entire disciplinary structure of the army, had to be founded upon mutual goodwill and recognition of the difficulties inherent in the relationship."[22] Again, in our examination of battalion hierarchy, we have seen both sides of the coin in the Highland regiments. And again, there is little or no reason to believe that the relationship between N.C.O.'s and men in the Highland regiments was exceptional. Like the relationship with their officers, it was another facet of morale in which they shared the common experience of the British soldier.

Support to our soldiers was also provided from sources outside the Army. The relationship with one's country was important. Patriotism was a factor not only in fuelling the cause, but also in providing identity and through that, additional moral cohesion. Highland soldiers could take pride in three 'national' allegiances; to Scotland, of course (though there were many Englishmen in the ranks), to Britain, and also to the British Empire. Patriotism was built on an awareness of national history, tradition and mythology, and could be inspired, perhaps particularly in Scotland, by thoughts of the country's rugged beauty. While Highland soldiers generally shared with their colleagues a certain commitment to Britain and the Empire, there is no doubt that a fierce sense of Scottish-ness was often central to their sense of identity. This identity was reinforced by the kilt and pipes, by songs and traditions, which lent their weight throughout training (military socialisation), and afterwards throughout a soldier's life in his battalion, whether on parade or at leisure. Perhaps equally important was the knowledge that the soldier in his mission had the support and understanding of the nation. Morale might be damaged when this assumption proved questionable, through strikes, civilian insensitivity, the apparent disconnection of the home world from the war, or the number of fit men of military age who did not volunteer. We have seen examples of anger and frustration expressed by Highland soldiers in these circumstances. But there can be little doubt that overall an exceptional sense of nationality was a correspondingly exceptional contributor to the morale of the Highland soldier.

Support from home came more particularly from the soldiers' own family and friends. The postal service to home was phenomenal, letters were exchanged with mothers, fathers, wives and sweethearts, and most touchingly, children, often weekly, sometimes almost daily. For those involved in such exchanges, love from home, though achingly distant, was never absent. Many soldiers effectively lived in two parallel worlds, coping with the extraordinary demands of their military life in the trenches while dealing with the often mundane but sometimes difficult affairs of home, if for example their parents were ill, the family business doing badly, or their father out of work. Those soldiers who indulged in regular correspondence with home were never out of touch with that alternative reality and were able to draw strength from thoughts of home and the love of their families. Of course, some soldiers did not benefit from these exchanges, and these men would need to rely more on the support of their comrades at the front. Sometimes too, news from home could be devastating; the loss of a loved one or simply being jilted, so the connection with home could be a double-edged sword. We have seen all these elements at play amongst our Highland soldiers. Again, there is no reason to believe that in the level of support to be derived from his friends and family at home, the Highland soldier was any different from his other Army colleagues.

---

22 Sheffield, *Command and Morale*, p.182.

Religion also provided support. In a much less secular world than our own, many soldiers had religious feelings, and those who truly believed could draw courage from their faith and from God's support. For many, faith in God effectively acted as another support mechanism. Of course, the carnage and suffering at the Front could lead some soldiers to question their faith. How, after all, could a merciful and omnipotent God permit such suffering? Those who lost their faith could then fall victim to disillusionment. But to many, faith remained constant throughout the war, and provided a solid rock of support.[23] Although we have commented on religious feeling in the study, we have not put it under the microscope, and so any conclusions we draw must be tentative. Nevertheless, we have seen these conflicting elements at play amongst our Highland soldiers, and it does seem unlikely that his experience in this respect was in any way unique compared with his British Army colleagues.

If we then consider morale as a whole, it is apparent that in many respects there is little or no reason to believe that there was any significant difference between the experience of the Highland soldier and his Lowland or English counterparts. Here, however, we need to inject a note of caution. While we have, in this study, endeavoured to identify those areas where the experience of the Highland soldier was unique, our evidence has been drawn almost totally from the experiences of the Highland soldiers themselves. This has not been a strictly comparative study. In some cases, we believe that we have conclusively demonstrated both normalcy and fallibility. In other areas, for example in relation to logistic support or religious experience, some may wish to question our assumption of normalcy or of similarity in behaviour between Highland troops and others. This is legitimate, but we would argue that the onus is on those critics to demonstrate that in such areas behaviours were so demonstrably different as to be significant.

There is nothing in this study to support the notion of unique inherent qualities, or exclusive pre-determinants of resilience. We have rejected the notion of the martial race and identified instead what we consider to be the normal unexceptional fallibility of the Highland soldier. We have identified an acceptance of patriotic duty, which, despite some disillusionment, persisted even after the introduction of conscription, but there is no reason to believe that these sentiments were unique to the Highland soldier. Similarly, while we do not claim to have examined Watson's 'coping strategies' in relation to the Highland soldier, it would be surprising if a comparative study were to reveal significant differences between Highland soldiers and others in this respect.

Of the two most important support mechanisms provided by the Army as a whole, military socialisation was common across the Army, and Highland soldiers shared many of its aspects with the rest of the Army, although they had the 'advantage' of the kilt and pipes. In particular, there is little indication that in regard to discipline, the behaviour of Highlanders was significantly better or worse than that of the Army as a whole. There is also no reason to believe that the overall logistical support provided to the Highland soldier was any better or worse than that provided to his colleagues in the Army, although, as we have demonstrated, he did suffer, in that the kilt was not really suitable for modern warfare. Regimental pride and strong regimental identity were common across all regiments of the British Army. There is little justification for

---

23 On religion see in particular Holmes, *Tommy*, pp.503, 522ff, and Watson, *Enduring the Great War*, pp.93-100.

assuming that it was greater in the Highland regiments than others. Similarly, the lower levels of battalion, company and platoon, the organisms in which soldiers fought, provided cohesion in similar ways across the Army as a whole. Crucially, at the lower level of comradeship, which we have identified as one of the principal props of morale, there seems no reason at all to believe that the experience of the Highland soldier was significantly different from his colleagues in the rest of the Army. Nor is there any reason to believe that the relationship between officers, N.C.O.'s and men in the Highland regiments was exceptional. It was another facet of morale in which they shared the common experience of the British soldier. Finally, it does seem unlikely that the Highland soldier's experience of support from religion was in any way unique compared with his British Army colleagues.

The differences we have suggested all relate to 'sense of identity,' that is that the Highland soldier had a stronger sense of identity than his colleagues. While Highland soldiers generally shared with their colleagues a certain commitment to Britain and the Empire, there is no doubt that a fierce sense of Scottish-ness was often central to their sense of identity. This could be considered part of upbringing. This identity was reinforced by the kilt, the pipes, songs and traditions. The kilt and pipes were central to the cadres in which military socialisation was achieved. Both appealed to national identity and the reputation and romantic history of the Highland regiments as a whole, and in this way contributed to the process by which a strong *esprit de corps* was built amongst Highland soldiers. This identity was reinforced at the regimental level by an awareness of regimental history, regimental uniforms, including tartans, and regimental pipe-tunes. The battalion and company were the practical formations in which these elements of identity found expression, and which also reinforced identity through arranging traditional games, dancing and feast days, and above all through the pipes. Indeed, in his moments of relaxation, some elements of the Highland soldier's experience were unique; his Scottish songs, Highland games, the pipes, dancing and his three special celebrations of the year. Whether these activities were simply informal, or arranged by company, battalion or higher formation, a significant amount of recreational activity actually promoted and fostered identity, both as a Scot and as a Highland soldier. On the down side, in 'logistical support,' as we have demonstrated, the Highland soldier did suffer, in that the kilt was not really suitable for modern warfare. Given the other undoubted benefits of the kilt for morale, in terms of pride, self-image, identity and esprit de corps, the key question is whether, in terms of morale, these benefits of the kilt outweighed its impracticality. In the Great War, it is probably true that they did.

Identity then seems to be the key moral advantage possessed by the Highland soldier. It may appear odd, therefore, that 'Identity' does not figure as an element of our model of morale mechanisms. Perhaps this is a flaw in the model. In fact, we find identity operating throughout the model, influencing both inherent characteristics, through upbringing, and support mechanisms, through national allegiance, home and family, military socialisation, the Regiment, the battalion and through recreation. It is, in fact, a powerful indicator of the significance of identity to see it operating in so many ways through so many mechanisms.

However, it is important to see this moral advantage in perspective. To begin with, a strong sense of identity was not unique to the Highland soldier. All regiments of the British Army had a strong sense of identity, be they Guards, Buffs, Royal Welsh Fusiliers or, for that matter, Royal Scots. It is simply argued that the identity of the Highland soldier was particularly strong and therefore perhaps a little stronger than others, although in the case of the Guards this is surely questionable. Secondly, as hopefully demonstrated in this chapter, identity was just one element amongst many affecting morale which generally affected all units of the Army in a similar manner. With respect to most of these elements, in particular the crucial area of comradeship, the principal characteristic of the Highland soldier was his normalcy. He was not unique. If indeed he had an advantage it was found in identity, and in this respect, the advantage lay only in the extent to which his sense of identity was greater, if at all, than his colleagues'. Having said which, in terms of moral advantage, how significant might be that 'little bit extra'?

Courage and morale are not identical, but we may apply Lord Moran's notion of the bank balance[24] equally to morale as well as courage. That 'little bit extra' morale in the balance might provide a little extra impetus in battle or, as the balance declines under the stress of campaigning, might save a soldier from breaking point for that little bit longer. If, indeed, the Highland soldier had that 'little bit extra', this was how it worked.

In most respects though, we should stress the normalcy of the Highland soldier. He was not a martial super-hero. He was, for the most part, an ordinary man, propelled out of his peace-time existence (even that in the Army) into the most trying circumstances, trying to cope and survive as best he might, displaying the range of human behaviours; in turn courageous and weak, joyous and sad, selfless and careless, compassionate and ruthless, but overall exhibiting basic human decency and fallibility. In other words, he was just like you or me.

We will close with two quotes, for reflection. The first is from Norman Macleod, brave soldier, commander of 6th and 7th Camerons, and fervent defender of the kilt.

> These men fought a war to end war, but their real victory was not accomplished, nor will the fight be ended until all people put the good of their fellow-men before ledger balances, comfort and ease.[25]

The second is from Lieutenant C.B. Anderson. Serving with 7th Seaforths, he had been commissioned thanks to the recommendation of his former Company commander in 1/20th Battalion London Regiment, Captain W.M.L. Escombe, under whom he had been known as 'Andy the Company runner'. The relationship had been close. At midnight 13 July 1916, 'Andy' wrote to Escombe, whom he described as Monsieur le Capitaine.

> Things have all been altered & we, my Coy, have a hell of a job. Something to be taken & held by us to the last man, 'fraid I shan't come through – if I do it will be the surprise of my life – anyway thanks awfully much Sir for having been such a pal to me, & Sir don't grieve, there are worse deaths than leading a platoon of Highlanders into action
> We go over in 3 hours
> Goodbye
> All love
> Yours faithfully ever,
> Andy[26]

---

24 Moran, Lord, *The Anatomy of Courage*, (London: Robinson, 2007) (first published 1945).
25 Macleod, *6th Camerons*, p.135.
26 IWM 7668 Escombe, letter from Anderson, 13 July 1916.

Bibliography

Published sources

Anon, *9th Royal Scots (T.F.) B Company on Active Service, from a Private's Diary February-May 1915* (Edinburgh: 9th Royal Scots, 1916)

Anon, *The 11th Battalion Gordon Highlanders*, (Glasgow: Maclure, Macdonald & Co., 1916)

Anon, *The 51st Battalion The Gordon Highlanders 1914-1920* (Mansfield: F. Willman, n.d.)

Anon, *The Royal Highlanders of Canada, allied with the Black Watch (Royal Highlanders)*, (Montreal, London: Hugh Rees Ltd, 1918)

Anon, *Souvenir Booklet 6th Cameron Highlanders*, (London: Spottiswoode & Co. Ltd, 1916)

Anon, *Souvenir Booklet of the Sixth Cameron Highlanders* (Glasgow: The Glasgow Herald', 1916)

Anon [Blampied, H. John] *With a Highland Regiment in Mesopotamia 1916-1917* (London: The Times Press, 1918)

Addison-Smith, Lt Col C.L., *10th Battalion The Seaforth Highlanders in the Great War* (Edinburgh: privately published, 1927)

Aiken, Alex, *Courage Past, A Duty Done*, (Glasgow: privately published, 1971)

Anderson, Brig. R.C.B., *History of the Argyll and Sutherland Highlanders 1st Battalion 1909-1929* (Edinburgh: Constable, 1954)

Allan, Stuart & Carswell, Allan, *The Thin Red Line* (Edinburgh: NMSE Publishing, n.d. [c.2000])

Andrews, Linton, *The Autobiography of a Journalist*, (London: Ernest Benn Ltd., 1964)

Andrews, William Linton, *Haunting Years*, (Uckfield: NMP reprint, n.d.)

Arthur, Max, *Forgotten Voices of the Great War* (London: Ebury Press, 2003)

Bannell, Charles Samuel, *His Offering. Poems by Charles Samuel Bannell, Seaforth Highlanders, Canadian Force (Killed in Action, October 30th, 1917)* (Liverpool: J.A. Thompson, n.d.)

Barber, Gordon, *My Diary in France* (Liverpool: Hay Young & Sons, Liverpool, 1917)

Barthomomew, G.H.F., *George Hugh Freeland Bartholomew, 8th June 1896 – 2nd Oct. 1917* (privately published, n.d.)

Baynes, John, *Morale* (London: Leo Cooper, 1987)

Baynes, John, *Soldiers of Scotland* (New York: Barnes & Noble, 1997)

Beal, George W., *Family of Volunteers*, (Toronto: Robin Brass Studio, Toronto, 2001)

Beattie, Kim, *48th Highlanders of Canada 1891-1928* (Toronto: 48th Highlanders of Canada, 1932),

Bewsher, Maj. F.W., *The History of the Fifty First (Highland) Division 1914-1918*, (Uckfield: NMP reprint, n.d.)

Bird, Derek, *The Spirit of the Troops is Excellent*, (Eastholme, Moray: Birdbrain Books, 2008)

Bird, Will R., *Ghosts have Warm Hands* (Ottawa, Canada: CEF Books, 1968)
Blaser, Bernard, *Kilts across the Jordan* (London: H.F. & G. Witherby, 1926)
Bogle, Kenneth R., *Walter Sutherland, Scottish Rugby Legend 1890-1918*, (Stroud: Tempus, 2005)
Boustead, Col. Sir Hugh, *The Wind of Morning*, (London: Chatto & Windus, 1971)
Brooke, *Poems by Brian Brooke (Korongo)*, (London: John Lane, 1917)
Brown, Malcolm, *Tommy goes to War* (Stroud: Tempus, 2005)
Brown, Malcolm & Seaton, Shirley, *Christmas Truce*, (London: Pan Books, 2001)
Bruce, Lt. Col. Walter, H., Turnbull, Lt. Col. William R. & Chisholm, Lt. Col. James, *Historical Records of the Argyll and Sutherland Highlanders of Canada etc., 1903-1928*, (Hamilton, Ontario: Robert Duncan & Co., 1928)
Buchanan-Smith, Alick, *The Gordon Highlanders Loos and Buzancy* (Aberdeen: University Press, 1981)
Buchanan Smith, George, *George Buchanan Smith 1890-1915* (Glasgow: privately published, 1916)
Burns, Robert, *Once a Cameron Highlander* (Bognor Regis: Woodfield Publishing, 2000)
Burrows, Rob, *Fighter Writer* (Derby: Breedon Books, 2004)
Butler, Ewan, *Mason-Mac, The Life of Lieutenant-General Sir Noel Mason-Macfarlane* (London: Macmillan, 1972) pp.1-14
Campbell, Colin, *Engine of Destruction: The 51st (Highland) Division in the Great War*, (Glendaruel: Argyll Publishing, 2013)
Campbell, Colin & Green, Rosalind, *Can't shoot a man with a cold*, (Glendaruel: Argyll Publishing, 2004)
Campbell, Ivar, Poems by Ivar Campbell, (London: A.L. Humphreys, 1917)
Campbell, Ivar, *Letters of Ivar Campbell written between May 1915 & January 1916*, (privately published, 1917)
Carswell, Allan, 'Scottish Military Dress,' in Spiers, Edward M., Crang, Jeremy A. and Strickland, Mathew J., *A Military History of Scotland* (Edinburgh University Press, 2014), pp.627-647
Carver, Field Marshal Lord, *The National Army Museum Book of the Boer War*, (London: Sidgwick & Jackson, 1999)
Cavendish, Brig Gen A.E.J., *An reisimeid chataich; The 93rd Sutherland Highlanders 1799-1927*, (Frome: Butler & Tanner, 1928)
Chambers, Heather (ed), *Diaries of World War 1 written by William Liddell Chambers June 1914-October 1916*, (Eglinton, Australia, c.2000),
Chartrand, Rene, *The Canadian Corps in World War 1* (Oxford: Osprey Men-at-Arms 439, 2007)
Clayton, Anne, *Chavasse Double VC*, (Barnsley: Pen & Sword, 1997)
Cluness, Alex, ed., *Doing his bit, A Shetland Soldier in the Great War*, (Lerwick: The Shetland Times Ltd, 1999)
Collins, Norman, *Last Man Standing* (Barnsley: Leo Cooper, 2002)
Corns, Cathryn & Hughes-Wilson, John, *Blindfold and Alone* (London: Cassell, 2005)
Corrigan, Gordon, *Mud, Blood and Poppycock*, (London: Cassell, 2003)
Cowan, Paul, *Scottish Military Disasters* (Glasgow: Neil Wilson, 2008)
Craig Barr, Lt Col J., *Home Service* (Paisley: Alexander Gardner, 1920)
Craig-Brown, Brig Gen E, ed., *Historical Records of the Queen's Own Cameron Highlanders*, Vols 3 & 4 (Edinburgh: William Blackwood & Sons, 1931)

Croft, W.D., *Three Years with the 9th (Scottish) Division*, (London: John Murray, 1919)
Darling, Sir William Y., *So it looks to me* (London: Odhams Press Ltd., n.d.)
David, Saul (ed), *Mud & Bodies, The War Diaries and Letters of Captain N.A.C. Weir, 1914-1920*, (London: Frontline Books, 2013)
Davies, Hugh, *The Compassionate War*, (London: Abbotsbury Publications, 1980)
Dinesen, Thomas, V.C., *Merry Hell!*, (Uckfield: NMP reprint, n.d.)
Dingwall Museum Trust, *Portrait of a Soldier, Sgt John Meikle, V.C., M.M., 4th Bn Seaforth Highlanders 1898-1918*, (Dingwall Museum Trust, Local Studies No.4, 1992)
Dunn, Capt J.C. *The War the Infantry Knew 1914-1919* (London: Abacus, 1994)
Ewing, John, *The History of the Ninth (Scottish) Division*, (London: John Murray, 1921)
Ewing, Maj. John, *The Royal Scots 1914-1919* (Edinburgh: Oliver & Boyd, 1925)
Fairrie, Angus, *Queen's Own Highlanders (Seaforths and Camerons) An Illustrated History* (Trustees of the Queen's Own Highlanders Amalgamation Trusts, 1998)
Falls, Cyril, *The Life of a Regiment, Vol.4, The Gordon Highlanders in the First World War* (Aberdeen: The University Press, 1958)
Fennah, Alfred, *Retaliation*, (London: Houghton, n.d.),
Ferguson, Niall, *The Pity of War* (London, Penguin, 1999)
Fetherstonhaugh, R.C., *The 13th Battalion Royal Highlanders of Canada 1914-1919*, (13th Bn Royal Highlanders of Canada, 1923)
Forrester, James & Crawford, Watson, *The War Diary of the 9th Argyll & Sutherland Highlanders, Dumbartonshire Men at the Front* (Glasgow: History Department, Jordanhill College, 1978)
Fowler, Captain Sir John, *Captain Sir John Fowler, Bart, Captain Alan Fowler* (Dingwall: Ross-shire Journal, n.d.),
Fraser, Edith, *Records of the Men of Lochbroom who fell in the European War 1914-1918* (Glasgow: Robert Maclehose & Co., 1922)
Fraser, Dr James Fowler, *Doctor Jimmy*, (Aberdeen: University Press, 1980)
Fraser, James F., 'War Diary, 1915', reprinted from the *Aberdeen University Review*, Vol.46, No.153, Spring, 1975, pp.32-44
Giblin, Hal, *Bravest of Hearts*, (Liverpool: Winordie Publications, 2000)
Gillespie, 2Lt A.D., *Letters from Flanders*, (London: Smith, Elder & Co., 1916)
Gilmour, Andrew, *An Eastern Cadet's Anecdotage*, (Singapore: University Education Press, 1974)
Goldsmith, Anne, ed., *Gentle Warrior, A Life of Hugh Grant, Soldier, Farmer and Kenya Administrator*, (Whitebridge, Inverness-shire: Anne Goldsmith, 2001)
[Gregory, John B.] *France 1916-1917-1918* (Crewekerne: Frank N. Parsons, 1924)
Grierson, Maj. Gen. J.M., *Records of the Scottish Volunteer Force 1859-1908*, (Uckfield: NMP reprint, 2004)
Haldane, Lt Col M.M., *History of the Fourth Battalion The Seaforth Highlanders* (London: H.F. & G. Witherby, 1927)
Hamilton, General Sir Ian, *Listening for the Drums*, (London: Faber & Faber, 1944)
Harrington, Peter, 'The Scottish Soldier in Art,' in Spiers, Edward M., Crang, Jeremy A. and Strickland, Mathew J., *A Military History of Scotland* (Edinburgh University Press, 2014), pp.688-705
Haworth, Christopher, *March to Armistice 1918* (London: William Kimber, 1968)
Hayes, Lt Col Joseph, *The Eighty-Fifth in France and Flanders*, (Halifax, Nova Scotia: Royal Print & Litho Ltd, 1920)

Henderson, Diana M, *Highland Soldier 1820-1920*, (Edinburgh: John Donald, 1989)
Holmes, Richard, *Tommy* (London: HarperCollins, 2004)
Horn, Robert, *Lieut.-Colonel Robert Horn, D.S.O., M.C., 1st Seaforth Highlanders, a Sketch by his Mother*, (privately published, 1933)
Horne, John & Kramer, Alan, *German Atrocities 1914, A History of Denial*, (Newhaven & London: Yale University Press, 2001)
Hunt, Capt M. Stuart, *Nova Scotia's Part in the Great War* (Uckfield, NMP reprint, no date) (first published c.1920)
Hutchison, Graham Seton, *Footslogger*, (London: Hutchinson, 1931),
Hutchison, Lt.-Col. Graham Seton, *Warrior*, (London: Hutchinson, 1931),
Ireland, Lockhart Landels, *Pte John Maclean of the Black Watch and other Stories*, (Kirkcaldy: The Fifeshire Advertiser, 1917)
Jackson, Frederick, 'Captain Noel Godfrey Chavasse, VC and Bar, MC,' *Army Medical Services Magazine*, Vol.24, No.3, 1970
Jones, Simon, *World War I Gas Warfare Tactics and Equipment*, (Oxford: Osprey Elite No.150, 2007)
Juta, H.C., *The History of the Transvaal Scottish*, (Johannesburg: Hortors Ltd, 1933)
Kruger, Rayne, *Goodbye Dolly Gray* (London: Pimlico, 1996) (1st published 1959)
Laband, John, *The Transvaal Rebellion*, (Harlow: Pearson Education Ltd, 2005)
Lauder, Harry, *A Minstrel in France* (London: Andrew Melrose, 1918)
Lehmann, Joseph, *The First Boer War* (London: Jonathan Cape, 1972)
Levyns, J.E.P., *The Disciplines of War*, (New York: Vantage Press, 1984)
Lewis-Stempel, John, *Six Weeks* (London: Orion Books, 2011)
Lindsay, Lt. Col. J.H., *The London Scottish in the Great War* (London: RHQ London Scottish, 1926)
Linklater, Eric, *Fanfare for a Tin Hat* (London: Macmillan, 1970)
Lloyd, Mark, *The London Scottish in the Great War* (Barnsley: Leo Cooper, 2001)
Longley, Michael, *Collected Poems*, (London: Jonathan Cape, 2006)
Lyon, Thomas M., *In Kilt and Khaki*, (Kilmarnock: The Standard Press, 1916)
Lyon, Thomas, *More Adventures in Kilt and Khaki* (Kilmarnock: The Standard Press, 1917)
McDermott, R.K. *Robert Keith McDermott, Captain 3rd Battn Seaforth Highlanders (attached 1st Battn)* (London: Walter McDermott, 1930)
Macdonald, Catriona M.M. and McFarland, E.W. (ed) *Scotland and the Great War*, (East Linton: Tuckwell Press, 1999)
Macdonald, Lyn, *1914* (London: Penguin, 1987)
Macdonald, Lyn, *1914-1918 Voices and Images of the Great War* (London: Penguin, 1991),
Macdonald, Lyn, *1915 The Death of Innocence*, (London, Penguin, 1997)
Macdonald, Martin, *Skye Camanachd, A Century Remembered*, (Portreee: Skye Camanachd, n.d.)
Macdougall, Ian, *Voices from War* (Edinburgh: Mercat Press, 1995)
McEvoy, Bernard & Finlay, Capt A.H., *History of the 72nd Canadian Infantry Battalion, Seaforth Highlanders of Canada*, (Vancouver: Cowan & Brookhouse, 1920)
McFarland, Elaine W., 'Scottish Military Monuments,' in Spiers, Edward M., Crang, Jeremy A. and Strickland, Mathew J., *A Military History of Scotland* (Edinburgh University Press, 2014) pp.748-775

McGilchrist, A.M., *The Liverpool Scottish 1900-1919* (Liverpool: Henry Young & Sons, 1930)

Mackay, John G., *The Romantic Story of the Highland Garb and Tartan* (Stirling: E. Mackay, 1924)

Mackay Scobie, Maj I.H., *Pipes and Pipe Music in a Highland Regiment* (Dingwall: Ross-shire Printing & Publishing Co., c.1934)

Mackenzie, Capt D., *The Sixth Gordons in France and Flanders* (Aberdeen: Rosemount Press, 1921)

Mackenzie, Gilbert M., *Diary and Letters written during the War in France, Belgium and Mesopotamia by the late Captain Gilbert M. Mackenzie, B.A., Cantab., 3rd Seaforth Highlanders*, (privately published, no date)

McKinnell, Bryden, Diary from November 1st, 1914 to June 14th, 1915 (privately published, n.d.)

Mackintosh, E.A., *A Highland Regiment*, (London: John Lane, 1918),

Maclean, Rev. Alexander Miller, *With the Gordons at Ypres* (Paisley: Alexander Gardner,1916)

Maclean, John, *On Active Service with the Argyll and Sutherland Highlanders in Belgium and France*, (Edinburgh: The Scottish Chronicle Press,, Vol 1, n.d. and Vol.2, 1926)

Macleod, John, Dunning, *Macedonian Measures*, (Cambridge University Press, 1919)

Macleod, John Dunning, *Poems* (privately published, 1958)

Macleod, Lt Col Norman, *War History of the 6th (Service) Battalion, Queen's Own Cameron Highlanders* (Edinburgh: Wm Blackwood & Sons, 1934)

McMillan, David, *Trench Tea and Sandbags* (R.McAdam, 1996)

Malcolm, Charles A., *The Piper in Peace and War*, (London: Hardwicke Press, 1993) (first published 1927)

Malcolm, Lt. Col. G.I., of Poltalloch, *Argyllshire Highlanders 1860-1960*, (Glasgow: Halberd Press, 1960)

Malcolm, Lt Col G.I., of Poltalloch, *The History of the Argyll and Sutherland Highlanders (Princess Louise's) 1794-1949* (Edinburgh: Mclagan & Cumming, 1949)

May, H.E., 'In a Highland Regiment,' in Lewis, Jon E. (ed), *True World War 1 Stories* (London: Robinson, 1999), pp.199-206

Maxwell-Scott, Susan, *Pa's Wartime Letters and This & That*, (privately published, 2010)

Ministry of Defence, *Army Doctrine Publications, Operations* (London: Ministry of Defence, 2010

Mitchell, William Fraser, *Off Parade and other Verses*, (Dundee: A.B. Duncan, 1919)

Monaghan, Lt. Hugh B., *The Big Bombers of World War 1*, (Burlington, Ontario: Ray Gentle Communications Ltd., n.d. c.1976), p.34

Montgomery, John, *Toll for the Brave*, (London: Max Parrish, 1963)

Moore-Bick, Christopher, *Playing the Game* (Solihull, Helion, 2011)

Moran, Lord, *The Anatomy of Courage*, (London: Robinson, 2007)

Morrison, A.D. (text), *7th Battalion The Great War 1914-1919* (Alva, Scotland, Robert Cunningham, n.d.)

Murray, David, *Music of the Scottish Regiments* (Edinburgh: Mercat Press, 2001)

Murray, Lt.-Col. D.J.S., 'The Great Highland Bagpipe and Scottish Military Music' in Baynes, John, *Soldiers of Scotland*, (New York: Barnes & Noble, 1997) pp.96-106

Newark, Tim, *Highlander, The History of the Legendary Highland Soldier* (London: Constable & Robinson, 2009),

Nicholls, Jonathan, *Cheerful Sacrifice* (Barnsley: Pen & Sword, 2003)
Nicholson, Col. W.M., *Behind the Lines* (London: Jonathan Cape, 1939)
Ogilvie, D.D., *The Fife and Forfar Yeomanry and 14th (F. and F. Yeo) Battn, R.H. 1914-1919* (London: John Murray, 1921),
O'Kiely, Elizabeth, *Gentleman Air Ace, The Duncan Bell-Irving Story*, (BC Canada: Harbour Publishing, 1992)
One of the Jocks [Capt Alex Scott], *Odd Shots*, (London: Hodder & Stoughton, 1916)
Orpen, Neil, *The Cape Town Highlanders 1885-1970* (Cape Town: The Cape Town Highlanders History Committee, 1970)
Pakenham, Thomas, *The Boer War*, (London: Weidenfeld & Nicolson, 1979)
Peel, Capt R.T & Macdonald, Capt. A.H., *The Great War 1914-1918 6th Seaforth Highlanders Campaign Reminiscences*, (Elgin: W.R. Walker & Co., 1923)
Pemberton, W. Baring, *Battles of the Boer War* (London: Pan Books, 1969)
Robertson, Donald, *Some Poems by the Kildary Bard*, (Balnagown, Kildary, 1918)
Rorie, Col David, *A Medico's Luck in the War* (Uckfield, NMP reprint, n.d.)
Rorke, F, *Roll of Officers 1st Dumbartonshire Volunteer Rifle Corps* (1937)
Ross, D.M., *A Scottish Minister and Soldier*, (London: Hodder & Stoughton, 1917)
Royal Scots RHQ, *9th Battalion (Highlanders) the Royal Scots (The Royal Regiment)* (Edinburgh: RHQ Royal Scots, 1925)
Royle, Trevor, *Fighting Mac* (Edinburgh: Mainstream,1982)
Royle, Trevor, *The Flowers of the Forest: Scotland and the First World War*, (Edinburgh: Birlinn, 2006)
Rule, Alexander, *Students Under Arms*, (Aberdeen: The University Press, 1934)
Sandilands, Col. J.W. & Macleod, Lt Col Norman, *The History of the 7th Battalion Queen's Own Cameron Highlanders*, (Stirling: Aeneas Mackay, 1922)
Schofield, Victoria, *The Highland Furies*, (London: Quercus, 2012)
Seton, Sir Bruce & Grant, John, *The Pipes of War*, (Glasgow: Robert Maclehose & Co., 1920)
Sheffield, Gary, *Command and Morale* (Barnsley, Praetorian Press, 2014)
Simpson, Cecil Barclay, *Cecil Barclay Simpson, A Memorial by Two Friends*, (Edinburgh: Turnbull & Spears, 1918)
Sommers, Cecil [Down, Norman Cecil Sommers] *Temporary Crusaders* (London: John Lane, London, 1919)
Sommers, Cecil [Down, Norman Cecil Sommers] *Temporary Heroes* (London: John Lane, 1917)
Sotheby, Lt.-Col. Herbert G., *The 10th Battalion Argyll and Sutherland Highlanders 1914-1919* (London: privately published, 1931)
Sotheby, Lionel, *Lionel Sotheby's Great War* (Athens, Ohio: Ohio University Press, 1997)
Spiers, Edward, 'The Scottish Soldier at War,' in Cecil, Hugh and Liddle, Peter H., *Facing Armageddon, The First World War Experience*, (Barnsley: Pen & Sword Select, 2003), pp.314-335.
Spiers, Edward M., *The Scottish Soldier and Empire, 1854-1902* (Edinburgh University Press, 2006)
Spiers, Edward M, 'Scots and the Wars of Empire,' in Spiers, Edward M., Crang, Jeremy A. and Strickland, Mathew J., *A Military History of Scotland* (Edinburgh University Press, 2014)
Springer, Shaun & Humphreys, Stuart, *Private Beatson's War*, (Barnsley: Pen & Sword, 2009)

Stewart-Smith, Dudley Cautley, *The Diaries of Lieutenant Dudley Cautley Stewart-Smith, 1918* (Taunton: Blue Guides Ltd., 2009)
Steel, Nigel & Hart, Peter, *Passchendaele* (London: Cassell, 2001),
Stewart, Lt Col J., & Buchan, John, *The Fifteenth (Scottish) Division 1914-1919*, (Edinburgh: William Blackwood & Sons, 1926)
Stothers, Steven, *Somewhere in France: The Letters of John Cannon Stothers 1916-1919* (Publisher not known, 2005)
Sutherland, Capt. D., *War Diary of the Fifth Seaforth Highlanders* (London: John Lane, 1920)
Sym, Col. John, ed, *Seaforth Highlanders* (Aldershot: Gale & Polden, 1962)
Thermaenius, Pehr, *The Christmas Match* (London: Uniform Press, 2014)
Topp, Lt Col C. Bereseford, *The 42nd Battalion, C.E.F., Royal Highlanders of Canada, in the Great War*, (Montreal: Gazette Printing, 1931)
Ugolini, Wendy, 'Scottish Commonwealth Regiments,' in Spiers, Edward M., Crang, Jeremy A. and Strickland, Mathew J., *A Military History of Scotland* (Edinburgh University Press, 2014), pp.485-505
Urquhart, Lt Col H.M., *The History of the 16th Battalion (The Canadian Scottish) Canadian Expeditionary Force in the Great War, 1914-1919* (Toronto: Macmillan, 1932)
Van Emden, Richard & Humphries, Steve, *Veterans* (Barnsley: Pen & Sword, 2005)
Wade, Maj. A.G., *Counterspy* (London: Stanley Paul & Co., 1938)
Walker, Tom, *Tom Walker Remembers* (privately published, n.d., c.1981),
Warwick, George W., *We Band of Brothers* (Cape Town: Howard Timmins, 1962)
Watson, Alexander, *Enduring the Great War* (Cambridge University Press, 2008)
Watt, Lauchlan Maclean, *In France and Flanders with the Fighting Men*, (London: Hodder & Stoughton, 1917)
Watt, Patrick, *Steel and Tartan* (Stroud: The History Press, 2012)
Wauchope, Maj Gen A,G,. *A History of the Black Watch (Royal Highlanders) in the Great War, 1914-1918* (London: Medici Society, 3 vols, 1925-1926)
Webster, J.A.C., *Mesopotamia 1916-1917, Letters from John Alexander Croom Webster, Second Lieutenant Seaforth Highlanders* (privately published, no date)
Weintraub, Stanley, *Silent Night*, (London: Simon & Schuster, 2001)
Weir, Alec, *Come on Highlanders!* (Stroud: Sutton Publishing, 2005)
West, Gary J, 'Scottish Military Music', in Spiers, Edward M., Crang, Jeremy A. and Strickland, Mathew J., *A Military History of Scotland* (Edinburgh University Press, 2014), pp.649-668
Westlake, Ray, *British Territorial Units 1914-1918*, (Oxford, Osprey Men-at-Arms 245, 1991)
Wheatley, Lawrence, ed., *Echoes from Hell Letters from the Western Front*, (Hitchin: The Dodman Press, 1982)
Wilson, Col Maurice J.H., *Biographical List of Officers (other than Regular, Militia and Territorial) The Queen's Own Highlanders* (published in Ten Supplements in each issue of the '79th News' from September, 1957, to September, 1960, inclusive)
Wood, Stephen, *The Scottish Soldier* (Manchester, Archive Publications Ltd, 1987)
Young, Derek, *Forgotten Scottish Voices from the Great War*, (Stroud: Tempus, 2005)
Zuehlke, Mark, *Brave Battalion* (Mississauga, Ontario: Wiley, 2008)

Archival sources

Argyll and Sutherland Highlanders Museum, Stirling [ASHM]
War Diary 1/6th Argylls,
N-E8.4	1/8th Bn Argyll & Sutherland Highlanders, Part 2 Orders, 1914-1916
N-E8.5	Anon, typescript account, 'At Beaumont-Hamel with the 8th Argylls, Nov. 13th, 1916
N-E2	Aiken, Sgt J, notes dated 18 December, 1914
N-E5	Bone, Robert, Alexandria, papers
N-E11	Bowie, LCpl J.M. diary
N-E5	Brown, Ronal, letters home,
N-E8	Campbell, George, typescript memoir, written 1935
N-E6	Clement, Lt. A.M., letters
N-E2	Collier, Frank, journal
N-E1	Dalziel, LCpl, diary
N-E7	Doig, Mrs, letter of condolence
N-E12	Fisher, Colin, typescript, 'The 12th Battalion Princess Louise's Own Argyll and Sutherland Highlanders,' written 1971, based partly on the memories of his grandfather, William Tennant
N-E7	Forbes, Alexander Bruce, letter of condolence
N-E10	Gairdner, Charles Dalrymple, letters
N-E6	Gardiner, Capt. Alister, postcard home, 2 January, 1918
N-E1	Herbert, Pte Tom, letters
N-E8	Humble, Lt. Alex. D., typescript diary
N-E2	Hyslop, Lt. Col. H.G., typescript war diary
N-E8	Jordan, Patrick, miscellaneous documents
N-E8	Kelly, Archie, letters
N-E2	Macfarlane, Cpl F.A., 'A brief sketch of my experience in the British Army from 11/5/09 to 21/1/21.' apparently written 12 March, 1921
N-E2	McGregor-Craig, Private S., typescript copy of manuscript 'History of 2nd Argyll & Sutherland Highlanders in World War' [from 9 August, 1914 to 15 October, 1915].
N-E8	McGuinness, Ernest, notebook
N-E11	MacIntyre, Sgt Dugald, undated letter (1918) extracted from Black, Nancy, *From a Hollow on the Hill* (1999)
N-E8	Maclachlan, Capt .T.K., letters
N-E12	Mclaren, Cpl John Malcolm, letters
N-E11	Macleod, George, letters
N-E2	MacMillan, Gordon H.A., notes written by him, 31 January, 1976
N-E6	MacPhie, Lt J., diary
N-E5	Main, Capt D.M., letters
N-E8	Munro, Hugh, letters
N-E6	O'Connor, Pte Daniel, letters
NE-10	Petrie, Sgt George Guthrie, manuscript memoir
N-E1	Pringle, 2Lt William B., letters

N-E8	Ritchie, letter from Pte James Campbell to his parents
N-E1	Robertson, Lt C.B., diary, letters, memoir
N-E2	Smith, Lt G.E., letter of condolence
N-E2	Todd, Capt H.B., manuscript memoirs

The Black Watch Museum, Perth [BWA]

BWA	Part 2 Orders, 1st Battalion The Black Watch, 1918
BWA	Nominal Rolls of A, B, C and D Companies, 10th Black Watch, c. June, 1916
BWA	Roll Book of No.13 Platoon, D Company, 1/4th Black Watch, last entry 21 November, 1914
BWA	Roll Book of 16 Platoon, D Company, 9th Black Watch
BWA	Various documents relating to concert parties of the Black Watch
BWA	Badenoch R.E., typescript memoir, 'My Recollections of the First World War 1914-1918', written 1978
BWA	Brown, George Murray, 'George Murray Brown His Story 1896-1980', privately produced, 2009
BWA	Cameron, William, manuscript memoir, 'Army Life & Trials of William G. Cameron'
BWA	Couston, William, letters
BWA	Cumming, Lt A.B., letters
BWA	Drummond, typescript memoir, 'A journey to India'
BWA	Dundas, Capt R.H., typed diary
BWA	Duke, A.W., letters
BWA	Forman, Charles, manuscript memoir, 'My Life', 1965
BWA	Gauldie, Lt K., letters
BWA	Gordon, Brig. Gen. C.W.E., notebooks containing letters from France, Vols 1-3
BWA	Guthrie, A.C., letters to wife
BWA	Hay, Albert A, manuscript memoir, 'Soldiering', written, 1935
BWA	Hitchman, Sgt Peter, diary
BWA	Junks, Herbert, 'The Diary of a Soldier in the Great War', typescript
BWA	Quekett, Hugh Scott, typescript memoir, 'Jottings of an ordinary man. From childhood to the end of the Great War 1914-1918'
BWA	Laing, Pte John, diary
BWA	Lloyd, Lt Col T.O., typescript 'Address by Lt.-Col. T.O. Lloyd commanding 9th Bn The Black Watch on 2-10-15'
BWA	Logie, Col. Marc James, papers
BWA	Macdonald, Coll, letters
BWA	MacGregor, Sgt Gordon, letters
BWA	McKay, Janet Haggard, typescript, 'Canadian Loyalty to Scottish Tradition and the British Empire', passed to Museum, 1965
BWA	Marshall, Pte James McGregor, manuscript reminiscences, written 1937
BWA	Muir, Cpl J., diary
BWA	Paul, Phil, letters

BWA	Sempill, Lord, papers
BWA	Stewart, Lt Col J., papers
BWA	Stratton, Sandy R., letters
BWA	Thomson, Alex, narrative
BWA	Young, Captain Thomas, field message book

Gordon Highlanders Museum, Aberdeen [GHM]

PB1892.3.30	*15th (Scottish) Division, Narrative of Operations from 15.7.18 to 7.8.18*, Appendices II & III
PB1699	Anon, 'As We Go Up the Line to Death, The Story of the University of Aberdeen Company of the 4th Battalion of the Gordon Highlanders in the Great War of 1914 1918'
PB2644	Anderson, James, letters
PB1506	Beaton, Capt D.B., 'A Concise History of the 50th Regiment (Gordon Highlanders of Canada) ', 1 page extract from *The Falcon* magazine, date not stated (received 1995)
Uncatalogued	Beaton, Norman, manuscript memoir
PB2370	*Bedfordshire Times and Independent*, 9th April, 1915
PB3112	Blinco, Sgt H.A., manuscript memoir, 'Rough Diary of a Voyage with D Coy 1st F.S. Garr. Battalion Gordon Highlanders to the Far East'
PB18	Boustead, Hugh, transcript letters
PB19	Blunt, Henry Staveley, papers
PB24	Brown, Brig Gen P.W., papers
PB1889	Brown, Capt W.N., letters, and typoscript memoir, 'The 20th Brigade on the River Piave, October, 1918',
PB1093	Brown, Capt. W.N., Photo album and scrap book, Programme of Events for the gathering of 24 September, 1918
PB29.2	Bruce, Maj Robert, diary,
PB2093	Crauford, Sir George Standish, letters
PB 580	D.C.B., 'The attack June 1918 at La Bassee Canal as remembered by Charles Crau'
PB1937	Dawson, Robert, letters
PB2788/1	Emslie, Henry, diary
PB1726	Fettes, Pte Charles, diary
PB97	Fraser, 2Lt. A.A., 'Manuscript Account of the 1st Bn the Gordon Highlanders in the Le Cateau area August 1914'
PB91	Flockhart, Sgt George, letters
PB102	Geddes, Godfrey Power, diary
PB2990	Gordon, Maitland Lockhart, miscellaneous documents
PB2790	Graham, Murdo, poem, 'Gordon Highlanders, 1914, aged 18'
PB1071	Grant, Arthur, diary
PB3253	Gray, John, manuscript memoir, written, 1920
PB1498	Hamilton, Ian B.M., POW diary 1914-1918
PB 1639	Kemp, Capt William, typescript memoir, 'The Great War 1914-1918 My Experiences'

PB2549	Leathem, Dr W.H., Chaplain to 1st Gordons, transcript of diary
PB564	Leslie, Jean, autograph book
PB1046	Lewis: Men from the Isle of Lewis, note by Charles Reid, 2009
PB149	Macbean, Lt D.G.F., letters
PB2025	McCurragh, Pte T., postcard published by the Bon Accord Press in Aberdeen, containing a poem by John Mitchell, entitled 'The Gay Gordons, posted 5 November, 1914
PB1892.3.18	McDonald, Lt.-Col. Sam, unpublished typescript, 'Uncle Harper's Duds'
PB161	Macgregor, Charles Lewis, letters
PB583	McKinnon, Capt R.L., manuscript memoir, 'Two years with the 4th Gordons in France'
PB2815	McWilliam, Pte John, letters
PB179	Marr, Joseph, record of service and miscellaneous documents
PB3279	Matthews, James, diary
PB2554/2	Mitchell, John, *Jock McGraw, The Tale of a Gay Gordon*, Wm Smith & Sons, Aberdeen, 1916
PB2586	Morrison, Col. William, biographical notes, and anonymous manuscript, 'A Dumfriesshire Soldier Lieutenant Colonel W.J. Morrison 1881-1932'
PB123	Mulligan, Pte John, diary
PB3712	Murison, William John, typescript recollections, written c.1985
PB1865	Neish, Maj. W, typescript, 'Benevolent Funds &c,' Aberdeen, 23 November, 1923
PB375	Pailthorpe, Maj D.W. ('Sassenach') typescript memoir, 'With the Highlanders'
PB493	Pearson, Maj. N.G., 'The 10th and 8/10th Battalions of the Gordon Highlanders August 1914 – June 1918,' written 1938
PB3309	Pelham Burn, Henry, biographical notes and letters
PB207	Pirie, Alexander, miscellaneous documents, and letters
PB1706/2	Robertson, H, diary
PB2366	Shadwell, Bernard, typescript poem, 'The Ladies fra' Hell'
PB3758	Shirreffs, James Dunn, diary
PB227	Sergeant, James, miscellaneous documents
PB234	Smith, Maj. G.A., diaries
PB1428	Spence, C.S.M. Robert, Account Book and Pocket Ledger
PB242	Stansfield, Lt.-Col. John Raymond Evelyn, extract from 'British Roll of Honour'
PB2021	Stewart, Peter, letters
PB2984	Strachan, Albert, diary
PB507	Wallace, Col. H.R., Diary 53rd Bn Gordon Highlanders
PB2183	Watson, Richard Jackson, typescript memoir, probably written 1943
PB 2459	Williams, Cpl J., 'Diary of my voyage from Plymouth 20/01/1917 to Bombay, India, 14/3/1917'
PB1253	Wood, Charles Hutchieson, autograph album.
PB1755	Young, Andrew, 'Memoirs of Captivity', printed in *Largs & Millport Weekly News*, June-August, 1929

PB2416/12   Young, Pte John, unattributed poem, 'The Charge of the Gordons'
PB1892.3.1   Youngson, Capt R.W., memoir, '1914-1919'

The Highlanders Museum, Fort George [THM]

Cameron Highlanders
                 'Letters from Cameron Highlanders Prisoners of war 1916-1919'
C90-122   Guidance for knitting hosetops for Q.O.C.H., n.d. [probably 1915]
C00-164   Letter from H.M. Office of Works to Mr J. Coutts, 22 May, 1917
C02-46   Notes, 'Cameron Highlanders March into Sherborne St John,' compiled by the Sherborne St John History Society, 2002
C80-13   Postcards from Bandsman Rossor and Pte Elder to Peking, 26 March, 1915
C89-44   Anderson, Brig. A., typescript memoir, 'A Well Trodden Path'
C91-46   Brownlie, John, letter
C85-9   Calder, Pte J., letters
C80-15   Chase, Pte Edwin Henry, letters & extract from Croydon newspaper, 30 March, 1915
C99-55   Coupar, W.A., typescript memoir, 'Memories of the Great War 1914-1919,' recording in 1999 info received in discussion with his father, William Waddell Coupar, who died in 1969
D242   Craig-Brown, Brig Gen E., papers, 'The Highland Soldier, as he is, & as he might be'
C81-7   Douglas, Archibald J A, typescript memoir, 'The Story of my Life'
C96-51   Douglas Hamilton, R.L., letter to Cpl W. Prime, 12 December, 1918
C91-62   Farmer, Donald D, typescript memoir, 'The Autobiography of Donald Dickson Farmer, VC', written after 1945
C90-62   Gibb, Capt E.J.C., typescript memoir, 'The German attack at Arras, March, 1918'
C02-58   Grant, Maj Gen I.C., letters
C502   Gunn, 'The Fine History of the Fighting Gunns', *Daily Sketch*, Mon., 11 Oct 1915
C102   Gunn, Lt Col. G., letters
C79-110   Hogg, Sgt J., untitled manuscript poem
C87-44   Hunter, Peter, letters
C02-40   Johnston, CSM Thomas, background notes
C96 52   Laidlaw, Petra, 'Grandpa's War, The War Correspondence of Thomas Douglas Laidlaw', written c.1996
C02-111   Leszczuk, J.A., Notes on various Cameron Highlanders
C85-91   Macadam, John. letter to father from battlefield of Festubert, May, 1915
C89-17   McFarlane, Daniel, typescript memoir, written 1969 1971
C93-123   McLeod, Pte Duncan, letter
C99-87   Macpherson, H., diary
C94-8   Mackay, Donald, ed, typescript 'Tell Them of Us; Ian and William Mackay, 4th Bn QOCH, letters from the trenches 1914-1918',

C81-203	Mackay, Ian, letters
C90-120	Mackay, Ian, letters
C91-7	Mackay, Maj. Ian, papers
C91-119	Macleod, Alexander/2Lt A.C. Macleod, documents
C10-25	Matheson, John, letters
C572	Panton, Howard, letters
C97-25	Reid, Pte Harold Wilson, letter to mother
C78-87a	Ross family, notes on service details, donated by Miss U. Ross
C97-22	Russell, S.C., of Aden, typescript memoir
C82-72	Sorel-Cameron, Maj. G.C.M., memoir, 'My Personal Experiences in the German War 1914-1915'
C94-99	Stewart-Murray, Capt Lord James, letters
C03-87	Tudhope, Pte J., letter about battle of Loos written from hospital [1915]
C93-35	Welsh, D, Typescript, 'Memoirs of an S.B'
C01-148	Wood, Pte David, letters

Seaforth Highlanders

	Laurie, John Emilius, diary
S81-181	4th Batt. Seaforth Highlanders, Clothing etc, worn by the Soldiers
S80-12	4th (Reserve) Bn Seaforth Highlanders, A Coy, No.4 Platoon Roll, 30th July, 1918
S81-36	7th Seaforths, B Coy, photograph
S02-138	Alexander, Pte Thomas, typescript diary
2013-072(S)	Braes, Alexander, typescript memoir, 'My Experiences during the Great War'
S98-11	Brooke, Frank C., typescript memoir, 'A Yorkshire Kiltie', written 1973
S796(R)	Cartmell, John, typescript memoir, 'Some memories of my service with the 'Seaforth Highlanders' during the Great War'
S81-2	Cooper, Leslie G., typescript memoir, 'Before I came of age'
S89-26	Crask, Lt William Gordon, diary and letters
S02-23	Dixon, 2Lt H.E.O., letters
S92-15	Frame, LCpl E., memorial song to him
S87-125	Heriz-Smith, Mrs, letters received
S87-141	Heriz-Smith, Mrs, photocopy extract from 'Noon Star', the family journal of Mrs Heriz-Smith
S05-87	Hope, A.H.C., typescript of diary,
S86-182	Innes, Cpl Arthur, memorial poem to him
S97-4	McDonald, Sgt Thomas, 'First World War Diary'
S91-27	McIntosh, Pte John, background notes
S81-180	Murray, Sgt George, letters
S89-122	Paterson, William, transcript of manuscript memoir, 'Life in the Army, Experiences at Home and Abroad', November, 1917
S07-42	Rowell, Miss, transcripts of letters sent to her from Dmr MacKenzie and Pte Thomson
S95-125	Sharp, Pte William, background notes

S84-117	Stewart, Pte J., diary, 30 November
S96-36	Tweddle, Archibald Thomas, manuscript 'Extracts from the letters of a Seaforth Highlander'; also manuscript account, 'The Son of the Father', written by his widow, Dorothy Tweddle, 1977
S84-65	Vickery, Cpl James, letters
S89-81	White, Pte Andrew, letters
S98-113	Wilson, Pte John, notebook
S01-25	Wood, Sgt Sidney V, DCM, letter
2013-072(S)	Braes, Alexander, typescript memoir, 'My Experiences during the Great War'

Imperial War Museum, London [IWM]

Books
Brooke, Frank C., typescript memoir, 'Wait for it'
Chavasse, Capt Noel, various papers
Cooper, John, 'Domi Militaeque', unpublished book written 1926
Haldane, M.M., 'A History of the 4th Battalion The Seaforth Highlanders 1914 to 1918,' drafts and typescripts
Parke, Capt C.G.A., typescript memoir, 'Memories of an 'Old Contemptible.'
Reid, Col. A.K., 'Shoulder to Shoulder, The Glasgow Highlanders 9th Bn Highland Light Infantry 1914-1918', unpublished typescript, 1988, edited by Alex Aiken
Stitt, Capt J.H., typescript 'History of the Sixth Gordons,' written 1933

Miscellaneous
Misc 234	Item 3338 Western Front Memories: 80 Years On Transcriptions, interview with Sgt Hal Kerridge and Robert Burns, 1998
15017 Misc	Wilson, G.L., *Lieutenant-Colonel Gavin Laurie Wilson, D.S.O., M.C., 11th Battalion Argyll and Sutherland Highlanders and later 1/8th Battalion Argyll and Sutherland Highlanders*, (privately printed, no date)

Private Papers (PP)
12392	Alexander, Thomas, diary, 10 June, 1916
114	Allen, Lt Col H.H., letters
3808	Anderson, Maj. A., manuscript memoir
2854	Bates, Maj J.V., letters
2221	Blount-Dinwiddie, extract from Ruvigny's *Roll of Honour*
576	Bowser, Lt H.F., papers including typescript memoir, written 1969
2528	Bradbury, S, typescript memoir written 1923
10819	Brittan, Stanley Victor,
13262	Bryden, R.E.C.
13263	Bryden, W.N.
12678	Burns, Robert, transcript of interview, 1998
8503	Byrom, Capt J.A., typescript memoir, 'Somewhere East of Suez'

15460	Chandler, Capt F.G., letters
1697	Chater, A.D.
4370	Christison, Sir Philip, typescript memoir, 'Life and Times of General Sir Philip Christison, Bt'
3449	Cordner, Charles, typescript memoir
14269	Couper, Capt Charles Miller, letters
862	Craig-Brown, Ernest, letters, diary, Field Message Books, and account of the action at Nonne-Boschen, written November, 1915
10909	Cunningham, Brig, J.C., typescript memoir,
12157	Dale, Lt J.L., letter to Aunt Edie, 31 May, 1917
6926	Dennis, R.V., typescript memoir,
4586	Douglas, J.A., manuscript memoir, 'Khaki Apron', 1578pp
20852	Drury, J.W., manuscript memoir, 'Experiences of the European Great War Aug 1 1914 – 1918 Nov 11th Armistice Day', begun 1919
5912	Elliott, J., manuscript recollections, written 1930s
7668	Escombe, Capt W.M.L., letters
12643	Ferrie, Capt. W.S.
15345	Fleming, J.G.G., typescript memoir, 'World War 1 and Other Army Memories,' written post 1945, 201pp
3563	Foulis, Capt J.B., letters
2483	Franklin, H.L., letter
2294	Fraser, J., letter to Gwen Howell, 12 September, 1916
13042	Frier, G.D., letters
612	Gameson, L., typescript memoirs
12205	Goodban, Pte M.S., diary
15990	Gunn, J.A., letters
7593	Harper, Cecil Gordon, transcription of *A Subaltern's Memoir of the 10th Battalion Gordon Highlanders, from July 1914 to July 1915*, edited by Beryl & Stuart Blythe, January 1998
16841	Harrison, D.C., letters
6873	Hendry, W.N., manuscript memoir, 'My Experience with the London Scottish 1914-1918', unpaginated
9885	Horsburgh, W, diary
4474	Johnston, Lt Col R.W.F., typescript memoir, 'Experiences in the Great War of 1914-1918,' written 1983
13593	Jolly, W., letter to mother
12678	Kerridge, Hal, Transcription of interview, 1998
15347	King, Capt H, typescript recollections
1713	Laurie, Maj Gen Sir John, typescript account of action of 1st July, 1916
8192	Lawson, R.K., letters
11637	Leppan, T.C., photocopy of 3 pages from *The Barkly East Reporter*, 20 and 27 September, 1997, with transcript of his diary
11125	Leys, C.G., memoir
11126	Liddell, Capt J.A., VC, diary
6993	Littlewood, M, diary & memoir

7408	Lorimer, Capt. J.B., typescript transcription of letters and memoir of his life by A.R.S.
6702	Low, Major C.J., papers
14340	McArthur, H, diary
15085	McDonald, Lce-Sgt George, diary
17133	McDougall, Duncan, letters
524	Macfarlane Reid, Sir Ranald, memoir 'Fly Past', written 1972
8592	Macgregor, Lt A.E., letters
21092	McGregor, Peter, letters
13511	Macgregor, Lt. R., letters
12688	MacKay, Maj. G.S., letters
11144	MacKay, Lt R.L., diary,
233	McKechnie, Maj. E.A., memoir, 'Reminiscences of the Great War 1914-1918'
926	Mackenzie, J.B., letters
16387	McLeod, Pipe Major Daniel Alexander, transcript diaries
3460	Macmillan, Wg Cdr N., diary, letters
3696	Macnaghten, Capt. A.C.R.S., Capt., letters
3008	McPake, R., diary
14335	Marr, J.R., word processed memoir
12311	Mason-Macfarlane, Lt Gen Noel, typescript memoir by Col David Mason-Macfarlane
7200	Maxwell-Scott, H.F., Maxwell-Scott, Susan, *Pa's Wartime Letters and This & That*, (privately published, 2010), Introduction
6656	Milligan, 2Lt A., letters to mother,
681	Mitchison, Naomi, letters
6933	Moir, K.P., letters
3249	Montgomerie, Maj. E.W., letters
2902	Munro, Lt. H.A., letters
15118	Murray, James Mossman, letters
21511	Nicol, Rev. D.B., letters
1375	Nimmo, P., letters
132	Paterson, W., typescript transcript memoir, 'Life in the Army, Experiences at home and abroad'
11255	Pennie, W., manuscript memoir, 'An account of my sojourn in France & Germany during the Great War'
11310	Prichard, Miss N., letters
16335	Racine, J., transcribed memoir, written 1920's
10533	Reid, Maj Gen D.W., manuscript memoir
2940	Ritchie, T.K., letters
11334	Robertson, William S, typescript memoir, 'Reminiscences of an Old Soldier', written 1983
5015	Ross, C., letter to MOD 12 May, 1981
1953	Ross, J.A., letter from Lt J.M. Reid to Mrs Ross (mother),
11739	Sangster, W.J.C., Memorial volume compiled by parents

1659	Scammell, F.H., letters
5821	Semple. M., letters
6444	Shewan, Capt. A.D.
14321	Small, P.M., letters
10529	Stanford, Lt.-Col. J.K., typescript memoir, 'Essays of a Non-Soldier', written c.1968.
17561	Steele, Thomas, V.C., poem by Geo. A Beattie, 'Sergeant Steele V.C.'
5525	Steven, Lieut S.H., MC, typescript extract from Rollo Steven's history of the Steven family
11923	Sutherland, J., letter to father
13432	Symington, Laurence, diary
4755	Taylor, H.S., typescript memoir
12968	Thomson, 2Lt J.S., letters
511	Thorburn, Lt M.M., letters home
18455	Turnbull, Dudley Ralph, letters
13230	Walker, A.R., typescript memoir, written 1978
19680	White, Mrs D.A, letters
15175	White, Capt. R., retrospective 'General Remarks on war'
156	Williamson, 2Lt A.J.N., extract from *The Bond of Sacrifice*, Vol.1, p.446
12007	Wilson, Capt. J.K., typescript memoir
430	Wimberley, Maj Gen D.N., typescript memoir, and unpublished paper, 'The Kilt & Modern War,' written 1979
3834	Wrench, A.E., diary
7508	Wyllie, Capt. A.T., diary
4576	Yarnall, G.S., diary

Recordings (Rec)

5251	Anderson, Ronald Charles Beckett, IWM interview, 1981
24887	Ashburner, Robert, interview, 1975
375	Bain, Andrew Ramsay, IWM interview, 1974
10117	Bartholomew, William George, IWM interview, 1987
22743	Burns, Robert, interview 1996
10038	Cadbury, Rachel, IWM interview, 1987
9	Clappen, Donald W., IWM interview, 1973
9833	Coates, Henry Bloomfield, interview, 1985
12043	Collins, Norman, IWM interview, 1991
4440	Croft, Oswald, IWM interview, 1979
374	Ditcham, Charles Harry, IWM interview, 1974
11047	Dixon, James, A.S.C., interview, 1989
4081	Douglas, Percy, BBC interview, 1963
43	Dunton, Arthur Naylor, IWM interview, 1973
24879	Fidler, John P., interview, 1975
16428	Gaffron, Horace, interview, 1995
15596	Gyton, S.G., interview, 1982
16455	Hay, William, interview 1984

10786	Hood, David L.S., IWM interview, 1989
13586	Johnston, R.W.F., interview with grandson James, 1975
10391	Jordan, Stewart, IWM interview, 1988
18836	Kerridge, Hal, IWM interview, 1999
10263	Knighton, Eric Leslie, interview, 1988
860	Mabbott, Henry, interview, 1976
10414	McGregor, James Wallace, IWM interview, 1988
24552	McLeavy, J.C., interview 1988
4173	Macmillan, Norman, BBC interview, 1963
9756	Manton, Charles Horace, IWM interview, 1987
24855	Newton, William James, interview, 1975
495	Pratt, James Davidson, IWM interview, 1974
20453	Pring, W., interview 1992
322	Reid, J.P.O., interview, 1966
373	Rodger, James Grant, IWM Interview, 1975
11965	Spencer, Robert Proctor, IWM interview, 1991
4771	Stitt, John Heslop, IWM interview, 1980
11460	Thomson, Alec, IWM interview, 1990
9930	Wells, Ronald Ewert, IWM interview, 1987

Liddle Collection, Brotherton Library, Leeds University [LC]

AIR
AIR 213A	Miscellaneous, Item A8, Anderson, P.W., photograph
AIR 258A	Low, P.V.C., extracts from typescript autobiography
AIR 258A	Recollections, Murray, H.G.F., typescript memoir

CO
CO 066	Murray, Albert Victor, letters

DF
DF 148	Campbell, Dr A.M., manuscript memoir
DF 105	Prior, A.E., 'Some Reminiscences of before, during, & after World War I,'
DF 148	Recollections, Samson, Dr H.P.

GALL
GALL 066	Nicol, 2Lt Alexander, letters

GS
GS 0030	Anderson, Brig. R.C.B., transcript of Tapes 338 and 382, interview with Liddle, 1976
GS 0084	Barclay, Brig. C.N., manuscript recollections, written 1973
GS 0132	Betteridge, Arthur H., typescript memoir, 'Combat in and over Delville Wood,' written 1974

GS 0158	Bolton, Sir Ian, typescript memoir, 'Reactions to First World War,' n.d. but post 1960
GS 0165	Boustead, Sir Hugh, transcript of interview with Liddle, 1976
GS 0177	Boyle, A.R., diary
GS 1843	Bradford David, poem by E.C.Melville, 1915
GS 0215	Bruce, I.R., letters
GS 0257	Cameron, W.G., Typescript memoir, written 20 July, 1918
GS 0259	Cameron Highlanders. Memoir by R.A. Muir
GS 0262	Campbell, J, diary compiled from letters
GS 0280	Chamberlain, Tom, interview with Liddle, 1978
GS 0298	Chavasse family, letters
GS 0315	Clark, H.J.D., Tape 356 Interview with Liddle, 1976
GS 0330	Clifton, J.G., diary
GS 0360	Coppard, E.F., manuscript recollections, undated
GS 0409	Cunningham, J.C., notes written 1976, and Tape 363, transcript of interview with Liddle, 1976
GS 0418	Dane, W.S., typescript diary
GS 0434	Dawson, Robert, diary
GS 0456	Dick, Rev Dr, typescript memoirs, pp59-70, diary, 7 November 1918 to 6 January, 1919
GS 0552	Ferguson, J.S., letters
GS 0588	Fraser, J.A., letters
GS 0627	Gilmour, Andrew, papers
GS 0731	Hay-Young, J, letters
GS 0771	Hirsch, F.B., papers
GS 0828	Imlah, A., letter to father, 28 December, 1914, reproduced in the *Banffshire Journal*, 5 January, 1915
GS 0875	Julian, F., diary
GS 0890	Kershaw, Kenneth R.B., letters
GS 0895	King, H., manuscript memoir, 'Recollections of the War'
GS 0972	Lloyd, A.B., letters
GS 0981	Low, LCpl J.B, letters to pen-pal Mary
GS 0993	Lynden-Bell, L.A., transcript of Tape 488, interview with Liddle, 1977, typed comments on the battle of Sannaiyat and memoir, 'The Effect on the Emotions', probably written c.1977
GS 1003	Macdermott, Lord, typescript recollections
GS 1008	Macdonald, W.S., diary & letters
GS 1021	Mackie, J.D., papers
GS M5	McLachlan, A, Cpl, diary
GS 1023	Maclaren, I, letters
GS 1026	Maclean, G.F., typescript memoir written from diary, 1977, and Tape 495, interview with Liddle, 1978
GS 1027	MacLeod, Lt. J.D., papers
GS 1124	Moffat, A., diary, 17 October, 1914
GS 1153	Murray, Maj. C.M., diary

GS 1203	Oldham, E.A.S., diary
GS 1367	Robertson, J.K. Argyle, manuscript book, 'Twelve months as a Platoon Commander in France & Belgium', written 1920, 61pp, pp.1-2, 6-7
GS 1422	Sanders, 2Lt Spence, diary
GS 1436	Scott, 2Lt J.G., letters
GS 1470	Silvester, Victor M, transcript of interview with Liddle, 1973
GS 1507	Sotheby, Lionel F.S., diary and letters
GS 1516	Stables, Sgt G., letter
GS 1534	Stewart, A.D.L., 'Memoir of the Late Captain Alexander Dugald Lorn Stewart, M.C., The Gordon Highlanders, Younger of Achnacone,' compiled by his father Lt.-Col. Alex. K. Stewart of Achnacone
GS 1535	Stewart, Brig. I.M., Tape 359, interview with Liddle, 1976
GS 1536	Stewart, G, letter
GS 1537	Stewart, W., letter to sister
GS 1549	Strachan, H.J., typescript memoir
GS 1551	Strang J.S., papers
GS 1579	Taylor, LCpl Harry S., typescript memoirs, 'Reminiscences' and 'Further Reminiscences of the Great War 1914/1918'
GS 1635	Turing, Sir John, privately published memoir, written c.1963
GS 1761	Wilson, Douglas J,B., typescript memoir, 'A Flanders Fling. A 1918 episode'
GS 1783	Wood, T.W., manuscript recollections, written 1970's, & Transcript Tape 310, interview with Liddle 1975

MES

MES 093	Recollections, Ballantyne, A.R., Tape 509, transcript of interview with Liddle 1978
MES 013	Bonar, Andrew, letters

Middlebrook Somme 1918

Crowder, W.H., manuscript memoir, written 1976
MacKay, D., letter to Liddle, 13 June, 1976
Savage, E.R., letters

POW

POW 031	Hain, John, letters
POW 056	Millar, W, manuscript memoir, 'My experience on the Somme & after at age 18', written c.1976
POW 056	Recollections, Sheppard, Dr H.J., typescript memoir, 'Dr Herbert James Sheppard, An Account of part of his life as recalled by his younger daughter Mrs Jillian Craig Peckham', 1984

SAL

SAL 059	Shipton, Charles Eldred Curwen, diary

Several Fronts Recollections
Judd, H,C., Transcript of Tape 1545, interview for Liddle Collection, 1997
Kingsley, E.D., typescript memoir, 'The Great War 1914-1918'
Munro, Archibald M., 'Recollections of the First World War with the Gordon Highlanders'

Tapes
Tape 963	Burns, Robert, interview 1994
Tape 1316	Burns, Robert, interview 1996
Tapes 636/653	Cowan, D.T., interview with Liddle, 1982
Tape 606	Douglas, Sir Sholto, interview with Liddle, 1980
Tape 744	Gaffron, Horace, interview with Liddle, 1989
Tape 700	Gilmour, Andrew, interview with Liddle, 1979
Tape 1618/1619	Kerridge, Hal, interview, 1998
Tape 630/647	Macdonald, W.S., interview with Liddle, 1981
Tape 922	McLean, Alexander, interview with Isobel Farrow, 1993
Tapes 481/519	Napier, Joseph, interview with Liddle, 1977
Tapes 621/641	Pollock, Henry, interview with Liddle, 1981
Tape 921	Stuart, Archie, interview with Isabel Farrow, 1993

Transcripts
Tape 364	Anton, C.S., interview with Liddle, 1976
Tape 432	Brown, G.W., interview with Liddle, 1976
Tapes 728/744	Davies, Harry, interview with Liddle 1989
Tape 592	Douglas, Sir Sholto, interview with Liddle, 1980
	Gammell, John Richard. Transcript of conversation between him, aged 90, and his son-in-law, Michael Wilson
Tapes 357/367	Hay-Young, Lt. Col. J., interview with Liddle, 1976
Tape 850	Henley, R.E., interview with Liddle, 1992
	Johnston, Lt Col R.W.F., typescript memoir, 'Some experiences of the Great War of 1914-1918', & Tape 992, Summary, interview with Johnston, 1975
Tape 324	Jordan, Charles Kenneth, interview with Liddle, 1976
Tape 619	McCrow, G.W., interview 1981
Tape 526	Macdonald, Donald, interview
Tape 526	McKay, D., interview with Liddle, 1978
Tape 99	Reynoldson, W., interview with William Redford
Tape 286	Wilson, J.K, interview with Liddle, 1975

Western Front Recollections
A9	Andrew, I.G., photocopied account
B28	Bradley, H.N., 'Signaller H.N. Bradley's Experiences at Poelcappelle 10th to 14th October, 1917'
C15	Cormack, E.W., typescript memoir, 'World War 1 Recollections, My Undistinguished Career,' written c.1970's
D8	Denham, Dr R.H.S.H., manuscript recollections

G5	Gillespie, Capt. Ronald Dave, typescript record of an interview by 'J'
	MacKenzie, Dr W., manuscript memoir, c.1980
M3	McLeavy, J.C., manuscript recollections, probably written 1970's
	Reece, E., typescript memoir, probably written 1970's
S18	Sloan, J.A.C., typescript memoir, 'Master of None,' written 1979

National Library of Scotland, Edinburgh [NLS]

Acc.6028	Addison Smith, C.L., biographical details
Acc.7658 No.2	Angus, Archie, Introductory notes
Acc.11627/86 & 87	Buchan Papers, Macmillan, Rev. Dr R.A.C.
MS 20248, 20249	Haldane, General Sir Aylmer, diary
MS 20655	Haldane, J.B.S., letters
MS 20234	Haldane, Dr J.S., correspondence
MS 10305	Jameson, Alastair, letters
Acc.9084, no.7	McLeod, Donald, letter to sister
Acc.9084 No.37	Macleod, George F., letters
Acc.9084 No.12	Macleod, Rev K.O., letters
Acc.7660	Raeper, Pte A., letters
MS 944-947	Ramage, George, diary
Acc.5415	Roy, James Stewart, typescript memoir, 'Recollections of an Intelligence Officer'
Acc.8802 No.4	Sellar, R.J.B., diary
Acc.12729	Wood, Lt Col J.B., letters
Acc.12872	Wood, Murdo, letters

Royal Scots Museum
Beatson, Cpl James, diary

Index

Index of People

Abercromby, Sir George 328, 456
Adamson, James 257, 272, 463
Alexander, Private Thomas 324, 343-344, 430
Alison, Sir Archibald 48
Allen, Hugh 26, 189, 194, 285, 288, 330, 357, 454
Anderson, Alfred 193
Anderson, Brigadier Andrew 20, 52, 198, 405
Anderson, Major A. 162, 201, 311
Anderson, Lieutenant C.B. 234, 481
Anderson, James 400
Anderson, Brigadier R.C.B. 442
Andrew, Ian G. 158, 249, 305, 309-310, 325, 347-348, 371, 374, 400
Andrew, Lieutenant Patrick Wright 153
Andrews, Linton 101, 109, 211, 250, 308, 314, 316, 321, 323, 331, 369, 371
Ashburner, Robert 91, 139, 342

Badenoch, Captain R.E., 179, 218, 448
Bain, Andrew 186
Bannell, Charles 379
Barclay, C.N. 109
Bartholomew, Hugh 181, 213, 297
Bates, Johnathan 108, 137, 210, 248, 271, 284-285, 327, 358, 414, 455
Beaton, Norman 158, 183, 221, 268, 295, 356, 459
Bell, C. Forbes 33
Bell-Irving, Duncan 376, 379
Betteridge, Arthur 139, 168, 170, 220, 325, 376, 425, 446
Bewsher, Major F.W. 407
Binks, Dicky 100-101
Blaser, Bernard 94, 251, 350, 352
Blount-Dinwiddie, James 139
Bodham-Wetham, Captain 333
Boustead, Hugh 139, 213, 308, 317, 396, 443, 460
Bone, Mr Robert 349
Bowie, Lance Corporal J.M. 84, 144, 147, 269, 273, 285, 299, 301, 310, 324, 343, 372, 385, 398, 399, 406, 421, 426, 429, 430, 433, 434, 452, 454, 461

Bowman, Charles 191
Bowser, Howard 97
Boyle, Captain 222
Bradbury, S. 144, 151, 190, 354, 373, 388, 424, 430
Bradley, H.N. 449
Braes, Alexander 111, 146, 191, 288, 313, 422, 428
Brodie, Douglas Edward 119
Brooke, Brian 91, 355
Brooke, Frank 89, 98-100, 103, 107, 142, 150-151, 160, 170, 197-198, 224, 250, 252, 254, 260, 305, 315, 317, 320-321, 346, 361, 369, 378, 396, 416-417, 426
Brooke, Captain H.V. 91
Brooke, Captain J.A.O. 91
Brooke, Rupert 95
Brown, Private Arrol 319, 338
Brown, George Murray 110-111, 168, 349
Brown, Ronal 414
Brown, Captain Willie N. 168, 211, 434
Bryce, Annan, M.P. 84
Bryden, William 203, 322, 456
Buchan, John 95
Burn, Henry Pelham 77, 104, 296, 377, 398, 413-414, 427
Burns, Robert 146, 164, 203, 226, 233, 343, 344, 348, 350, 401, 433, 442, 461
Byrom, Captain Allan 169

Calder, Private J. 320
Cameron of Lochiel, 31, 125, 126, 152, 244, 340, 378, 393
Cameron, D.C. 29
Cameron, William G. 110, 147, 221, 320
Campbell, Dr A.M. (Alex) 78, 80, 100, 343-344
Campbell, Ivar 208, 296, 373
Campbell, Private James 175, 255, 316, 321-322
Campbell of Kilberry, John 26
Carter, Lance-Corporal 185
Cartmell, Private John 182, 448
Chamberlain, Tom 448

Index 505

Chambers, William 201, 325-326, 359, 361, 422, 430
Chandler, Captain Frederick 137, 261, 412-413, 417
Charker, Private Arthur 262
Chavasse, Noel V.C. and Bar 202, 294, 366, 421, 455
Christison, Philip 120, 135, 176, 217-218, 233, 240, 264, 273, 300, 385, 423
Clappen, Donald 375-376
Clark, H.J.D. 19, 52, 53, 173, 332
Clement, Lieutenant A.M. 352
Coates, Henry 97, 195, 274
College, Captain, 5th Camerons 329, 457, 460
Collier, Private Frank 427
Collins, Norman 106, 109, 117-118, 146, 149, 151, 157-158, 162, 176, 185, 194, 197, 224, 416, 428, 433, 442, 454
Cooper, John 88, 108, 156, 158, 201, 227, 238, 248, 253, 259, 272, 278, 287, 289, 301, 305, 314, 317, 324, 351, 364-365, 368, 399
Cooper, Lieutenant Leslie 224, 276, 332, 376, 458
Cordner, Charles 101, 144, 317, 348
Corstophine, Peter 148
Couper, Captain Charlie 413, 416, 454
Couston, Private William 185, 187, 195, 292, 321, 351, 358, 421, 452, 456
Cowan, Lieutenant 443
Craig-Brown, Ernest 137, 152, 173, 188, 196, 230, 240, 286, 288, 290, 381, 389, 395, 446, 464
Cran, Private Charlie 429
Crask, Gordon 117, 161, 288, 313, 351, 374, 402
Crauford, Standish 95, 375, 412
Croft, Oswald 80, 93, 177
Cumming, Lieutenant Bryant 286, 333, 453, 459
Cunningham, James 18, 19, 106, 109, 171, 205, 270, 334, 436, 437
Currie, Sir Donald 32
Currie, Lieutenant-Colonel John 465

Dale, Lieutenant Jim 293
Dalziel, Lance-Corporal 184, 194, 382
Darling, William 96, 378
Davies, Hugh 164
Dawson, Robert 166, 236, 241, 252, 319, 395
Denham, Dr R.H.S.M. 109, 301
Dennis, R.V. 147, 164, 195, 248, 367
Dick, D. 104, 109, 304
Dick-Cunningham, Lieutenant Colonel, V.C. 47
Dinesen, Thomas 149, 151, 154, 160, 161, 164, 192, 223
Ditcham, Harry 20, 229-230, 254
Dixon, Jimmy 174, 230, 262
Douglas, J.A. 110-111, 129, 135, 137, 153, 157, 159, 169, 176, 189, 203, 210, 212-213, 218, 219, 276, 287, 288, 294, 299, 305, 312, 318, 321, 324, 338, 342, 360, 365, 408, 427, 433, 443, 445, 454

Douglas, Lieutenant Sholto 169
Down, Norman 250, 400
Drummond, Private Alex 318, 349
Drury, J.W. 100
Dunn, Captain J.C. 220
Dunlop, Sir Thomas 83

Edward VII, King 30, 32, 34, 48
Elcho, Lord 24
Elliott, Jim 395
Escombe, Captain W.M.L. 481
Ewart, Ronald 147

Farmer, Donald, V.C. 27, 118
Fennah, Alfred 79, 261, 306, 324, 353, 459
Ferguson, Lionel 110
Ferguson, Lieutenant Scott 292, 381, 403
Fergusson, Sir Charles 403
Ferrie, William 104, 156, 158, 374
Fettes, Charles 104, 312
Fidler, John 150
Findlater, Piper 34-35, 107, 228, 233, 475
Fleming, Grant 92, 99, 187, 213, 296, 366
Fleming, R.S.M. Robert 303, 304
Forman, Charles 101, 107, 123, 428, 430
Foulis, Jim 254, 411
Fowler, Private, 1/8th Argylls 257, 269
Fowler, Alan 19
Fowler, Sir John 19, 299, 343
Fraser, Hon. A.A. 20
Fraser, James 98, 201, 227
Fraser, Private John 262
Fraser, Lieutenant John, 356
Frier, Private G.D. 254
French, Sir John 98, 403

Gaffron, Horace 210
Gairdner, Charlie 167
Gammell, John 396
Gauldie, Lieutenant Ken 284
George V, King 30, 32
Gibb, Captain E.J.C. 290
Gibbs, Philip 232
Gillespie, Douglas (a.k.a. Alex) 19, 94, 99, 153, 178, 181, 188, 208, 222, 252-253, 291, 397, 406, 413-414
Gilmour, Andrew 183, 271, 373
Goodban, Private Monty 427
Gordon, Colonel, V.C. 466
Gordon, Colonel C.W.E. 284-285, 287, 330, 332, 366, 368, 374
Gordon, General Hamilton 107
Gough, General 273-274
Grant Sir Arthur 57, 77, 79, 295
Grant, Sir Hope 24
Grant, Hugh 116

Grant, Ian 184, 372
Gregory, John 167
Greig, Robert 105, 269
Gunn, Lieutenant Colonel G. 83
Gunn, Jack 124, 151, 393
Guthrie, Sergeant Alick 76, 79, 82, 159, 194, 276, 310, 359, 414, 418, 457
Gyatt, Ernest 80
Gyton, S.G. 80

Haig, Lieutenant Colonel 83
Haig, Sir Douglas 228
Hamilton, General Ian 148, 162
Hamilton, Captain Ian, 222, 390
Harper, Cecil 99, 107, 128, 145, 156, 251, 289, 316, 400
Harper, Major-General 226
Harrison, Dave 97
Haworth, Christopher 209
Hay, Albert 111, 147, 221, 353, 419
Hay, William 159, 175, 197, 209
Hay-Young, Captain John 206, 334, 375, 436, 457
Hendry, Neil 299, 408
Henley, Roy 274, 430
Hodges, Cecil 157-158
Hood, David 101, 226
Horn, Robert 105, 447
Hughes, Sir Sam 63, 64, 363
Hunter Weston, Lieutenant general Sir Aylmer 264
Husband, Ross 95, 412, 416
Hutchison, Graham Seton 98, 210, 219, 248, 263, 278, 302, 330-331, 401, 416, 430
Hyslop, Captain 173, 177, 198, 230, 327, 381

Jackson, Frederick 437
Jameson, Lieutenant Alastair 186
Johnson, Harry 100, 107
Johnston, R.W.F. (Robert) 27, 188, 266, 376
Jordan, Charles 110-111
Jordan, Private Patrick 354
Jordan, Stewart 85, 158, 402
Judd, Harold 108, 288, 434
Junks, Herbert 312, 450

Kelly, Major-General 90
Kemble, Major 83
Kemp, Captain William 158, 162, 209, 215, 219, 242, 290, 292-293, 296, 330, 331, 402, 424, 442, 457
Kerridge, Hal 101, 108, 137, 149-150, 158, 161, 164, 172, 184, 241, 367, 407, 417-418, 447
King, H. 110-111
Kitchener, Lord 57, 59, 63, 98-99, 144, 152, 162, 244, 363
Knighton, Eric 211
Knowles, John Forbes 277

Laing, Private John, 1st Black Watch 267, 291
Langlands, Chaplain Fred 357
Lauder, Harry 99, 101, 332-333, 344-346, 362, 385, 420
Lauder, John 332-333, 345, 420
Laurie, Pipe Major Willie 277
Lawson, Bob 86, 193, 383, 415
Leathem, Dr W.H., chaplain 359
Leckie, Captain 30
Lee, Joe 314, 321
Leith-Buchanan, Sir Alexander 26
Levyns, J.E.P. 93, 110, 139, 185, 222, 321-322, 361, 375, 442
Leys, George 236, 241
Liddell, Adrian 201
Linklater, Eric 170, 175-176
Lloyd, Lieutenant Colonel 284, 353
Logie, Marc James 98
Lorimer, Captain J.B. 279
Low, Claud 77, 78, 279, 323, 331, 356, 367, 397, 405, 412, 418, 435, 449, 456, 460
Low, J.B. (Jock) 103, 353
Lynden-Bell, L.A. 89, 223, 334, 373, 445
Lyon, Thomas 99, 164, 180, 190, 406-407

Mabbutt, Henry 232
Macadam, Private John 362
McArthur, H. 374
Macbean, Captain Duncan, 298-299
McCallum, Sergeant Alex 305
McDermott, Keith 206, 372, 381
McDermott, Tommy 101
Macdonald, Captain A.H. 105
MacDonald, Coll 108, 153, 183, 357-359, 392, 396, 415, 420, 458
Macdonald, Donald 21
MacDonald, Sir Hector 39, 45, 48, 49, 98, 116
McDonald, Private J. 352, 434
MacDonald, John, piper 36, 229
MacDonald, W.S. 100, 185, 460
McDougall, Duncan 89
McFarlane, Daniel 144, 276, 436, 458, 465
MacFarlane, David 128
Macgregor, Private 257, 265
Macgregor, Lieutenant A.E. (Guy) 103, 117, 118, 194, 203, 227, 292, 296, 328, 370, 381, 411, 415, 417, 434, 435, 457
Macgregor, Lieutenant Charles 303
McGregor, Peter 151, 156-157, 161, 312, 315, 320, 351-352, 384, 399, 402, 405
Macgregor, lieutenant Rory 387
McGuinness, Ernest 124
Macintyre, Donald 120
MacIntyre, Sergeant Dugald 399
McIntyre, Ross 90-91
McKay, Private D. 449

Index   507

McKay, Private Donald 22, 304
Mackay, Captain G.S. 375, 460
Mackay, Ian 26, 159, 173, 190, 408
Mackay, Lieutenant Robert Lindsay 84, 212, 221, 235, 289, 328, 377, 413, 418, 458
Mackay, William 26, 239
Mackay Scobie, Ian 229, 233, 239-240
McKechnie, Lieutenant 375
Mackenzie, Duncan 418, 426
Mackenzie, Private Jack 293
Mackenzie, W. 376, 458
McKinnell, Bryden 335, 342, 394, 397, 418, 420, 435
McKinnon, Captain R.L. 85, 96-97, 236, 400
Mackintosh, Alan (E.A.)117, 135, 249, 326, 333-334, 355, 380, 384, 393, 417, 425, 442
McLachlan, Adam 173
McLaren, Private William 303
Maclean, Alexander, chaplain 368
Maclean, G.F. 205-206, 334
McLean, Colonel, C.O. 6th Gordons 76, 289
McLeod, Piper Daniel 195, 229, 231, 235, 238-239, 241, 389
Macleod, Donald, piper 389
McLeod, Donald, chaplain 358, 426
Macleod, John Dunning ('Jock'), officer 2nd Camerons 94, 120, 196, 205-206, 246, 324, 356, 371, 376, 380, 399, 404, 414, 417
McLeod, Jock, private, 5th Camerons 158, 211, 238, 248, 365, 394, 402-403, 413
Macleod. George 205, 361, 415
Macleod, Lieutenant Colonel Norman 160, 172, 176, 185, 210, 216-217, 227, 261, 268, 279, 481
McMillan, Private 257, 262
Macmillan, Alex ('Sandy') 89, 144, 198, 302, 317, 338, 347
McMillan, David 154, 309, 320, 344, 364, 445, 453, 463
Macmillan, Norman 56, 57, 178, 188, 280, 295, 306, 309-310, 313, 319, 323, 325, 360, 376, 380, 452, 461
Macmillan, Reverend Dr. Robbie 95, 187, 358-360
Macmillan, William 160, 189, 311, 342, 348, 351, 355, 361
Macnaghten, Angus 20, 88, 135, 291
MacNeill, Father 135, 360
McPake, Private 180
McPherson, Private 257, 266
Macpherson, Sergeant H. 52, 174, 341
Main, Captain Don 104, 129, 300
Maitland, Captain 77
Manton, Horace 219
Marr, James 146, 199, 457, 460
Marshall, Private James McGregor 277
Martin, George 102
Mason-Macfarlane, David 26, 28

Matheson, John 84
Maxse, General 404
May, Sergeant H.E. 175, 217
Meikle, Sgt John, V.C. 441
Methuen, Lord 45
Millar, Private Billy 365
Milligan, Alistair 331
Milne, Major General 266
Milne, piper 34
Milne, G. Forbes 25
Mitchell, William Fraser 121, 315
Moffat, Alex 167, 273
Monaghan, Hugh 376
Moncrieffe, Sir Robert 76, 289
Montgomerie, Major 137
Morrison, William 114
Munro, Archie 423
Munro, Hugh 125, 348, 384, 447
Murison, Wullie 124, 142, 223
Murray, Major Charles 400
Murray, Francis 257
Murray, George 81, 188, 196, 197, 397, 452, 457
Murray, C.S.M. Jim 226
Murray, Lieutenant Colonel Wolfe 428

Neish, Lieutenant-Colonel 466
Newton, William 106, 127, 164, 398
Nicholson, Colonel W.N. 226, 382, 453
Nimmo, Peter 143

Ogilvie, D.D. 85, 86
Oldham, Lieutenant F. A.S. 207, 375, 427

Pailthorpe, Captain D.W. 298, 303-304, 370, 372, 374, 403, 422, 433, 439, 448, 450, 463
Panton, Howard 394, 422, 428
Parke, Charlie 20, 148
Paterson, Jim 151
Paterson, William 88, 108, 118, 314, 323, 358, 360, 456
Paul, Piper, Canadian Scottish 236
Paul, Phil 158, 161, 365, 379-380, 459 460
Peck, Lieutenant Colonel C.W. 236
Philip, John 76
Pirie, 2nd Lieutenant Alexander 333
Pollock, James Dalgleish, V.C. 119
Powell, Private 257, 272, 463
Prior, Audrey 166, 450

Quckett, Hugh 76, 117, 137, 177, 328, 339

Racine, James 80, 144, 291, 381, 437, 454, 462
Raeper, Private Alick 319
Ramage, George 93, 130, 312, 314-315, 346, 361, 366, 394, 402, 427, 462
Rathbone, Basil 213

Reed, Major General, V.C. 403
Reid, Captain 79
Reid, D.W. 147, 149, 330, 374
Reid, Percy 184, 187, 188
Richardson, Piper, V.C. 234. 236
Ritchie, Tom 305
Roberts, Lord 98
Robertson, Lieutenant C.B. 184, 455
Robertson, Donald 370, 393, 401
Robertson, Corporal Harry 198, 209, 429, 448, 461
Robertson, J.K. 97, 104
Robertson, William 53, 226
Rodger, James 28, 76
Rose-Miller, G.P. 463
Ross, Hugh 19
Rowan, Captain 214-215
Roy, James 149
Rule, Alexander 106, 148, 165, 203, 250, 253, 400
Russell, Captain S.C., of Aden 22, 102, 212, 250, 293, 375

Samson, H.P. 89, 146, 374
Sanders, Lieutenant Spence 197, 306
Sangster, Jack 368
Savage, Private E.R. 110, 187, 261
Scott, Captain Alex 270, 309
Sellar, Private R.J.B. 191
Sempill, Colonel Lord 329, 369
Shewan, Alan 90, 102, 303
Shireffs, Jim 262, 276, 280
Silvester, Victor 444, 446, 464
Simpson, Cecil Barclay 95
Skinner, David 394, 457
Sloan, James 92, 106, 176, 218-219, 324, 367
Small, Pete 325
Smith, Albert 218, 321, 324
Smith, Lieutenant G.E. 357
Smith, Major G.A. 215
Smith, John 81
Smith, Miss Sybil 352
Sotheby, Herbert 234
Sotheby, Lieutenant Lionel 94, 96, 176, 183, 280, 293, 351, 402, 418
Stables, George 155, 190, 304, 323, 445
Stanford, J.K. 99, 171, 375
Stansfield, Colonel John 137, 350, 367, 370, 374, 458
Steven, Harvey 117
Steven, Lieutenant Sidney 296
Stewart, Alexander 18, 19
Stewart, Colonel C.E. 365
Stewart, Brigadier I.M. 28, 170, 440, 459
Stewart, Private J. 298
Stewart, 'Jack' 207, 264, 275, 283-286, 288, 335, 353, 360, 365, 367, 371, 456
Stewart, Piper James 35

Stewart, Peter 91, 92, 290, 291, 338, 342, 371, 412, 440
Stewart-Smith, Lieutenant Dudley 159
Strachan, Albert 28, 56, 76-77, 148, 161, 173, 289, 419, 466
Strachan, Harry 77, 126, 150, 299
Strang, Johnnie 80
Sutherland, Captain 310, 356
Sutherland, Jim 427, 447
Sutherland, Walter S. 109, 458

Taylor, Harry 93, 109-110, 197, 217, 250, 323
Taylor, Private Percy 105
Thomson, Alec 146, 189, 266-267, 287
Thomson, Stewart 104, 212
Thomson, Corporal W. 298
Thorburn, Lieutenant Malcolm 169, 234, 337
Todd, Captain H.B. 322
Tullibardine, Marquis of 31
Turing, Lieutenant John 151, 252, 289, 371, 429, 446, 451
Turnbull, Major 370
Tweddle, Archie 80, 326, 425

Unthank, Lieutenant Colonel 366

Veitch, Private, South African Scottish 139, 317

Wade, Major A.G. (Alec) 21, 308
Walker, A.R. 80
Walker, Tom 223
Wallace, Lieutenant Colonel 287, 442
Warwick, George 171
Watson, Richard 171, 429, 462
Watt, Chaplain Lauchlan Maclean 136, 238, 253, 426,
Watts, Alan 20
Wauchope, 'Andy' 45
Wauchope, Lieutenant Colonel 286, 293-294
Webster, John 206, 210, 240
Weir, Captain Neil 234, 240, 327, 429
Wells, Ronald 151, 185, 194
Wells, Colonel William 83
Welsh. Private D. 186, 317, 436, 455
White, Private Andrew 190
White, Captain Robert 212, 444
Wilson, Douglas 179, 201, 213, 219, 220, 232, 234, 268, 281, 284, 292, 294, 304, 325-326, 335, 376, 397, 435, 452-453, 454
Wilson, Lieutenant Colonel G.L. (Laurie) 114
Wilson, Jim 81
Wilson, Rachel 202
Wimberley, Douglas 116, 160, 165, 172, 180, 185, 189, 195, 210, 216, 227, 238, 364, 423-424, 431-432, 452
Wood, Charles Hutchieson 370

Wood, Private David 422, 427
Wood, Johnnie 398, 429, 432, 449, 457
Wood, Sergeant Sidney 433
Wrench, Arthur 102-103, 188, 192, 223, 246, 265, 288, 291, 294, 299, 301, 312, 354, 396, 403, 408, 413, 415, 427, 434, 443

Wyllie, Captain Alistair 62, 204, 238, 254, 270, 285, 297, 443, 451

Young, Andrew 406
Young, Captain Thomas 258-260, 263, 265
Youngson, Captain 178, 244, 347, 378, 395

Index of Places

Abbeville 167, 199
Aberdeen 18, 27, 40, 47, 83, 91, 106-107, 109, 111, 146, 148, 154, 289, 331, 370
Aberdeenshire 95, 98, 111,
Aberfeldy 24, 40
Achmonie 26
Afghanistan 38, 44
Agra 53, 333
Aisne, river 131
Aldershot 51, 69, 88, 107, 145-146, 158, 160, 313, 327, 351, 365, 373, 377-378, 384, 411
Alexandria 65, 69, 104, 241, 273, 285, 349
Alford 24, 77, 124
Alloa 47-48, 469
Alness 24
Amiens 421
Angus 23, 123
Ardersier 259
Argentina 90, 281
Argyllshire 23, 25, 260
Arras 95, 102-103, 187-189, 209, 212, 223-224, 247, 251, 253, 260, 262, 276, 290, 305, 321-322, 324-326, 346, 360-361, 369, 377, 398, 402-403, 417, 419, 423, 426-427, 429-430, 455, 462, 465
Atbara 35, 42, 107
Aubers Ridge 89, 96, 223, 235, 287, 293, 320, 420, 447, 449, 458
Auchterarder 28
Aveluy 180

Baghdad 169, 240, 373, 445
Ballachulish 277
Ballynovare 75, 390
Balquhidder 21
Banchory 77, 125, 299
Bangalore 16
Bannockburn 33
Bareilly 53
Barra 22
Basingstoke 145, 273, 347
Basra 459
Batum 75
Beaumont-Hamel 85, 224, 235, 272, 369, 380, 395, 396, 423, 425, 428, 433, 463, 469
Bedford 54-57, 76-77, 79-81, 96, 124, 136, 144, 149-151, 161, 165, 173, 229, 241, 247, 249, 252, 257-258, 260, 262-264, 277, 291, 295, 299, 345-348, 352, 378, 380, 393, 434
Belfast 26, 314
Belgium 87, 92, 94-98, 167, 315, 412, 473
Benbecula 126
Birmingham 139, 346
Birr 75
Bordon 65, 322, 394
Bouchavesnes 181, 193
Boulogne 27, 70, 96, 170-171, 198, 218, 294, 458
Bouzincourt 178
Bradford 100, 313-314, 351
Bramshott 151, 154, 161, 249, 309
Brighton 135, 342
British East Africa 90-91, 355
Brodie Castle 119
Bromley 107, 124
Broughty Ferry 108, 149
Bulgaria 62, 72
Burton-on-Trent 107, 123
Butte de Warlencourt 213, 293, 370, 424
Buzancy 403-404

Cairo 46, 53, 285
Caithness 23
Calais 111, 132, 147, 219, 433
Cambrai 187, 221, 235, 333, 360, 369, 396, 402, 415, 423-424, 431-432
Cambuslang 89, 317
Campbeltown 84
Canada 89, 90, 97
Cape Town 110, 244
Carradale 97
Catterick 161, 317
Ceylon 18, 49, 91, 139
Chelford 116
China 43, 90
Cirencester 145, 347
Clackmannan 23
Clapham 102
Clyde, river 354-355
Constantinople 62, 72, 75, 201, 204, 242, 254, 259, 274, 289, 364, 387, 399
Constanza 62, 72, 297, 387, 390
Corgarff 24
Courcelette 175, 183, 186, 193, 436

Crimea 38, 43
Cromarty 329, 371, 451
Cromer 165-166
Cuinchy 232
Culloden 32, 116
Curragh 75, 148

Dakar 168
Dargai 34-35, 42-43, 107, 228, 233, 475
Delville Wood 71, 140, 245, 304, 425, 448, 461
Denver, South Africa 44
Devonport 65
Dewsbury 100
Dickebusche 184
Dinapore 53
Dingwall 23, 48-49, 149, 299, 313, 344, 351, 402, 441, 469
Donegal 125, 354
Dorking 171, 375
Drumossie 105
Dublin 26, 75
Dum Dum 53
Dumbarton 104, 129
Dumfries 110
Dunbartonshire 23, 83
Dunblane 37, 47
Dundee 18, 23, 88, 95-96, 101, 108-109, 123, 125, 129, 211, 249, 267, 311, 314
Dunderave. Antrim 21
Dunfermline 126
Durban 168, 244, 342, 349
Durham 127, 128, 316

East Sheen 108, 137
Edinburgh 25, 37, 39, 47-49, 51, 79, 95, 100, 105, 120, 126, 142, 148, 150, 165, 196, 311, 340, 344-345, 354, 360, 469
Egypt 32, 38, 58, 69, 72-73, 107, 170, 184, 207, 242, 270, 301
Elandslaagte 91
Elgin 23, 95
Eski-Chehir 239, 243
Étaples 70, 110, 137, 198, 238, 242, 257, 259-260, 262, 271, 273, 304, 344, 376, 388, 399, 457-458

Falkirk 19, 48
Festubert 108, 124, 136, 362, 418-419
Fife 18, 23, 27, 109, 123, 125, 127, 129
Fillievres 162
Folkestone 104, 378
Forfar 292
Fort George 18, 51, 111, 161, 252, 288, 301, 312-314
Freetown, Sierra Leone 244
Fremicourt 188
Frensham Common 162

Gailes 96, 144
Gairloch 23
Gallipoli 58, 67, 69, 72-74, 92, 104, 148, 349
Gaza 94
German East Africa 66, 73
German South West Africa 65, 72, 91
Givenchy 159
Glasgow 19, 24, 78, 81, 99-101, 111, 120, 125, 127-128, 300, 302, 311-312, 344, 354, 367, 380
Glenbuchat 24
Glenmoriston 116
Golspie 23, 109
Greenock 109, 349, 356
Guildford 80, 381

Hamilton, Ontario 29
Hampstead 80
Harris 22, 126
Hartlepool 117, 127, 348
Hawick 109
Hexham 110
High Wood 131, 245, 382, 403, 427, 430
Hill 70 222, 236, 394, 398, 424
Hindhead 161
Holland 168
Hong Kong 90, 349
Hull 109
Huntly 106

India 18, 21, 91-92, 116, 120, 148, 184, 244, 270, 272, 275, 277, 290, 333, 338, 342, 349, 355, 371, 373, 385, 459-460
Invergordon 23, 102, 128, 161, 165, 196, 238-239, 343-344
Inverness 18, 20, 36, 40, 77, 83-84, 116, 126, 128, 147, 229, 340-341, 343
Inverness-shire 23, 83, 126
Ireland 59, 73, 75, 127, 138-139, 354, 388, 400, 460
Islay 25-26, 78, 80, 100
Italy 67-69, 73, 168, 175, 186, 211, 243, 245, 374, 387-388, 456

Jacobsdal 46
Johannesburg 43
Jubaland 91

Keith 77
Kelso 106
Kemmel 167
Kensington 95
Kilwinning 110
Kinross 23
Kinsale 75

La Bassée Canal 428-429
Ladysmith 47, 91, 107

Lagny-Thorigny 67
Lairg 19
Lanarkshire 126-127
Lancashire 91, 126, 139, 311
Le Cateau 379, 406, 419, 440, 466
Le Crotoy 186-187, 287
Le Havre 53, 60, 176, 183, 189, 191, 197, 230, 244, 324, 405
Le Sars 183
Le Touquet 210, 219, 332
Leeds 89, 98-99, 107, 250, 317
Lewis 19, 21, 22
Lillers 195
Limerick 75
Lochaber 126
Lochbroom 19, 344
London 24, 56, 79-81, 85, 93, 97, 117, 124. 136, 150-151, 164, 171, 345, 357, 365, 414
Longueval 232, 234, 237, 241, 284, 368, 429, 456
Loos 84, 92, 119-120, 125, 128, 131, 222, 231, 233-235, 287-288, 296, 316, 322, 324-325, 335, 348, 357, 369-371, 373, 375, 385, 392-394, 398-400, 402-403, 406, 419, 421-422, 426-429, 437, 447, 466
Lucknow 107

Mafeking 47
Magersfontein 35, 45-46, 48, 50, 107
Mainz 169
Maizieres 165
Majuba Hill 40-42
Malay States 90, 116
Malta 34, 246, 324, 414, 417
Mametz 91, 221, 455
Manchester 124, 150
Marseilles 53-54, 65-66, 166-167, 171
Martinpuich 303, 430, 432
Maryburgh 24
Maud 111
Mesopotamia 67-68, 72-74, 85, 98, 168-169, 201, 203-204, 206-207, 210-211, 231, 234, 238-242, 264, 275, 283, 286, 332-333, 348-349, 355, 367, 369, 372-373, 386-388, 393, 436, 445, 456, 459-460
Meteren 232, 263, 284, 292, 397, 435, 453-454
Modder River 35, 107
Mome Gorge 43
Mons 173-174, 198, 230, 262, 420
Montreal 149, 154, 164
Mooltan 162
Morayshire 23
Mull 135
Munlochy 23

Naours 198
Natal 36, 43-44

Neuve Chapelle 124, 233, 240, 296, 370, 398, 403, 418-419, 426, 458
New York City 98
Nigg 90, 293
Nonne-Boschen 395, 464
North Uist 126
Norwich 111
Nova Scotia 31, 64, 135

Omdurman 38-39, 45
Ontario 90
Oxford 95

Paignton 106
Paisley 20, 26, 143
Palestine 59, 69, 71-73, 94, 168, 201, 203-204, 207, 231, 242, 249, 251, 288, 299, 350, 371, 408
Paris 49, 167, 246-247
Passchendaele 175-176, 179, 215-216, 379, 392, 402, 419-421, 423, 430, 434
Peking 43, 349
Perth 18, 76, 98, 148, 164, 293, 377
Piave, river 423, 434
Pietermaritzburg 43
Ploegsteert Wood 177
Plymouth 51, 243, 312
Poona 53, 355
Portree 125
Portuguese East Africa 90
Potchefstroom 65, 139, 321
Pretoria 43, 47

Quatre Bras 39
Queenstown 75

Rawalpindi 61
Regina Trench 234, 344
Renfrew 23, 129
Richmond, Yorkshire 144
Ripon 59, 100, 103, 107, 124, 129, 135-137, 144, 150-151, 157, 170, 212, 238, 250, 259, 261, 264, 272, 287, 289, 294, 301-302, 305, 312, 317-318, 346, 369, 384, 448-450, 459-460
Romsey 110
Ross-shire 19, 23
Rouen 218-219, 260, 366, 373, 402, 458, 460
Rumania 62, 72, 75
Ruschuk 72, 75, 386
Rushmoor 145

Sailly-Saillisel 182
St Omer 116
St Petersburg 90
St Quentin 159
Salisbury Plain 64, 377
Salonika 58, 62, 67 72, 75, 95, 154, 175, 201,

203-207, 210, 234, 238-242, 246, 264, 267, 270, 285, 300, 324, 371-372, 375, 385-388, 390, 399, 404-405, 408, 443, 451, 460
San Francisco 124
Sandhurst 18, 20, 89, 106, 121, 334
Sanniyat 210
Scarpe, river 215
Selkirk 29, 33, 162
Sevastopol 43
Sheffield 44
Shorncliffe 51
Skye 22, 125, 126, 136
South Africa 89, 91, 93
South Queensferry 76
South Uist 21, 22, 126
Southampton 287, 295
Stirling 18, 20, 48, 128, 144
Stirlingshire 23
Stornoway 19
Strathdon 24, 76, 79
Strathspey 126
Struma, river 62, 203-205, 239-240
Sudan 19, 38, 90, 117
Sunderland 110
Sutherland 23
Sutton Coldfield 162

Tain 23, 164, 241, 279, 343
Tamai 42, 379
Tamines 412
Tebay, Westmoreland 103, 353
Tel-el-Kebir 35, 38-39, 43, 107, 473
Tiflis 75
Tinques 246, 388, 473
Torquay 106, 127
Tralee 73, 75

Trans-Caucasia 72, 75
Turkey 72, 239, 243, 270, 372, 390

Ullapool 23, 95, 344
Ulster 21, 44, 124
United States 90, 138
Upminster 81

Valcartier 155
Vancouver 29, 117, 379
Vardar, river 203, 205
Varna 239, 297
Vendresse 188
Venice 168
Vera Cruz 98
Victoria, British Columbia 29
Vimy Ridge 70, 236, 369, 396

Wales 127, 129, 139, 147, 151
Walker-on-Tyne 110-111, 137, 318, 338, 342
Walthamstow 108
Warminster 166
Waterloo 32, 38-39, 107, 110, 368
West Hartlepool 128, 316
Wick 88, 108, 118, 125, 311
Wiesbaden 169
Winnipeg 29, 31, 260, 364
Wormhoudt 195

Yorkshire 59, 117, 129 136-137, 320, 346, 388, 394-395
Ypres 88, 102, 131, 148, 179, 209-210, 214-215, 223, 247, 273, 333-334, 360, 398-399, 413, 429, 452, 463, 465

Zeebrugge 53

Index of Military Formations & Units

British Army

General
Army organisation pre-War 15-28
First Corps 412
Garrison Battalions 61-62
Graduated Battalions 61
Indian Army 116, 375, 460
Labour battalions 60, 66, 69-70, 190-191
Militia 20-21, 38, 46, 106, 114-115, 118-119
New Army (Kitchener's Army) 59-61, 63 113-115, 117, 119, 121-122, 125-131, 141, 143-145, 152, 229, 277, 279, 330, 346, 363, 368, 468
Pioneer battalions 190, 194
Regimental Depots 54
Regular Army 15-20, 51-53, 114-119
Reservists 21, 52-53, 114-115, 122-123, 140, 174
Special Reserve 20-22, 54, 113-115, 119, 122-123, 131
Territorial Force 22-28, 54-59, 63, 113-115, 117-119, 123-125, 129, 346, 368, 468-469
  Second-line battalions 59, 83, 113, 115, 229
  Third-line battalions 59, 83, 113, 115, 229
Third Army 226
Volunteers 22-23, 33, 38, 46-47, 98, 119

Divisions
1st Division 85, 402
2nd Highland Division (subsequently 64th Division) 59
3rd Division 85, 400
5th Division 68, 190

Index   513

6th Division 399
9th (Scottish) Division 60, 65-66 69-71, 153, 234, 382, 396
15th (Scottish) Division 60, 66, 69-70, 84, 131, 185, 195, 215, 247, 382, 388, 398, 402-404, 406, 432
17th Division 382
21st Division 399
26th Division 60, 69, 71
27th Division 68, 72, 377
33rd Division 219
40th Division 193
51st (Highland) Division 58, 68, 70, 84-85, 131, 150, 172, 175, 178, 186, 190, 193-194, 221, 226, 247, 252, 274, 280, 287, 365, 370, 382, 384, 388, 395-398, 400, 404, 407, 409, 424-425, 427, 432, 452, 457, 469
52nd (Lowland) Division 58, 72-73, 382
55th Division 85
56th Division 85, 195, 402
63rd Royal Naval Division 396
64th (Highland) Division 59
Highland Division (subsequently 51st Division) 55, 57-58, 66, 68, 79-81, 136-137, 247, 346, 352
Meerut Division 68, 73, 85

Brigades
8th Brigade 400
44th Brigade 398
45th Brigade 404
81st Infantry Brigade 240
152nd Brigade 58, 398, 427
153rd Brigade 58, 396
154th Brigade 396
191st (Highland) Brigade 165
'Lancashire Brigade' (attached to 51st Division) 58, 68

Highland Regiments and Battalions
Argyll & Sutherland Highlanders 15-18, 30, 40, 89, 101, 109 111, 129, 135, 156, 158, 167, 246, 248, 252, 266, 287, 328, 365, 401, 415
    1st Battalion 17, 34-35, 53, 67, 72, 75, 171, 184, 194, 204-206, 222, 234, 240, 242, 254, 260, 267, 270, 334, 352, 373, 375, 377, 382, 436, 455, 457
    2nd Battalion 17, 18-19, 34, 51-52, 67, 94, 98-99, 137, 153, 170, 173-174, 177-178, 181-183, 188, 198, 201-202, 208, 215, 219-220, 222, 226, 229-230, 235, 254, 261-263, 278, 291, 302, 317, 322, 327, 331-332, 348, 357, 369, 377, 381, 397, 400, 405-406, 410, 412-414, 416, 427, 435-436, 440, 443, 459, 464
    3rd Battalion 20, 75, 104, 373
    4th Battalion 20
    5th Battalion 22, 204, 207, 241, 243, 349, 414

1/5th Battalion 58, 69, 72-74, 104, 300
3/5th Battalion 125
5th (Reserve) Training Battalion 129, 294, 318
6th Battalion 22, 190, 194, 203, 227, 243, 245, 411, 434, 436
1/6th Battalion 58, 68-69, 73, 103, 265-266, 269, 292, 296, 316, 352, 370, 375, 448, 457
2/6th Batalion 143, 154
7th Battalion 22, 27, 180, 186, 193, 222, 270, 415, 436
1/7th Battalion 58, 68, 142, 309, 331, 389, 444, 464
8th Battalion 22-23, 26, 78-80, 124, 134, 140, 332, 345, 415, 447, 469
1/8th Battalion 56, 58, 68, 70, 77, 81-82, 84, 114, 125, 151, 256-260, 262-263, 265-269, 271-272, 275, 277, 288, 346, 348, 354, 374, 379, 384, 393, 406, 463
2/8th Battalion 56, 328
9th Battalion 22, 26, 117, 265, 442, 450
1/9th Battalion 58, 68, 83
2/9th Battalion 117, 381
3/9th Battalion 104
10th Battalion 60, 128, 160, 167, 234, 240, 327, 347, 377, 393, 419, 424, 429, 456
11th Battalion 60, 70, 84, 90, 102, 114, 145, 147, 195, 205, 210, 212, 221-222, 235, 257, 264-265, 269, 273, 276, 285, 289, 299, 303, 306, 310, 312, 324, 328, 342-343, 361, 372, 373, 375, 377, 399, 411, 418, 421, 427, 429, 433-434, 452, 454, 458, 461, 463
12th Battalion 60, 69, 72, 75, 201, 204-205, 210, 227, 246, 259, 274, 289, 300, 314, 364, 399
13th Battalion 144, 317
14th Battalion 60, 66, 69, 86, 100, 104, 109, 127, 128, 151, 156-157, 161, 181, 183, 185, 193, 198, 209, 213, 271, 287, 297, 304, 312, 320, 351, 373, 383-384, 399, 402, 405, 415, 419, 458, 460
15th Battalion 60, 144, 317
16th Battalion 60, 157
17th Battalion 60, 69

Black Watch 15-19, 30, 34, 39-40, 42, 45, 48, 55, 85-86, 88, 90, 97-98, 101, 104, 106-111, 116, 129, 132, 148-149, 156-158, 161, 168, 174, 238, 254, 289, 305, 314, 316, 318, 328, 364-366, 373, 379, 386, 395, 402, 406, 408, 416, 426, 429, 450, 459-460, 463, 465, 475
    1st Battalion 17, 19, 42, 51-52, 67, 88, 90, 96, 111, 116, 135, 147, 159, 221, 232, 245, 256-259, 262, 265, 267, 269, 275, 280, 291, 293, 300, 351, 353, 358, 365, 382, 419-420, 426
    2nd Battalion 17, 53-54, 67, 72-73, 94, 96, 116, 148, 169, 204, 206-207, 231, 234, 243, 264,

275, 277, 283, 285-286, 288, 330, 333, 339, 349, 367, 369, 371, 374, 453, 456, 459
3rd Battalion 20, 54, 75, 88, 274, 293
4th Battalion 22, 109, 124, 189, 191, 195, 211, 231, 235, 238-239, 241, 413
1/4th Battalion 58, 68, 84, 123, 231, 266, 269, 287, 294, 296, 308, 321, 331, 369, 371, 454, 464
3/4th Battalion 108, 238, 248, 272, 287, 312, 368
4/5th Battalion 60, 68-70, 175-176, 179, 193, 215, 218, 229, 235, 238-239, 241, 389, 456-457
5th Battalion 22, 27, 76, 117, 137, 177, 184, 193, 339, 394
1/5th Battalion 58, 68, 231
6th Battalion 22, 26, 28, 76, 159, 180, 193, 194, 221, 227, 238, 248-249, 414, 418, 457
1/6th Battalion 57-58, 79, 82, 267, 276, 278, 301, 310, 317, 324, 359, 364, 399
2/6th Battalion 79
3/6th Battalion 258-260, 263, 265
7th Battalion 22-23, 26-27, 110, 125, 147, 187, 189, 193-195, 221, 264-265, 285, 288, 292, 330, 365, 421, 454
1/7th Battalion 57-58, 131, 320-321, 357, 448, 452, 456
8th Battalion 60, 108, 129, 134, 137, 153, 159, 169, 176, 183, 189, 203, 210, 212-213, 218, 248, 267, 269, 271, 284-285, 287-288, 294, 299, 318, 321, 324, 327-329, 338, 357-360, 365, 368-369, 392, 408, 414-415, 428, 430, 455-456, 458-459
9th Battalion 60, 69-70, 128, 187, 261, 284-285, 335, 353, 360, 365, 376-378, 456, 458
2/9th Battalion 60, 69
10th Battalion 60, 69-70, 72, 127, 154
11th Battalion 60-61, 158, 161, 165, 365, 379
12th Battalion 60, 69
13th Battalion 58, 59, 69, 72
14th Battalion 59, 69, 72, 204, 207, 372

Cameron Highlanders 15-18, 20 34-35, 40, 42, 116, 129, 132, 134, 144, 146, 152, 158, 202, 266, 328, 340, 354, 364, 369, 385, 388, 469
1st Battalion 44, 51-52, 67, 84, 102, 120, 131, 137, 152, 173-174, 177, 180, 186, 188-189, 194, 196, 198, 201, 230-231, 235, 240, 245, 269, 286, 288, 290, 293, 320, 326, 341, 359, 361, 365, 369, 375, 378, 381-382, 389, 395, 405, 422, 427, 430, 446-448,451, 455, 463-464
2nd Battalion 16-18, 19, 43, 53, 67, 72, 75, 95, 120, 184, 196, 204-206, 232, 240, 246, 293, 324, 356, 358, 371-372, 376, 379-380, 388, 399, 404, 417

3rd Battalion 21-22, 75, 102, 125, 128, 149, 161, 165, 196, 211, 238-239, 248, 250, 343, 386, 390, 461
4th Battalion 22, 23, 26, 77, 79-80, 173, 190, 239-240, 249, 262, 378, 380, 397, 418, 426
1/4th Battalion 58, 68, 84, 124, 136-137, 159, 229, 362
3/4th Battalion 83, 124, 137, 144, 151, 373
5th Battalion 60, 126, 131, 135, 145, 179, 201, 211, 213-214, 219-220, 232, 235, 244, 254, 264, 281, 284, 290, 292-294, 304, 325, 329, 325, 360, 365, 367, 376, 387, 393-394, 399, 402-403, 411, 413, 435, 448, 452, 454, 457, 460
6th Battalion 60, 70, 84, 120, 126-127, 145, 155-156, 172, 175, 214-215, 217, 233, 240, 249, 255, 261, 264, 268, 273, 279, 300, 305, 309, 316, 321-322, 325, 360, 367, 369, 371, 375, 394, 398, 400, 403, 406, 408, 481
7th Battalion 60, 69-70, 83-84, 126-127, 145-146, 164, 203, 212, 226, 233, 257, 262, 272, 276, 279, 290, 325-326, 343, 347, 350, 367, 378, 401, 422, 427-428, 433, 458, 463, 465, 481
8th Battalion 83, 126, 128, 153, 279, 329, 343
9th Battalion 60, 69, 190
10th Battalion 58, 69, 72
11th Battalion 60, 69-70, 148, 164, 190-191, 195, 248, 367

Gordon Highlanders 15-18, 30, 34-35, 39-43, 46-47, 86, 89, 91, 107, 114-116, 134, 137, 146, 148, 155-156, 158, 162, 164, 171, 175, 191, 209, 217, 224, 228-229, 262, 264, 328, 332, 355, 366, 370-371, 376, 379, 398, 402-403, 407, 426, 460, 475
1st Battalion 17-18, 44, 51-52, 67, 85, 92-93, 104, 130, 137, 149, 158, 161, 184. 187, 191, 198, 209, 213, 222, 241, 296, 312. 314, 319, 333, 359, 361, 366, 368, 377, 379, 390, 394, 406, 413, 417-418, 427-428, 447-448, 454, 461, 464, 466
2nd Battalion 17, 53, 67, 73, 91, 132, 148, 168, 211, 214, 221, 298, 303, 330, 350, 367, 370, 372, 374, 388, 412, 421, 423, 433-435, 439, 448, 450, 455-456, 458, 463
3rd Battalion 20-21, 330
4th Battalion 22, 27, 55, 107, 109, 146, 148, 165, 166, 173, 199, 201, 203, 227, 236, 241, 250, 252-253, 265, 301, 314, 319, 383
1/4th Battalion 55, 58, 68, 85, 96, 104, 106, 277, 312, 368, 395, 400
2/4th Battalion 55
3/4th Battalion 55
5th Battalion 22, 57, 77, 79, 178, 215, 219, 244, 246, 295, 325, 347, 357,368, 373, 378, 395

Index 515

1/5th Battalion 58, 68, 70, 131, 274-275, 280, 378
6th Battalion 22, 24, 28, 76-77, 79, 148, 161, 164, 173, 184, 187-188, 190, 197, 210, 213, 215, 223, 244, 247, 268, 289, 296, 306, 378, 419, 435, 444, 466
1/6th Battalion 56, 58, 68, 69, 83, 124, 155, 403
2/6th Battalion 83, 143, 370, 463
3/6th Battalion 83
6/7th Battalion 68, 304
7th Battalion 22, 77, 124, 150, 183, 221, 299, 357, 443, 459
1/7th Battalion 58, 68-69, 131, 268, 295, 356-357, 369, 378, 464
8th Battalion 60, 69, 84, 91, 126-127, 131, 284, 287, 290-291, 332, 338, 342, 366, 371, 377, 412, 440, 457
8/10th Battalion 69-70, 209, 213, 242, 251, 253, 290, 292-293, 329, 331, 370, 424, 429, 462
9th Battalion 60, 103, 126-127, 190-191, 215, 257, 353
10th Battalion 60, 69, 84, 107, 126-128, 131, 145, 156, 287, 289, 295, 316, 369, 398, 400, 429, 442, 449, 457-458
11th Battalion 330
1st Garrison Battalion 61, 244, 349, 385
51st Graduated Battalion 61, 75, 153, 241
52nd Graduated Battalion 61, 75, 153
53rd Young Soldiers Battalion 61, 75

Highland Light Infantry (H.L.I.)
6th Battalion 24, 26, 33, 364
1/6th Battalion 58, 69, 72-73
2/6th Battalion 59, 75
9th Battalion (Glasgow Highlanders) 24-25, 27, 33, 99, 110, 131-132, 164, 178, 180, 186, 188, 190, 211, 213-214, 219-20, 248, 309, 313, 319, 323, 360, 364, 376, 405-406, 408, 425, 427, 452, 461, 464
1/9th Battalion (1st Glasgow Highlanders) 56, 58, 83, 264-265, 280, 295, 300, 306, 313, 322
2/9th Battalion (2nd Glasgow Highlanders) 56, 59, 75, 313, 322

Liverpool Scottish 24, 25, 27, 33, 46, 56, 77, 79, 93, 110, 124, 185, 196-197, 202, 213, 215, 217, 250, 335, 389, 394, 397, 418, 420, 435, 437
1st Battalion 27, 58, 68, 85, 269, 294, 323-324, 342, 353, 366, 455
2nd Battalion 59, 66, 68, 261, 293, 306, 459

London Scottish 24, 27, 46-48, 54, 56, 77-81, 97, 101, 106, 108-109, 124-125, 136-137, 144, 147, 149-150, 158, 161, 163-164, 167-168, 171-172, 184, 225, 241, 364, 367, 375, 394, 397, 407
1st Battalion 58, 85, 92, 104, 132, 167, 176, 195, 203, 212, 215, 218-219, 273-274, 279, 322-323, 331, 356, 367, 397, 402, 405, 412, 418, 444, 449, 456, 460
2nd Battalion 59, 66-67, 69, 72-73, 94, 175, 204, 207, 244, 251, 267, 288, 299, 350, 375, 408, 434

Royal Scots
9th Battalion ('The Dandy Ninth') 24-27, 33, 46, 124, 147, 150-151, 175, 185, 188, 193, 194, 197, 201, 209, 266, 311, 376, 395
1/9th Battalion 58, 68, 70, 79, 159, 311
2/9th Battalion 59, 75, 79, 162, 267

Seaforth Highlanders 15-19, 30, 34, 40, 47, 48, 89, 95, 100, 109, 111, 116, 124, 126, 128, 134, 142, 146, 149-151, 157-158, 160, 169-170, 197, 249-250, 258, 288, 312-313, 317-318, 350, 365, 370, 378, 402, 408, 429, 433, 441-442, 469
1st Battalion 17, 19, 43-44, 46, 53, 67, 72-74, 85, 89, 106, 190, 204, 206-208, 210, 223, 226, 229, 231, 233-234, 239-240, 249, 272, 275, 286, 296, 332, 334, 348, 355, 372-373, 388, 436, 445 447
2nd Battalion 17, 19, 46, 51, 67, 95, 105, 111, 174, 269, 298, 318, 343, 377-378, 435, 448
3rd Battalion 46, 371, 451
4th Battalion 22-23, 26, 28, 79-80, 188, 192, 196-198, 212, 217, 223-224, 245, 254, 299, 315, 343, 366, 397, 416-417, 425-428, 433-434
1/4th Battalion 58, 68, 81, 85, 100, 102, 121, 160, 165, 262, 274, 292, 294, 299, 301, 315, 320, 326, 343, 369, 381, 396-397, 403, 449, 452, 457
3/4th Battalion 59, 107, 146, 157, 161, 402
4th Reserve Training Battalion 59, 129
5th Battalion 22-23, 79-81, 88, 93, 118, 135, 144, 260, 265, 291, 310, 326, 332, 354-356, 364, 373, 380-381, 384, 424-425, 427, 430, 437
1/5th Battalion 58, 80, 114-115, 137, 288, 375, 454, 462
2/5th Battalion 117
3/5th Battalion 59, 98, 103, 109, 314, 323
6th Battalion 22-23, 79, 105, 187, 213, 224, 352, 423, 442
1/6th Battalion 58, 95, 117, 124, 329, 358
3/6th Battalion 59
7th Battalion 60, 152-153, 182, 189, 207, 217, 234, 237, 276, 291, 311, 342, 348, 351, 361, 376, 481
8th Battalion 60, 146, 149, 191, 252, 288-289, 324, 330, 371-372, 422, 428-430, 436, 446, 451, 464
9th Battalion 60, 190, 262, 267, 276, 332, 376
10th Battalion 143, 229, 343

1st Garrison Battalion 61-62, 72, 75, 175, 204, 238-239, 242, 264-265, 270, 285, 297, 372, 375, 443, 451, 460

Other British Regiments
Border Regiment 399
Buffs 480
Cameronians (Scottish Rifles) 375
Connaught Rangers 221
Durham Light Infantry 366
East Surrey Regiment 101
Fife & Forfar Yeomanry 59, 85-86, 207, 328
Grenadier Guards 111, 400
Guards 253, 367, 398, 406, 480
Hertfordshire Regiment 231
Highland Light Infantry 101, 186, 229
Imperial Yeomanry 21, 46, 81
King's Royal Rifle Corps 147, 195, 368
King's Shropshire Light Infantry 222
Lanarkshire Yeomanry 186
London Regiment 254-255, 400, 481
Lothian and Border Horse 109, 458
Lovat Scouts 58, 132
Manchester Regiment 158
Middlesex Regiment 400
Queen's Regiment 248
Royal Fusiliers 398
Royal Scots 108, 255, 427, 376, 400, 480
Royal Scots Fusiliers 111, 157
Royal Welsh Fusiliers 220, 480
Royal West Kent Regiment 101
Scots Guards 146, 178, 212, 375, 395
Scottish Horse 31, 58, 86, 110-111, 132, 147
South Staffordshire Regiment 330, 374
Suffolk Regiment 254-255, 375, 400
West Yorkshire Regiment 221
Wiltshire Regiment 355
Worcestershire Regiment 248

Miscellaneous Formations/Units
3rd Scottish Provisional Battalion 157
81st Composite Regiment 205
Army Pay Corps 458
Army School of Piping 36
Army Service Corps (A.S.C.) 110, 174, 230, 262
Entrenching Battalions
    2nd Entrenching Battalion 190, 373
    4th Entrenching Battalion 153
    11th Entrenching Battalion 131
Machine Gun Corps 147, 158, 205, 365, 371, 374-376, 458-459
Officer Cadet Battalions
    9th Officer Cadet Battalion 96
    Inns of Court O.T.C. 95-96, 121
Royal Army Medical Corps (R.A.M.C.) 194, 218, 239, 366,

Royal Engineers 27, 111, 125, 179, 214, 312, 374, 376, 458
Royal Flying Corps 110-111, 218, 375-376, 458, 461
Royal Garrison Artillery 149
Royal Horse Artillery 461
Tank Corps 111, 458-459
Training Reserve Battalions 60
    38th Training Reserve battalion 60-61, 153
    40th Training Reserve battalion 153

Canadians
Canadian armed forces
    organization pre-War 15, 28-31
    organization wartime 62-65, 363

Canadian Expeditionary Force 63-66, 70, 192-193, 229, 261, 274, 281-282, 319-320, 338, 344-345, 363, 377-379, 387
2nd Canadian Field Artillery
2nd Canadian Infantry Brigade 465
3rd Canadian Infantry Brigade 247, 388
13th Battalion (Royal Highlanders of Canada) 63-65, 138, 154, 173, 192, 229, 247, 262, 275, 281, 365, 377, 380, 384, 386
15th Battalion (48th Highlanders of Canada) 63-65, 154, 167, 192, 203, 217, 229, 243, 322, 386, 465
16th Battalion (Canadian Scottish) 63-65, 71, 97, 138-139, 154-155, 192, 233-234, 236, 243, 246, 274, 282, 364, 389, 415, 421, 423-424, 437, 450, 465
42nd Battalion (Royal Highlanders of Canada) 63-65, 151, 154, 160-161, 192, 215-216, 274, 365, 385, 421, 430
43rd Battalion (Cameron Highlanders of Canada) 63-65, 138, 154, 261, 309, 320, 344, 364, 378, 444, 453, 463
72nd Battalion (Seaforth Highlanders of Canada) 63-65, 97, 192, 377-379
73rd Battalion (Royal Highlanders of Canada) 63-65, 70, 319, 338
85th Battalion (Nova Scotia Highlanders) 63-65, 70, 192
92nd Battalion 143
Nova Scotia Highland Brigade 64, 135, 261

Canadian Militia Regiments 15, 28-31, 62-64, 228, 468
5th Royal Highlanders of Canada 29, 30, 64, 138, 149, 154. 164, 229, 367
48th Highlanders of Canada 28, 30, 31, 43, 46, 64, 229
50th Gordon Highlanders 29, 33, 64, 155, 468
72nd Seaforth Highlanders 29-31, 64
78th Pictou Highlanders 28

79th Cameron Highlanders of Canada 29-31, 64, 260, 376
91st Canadian Highlanders 29, 30, 64,
94th Victoria Regiment, Argyll Highlanders 28, 31

South Africans
9th South African Infantry Battalion 66, 73
Active Citizen Force 15, 32, 65
Cape Town Highlanders 31-32, 36, 43-44, 46, 65, 72, 228
Natal Active Service Contingent (1906) 43
Natal Rangers (1906) 43
South African armed forces
  organization pre-War 15, 31-32
  organization wartime 65-66
South African Brigade 65, 70-71, 245, 401
South African Field Ambulance 400
South African Scottish (4th South African Infantry Battalion) 65-66, 70-73, 91, 93, 110, 139-140, 163, 166, 168, 170-171, 185, 220, 222, 224, 245, 273, 308, 317, 321, 325, 342, 375-376, 425, 431, 442, 446, 468
Transvaal Scottish 31-32, 36, 43-44, 48, 65-66, 72-73, 139, 228
  1st Transvaal Scottish 65
  2nd Transvaal Scottish 65

Index of General & Miscellaneous Terms

Anatolian Railway 62
active service experience, pre-war 19
affiliation to Old Country regiments 30, 377-378
amalgamations and reductions 68-70, 82-84
American Expeditionary Force 98
Ashanti campaign 38
atrocities, German 92, 410-415, 418-420, 437, 473
avoiding the trenches 456-462, 466, 472

bayonet, use of
  pre-War 39
  self-image 393-394
  wartime 422-423, 426-427, 431, 437, 472
Black Week (1899) 46
Blighty wounds 462
Boer Rebellion (1914) 65, 73
Boy Scouts 343-344
Burns' Night 385, 391, 473

Caledonian Societies 29, 31, 65
Camp Coffee 39
Childers reforms (1881) 17-18, 20, 23, 32, 38, 50
church ministers 95-96
Christmas Truce 435, 438
Clyde, unrest 354-355
comforts, provision of 196, 288, 318-319, 332, 337-343, 475-477
commanding officers 113-115, 283-289
  relationship with officers 284-286
  relationship with men 286-289
commissioning from ranks 116-119
community support 341-349
comradeship 79, 84-86, 308-336, 475-476, 480-481
  N.C.O.s and men 309-326
  officers 326-335
conscripts 61, 87, 122-123, 129-130, 140, 275, 279
courage 439-442, 466-467, 470, 472
cowardice 257, 272, 439, 462-466, 472

deployment 53, 57-62, 65-75
Derby scheme 87-88, 108, 110-111, 122-123, 129-130, 140, 146
discipline 256-282, 283, 469, 474-475, 479
  absence 257-261
  Canadians 281-282
  censorship infringements 267-268
  compassion and leniency 280-282
  courts martial 256-282 passim, 454, 463
  deprivation of rank 276-278
  desertion 37, 257-259, 278, 458, 474
  disobedience 257-260, 265-266, 280-281
  drunkenness 37, 257-259, 261-265, 275-276, 278-280, 285, 312, 454-455
  executions 257
  field punishment 256-282 passim
  gambling 272
  looting 268-269, 281
  mutiny 132, 273-274
  neglect 257-258, 266-267
  pre-War 36-37
  prostitution 272, 312, 473
  scrimshanking 257, 270-271, 287, 462
  self-inflicted wounds 269-270, 462, 474
  sleeping on sentry 266-267
  theft 257, 269
disillusionment 102-105, 473
Duchess of Westminster's Hospital 210, 332
dug-outs (personnel) 130-131, 329, 331-332, 460

English, attitude towards 399-401
enlistment, reasons for 87-112
  boyhood influences 98-99
  duty 87-92, 472, 476, 478-479
  family connections 109
  friends, influence of 99-100, 109-111
  justice of cause 92-96, 472, 476
  kilt and uniform, attraction 105-106

local regiment 108-109
naïve enthusiasm 96-97, 473
patriotism 98
pestering 100-101
reputation 106-108
Scottish ancestry 109
self-image 99
unemployment 101
esprit de corps 84-86, 133, 141-142, 160, 171-172, 200, 227, 248, 255, 290, 306, 309, 322-323, 327, 363, 367, 370, 374, 378, 382, 391, 396, 404, 474-475, 480. *See also under kilt and pipes.*
expatriate Scots 349

fear 440-446, 466-467, 472
foreign adventurers 98
Friends Ambulance Unit 202
frost-bite 104, 181-186, 199

Gaelic speakers 18, 19, 22, 25, 31, 120, 126, 134-136, 140, 381, 391, 469
gas, general 413, 415. *See also kilt/mustard gas*
German opinion of Highlanders 405-408, 431, 437
Glasgow Evening News 33
Glasgow Stock Exchange 126, 128
gold field strikes (1907) 43

Haldane reforms (1908) 20
hatred 410-421, 437
headwear 173, 199
Highland dancing 389-391, 473, 480
Highland games 388-389, 391, 473, 480
Highland Society of London 21, 24, 33
Highlandism 38
Hogmanay 387-388, 391, 473
Home Defence, T.F. 22, 50, 54-56, 459
Home Service, Regular battalions 17, 51
humanity, German 420-421
humanity towards enemy 416-417, 431-435, 437, 438

identity
    Canadian 379-380, 391
    pre-War 36, 38, 50
    regimental 132-133, 171, 228, 255, 363-379, 391, 471, 473-475, 479-481
    Scottish 379-91, 470-474, 478, 480-481
    wartime 363-391
    See also under kilt and pipes
Imperial Order of the Daughters of the Empire 29
Indian Mutiny 38, 40, 42, 116
industrial agitation, S. Africa (1914) 44
Irish troubles 354

kilt
    abolition, attempt 226
    attitude of public 165-171
    attraction for enlistment 105-106
    barbed wire 161, 208-212, 226
    battle 223-225
    bicycle-riding 162-163, 191-192
    chafing 175, 178, 187-188, 198-199
    cold 161-162, 181-189
    cuts and abrasions 161, 208-213, 226
    deception 220-222, 226
    decorum 164-165
    delayed issue 142-145
    drawers (or not) 148-151, 170-171, 194-197, 199, 205-206, 219-220
    esprit de corps/morale 142, 160, 171-172, 227
    flies 208
    German use of 222
    heat 197-199
    horse-riding 162-163
    ice 187-189
    identity 171, 364, 391, 468-469, 474-475, 478-480
    initiation 145-148, 151
    khaki kilts 152-155
    lice 103, 197, 199-203, 225, 227, 376
    marching 160-161
    mosquitoes 203-208, 225
    mud 177-181, 199
    mustard gas 172, 200, 214-220, 226
    natural functions 222-223
    pride 155-160, 171
    raids 200, 213-214, 221
    rise to dominance pre-War 32-33
    labour battalions 60, 70
    sleeping 222
    sports 163-165
    trench waders 189-191, 199
    trousers, use of 155-156, 190-194, 199, 205-207, 213, 220-221, 226
    water 174-176, 199
    Yeomanry conversions 58, 59

"Ladies from Hell" 405-406
letters from home 349-354, 478
"live and let live" 436-438
Llandovery Castle, hospital ship 414-415
Lusitania 93, 94, 414

malaria 62, 203-207, 226, 372, 460
martial race 393-394, 472, 479, 481
military disasters, pre-War 40-42, 45
mobilisation 52-55, 62-63, 65, 78, 230
Mohmand expedition (1908) 19, 43, 44
monuments 39-40, 45, 47-48, 469
morale 468-481 *See also esprit de corps*

nerves 446-456, 466, 472

newspapers 354, 397-399
North-West Frontier 19, 38, 43

officers, pre-War 18, 20-21, 26
officers' servants 302-303
officers' wives, role 283, 285, 287-288, 295-296, 302
other ranks, pre-war 19-20
overseas recruits 89-93
overseas service,
    Regulars, pre-War 17, 53
    T.F., pre-War 22
    T.F., wartime 55-57, 75-79, 88, 123

pacifists 355-356, 417
paintings 39, 45
Peninsular War 38
pioneer battalions 60, 68, 190, 376, 457-458
pipes
    arrivals 243-244
    battle, use in, pre-War 34-35
    battle, use in, wartime 232-237, 250-251, 254-255, 476
    funerals 244-245, 253
    entertainments and concerts 245-246, 473
    esprit de corps 248, 255
    hospitals 246
    identity 228, 248, 255, 366, 391, 468-469, 478, 480
    marching 241-242, 249, 251 253, 377, 476
    mobilization 229
    morale 248-255
    officers' mess 238-239
    parades and inspections 244
    pipe-bands, reconstitution and maintenance 229-231
    pipe-calls 238, 252
    Pipe President 239-240
    pipe-tunes, pre-War 35
    pipe-tunes, wartime commemorative 240
    receptions 242
    remembrance 245
    Retreat 231, 241-242, 248-249, 252, 471, 473, 476
    role in regiment, pre-War 34-36
    role in regiment, wartime 228, 247-248, 474, 479
    role of officers 35, 239-240
    send-offs 240, 242-243, 249-250
    simulating barrage 247
    special occasions 246
    sports days and gatherings 247
    swank 253
    Tattoo 231
poetry 91, 94, 105, 121, 225, 228, 249, 303, 308, 315-316, 324, 326, 334, 354, 355, 359, 370, 379-381, 393, 395-396, 401, 417, 426, 442
prisoners, enemy 299, 407-408, 41, 415, 421-422, 424-434, 437

prisoners, Highland 159, 319, 339-340, 365, 420

Queen Alexandra Hospital, Dunkirk 202

red hackle 364-365
recruiting
    English 136-137
    London 56, 79-81, 124, 136
    pre-War 17
    wartime 56, 68, 82-84, 99, 101, 106, 109, 123-125, 127-129, 133, 345
    Yorkshire 124, 136
Regimental associations 37, 340
regimental districts 18, 23, 33, 50
regimental family, pre-War 37
regimental support 339-340
regional and national origins 109
    Canadians 30-31, 138-140
    officers, pre-War 18, 20-21, 26
    officers, wartime 116-117, 119-120, 140
    other ranks, pre-War 19-20, 21, 36-27
    other ranks, wartime, 79-81, 123-127, 129, 140
    South Africans 139-140
relations between ranks 52-53, 469-470, 474, 477-478
    N.C.O.s and men 303-306
    officers and C.O. 284-286
    officers and men 291-303
    officers and N.C.O.s 289-291
    pre-War 37
religion 322, 356-362, 474, 479-480
reputation
    pre-War 38-43, 45, 49, 106-108
    wartime 403-409, 438, 472, 480
Royal Army Clothing Department 341
Royal Volunteer Review, Edinburgh (1905) 48
ruthlessness and brutality 421 434, 437

St Andrews Day 385-386, 391, 473
Sault Saint Marie riots (1903) 31, 43
Schools
    Dulwich 314
    Eton College 351
    Glenalmond 120
    Queen Victoria School, Dunblane 37, 47
    Robert Gordon's College Aberdeen 89
    Rugby School 89, 120
    St Paul's 135
Scottish Churches Hut 357
Scottish Naval and Military Veterans Residence 37, 47
self-image 392-403, 409
Senussi campaign 65, 72, 139, 317
shirkers 355-356
shoes and spats 173-174, 177, 183-184, 199
snipers 27, 125, 425, 434

snobbery (towards Temporary Officers) 329-331
social composition
   officers, pre-War 18, 20, 26
   officers, wartime 115-118, 120-121
   other ranks, pre-War 20-21, 27
   other ranks, wartime 125, 127-129
songs 366-367, 383-385, 391, 473, 478, 480
South African Hospital, Richmond 322, 342, 361
South African War (1899-1902) 19, 25, 27, 29, 31, 33, 38, 43-48, 50, 91, 98-99, 107, 291
"sticking it" 104-105
suicide 270, 353, 454

tartans, arbitrary selection of, 29-30, 33, 65
temporary uniforms 143-145
time-expired men, T.F. 81-82
Toronto Railway Company strike (1902) 31, 43
tradition, invention of 29, 32-33, 63, 475
training 474-475, 478-480
   Graduated battalions 60
   New Army 60
   Special Reserve, 21-22, 54
   T.F., 27-28, 55-57, 59
trauma (shell-shock) 439, 446-451, 466

trench-foot 104 181-186, 199
tunnellers 27, 125

Universities
   Aberdeen 27, 89, 301, 314
   Cambridge 120
   Glasgow 126, 128, 305, 309, 325, 367, 371, 375
   Oxford 95, 120, 135-136
   St Andrews 109

Victoria Cross 91, 119, 228, 233-234, 236

war-profiteers 355-356
white feathers 100

Y.M.C.A 343
Yeomanry conversions 58-59, 85-86, 132
young recruits
   pre-War 20, 27
   wartime 89, 100-101, 106, 133-134, 140

Zakha Khel expedition (1908) 19, 43
Zeppelins 414
Zulu Rebellion (1906) 36, 43